The Meaning of

Biosocial Encounters

Edited by
Dona Lee Davis and Anita Maurstad

LONDON AND NEW YORK

First published 2016
by Routledge
2 Park Square, Milton Park, Abingdon, Oxon OX14 4RN

and by Routledge
711 Third Avenue, New York, NY 10017

First issued in paperback 2017

Routledge is an imprint of the Taylor & Francis Group, an informa business

British Library Cataloguing in Publication Data
A catalogue record for this book is available from the British Library

Library of Congress Cataloging in Publication Data
A catalog record for this book has been requested

ISBN 13: 978-0-8153-4671-5 (pbk)
ISBN 13: 978-1-138-91455-1 (hbk)

Typeset in Goudy
by Taylor & Francis Books

The Meaning of Horses

The Meaning of Horses: Biosocial Encounters examines some of the engagements or entanglements that link the lived experiences of human and non-human animals. The contributors discuss horse human relationships in multiple contexts, times and places, highlighting variations in the meaning of horses as well as universals of 'horsiness'. They consider how horses are unlike other animals, and cover topics such as commodification, identity, communication and performance. This collection emphasises the agency of the horse and a need to move beyond anthropocentric studies, with a theoretical approach that features naturecultures, co-being and biosocial encounters as interactive forms of becoming. Rooted in anthropology and multispecies ethnography, this book introduces new questions and areas for consideration in the field of animals and society.

Dona Lee Davis is Professor of Anthropology at the University of South Dakota, USA.

Anita Maurstad is Professor of Cultural Science at University of Tromsø The Arctic University of Norway.

To Svein, a man who loved horses

Contents

Contributors

Dona Lee Davis received her Ph.D. in Anthropology from the University of North Carolina at Chapel Hill. She is currently Emeritus Professor of Anthropology at the University of South Dakota. Her areas of research and publication include maritime, psychological and medical anthropology as well as gender studies. She has conducted research in Canada, Norway and the United States. Her most recent book is *Twins Talk: What Twins Tell Us about Person, Self and Society* (Ohio University Press, 2015).

Anita Maurstad, Ph.D., is Professor of Cultural Science at University of Tromsø The Arctic University of Norway. She received her doctorate from the Norwegian College of Fishery Science at UiT The Arctic University of Norway. Areas of research and publication include horse human relationships, materiality, expertise and museology, as well as small-scale fishing and resource management.

Kristin Armstrong Oma is an archaeologist and is currently head of the education and visitor service department at the Museum of Archaeology, University of Stavanger. She holds a Ph.D. in Archaeology from the University of Southampton from 2006 and completed a postdoctoral fellowship at the University of Oslo in 2013. Her main research focus is human animal relationships in past societies, and she works in the cross-disciplinary field of Human Animal Studies in order to study interactions between humans and animals from a perspective of time depth. In addition to her study of horses, she has worked on exploring the dynamics between sheep, dogs and shepherds, and on mutual becomings in households with human and animal members that lived under the same roof.

Christoph Lange studied Social Anthropology and Middle East Studies at the University of Leipzig from 2004 to 2011. From 2008 to 2012 he worked for the German state-funded Collaborative Research Center CRC 586 "Difference and Integration" at the universities of Leipzig and Halle/ Lutherstadt Wittenberg where he conducted his first ethnographic research about authenticity of Bedouin representations in Syrian television dramas and Arab media discourses. Since 2014 he has worked as a doctoral researcher at the Research Lab "Transformations of Life" at the a.r.t.e.s. Graduate School for the Humanities Cologne. He is currently conducting his Ph.D. research on the breeding, standardization and circulation of Arabian thoroughbred horses with an ethnographic focus on Egypt and Arab actors within the global breeding industry.

Riitta-Marja Leinonen is a university teacher of Cultural Anthropology at the University of Oulu in Finland, where she also received her Ph.D. in Cultural Anthropology. Her areas of research include the human horse relationship, especially in horse logging, in World War II and in leisure. She has also studied conceptions and narratives about horses, nationalistic representations of the Finnhorse, horsemanship skills, the death of a horse and horses in mythology. She has presented papers in international conferences in Estonia, Finland, Greece, Italy, the UK and the US, and conducted research in Finland, Canada and the US.

Claire J. Brown is a doctoral candidate in the Anthropology Department at Binghamton University, State University of New York, and a National Science Foundation Graduate Research Fellow. She is currently conducting fieldwork in the West of Ireland for her doctoral dissertation, as she continues to study the social and cultural contexts of owning, breeding, showing and selling Connemara ponies. Her research interests lie in exploring new ways to theorize relationships between humans and animals in anthropology, through perspectives such as biosociality and multispecies ethnography.

Katherine Dashper, Ph.D., is senior lecturer in events management at Leeds Beckett University, UK. Her research interests include gender and sexuality within sport, leisure and tourism, with a particular focus on equestrianism and rural recreation. She is currently researching human animal relationships within rural leisure spaces. She has published in a variety of international peer review journals and is editor of *Rural Tourism: An International Perspective* (Cambridge Scholars, 2014), *Sports Events, Society and Culture* (Routledge, 2014; with Thomas Fletcher and Nicola McCullough) and *Diversity, Equity and Inclusion in Sport and Leisure* (Routledge, 2014; with Thomas Fletcher).

Charlotte Marchina is a Ph.D. candidate in Anthropology and lecturer at INALCO (National Institute of Oriental Languages and Civilizations, Paris), where she teaches Mongolian Language and Anthropology of Mongolia. Her doctoral research focuses on human animal coexistence, communication and collaboration in nomadic pastoralism among the Mongols in Mongolia and Buryatia (southern Siberia, Russia). Affiliated with the research team ASIEs (INALCO – EA 4512) and the Laboratoire d'Anthropologie Sociale (Collège de France, EHESS, CNRS – UMR 7130), Marchina is also a scientific member of the International Research Group "Nomadism, Society and Environment in Central and Northern

Asia" (a collaboration between France, Russia and Kirghizstan), and of the Monaco–Mongolia joint archaeological expedition. Her current research includes a diachronic study of Mongolian nomadic pastoralism in a multidisciplinary approach (social and cultural anthropology, archaeology, archaeozoology, biochemistry) in collaboration with the French National Museum of Natural History and the Mongolian Academy of Sciences.

Susan M. DiGiacomo is Professor of Anthropology at the Universitat Rovira i Virgili in Tarragona (Catalonia) and a member of the university's Medical Anthropology Research Center. She received her Ph.D. in Cultural Anthropology in 1985 from the University of Massachusetts at Amherst. Her dissertation explored the (re)construction of a Catalan national project in the context of the transition to democracy in Spain in the late 1970s and early 1980s, a process she continues to follow both as a social analyst and a political activist. A biographical coincidence – a diagnosis of cancer during her doctoral fieldwork in 1980 – led her to the cultural study of biomedicine. A nearly lifelong rider, she gets to the barn as often as possible.

Nora Schuurman, Ph.D., is a researcher at the University of Eastern Finland, Joensuu campus. Her research interests include conceptions of animals, animal-related practices, discourses of animal welfare, and the role of the horse in Western society. Her current research is focused on the affective and performative dimensions of human horse relationships, in the contexts of leisure horse keeping, equine trade and horse training, and the practices and conceptions concerning animal death.

Maarit Sireni is a senior researcher at the Karelian Institute, University of Eastern Finland. She has a Ph.D. in Human Geography, and she is an adjunct professor of Social Geography at the University of Eastern Finland. Her research interests include women and agriculture, changing gender relations on family farms, and motherhood and childcare in rural contexts.

Amelia-Roisin Seifert is a Ph.D. candidate in Social Anthropology at Queens University Belfast, Northern Ireland. Her wider thesis is a restudy of Native American Horse Culture in the 21st century based on a year living and riding with families on three inter-related reservations – the Nez Perce, Umatilla and Colville Reservations, respectively. Her work seeks to honor the contemporary dynamism of native people and the animals in their lives through a participant-led post-colonial multispecies ethnographic approach.

Ana C. Ramírez received her Ph.D. in Social Anthropology from el Colegio de Michoacán, Zamora, Mexico. Her dissertation is entitled *The Brave Game: Men, Women and Beasts in Charreria (1923–2003)*. She is a former *escaramucera* and judge of *escaramuzas*. Her areas of research and publication include riding technologies and their impact upon complex societies with a special emphasis on how animal agencies shape and are shaped by history, geography, gender relations, economics and politics. She is currently a professor in the Philosophy Department, Michoacana University of Saint Nicholas of Hildago, Mexico.

Sarah Dean graduated with a B.A. in Anthropology and Spanish from the University of South Dakota. As an undergraduate student, she participated in research on human animal relationships. She is the co-author (with Dona Lee Davis and Anita Maurstad) on a number of recent publications on horse human relationship. She is currently opening an online tutoring business in Las Vegas, Nevada, where she lives with her family.

Preface

Anita and I have been colleagues for over 20 years. At our original meeting in Tromsø, Norway, as two academics, we shared interests in fish, fishing and the study of North Atlantic maritime cultures. Little did we realize, when we first met, that our mutual leisure-time interests in horses would not only cement our friendship but also develop into a shared area of academic expertise. Stimulated by recent publications outlining a field of multispecies ethnography, we embarked on a joint research project focused on horse human relationships. With my student Sarah Dean, we collected narrative data from riders who participate in a range of equestrian sports and activities in the American Midwest and north Norway. Initially seeing the project as a way to get together and present papers at conferences, we had not anticipated how rich the data we had collected would be. With a number of excellent studies of human horse relationships to inspire us, we tentatively moved into the field. Anticipating that we had entered a new field of study (animals and society), we were surprised at how well our "new" data fit into our already established interests in gender, ageing, medical/psychological anthropology, practice and performance, relational materialities and exploration of the variety of ways in which nature and culture intra-act with each other.

In 2013 I organized a session on "Anthropologies of Living with Horses and Equine Sports" at the American Anthropological Association Meetings held in Chicago. The session was held at 8:00 a.m. on a Sunday morning, but the session room was overflowing and it was very clear from the lively discussion that followed that anthropologists from equestrian backgrounds were very interested in what we were doing. Hoping that we had the beginnings of an edited book, we sought to expand our collection of chapters by also organizing a session on "The Meaning of Horses" at the European Association of Social Anthropologists meetings held in Tallinn, Estonia, during the summer of 2014. Both sessions allowed us to connect with well-established scholars and those who, like us, were relative newcomers to the field of horse human relationships. In advance of the EASA conference, Katherine Ong, a commissioning editor with Routledge, contacted us and with Katherine's encouragement our edited book project was underway.

The contributors to this volume are drawn from the two conference sessions. We would like to thank them for their continued interests in and support of this project and for meeting our exacting deadlines. We would also like to thank Katherine Ong for her initial encouragement and support. Lola Harre, our Routledge editorial assistant, has been most helpful and supportive with her guidance and immediate responses to all of our questions. We would also like to thank our respective universities for providing travel funds for attending the two conferences. Lastly, we would like to thank the horses we have lived with past and present. Without them we would probably still be writing about fish. Writing about horses has rewarded us with new ways of treasuring and respecting them.

1 Meaning of Horses

Dona Lee Davis and Anita Maurstad

Human Animal Studies have recently emerged as a topical, popular, controversial, cross-disciplinary arena of research, theory and practice that calls for innovative ways of understanding human animal relationships (DeMello 2012; Hurn 2012). Just as the 1960s and 1970s brought women from the periphery to the center of analysis, today's researchers are exploring new ways of thinking about human animal relationships. Three theoretical frameworks dominate the new field of human nonhuman animal studies. Posthumanism seeks to decenter the human from human animal studies (Wolfe 2010). Multispecies ethnography advocates a more nuanced focus on the contact zones, or types of entanglements and engagements, that link lived experiences of human and nonhuman animals (Haraway 2008; Hamilton and Placas 2011). An innovative movement in biosocial anthropology (Ingold and Pálsson 2013) proposes (Ingold 2013) new ways of thinking about creatures as individual, biological and social beings that, through interspecies practices and interactions or biosocial encounters, mutually create their selves. Within each of these theoretical frameworks, horses and human horse interactions as a topic of study invite a broad perspective of analytic themes and frameworks. By bringing horses from the periphery to the center of analysis, the book's contributors demonstrate the utility of an ethnographic perspective as they describe and discuss horses in multiple specific and situated contexts, times and places. As a whole this collection identifies and explores a variety of horse human entanglements that not only center the horse and bridge or challenge the nature–culture divide but also focus on the complexities of horse human relationships as forms of meaning making.

Although our focus on the horse draws from broadly defined ethnographic methods and case studies to contribute to the animals and society literature, we also assert that horses are not like other animals. They are partner (Birke 2008) rather than companion animals. Horses' very nature, history, morphology and function set them apart from other kinds of animals in important ways. The practice of horse riding provides new dimensions of meaning to concepts such as co-being (Haraway 2008, 3), forms of "we" (Haraway 2008, 11) or "contact zones" (Haraway 2008, 5). The human riding with horse (Argent 2012) becomes the centaur (Game 2001) and a form of a "knotted being" (Haraway 2008, 15). The very act of riding is a process of "becoming with" (Haraway 2008, 16). Together rider and horse flatten or bridge not only the divides of animal/human but also those of nature/culture. Moreover, in addition to their use in riding and hauling as forms of transport, the speed, mobility, longevity and stamina of horses as well as their ability to survive in a variety of terrains and climates has had profound effects in human histories locally and globally and in both the long and short term (Kelekna 2009).

The contributors to this volume are situated in a variety of cultures that enable a focus on local variations in meaning of horses as well as on universals of 'horsiness.' The chapters draw from an international collection of authors and cover topics in a wide range of national, indigenous or cultural settings including Mongolia, Egypt, Finland, Norway, Ireland, Mexico, Spain, the US and the UK. Taken together, the contributors bridge dichotomies between nature and culture in ways that support developments of new theoretical language of nature-cultures and biosocial becomings (Ingold and Pálsson 2013; Kirksey and Helmreich 2010; Haraway 2008; Hurn 2012) but also intersect with an existing social science literature that has ascribed meaning to horses and horse human relationships in a multiplicity of ways. Although there is considerable overlap among the chapters, each chapter stands by itself and chapters can be read in any order.

In this chapter we set the scene for what follows with an introductory overview of key themes or topics of inquiry that characterize contemporary literatures on the meaning of horses. We return to a more detailed assessment of horse human relations as biosocial encounters in our conclusion (Chapter 13). Although we cover a wide range of topics, the review is illustrative rather than comprehensive. The goal, aside from introducing the chapters of this book, is to demonstrate the various meanings in terms of significance or import that horses have had as they have been situated in a variety of genres of academic writing. Although the focus is on anthropology and works by anthropologists, rather than set, rigid academic boundaries, many non-anthropologists who employ an ethnographic perspective and are influential in the field are also included. The review is divided thematically into sections on the meaning of horses in reference to:

1 evolution and history;
2 harm and health;
3 embodiment, mutuality and communication; and
4 horse cultures and the ethnography of sport.

Evolution and history

The meanings of horses can be shaped through analysis of their roles and function in historical and evolutionary contexts. Anthropology is a four field discipline that includes cultural anthropology, biological anthropology, archaeology and linguistics. Archaeologists and biological anthropologists (Olsen et al. 2006) have shown a continuing interest in both the evolution of horses and their role in prehistorical and historical cultures of the past. Without horses the history and culture of humans would be very different (Lawrence 1988). For example, Sandra Olsen (1995, 2006a, 2006b) has studied human horse relationships from the Pleistocene past to current day herders in Kazakhstan (Olsen et al. 2008; Shnirelman and Olsen 1995). An archaeologist, Olsen documents the variety of relationships that have existed between horse and humans over the millennia. The horse was originally exploited for meat by Paleolithic hunters spreading across Europe and Asia and probably domesticated around 4,000 BC. Since that time, the horse has had not only multiple occupations but also a tremendous impact on geopolitics. Kelekna (2009, 1) describes the emergence of "horse power" in human history and documents the important roles that horses have played throughout a wide variety of regional and cultural contexts (see also Chamberlin 2006; Clutton-Brock 1992; Digard 2003; Hansen 2014). Kelekna's (2009) study is interesting because the focus on horses moves analysis of key developments in human history and prehistory from the centers of sedentary agricultural civilizations to the margins and peripheries or the steppes and deserts of Europe, Asia and North Africa. Being the fastest long distance quadruped on Earth, long lived, able to run on hard surfaces, and having strength and stamina, horses became the basis of mobile equestrian cultures active in trade and a highly effective warfare that functioned to spread Indo-European languages, religion and writing through large areas of the old and new worlds. Taking a more literary turn, Raber and Tucker (2005) describe the role of the horse in defining the early modern world (Middle Ages to the 18th century) in Europe, Russia and Africa, where horses become associated with aristocratic, masculine, military and national identities. Returning to ethnography, Lawrence (1988) notes the readiness with which people throughout history have embraced horses and how mounted societies are characterized by pride and a sense of independence and superiority.

Of the contributors to this volume only Kristin Armstrong Oma, in Chapter 2, takes a specifically archaeological/historical perspective. Although she notes the importance of the horse for meat and transport among Iron Age Viking cultures in Scandinavia, Oma's focus is on the more symbolic aspects of horses as vehicles for transport between the realms of the everyday and the supernatural. Nevertheless, Oma's analysis is also embedded in discussions of culture change and state formation implicating the role and life of the horse as enmeshed in each. Charlotte Marchina, in Chapter 7 on Mongolian horsemanship, focuses on the contemporary Mongolians or modern day descendants of the horse cultures that figure so prominently in the accounts of historians like Kelekna (2009). Narrowing their analytic frameworks to the last two centuries, a number of contributors also take a historical turn, where the horse becomes a dynamic intermediary between traditional and modern. In Chapter 10, Amelia-Roisin Seifert takes Lawrence's (1985,

1988) ethnography of North American Plains Indians, like the Crow, into a more contemporary setting by looking at the shifting but vital roles horses have come to play as keystone species and potent symbols in the biopolitical sphere. Seifert shows how traditional equestrian practices and meanings co-occur among those that are more modern or contemporary. Similarly, Claire Brown, in Chapter 5, demonstrates how the modern Connemara pony has become an admixture of traditional and modern in current-day Ireland. Others, for example Riitta-Marja Leinonen (Chapter 4) and Christoph Lange (Chapter 3), take a historical approach to changing uses and meanings of a particular regional or national breed of horse in Finland and Egypt, respectively. While Leinonen focuses on the changing functions of the Finnish horse, Lange traces the impacts of first colonialism and then globalization on the breeding of Arab horses in Egypt. Today the Connemara pony has become an athlete, the Finnish horse a therapist and the Arab horse a work of art. All of these contributors share an interest in the changing functions and morphologies of the horses who are subjects of their studies. In particular, Seifert, Brown, Leinonen and Lange all agree that as horses' significance in work and subsistence decreases, their symbolic significance increases.

Harm and health

While McShane and Tarr (2006) assert that it is questionable if the horse would have actually survived without human intervention, Cassidy (2013, 2) refers to "the costs of our entanglements with animals" in terms of harm to the animal. Any discussion of the human horse interactions, past or present, raises issues of what potentials for harm exist in the case of the horse and for help or health in the case of the human. Tuan (1984), writing about human histories of hunting and domestication of animals in general, describes human animal relationships as characterized by cruelty, power and dominance. Gilbert and Gillet's (2014) edited book on the use of animals in sport contains an entire section on violence towards and the unethical treatment of animals. Young and Gerber (2014) describe the cruelty to horses that occurs in chuck wagon racing at the Calgary Stampede. According to Hurn (2012), the breeding and commercial sales of Welsh cobs is a kind of sex trade where obese horses are enslaved to human ideals of what features should characterize the breed. Lange in this volume sets forth similar arguments for the case of the *asil* Arab horse where breeding for form trumps function. American rodeo (Lawrence 1982; Rollin 1966) is often portrayed in terms of abusive practices towards animals including horses. Dalke (2010) describes how herd culling policies for management of mustang herds must juggle images of historical icon, object of beauty and pest. We, like other contributors to this volume, have attended animal and society conferences where members of the audience vocally object to any form of riding, stabling or domestication of the horse as a form of abuse.

More nuanced approaches to the ethical treatment of horses, however, also occur both in terms of domestication and sport. Rather than view domestication as a form of human control, exploitation and dominance, Cassidy (2007a) characterizes domestication as a more symbiotic, mutual co-evolution or exchange between humans and animals in general. Similarly, Argent (n.d.) and Goodwin (1999) caution against emphasizing dominance over co-operation in horse human relationships. The importance of animal ethics and welfare in sports is noted by Rollin (1966), as are safety concerns or accident/injury prevention in a variety of equestrian sports (Bryant 2008; Murray et al. 2005; Odberg and Bouissou 1999; Thompson and Adelman 2013). Dashper (2014), while noting that the horse does not choose to participate in equine sports, like Birke (2004), sees human horse interactions as a kind of partnership rather than a form of exploitation. Smith (2014) fine tunes her discussion of horse human riding partnerships, with an elaborated distinction of what constitutes good and bad dressage as a difference between a responsive horse and a controlled horse.

As there is a literature on harm to horses, there is also a literature on the benefits of health and well-being that horses bring to humans. Although problematic when it comes to efficacy studies (Davis et al. 2015; Kruger and Serpell 2010), horses do bring healing benefits to humans. Equine assisted therapy (EAT) or, more broadly, equine assisted activities, include physical and psychological benefits from riding or just being around horses. Although EATs are focused on those who suffer some sort of impairment (Michalon 2014), horse human alliances are also considered to give pleasure to their human partners and the depth of emotional connection people feel with their horses is said to exceed that of the client/therapist relationship (York et al. 2008). Keaveney (2008), Gilbert (2014) and Lawrence (1988) summarize these benefits as the physical pleasures of grooming or touching a horse; a sense of connection, partnership and mutual trust that arises in the shared embodiments of riding: feelings of happiness, relaxation, escape, freedom, transcendence, communion with nature and spirituality; a sense of community in the barn; and a sense of accomplishment and self-actualization or confidence. According to Lawrence (1988) the qualities of the horse as healer in modern society reside in his or her nobility, beauty and grace; patience and kindness; the rhythm and power of his movements. A horse's tractable personality and willingness to work, according to Hansen (2014), are traits resulting from 600 years of genetic selection and selective breeding or as Argent (n.d., 2), rather succinctly claims: "Horses and humans take care of each other."

Although none of the contributors specifically focus on animal rights and abuse issues, issues of cruelty such as severe bits and spurs are addressed in Ana C. Ramírez's (Chapter 11) discussion of *escaramuzas charras* or female equestrian skirmish/drill teams who perform at traditional Mexican rodeos. Leinonen discusses both intentional, calculated abusive practices in the past towards the Finnish horse in logging operations as well as a kindly meant but harmful feeding practices among farmers. Leinonen also notes how forms of horse use have changed over time. Among contemporary horse hobbyists the horse's role has changed from one of workmate to therapist or playmate. Taking issue with the whole horse as therapist approach, in Chapter 8, Susan M. DiGiacomo focuses on the feeling of well-being and artistry that comes with being on a horse, while (like Keaveney 2008) refusing to resort to a medical language or over-medicalized interpretation of riding. Nora Schuurman and Maarit Sireni (Chapter 9) also discuss the mixed meanings of 'healthy' riding when it comes to a woman's decision-making about how long through her pregnancy it is safe to ride. Although DiGiacomo and Schuurman and Sireni problematize issues of risk, sickness and health, they recognize the importance of a sense of embodied mutuality, partnership and interspecies communication as being essential to the formation of the human horse bond. Even Ramírez, who offers a very interesting example of some women who do not care for or bond with their horses, argues that they would ride more effectively and more humanely if they did.

Mutuality, embodiment and communication

Unlike household pets, horses cannot be cuddled in your lap (Keaveney 2008), but this does not preclude a strongly felt sense of mutuality or intimate contact with them. At the horse human interface boundaries of two species open up to and even support each other (Clark 2007, Serpell 2003, Wipper 2000). Horse human relationships entail a kind of prosocial empathy (Tymowski 2014) where intersubjective worlds of horsiness and humanness are shared as they register, respond and bond to each other as individuals (Argent n.d.; Birke et al. 2004; Brandt 2004). Embodiment and the shared act of riding bring a special dimension of sensorial experience to the horse human relationship. This relationship has been described variously as embodying the centaur (Game 2001), somatic modes of attention and co-being (Maurstad et al. 2013), intercorporeality (Thompson and Adelman 2013) and anthropozoogenesis as in forms of attunement that differ from cause and effect thinking (Despret 2004). Much is also said about communication. Gala Argent (2012, 2010) focuses on everyday, working riders, who ride with their horses and experience long term human horse interactions. She privileges nonverbal communications with horses (what she calls embodied language or kinesics, haptics and proxemics) and stresses intersubjectivity and mutual trust as well as understanding and responsiveness in human horse relations. Patton (2003) likens training in dressage to a kind of negotiated body language between horse and rider that enhances feelings of power in both horse and rider. Birke (2007), referring to jumping and dressage, notes how these do-it-together activities unlock something in both horse and rider to form a partnership that communicates in deep and nonverbal ways. Similarly Hansen (2014) and Brandt (2004) describe horse training as a co-creative process of embodied communication wherein human and horse develop a mutually intelligible language. Hearne (2007, 108) terms this conversation the "art of horsemanship." Within these frames of analysis horses are viewed as agentive social beings, as individuals with their own biographies and as having their own temperaments and talents (Argent n.d.; Birke 2004).

The contributors to this volume grapple with issues of communication and relation in a number of ways. DiGiacomo's account is certainly a very special and personal celebration of the kinds of experiential co-being that may emerge between horse and rider. What is unique to the contributors in this volume (including DiGiacomo, who privileges two different horses in her analysis) is that they go beyond a simple horse human dyad to include multiple dimensions of communication and relationship. Katherine Dashper in her study of riding lessons in Britain (Chapter 6) explores the dynamics of a triangular relationship that involves rider, instructor and horse (and we might add herself as observer) as it is developed and enacted by all three participants during a riding lesson. Dashper's analysis also takes on embodiment or intercorporeality with a focus on movement, *feel* and the shared sensorial processes that occur between horse and rider. Marchina's tripartite analysis includes the Mongolian herder, the horse he rides with and the 'wild' horse that is being lassoed or captured. Moreover, she describes how the ridden horses alternate between capturer and captured. Schuurman and Sireni's analysis of a pregnant women's blog in Finland introduces the fetus and new-born child into a threefold analytic framework. Oma, in her chapter on relationship to horses in the Iron Age Viking culture, looks to the mythical and spiritual realms where mutuality involves horses integrated into meshworks (Ingold 2013) or threads woven into webs of practice and meaning. In Chapter 12, Anita Maurstad, Dona Davis and Sarah Dean go beyond the physicality of movement or riding to introduce the concepts of objectified meaning and objects. They are interested in the various kinds of objects and things (tangible and intangible as well as predictable and idiosyncratic) that riders refer to as depicting their relationships to or connections with their horses. Interesting also are the null cases. For example, Lange describes the *asil* Arab horse as subject to a critical aesthetic gaze but unridden and Ramírez describes the lack of feeling or connections between the *escaramuzas charrerias* and their horses, where horses are sat upon but not felt.

Horse cultures: Ethnography and sport

Although multispecies ethnography has emerged as a new field of study there is an already well-established substantial body of anthropological literature on horse cultures. Unlike the literature that focuses on the human horse pair in terms of mutuality or co-embodiment of riding with the horse, these ethnographically focused sources take a broader, more culturally inclusive view of equestrian or horse cultures. Clutton-Brock (1992), Digard (2003) and Kelekna (2009) share an interest in charting the history of horse cultures at different times in various wide-scale geographical or cultural areas of the world. Lawrence (1988) and others (Ewers 1955; Haines 1938; Wissler 1914) have described horse cultures in native America. Shnirelman and Olsen (1995) offer an ethnographic description of contemporary horse pastoralists in Kazakhstan. There also exists a contemporary literature on horse cultures as defined by specific equestrian sport communities. These include depictions of rodeo culture (Allen 1998; Arluke and Bogden 2014; Lawrence 1982; and Penaloza 2011) and horse racing cultures associated with harness racing (Helmer 1991), thoroughbred racing in Brazil (Adelman and Moraes 2008), racing in the US and Great Britain, as well as race horse breeding in the global village (Cassidy 2003, 2007b, 2013; K. Fox 2005; R. Fox 2006). Associations of horses and horsemanship skills with military and colonial elites in the era of British imperialism are topics of studies by Riedi (2006) and Landry (2001). Rose (1990) offers a critical view of the elite sport of fox hunting in Eastern US. Gilbert and Gillett's (2014) recent edited volume, on the use of animals in sport, features analyses of particular equestrian sports as subcultures. Their book includes chapters on horses as athletes in a number of interspecies sports including horse jumping in Europe (Thompson and Birke 2014) and Canada (Coulter 2014), dressage (Smith 2014), and disabled riders in the Olympics (Larnby and Hedenborg 2014). Stable labor and stable as cultural place are also subjects of ethnographic study (Gilbert 2014; Hedenborg 2014). Adelman and Knijnik (2013) in another recent book focus on the intersections of race, gender and class in equestrian sports as communities of practice. This includes Grand Prix jumping in Canada (Coulter 2013) and Britain (Dashper 2013), stable labor in Great Britain (Butler 2013), dressage in Brazil (Knijnik 2013) and women in rodeo (Adelman and Knijnik 2013). Thompson (2011, 2013) also explores intersections of gender and class in the Spanish bullfight. Biographies of or tributes to horses as individuals with their own life histories are presented by Crawford (2007) and represent a new trend in writing animal biographies (Nance 2014; see also Birke 2004). As the above explore the intersections of interspecies sports and gender, Helgadóttir (2006) explores the intersections of cultures of horsemanship and tourism in Iceland, taking a stance that cross cuts various horse cultures. Others (e.g., Birke, 2007; et al. 2004; Latimer and Birke 2009) demonstrate how different cultures of horsemanship such as traditional British and American-based natural horsemanship cultures influence the way in which people think about horses. Borneman (1988) takes a culturally informed stance in his comparison of the cognitive constructions of light horse breeds in the US and Europe.

Well-known equestrian horse cultures are subjects of chapters by Marchina on the Mongolian herders, Ramírez on Mexican rodeos, and Seifert on indigenous North America. Yet, each of these studies focuses on a particular equestrian activity. Marchina describes skills and strategies used for the roping or lassoing of horses. Ramírez focuses on the performance of women's riding team events in traditional Mexican rodeo. Seifert describes the contemporary native sports of racing and co-option of horses in ceremonial activities. Lange's portrayal on the Arabian horse in Egypt, as well as Brown's on the Connemara pony in West Ireland and Leinonen's on the Finnish horse depict how a particular breed of horse has come to figure prominently in terms of regional or national identity. Each author's account not only demonstrates how form and function of the horse changes through time but also documents the important roles that socioeconomic and political factors come to play in the process. Additionally, although there is a considerable body of literature on equestrian sports, Thompson and Adelman (2013) have noted a lack of data on pleasure or leisure riders who make up the vast majority of any equestrian sport or activity. In this volume, Dashper; Maurstad, Davis and Dean; Schuurman and Sireni; and DiGiacomo all focus on leisure riders in a Euro-American context.

As a review of the horse and human, and of horse human relationship literature, the topical categories discussed above represent just one of many ways of approaching the subject or schemas for meaning making in today's rapidly expanding literatures. While we have organized our review as an introduction to this body of literature, the chapters of this book call forth other strategies for meaning making. The genesis of this book came from two paper sessions organized first for the meetings of the American Anthropological Association held in Washington, DC, in 2013 and the European Association of Social Anthropology Meetings held in Tallinn, Estonia, during the summer of 2014. The former session was titled *Anthropologies of Living with Horses and Equine Sports* and the latter *The Meaning of Horses*. Contributors to this volume were selected from these two sessions. Although they show overlap with the more traditional approaches we have so far described in this chapter, they also invite a different mode of ordering and presentation. These we have titled Part I Commodification and Identity; Part II Communication and Relation; and Part III Performance, Practice and Presentation. With these parts in mind an overview of the volume follows.

Part I: Commodification and identity

Part I focuses on commodification and identity. In various ways horses become instrumental in the self-construction as horse and human conjointly make each other up (Birke et al. 2010; Davis and Davis 2010). Horses are implicated in the formation and enactment of national, cultural, gender, age-graded and particular sports' subculture identities (Adelman and Knijnik 2013; Dashper 2012a, 2012b; Davis et al. 2014, 2015; Forsberg and Tebelious 2011; Lawrence 1982, 1988). Moreover, as participants in interspecies sports, horses have developed or been ascribed with particular or distinguishing identities in terms of commodity values. Sport and show horses can now be bred for particular characteristics in morphology and temperament that enhance their monetary value on international markets (Cassidy 2013; Gilbert and Gillett 2012). The chapters in this section focus on changing meanings of the horse through time within a particular cultural or national context. Taken together, the chapters grapple with entanglements such as the religious or symbolic functions of the horse; the horse as companion, family member and workmate; the horse as national or regional icon; and as an internationally marketed commodity. In Chapter 2, Oma engages symbolic and political forms of analysis. She describes how in pagan Scandinavia, horses were real-life companions with spiritual properties and magical abilities. Consumption of horsemeat and the deposit of horses or tokens of them in graves facilitated passage through the borderlands of life and death and the real and divine. With the onset of Christianity from late 900 AD, however, pagan burials and the consumption of horsemeat were banned. Oma proceeds to argue that authorities in the new fledgling states sought to eradicate the horse cult as it was seen to be in direct conflict with a new ideology of Christ the savior. Lange, in Chapter 3, demonstrates the cosmopolitan nature of the Arab horse as a valuable commodity in a global marketplace. His discussion on the breeding and changing morphology of the Egyptian Arabian horse pays particular attention to how constructions of identity in terms of function, performance and aesthetics of the Arabian horse have shifted with pre-colonial, colonial and post-colonial sociopolitical contexts. As centers for breeding of the Arab horse have moved to America, Lange engages current debates about what constitutes an authentic Arab horse. In Chapter 4, Riitta-Marja Leinonen draws on narrative accounts from interviews and written stories of the Finnish people to describe how cultural models of the Finnish horse have changed over the last 100 years as the horse has moved from servant, machine, hero and performer to therapist. Yet, throughout these periods of change the horse has continued to be regarded by the Finnish people as a cognitively gifted, sentient animal who is both an active agent and a friend. Claire Brown, in Chapter 5, also focuses on the evolving nature of the regional horse as a kind of hoofed commodity as she explores local and global perspectives on the breeding, showing and marketing of the Irish Connemara pony. Brown examines the sociocultural complexities in construction of value for the Connemara pony as an international commodity exported from its native home in Western Ireland to breeders around the world. Brown describes not only how symbol, meaning and value are negotiated through time in a local and a global context, but also depicts the roles the ponies take as active agents in the process. Taken together these economically, politically and historically informed accounts evidence the dynamic temporal aspects of horse human encounters and how they change over time and place. As symbols of past identity (Oma) or as commodities exchanged on national (Leinonen) or international (Lange and Brown) markets, horses emerge as contested units of value that represent both traditional and modern identities (Lange, Brown, Leinonen) in a process whereby their authenticity is challenged and the roles that their form and function come to play in human culture become renegotiated.

Part II: Communication and relation

As we read in the section on embodiment, mutuality and communication, horses as partner species and the embodied practices of riding with them have challenged researchers to explore new avenues for understanding and articulating interspecies relationships and of recognizing agency of the horse in these relations (Argent 2012, n.d.; Thompson and Birke 2014). The practices of training, learning to ride, riding with and being in the company of horses comprise a kind of embodied mutuality that has received much note in the literature (Maurstad et al. 2013; West and de Braganca 2012) and holds much promise for future researchers. The notions of the pleasurable and therapeutic value of horses for humans, both functioning and impaired, have also been the topic of controversy and discussion (Anestis et al. 2014; Davis et al. 2015). In Part II, contributors both take issue with and expand on issues raised in this body of literature. In Chapter 6, Dashper, a well-established scholar in both the fields of sports sociology and equestrian cultures within the UK, describes the systematic training of horse rider partnerships through formal horse-riding lessons. She considers how communication and meaning are transmitted, negotiated, understood and misunderstood across species. Dashper's concern is with spatial and sensory boundaries that involve not just the commonly referred to dyad of rider and horse but a triad of rider, horse and instructor. She describes how harmony and shared purpose in horse human relations is deeply felt but must be learned and negotiated in a constant series of feedback loops involving the horse, the rider and the riding instructor. In Chapter 7, Marchina draws on her field-work with Mongolian horse pastoralists to explore a triad of horse human relationships. Referring to the skills involved in the practice of lasso-poling as a form of horse capture in an almost fenceless environment, Marchina not only describes the fine-tuned coordination and collaboration between trained horse and rider but discusses the processes whereby herders give agency to the horse, encouraging the horse to take the initiative. Marchina's account, however, also introduces a third actor to the encounter. This is the horse being lassoed. DiGiacomo, in Chapter 8, reflects on the important role that horses came to play during a personal life crisis to argue that her horse is *not* her therapist. She provides an autoethnographic account of how the embodied communicative practices of dressage restored to her the use of her body after treatment for Hodgkin's lymphoma. Rejecting the medicalized reduction of her experience to 'therapy,' she goes on to explore her human horse relationships as a way of being in the world where one's body is completely alive to another body. In the final chapter of Part II, Schuurman and Sireni take notions of mutuality to task with a case study of conflict and disharmony in human horse relationships. They ask how two bodily states, the human horse relationship and pregnancy, affect each other. Basing their analysis on a blog kept by a Finnish mother and horse owner, the study expands into debates over how far into her pregnancy a woman should ride.

Analysis is informed by recent discussions within human, animal and feminist studies about embodiment, performativity and rationality, and the production of gender in the context of equestrianism. Whether positioned as an account of a single individual's auto-ethnography or blog, an accomplished equestrian's view of a rider/horse/instructor triad, or an ethnographer's description of a cultural practice, the chapters in this section combine to provide a more situated and nuanced understanding of what is too often unproblematically referred to as human horse relationships.

Part III: Performance, practice and presentation

This section features a closer look at the role that heritage, performance and sport activities as well as objects and regalia can play in the bringing of meaning to, the celebration of, and the re-invention of cultural traditions. Different equestrian traditions have been recognized as definitive of national equestrian cultures [for example, classical dressage in France, forward seat jumping in Great Britain (Raber and Tucker 2005), mounted bull fighting in Spain (Thompson 2012), or rodeo in the American west (Lawrence 1982), the five gated Icelandic horse in Iceland (Helgadóttir 2006)]. Here, however, we introduce relatively unexplored examples of dimensions of performance, presentation and practice of human horse relations as a kind of nature–culture or interface of heritage, identity, place, past and present. Seifert, in Chapter 10, uses the terms living heritage and keystone species to describe both a powerful interspecies bond and range of roles for horses among contemporary Native Americans living on the U.S. Western Plateau. Seifert describes three types of contemporary horse activities. These include breeding a keystone species or a new type of Appaloosa horse among the Nez Perce, horse as culture bearer or parading of horses in native regalia, and the Indian sports of suicide, relay and bush track flat racing. All are seen as manifestations of cultural survival, as rites of passage and as markers of masculinity. Yet, Seifert also depicts how this revitalization of horse cultures is compromised by issues of what to do with excess, feral range horses. Ramírez, in Chapter 11, provides a complex account of *escaramuzas charras*, adolescent and young girls who perform at Mexican rodeos in an aggressive and competitive women's sport that predates the North American rodeo. Although overtly associated with a strong sense of nationalism with an intense cult of virility, these synchronized equestrian performances by all women teams have their own cultural logic that recombines traditional aspects of father daughter relations and femininity and masculinity in rather convoluted ways. Based on fieldwork conducted in Mexico and California, Ramírez's study also provides interesting revisions to literatures on the formation of the horse human relationships and bonds and notions of embodiment and partnerships in riding. Part III concludes with Anita Maurstad, Dona Davis and Sarah Dean's discussion of how (and if) traditional museum instruments as material objects can be used to capture the less objective, less palpable, subjectively felt meanings that develop through the practice of horse human relationships. Based in the analysis of narrative data collected from riders in Norway and the Midwestern United States, the authors demonstrate how objects associated with horses can resonate with typical expectations of museum collections, but meaning as communicated through horse people's narratives can also be atypical, idiosyncratic and highly personal. The authors also focus on how objects can show agency in ways that both engage and transform horse human relationships. While Part II features the experiential complexities in personal and interpersonal aspects among actors in different locales or environments of human horse relationships, Part III, with its emphasis on performance, practice and presentation, features the positioned or situated cultural complexities involved in depictions of past and present, processes of engendering masculinity and femininity, and subjectivity and objectivity in equestrian cultures as enveloped within more widely shared cultural meaning systems.

In the final Chapter 13, we (Maurstad and Davis) focus on how the contributors individually and collectively contribute to the emergent field of multispecies ethnography. In particular, we revisit the variety of horse human relationships discussed in the volume and rather than passively regard them as forms of we, co-beings, or entanglements we engage these relationships as dynamic forms of *intra-action*. By rephrasing these intra-actions as forms of biosocial encounters and/or biosocial becomings (Ingold 2013, 9), our goal is to advocate an approach that engages horses and humans not so much in terms of who they *are*, but in terms of what horses and humans *do* and experience as they collaborate and interact (in practice as well as meaning) to shape their selves.

Our aim in this introductory chapter is to provide a wide ranging literature review that targets a variety of audiences. These include riders or those who love and work with horses, academics and those interested in the more general field of human animal studies, and researchers who are part of this rich, diverse and growing body of academic literature on horses and humans. This review on the meaning of horses features a topical approach and offers a sampling of this body of literature and in the review process, situating our own book within it. By doing so, we contribute to the multiplicity of meanings that already exist in the field. As a whole, this book about the meaning of horses, human horse interactions, practices and relationships provides and develops temporally and cross culturally informed perspectives by bringing animals, in this case horses, to the center of analysis. The collection aims to identify and explore how a variety of nuances and entanglements, some concrete, some more ephemeral, come to influence horse human relationships.

References

Adelman, Miriam and Fernanda Moraes. 2008. "Breaking Their Way in: Women Jockeys at the Racetrack in Brazil." *Advances in Gender Research* 12: 99–123.

Adelman, Miriam and Jorge Knijnik. 2013. *Gender and Equestrian Sport: Riding around the World*. New York: Springer.

Allen, Michael. 1998. *Rodeo Cowboys in the North American Imagination*. Reno & Las Vegas: University of Nevada Press.

Anestis, Michael, Joye Anestis, Laci Zawilinski, Tiffany Hopkins and Scott Lilienfeld. 2014. "Equine-Related Treatments for Mental Disorders Lack Empirical Support: A Systematic Review of Empirical Investigations." *Journal of Clinical Psychology* 70(12): 1115–1132.

Argent, Gala. 2010. "Do the Clothes Make the Horse? Relationality, Roles and Statuses in Iron Age Inner Asia." *World Archaeology* 42(2): 157–174.

Argent, Gala. 2012. "Toward a Privileging of the Nonverbal: Communication, Corporeal Synchrony and Transcendence in Humans and Horses." In *Experiencing Animal Minds. An Anthology of Animal–Human Encounters*, edited by Julie Smith and Robert Mitchell, 111–128. New York: Columbia University Press.

Argent, Gala. (forthcoming). "Killing (Constructed) Horses: Interspecies Edlers, Empathy and Emotion, and the Pazyryk Horse Sacrifices." In *Ethnozooarchaeology: Global Perspectives*, edited by Lee. G. Broderick, forthcoming for 2015. Oxford: Oxbow Books Ltd.

Arluke, Arnold and Robert Bogden. 2014. "Taming the Wild: Rodeo as a Human–Animal Metaphor." In *Sport, Animals, and Society*, edited by James Gillett and Michelle Gilbert, 15–34. New York: Routledge Research in Sport, Culture and Society.

Birke, Lynda. 2004. "Dreaming of Pegasus, or Quin's Story." In *Horse Dreams: The Meaning of Horses in Women's Lives*, edited by Jan Fook, Susan Hawthorne and Renate Klein, 207–208. Melbourne: Spinifex Press.

Birke, Lynda. 2007. "Learning to Speak Horse: The Culture of Natural Horsemanship." *Society & Animals* 15(3): 217–239.

Birke, Lynda. 2008. "Talking about Horses: Control and Freedom in the World of Natural Horsemanship." *Society & Animals* 16: 107–126.

Birke, Lynda, Mette Bryld and Nina Lykke. 2004. "Animal Performances. An Exploration of Intersections between Feminist Science Studies and Studies of Human/Animal Relationships." *Feminist Theory* 5(2): 167–183.

Birke, Lynda, Joanna Hockenhull and Emma Creighton. 2010. "The Horse's Tale: Narratives of Caring for/about Horses." *Society & Animals* 18: 331–347.

Borneman, John. 1988. "Race, Ethnicity, Species, Breed: Totemism and Horse-Breed Classification in America." *Comparative Studies in Society and History* 30(1): 25–51.

Brandt, Keri. 2004. "A Language of Their Own: An Interactionist Approach to Human–Horse Communication." *Society & Animals* 12(4): 299–316.

Bryant, Jennifer. 2008. *Olympic Equestrian: A Century of International Horse Sport*. Lexington, KY: Eclipse Press.

Butler, Deborah. 2013. "Becoming 'One of the Lads': Women, Horse Racing and Gender in the United Kingdom." In *Gender and Equestrian Sport: Riding around the World*, edited by Miriam Adelman and Jorge Knijnik, 55–72. New York: Springer.

Cassidy, Rebecca. 2002. *The Sport of Kings: Kinship, Class and Thoroughbred Breeding in Newmarket*. Cambridge: Cambridge University Press.

Cassidy, Rebecca. 2003. "Turf Wars: Arab Dimensions to British Racehorse Breeding." *Anthropology Today* 19(3): 13–18.

Cassidy, Rebecca. 2007a. "Introduction: Domestication Reconsidered." In *Where the Wild Things Are Now: Domestication Reconsidered*, edited by Rebecca Cassidy and Molly Mullin, 1–26. Oxford: Berg.

Cassidy, Rebecca. 2007b. *Horse People: Thoroughbred Culture in Lexington and Newmarket*. Baltimore: Johns Hopkins University Press.

Cassidy, Rebecca. 2013. "Introduction." In *The Cambridge Companion to Horseracing*, edited by Rebecca Cassidy. 1–12. Cambridge: Cambridge University Press.

Chamberlin, J. Edward. 2006. *Horse: How the Horse Has Shaped Civilizations*. New York: Bluebridge.

Clark, Nigel. 2007. "Animal Interface: The Generosity of Domestication." In *Where the Wild Things Are Now: Domestication Reconsidered*, edited by Rebecca Cassidy and Molly Mullin, 49–70. Oxford: Berg.

Clutton-Brock, Juliet. 1992. *Horse Power: A History of the Horse and the Donkey in Human Societies*. Los Angeles: Natural History Museum Publications.

Coulter, Kendra. 2013. "Horse Power: Gender, Work and Wealth in Canadian Show Jumping." In *Gender and Equestrian Sport: Riding around the World*, edited by Miriam Adelman and Jorge Knijnik, 165–182. New York: Springer.

Coulter, Kendra. 2014. "Herds and Hierarchies: Class, Nature, and the Social Construction of Horses in Equestrian Culture." *Society & Animals* 22(2): 135–152.

Crawford, Scott. 2007. "Foxhunter and Red Rum as National Icons: Significant Equestrian Episodes in Post Second World War British Sports History." *Sport in History* 27(3): 487–504.

Dalke, Karen. 2010. "Mustang: The Paradox of Imagery." *Humanimalia* 1(2): 97–117.

Dashper, Katherine. 2012a. "Dressage Is Full of Queens! Masculinity and Sexuality within Equestrian Sport." *Sociology on Behalf of British Sociological Association* 46(6): 1109–1124. doi:. DOI: 10.1177/0038038512437898 (online article available at http://soc.sagepub.com/content/46/6/1109).

Dashper, Katherine. 2012b. "Together yet Still Not Equal? Sex Integration in Equestrian Sport." *Asia-Pacific Journal of Health, Sport and Physical Education* 3(3): 213–225.

Dashper, Katherine. 2013. "Beyond the Binary: Gender Integration in British Equestrian Sport." In *Gender and Equestrian Sport: Riding around the World*, edited by Miriam Adelman and Jorge Knijnik, 37–53. New York: Springer.

Dashper, Katherine. 2014. "Tools of the Trade or Part of the Family? Horses in Competitive Equestrian Sport." *Society & Animals* 22(4): 352–371.

Davis, Dona and Dorothy Davis. 2010. "Dualling Memories: Twinship and the Disembodiment of Identity." In *The Ethnographic Self as Resource: Writing Memory and Experience into Ethnography*, edited by Peter Collins and Anselma Gallinat, 129–149. Oxford: Berghahn.

Davis, Dona, Anita Maurstad and Sarah Dean. 2014. "'I'd Rather Wear Out than Rust Out': Autobiologies of Ageing Equestriennes." *Aging & Society*, doi 10.1017/S0144686X14001172, published online 4 November.

Davis, Dona, Anita Maurstad and Sarah Dean. 2015. "'My Horse Is My Therapist': The Medicalization of Pleasure among Women Equestrians." *Medical Anthropology Quarterly* 29(3): 298–315.

DeMello, M. 2012. *Animals and Society: An Introduction to Human–Animal Studies*. New York: University of Colombia Press.

Despret, Vinciane. 2004. "The Body We Care For: Figures of Anthropo-zoo-genesis." *Body & Society* 10(2–3): 111–134.

Digard, Jean-Pierre. 2003. *Une Histoire du cheval: art, technique, société* [A History of the Horse: Art, Technique and Society]: Arles: Acta Sud.

Ewers, John. 1955. *The Horse in Blackfoot Indian Culture: With Comparative Material from Other Western Tribes*. Washington, DC: The Smithsonian Institution Press.

Forsberg, Lena and Ulla Tebelious. 2011. "The Riding School as a Site for Gender Identity Construction among Swedish Teenage Girls." *World Leisure Journal* 53(1): 42–56.

Fox, Kate. 2005. *The Racing Tribe: Watching the Horse Watchers*. London: Metro.

Fox, Rebecca. 2006. "Animal Behaviors, Post Human Lives: Everyday Negotiations of the Animal–Human Divide in Pet-Keeping." *Social and Cultural Geography* 7(4): 525–537.

Game, Ann. 2001. "Riding: Embodying the Centaur." *Body & Society* 7(4): 1–12.

Gilbert, Michelle. 2014. "Young Equestrians: The Horse Stable as a Cultural Space." In *Sport, Animals, and Society*, edited by James Gillett and Michelle Gilbert, 233–250. New York: Routledge.

Gilbert, Michelle and James Gillett. 2012. "Equine Athletes and Interspecies Sport." *International Review for the Sociology of Sport* 47(5): 632–643.

Gilbert, Michelle and James Gillett. 2014. "Sport, Animals and Society." In *Sport, Animals, and Society*, edited by James Gillett and Michelle Gilbert, 3–14. New York: Routledge.

Goodwin, D. 1999. "The Importance of Ethology in Understanding the Behavior of the Horse." *Equine Veterinary Journal* 28: 15–19.

Haines, Francis. 1938. "The Northward Spread of Horses among Plains Indians." *American Anthropologist* 40(3): 429–437.

Hamilton, Jennifer and Aimee Placas. 2011. "'Anthropology Becoming…'? The 2010 Sociocultural Anthropology Year in Review." *American Anthropologist* 113(2): 246–261.

Hansen, Natalie. 2014. "Embodied Communication: The Poetics and Politics of Riding." In *Sport, Animals, and Society*, edited by James Gillett and Michelle Gilbert, 251–267. New York: Routledge.

Haraway, Donna. 2008. *When Species Meet*. Minneapolis, MN: University of Minnesota Press.

Hearne, Vicki. 1986 [2007]. *Adam's Task: Calling Animals by Name*. New York: Skyhorse Publishing.

Helgadóttir, Guðrún. 2006. "The Culture of Horsemanship and Horse-based Tourism in Iceland." *Current Issues in Tourism* 9(6): 535–548.

Helmer, James. 1991. "The Horse in Backstretch Culture." *Qualitative Sociology* 14(2): 175–195.

Hurn, Samantha. 2012. *Humans and Other Animals: Cross-Cultural Perspectives on Human–Animal Interactions*. London: Pluto Press.

Ingold, Tim. 2013. "Prospect." In *Biosocial Becomings: Integrating Social and Biological Anthropology*, edited by Tim Ingold and Gisli Pálsson, 1–22. Cambridge: Cambridge University Press.

Ingold, Tim and Gisli Pálsson. 2013. *Biosocial Becomings: Integrating Social and Biological Anthropology*. Cambridge: Cambridge University Press

Keaveney, Susan M. 2008. "Equines and Their Human Companions." *Journal of Business Research* 61(5): 444–454.

Kelekna, Pita. 2009. *The Horse in Human History*. Cambridge: Cambridge University Press.

Kirksey, S. Eben and Stefan Helmreich. 2010. "The Emergence of Multispecies Ethnography." *Cultural Anthropology* 25(4): 545–576.

Knijnik, Jorge. 2013. "The Black, the White, the Green: Fluid Masculinities in Brazilian Dressage." In *Equestrian Sport: Riding around the World*, edited by Miriam Adelman and Jorge Knijnik, 183–194. New York: Springer.

Kruger, Katherine and James Serpell. 2010. "Animal-Assisted Interventions in Mental Health: Definitions and Theoretical Foundations." In *Handbook on Animal Assisted Therapy: Theoretical Foundations and Guidelines for Practice*, edited by Aubrey Fine, 33–48. Amsterdam: Elsevier.

Landry, Donna. 2001. "Horsey and Persistently Queer: Imperialism, Feminism and Bestiality." *Textual Practice* 15(3): 467–485.

Larnby, Marie and Susanne Hedenborg. 2014. "(Dis)abled Riders and Equestrian Sports." In *Sport, Animals, and Society*, edited by James Gillett and Michelle Gilbert, 192–208. New York: Routledge.

Latimer, Joanna and Lynda Birke. 2009. "Natural Relations: Horses, Knowledge, and Technology." *The Sociological Review* 57(1): 1–27.

Lawrence, Elizabeth. 1982. *Rodeo: An Anthropologist Looks at the Wild and the Tame*. Chicago: University of Chicago Press.

Lawrence, Elizabeth. 1985. *Hoofbeats and Society: Studies of Human–Horse Interactions*. Bloomington, IN: University of Indiana Press.

Lawrence, Elizabeth. 1988. "Horses in Society." In *Animals and People Sharing the World*, edited by Andrew Rowen, 95–114. Hanover: University Press of New England.

Maurstad, Anita, Dona Davis, and Sarah Cowles. 2013. "Co-being and Intra-action in Horse–Human Relationships: A Multi-species Ethnography of Be(com)ing Human and Be(com)ing Horse." *Social Anthropology* 21(3): 322–335.

McShane, Clay and Joel Tarr. 2006. "The Horse as Technology – The City Animal as Cyborg." In *Horses and Humans: The Evolution of Human–Equine Relationships*, edited by Sandra Olsen, Susan Grant, Alice Choyke and László Bartosiewicz, 365–375. Oxford: Archeopress.

Michalon, Jerome. 2014. "From Sport to Therapy: The Social Stakes in the Rise of Equine-Assisted Activities." In *Sport, Animals, and Society*, edited by James Gillett and Michelle Gilbert, 85–100. New York: Routledge.

Murray, Jane, E. R. Singer, K. L. Morgan, C. J. Proudman and N. P. French. 2005. "Risk Factors for Cross-Country Horse Falls at One Day Events and Three Day Events." *Veterinary Journal* 170(3): 318–324.

Nance, Susan. 2014. "A Star Is Born to Buck: Animal Celebrity and the Marketing of Professional Rodeo." In *Sport, Animals, and Society*, edited by James Gillett and Michelle Gilbert, 173–191. New York: Routledge.

Odberg, F. O. and M. Bouissou. 1999. "The Development of Equestrianism from the Baroque Period to the Present Day and Its Consequences for Welfare of Horses." *Equine Veterinary Journal* 31 (S28): 26–30.

Olsen, Sandra. 1995. "Introduction." In *Horses through Time*, edited by Sandra Olsen, 3–9. Boulder, CO: Rinehart Institute.

Olsen, Sandra. 2006a. "Introduction." In *Horses and Humans: The Evolution of Human-Equine Relationships*, edited by Sandra Olsen, Susan Grant, Alice Choyke and László Bartosiewicz. 1–8. Oxford: Archeopress.

Olsen, Sandra. 2006b. "Early Horse Domestication: Weighing the Evidence." In *Horses and Humans: The Evolution of Human-Equine Relationships*, edited by Sandra Olsen, Susan Grant, Alice Choyke and László Bartosiewicz. 81–114. Oxford: Archeopress.

Olsen, Sandra, Susan Grant, Alice Choyke and László Bartosiewicz. 2006. *Horses and Humans: The Evolution of Human–Equine Relationships*. Oxford: Archeopress.

Olsen, Sandra, Susan Grant, Alice Choyke and László Bartosiewicz. 2008. "Women's Attire and Possible Sacred Role in 4th Millennium Northern Kazakhstan." In *Are*

All Warriors Male?, edited by Katheryn Linduff and Karen Rubinson. 35–51. Walnut Creek, CA: Alta Mira Press.

Patton, Paul. 2003. "Language, Power and the Training of Horses." In *Zoontologies: The Question of the Animal*, edited by Cary Wolfe, 83–99. Minneapolis, MN: University of Minnesota Press.

Penaloza, Lisa. 2011. "Consuming the American West: Animating Cultural Meaning at a Stock Show and Rodeo." *Journal of Consumer Research* 28(4): 369–398.

Raber, Kate and Treva Tucker. 2005. *The Culture of the Horse: Status and Discipline in the Early Modern World*. New York: Palgrave.

Riedi, Eliza. 2006. "Brains or Polo? Equestrian Sport, Army Reform and the Gentlemanly Officer Tradition, 1900–1914." *Journal of the Society for Army Historical Research* 84: 236–253.

Rollin, Bernard. 1966. "Rodeo and Recollection: Applied Ethics and Western Philosophy." *Journal of the Philosophy of Sport* 1(23): 19.

Rose, Dan. 1990. "Quixote's Library and Pragmatic Discourse: Toward Understanding the Culture of Capitalism." *Anthropological Quarterly* 64(4): 155–168.

Serpell, James. 2003. "Anthropomorphism and Anthropomorphic Selection – Beyond the Cute Response." *Society & Animals* 11(1): 83–100.

Shnirelman, Victor and Sandra Olsen. 1995. "Hooves across the Steppes: The Kazak Life Style." In *Horses through Time*, edited by Sandra Olsen, 131–152. Boulder, CO: Rinehart Institute.

Smith, Stephen. 2014. "Human–Horse Partnerships: The Discipline of Dressage." In *Sport, Animals, and Society*, edited by James Gillett and Michelle Gilbert, 127–148. New York: Routledge.

Thompson, Kirrilly. 2011. "Theorizing Rider–Horse Relations: An Ethnographic Illustration of the Centaur Metaphor in the Spanish Bullfight." In *Theorizing Animals: Rethinking Humanimal Relations*, edited by Nik Taylor and Tania Signal, 221–253. Leiden: Brill.

Thompson, Kirrilly. 2013. "Cojones and Rejones: Multiple Ways of Experiencing, Expressing and Interpreting Gender in the Spanish Mounted Bullfight (Rejoneo)." In *Gender and Equestrian Sport: Riding around the World*, edited by Miriam Adelman and Jorge Knijnik. 127–148. New York: Springer.

Thompson, Kirrilly and Miriam Adelman. 2013. "Epilogue: A Research Agenda for Putting Gender through Its Paces." In *Gender and Equestrian Sport: Riding around the World*, edited by Miriam Adelman and Jorge Knijnik. 195–211. New York: Springer.

Thompson, Kirrilly and Lynda Birke. 2014. "'The Horse Has Got to Want to Help': Human–Animal Habituses and Networks of Relationality in Amateur Show Jumping." In *Sport, Animals, and Society*, edited by James Gillett and Michelle Gilbert, 69–84. New York: Routledge.

Tuan, Yi-Fu. 1984. *Dominance and Affection: The Making of Pets*. New Haven, CT: Yale University Press.

Tymowski, Gabriela. 2014. "The Virtue of Compassion: Animals in Sport, Hunting as Sport, and Entertainment." In *Sport, Animals, and Society*, edited by James Gillett and Michelle Gilbert, 140–154. New York: Routledge.

West, Daune and D. Francisco de Bragança. 2012. "A Systemic Approach to Eliciting and Gathering the Expertise of a 'Knowledge Guardian': An Application of the Appreciative Inquiry Method to the Study of Classical Dressage." *Systemic Practice and Action Research* 25(3): 241–260.

Wipper, Audrey. 2000. "The Partnership: The Horse–Rider Relationship in Eventing." *Symbolic Interaction* 23(1): 47–70.

Wissler, Clark. 1914. "The Influence of the Horse in the Development of Plains Culture." *American Anthropologist* 16(1): 1–25.

Wolfe, Cary. 2010. *What Is Posthumanism?* Minneapolis, MN: University of Minnesota Press.

York, Jan, Cindy Adams and Nick Cody. 2008. "Therapeutic Value of Equine–Human Bonding in Recovery from Trauma." *Anthrozoos* 21(1): 17–30.

Young, Kevin and Brittany Gerber. 2014. "Necropsian Nights: Animal, Sport, Civility and the Calgary Stampede." In *Sport, Animals, and Society*, edited by James Gillett and Michelle Gilbert, 155–172. New York: Routledge.

Part I

Commodification and Identity

2 From Horses to Jesus

Saving Souls in the Transition from Pagan to Christian Scandinavia

Kristin Armstrong Oma

The mythology of the past has an afterlife as one of several frames of reference and identity for the Western world, and is even formative for deep-seated current practices, such as the common unease surrounding consumption of horsemeat in Norway and the United Kingdom. Pagan Scandinavia is brought back to life not only through the sagas of the Icelanders, but also by way of magnificent archaeological finds. Lately, silver screen productions such as *Vikings* and *Thor* are giving us their very own spin of how to understand the world of these women and men from the not-so-distant past.

By probing into both the literary sources and the archaeological material, we are able to go beyond the surface of the myths of marauding Northmen and looters and touch at some of their core beliefs, deeply seated in their pagan worldview. The horse has proven to be a fitting vehicle for doing so. In untangling the meaning of horses, the horses of the past have a role to play. By way of their agency, horses co-authored the lifeworld of the pagan Scandinavian past (Armstrong Oma 2011).

In pagan Scandinavia, horses as real-life companions with spiritual properties and magical abilities hold great time-depth, probably from their introduction in the Bronze Age (1800 BCE; see Armstrong Oma 2013; Kristoffersen and Armstrong Oma 2008, 60–61) until the onset of Christianity around 900–1030 CE. Throughout this period, horses lived both with humans inside their longhouses (Nielsen 2002) and also in the wild (Armstrong Oma 2011, 55–57; Sundkvist 2001, 2004) and they accompanied and transported humans through the dangerous wilderness. Throughout the Iron Age (500 BCE–1000 CE) horses – real or symbolic – also accompanied the deceased in graves, possibly transporting the dead from the world of the living to the world of the dead. In Norse mythology, there are several separate places where the dead could go: realms of death are Niflheim and Helheim, and dead warriors could go to Valheim (Aukrust 1995). According to pagan beliefs, consuming horseflesh or depositing horses or tokens of them in graves ensured the help of horses in traversing spheres that would normally not communicate, such as the different worlds of divine beings or the borders between life and the worlds of the dead.

With the onset of Christianity from late 900 CE and onwards, the transitional role of the horse was ritually terminated by the Church and the state. Pagan burials were banned according to the oldest of the law texts, the Gulathing law, and likewise the consumption of horseflesh. Eating horsemeat on Fridays, on feast days and during the fast was punished with loss of all lands and property and banishment from the kingdom. I therefore contend that the authorities of the new, fledgling states tried to eradicate the horse cult since it was in direct conflict with the new ideology – Christ the savior.

To set the scene I explore what kind of ontological status horses had, and how their agency lent them a particular status in two related, yet different, historical situations: Pagan Iron Age tribal Scandinavia (500 BCE-ca. 1000 CE) and the subsequent Christian early state (1000 CE onwards). I will briefly set out how ontological status emerges from a web of meaning, before I delve into how those webs of meaning changed in the transition from pagan practices to Christianity as Norway was at the cusp of becoming a fledgling state. Further, I will explore how horses came to play a crucial part in the political power struggle that ensued. The transition itself took place during the Viking period (800–1030 CE); however, I will go further back in time into the earlier parts of the Iron Age to set out how horses and their entangled webs of relationality were manifested materially.

The data are discussed with regard to new theoretical approaches to human horse relationships found in the cross disciplinary field of human animal studies that include sociology, philosophy and biology (e.g., Argent 2010, 2012; Birke et al. 2004; Brandt 2004; Evans and Franklin 2010; Game 2001; Hearne 1987; Thompson 2011). I will briefly outline the long-term development of the roles of horses in the Iron Age to investigate the enduring structures that horses are part of. Following this, I will attempt to investigate the core of the human horse relationship.

Ontology in the Scandinavian Iron Age

The Scandinavian Iron Age (500 BCE–1030 CE) spans some 1500 years, and was a period of great changes and upheavals. Still, there were stable elements to society. Notable amongst these is what I call a flat ontology. By this, I mean that there probably was no hierarchy of being such as that which was established at the onset of Christianity. The rationale that was underlying society, ways of living and beliefs was based upon some common structuring principles.

Ontology is the study of, and inquiry into, that which is. By this I mean that it grapples with the very foundational building blocks of the world – and moreover, how these building blocks are perceived by different cultures. Ontology is, then, not by its own nature fixed and stable, but it appears so by the way it is situated in time-space, within its own historical-cultural context. An often discussed example is the Cartesian worldview that considered humans as beings with souls whereas animals were seen to be like machines, *automaton*.

Recently, there has been a return to inquiry into ontology in anthropology, and to a minor degree in archaeology – frequently referred to as the ontological turn. Proponents of this school of thought have emerged from the outside of Anglo-American anthropology, foremost by way of Eduardo Vivieiros de Castro (1998, 2004), Bruno Latour, with his online project www.modesofexistence.org (see also Latour 2013), and Eduardo Kohn (2013). For example, in his groundbreaking book *How Forests Think*, Kohn (2013) explores ontology as an interconnected web of emergent meanings. It is the web of meanings that give ontological status to beings. This is often termed a relational ontology, meaning that ontological status springs from the sum of threads in the web – what Ingold (2011) refers to as meshwork. A bounce on the web travels along the threads and affects various entities.

A core idea is that the nature of the world (ontology) is constructed just as much as knowledge (epistemology) is constructed. In a discussion article on the ontological turn, Fowles (Alberti et al. 2011, 898) argues that ontology springs from an understanding of origins and that ontology is anchored in narrative; "The world is as it has come to be." Instrumental to this development has been Viveiros de Castro's (1998, 2004) work on perspectivism amongst Amerindians. In his case studies, he is able to demonstrate that humans and animals are interchangeable, and that humans can take on the perspective of animals (i.e., be in the world through the body of an animal). Thus, Amerindians perceive animals as possessing an inner, human form that is hidden by their bestial bodily form. In comparison with the Cartesian worldview, the nature of being is turned on its head: humans exist in and from animal form, and animals exist in human form, and the diversity of animal bodies has evolved out of humanness. Similarly, the Norse myth of origins recounts how the world and all beings in it was made from the bestial shape of the giant Yme, who lived off milk from the cow Audhumbla (Holtsmark 1989). I argue that de Castro's finding opens up the field of ontological inquiry and makes possible a range of understandings of agency, personhood and ontological status in all societies, past and present. I follow Alberti et al. (2011, 900), "I conceive of ontological inquiry as a means to insert a difference (...) in the present and in our accounts of pasts."

Taking other-than-human animals seriously as participants in forming relationships (e.g., Birke and Hockenhull 2012) entails not collapsing them within a single frame of reference (i.e., as The Animals). Although animal is useful as a broad category, to truly understand and appreciate their different roles, I suggest that their ontological status within historically specific societies should be studied. By ontological status I mean how the different beings' place in the web of life was understood and formed by the emergence of particular – acted out as well as materialized – relationships. Returning to the idea of meshwork (Ingold 2011), relating – and shaping ontological statuses – emerges out of the lines that connect the web. The way life-worlds are and were co-shaped between entities lent those entities their ontological status, by mutually becoming in a back-and-forth interchange of action, situatedness and conviviality.

Horses in the pagan world

There is evidence to suggest that horses held a particular ontological status in the Iron Age, with the ability to communicate with humans and wield their agency in conjunction with humans, as well as bonding deeply at individual levels. Both literary sources and archaeological evidence suggest great proximity between humans and horses.

Horses were first introduced as domesticates to Scandinavia in the early Bronze Age. During the Bronze Age, it became increasingly obvious that horses were given a special status compared to other animals (e.g., Armstrong Oma 2013; Kaul 2004; Ullén 1994, 1996; Østmo 1997). However, horses are best known from Iron Age contexts (i.e., 500 BCE–1000 CE). Throughout this period, horses appear in a wide array of archaeological contexts, including bog sacrifices, ritual contexts and graves, as well as on iconography and in the Norse textual sources. Within these categories, a rich variety is found. I have previously pieced together the material pertaining to horses in a contextual analysis (Armstrong Oma 2011; Oma 2000, 2001, 2004, 2005), and I found that horses are present as the primary sacrificial animal in large collective bog sacrifices, in smaller, more private sacrificial contexts, and as a gift to the deceased in graves. Further they are depicted on jewelry such as brooches, bracteates, on fittings and trappings, in many cases hidden in the Animal Styles, on pictorial or rune stones, rock carvings, and on woodwork and textile where such has been conserved. The Eddas and the earliest laws inform us about the horse and the structures surrounding it, and give valuable insights into how horses were used and also beliefs attached to them. In summary, the horse appears in sundry sources through a long span of time. Comparing the various material categories and pieces of information will disclose the structures underlying beliefs and ways of living as well as the ontological status of horses.

I have previously argued (Armstrong Oma 2011; Oma 2000, 2001, 2004, 2005) that horses held a particular ontological status throughout the Iron Age, from 500 BCE to 1000 CE. The foundation of this status was their symbolic role as transporters from one realm to another, from the world of humans (Middle-earth) to the different abodes of the gods, and from the realm of life to the worlds of the dead. Their role as transporters can be extrapolated from depositional patterns such as horse offerings in graves and wetlands, and the way horses are depicted in art. The archaeological data is presented below. Further, the Eddic poems tell of horses as the only means to cross the dangerous in-between zones, the wilderness. I will present these findings briefly to highlight the fundamental nature of the transition from a pagan to Christian worldview.

A general reading of both the written sources concerning the Iron Age, as well as the landscape and pattern of resources used, shows a society that was divided by borders (Fabech 1994; Hedeager 1999, 2011; Lund 2008; Wiker 2000). Theories on liminality inform us that borders are dangerous areas, and can be difficult and hazardous to cross (Turner 1967; van Gennep 1960). This reflects a fear of being stuck in the twilight, the "grey zone," betwixt and between. In the Eddas this zone is often described as *Mørkskog*, Mirkwood, which is a very dangerous place to cross. The only way of doing so is to ride through it; people never simply walk through. The Eddas describe the passage of such borders as being performed by horses. The only safe means of passage is to be carried across by a horse. This reflects a fear that is well founded; in those days wolves, bears and other wild animals were roaming the forest. Crossing such liminal zones is something that really sets the horse apart from the other animals. In Norse folklore horses are often given the role of the pathfinder; they will always find the way home. These capabilities would explain why they attained such a high status, since this quality is important to possess and control.

A relational entity: Communicating with the divine by wetland sacrifices

Such prowess could explain why horses are the most frequently sacrificed animals in the liminal zones of bogs and lakes in the early Iron Age; examples are the wetland areas of Skedemosse (Hagberg 1963) and Rislev (Ferdinand and Ferdinand 1961; Møhl 1961), and also war booty sacrifices in bogs such as Ilerup Ådal (Ilkjær 1997), Thorsbjerg (Randsborg 1995) and Ejsbøl Nord (Ørsnes 1984). Remains from other domestic animals are also recurrently found, but these are represented by skeletal elements from meat-rich parts of the body, and the bones are frequently split for marrow extraction. In the pre-Roman period a few such deposits are found – for example, the bog sacrifice of Hjortspring on the Danish island of Als, where a whole horse was deposited in the bog and a tibia placed in its mouth, with the famous boat overlying (Randsborg 1995; Rosenberg 1937).

The early Iron Age spans a period of roughly 1000 years (500 BCE–550 CE) and the people left a rich legacy of objects and contextual data. Throughout this period, remains of horses are found in wetland areas, sacrificed in bogs and lakes. A vast array of material culture has been found in wetland sacrifices, ranging from braids of human hair to butter, wagons, statuettes of deities and boats. Most common, however, are skeletal remains both from humans and animals (Hagberg 1963; Monikander 2006; Møhl 1961). Regarding animal remains, horses are frequently found, but their pattern of deposition sets them apart from the other animals. In many instances, the skeletal remains of horses stem from the skull, the lower legs and sometimes the tail bone. In several bog sacrifices in Denmark, finds of these skeletal elements from horses have been found in lakes where other animals also have been deposited (Ferdinand and Ferdinand 1961; Møhl 1961), reminiscent of a larger, European tradition of sacrificing heads and hooves of horses (Klindt-Jensen 1967; Mallory 1981; Piggott 1962). A particular aspect regarding the bones from horses is that they are found in closed contexts (i.e., that the bones are positioned on top of each other). The leg bones (phalanges) are found under the skull, and in some instances the tongue was cut out and the tail cut off and placed inside the mouth (Ferdinand 1961; Møhl 1961). The other animal remains have drifted apart, indicating that whole carcasses have been deposited, and the skeletal elements have drifted apart according to movements in the lake after decomposition. The excavator (Møhl 1961) suggests that the horse bones were placed in their particular position and then possibly wrapped up in the horse's hides. This would explain why the bones were found together.

Water is an element that is particularly laden with mystery and is often seen as an entrance to another world. Sacrificing these particular parts in bogs and lakes demonstrates a will to communicate with the gods and, further, to traverse these borders.

Thus, the pagan Norse women and men handled remains from horses with particular care. This could be because they revered the horse above the other animals, and goes some way towards substantiating a claim made by the Roman historian Tacitus. In *Germania*, he wrote about German tribes around the time of the start of the CE, and in a passage on horses, he made it clear that in pagan Germania, horses held a particular position:

> [...] but it is peculiar to them to derive admonitions and presages from horses also. Certain of these animals, milk-white, and untouched by earthly labor, are pastured at the public expense in the sacred woods and groves. These [...] are accompanied by the priest, and king, or chief person of the community, who attentively observe their manner of neighing and snorting; and no kind of augury is more credited, not only among the populace, but among the nobles and priests. For the latter consider themselves as the ministers of the gods, and the horses, as privy to the divine will.
>
> (Book 1, verse 68–69)

In light of this text it is likely that the sacrifice of horses, and the particular treatment of their bones, was meant to lead the horses into the otherworld to send messages to the gods. Thus humans, in their need to reach out to the powers beyond, put forth the horse as the one that traveled along the lines of the web and acted as a channel for human–divine relationships.

Voyages to otherworlds: In graves and on art

This practice did not entirely end around 500 CE, but became less common. From ca. 500 CE until 1000 CE, horses became embedded in another kind of journey into the otherworld, namely burial rituals. Infrequently, tokens of horses such as horse equipment or spurs have also been found in graves prior to this period, but in small numbers and faunal remains occur merely on a sporadic basis. However, from 550 CE onwards, either faunal remains from horses or pieces of horse equipment frequently follow men and women in their graves. In Sweden, horses are found in the grand boat graves in the Mälar Valley from 500–700 CE (Arwidsson 1954, 1977; Arrhenius 1983). In many instances, horses have been killed by a blow to the head and are placed close by the bows of the boats, mostly placed in the same directions as the boats, thus indicating their role in an imagined journey into the otherworld. The horses bounced on the web and leapt along the threads that joined the different spheres.

This role of traveler and traverser is also glimpsed in Iron Age art that depicts horses, such as on freestanding pieces of jewelry. The brooches with horses usually depict them as being in motion, as going somewhere. One beautiful example is the exquisite Veggerslev horse from ca. 600 CE, found in Veggerslev on Djursland in Denmark (Gjessing 1943). Also in the so-called Animal Styles, both around 400–550 CE, and later, in the Viking period (800–1000 CE), horses appear to be rendered in a state of transformation, moving from one state of being to another (Kristoffersen 1995, 2010). Such art is often found in the graves.

Similar to the sacrificial contexts in the early Iron Age, heads and hooves are found in Viking period graves (Armstrong Oma 2011; Braathen 1989; Meling 2014). The head is very often found. Decapitation seems to have been a common way of fitting horses into cramped grave chambers. This indicates that parts of the horse could stand in for their symbolic ontological status as travelers along the web. High-quality harnesses with fittings made of gold, silver or bronze are found in a number of contexts, such as in the Gausel graves. Frost nails found close to the dead often represent the hooves. Towards the end of the Viking age the practice of sacrificing horses in graves becomes standardized, before it disappears at about 1050 (Armstrong Oma 2011; Braathen 1989).

In the graves, either whole or parts of horses are found, as well as horse bits and other equipment pertaining to horse riding or horse and driver, such as spurs, studs for hooves (for use in winter) and various bits belonging to the saddle or the wagon. There is no real logic to what goes in the grave. One horse might have one frost nail and two harnesses. Tree stirrups may also be thrown into the grave. It seems to be a case of both *pars pro toto*, and you give what you have.

These archaeological finds present us with a Norse pagan universe as one of beliefs in the powers beyond, and in which certain beings can communicate with those powers, the horse being one of these. But how did humans and horses, from the perspective of interspecies relationality, connect to one another in real life? What do such stories look like?

Becomings with horses

The evocative Norse Eddic poems present several narratives that reveal structures pertaining to the pagan Norse perceptions of the inner lives of horses. A poignant example is the death of Sigurd, the dragonslayer, as it is described in the poems "The Second Lay of Guðrún" and "Fragment of a Sigurd Lay." In "The Second Lay of Guðrún," verses 4 and 5, Guðrún recounts how it happened that she found out that her husband Sigurd was dead:

> 4. From the Thing ran Grani with thundering feet,
> But thence did Sigurth himself come never;
> Covered with sweat was the saddle-bearer,
> Wont the warrior's weight to bear.

Guðrún held the rein of the horse and began to cry, as she understood what had happened:

> 5. Weeping I sought with Grani to speak,
> With tear-wet cheeks[1] for the tale I asked;
> The head of Grani was bowed to the grass,
> The steed knew well his master was slain.
> (The Poetic Edda 1936b)

Also in the poem "Fragment of a Sigurd Lay," the following line in verse 7 refers to Grani mourning Sigurd: "The gray horse mourns by his master dead" (The Poetic Edda 1936a).

The story demonstrates that human horse bonds were deemed possible, and that horses were not only seen as sentient, but also held the potential agency to both have and express strong feelings. The description of how Grani ran to Guðrún and grieved in front of her is remarkable. This reveals a belief in horses having the ability to understand human relationships. Grani seeks out the wife of Sigurd to mourn together with her, and to thus facilitate a mutual recognition of the love they both bore for Sigurd. It is a recognition in which they can find solace, as two persons who loved this man deeply and miss him dearly. A similar argument has been proposed by Gala Argent (2010, 162), suggesting that "horses can and do bond deeply with specific people; horses, too, can choose particular people as their 'person of a lifetime'." This bonding is exemplified by the account of Alexander the Great and his renowned horse Bucephalos.

The telling of Grani's reaction could be seen as an example of anthropomorphism. Guðrún mourns with the horse, and she might project her own feelings onto Grani. The real truth is beyond reach, but clearly, this points to a perception of an emotional component to the human horse relationship in the Scandinavian Iron Age, considering that the mourners have placed horses – or tokens of them – with their dead (Armstrong Oma 2011; Oma 2000, 2001, 2004).

The Christianization of Norway: From tribes to states

Having established that the horse was vital to transcend liminal zones and boundaries between the different worlds, I will now turn specifically to the historical events of Norway, and the way in which the horse as a living symbol was used to make a stand of allegiance in a political struggle for power.

Pagan Norway consisted of a mosaic of tribal communities. In this society, horses held a very special role as those who transported the dead into the realm of death. Networks of chieftains – earls – who pledged allegiance to each other through the practice of gift giving and a strong code of honor upheld this society. In the centuries leading up to the religious conversion in 1030 CE, various chieftains tried to take control over larger areas, with varying success. According to the Icelandic bard Snorre Sturlason, who famously narrated these events, none managed to sufficiently consolidate their power to retain enduring kingship beyond a few generations.

With the onset of Christianity, such men who sought power by way of kingship finally possessed a framework for seizing and holding power on a more permanent basis. In Norway, Olav Haraldsson, after his death known as Saint Olav, gathered all of Norway into one kingdom and violently enforced Christianity as the new religion of the state. The earliest Christian law, the law of the Gulathing, demonstrates how pagan practices were either forbidden by law or usurped by Christianity. For example, the pagan Yule *blót*, in which horses were sacrificed, eaten and their blood sprinkled inside pagan shrines and also on the religious practitioners (The Saga of Håkon the Good), became the Christian Christmas. On such feast days, the Gulathing law strictly forbade the consumption of horseflesh: "he who consumes horse flesh on feast days or during the fast, shall forfeit his lands and all possessions and hereforewith be banished from the country."[2]

The fundamental differences between the pagan religion and Christianity concerning ontological worldviews become disclosed in the meeting between them, and in the changes that emerged as a result of the conversion. The era of the Vikings ended with their conversion to Christianity, and a set of laws forbade the religious practices of the Iron Age society. Several such rules are known from the Gulathing law. In order to successfully convert the people to the new religion, the Iron Age cults and religious practices had to be eradicated. The people must stop their feasting on horseflesh in honor of the old gods, Thor and Odin.

Håkon the Good and the *blót*

I will relate one story from Snorre Sturlason to demonstrate how horses came to play such a poignant role during the conversion to Christianity. The

Saga of Håkon the Good is our foremost literary source of the phenomenon known as *blót* – religious feasting. *Blót* was a feast devoted to the gods and the communication with them. It could be a large communal rite, feasting for a bountiful harvest and for peace: "*till àrs ok friðar*" (for a good and peaceful year). Mostly the feasting was on horseflesh, which was cooked in large pots and consumed during the *blót*.

The English king Aethelstan fostered Håkon the Good. Håkon's foster father converted him to Christianity and taught him how to be a good Christian. When Håkon returned to Norway, he found himself in a religious minefield. His saga relates how Håkon was frustrated by the practice of *blót* and its frequency, and he wanted no part in it. Rather, he observed the Christian customs, such as keeping the Sabbath and fasting on Fridays. At the same time, he attempted to keep his head down so as to not get involved with the battle between the pagan religion and Christianity. But he did not always succeed in staying out of trouble. One of the earls, Sigurd Ladejarl, held great *blóts*, gathering all of the farmers from wide and far. Horses and cattle were butchered and the blood was gathered up in large cauldrons. A sort of wisp was used to sprinkle the blood on the walls of the shrine, and the walls of the stables, leaving the walls red with blood. One winter Håkon the Good arrived during such a *blót*. Håkon would normally try to sneak off and eat in another house, but the men refused him this. Eating together was an act of social recognition. The men made Håkon sit in the high seat and demanded that he join the party. The first day the king was bound to drink to Odin, but got away with it by marking his cup with a cross. The following day was trickier:

> The next day, when the people sat down to table, the farmers pressed the king strongly to eat of horseflesh; and as he would on no account do so, they wanted him to drink of the soup; and as he would not do this, they insisted he should at least taste the gravy; and on his refusal they were going to lay hands on him. Earl Sigurd came and made peace among them, by asking the king to hold his mouth over the handle of the kettle, upon which the fat smoke of the boiled horse-flesh had settled itself; and the king first laid a linen cloth over the handle, and then gaped over it, and returned to the high seat; but neither party was satisfied with this.
>
> (*Håkon the Good's Saga*, Chapter 18)

This conflict between Håkon the Good and the farmers escalated until Håkon was bound to desert his mission of Christianization. The text recounts the great resistance to Christianity amongst the Norwegians. Yet in the long run, Christianity was victorious. This story about Håkon the Good serves as an example of how horses and horseflesh came to represent and embody the pagan practices in this conflict between religions. To Håkon, horseflesh was the pinnacle of everything pagan, and he did not want to contaminate his body by allowing horseflesh to pass his lips.

After the conversion to Christianity, any kind of *blót* was forbidden. As mentioned above, this prohibition is set down in the Gulathing law. This law is the oldest that is known from Norway; it dates back to the Viking period and is thus originally a pagan law (the final part of the Iron Age, ca. 800–1030 CE), but the version we know dates from the early Middle Ages, from the fledgling Christian state. It clearly has a Christian orientation, and refers to deeply embedded Christian institutions. It acts as a counter-weight to the pagan religion, as to how paganism is narrated in the Saga of Håkon the Good.

Consuming horseflesh became strictly forbidden. Simply consuming horseflesh meant that a fine must be paid to the bishop, as well as a confession given. But, as outlined above, eating horseflesh on feast days and particularly during Lent meant the loss of property and banishment. It is compared to the pagan custom of setting babies out in the woods to die.

From horses to Jesus – the aftermath

Why were the pagan practices linked to horses outlawed? I claim that a comparison between the symbolic roles of horses in the pagan world and Christ in Christianity is enlightening and can lead to the heart of the matter (Armstrong Oma 2011; Oma 2000, 2001, 2004). The horse holds dominion over the cosmological landscape and traversing the boundaries between different spheres, the same as Jesus, who conquered death and came back from the dead. Each in their way, they both safeguard the passage into the realm of death. From this perspective it makes sense that rituals involving horses were forbidden by law, particularly considering the fact that the pagan religion was based upon practices rather than faith and confession. The practice of feasting on horseflesh to communicate with the gods and to place horses in graves to lead the dead to the otherworld was simultaneously an offense to, and a strategic undermining of, the Christian faith and the Holy Communion. The horse became a grave challenge to the Christian dogma, and a serious threat against the consolidation of Christianity. Not only did this ontological status of horses threaten the Church, but it also undermined the very foundation of the young state, founded as it was upon the Christian laws. Thus, the horse needed to give way to Jesus, who could not tolerate competition: "Thou shalt have no gods but me!" Thus, Jesus usurped the role as the mediator of boundaries, and of life and death.

Saving souls, by which I mean bringing the dead to the otherworld, was no longer the task of the swift steed. The relational ontology of pagan Scandinavia was renegotiated, and in this renegotiation, the horse lost his ground, the web was diverted so as to tame the importance of horses within the meshwork.

This is aptly demonstrated by the Gulathing law, which represents the young Norwegian state's official post-conversion stance towards the pagan religion. Consuming horses, the physical manifestation of their particular ontological status, was banned. However, there are other stories that allow us to glimpse other layers of society, probably closer to how the common people lived. One of these is known as Volsatottr, and is found in the medieval text known as Flateyarbok. It tells the tale of a strange custom in which a severed horse penis (named Volsi) was worshipped like a deity in a private household cult by all members of a family, presumably after the conversion to Christianity. In the story, Saint Olav happened to drop in on this family on one of his travels, and was shocked by this custom. Whether or not there is historical truth to this narrative, the text demonstrates that not all layers of society abandoned the old ways and the pagan world-order. Likewise, an archaeological find supports the practice of horse cults after the conversion. Faunal remains from Kaupang dating to the early medieval period have cut marks consistent with butchering. These bones are clearly the remains of meals (Betti 2007). It seems likely the symbolic role of horses, and with it, the ontological status as facilitator for change and crossing thresholds, lived on but in secret.

Nonetheless, the materialization of the ontology of Christianity, for example by way of burial, demonstrates that the ban on horses extended to dealing with death. No horses are found in medieval, Christian graves, following the Christian law that banned the custom of giving the dead grave goods. The consequence for the people was that they lost access to the powerful pathfinder between the worlds, and lost most of the ways to communicate with the divine. The people were robbed of the paraphernalia of the horse in their ritual practices. The Christian state was structured so that the clergy were responsible for communicating with the divine, and the common people could hear the word of the book, in a foreign language (Latin) on Sundays. The pagan meshwork, a system of beliefs and practices that was available to all by way of sacrifices, consuming horseflesh and placing tokens of horses in graves, crumbled. The divine was redefined and access to it restricted to an educated elite. Throughout this transition, the horse and the practices surrounding him became important symbols, and studying archaeological traces of practices demonstrates how horses' changing ontological status was tied up with greater historical changes in society.

Acknowledgments

Thanks a million to the editors for their very helpful comments. The research leading to these results has received funding from the Norway Financial Mechanism 2009–2014 under project contract no. EMP151.

Notes

1 In the original Norse *Guðrúnarkviða* II, it is ambiguous which of the two has tear-wet cheeks. Even though the English translator has chosen to let Guðrún's cheeks be covered in tears, two Norwegian translators understand the text as that Grani has tears in his eyes.
2 Translation by author.

References

Alberti Benjamin, Severin Fowles, Martin Holbraad, Yvonne Marshall, and Christopher Whitmore. 2011. "'Worlds Otherwise'. Archaeology, Anthropology and Ontological Difference." *Current Anthropology* 52(6): 896–912.

Argent, Gala. 2010. "Do the Clothes Make the Horse? Relationality, Roles and Statuses in Iron Age Inner Asia." *World Archaeology* 42(2): 157–174.

Argent, Gala. 2012. "Toward a Privileging of the Nonverbal: Communication, Corporeal Synchrony and Transcendence in Humans and Horses." In *Experiencing Animal Minds: An Anthology of Animal–Human Encounters*, edited by Julie A. Smith and Robert W. Mitchell, 111–128. New York: Columbia University Press.

Armstrong Oma, Kristin. 2011. *Hesten: en Magisk Følgesvenn i Nordisk Forhistorie* [The Horse: a Magical Companion in Nordic Prehistory]. Oslo, Norway: Cappelen Damm.

Armstrong Oma, Kristin. 2013. "Bronze Age Horses – beyond Dualist Explanations." In *Counterpoint: Essays in Archaeology and Heritage Studies in Honour of Professor Kristian Kristiansen*, edited by Sophie Bergerbrant and Serena Sabatini, 141–146. Oxford: Archaeopress.

Arrhenius, Birgit. 1983. "The Chronology of the Vendel Graves." In *Transactions of the Boat-Grave Symposium*, edited by Lamm, Jan Peder and Hans-Åke Nordström, 39–70. Stockholm, Sweden: Statens historiska museum.

Arwidsson, Greta. 1954. *Valsgärde 8*. Uppsala, Sweden.

Arwidsson, Greta. 1977. *Valsgärde 7*. Uppsala, Sweden.

Aukrust, Olav O. 1995. *Dødsrikets Verdenshistorie: Menneskehetens Forestillinger og Kunnskaper om Livet etter Døden*. [The World History of the Realm of Death: Humankind's Perceptions and Knowledge of Life after Death], Vol. 1. Stavanger, Norway: Dreyer Forlag.

Betti, Marianna. 2007. "Animals and the Christianisation of Norway." Conference paper presented at Nordic Theoretical Archaeology Group in Aarhus, 11 May 2007.

Birke, Lynda, Mette Bryld, and Nina Lykke. 2004. "Animal Performances. An Exploration of Intersections between Feminist Science Studies and Studies of Human/animal Relationships." *Feminist Theory* 5(2): 167–183.

Birke, Lynda and Joanna Hockenhull. 2012. "On Investigating Human–Animal Bonds: Realities, Relatings, Research." In *Crossing Boundaries. Investigating Human–Animal Relationships*, edited by Lynda Birke and Joanna Hockenhull, 15–36. Leiden & Boston: Brill.

Braathen, Helge. 1989. *Ryttergraver. Politiske Strukturer i Eldre Rikssamlingstid*. [Riders' Graves. Political Structures in the Early State-Formation Period]. Oslo, Norway: Universitetets Oldsaksamling.

Brandt, Keri. 2004. "A Language of Their Own: An Interactionist Approach to Human–Horse Communication." *Society & Animals* 12(4): 299–316.

Evans, Rhys and Alexandra Franklin. 2010. "Equine Beats: Unique Rhythms (and Floating Harmony) of Horses and Their Riders." In *Geographies of Rhythm: Nature, Place, Mobilities and Bodies*, edited by Tim Edensor, 173–188. Manchester: Ashgate.

Fabech, Charlotte. 1994. "Society and Landscape. From Collective Manifestations to Ceremonies of a New Ruling Class." In *Iconologia sacra. Festschrift für Karl Hauch*, edited by Hagen Keller and Nicolaus Staubach, 132–143. Berlin & New York: Walter de Gruyter.

Ferdinand, Johs and Klaus Ferdinand. 1961. "Jernalderofferfund i Valmose ved Rislev." [Iron Age sacrificial finds in Valmose by Rislev], *Kuml*, 47–90.

Flateyarbok http://www.northvegr.org/sagas%20annd%20epics/miscellaneous/the%20flately%20book/index.html, accessed 15 February 2015.

Game, Ann. 2001. "Riding: Embodying the Centaur." *Body & Society* 7(4): 1–12.

Gjessing, Guttorm. 1943. "Hesten i Førhistorisk Kunst og Kultus." [The Horse in Prehistoric Art and Cult], *Viking: The Journal of Northern Archaeology* 7: 5–143.

Hagberg, Ulf E. 1963. "Blotare i Skedemosse." [Feasters in Skedemosse], *Tor* I (IX): 144–162.

Hearne, Vicki. 1987. *Adam's Task: Calling Animals by Name*. London: Skyhorse Publishing.

Hedeager, Lotte. 1999. "Sacred Topography. Depositions of Wealth in the Cultural Landscape". *Glyfer och arkeologiska rum. In honorem Jarl Nordbladh*. [Signs and Archaeological Rooms. In honor of Jarl Nordbladh], edited by Anders Gustafsson and Håkan Karlsson, 229–252. Gothenburg, Sweden: University of Gothenburg.

Hedeager, Lotte. 2011. *Iron Age Myth and Materiality. An Archaeology of Scandinavia AD 400–1000*. London & New York: Routledge.

Holtsmark, Anne. 1989. *Norrøn Mytologi : Tru og Myter i Vikingtida*. [Norse Mythology: Beliefs and Myths in the Viking Period]. Oslo, Norway: Det Norske Samlaget.

Håkon the Good's Saga. English translation: http://www.sacred-texts.com/neu/heim/05hakon.htm, accessed 11 March 2015.

Ilkjær, Jørgen. 1997. "Gegner und Verbündete in Nordeuropa während des 1. bis 4. Jahrhunderts". *Military Aspects of Scandinavian Society in a European Perspective, AD 1–1300*. Studies in Archaeology and History Vol. 2: København. København, Denmark: Publications from The National Museum.

Ingold, Tim. 2011. *Being Alive: Essays on Movement, Knowledge and Description*. London and New York: Routledge.

Kaul, Flemming. 2004. *Bronzealderens religion: Studier af den nordiske bronzealders ikonografi*. [Bronze Age Religion: Studies of the Iconography of the Nordic Bronze Age]. København, Denmark: Det Kongelige Nordiske Oldskriftselskab.

Klindt-Jensen, Ole. 1967. "Hoved og Hove." [Head and Hoofs], *Kuml*, 143–149.

Kohn, Eduardo. 2013. *How Forests Think: Towards an Anthropology beyond the Human*. Berkeley, Los Angeles and London: University of California Press.

Kristoffersen, Siv. 1995. "Transformation in Animal Art." *Norwegian Archaeological Review* 28: 3–15.

Kristoffersen, Siv. 2010. "Half Beast – Half Man. Hybrid Figures in Animal Art." *World Archaeology* 42(2): 261–272.

Kristoffersen, Siv and Armstrong Oma, Kristin. 2008. *Solens reise. Rogaland i europeisk bronsealder*. [The Journey of the Sun. Rogaland in the European Bronze Age]. Stavanger, Norway: Arkeologisk museum i Stavanger.

Latour, Bruno. 2013. *An Inquiry into Modes of Existence: An Anthropology of the Moderns*. Cambridge: Harvard University Press.

Lund, Julie. 2008. "Banks, Borders and Bodies of Water in Viking Age Mentality." *Journal of Wetland Archaeology* 8: 53–72.

Mallory, James P. 1981. "The Ritual Treatment of the Horse in the Early Kurgan Tradition." *The Journal of Indo-European Studies* 9(3 and 4): 205–226.

Meling, Trond. 2014. To Graver med Hest og Hesteutstyr fra Tu. Maktpolitiske Forhold på Sørvestlandet i Yngre Jernalder. [Two Graves with Horse and Horse Equipment from Tu. In Power and Politics in South Western Norway in the Late Iron Age]. *Et Akropolis på Jæren? Tinghaugplatået gjennom Jernalderen*. [An Acropolis at Jæren? The Tinghaug Plateau through the Iron Age], edited by S. Kristoffersen,

M. Nitter and E. Solheim Pedersen, AmS Varia 55: 107–115. Stavanger, Norway, Universitetet i Stavanger.

Møhl, Ulrik. 1961. "Rislevsfundets Dyreknogler." [Faunal Remains from the Rislev Find], *Kuml*, 96–106.

Monikander, Anne. 2006. "Borderland-Stalkers and Stalking-Horses. Horse Sacrifice as Liminal Activity in the Early Iron Age." *Current Swedish Archaeology* 14: 143–158.

Nielsen, Jens N. 2002. "Flammernes Bytte." [Perished in Flames], *Skalk* 6: 5–10.

Oma, Kristin. 2000. *Hesten i Nordisk Jernalder. Ei Kontekstuell Analyse Av Den Symbolske Sfære Kontra Den Materialle Røynda.* [The Horse in the Norse Iron Age. A Contextual Analysis of the Symbolic Sphere versus the Material Reality], Unpublished MA dissertation / Hovudfagsoppgåve: University of Oslo, Norway.

Oma, Kristin. 2001. "Hesten i Jernalderen – i Brytningspunktet mellom 'Seige Strukturar' og Endring i den Materielle Kulturen." [The Horse in the Iron Age – Breaking Points between Resilient Structures and Changes in the Material Culture], *Primitive Tider* 4: Primitive Tider.

Oma, Kristin. 2004. Hesten og det heilage. Materialiseringa av eit symbol. [The Horse and the Holy. The Materialization of a Symbol]. *Mellom himmel og jord. Foredrag fra et seminar om religionsarkeologi, Isegran 31. januar – 2. februar 2002.* [Between heaven and earth. Papers from a seminar on the Archaeology of Religion at Isegran, 31 Jaunary – 2 February 2002], edited by Lene Melheim, Lotte Hedeager and Kristin Oma, 2: 68–81. Oslo, Norway: Universitetet i Oslo.

Oma, Kristin. 2005. Hestetenner i kokegroper – på sporet av blot? Eit perspektiv frå Veien. [Horse Teeth in Cooking Pits – traces of ritual feasting], Perspective from Veien. De Gåtefulle Kokegroper. [The Mysterious Cooking Pits], edited by Lil Gustafson, Tom Heibreen and Jes Martens. *Varia*. 58: 243–259. Oslo: KHM [Kulturhistorist Museum].

Ørsnes, Mogens. 1984. *Sejrens pris. Våbenofre i Ejsbøl Mose ved Haderslev.* [The Price of Victory. Weapon Sacrifices in Ejsbøl Mose by Haderslev], Haderslev Museum.

Østmo, Einar. 1997. "Horses, Indo-Europeans and the Importance of Ships." *Journal of Indo-European Studies* 3&4: 285–326.

Piggott, Stuart. 1962. "Heads and Hoofs." *Antiquity* 36: 110–118.

Randsborg, Klaus. 1995. *Hjortspring. Warfare & Sacrifice in Early Europe.* Aarhus: Aarhus University Press.

Rosenberg, Gustav. 1937. "Hjortspringfundet." [The Hjortspring Find], *Nordiske Fortidsminder* 3(1).

Sundkvist, Anneli. 2001. *Hästarnas Land. Aristokratisk Hästhållning Och Ridkonst I Svealands Yngre Järnålder.* [The Land of the Horses. Aristocratic Horse-Keeping and Riding in the Late Iron Age of Svealand]. Uppsala, Sweden.

Sundkvist, Anneli. 2004. "Herding Horses: A Model of Prehistoric Horsemanship in Scandinavia – and Elsewhere?" *Man and Animal in Antiquity. Proceedings of the Conference at the Swedish Institute in Rome, 9–12 September 2002.* B. Santillo Frizell. Rome: Swedish Institute in Rome. 1: 241–249.

Tacitus. *Germania.* http://www.sacred-texts.com/cla/tac/g01010.htm, accessed 11 March 2015.

The Poetic Edda. 1936a. "Fragment of a Sigurd Lay." H. A. Bellows (translator), http://www.sacred-texts.com/neu/poe/poe26.htm, accessed 11 March 2015.

The Poetic Edda. 1936b. "The second lay of Guðrún." H. A. Bellows (translator), http://www.sacred-texts.com/neu/poe/poe31.htm, accessed 11 March 2015.

Thompson, Kirrilly. 2011. "Theorizing Rider–Horse Relations: An Ethnographic Illustration of the Centaur Metaphor in the Spanish Bullfight." In *Theorizing Animals: Rethinking Humanimal Relations*, edited by Nik Taylor and Tania Signal, 221–253. Leiden & Boston: Brill.

Turner, Victor W. 1967. *Forest of Symbols*. Ithaca: Cornell University Press.

Ullén, Inga. 1994. "The Power of Case Studies. Interpretation of a Late-Bronze-Age Settlement in Central Sweden." *Journal of European Archaeology* 2(2): 249–262.

Ullén, Inga. 1996. "Horse and Dog in the Swedish Bronze Age. A Close-Up Study of the Relation of Horse and Dog to Man in the Bronze Age Settlement of Apalle." *Archäologisches Korrespondenzblatt* 26: 145–166.

van Gennep, Arnold. 1960. *The Rites of Passage*. Chicago, IL: University of Chicago Press.

Viveiros de Castro, Eduardo. 1998. "Cosmological Deities and Amerindian Perspectivism." *The Journal of the Royal Anthropological Institute* 4(3): 469–488.

Viveiros de Castro, Eduardo. 2004. "Exchanging Perspectives. The Transformation of Objects into Subjects in Amerindian Ontologies." *Common Knowledge* 10(3): 463–484.

Wiker, Gry. 2000. "Gullbrakteatene – i Dialog med Naturkreftene." [The Gold Bracteates – Dialogue with the Forces of Nature]. Unpublished MA dissertation, Oslo, Norway: Oslo.

Xenophon. 2002 [1894]. *The Art of Horsemanship*. M. H. Morgan (translator). London: J. A. Allen.

3 Purity, Nobility, Beauty and Performance

Past and Present Construction of Meaning for the Arabian Horse

Christoph Lange

The *Classic Arabian Horse*[1] is generally seen as the result of breeding activities of Arab Bedouin from the northern Arabian Peninsula and Syrian steppe desert over hundreds of years. While the exact origin of the breed is vague and still a matter of controversial discussion, it is broadly accepted that the breed was already fixed in the middle of the second millennium BC and from then on mostly bred by Bedouin tribes, with Nejd in the northern Arabian Peninsula as "the most significant center" (Derry 2003, 104). Therefore, talking about *the* Arabian horse in terms of ancestry and origin generally refers to the Bedouin horse or desert horse of the Bedouins who managed to hold the traditional breeding monopoly for centuries.

With the beginning of the 20th century the centers of Arabian horse breeding mostly shifted to Western Europe[2] and the United States. There, new breeding programs were established, based on direct and indirect imports of Arabians from the Arab Middle East, and evolved into a global Arabian horse industry. European and US horse breeders and traders created a transatlantic commodification system of registration and certification for their modern Arabian horses, resulting in the separation of Arabian horses into a Western certified closed group of Arabian pedigrees. These were recognized as the only authentic Arabian purebred horses and distinguished from the group of horses with unaccepted or unreliable Arabian bloodlines. This directly connects to an enormous cultural production. The medial representation of horses, organizations and studs through publications, the internet and in performative show events and championships are markers of persistently fought-over discourses about the origin, purity of blood and aesthetics of the animals.

In this chapter I will develop an ethnographic approach to analyze these translocal connections within the global network of contemporary Arabian horse breeders. The focus thus lies on the horses and specific locally-situated work and practice, not only connecting the horses with their human counterparts but also on the different groups of actors and their relations among each other. Methodically, I draw on theoretical concepts from the field of anthropology, traditionally concerned with human–animal–nature entanglements. These entail a consideration of domestication studies and studies of nomadic pastoralists (e.g., Cassidy and Mullin 2007; Ingold 1988, 2011 [2000]; Grasseni 2009; Leder and Streck 2005). Additionally I draw on concepts influenced by human animal studies such as multispecies ethnography. Last but not least, I draw on concepts associated with the French tradition of science and technology studies. I chose Egypt's scene of Arabian horse breeders as the ethnographic center of this analysis. In the first section I elaborate on the theoretical and conceptual approaches of what one could summarize with the slogan "Follow the Horses." In the next section I present a historical contextualization of the emerging global Arabian horse industry and its dominant actors that will be followed by an overview of the collected ethnographic material.

Anthropological perspectives on human animal histories of entanglement

In recent work in the field of human animal studies and multispecies ethnography (Birke and Hockenhull 2012; Cassidy 2002a, 2007; Descola and Pálsson 1996; Grasseni 2009; Haraway 2008; Kirksey and Helmreich 2010; Maurstad et al. 2013; Shapiro and DeMello 2010) the authors invoke a new and radical recentering and renegotiating of the position and role of animals in social science research and conceptualize them as actors with the potential agency to create and transform social relations. Furthermore, these approaches are directly connected to the French tradition of science and technology studies at the Centre de Sociologie de l'Innovation (CSI) in Paris that is mainly represented by the work of Michel Callon, Antoine Hennion, Bruno Latour, and their long fight for objects' symmetric place in social science theory. I will show how a combination of key conceptual tools of both traditions provides a methodological approach for explaining and dealing with the world of modern Arabian horses and their breeders, lovers and traders, and, in particular, how specific practices of bonding/attachment between human and horse constitute different transnational communities within the global network. In addressing this, I will focus on concepts developed in Actor-Network-Theory, namely the concepts of "obligatory passage point" (OPP) (Callon 1986, 204), "centers of calculations" (Latour 1993, 37) and "immutable mobiles" (Latour 1999, 306). I will also account for the significance of ethnographic research: Malinowski drew on the importance of understanding the Kula by "follow[ing] the natives on one of their overseas trips, describing it in all details" (Malinowski 2002 [1922], 79). This not only evokes the ANT slogan "Follow the Actors" but also leads to Hennion's concept of "attachment," (Hennion 2007, 109), fruitful in the sense that he analyzes the specific processes of how people become amateurs, lovers and experts in their fields of interest through practices *in situ*. In doing so, the actors not only discursively create the meanings of objects or animals, but develop a deep attachment based on their bodily experience with them. This brings Tim Ingold's "skilled practices" (Ingold 2011, 5) and "taskscapes" (Ingold 2011, 154) to mind and the "fact that one of the outstanding features of human technical practices lies in their embeddedness in the current of sociality" (Ingold 2011, 195). Cristina Grasseni, for example, combines Ingold's concepts with the idea of "communities of practice" (CoP) by Lave and Wenger (1991, 53) and elaborates them further in her ethnography on contemporary cattle breeders in the Italian Alps (Grasseni 2009). The resulting "ecology of practice" (Grasseni 2009, 128) focuses on the practices of visual apprenticeship or "skilled vision" (Grasseni 2009, 129) of the cattle breeder community members. It also addresses questions of how to train the eye in developing the skills to judge the good from the bad in their breeding activities and consequently raises issues of how to constitute the community itself: "The local construction of skilled knowledge, through the training of expert eyes, hands, discourses and sensibilities, actually contributes to establishment and maintenance of hegemonic, often global, standards of practice through which we perceive, order and manage the world" (Grasseni 2007, 7–8).

In the case of Arabian horses, one might ask how and by what means do Arabian horse breeders and lovers deploy their locally constituted ecologies of practice in the global world of the Arabian horse trading industry and international breeders' presentation shows? And, thus, by what means do different groups of actors constitute diverse, often competing sets of meaning through their specific 'attachments' to Arabian horses, defining what an authentic Arabian horse should be and thus recursively producing and/or altering established "hegemonic, often global, standards of practice" (Grasseni 2007, 7)? Consequently, the localized discursive and interactional practices of actors and horses are entangled in a twofold manner. Firstly, the practices compose the modern Arabian horse in arenas of different scale and through this also give meaning to themselves as individual subjects, as well as members of the Arabian horse lovers' communities. Rebecca Cassidy, in her ethnography on the English thoroughbred race horse industry, puts it this way: "[W]omen and men in the racing industry imagine their lives and those of others through the lives of horses, not to mention the lives of horses through their own" (Cassidy 2002b, 168).

As a consequence, the Arabian horse (and its circulation) constitutes the network and connects all actors and practices with each other; the horse is 'mediator' and medium for the transnational interrelations of Arabian horse breeders and lovers. With Hennion's (Gomart and Hennion 1999) "sociology of attachment," this process of 'mediation' can be described as a bodily experienced interaction of human and animal/horse. Gomart and Hennion (1999, 220) call this "attachment" (where somebody else might say bonding). Attachments always realize themselves locally and are situated: in the case of my study in the contact with and handling of horses. Like Grasseni's "skilled knowledge" above, attachments are also influenced by, multiplied and spread through material and media objects into global arenas of social practice: "They [taste and pleasure] are the results of a corporeal practice, collective and instrumented, settled by methods that are discussed endlessly, oriented around the appropriate seizing upon of uncertain effects. It is for this reason that we prefer to speak of attachments" (Hennion 2007, 108–109). A last conceptual notion in this regard is the idea of the *living sculpture*, which struck my mind during my first observations of Arabian horses at show events and during their training. I have borrowed the term from a debate in art history about the beginnings of performance art. It originally relates to the work of the artist duo Gilbert and George in the 1960s who presented themselves and their daily life as artwork and called it a *living sculpture*. I use the term in my analysis to denote the culmination point of all practices relating to the Arabian horse – the moment at which all efforts and attachments are designated. It is the climax of every Arabian horse presentation performance, namely the very short moment when the horse freezes in perfect position and shape in front of the audience and judges.

Origins of the Arabian horse

Together and in alliance with camels, horses allowed for a high level of mobility and therefore were essential for the traditional nomadic and pastoralist patterns of Bedouin livelihood. They were used in warfare and raids where "the superior qualities of the horse give the rider incalculable advantages over his enemies" (Burckhardt 1831, 134). However, not all Bedouins bred horses. Rather, the breeding and possession of Arabian horses had always been a marker of social distinction, so that Arabian horses were mostly and exclusively bred by the 'noble' Bedouin tribes. These constituted a sort of aristocracy of the desert, due both to their prestige and to the economic advantages of camel herding (Chatty 1996).[3] Moreover, Arabian horses served as an important good for trading with the sedentary population and merchants in the region. From the 13th to the 18th centuries, these merchants established a flourishing oversea trade of Arabian horses, from south Arabian coast ports to India (Lancaster 2011). In connection with these pastoral–sedentary relations, this special breed of Bedouin horses attracted different ruling state authorities in the region, such as the Ottoman sultans in Istanbul or Mamluks and Egyptian pashas in Cairo, who purchased large numbers of horses for their stables. State authorities and urban elites accordingly maintained special relations to Bedouin in their capacities as horse breeders, caretakers and trainers at the royal stables (see Aharoni 2007; Shwartz 2011).

Arabian horses are not only of central economic importance to Bedouin society; they also, and as a consequence of the latter, are significant for the construction of Bedouin cultural and social identity. Arabian horses were incorporated into Bedouin society in different ways and were treated as if they were human members of the society. On the one hand, they were subjects of the same genealogical systems that dominated parts of Bedouin and Arab society. They thus played an important role in the world of meanings – for example, horse were central in the moral economy of honor and social hierarchy as well as regarding intertribal communication and exchange systems. Additionally,

Emrys Peters highlights the function of the horse as status symbol for the Bedouin of Cyrenaica: "In the ordinary run of daily life, it is impossible to distinguish between patrons and clients. [...] There are rich and poor in both statuses, and the prime symbol of wealth, the horse, is to be seen tethered in front of the wealthy client's tent, as well as the wealthy nobleman's tent" (1990, 55). Peters also stresses the role of the horse as a mount for a tribal leader or *shaikh* to fulfill his duties and ensure authority and control over his group. On the other hand, we find a deep bond and attachment of pastoralists and their animals that went far beyond admiration and appeared in a range of shared daily practices: the common drinking of camel milk, same treatments for illnesses, and soft and gentle caretaking such as interpersonal interaction (Blunt 1879).

Like any society, Arab Bedouin societies have always been in transition and subjected to social, economic and political changes. Internal competition for pastures or wells and tribal rivalries caused constant migrations. Shifting relations and alliances with ruling (state) authorities continuously affected Bedouin life, wealth and income. Bedouni were always integrated in the wider "external economy" and thus "have been competitive producers and also developed some types of conspicuous consumption, such as keeping horses and the exercise of lavish hospitality" (Marx 1984, 4). Yet, throughout history, the Bedouins never had to adapt to transformational processes like those that confronted the people of the Arab Middle East in the 19th and 20th centuries, and that had wide-ranging consequences for nomadic patterns of livelihood. The Western colonial encounter initiated processes of industrialization and modernization throughout the whole Middle Eastern region that manifested in railroads, trucks, mechanized warfare and expanding nation states. The horse- and camel-breeding Bedouin nomads were most affected by pacification campaigns of the desert by means of advanced weaponry (especially the deployment of war planes), the mechanization of transportation and the emerging nation states with their national borders and sedentarization programs. Important traditional forms of income became obsolete – for example, security and protection services of the main trading and pilgrimage routes and the camel caravan trading system. Intertribal warfare was reduced to a minimum due to the monopolization of force, first by the colonial powers and later by the new nation states. By the middle of the 20th century most of the camel-herding and horse-breeding 'noble' Bedouin tribes had abandoned their herding activities and shifted to small stock animals such as sheep or goats. As there no longer were constant threats of attack by neighboring tribes or the need to offer protection services to caravans, the economic value of horses drastically decreased. Moreover, the declining importance of the cavalry in modernized armies and their military campaigns further diminished the general demand for horses. With the loss of their economic function, Arab Bedouins held and bred the few remaining Arabian horses only for matters of prestige and cultural heritage.

Arabian horses in an emerging global market

Since the late 17th century, Arabian horses – especially stallions – were used in European state-run breeding programs for the enhancement of local breeds, particularly for military purposes. Margaret Derry brings the connection between Europe, the Arabian horse and its meaning for war to the point:

> Certain earliest developments in the French Haras [Europe-wide, state-run war horse breeding and regulation program, initiated by Louis XIV in 1665] indicate the importance of the Arabian to European warfare as early as the late seventeenth century. War and the Arabian [horse] had a long interrelated history by that time in other parts of the world. While the Arab people first relied on the horse in tribal combat and in campaigns of conquest, it was the Ottoman Empire that initiated what would become the global spread of Arabians.
>
> (Derry 2006, 105–106)[4]

In the second half of the 18th century major transformational processes began to change British agricultural economy. These were primarily connected to the establishment of new selective breeding systems for the improvement of horses, cattle and sheep. The new systems were based on intensive pure-, cross- and inbreeding techniques invented by English breeders such as Robert Bakewell, who became famous for the creation of his New Leicester sheep. The experiments of Bakewell and his fellow breeders were dominated by a fascination for the creation of new and unique breeds with distinct inheritable features. These early stages of selective breeding methods did not only lead to some rather grotesque new breeds (like the Durham Ox) but also to the establishment of a new system of public standardized registries. The new system, introduced at the beginning of the 19th century, was designed to control and market the new breeds in an emerging transatlantic agricultural trading system. Derry points to the link between these newly created public registries for pedigrees and their first and only precursor, *The General Stud Book* (GSB) for thoroughbred horses in Britain. The GSB was initiated in the late 18th century in order to control and register horses involved in the racing industry and thus was an attempt to regulate the racing business (Derry 2003). In the terms of Latour and Callon, *The General Stud Book*, productive livestock registries and their regulating technologies of certification can be seen as the institutionalized origins of the future "centers of calculation" (Latour 1993, 37) and thus "obligatory passage points" (Callon 1986, 204) in the global Arabian horse industry.

In the beginning of the 19th century, Europe and the USA developed an increasingly specialized demand for purebred Bedouin Arabian horses. This has to be seen in the context of the above-mentioned developments, since Arab Bedouin breeding traditions suddenly exactly met the desires of this new generation of British breeders. Derry holds that:

> The Arab people were known to have practiced intense selective breeding on this animal for hundreds of years, thereby enhancing a natural tendency for these horses to breed consistently to a type not found in northern Europe. Arabians were lighter, faster, and smaller than their European counterparts, and these differences, along with their ability to stamp their style on progeny, impressed British horse breeders. The trueness to type re-enforced certain ideas about the nature of heredity itself.
>
> (Derry 2006, 31–32)

So, in the course of the colonial opening and *Pax Britannica* in the Arab East, Western travelers encountered Arab Bedouins and their horses in the Syrian steppe and northern Arabian desert just before the massive social and economic transformations that caused the disappearance of the (Bedouin) Arabian horse. Motivated by their search for the origins of humankind and attempts to escape the noise of European industrialization, those from the West returned home not only with material for numerous books spreading romantic clichés about Bedouin desert life (and, of course, some excellent ethnographic observations as well), but also with exclusive specimens of pure desert-bred Arabian horses (e.g., Blunt 1879, Davenport 1909). The horses that found their way to Europe and the United States were not exclusively direct acquisitions from Bedouins, but many came from the royal stables of Egypt.

Thus, Western breeders and horse lovers of the late 19th century took up and adopted a local (breeding) practice that had been orally passed down by Arab Bedouins over hundreds of years. From the beginning, Western breeders shared the Bedouin concern with pure (arab. *asil*) horses with proven pedigrees. I call this the *asil paradigm* of Arabian horse breeding.[5] Western breeders incorporated *asil* horses into the registration and control mechanism of the established transatlantic trade system, opening a special section for Arabian horse pedigrees in the British *General Stud Book* in 1877 (Derry 2003), and by the mid-20th century we find the contemporary regimes of registration and standardization taking effect. The emerging global market for Arabian horses also attracted Arab elites, mainly from the Arabian Peninsula and the Gulf countries. Their considerable wealth and the newly resurfacing discourses of cultural heritage meant that the Arab elites entered the world market of Arabian horses as powerful players. Rebecca Cassidy (2003) examines the irritations that the strong position of the Arab elites generated in the British thoroughbred market.

National and international Arabian horse organizations with their restricted member lists, horse registries and stud books dictate the globally accepted standards of breeding, keeping and presenting Arabian horses in show events. They constitute what Latour (1993, 37) calls "centers of calculations" – that is, the control and administration centers of our Western discourse with its focus on enlightenment and modernity. It is their task to enforce the *asil paradigm* of all as purebred-labeled Arabian horses. Moreover, these centers represent the global breeders' key technologies of exclusion and inclusion by negotiating memberships and particular interests and thus managing cooperation in and access to the global market. The different horse organizations and their agendas of promoting, regulating and marketing Arabian horses thus maintain a restrictive network with "obligatory passage points" (Callon 1986, 204) that every Arabian horse and breeder has to pass through in order to participate. A basic requirement for any circulation in the network is the transformation of the Arabian horse from a unique complex living creature into an "immutable mobile" (Latour 1999, 306) – the transformation of a complex (natural) entity into "a sign, an archive, a document, a piece of paper, a trace" (Latour 1999, 306) in order to use the horse for argumentation and mobilization without any need for adjustment in different social contexts. These transformations differ according to actors' local practices: their breeding decisions, horse keeping, presentations and the production of specific meanings and publics through media and discourse.

The composition of the modern Arabian horse as a living sculpture for a global industry

I choose Egypt as a site of ethnographic reconstruction and analysis of the dynamics of the transnational circulation networks of Arabian horses since no contemporary ethnographic material is available on this aspect of horse human interaction. Moreover, Egypt's paradoxical position within the global network, as a historically important center for Arabian horses that is now peripheral, allows tracing of locally situated controversies about authenticity, recognition and participation. I therefore focus on central questions about the potential for interaction and cooperation that transnational Arabic groups hold when trying to engage with and improve their standing in the Western-dominated global industry of Arabian horse breeding and trading.

The field of Egyptian horse breeders is elaborate and professional. My first point of contact was the stud owner and breeder Dr. Nasr Marei (<http://www.albadeia.net>). Marei is a third-generation Arabian horse breeder; his father and grandfather laid the foundations for Egypt's modern breeding of Arabian horses, dating back to 1935. Marei himself is a well-known international judge for Arabian horse shows, a professional photographer of Arabian horses, and he published the book *Arabian Horse of Egypt* (Marei and Culbertson 2010). When looking for his stud, located next to the pyramids in Giza, I was convinced that such a big and traditional stud could not be missed. Yet, *Albadeia* was not easy to find or ask for. I was lucky to meet Ahmed, a former tourist guide, who promised to show me the way to Dr. Marei's stud and also offered to arrange meetings with other horse breeders. At the meetings he introduced me as a potential buyer of Arabian horses and explained that this misinformation was necessary since otherwise the owners would not open their gates for us. I visited four studs of different sizes in the course of two days. The first stud was owned by Abd al-Wahab, a cousin or friend of Ahmed. It was the smallest stud I visited, with approximately 15 horses cared for by two or three grooms. My cover identity as potential buyer was instantly blown as Abd al-Wahab immediately discovered that I knew nothing about Arabian horses. When he and his staff presented his horses and asked for my judgment of age and beauty, I even failed to determine the right sex. Although realizing that I lacked Grasseni's (2009, 1) "skilled vision" in judging Arabian horses, Abd al-Wahab was kind enough to tell me that I had some sort of connection with the horses and offered to teach me how to know and understand Arabian horses.

The visits to the other three studs did not recreate the intimate atmosphere of the first one but nevertheless yielded important insights into the Egyptian practices of keeping and breeding Arabians. Two of the studs, both holding over 100 Arabian horses in big stables, are considered to be the most influential and economically successful studs in Egypt. Here I understood why Ahmed told me that the gates would not open for just anyone. The studs are worlds of their own, with luxury villas, huge areas of green, palm trees and a small farming business next to the paddocks, stables and houses for the grooms. In these surroundings I met a French trainer for Arabian horses who is working for an international training center for Arabian horses, including personal training of horses at studs all over the world. He trains horses that were chosen to participate in a breeders' presentation show, working on the correct standing and positioning of legs, neck and head, that are all crucial to gain a high ranking by the judges. The training session takes about ten minutes per horse, after that the horse's attention span is exhausted. This time, he would stay in Egypt for ten days and train the horses for a local show and then travel to the World Championship of Arabian Horses in Paris. Asked if he rides horses, his surprising answer was that he hates riding but loves training and working with horses on the ground.

This, as I realized, was a central point: the unexpected use (or, better, non-use) of Arabian horses, employing them only for breeding and mostly rejecting all riding activities. I did not find a single Arabian horse that was trained for riding on any of the studs. Everyone I talked to rejected the very idea. I first surmised that this was a market-driven consequence of the Egyptian horse breeders' world; but I discovered that most of the Arabian horses worldwide are bred for their beauty and unique aesthetics. While watching the highly professional and skillful horse training I concluded that it all comes down to an artistic act: the composition of a perfect *living sculpture*. The first Arabian horse halter shows I attended strengthened this impression. The horse's performance in the ring reaches its climax when horse and trainer meet in the center and perform the perfect stand up, and the horse freezes into the admired sculptural form for less than a second. This is the moment when the audience starts to cheer and applaud, and the judges write down their points. To use the theoretical terms of Hennion and Grasseni, Abd al-Wahab and the French horse trainer showed me how the "skilled knowledge" (Grasseni 2007, 7) of the beauty of an Arabian is crucial for deciding who is an "amateur" (Hennion 2007, 103) and therefore who is part of the in-group.

This episode also revealed how, where and by whom the sets of aesthetic standards are negotiated through bodily inscriptions in the direct interaction of horse and human. Moreover, when the judges write down the scores, they transform the Arabian horse from a complex living creature into a commodified, transferable good that is represented by numbers in five aesthetic categories (1 type; 2 head and neck; 3 body and tail; 4 legs; 5 movement). This locally defined reduction to numbers for the purpose of global circulation perfectly fits the concept of Latour's (1999, 307) "immutable mobiles [...] that focuses on the movement of displacement and the contradictory requirements of the task."

A closer look into the different groups of actors in the Egyptian Arabian breeders' world will show the contrasting politics and interests involved in the transformation of the Arabian horse into an immutable mobile.

During a second stay in Egypt, I spent more time with breeders, meeting them on their studs, visiting a local breeders' championship show and a private auction of Arabian horses, and going to El Zahraa, the state stud run by the Egyptian Agricultural Organization (EAO). I also talked to Egyptians in the streets or taxi drivers about my interest in Egyptian Arabian horses. Throughout these small talk situations my conversation partners mentioned a particular region in the Nile Delta, called al-Sharqiya, where I would find the finest and purest Arabian horses that are still bred by Bedouin. I established contact with the Tahawi Bedouins, who became settled in the al-Sharqiya region as a reward for their support in military campaigns under Muhammad Ali during his land reforms in the 1830s (Aharoni 2007). The Tahawi were well-known and famous Arabian horse breeders and had good connections to other horse-breeding Bedouin in Syria and the Arabian Peninsula. From them they purchased desert-bred Arabian horses for their own breeding programs and delivered the offspring to the royal stables in Cairo. As a consequence of the events of the 19th and 20th centuries, the unique Tahawi breeds of *asil* (pure) Arabian horses are now nearly extinct. As far as I could gather, most of the Tahawi horses were excluded from official registrations in the 1970s when the EAO introduced a new registration process of Egyptian Arabian horses to meet new international registration standards.

A listing in the national EAO *General Stud Book* is the essential requirement for being accepted by the World Arabian Horse Organization (WAHO). The WAHO, founded in 1974, regulates on an international level which horses count as purebred Arabian horses. Until today the Tahawi horses remain largely unaccepted and therefore excluded from the international Arabian horse world. Dr. Marei warned me that the Tahawi have a lot of non-*asil* half-bred horses. Despite the reservations that his cautioning shows, a small group of Tahawi fights for the survival and international recognition of their last remaining horses. To that end, they have built an international network of supporters through social and electronic media, running a cultural heritage website and Facebook page.[6] Small victories for the Tahawi were the recognition as "horses of interest" by the US-based al-Khamsa organization in 2011 and the opening of a special EAO registry for the Tahawi horses as the "Asil Bedouin Egyptian Arabian Horses" in 2013.

For the Tahawi, horse breeding and dealing with horses is a cultural tradition that should be continued after the fashion of 'the old days.' During a short trip to al-Sharqiya and a visit to some members of Tahawi and the breeders' preservation initiative, it became clear that they follow a concept of horse-breeding and value judgment that differs from the one I encountered in the Egyptian breeders' community in Cairo. Holding up to the centuries-old Bedouin traditions of breeding, they still value riding and performance qualities of their horses over aesthetic aspects and therefore reject the international beauty contests that dominate most of the international Arabian horse world. Thus, their main breeding activities today focus on the local horse racing industry and the main racetracks in Alexandria and Cairo. They also continue to have their horses integrated in social activities and public events such as weddings, fantasias and riding parties of young men into the desert. Their culturally motivated attachment to their horses not only creates specific sets of meaning but also constitutes the Tahawi as a group in contrast with the mainstream establishment of the global Arabian horse world.

Yet, with their rejection of the international halter show business, the Tahawi do not simply oppose their influential fellow Egyptian breeders. They also seek to establish alliances with Arabian horse lovers who follow similar attachments (such as representatives of the US al-Khamsa organization or the German Asil Club). Within the breeders' group of wealthy, well-connected businessmen, there also exists a small group of horse lovers and breeders who reject the show business and do not perform or show their horses in the ring. The Egyptian breeder Philippe Paraskevas openly opposes the international halter shows (Paraskevas 2010, 2012). He follows a double strategy. He criticizes the Western dominance in the world of Arabian horses, including the setting up of regulations and dictating of breeders' decisions through promoting only a few Western-bred elite bloodlines (and intensive inbreeding). His critique aims at a reorientation of the international breeders' network away from a profit-oriented industry towards a global program preserving the diversity of the Arabian horse population at large. He calls this the "safe-havens" for the last remaining *asil* Arabians (Paraskevas 2012, 424). These preservation efforts are intertwined with a political agenda to strengthen the Arab countries as the traditional origin of Arabian horses. Egypt with the El Zahraa stud should therefore take a central role in the global preservation of the Arabian horse. On a practical level, the breeders are encouraged to integrate horses into their breeding programs that are unknown or unrecognized but proven to be 100 percent desert-bred Arabians. Paraskevas (2012) sees the integration of Tahawi bloodstock as one possibility to achieve a new diversity in Arabian horse population.

Conclusion

The different Egyptian breeding communities, Tahawi and wealthy business breeders, have to deal with established global standards, ranging from preferred bloodlines of horses to aesthetic ideals to registration regulations and presentation rules. The diverse Egyptian breeding communities radically differ in their levels of integration and participation in the global market for Arabians, not just regarding their means of resources but also by their willingness to commit themselves to established regimes of certification and the dominance of the global halter show business. In interviews and visiting talks, members of the Tahawi breeders' initiative rejected the standards and preferences of this global industry as not compatible with their traditional Bedouin practices. On the other hand, they obviously seek alliances within the global world of Arabian horse lovers and fight for the recognition of their horses by the official horse organizations on national and international levels. They have already found potential associates and advocates, for example, in the US al-Khamsa organization and the German Asil Club. It seems that the only way to save the few remaining *asil* Tahawi horses from extinction is to create an effective public for their concerns through the use of social electronic media and cooperating with the established structures of the Arabian horse world. The main theme of public presentation is the Tahawis' unique tradition as Bedouin horse breeders and their preservation of a cultural heritage that the majority of the Egyptian breeders cannot access. It remains an open question whether the current activities will successfully mobilize powerful supporters and open alternative passage points. At the moment, however, the EAO still embodies the localized needle eye or "obligatory passage point" (Callon 1986, 204) that every breeder and Arabian horse in Egypt has to pass. This study, with its focus on the Arabian horse as the overall connecting 'object of dispute' provides a basis that enables further research on how different Egyptian groups of actors deploy their respective opportunities of action, resources and forms of (forced) cooperation to gain access to the global Arabian horse market, change established structures and create their own new obligatory passage points.

Notes

1 The term refers to Judith Forbis's (1976) book which is very influential within the Arabian horse breeders' community.
2 "Western" or "Westerner" is used throughout the chapter as a mainly geographical category to include various European and US-American actors who share certain social and economic characteristics.
3 For further discussion of the social differentiation of the Bedouin tribes into "noble" and "non-noble" – based on their identities as camel or sheep herders – see Katharina Lange (2005).
4 The most popular non-military breeding example involving Arabian horses is the creation of the English racing thoroughbred with its three founding stallions

Darley Arabian, Godolphin Arabian and Byerly Turk. For a detailed history of the English thoroughbred see, for example, Eversfield and Ahnert (1970).

5 See, for example, the quote and official definition of purebred Arabian horses that is used by the German Asil Club, the International Association for the Preservation and Rearing of the Asil Arabian: "The ASIL ARABIAN is a horse whose pedigree is exclusively based on Bedouin breeding, without any crossbreeding with non-Arabian horses at any time. The word 'aṣīl' is derived from the Arabic language and means pure, true, noble and genuine. The ASIL ARABIAN horse should have the riding qualities and the characteristics of type that distinguish the desert Arabian" (Olms 1985, 52).

6 The tribal heritage website is in Arabic (<http://www.eltahawysaoud.com>). For the English-run Facebook page and the *Tahawi Horses Newsletter* see <https://www.facebook.com/TahawiHorses/timeline>.

References

Aharoni, Reuven. 2007. *The Pasha's Bedouin – Tribes and State in the Egypt of Mehemet Ali, 1805–1848*. London: Routledge.

Birke, Lynda and Jo Hockenhull. 2012. "Introduction: On Investigating Human–Animal Relationships." In *Crossing Boundaries. Investigating Human Animal Relationships*, edited by Lynda Birke and Jo Hockenhull, 1–12. Boston: Brill (Human–Animal Studies).

Blunt, Lady Anne. 1879. *Bedouin Tribes of the Euphrates*. New York: Harper and Bros.

Burckhardt, John Lewis. 1831. *Notes on the Bedouins and Wahabys*, Vol. 1. London: Henry Colburn and Richard Bentley.

Callon, Michel. 1986. "Elements of a Sociology of Translation: Domestication of the Scallops and the Fishermen of St Brieuc Bay." In *Power, Action and Belief: A New Sociology of Knowledge?*, edited by John Law, 196–233. London: Routledge.

Cassidy, Rebecca. 2002a. *The Sport of Kings. Kinship, Class and Thoroughbred Breeding in Newmarket*. Cambridge/New York: Cambridge University Press.

Cassidy, Rebecca. 2002b. "The Social Practice of Racehorse Breeding." *Animals & Society* 10(2): 156–171.

Cassidy, Rebecca. 2003. "Turf Wars: Arab Dimensions to British Racehorse Breeding." *Anthropology Today* 19(3): 13–18.

Cassidy, Rebecca. 2007. *Horse People: Thoroughbred Culture in Lexington and Newmarket*. Baltimore: Johns Hopkins University Press.

Cassidy, Rebecca and Molly Mullin. 2007. *Where the Wild Things Are Now: Domestication Reconsidered*. New York/Oxford: Berg.

Chatty, Dawn. 1996. *Mobile Pastoralists: Development Planning and Social Change in Oman*. New York: Columbia University Press.

Davenport, Homer. 1909. *My Quest of the Arab Horse*. New York: Dodge & Company.

Derry, Margaret. 2003. *Bred for Perfection – Shorthorn Cattle, Collies, and Arabian Horses since 1800*. Baltimore: Johns Hopkins University Press.

Derry, Margaret. 2006. *Horses in Society – A Story of Animal Breeding and Marketing, 1800–1920*. Toronto: University of Toronto Press.

Descola, Philippe and Gísli Pálsson. 1996. *Nature and Society: Anthropological Perspectives*. London: Routledge.

Eversfield, Martin E. and Rainer L. Ahnert. 1970. *Thoroughbred Breeding of the World – L'Elevage Mondial du Pur Sang – Die Vollblutzucht der Welt*. Dornheim: Podzun-Verlag.

Forbis, Judith. 1976. *The Classic Arabian Horse*. New York: Liveright.

Gomart, Émilie and Antoine Hennion. 1999. "A Sociology of Attachment: Music Amateurs, Drug Users." In *Actor Network Theory and After*, edited by John Law and John Hassard, 220–247. Oxford/Malden: Blackwell.

Grasseni, Cristina. 2007. *Skilled Visions: Between Apprenticeship and Standards*. EASA Series 6, New York/Oxford: Berghahn Books.

Grasseni, Cristina. 2009. *Developing Skill, Developing Vision: Practices of Locality at the Foot of the Alps*. New York/Oxford: Berghahn Books.

Haraway, Donna. 2008. *When Species Meet*. Minneapolis: University of Minnesota Press.

Hennion, Antoine. 2007. "Those Things That Hold Us Together: Taste and Sociology." *Cultural Sociology* 1(1): 97–114.

Ingold, Tim. 1988. "The Animal in the Study of Humanity." In *What Is an Animal?*, edited by Tim Ingold, 84–99. London: Routledge.

Ingold, Tim. 2011 [2000]. *The Perception of the Environment – Essays on Livelihood, Dwelling and Skill*. London: Routledge.

Kirksey, S. Eben and Stefan Helmreich. 2010. "The Emergence of Multispecies Ethnography." *Cultural Anthropology* 25(4): 545–576.

Lancaster, William and Fidelity Lancaster. 2011. *Honour is in Contentment: Life before Oil in Ras al-Khaimah (UAE) and some Neighbouring Regions*. Berlin: Walter de Gruyter.

Lange, Katharina. 2005. "Shawâyâ: Economic Mélange, Pure Origins? Outsiders' and Insiders' Accounts of Tribal Identity in Northern Syria." In *Shifts and Drifts in Nomad–Sedentary Relations*, edited by Stefan Leder and Bernhard Streck, 99–122. Wiesbaden: Reichert.

Latour, Bruno. 1993. *We Have Never Been Modern*. Cambridge, MA: Harvard University Press.

Latour, Bruno. 1999. *Pandora's Hope: Essays on the Reality of Science Studies*. Cambridge, MA: Harvard University Press.

Lave, Jean and Etienne Wenger. 1991. *Situated Learning: Legitimate Peripheral Participation*. Cambridge/New York: Cambridge University Press.

Leder, Stefan and Bernhard Streck. 2005. *Shifts and Drifts in Nomad–Sedentary Relations*. Wiesbaden: Reichert.

Malinowski, Bronislaw. 2002 [1922]. *Argonauts of the Western Pacific*. London: Routledge.

Marei, Nasr and Cynthia Culbertson. 2010. *The Arabian Horse of Egypt*. Cairo: American University Press.

Marx, Emanuel. 1984. "Economic Change among Pastoral Nomads in the Middle East." In *The Changing Bedouin*, edited by Emanuel Marx and Avshalo Shmueli, 1–14. New Brunswick: Transaction Books.

Maurstad, Anita, Dona Davis, and Sarah Cowles. 2013. "Co-being and Intra-action in Horse–Human Relationships: A Multi-species Ethnography of Be(com)ing Human and Be(com)ing horse." *Social Anthropology* 21(3): 322–335.

Olms, W. Georg. 1985. *Asil-Araber. Arabiens Edle Pferde. Eine Dokumentation*. [Asil Arabians, the Noble Arabian Horses. A Documentation]. With assistance of Sigrid Eicher. 3rd ed. Hildesheim/Zürich/New York: Olms.

Paraskevas, Philippe. 2010. *The Egyptian Alternative: Breeding the Arabian Horse*, Vol. 1. Obelisque Publications: Cairo.

Paraskevas, Philippe. 2012. *The Egyptian Alternative: In Search of the Identity of the Egyptian Arabian Bloodlines*, Vol. 2. Obelisque Publications: Cairo.

Peters, Emrys L. 1990. *The Bedouin of Cyrenaica: Studies in Personal and Corporate Power*. Cambridge: Cambridge University Press.

Shapiro, Kenneth and Margo DeMello. 2010. "The State of Human–Animal Studies." *Society & Animals* 18(3): 307–318.

Shwartz, Igal. 2011 [1987]. *Die Beduinen in Ägypten in der Mamlukenzeit*. [The Bedouin in Egypt during the Mamluk Period]. Working translation published by Kurt Franz and translated from Hebrew by Leonhard Becker. CRC 586 Difference and Integration: Halle/Saale, <http://www.nomadsed.de/b1/shwartz>, last accessed 14 December 2014.

Online references

Website of *alBadeia* stud: <http://www.albadeia.net>, last accessed 27 January 2015.

Tahawi Horses Facebook: <https://www.facebook.com/TahawiHorses/timeline>, last accessed 27 January 2015.

Tahawi cultural tribal heritage website <http://www.eltahawysaoud.com>, last accessed 27 January 2015.

4 From Servant to Therapist

The Changing Meanings of Horses in Finland

Riitta-Marja Leinonen

In Northern Europe the horse has occupied a variety of equine roles and participated in a variety of human horse relationships during the last 100 years. Throughout the 20th century Finnish society experienced a rapid change from an agrarian to an information society. Industrialization and urbanization transformed the economic structure radically throughout the 1950s and 1970s. As a result, the number of horses collapsed from 400,000 to 40,000 (Finnish Trotting and Breeding Association 2015). At the same time, the human–animal relationship changed as the relationship to primary production changed (Ylimaunu 2002). The working horse culture that was present almost everywhere in agrarian society became reduced to equestrian subcultures of trotting and riding at the margins of the information society. Currently, the number of horses is rising again along with their popularity in recreation and sports.

This chapter explores the meanings that Finnish people give to their horses, how these meanings have changed over time and how they are displayed both in terms of the handling of the horse and ideas about human horse relationships. Drawing upon the perspectives of cognitive anthropology (D'Andrade 2000; Quinn 2005a), I will analyze personal narratives that reveal cultural models of human horse relationships. The power of stories lies in the compelling interpretation they offer to life and its different occasions. Personal narratives are often applied in cognitive anthropology because of the knowledge and meanings they convey. Cognitive anthropology investigates the relationship between human mind and culture. In other words, we want to know how the knowledge of individuals becomes culture, or shared knowledge, and what people think about things and phenomena that make up their perceptual worlds.

This research consists of narrative data I collected from 23 interviews between 1995 and 2005. My sample includes Finnish horse loggers, farmers and trotting (horse) people. In addition to participant observation fieldwork, I draw on 125 personal narratives and memories from the Folklore archives of the Finnish Literature Society.[1] In the interviews I focus on memories and experiences of working with horses in agriculture and forestry. The data from the Folklore archives are also a valuable resource, in that they stem from a writing competition[2] announced in newspapers and horse magazines in 2003. The competition invited people to write about their experiences of horses "in the olden days," today and as professionals. The interviewees are all men born between 1904 and 1964. The Folklore archive data consists of the narratives of 89 women and 36 men born between 1918 and 1989. Men figure prominently in my own interviews because I presumed that men had most knowledge about working horses. Moreover, male informants tended to refer me to other men as good horse handlers worth interviewing. Since I conducted my own interviews before I read the archive narratives, it was only later that I began to appreciate that many women born before 1960 actually had a vast knowledge of and considerable experience with horses. Finnish women, as well as men, had been handling horses from childhood. Reading the archives helped me to understand how more pronounced cultural models of the companionship of man and horse acted to overlook or silence the voice of women.

Cultural models of horse human relationships

The meanings we give to animals affect the way we interact with them (Dutton 2007; Lawrence 1994; Stibbe 2001). That is why we treat lab rats differently from pet rats. Meanings change with time, livelihoods and ideologies (Ylimaunu 2002). Lawrence (1985, 293) holds that:

> Where cultural perceptions determine that animals and people share many important qualities and can cooperate and communicate, it follows that the treatment of animals generally is based on respect. In human-animal interactions, the degree of awareness attributed to the beasts works in dynamic equilibrium: the more an animal is downgraded as an object whose worth is measured only by usefulness to mankind, the less it is possible for that animal to have meaningful input into a relationship with people.

What Lawrence (1985, 293) calls "cultural perceptions," I call cultural models. Cultural models are affected by the media, literature and interaction with other people. They are constructed socially with other people. In Finland, this can be seen in the ways that different generations of people tell about their lives and their relationship to animals. Cultural knowledge and cultural models are hardly exact representations of the animals people have encountered; rather they are more flexible generalizations of the animal and the things that are associated with it (Quinn 2005b; Shore 1996).

I analyzed the three sets of data to find the most common concepts given to horses and the associations connected to them. I paid particular attention to what the horses were called, how their physical and mental qualities were described and how the human horse relationship was described. My analysis illustrates that even though the cultural models of the horse change more slowly than the use of horses, they too do change gradually. The working horse was seen as a servant and even as a machine until the 1960s. During World War II, the war horse emerged as a hero. From the 1970s onward the cultural model of the horse gradually changed to that of a performer in sport and therapist in leisure. In the following sections, I identify and present a series of different cultural models of horses and of human horse relationships. Data will be used to identify and discuss core principles on which people base their interaction with the horse. Cultural models included are horse as servant, horse as machine, horse as hero, horse as performer and horse as therapist.

Horse as a servant

The period of fast modernization in agriculture and forestry lasted only one hundred years (from the 1860s to 1960s) in Finland. This was a period when cultivating methods intensified and the forest industry grew rapidly. During this time, horses were used intensively in agriculture and forestry. They were also essential for traveling and played important roles in the army. Most Finns considered horses to be faithful servants. One informant expresses this sentiment as follows: "Horses like it when you work with them, because they were created as servants for humans. And they will serve humans as long as they have the right personality for it and they are used well" (Interviews 1997: man b. 1924).

Cultural models and metaphors, however, are not value free (Goatly 2006) and calling the horse a servant entails the existence of uneven power relations between a horse and a human. Servant themes, however, also include affection towards and usefulness and agency of the animal. The data show that people who were born during the agrarian era – that is, until the 1950s – share a very similar model of the horse as a servant to humans. Finns value work (Silvasti 2003, 144–145) and horses were valued for "working together" with humans. When remembering their childhood, youth and working years, informants portrayed the horse as instrumental in creating prosperity. The horse was a helper and a coworker in cultivating the land. Horses' labor was a source of cash brought for those who used them to work logging sites. Finnish farms, mostly self-sufficient, were small family farms. Every family member, including animals, had their place and their work to do. Horses were at the top of the farm animal hierarchy because they were considered to be men's working-companions, but also occupied a status of friend. Utilitarian and empathic attitudes to farm animals are not exclusionary (Bokkers 2006). In the servant model of the horse, both horse and human shared a kind of moral duty and work effort. Farmers saw themselves as having a moral duty to take care of animals. In the interviews horses are presented as "creatures of nature." This implies both a subordination to humans and a farmer's responsibility to take care of animals. It is the responsibility of the horse to work for the human. Informants say that horses liked working with humans as long as the workload was reasonable. This kind of thinking can be seen as a Christian idea of humans being responsible for the animals that were created for them (Silvasti 2003).

The narratives depict a good working horse in terms of physical features such as being tall, heavy and strong. Horses who were fast walkers with long strides were preferred. Geldings and mares were favored as being easier to handle than stallions. Valued mental features of horses were also mentioned. These include the horse as a wise, sentient and moral being, who has a good memory and an advanced capacity to sense human feelings. Each horse was also perceived to have its own personality, as versatile as is the case for humans. All working horses were Finnhorses, who are, like other native breeds, adapted to the environment and have been bred and shaped by the people for human use or purpose (Walker 2008). The Finnhorse has strong symbolic meanings for Finns and the identity of the Finnish people.[3] The horse is seen as an equal partner in the history of the nation. Just like its owners, the horse is deemed hardy, stubborn and independent.

Treatment of working horses depended on perceptions of them as wise and sentient servants. In various cultures, people and working animals develop a close bond that is based on mutual regard with a high level of mutual awareness. The relationship is, nevertheless, primarily one that is instrumental and hierarchical (Knight 2012; van Dierendonck and Goodwin 2005). Narratives show that while working horses were expected to obey people there was usually a sense of genuine communication between the master and the servant. I analyzed the narratives for indications of what exactly makes a good human working horse relationship and found five factors. These are expressed as trust, human leadership, matching personalities, mutual understanding and time spent together. In previous research, trust is often considered an essential part of the human horse relationship (Armstrong Oma 2010; Keaveney 2008; Maurstad et al. 2013; Robinson 1999; van Dierendonck and Goodwin 2005). My data make no exception. One interviewee explained that to gain the trust of a horse one must treat the horse "consistently, calmly and decisively without demanding too much of the horse" (Interviews 1997: man b. 1957). According to animal trainer and philosopher Vicki Hearne, trust builds on functioning communication and given rules. The better the animal has been trained, the greater its "vocabulary" is, the better is the trust between a human and an animal (Hearne 2007, 21). A well-treated and taught horse is said to be "like a master's thought." The horse wants to please his master so it has to be treated with love and compassion.

In terms of functionality, in the servant model, the horse requires absolute human leadership. According to the research materials, leadership is roughly divided into two types: dominant and caring. Leadership is always associated with perceptions of power and responsibility and it requires interaction skills. If the person does not have them, the interaction with the animal is prone to failure. As performance pressures increase, human behaviors may become increasingly dominant and violent (Knight 2012; van Dierendonck and Goodwin 2005). A caring leader will assume responsibility for the animal and treat the animal well. He/she is also able to temporarily hand over the leadership position to the horse, in tasks where the horse performs better than people, for example, finding the load-bearing path in the snow.

A working relationship is also said to presuppose matching personalities in interspecies relationships. This includes the idea that humans and horses can "think accordingly" thus making working together a successful endeavor. Interviews also reveal the idea that there are only some people with which the horse gladly works. In other words, the horse needs someone he or she can respect. This, in the informant's discourse, would be someone who likes the horse and shows empathy towards it. People state that it is good for the horse if there is only one person at a time communicating with it, otherwise the horse will shut itself down and listen to nobody.

In the working horse narratives, the human horse relationship is also associated with a sense of time. In times of rapid sociocultural change, time can be taken or slowed down. One sense of time comes from taking the time to capture or savor a moment. Here, time slows down as one sits on the horse-driven sleigh and has time to think and to observe the environment. On the other hand, a longer range may entail the period of time that it takes to breed and train a horse. This usually takes years to achieve. That is why foals were handled from early on in agrarian societies (Knight 2012). It is said to make the horse more co-operative over his or her lifetime.

Horse as a machine

Not all workhorses were treated with empathy and patience. The human horse working relationship is open to abuse when economic ambitions combine with handlers who are less skillful and empathetic (van Dierendonck and Goodwin 2005). In the data, the stories of cruelty are mostly associated with hard work such as logging in the huge wintery logging sites. For example:

> It was the horse that suffered the distress, laziness, ignorance and poverty of its driver. There were men who did not feed their horse any oats in the evening. The hay they gave was damp and of poor quality. Even if the horse was old, small in size, toothless or emotionally cripple, the sick driver always wanted the best performance. It is a horse, it has to be able.
> (SKS KRA. HT man b. 1928, 2003)[4]

The last sentence in this quote refers to the idea that the horse is a strong animal and can thus always perform, no matter what the conditions are like. Most men took good care of their horses in the logging sites, but the reason abuse is mentioned in this context is probably because some men purchased horses for just one winter's logging. Horses either lasted for only that season or were sold in poor condition in spring to horse dealers who, in turn, sold them back to loggers the following fall.

Horses were compared to slaves in some of the narratives. Here, working horses become the objects of control and exploitation just like nature. The machine model evidences a negative attitude towards horses, with terms like fear, aversion or indifference (Kellert 1997). The comparison of the horse to a machine is partly connected to a developing enthusiasm for new technologies and machinery that characterized the late 1800s. One manifestation of this is the emergence of a desire or need to measure the horse's performance and compare it with machines. This makes the horse an object and instrument and relates to Cartesian and modernist interpretation of the horse as machine and/or kind of "biotechnology" (Schuurman 2012, 184; Greene 2008, 4, 5).

People for whom the horse is like a machine or a slave treat it accordingly. The machine horse is expected to work as long as it can stay on its feet. This kind of thinking creates a human horse relationship based on instrumentality, suspicion, indifference, dominance and ignorance. Instrumentality is visible in the notion of the horses as tools and bad ones if they do not perform. Relationship with the horse is characterized by lack of empathy, that is, these people are unable to see horses as sentient beings and are too indifferent to take care of them properly.

Suspicion towards horses grows from the lack of trust, as neither the horse nor the human has positive experiences about working with one another. Horses' personalities are not considered or even thought to exist. All horses are treated the same way. Indifference towards the horse seems to increase particularly if the horse is cheap. Not everyone liked horses; they just wanted to get the job done. Mechanistic and negative understanding of the horse made people see horses as angry, lazy or restive and disobedient to people. Like slaves horses can be beaten into obedience. The horse's strength and ability to pull heavy loads is appreciated but not his or her efforts to communicate.

The need to dominate is often connected with masculinity (DeMello 2012). Perpetrators of violence come through in the data. For example, a few men admit that in their youth, they caused pain to horses, because they did not yet understand that the horse had the ability to suffer. The human capacity for empathy increases with age, and some studies have shown that women tend to express more empathy than men (van Dierendonck and Goodwin 2005). Being violent towards animals can be influenced by multiple factors such as mental and physical violence experienced in childhood and daily stress (Henry and Sanders 2007, Taylor and Signal 2005). Wider sociocultural factors such as class, sexism, racism and slavery can also be linked to systems of abuse that also affect animals (DeMello 2012). Abusive practices are associated with the subordination of women and children and the lower echelons of agrarian society. Animal subordination is also explained with social dominance theory, according to which the ones that identify themselves to be at the top of the social hierarchy, create and maintain the "legitimate myths" to justify the exploitation of others (DeMello 2012, 261).

No one in my data boasts about being violent towards horses; but hitting a horse is talked about openly in the interviews. Although generally accepted, up to a point, if the beating is considered severe, people will interfere and report it to the police.

The machine model can also be ascribed to ignorance and misunderstanding, by which I mean that the horse is not intentionally mistreated, but one does not know how to take care of it. For example, it was commonly thought in Finland that feeding horses rye flour made them strong. As a matter of fact, however, it could be lethal (Leinonen 2012). The horse is perceived to be in working condition, as long as it was "intact," that is, it did not have any externally visible injuries. Yet, the horse could be so weak from poor feeding, that he or she scarcely kept on his or her feet. It was a daily challenge first to get the horse on its feet and then to keep it on its feet. A quote from the archival narratives elaborates this further:

> In the morning, it was difficult for the horse to get up on its feet. Voikko[5] could get up if its head was towards the door. There was a larger space there. Once I spent the whole morning until noon trying to get Voikko's head towards the door but I couldn't do it because I didn't have enough strength. Finally I took down the whole wall, and got Voikko to its feet. The stable was made of moss so it was easy to take the wall down. It was not until after the (Second World) war that a cowshed with a stable was built with logs.
>
> In the winter it was difficult to get the hay from the barn. I once had to come back with an empty sleigh because Voikko couldn't make it to the haystack. It fell to the ground on its side. I tried to entice it to get on its feet and I pulled it up from its tail, and managed to turn it to the direction where we came from.
>
> (SKS KRA. HT man b. 1928, 2003)

Horse as a hero

During World War II, as the civilian workhorses were taken to war, the conception of the horse as a hero was born (Leinonen 2012). In the war the horse's role as a servant was taken to the extreme. People felt gratitude, sorrow and guilt for the fate of the horses. Veteran horses were respected and were treated very well if they made it back home. If the horse died, the death was a cause of great grief in the family. Horses were remembered and stories of them were told to future generations. Two excerpts from the archive narratives illustrate the hero model:

> At the front I was constantly working with horses. At Rukajärvi my eyes got sick. I rode to Tieksa and back to Rukajärvi to get papers that gave me permission to treatment in Hyks.[6] I was grateful to the horse that carried a blind man for tens of kilometres.
>
> (SKS KRA. HT man b. 1921, 2003)

> Even years later we were remembering how Poju[7] left for war. As Poju left from our yard, everyone was there to see it as long as we could see it. And everyone had tears in their eyes, even men. Our milkmaid cried for days though she tried to hide it. Separation from Poju was hard.
>
> (SKS KRA. HT woman, 2003)

During World War II, the horse was a convenient, and often the only means of transport in the Finnish and Soviet borderlands. A war horse's physical characteristics were determined by the army. Horses considered to be in their prime were workhorses – 5- to 18-year-old mares and geldings. The officers had warm blooded riding horses but the artillery and maintenance used almost exclusively Finnhorses.

The idea of a war horse as hero and victim makes for a relationship based on affection, respect and patience. Horses are thanked, honored and pitied for their sacrifices in war. War horses are anthropomorphized more than other models of horses presented in the narratives. They are called heroes, brothers in arms, veterans, defenders of the country and fellow-sufferers in the cruel war conditions. They are even said to make the war more humane (Leinonen 2012). Shared risks and dangers gave men a sense of solidarity with their horses (Lawrence 1989). If the horses lacked feed, the soldiers gave them their own bread portions and when it was cold they gave their blankets to their horses. Horses were pitied, because they had to suffer for the insanity of men. The horses were seen as innocent victims. The relationship between the war horse and its human caretaker was often a very affectionate one.

For the most part the narratives do not include many recollections about the horrors of war. Instead, the memories concentrate on the human horse partnership. Memories feature the worry, grief, and anticipation felt by the people on the home-front and delight of reunions experienced after the war. Each war horse was designated a caretaker among the soldiers, who often started a correspondence with the owners of the horse, telling how he or she was doing. Owners sent care packages to the war-front. The relationship of women and horses also changed during the war. Women did the farm work with horses when the men were at the front. Some women worked in horse hospitals at the front, thus gaining knowledge and skills that they would find useful after the war.

Horses that were returned by the army to their owners after the war came galloping and neighing to their home yard, if they could. As they were regarded as heroes and were respected, they were fed better and were taken into account more than other horses on the farm. Although continuing to work on the farm, they were also given space to rest and recover. Even though horses were in bad shape physically after the war and suffered from mental traumas, people report understanding them and handling them with patience.

Horse as a performer

There are about 75,000 horses in Finland today (Finnish Trotting and Breeding Association 2015). About half are trotting horses. Trotting races are the most popular horse sport in Finland. Most of these sport horses are Standardbreds and Finnhorses. Finnhorses are also used for competitive and recreational riding. A typical sport horse is young, athletic, lightweight, muscular and suitable for show jumping and dressage. Informants characterize sport horses as having strong personalities, being tough, energetic, determined and fiery. A horse's abilities, behavior and temperament can be attributed to either inheritance or training. These two models resonate with the nature and nurture debates (Macbeth 1989). The meaning of inheritance is emphasized for the owners of sport horses, who are mostly professionals and who say that a horse is born with either good or bad qualities: "You can ruin a good horse, but you cannot make a poor one good" (Interviews 1995: man b. 1930). For example, humility of the horse is thought of as an inherited trait that is said to make training easier. Those who emphasize nurture speak of the importance of training and treatment of the sport horse.

Horse professionals are practical. Their passion or love for horses is tempered by a sense of utility or instrumentalism. Professionals employ a species-specific knowledge of horse behaviors as a guide to training a particular horse. Yet, professionals must also be able to handle horses with different abilities, temperaments and ages. Horse professionals handle several horses a day and many of their horse relationships are short in duration. Nature, as inherent abilities, here, trumps nurture as professionals do not want to waste resources on horses that are not suitable for sport use. Instead, unsuitable horses are sold or taken for slaughter.

Training or nurture is also an important theme that emerges in the narratives. All professionals in my data talk about gaining the horse's respect with consistent treatment. According to the consistency model, professionals have to work in a goal-oriented, determined and calm way in order to get the horse into competition condition. These trainers draw on a leadership model that is based on a conception of the horse as a hierarchical herd animal, and willing to please its leader.

Nature and nurture also combine when professionals emphasize that one has to know how to read a horse and to know its habits, to be able to train it successfully. Trainers plan the daily training according to the condition of the horse. Grooms take care of the horses, always thinking primarily of what the horse needs. Reluctant and ill horses are not strained, because the horse is seen as a top athlete, and if strained, it might lead to a longer sick leave or be fatal to the animal. Horses are considered as individuals, and top horses are given privileges.

Those who participate in Finnhorse and Standardbred trotting horse sports typically feel that their love for the sport is rooted in nature, as "in their blood." This means that their family has owned horses for generations.

Most of the professionals are content with their work, even though it is hard, with long working hours and bad wages. They say that they would not be able to do it without the love for horses and the sport:

> [...] such a great care is taken of these sport horses that the personal well-being of the trainer or groom is not important. It is the horse and nothing else. Everything is done that can be done. And it takes a lot of attachment and love because there usually is no reward for it.
>
> (Interviews 1995: man b. 1930)

Professionals and goal-oriented hobbyists are ambitious about their horses. They want to succeed, whether it is about breeding a prize pony, winning the championship race for Finnhorses or the show jumping derby. Everything is aimed at winning and success at competitions. The horse is bred and trained for specific sport activities. Sport horses are taken care of as well as possible in order to keep competing successfully. The sport horse thus becomes an instrument of human competitive instinct and ambition (Schuurman 2012).

Horse as a therapist

> As hard values shape the world
> colder and crueler
> it is good then for someone disappointed in life
> to lean to the soft muzzle of the horse.
>
> (SKS KRA. HT man b. 1933, 2003)

These lines are a part of a poem written by a man who used to work with horses in his youth and later became a trotting horse hobbyist. He sees the meaning of the horse today as a friend and a therapist, a counterbalance to "the hard values of today's society." The view of the horse as a therapist comes through in interviews with riding school customers, horse owners and trotting hobbyists. Increased free time, wealth and urbanization have resulted in a leisure horse culture that provides thrills and serves as a way to cope with everyday life.

Unlike the case for work and sport, in Finland, horses used for leisure activities come in a variety of breeds. The physical character of the horse and its ability to perform, however, are still a central focus of concern. The breed of the leisure horse is selected in terms of what he or she will be used for and the needs of the owner. Children have ponies for riding and trotting. Adults also have horses of various breeds. The horses come in all ages and mares and geldings are preferred.

When the horse is seen as a leisure companion and therapist, the human horse relationship becomes based on needs for mutual understanding and well-being. Among the hobbyists of the 21st century, these needs are expressed as nurture, friendship, cooperation and trust, powerful experiences and an ability to follow the human lead. Leisure riders tend to come from urban environments rather than from traditional farm or horse families. Their encounters with horses are limited to one or two times a week at a riding school. They tend to lack experience with and knowledge about horses. On the other hand, there is a wealth of knowledge today and it is easily accessible online, in books and through taking lessons. Leisure riders aspire to see the world from the horse's perspective. Their goal is to understand and adjust their behaviors, in terms of communication and bodily messages, in ways that take into account how the horse responds to them as humans. Maurstad et al. (2013, 324) refer to this as "co-shaping and co-domesticating each other."

A contradiction of ideas in handling the horse is obvious in the leader/friend model. Those who believe that the human has to be the leader base their belief on what they perceive to be a biological and natural law that attributes herd survival to a wise, effective and responsible equine leader. Just as horses follow the leader horse in the wild, they must learn to accept a human leader. Horses who obey humans are safer to be around. The friend model of human horse relationship asserts that being with a horse is like "equal friendship." While this view holds that the horse can reciprocate friendship, it is the human who ultimately has to take the responsibility or the dominant role in the friendship. Leadership and safety are often connected with trust. To be able to work with and control the horse one needs to have mutual trust (Maurstad et al. 2013). This, in turn, requires self-confidence as a handler and an interpreter of horse behavior. Gaining trust takes time but achieving it creates an affinity between a human and a horse.

Well-being and nurture are considered to be mutual. People want to take good care of their horses and they are keen on giving the horse a life worth living. Taking good care of horses is considered to improve the human's own sense of well-being. Many informants described their relationship to horses as being therapeutic. This is especially true for teenagers when they are having crises in their lives. Going to the stable or taking a ride into the woods can restore balance to everyday life. Horses are considered to carry the worries of people.[8] Women, in particular, say that all their worries are forgotten when they are with horses. Additionally, some informants feel that horses were taking care of them. Getting powerful experiences are also considered part of the leisure horse culture. Horses help women to transcend the daily grind of routine living and responsibility – at least for a while. Experiencing nature on horseback, sensing the horse's power, speed, movements and the affection shown by the horse are all considered to be positive experiences. Succeeding in handling a difficult horse gives feelings of accomplishment and empowerment. Working with horses also leads leisure riders to a respect for other horse people. This is how the experience of riding is described:

> [...] in my mind I am already sitting on horseback getting fine experiences that are impossible to describe to people that have never ridden a

> horse. When you are riding you have to be sensitive, demanding, receiving, and accurate all at the same time.... To be able to control your body and the horse's body on every step. Riding is like ballet dancing.
>
> (SKS KRA. HT woman b. 1967, 2003)

Conclusions

My analysis of cultural models of horses over the last century illustrates that the meaning of horses is variable and changeable through time. At its most extreme the cultural model of the horse has transformed from that of a man's slave to a woman's therapist. Behind these changes from servant, machine and hero to performer and therapist lies the transformation from communal agrarian culture to more individual and hedonistic leisure cultures. A different kind of interaction has been emphasized in different eras in the human horse relationship depending on the use of the horse.

Cultural models often seem obvious but when we take a closer look they gain multiple meanings in different temporal and socioeconomic contexts. The Finnish models do overlap and are connected to each other. Despite these perceptual differences or models concerning the nature of the human horse relationship, the idea of the horse as a cognitively gifted and sentient animal, an active agent and a friend has persisted throughout the 20th century.

Trust is an example of an element of the human horse relationship that has changed in the last decades. In the agrarian era, the horse was given more responsibility and freedom. Horses were trusted to get their wounded soldier rider home to the base in war time or their sleeping, or drunken farmer rider safely back to home in times of peace. Horses were trusted to navigate through the most difficult terrain and to roam free in the farm yard or in forests in summertime. Today the lives of sport and leisure horses are more restricted as they spend most of their lives in their stalls, leaving them only for a brief exercise or a few hours in a pen. The practices of horse keeping have changed as have notions of well-being and nurture. Many working horses were not brushed, washed, regularly shod or taken to the vet before World War II. Today's horses are well taken care of and covered with blankets, fed a fancy diet and have the services of a masseur, a vet and a trainer.

Ideas of leadership are shifting from dominant master–servant ideas to more scientific and equal ways of perceiving the human horse relationship where the human is seen less as leader but more as teacher. The servant model is still alive, however, with people who work with horses. Also the sense of time has changed with the shift from work use to recreational use of the horse, as the amount of time spent with them has changed. Working with a horse during a whole day in the slower pace of the agrarian society has changed to a quick visit to the stables after work. On the other hand, the contact with leisure horses is usually relaxing as there is no pressure of subsistence or daily survival.

The narratives and interviews of Finnish horse people in my data have served as abundant sources for the diverse schemes of meaning-making that have both changed and remained consistent over time. Memories make us who we are, and most of the stories begin with memories and experiences from childhood. Childhood experiences form the worldview and relationship to nature and animals for each generation. The cultural models learned in childhood are relatively stable through life, even though horse use and roles have changed through urbanization. Horses used to be symbols of masculinity, and boys wanted to grow up to be good horsemen. Boys wanted to handle and drive horses from early on and wanted to be like the men who were role models for their future. If there were no boys in the house, girls helped their father with the horses. Girls handling horses were considered daring and to be crossing more conventional gender practices. Yet, when these girls became women other demands on their time precluded their ability to take the time needed for horse care.

Girls today can go to the riding stables and learn that horses are a part of feminine space and culture.[9] Riding is considered a very feminine hobby and it is the boys now who need to cross the gendered practices to ride horses. Today, most boys do not want to risk getting the stigma of a girl's hobby even if they are interested in horses. Trotting stables have more men working in them but here too it is the women who usually take care of the horses. However, for today's children horses and ponies represent leisure time, an exciting hobby, a friend and a pet. Hard work and responsibility is only present if they have a horse/pony of their own or they are helpers and grooms at the stables. The work is done *for* the horses, not *with* them, making humans sometimes feel like they are now servants to horses.

Changing models of horse human relationships invite further investigation for they can contribute to the formation of new knowledge in handling horses. This is a knowledge that combines experience and science. It combines effective consistent horsemanship with the empathy of horse-*woman*ship. Although notions of utility or service and domination of the horse continue to be associated with present-day horse handling, new ways of knowing and being with the horse, in this case the Finnhorse, are emerging.

Notes

1 The Finnish Literature Society is an international research institute, national memory organization and national cultural organization founded in 1831. It consists of literary and folklore archives, library, publishing house and a research department.

2 Writing competitions are an established way of collecting folk knowledge in Finland that dates back to the end of the 1800s.

3 It was named the National Horse of Finland in 2007. Its story is part of "the great national story" of Finland with wars and rebuilding, development of agriculture and forestry and building of the welfare state.

4 Archive references: SKS means Suomalaisen Kirjallisuuden Seura [Finnish Literature Society]; KRA means Kansanrunousarkisto [Folklore Archives]; HT means Hevostarina [Horse Narrative Collection]; man b. 1928, 2003 means male born in 1928, narrative collected 2003.
5 The name of the horse refers to its coloring, palomino.
6 Hyks refers to a hospital in Helsinki.
7 *Poju* means boy.
8 This idea goes back for centuries as it is mentioned already in the old poetry of Kalevala, the national epic of Finland.
9 Ninety-four percent of the members of the Equestrian Federation of Finland are women (Equestrian Federation of Finland 2015).

References

Armstrong Oma, Kristin. 2010. "Between Trust and Domination: Social Contracts between Humans and Animals." *World Archaeology* 42(2): 175–187.

Bokkers, Eddie A. M. 2006. "Effects of Interactions between Humans and Domesticated Animals." In *Farming for Health*, edited by Jan Hassink and Majken van Dijk, 31–41. The Netherlands: Springer.

D'Andrade, Roy. 2000. *The Development of Cognitive Anthropology*. Cambridge: Cambridge University Press.

DeMello, Margo. 2012. *Animals and Society: An Introduction to Human–Animal Studies*. New York: Columbia University Press.

Dutton, Diane. 2007. "Metaphors in Constructing Human–Animal Relationships." In *Encyclopedia of Human–Animal Relationships Vol 3*, edited by Marc Bekoff, 1065–1068. Westport, CT: Greenwood Press.

Equestrian Federation of Finland. 2015. "Facts and Figures: Equestrianism in Finland." Accessed 30 January 2015, http://www.ratsastus.fi/.

Finnish Trotting and Breeding Association. 2015. "Hevosten lukumäärän kehitys 1910-.[Development of the Number of Horses (from 1910 to present)]." Accessed 26 February 2015, http://www.hippos.fi/files/4481/Hevosmaara_kokon_1910.pdf.

Goatly, Andrew. 2006. "Humans, Animals and Metaphors." *Society & Animals* 14(1): 15–37.

Greene, Ann Norton. 2008. *Horses at Work. Harnessing Power in Industrial America*. Cambridge, MA: Harvard University Press.

Hearne, Vicki. 2007. *Adam's Task: Calling Animals by Name*. New York: Skyhorse.

Henry, Bill and Cheryl E. Sanders. 2007. "Bullying and Animal Abuse: Is There a Connection?" *Society & Animals* 15(2): 107–126.

Keaveney, Susan M. 2008. "Equines and their Human Companions." *Journal of Business Research* 61(5): 444–454.

Kellert, Stephen R. 1997. *The Value of Life. Biological Diversity and Human Society*. Washington, DC: Island Press, Shearwater Books.

Knight, John. 2012. "The Anonymity of the Hunt: A Critique of Hunting as Sharing." *Current Anthropology* 53(3): 334–355.

Lawrence, Elizabeth A. 1985. "Human Perceptions of Animals and Animal Awareness: The Cultural Dimension." In *Advances in Animal Welfare Science 1985/86*, edited by M. W. Fox and L. D. Mickley, 285–295. Washington, DC: The Humane Society of the United States.

Lawrence, Elizabeth A. 1989. *His Very Silence Speaks: Comanche – The Horse Who Survived Custer's Last Stand*. Detroit: Wayne State University Press.

Lawrence, Elizabeth A. 1994. "Conflicting ideologies: Views of Animal Rights Advocates and their Opponents." *Society & Animals* 2(2): 175–190.

Leinonen, Riitta-Marja. 2012. "Finnish Narratives of the Horse in World War II." In *Animals and War: Studies of Europe and North America*, edited by Ryan Hediger, 123–150. Boston: Brill.

Macbeth, Helen M. 1989. "Nature/Nurture: The False Dichotomies." *Anthropology Today* 5(4): 12–15.

Maurstad, Anita, Dona Davis, and Sarah Cowles. 2013. "Co-being and Intra-action in Horse–Human Relationships: A Multi-species Ethnography of Be(com)ing Human and Be(com)ing Horse." *Social Anthropology* 21(3): 322–335.

Quinn, Naomi. 2005a. "Introduction." In *Finding Culture in Talk. A Collection of Methods*, edited by Naomi Quinn, 1–34. New York: Palgrave Macmillan.

Quinn, Naomi. 2005b. "How to Reconstruct Schemas People Share, From What They Say." In *Finding Culture in Talk. A Collection of Methods*, edited by Naomi Quinn, 35–82. New York: Palgrave Macmillan.

Robinson, I. H. 1999. "The Human Horse Relationship: How Much Do We Know?" *Equine Veterinary Journal*, 31: 42–45.

Schuurman, Nora. 2012. *"Hevoset hevosina": Eläimen ja sen hyvinvoinnin tulkinta* ["Horses as Horses": Interpreting the Animal and Its Welfare]. Publications of the University of Eastern Finland, Dissertation in Social Sciences and Business Studies No 37.

Shore, Brad. 1996. *Culture in Mind. Cognition, Culture and the Problem of Meaning*. New York: Oxford University Press.

Silvasti, Tiina. 2003. "The Cultural Model of 'The Good Farmer' and the Environmental Question in Finland." *Agriculture and Human Values* 20: 143–150.

Stibbe, Arran. 2001. "Language, Power and the Social Construction of Animals." *Society & Animals* 9(2): 145–161.

Taylor, Nik and Tania D. Signal. 2005. "Empathy and Attitudes to Animals." *Anthrozoös* 18(1): 18–27.

van Dierendonck, Machteld and Debbie Goodwin. 2005. "Social Contact in Horses: Implications for Human–Horse Interactions." In *The Human–Animal Relationship: Forever and a Day*, edited by F. H. De Jonge and Ruud van den Bros, 65–81. Assen: Uitgereij Van Gorcum.

Walker, Elaine. 2008. *Horse*. London: Reaction Books.

Ylimaunu, Juha. 2002. "Elinkeinot ihmisen ja eläimen suhteen muokkaajana." In *Eläin ihmisen mielenmaisemassa* [The Animal in the Mindset of the Human], edited by Henni Ilomäki and Outi Lauhakangas, 115–133. Helsinki: Suomalaisen Kirjallisuuden Seura.

5 From Working to Winning

The Shifting Symbolic Value of Connemara Ponies in the West of Ireland

Claire J. Brown

In the town of Clifden, County Galway, located on the west coast of Ireland, the local lives of Connemara ponies and their owners intersect with global processes of commodification, globalization and modernization. Connemara ponies are symbolic markers and active agents of change over time in processes of status negotiation and economic power in the lives of their owners. Similar to other forms of cultural performance in Ireland, Connemara ponies and their competitions are "symbols and rituals which transcend differences among people in a society, serving to integrate disparate classes, occupations, ethnic groups, regions and religions" (Donnan and Wilson 1999, 67). Creating a "symbolic vocabulary" (Cohen 1985, 28) for the Connemara pony does not imply a disregard for the agentic qualities of the animal, as the ponies themselves act as catalysts for social interactions amongst diverse populations. "Animal 'objects' can also become active subjects with the capacity to impact the relationships between the humans involved" (Hurn 2012, 125).

In light of these complexities in evaluating the animal as a symbol, this research considers the Connemara pony as a functioning symbolic agent in representing the history and heritage of the Connemara region while simultaneously heralding modernity and progress in its marketing and sales. This analysis articulates the ways in which the Connemara pony itself is a social, political and economic symbol that is recognized at local, regional, and national levels. By treating Connemara ponies as simultaneously "parts of human society," as well as "symbols of it," this work bridges a symbolic and agentic perspective of human–animal relations (Knight 2005, 1). The symbolic power of individual equines translates into an even stronger material function of horse and pony breeds in constructing national identity. Horses and ponies often physically embody culturally valued traits such as strength, stamina and adaptability to the landscape, and have been interpreted as markers of national identity in Australia (Peace 2009), the Sakha Republic (Maj 2009), Spain (Thompson 2011), Ireland (Latimer and Birke 2009), Wales (Hurn 2008a,b), England (Cassidy 2002a, 2002b, 2003, 2005), Kyrgyzstan (Cassidy 2009), and Iron Age Pazyryk (Argent 2010). As these works illustrate, considering horses as symbols does not reduce their agency; rather, the strong material value attributed to these animals allows them to significantly impact the lives of their owners. This chapter argues that the changing morphology and commodification of the Connemara pony acts as a material culture vehicle that is the means for ideology, people, and local identities to move across multiple borders at home in Ireland and more globally (Wilk 2004).

Situating the Connemara pony: Symbol, agent, commodity

The definition of 'symbol' and the notion of a 'symbolic vocabulary' used in this chapter draw upon the work of Cohen (1985, 28), who notes that although symbols are held in common by members of a society, they also vary with members' different orientations to their meaning. According to Cohen (1985, 15), symbols "do not so much express meaning as give us the capacity to make meaning." Symbols are malleable and adaptable to different spatial and temporal contexts, as symbolic meaning is determined by individuals' orientations to the symbol. This analysis considers not only the symbolic ideological qualities of Connemara ponies, but also their materiality and multiple morphologies resulting from their changing roles as commodities in Connemara society. It is important to give equal weight to a symbol's physical features and form as one does to the meaning that is abstracted from it; as Eipper (2007, 256) argues, "we too often neglect the materiality of the symbol in favour of its meaning."

Anthropologists applying this symbolic perspective to the physical features and forms of animals advocate that animals are "good to think" (Hurn 2012, 85), and perceive animals as symbols whose multiple morphologies reflect changing social and cultural aspects of human life. In appreciating the materiality of the symbol, one must also consider the impact that a symbol can have in its own right. Animals are sentient beings that directly influence the humans who come into contact with them; therefore the very act of according symbolic status to an animal in turn requires that the animal influences the actions and thoughts of humans. This analysis therefore considers the agency of Connemara ponies in tandem with their symbolic qualities, and the ways in which pony owners respect and represent their individual ponies as symbolic agents.

While human–animal researchers in anthropology largely argue against anthropologists portraying animals as "entities for the benefit of humans, whether for economic or symbolic purposes" (Overton and Hamilakis 2013, 114), this chapter considers a symbolic perspective valuable as long as our informants themselves consider the animal as a symbol. Anthropologists must examine the ways in which the people we study actually view animals at the ground level if we hope to achieve a full understanding of the intersections between human and animal lives in our research (Hurn 2012, 134). Therefore anthropologically considering animals as symbols and agents is best understood through the perceptions of research respondents, who often accord animals both object and subject status (Cassidy 2002a, 2002b). As Hurn (2012, 103) observes, while anthropologists have criticized the symbolic reductionism of animals, "it is also true that many humans who are not theoretically engaged with the issue will continue to see animals, including their own animals, as symbols."

Fieldwork in Connemara

The Connemara pony is inextricably linked with the Connemara region through not only its name, but also as a reminder of the agricultural heritage, rural character, and general hardiness of the region. Animals are often used as symbolic indicators of place or as guardians of boundaries within human cultural constructs, and the Connemara pony in Ireland is no exception (Wessing 2006, 206). A sense of place and landscape plays a critical role in the constitution of human–animal relationships, rather than merely existing as a background setting (Marvin 2003, 2005). The place and landscape at the forefront of this analysis is the town of Clifden, County Galway, which is widely considered to be the 'capital of Connemara,' as well as the 'capital of Connemara ponies.' Clifden is also home to the headquarters of the national Connemara Pony Breeders' Society. Breeding and showing performance Connemara ponies in Clifden creates a social, economic, and political context in which rural social relations are defined and local identities are established. Clifden is therefore an ideal location for "telling a global story from the point of view of one tiny place" (Wilk 2006, 23).

This research derives from fieldwork conducted within the Connemara pony industry during the summers of 2009–2013, through my immersion in the social and economic Connemara pony world while living and working in Clifden. Much like Rebecca Cassidy's experience in becoming 'one of the lads' during her ethnographic study of Thoroughbred racing culture in Newmarket, I became one of the local 'pony girls' in the Clifden scene (Cassidy 2002a). A critical factor in breaking into the local pony scene was my participant observation working as a 'pony girl' at Errislannan Manor, a local pony breeding and trekking center. Working at the yard involved assisting in organizing Pony Club camps, leading treks, grooming and tacking the ponies, feeding, assisting the trainers during lessons and organizing paperwork on the business side of the trekking center. By showing knowledge of caring for and riding ponies, working at Errislannan gave me the social credentials to enter into the Connemara pony community.

This involvement at Errislannan enabled crucial social contacts with noted breeders, judges and exhibitors throughout Connemara, with whom I conducted interviews, as well as spent casual time while taking care of their animals and engaging in 'pony chat.' As the years of my fieldwork progressed I also came into contact with active members of the Clifden heritage council as well as international pony breeders, and held interviews with them as well. Over the years 30 interviews were conducted in this manner in various locations, as well as over 50 informal conversations in cafes, pubs, shops, fields and ringside at pony shows.

Attending local pony shows throughout the area was critical to my fieldwork, as it gave me the opportunity to watch the politics of judging play out firsthand through the results of each class. Spectators around me discussed the ponies in the ring, their owners, the ponies' respective pedigrees and, most importantly, the spectators' reactions to the judges' decisions. Every fellow spectator holds his or her own opinions about the ponies on display. Inquiring as to which pony people felt deserved to win provided fascinating conversation and insights into the showing world. In the weeks following a show, I would ask people in the community how they felt about the show, the judging results, etc. These post-show discussions were the most politically charged, as people were willing to discuss society politics while still in a reactionary state about the show results. Many of these discussions form the basis for my arguments that will appear later in this chapter, as well as provide critical background information regarding the development of the breed and its associated societies.

Tradition and modernity in Connemara and its pony

The following section examines the symbolic aspects and consequent impact of the Connemara pony in Irish society as a symbol representing the history and heritage of the region while at the same time heralding modernity and progress in its marketing and sales. In studying how tradition and modernity intersect in a dynamic relationship, this analysis also presents the people and the ponies in Connemara as inextricably intertwined in a relationship that is both symbolic and mutually constitutive. Connemara ponies and their associated social worlds illustrate "how the forces of tradition and modernity, the global and the local, and the authentic and the commodified have impacted and been reflected in contemporary Irish cultural performance" (Wilson and Donnan 2006, 112). This analysis avoids delineating the actants in the Connemara pony world as either traditional or modern; rather, various aspects of their lives are traditional, or modern, or an admixture of both. Notions of tradition and modernity are important themes included within discussions of symbols and identity in the anthropology of Ireland. Concerns with modernity and modernization characterized anthropological work in Ireland from its earliest days, starting with Arensberg (1937) and Arensberg and Kimball's (1948) seminal research on tradition and change in Irish communities (Wilson and Donnan 2006).

The working pony

Connemara lies on the western coast of Ireland, occupying the southerly portion of western Connacht between Galway Bay and the counties of Galway and Mayo (Robinson 1997). The Connemara landscape not covered by bogland is extremely rocky and difficult to cultivate, as much of the region does not have soil as a ground cover (Robinson 1997). Farms during the nineteenth and twentieth centuries were centralized within the family unit, and larger scale agricultural labor featured cooperation between neighbors when extra help was needed for mowing, harrowing, and ploughing (Arensberg 1937). A settlement pattern of clustered farmsteads was therefore linked with social organization and mutual agricultural labor for shared field systems in rural Ireland (McCourt 1971).

The horse and pony were essential tools in this small-scale agricultural production on the Irish farm during the nineteenth and twentieth centuries and were central to rural livelihoods. In 1912 nearly every farm had a horse or pony and cart and most had a plough and harrow (O'Neill 1983), making horses and ponies key contributors in shaping the Irish rural landscape. Such farming practices and community-focused livelihoods contributed to the popular consideration of the West of Ireland as the bastion of 'traditional' Irish life, where the "real Ireland and the Irish" could be found (Wilson and Donnan 2006, 20). Connemara's reputation as the 'real Ireland' persists in the present day, making it a popular tourist destination for those wishing to receive an 'authentic' Irish experience (Kockel 1994, 250).

Equines and subsistence were inextricably linked in Irish communities, which established the horse and pony as crucial factors in both social and economic frameworks in Irish history. The Connemara pony is one such breed of equine native to coastal Connemara in the West of Ireland, and is marked by its hardy and reliable nature that allows it to thrive in mountainous and boggy landscapes. The ponies are "renowned for their strong constitutions, as only the strongest could survive" (Petch 1998, 1) in the harsh Connemara weather and were thus an important asset to farmers in the nineteenth and twentieth centuries. Their strength and stamina for transporting people and materials was paramount, as farmers used ponies to haul turf, timber, and produce from the farmland over the rocky landscape and to roads for transportation between towns (Lyne 1984; MacLochlainn 2010). The Connemara pony's working history is still prominent today in both private conversations as well as in public displays of the breed in Clifden. For example, a museum dedicated to the Connemara pony in Clifden is located near the show grounds and features informative plaques and farming paraphernalia reflecting the agricultural history of the pony. Nearly all breeders reference this history when discussing the pony, with comments like "I look for ponies that could do the working of the farm; pulling carts with turf and seaweed, etc. That is how the ponies originated, so that is what I look for," and "the pony is meant to be bloody working."

In 1923 the Connemara Pony Breeders' Society (CPBS) was established, which created breed standards, conducted classification inspections, and established an official Connemara Pony Studbook in 1926 (Lyne 1984). Two breeding goals shaped the society at this time: 1) increase the bone of the pony and 2) improve the make or conformation without destroying the hardiness, vigor, stamina, and docility of the pony (Petch 1998). Farmers regarded the pony as an animal for labor as well as pleasure during the first half of the twentieth century and it continued to be used for work on the farm and the bog until the 1960s (Brooks and Mannion 2002). The Connemara pony also played a critical role in organizing the summer event calendar in the West of Ireland that featured pony races and shows as key social events of the season. Races and shows provided the Irish countrymen and women with a day out for social activities, and focused upon leisure and pleasure rather than intense competition (Lyne 1984). An astounding two thousand people attended the first official Connemara pony show in 1924, with some traveling more than twenty miles for the single-day event (Petch 1998).

This symbolic connection between the present-day pony and past rural life is supported by a study from the National Development Plan that found 54 percent of those involved with native horses in Ireland feel that it brings them into closer contact with rural life and rural communities (Quinn and Hennessy 2007). Therefore it is evident that owning a native breed such as the Connemara pony is often tied to concerns of a regional identity with rural connotations and that the symbol of the working Connemara pony does not simply reflect a certain style of breeding, but more importantly represents a former way of life. The breed as a whole symbolizes both Connemara heritage as well as the unique 'nature' that exists in those who live in the region, due to the 'tough' reputations that Connemara people gained from surviving in the difficult landscape. During interviews breeders often equated the hardiness of the pony with the hardiness of the people of Connemara, stating that the ponies "lived in an environment that suited them before the breed changed. Now they don't survive as well. Like the people too." In a separate interview, a trainer not only compared the 'toughness' of humans and ponies, but also their vulnerability in a shared history. While discussing the difficulty of farming the landscape in the early twentieth century, she remarked, "Connemara was very poor. People were thin, ponies were thin, and cows were thin. There was no food and no money." She then went on to speculate that this shared history of poverty is why overweight ponies are now valued by Connemara owners, stating, "It must be some inherent thing that if you produce something fat, it will do well and survive."

The value placed on the physiology and personality of a native breed symbolizing the hardiness and ecology of a region is also present in the case of wild ponies in Australia (Peace 2009) and Welsh Cobs in Wales (Hurn 2008b). In this sense the symbolic significance of the pony is increasing in proportion to its decreasing role as an integral component to the household farming economy (Maj 2009). Therefore the Connemara people are both "symbol producers and symbol users" (Kertzer 1988, 8) in presenting the pony as a historical referent, and also in the deep connection that people in Connemara feel through their shared history with the Connemara pony.

Multiple morphologies: Changing form and function of the Connemara pony

The Connemara pony's status as a working animal began to change in the mid-20th century along with the broader change in Irish farming practices. Mechanical means of production replaced the labor of humans and horses, and largely removed working horses and ponies from the Irish landscape (Gillmor 1989). Rendered obsolete as a farm animal by the introduction of the tractor and large scale farming equipment to Western Ireland, a new use for the pony as a riding animal emerged in the 1970s. Local pony shows introduced riding classes in 1933, but these classes were slow to become popular as people still saw the pony as a working animal at that time (Petch 1998). However, by the 1970s, riding classes were *de rigueur* at every show, and the Connemara pony slowly garnered a reputation for being an excellent animal for equine sports such as jumping and endurance riding. The Breeders' Society began actively campaigning for an increase in performance ponies in 1979 with the introduction of the Ridden Connemara Pony of the Year Award Scheme (Petch 1998). This scheme was a marked effort by the society to market the Connemara pony as a versatile riding animal, thereby creating a new market for the sale of the pony after it was rendered obsolete as a farming animal.

Promoting the Connemara pony as a riding animal continued and strengthened over time, to the extent that most local shows have added extra show days to accommodate the increase in riding and jumping classes and exported ponies are typically for riding rather than breeding purposes. The modern market now favors a "quality athletic pony, of necessity lighter in bone and general structure" (O'Hare 2008, 8). Full and halfbred Connemara ponies are extremely common on the equestrian performance circuit. For example, the halfbred Connemara pony 'Portersize Just a Jiff' represented Ireland on the three-day eventing team at the 2012 London Olympics (Connaughton 2012). The morphology of the pony is changing to suit the needs of this riding public, to such an extent that there are now two 'types' of Connemara pony that are bred. The first is the 'old type,' that describes a pony with a good amount of 'bone' (thick bone in the lower legs) that is stocky and robust, like the farming ponies of the nineteenth and early twentieth century. The 'new type' is more streamlined and lighter, and is suited to athletic pursuits in riding activities.

A judge explained the shift in type in the following manner: "In earlier years, ponies were for work. They were for a farmer for cutting turf. They were a work type, and breeders looked for strong bone. Now you need a different type for performance. We have to protect our type, because if you lose the type, you lose the pony." The shift from old type to new type ponies is both an ideological and a physical issue, for a loss of the old type constitutes an equivalent symbolic loss of regional Connemara identity. If the morphology of the breed no longer reflects this unique heritage and the breed becomes indistinguishable from the numerous other breeds of sporting ponies, an integral part of the region's identity could be lost. Several breeders reiterated this point during interviews, as they often remarked that if the bone of the old type pony is lost, the Connemara pony is lost as well. In one trainer's words, choosing to have a Connemara pony that embodies the traits of the new type means "you might as well have any pony [...] don't forget why you went for Connemaras in the first place. Please don't treat them like normal ponies." Therefore the substance and materiality of the pony itself embodies a symbolic value as a reflection of past work and values for the residents of Connemara (Eipper 2007).

Pony 'type' is maintained through biannual breed inspections held in the spring and the autumn at local equestrian centers. These inspections began in the late twentieth century, and the Connemara pony is one of the few equine breeds today in which each animal must be inspected by a board of certified breed inspectors in order to be registered with the Breeders' Society. Any breeding, selling, or showing transaction involving a pony requires a registration 'passport'; therefore a pony must be inspected if it will have any purpose other than standing in a family field. Inspectors organize ponies into three classes of quality. Class 1 is the highest class, and a pony must be in this class in order to be shown in general classes or bred. Class 2 ponies can be shown in specific classes that are reserved for lower quality ponies, and ponies classified as Class 3 are essentially 'worthless.' Inspections are inherently political, as the inspectors are "manipulating 'norms' which are neither consistent nor fully coherent, as they pursue their ambitions and personal interests" (Gledhill 2000, 132).

Breeding and selling practices concurrently shifted along with inspection policies in the late twentieth century, by transitioning from local pony fairs to large-scale market auctions. In the nineteenth and early twentieth centuries, selling ponies occurred at scheduled street fairs held annually in small towns throughout the West of Ireland. Like the shows and races, pony fairs were some of the most important events of the year as a setting where "town meets country," and farmers mixed and mingled with the people from the town (Mullins 2008, 7). As automotive transport became more widespread in Ireland during the second half of the 20th century, streets became increasingly congested and put the safety of roadside fairs in jeopardy. Some buyers also desired a regulated atmosphere for making deals that was more modern, cosmopolitan and economically rational (Saris 1999). For these reasons livestock fairs' predominance gradually declined from the 1960s onward and large-scale buying and selling is now almost exclusively in the form of auctions in marts and markets (Curtin and Varley 1982).

The central stage for selling Connemara ponies at present is the Clifden Connemara Pony Mart. The largest Connemara pony show in the world is also held in Clifden each August. The Clifden mart is located near the site of the show and was the first permanent mart established exclusively for selling Connemara ponies. The first auction held at the mart was in 1991, and there are now four auctions held at this site each year (Petch 1998, 244). The auctions held in Clifden are annual events in February, May, August, and October, and are reminiscent of the old fair days with their importance in the local social calendar. Between these sales and the shows in Clifden and surrounding areas, approximately ten weekends out of the year in Connemara prominently feature the Connemara pony in economic activity. The sales showcase ponies for both local and international buyers and bring valuable outside revenue into the area. The pony's increasing performance status introduces a new group of buyers to the mart landscape who are external to the ridden pony market in Ireland. The Connemara pony's popularity abroad experienced a boom in recent years, with a total of seventeen international societies established in Australia, Austria, Belgium, Canada, Denmark, Finland, France, Germany, Great Britain, Ireland, The Netherlands, New Zealand, Norway, South Africa, Sweden, Switzerland and the US. Members of these international societies frequent the Clifden mart, and use the sales to establish their own breeding lines in their respective countries. Based upon sales data from the four sales held each year in the Clifden Mart, in 2010 the highest-priced pony in three of the four sales sold to a buyer living outside of Ireland (February sale: €3,600; August sale: €4,000; October sale: €5,000). In 2011, two out of the four highest priced ponies sold to buyers outside of Ireland (February sale: €2,500; May sale: €4,600). The dynamic of these sales is an integral component to the shift towards more progressive and modern forces in the pony community.

New strategies in pony commodification

The morphological and recreational changes occurring in the Connemara pony concurrently impact its symbolic status, as the pony is now a symbol of progress and modernity as much as it is one of heritage and history. This process is parallel to Wessing's (2006) findings while studying the symbolic status of animals in Indonesia, in that animals can simultaneously be symbolic indicators of both human transition as well as guardians of place. In the case of Connemara, the human transition is one of a shift towards an international riding market, and the guardian of place is that of the pony as a symbol of the region's agricultural past. Thus the Connemara pony is not only a symbol of power relations, but also of changing power relations (Kertzer 1974). This malleability and versatility of the symbolic status of the Connemara pony is a hallmark of symbolic construction, as symbolic form can stay largely the same while its associated meaning is altered (Cohen 1985). In this case, a shift from symbol to commodity is also evident in the cases of dance and sport in Ireland, as these cultural products are "squeezed between the local and the global, the past and the present, with the forces of tradition apparently pitted against those of modernity as Ireland strives to reinvent itself" (Wilson and Donnan 2006, 100).

The increasing demand in the international market for Connemara ponies as ridden commodities is rapidly changing the way that people do business in the Connemara pony industry. Such effects are evident in Clifden. Over the course of myfieldwork from 2009 to 2013 the Clifden Connemara Pony Mart introduced webcams to pony sales, the CPBS launched an electronic studbook, the International Committee of Connemara Pony Societies established an online society database, the CPBS created a Performance Training Day, and the Clifden show committee added two new riding days to the Clifden Championship Show calendar. The first three examples of change are the most drastic, for they reflect a technologizing of the pony that is unprecedented in the history of the breed.

The first example of change, introducing the webcam at the Clifden Mart, occurred in 2012. The webcam allows for pony sales to be streamed live on the mart's website (www.connemaraponysales.com) and viewers can use their credit card to bid upon and buy ponies remotely from anywhere in the world. Sales are not limited to local buyers and involve national and international buyers at the click of a mouse. The electronic studbook and the online society database have similar functions and were implemented from 2008 onward. Just as Wilson and Donnan (2006) observed in the case of the spread of Riverdance, changing electronic forms of media and increasing migration have altered the ways in which the cultural performance of buying and selling ponies is played out in Ireland.

Before being replaced by electronic versions, the Connemara pony studbooks were traditionally small, red hardbound books listing all registered Connemara ponies in Ireland, as well as their lineages (i.e., sires, dams, grandsires, grand-dams). It is not uncommon to see studbooks lining the shelves at pubs in Clifden and most of the homes belonging to pony owners have bookshelves dedicated to these books. All of this is now available online, and the CPBS published the last printed version of the studbook (Volume 21) in 1999. The online society database links the studbook in Ireland with studbooks from the other international breeders' societies so that the pedigree of any Connemara pony around the world can be researched by any breeder from around the world. This database also houses the details of the council and members from each society, in order for people in the global Connemara pony community to look up and contact other breeders electronically.

While the pony still symbolizes history and heritage, these new technological changes surrounding the breed also add a symbolic dimension of modernity and progress to the social identity of the Connemara pony. These technologizing social forces therefore increasingly alter the symbolic system of the Connemara pony (Kertzer 1988). Digitizing the Connemara pony in the case of the mart webcam illustrates not only the ongoing modernization of the mart but also the increasing globalization of the Connemara pony; as one of my informants said, "now you can get it [the sale] from Clifden to Colorado." The local and regional pony markets depend upon their visibility and attractiveness to outside buyers, and thus local breeders learned to counter global pressures with social creativity and collective inventiveness through innovations such as the webcam (Peace 1996). The webcam is a further move away from the traditional livestock fairs that involved intensive face-to-face interaction and "confrontation between the individual buyer and seller who higgled over price in public view and, if a bargain was struck, sealed the deal by a symbolic clasping of hands" (Curtin and Varley 1982, 349).

Using modern technology rather than the personal interactions that used to characterize the pony industry is also common with individual breeders outside of the mart. During several interviews in 2012 breeders identified Facebook as a valuable tool for selling ponies to international buyers, as "Facebook is great because you can trace how they're [the ponies] going." This trend in 2012 is particularly interesting due to the fact that during interviews for this research in 2009 breeders never mentioned using the Internet, particularly Facebook, as a way to negotiate pony sales. These testaments illustrate that economic globalization has reached the Connemara pony, as the new global currents of "rapidly changing technologies, increased communications, heightened flows of information, the blurring of state boundaries and the increased effects of others' actions on ourselves" (Gudeman 2001, 144) drastically change the ways in which the buyers and sellers of Connemara ponies do business.

The modern and progressive symbolic aspects of the Connemara pony due to new technological savvy by the Breeders' Society and its members are not universally accepted in the Clifden community. The online studbook is a highly contentious topic, for what used to be a tangible piece of pony history and authority moved to an intangible online database. The issue is not the economic value of the studbooks themselves, but the qualities and sentiments they embody to the breeders in terms of history and tradition (Eipper 2007). One breeder stated: "It is not right that the book has been replaced by a computer. The studbook was a bible. You can't bring a computer to a fair or the field. The book was valuable."

A more accepted development in the modern Connemara pony world is directing breeding for ponies as riding and performance animals. The increase in riding classes and the introduction of a Performance Training Day are part of the Breeders' Society's efforts to market the Connemara pony as a versatile riding animal and to increase public interest in the possibilities that ponies can achieve as performance animals, such as the puissance jumping competition. Nicholas O'Hare (2008, 7), a breed historian, summed up this shift in the following way: "The buyer these days wants a pony that can jump. The in-hand culture which dominated pony breeding for seventy years has been pushed back." The CPBS council considers performance ponies as 'ambassadors of the breed,' thereby making the ridden Connemara pony physically and symbolically embody notions of progress, modernity, and the future of the breed.

Conclusion

Using Cohen's (1985) definition of the symbol and symbolic construction, I argue for considering the pony as a complex, multidimensional symbolic agent representing social, political, and economic forces at work in the local community over time. Breeding, selling, and showing Connemara ponies creates a 'symbolic vocabulary' through which people in Western Ireland communicate not only with each other, but also with international customers. Forces of commodification, globalization, and modernization impact the symbolic status of the Connemara pony in ways which reflect larger identity negotiations within the Connemara region and Ireland as a whole. In this regard modernizing the Connemara pony is a similar cultural phenomenon to Wilson and Donnan's (2006, 96) account of modernizing Irish dance, as the breed is "standing at the intersection of the local and the global, the present and the past, and of tradition and modernity, it is a powerful illustration of how notions of Irishness are truly at a crossroads."

As previously stated, symbolic analysis is alive and thriving in the anthropology of Ireland, but studies of human–animal relations in local Irish communities have fallen out of favor in the new millennium. In contrast, within the broader anthropological discipline research focusing upon human–animal relationships is a rapidly growing area of interest (Hamilton and Placas 2011). Theoretical renegotiations of the relationships between humans and animals appeared in anthropology in the early 2000s. Until the late 1990s and even into the new millennium sociocultural anthropologists commonly viewed animals as "a convenient window from which to examine a great many other aspects of human societies" (Mullin 1999, 219). Anthropologists negotiating with non-human animals, prior to what John Knight (2005, 1) calls the "animal turn," did so primarily in terms of animals as objects rather than subjects, symbols of human society rather than parts of it and representations of animals rather than describing human interactions and relationships with them.

Research on human–animal relationships developing after the 'animal turn' calls for a reversal of these considerations of animals, thereby renegotiating the boundaries of animal personhood and the possible intersubjectivities between humans and animals. Rebecca Cassidy (2002a, 2002b) defines intersubjectivity as the notion that animals (particularly companion species such as horses) hold similarities with humans because of their shared origination in nature. Such similarities create an intersubjective relationship in which humans and animals are not explicitly equal, but rather are engaged in "the conjoined dance of face-to-face significant otherness" (Haraway 2003, 41). This perspective takes into account the multitude of ways in which humans and animals inter-relate with one another and introduces considering animals as capable of impacting human behavior. Such approaches intend to "reveal the dependence of man, human, humanity, and subjectivity on animal, animals, and animality" (Oliver 2009, 5).

The theoretical negotiations with human–animal relations briefly outlined here are not fundamentally opposed to the symbolic analysis presented in this chapter. In contrast, many of the ways in which people symbolically consider their Connemara ponies in Clifden (i.e., pony hardiness, stallion ownership, and owner connection with pony) directly draw upon the so-called 'animal turn' themes of intersubjectivity, animals as active agents within society, and the individual identities of animals. The tradition of interpreting animals as symbolic agents for their owner's individual status or social capital is alive and well in studies of human horse relations, as evident in the works of Gala Argent (2010), Rebecca Cassidy (2002a, 2002b), Samantha Hurn (2008a), Anita Maurstad, Dona Davis and Sarah Cowles (2013), and Kirrilly Thompson (2011).

The interaction between an owner and her pony (whether in the context of a show, riding, or breeding) is never solely mediated by the human. As Hurn (2012, 134) states, "the actual outcome of the interaction between all of these actants, human and nonhuman, 'animate' and 'inanimate' is by no means predetermined precisely because of the individual 'agency' of all actants within the network and their respective abilities to impact on the actions of the others involved." To entirely disregard the symbolic aspect of the Connemara pony would ignore a critical human component of this ethnography: the people of Connemara see the pony as a symbol. Thus the notion of the pony as a "symbolic real" is not constructed by this anthropologist, but rather is already present in Connemara society (Hamilton and Placas 2011, 253).

Because of these theoretical intersections, this research merges the strong trend of symbolic anthropology in Ireland with the new widespread trend of human–animal research in anthropology as a whole. In recognizing symbols as "products of nature" as well as "products of human creation" (Kertzer 1988, 4), this project brings a newfound interest to the symbolic capabilities that exist in studying animals in Ireland. As Anthony Buckley and Mary Kenney (1995, 22) state, "to explore identity in all its richness [...] one must study within particular worlds." Studying within the particular world of the Connemara pony provides fascinating and significant insights into the richness of identity construction in the West of Ireland.

References

Arensberg, Conrad M. 1937. *The Irish Countryman: An Anthropological Study*. Cambridge: Macmillan.

Arensberg, Conrad M. and Solon Kimball. 1948. *Family and Community in Ireland*. Second Edition. Cambridge: Harvard University Press.

Argent, Gala. 2010. "Do the Clothes Make the Horse? Relationality, Roles and Statuses in Iron Age Inner Asia." *World Archaeology* 42(2): 157–174.

Brooks, Stephanie and Karen Mannion. 2002. *Seahorses: Connemara and Its Ponies*. Pisa: Meredith Praed.

Buckley, Anthony D. and Mary Catherine Kenney. 1995. *Negotiating Identity: Rhetoric, Metaphor, and Social Drama in Northern Ireland*. Washington, DC: Smithsonian Institution Press.

Cassidy, Rebecca. 2002a. *The Sport of Kings: Kinship, Class and Thoroughbred Breeding in Newmarket*. Cambridge: Cambridge University Press.

Cassidy, Rebecca. 2002b. "The Social Practice of Racehorse Breeding." *Society & Animals* 10(2): 155–171.

Cassidy, Rebecca. 2003. "Turf Wars: Arab Dimensions to British Racehorse Breeding." *Anthropology Today* 19(3): 13–18.

Cassidy, Rebecca. 2005. "Falling in Love with Horses: The International Thoroughbred Auction." *Society & Animals* 13(1): 51–67.

Cassidy, Rebecca. 2009. "The Horse, the Kyrgz horse and the 'Kyrgz horse'." *Anthropology Today* 25(1): 12–15.

Cohen, Anthony P. 1985. *The Symbolic Construction of Community*. New York: Routledge.

Connaughton, Aislinn. 2012. "From Rosmuc to London – How the Connemara Ponies Made Their Debut 100 Years Ago." *Galway Advertiser*. Accessed 13 December 2012, www. advertiser.ie/galway/article/57228/from-rosmuc-to-london-how-the-connemara-ponies-made-their-debut-100-years-ago.

Curtin, Christopher and Anthony Varley. 1982. "Collusion Practices in a West of Ireland Livestock Mart." *Ethnology* 21(4): 349–357.

Donnan, Hastings and Thomas M. Wilson. 1999. *Borders: Frontiers of Identity, Nation and State*. New York: Berg.

Eipper, Chris. 2007. "Moving Statues and Moving Images: Religious Artifacts and the Spiritualization of Maternity." *The Australian Journal of Anthropology* 18(3): 253–263.

Gillmor, Desmond. 1989. "Land, Work and Recreation." In *The Irish Countryside: Landscape, Wildlife, History, People*, edited by Desmond Gillmore, 161–196. Dublin: Wolfhound Press.

Gledhill, John. 2000. *Power and Its Disguises*. Second Edition. London: Pluto Press.

Gudeman, Stephen. 2001. *The Anthropology of Economy: Community, Market and Culture*. Malden, MA: Blackwell Publishers.

Hamilton, Jennifer A. and Aimee J. Placas. 2011. "Anthropology Becoming…? The 2010 Sociocultural Anthropology Year in Review." *American Anthropologist* 113(2): 246–261.

Haraway, Donna. 2003. *The Companion Species Manifesto*. Chicago: Prickly Paradigm Press.

Hurn, Samantha. 2008a. "The 'Cardinauts' of the Western Coast of Wales." *Journal of Material Culture* 13(3): 335–355.

Hurn, Samantha. 2008b. "What's Love Got to Do with It? The Interplay of Sex and Gender in the Commercial Breeding of Welsh Cobs." *Society & Animals* 16: 23–44.

Hurn, Samantha. 2012. *Humans and Other Animals: Cross-Cultural Perspectives on Human–Animal Interactions*. London: Pluto Press.

Kertzer, David I. 1974. "Politics and Ritual: The Communist Festa in Italy." *Anthropological Quarterly* 47(4): 374–389.

Kertzer, David I. 1988. *Ritual, Politics and Power*. New Haven, CT: Yale University Press.

Knight, John. 2005. "Introduction." In *Animals in Person: Cultural Perspectives on Human–Animal Intimacies*, edited by John Knight, 1–14. Oxford: Berg.

Kockel, Ullrich. 1994. *Culture, Tourism, and Development: The Case of Ireland*. Liverpool: Liverpool University Press.

Latimer, Joanna and Lynda Birke. 2009. "Natural Relations: Horses, Knowledge, Technology." *The Sociological Review* 57(1): 1–27.

Lyne, Pat. 1984. *Shrouded in Mist: The Connemara Pony*. Presteigne: Combe Cottage.

MacLochlainn, Tom. 2010. *The Moycullen Ponymen: From Working Ponies to International Stars*. Ballinsaloe, Ireland: Ashbrook Connemara Pony Stud.

Maj, Emilie. 2009. "The Horse of Sakha: Ethnic Symbol in Post-Communist Sakha Republic (Iakutiia)." *Sibirica* 8(1): 68–74.

Marvin, Garry. 2003. "A Passionate Pursuit: Foxhunting as Performance." *Sociological Review* 52(2): 46–60.

Marvin, Garry. 2005. "Sensing Nature: Encountering the World in Hunting." *Etnofoor* 18(1): 15–26.

Maurstad, Anita, Dona Davis and Sarah Cowles. 2013. "Co-Being and Intra-Action in Horse–Human Relationships: A Multi-Species Ethnography of Be(com)ing Human and Be(com)ing Horse." *Social Anthropology* 21(3): 322–335.

McCourt, Desmond. 1971. "The Dynamic Quality of Irish Rural Settlement." In *Man and His Habitat: Essays Presented to Emyr Estyn Evans*, edited by Ronald Hull Buchanan, Emrys Jones, and Desmond McCourt, 126–164. New York: Barnes and Noble Incorporated.

Mullin, Molly. 1999. "Mirrors and Windows: Sociocultural Studies of Human–Animal Relationships." *Annual Review of Anthropology* 28: 201–224.

Mullins, Noel. 2008. *The Origins of Irish Horse Fairs and Horse Sales: 3,000 Years of Selling Irish Horses*. Skerries: NDM Publications.

Oliver, Kelly. 2009. *Animal Lessons: How They Teach Us to Be Human*. New York: Columbia University Press.

O'Hare, Nicholas. 2008. *Great Connemara Stallions*. Eastbourne: Harkaway.

O'Neill, Tim. 1983. "Tools and Things: Machinery on Irish Farms 1700–1981." In *Gold Under the Furze: Studies in Folk Tradition*, edited by Alan Gailey and Dáithí Ó Hógáin, 101–114. Dublin: Glendale Press.

Overton, Nick J. and Yannis Hamilakis. 2013. "A Manifesto for a Social Zooarchaeology: Swans and Other Beings in the Mesolithic." *Archaeological Dialogues* 20(2): 111–136.

Peace, Adrian. 1996. "When the Salmon Comes: The Politics of Summer Fishing in an Irish Community." *Journal of Anthropological Research* 52(1): 85–106.

Peace, Adrian. 2009. "Ponies Out of Place? Wild Animals, Wilderness, and Environmental Governance." *Anthropological Forum* 19(1): 53–72.

Petch, Elizabeth. 1998. *Connemara Pony Breeders Society 1923–1998*. Middleton, Co Cork: Litho Press.

Quinn, Katherine and Karen Hennessy. 2007. "Profile of the Irish Sport Horse Industry." National Development Plan. Dublin: University College Dublin.

Robinson, Tim. 1997. "Connemara Co. Galway." In *Atlas of the Irish Rural Landscape*, edited by F.H.A. Aalen, Kevin Whelan and Matthew Stout, 329–344. University College Cork: Cork University Press.

Saris, A. Jamie. 1999. "Producing Persons and Developing Institutions in Ireland." *American Ethnologist* 26(3): 690–710.

Thompson, Kirrilly. 2011. "Theorizing Rider–Horse Relations: An Ethnographic Illustration of the Centaur Metaphor in the Spanish Bullfight." In *Theorizing Animals: Re-thinking Humanimal Relations*, edited by Nik Taylor and Tania Signal, 221–254. Boston: Brill.

Wessing, Robert. 2006. "Symbolic Animals in the Land between the Waters: Markers of Place and Transition." *Asian Folklore Studies* 65(2): 205–239.

Wilk, Richard. 2004. "Miss Universe, the Olmec, and the Valley of Oaxaca." *Journal of Social Archaeology* 4(1): 81–98.

Wilk, Richard. 2006. *Home Cooking in the Global Village: Caribbean Food from Buccaneers to Ecotourists*. New York: Berg.

Wilson, Thomas M. and Hastings Donnan. 2006. *The Anthropology of Ireland*. New York: Berg.

Part II

Communication and Relation

6 Learning to Communicate

The Triad of (Mis)Communication in Horse Riding Lessons

Katherine Dashper

The relationship between a horse and rider is one of reciprocal dependence, collaboration and mutual becoming (Oma 2010; Maurstad et al. 2013). These multispecies relations are commonly described as 'partnerships' (Wipper 2000) and understood as dyadic, involving two beings – horse and rider. However, horse riding is a complex activity involving interspecies communication and a variety of athletic skills and competencies, and thus both horse and rider need to learn how to ride and how to perform together. Learning to ride is not a simple process, and takes a lifetime to master (West and de Bragança 2012). All riders, regardless of their level of experience and expertise, benefit from training sessions with a knowledgeable instructor who can help them develop their skills, improve communication with the horse and boost performance. Such training sessions, referred to as 'riding lessons' throughout this chapter, expand the human horse relationship beyond the dyad of horse and rider. The presence of the instructor, positioned in this relationship as an 'expert' in horse human partnerships, expands these interspecies collaborations and draws attention to the complexity of learning, communicating and performing across species, temporal, spatial and sensorial boundaries.

The argument developed here is based on an eight-year multispecies ethnography conducted in the UK in which I explored various facets of human horse relationships that manifest through equestrian sport and leisure. Equestrian cultures vary around the world and even within the UK, the context for this study, there are different horse and riding social worlds. For example, there are many differences between the practices of natural horsemanship and more sport-related riding cultures (see Birke 2007; Latimer and Birke 2009; Dashper 2014). This project was based within the sport-related equestrian culture of the UK. Participants within this equestrian culture tend to be highly committed to horses and riding and identify themselves as 'horsey people.' Investing significant resources in terms of time, money and emotional commitment, participants in this equestrian subworld are predominantly female (although proportions of men increase at the higher competitive levels) and look to form close partnerships with their horse(s) (see Dashper 2012, 2013, 2014, 2015a, 2015b). Riding lessons form an important element in the forging of interspecies relationships for the human participants in this particular equestrian subworld.

This chapter is based on a combination of ethnographic methods that include my own embodied experiences, observations of other people's riding lessons, interviews with riders and instructors, and analysis of equestrian training texts. I use these sources to develop my ideas and arguments about the complexities of interspecies communication that are manifest within the horse riding lesson.

Dyadic relationships: Horse and rider

The expanding field of human–animal studies encourages researchers to explore the 'contact zones' between humans and nonhumans in order to consider how we interact, intermingle, and entangle with others and the wider environment (Haraway 2008; Kirksey and Helmreich 2010). The relationship between humans and horses is one such contact zone and one that is based around intimate body-to-body contact and collaboration. Horses and humans interact in a variety of different ways but, due to the focus of this chapter, I will concentrate here solely on interspecies communication and collaboration that is achieved through riding.

The fact that humans ride horses has a profound effect on human horse relationships. There is no other creature with whom humans share a closer, more embodied form of connection than with the riding horse. Communication between horse and rider occurs through the bodies of both partners, requiring sensitivity, emotion and kinetic intelligence (Brandt 2004; Maurstad et al. 2013). Riding is a unique form of interspecies encounter in which both actors – horse and human – act, respond and affect the other (Birke et al. 2004; Oma 2010).

The ultimate goal of riding is to achieve "a oneness with the horse, a kind of fluid intersubjectivity" (Birke and Brandt 2009, 196). This 'oneness' is brought about through body-to-body contact and communication that goes beyond verbal language. Game (2001, 8) describes riding as "a mindfully embodied way of being" and the rider has to respond to the horse with and through her body, in a way that builds on her mindful knowledge of *how* to ride and *what* to do, but transcends this intellectual know-how and is instead felt, lived and experienced through the body. Samudra (2008, 671) argues that "[k]nowing the structure of movement is not the same as knowing the sensation of movement" and an important concept in horse riding is that of 'feel.' 'Feel' is an elusive concept, much like the idea of '*känsla*' that Bäckström (2012, 754) describes in relation to skateboarding as "sensuous experience, affect, descriptions of affect and, moreover, knowing its cultural and social settings."

'Feel' is thus an embodied experience, felt and negotiated through intimate body-to-body communication, developed within the wider context – historical and contemporary – of equestrianism. To date, most researchers have focused on this as a two-way relationship, between horse and rider. The language of partnership, or working together to achieve harmony, is often invoked when trying to describe the interspecies encounter of humans riding horses (Savvides 2012; West and de Bragança 2012). Very often this is a two-way relationship, however due to the complexity of riding and the elusiveness of the concept of 'feel' many riders require regular training to improve their performance, sensitivity and communication with the horse. Training, in the form of riding lessons, expands the dyadic relationship between horse and rider to include a third actor, the instructor, who enters the communicative milieu and tries to bridge the gap between knowing what to do, feeling what is happening, communicating between horse and rider, and producing a visually appealing performance often with the goal of sporting competition.

The triad of horse, rider and instructor

Horse riding is a complex mix of intricate interspecies communication and athletic skill and competence. Horse and rider are constantly communicating with each other, through embodied intra-action, and both also pick up on external cues. The demands of different equestrian sport practices, such as dressage or show jumping, require the development of different riding skills and performance attributes, further complicating the notions of learning to ride and to perform. Some commentators suggest that the pressures of sporting competition may lead to breakdown in communication between horse and rider, as the desire for competitive success may encourage a focus on quick, quantifiable results rather than taking the time to develop a true partnership between horse and rider, based on mutual trust and respect (Gilbert and Gillett 2012; Savvides 2012). However, although the pressures of sporting competition may complicate the riding process further, most riders recognize that it is easier to work with a willing, happy equine partner, and that this is much more likely to lead to riding and competitive success, than trying to force a horse to act against his will (Wipper 2000; Dashper 2015a). Riding is thus a complex and intricate process that requires constant learning from both horse and rider. As a result, many riders turn to professional trainers, called 'instructors' throughout this chapter for clarity, in order to try and improve their understanding and performance.

Learning is itself a complex process and can be understood as corporeal and experienced in and through the body (see Evans et al. 2009). All learning takes place within particular situated social practices (Lave and Wenger 1991) and in this case within the framework of horse riding lessons. These lessons, in turn, are situated in contexts that draw on centuries of equestrian tradition, noted, documented and passed on to new generations and transformed to accommodate changing conditions, such as the specific requirements of modern equestrian sport.

Riding lessons are a medium through which riders attempt to learn more about riding, tapping into this rich equestrian heritage and improving their performance in equestrian sport and/or leisure. The purpose of a riding lesson will vary depending on factors such as the stage of training of both horse and rider, the competitive goals of the rider, particular problems horse and/or rider may be experiencing in training or competition and the expertise of the instructor. The overall goal of these lessons is, however, broadly similar. Riders hope that, through the expertise of the instructor, they will improve communication between themselves and their horse leading to better performance in whatever task or discipline they perform in, such as dressage, jumping or trail riding.

There are three key actors in the learning situation of the riding lesson – instructor, rider and horse. Each has a different role, purpose, disposition and sensory apparatus which impacts on the learning process. The instructor's role within this triadic relationship is that of 'expert' or 'knowledge guardian' or an individual who possesses culturally embedded knowledge about riding that has been passed on for generations through apprenticeship, that is, through riding themselves (West and de Bragança 2012). Riding instructors are almost always experienced riders in their own right, as the level of kinesthetic knowledge required to teach such elusive sensory concepts as 'feel' and successful interspecies communication requires the instructor to have felt those sensations for herself. However, being able to do something does not automatically make an individual a good teacher and the instructor has to have the ability to transform their kinesthetic knowledge of riding into verbal form that the riding student can understand (Fortin and Siedentop 1995).

The instructor is thus involved in a complex mesh of sensory and communicative processes. The instructor observes the horse and rider partnership and makes judgments of that performance, and what techniques might be effective to improve the performance, based on a combination of what she sees from her external vantage point, what she hears from the rider's verbal explanations of what she is doing and feeling, what she perceives from the horse's way of going and demeanor and reactions, and from the rider's bodily performance and responses. This complicated array of sensory stimuli is constantly received by the instructor throughout the course of the lesson. The instructor then relies upon her own corporeal knowledge and kinesthetic empathy (Parviainen 2002) to understand the embodied experiences of the horse–rider partnership, even though the instructor cannot feel that riding partnership herself. The instructor then has the difficult task of translating into words her embodied knowledge of what the rider should do to try and improve riding performance. Words are often inadequate at translating kinesthetic knowledge into a form that a third party (in this case, the rider) can understand (Sklar 2000). The instructor thus has a difficult job, and the potential for miscommunication and misinterpretation of this diverse set of sensory inputs is considerable.

The second key actor in the context of the riding lesson is the rider herself. The rider is a 'student' in the triadic relationship of the riding lesson. She is an active player in the learning experience but is positioned asymmetrically in relation to the instructor, who is more knowledgeable about the practice of riding/training/competing. However, the rider does often have considerable knowledge and experience herself. Many riders have been riding, training and competing for years and so they have relatively well developed kinesthetic, bodily knowledge of riding and are looking to the instructor to help develop these skills further. Consequently the rider does not just receive information, instruction and advice from the instructor and try to apply this to her riding. Rather, the rider contributes her own embodied skill and knowledge to the learning encounter and is thus part of a 'community of practice' (Lave and Wenger 1991; Bäckström 2012) of riding and training in concert with the instructor, albeit the instructor is positioned as more experienced and knowledgeable than the rider.

The rider is in constant communication with the horse and is continually giving the horse instructions and sensory cues (both intentional and unintentional on the part of the rider) and is receiving information from the horse's body. Some of this communication is apparent to the watching instructor, but much of it is not visible to the observer but is felt by both rider and horse. The rider is thus communicating bodily with the horse, but at the same time attempts to tell the instructor what she is feeling as she rides. This requires the rider to attempt to translate into words the kinesthetic experiences of riding and interspecies communication, embodied sensations that can be difficult to express in words. The rider is thus enmeshed in embodied communication with the horse – through her body and the horse's body – and verbal communication with the instructor. The rider also has to listen and respond to the verbal cues of the instructor and translate word-based ideas and instructions into nonverbal communication with the horse. There are thus many demands on the rider at any time during the course of the lesson.

The horse makes up the third part of the communicative triad of the riding lesson. As a different species horses sense, react and communicate very differently to humans (Keaveney 2008). Unlike the human rider and instructor, the horse is not aware of the purposes of the riding lesson, such as competition requirements and goals. However, although the horse is placed in a relatively subordinate position in relation to the two human players, the horse is still an active participant in the riding lesson encounter. The horse can and does act and have agency within the riding lesson, even though that agency is somewhat limited by the horse's position within human-centric power relations between humans and horses (Carter and Charles 2013; Dashper 2015a). The horse does not have the freedom to choose whether or not he wants to participate in the riding lesson as the human rider and instructor both dictate that he will. However, he can decide whether or not he wants to be responsive to the rider's commands or generous to any mixed messages coming from the rider and so can exercise some limited agency in the context of the riding encounter. The horse's personality and mood impact on the riding lesson and the learning encounter, demonstrating that the horse is an active player within this communicative triad.

The horse, as with the instructor and the rider, is subject to a barrage of sensory stimuli over the course of the lesson. First, and most directly, the horse is in body-to-body communication with the rider. Horses are highly sensitive to small changes in the rider's balance and pick up on tension and stress in the rider's body. The horse may also be subject to occasional reprimand by the rider's whip. The whip is an external 'aid' the rider may use to prompt the horse to respond more quickly or with more energy to a command given initially through the rider's body. The horse is also attuned to the instructor, as examples below illustrate. Finally, the horse's natural disposition as a prey animal makes him highly attuned to his environment, constantly on the lookout for potential threat and danger. It is useful to understand the riding lesson through the concept of 'emplacement,' especially in relation to the horse and the horse's responses to stimuli. Emplacement focuses on the interrelationship between body, mind and environment (Pink 2011) and the horse (and rider and instructor) is within a physical environment that is always changing with weather, time, light, sound, smell and a wide variety of other factors. Horses are very sensitive to these changes, and these external stimuli can sometimes overpower the horse, who will respond more to a change in the environment than to communication from his rider.

All three players within the communicative triad of the riding lesson are thus subject to a wide array of sensory stimuli and are communicating simultaneously across diverse spatial, temporal and sensory forms, as well as across species boundaries. These are highly complex communicative relationships and in the next sections I consider various ways in which such communication is managed, negotiated and sometimes misunderstood within the triad of instructor, rider and horse within the horse riding lesson.

Translation across senses

Learning anything, be that a language, how to dance, or how to ride, is an embodied experience. Ellsworth (2005) uses the phrase 'pedagogies of sensation' to capture learning processes that recognize us as bodies, where movement and sensation are central to the experiences of learning. Fors et al. (2013, 181) argue that learning should be understood as "a full-embodied emplaced experience." They urge researchers to pay attention to the multi-sensoriality of learning experiences, focusing on the inseparability of the senses in learning and developing skills, and the cultural specificity of how we experience and learn through our senses. This is important for trying to understand learning and interspecies communication within riding lessons. Instructor, rider and horse have to work together if learning and improved performance are going to be achieved within and beyond the context of the lesson. Such three-way collaboration requires communication across sensory boundaries, but this is not a clear-cut case of translation of visual stimuli (what does the horse–rider partnership look like, to the instructor) into verbal stimuli (the instructor directs the rider how to improve performance, using language) into aural stimuli (what the rider actually hears and understands of the instructions) into kinesthetic stimuli (what the rider does through her body to communicate to the horse through his body). This communicative chain is complex enough, yet it still oversimplifies the learning and performing processes that happen in the lesson. These stimuli and communicative strategies (along with others from the external environment, such as wind or noise, and internally for each actor, such as fatigue on the part of the rider) do not happen in a chain. They occur simultaneously, and impact upon each other, in a multi-sensorial manner. The following example illustrates some of the interplays between different sensory experiences, stimuli and communicative strategies.

I was struggling to teach my horse how to do 'medium trot,' a movement required in many dressage competitions. Medium trot is defined by the FEI (the international sports governing body for equestrian sport) (2007) as follows: "The horse goes forward with clear and moderately lengthened steps and with obvious impulsion from the hind quarters [...]. The steps should be even and the whole movement balanced and unconstrained." I knew what medium trot should look like, having seen many riders perform it successfully. I even knew what it should feel like, having ridden medium trot on other horses. I therefore also should have known 'how to' ride medium trot on my horse, as I knew the aids to apply to communicate my wishes with him. Yet it wasn't happening. "No," my instructor said again, after another messy attempt at medium trot strides. "No, he's just running. You need to hold him more through your middle, sit up and back and power through from behind." Right, power through from behind. I set my horse up for our next attempt. Sitting tall, taking my weight a little further back, a small squeeze down the reins, legs on his side, and go! "No," my instructor again. "Too quick. You're letting him fall onto his shoulder." "But I'm doing what you said," I argue. "You're not," she replies bluntly. "You set him up and then you drop him. Make sure you tell him what you want." I thought I was doing that but the responses of both my horse and instructor suggest otherwise. I take a deep breath, determined this time. I think it all through. I try and envisage his back legs stepping more under his body. I grow up tall. I think medium trot and this time [...] we do it! I know that was it, I felt it! This time was different, this time my horse and I understood each other, worked together and we did it! "Well done, that's it!" my instructor is smiling now. But I don't need her to tell me, I already know that this time we nailed it!

In this example no one sensory apparatus was dominant. I needed to use my knowledge of medium trot, to listen to what my instructor was saying, to feel what my horse was doing with his body and to tell him what I wanted him to do instead, to sense my own body and to communicate physically the movement I wanted to achieve. When we got it right, it felt right and it also looked right. This was a multi-sensorial learning experience (Fors et al. 2013) in which the intermingling of diverse and overlapping sensory information was essential in achieving a successful outcome. Once I had *felt* my horse and I got it right once, we could achieve it again. But until I felt it, and until he understood what I was trying to ask him to do and how to convert that request into bodily action, we kept on making mistakes. All three actors in the lesson were essential to this learning encounter: myself and my horse had to learn to understand each other in this slightly new way, and to perform a different physical movement in partnership, and my instructor was essential in giving me the motivational and conceptual tools to understand why my earlier requests for medium trot were unsuccessful, and to keep on asking until we got it right.

The learning of many sports and physical practices, including skateboarding, dance and martial arts, involves processes of imitation (Wuff 2001; Downey 2005; Bäckström 2012). An expert, usually the teacher or instructor, demonstrates a skill or a required movement and students try to imitate that performance, receiving feedback and critique as they do so. Horse riding is somewhat different. Although there is certainly much to be gained from watching other people ride, and seeing how they position themselves and their horse in different movements and conditions, a process of imitation does not work when learning to ride. This is because very often it is not visibly apparent what the rider is doing to communicate with the horse and the more skilled the rider, the less visually discernible are her actions. This has implications for learning and improving performance within the context of the riding lesson as the instructor cannot simply show the rider what to do and the rider then try to imitate that.

Numerous times I observed an instructor telling the rider to dismount and let her ride the horse instead. This usually happens when horse and rider are having problems in communication, or when the rider cannot grasp the details of what the instructor is trying to get her to do. The instructor choosing to get on the horse herself during a lesson creates an interesting dynamic in the triadic relationship. The horse often seems to recognize the authority of the instructor in the lesson situation (over and above that of the rider) and will respond more swiftly to the instructor's commands. As the instructor rides the horse herself, she talks to the rider who is now standing on the ground watching. The instructor explains to the rider what she is feeling from the horse, what she, the instructor, is doing to communicate with the horse, and how she can feel the horse responding. The watching rider is listening to the instructor, is watching what the instructor is doing and also monitoring the reactions and performance of the horse. The rider then compares these visual and aural cues with how she herself felt when she was riding the horse, and how the horse responded to her attempts at communication. Invariably, as a result of the instructor's expertise, experience and skill the horse responds well to the instructor riding him and eventually reacts as required and executes the movement or performs to the desired standard. The rider then remounts. Some imitation goes on here as the rider tries to recreate what she saw the instructor achieve moments before. However, this is not simple imitation, as the rider could not fully understand what the instructor had done just by watching. The verbal cues the instructor gave whilst she was riding are helpful, as are the verbal cues the instructor now gives the rider from the ground. These verbal cues may be more detailed and insightful than previously as the instructor has herself felt how the horse responds and so has kinesthetic empathy with the rider (Parviainen 2002). The rider is now also helped by the horse, who has just experienced effective communication (from the instructor) and understands the task required of him and so is more willing and helpful to the rider than previously. In all the cases I observed and experienced, horse and rider performance was better after the instructor had ridden the horse as communication between the three actors in the lesson had improved as each had experienced different forms of multisensory collaborative sensations.

These two examples illustrate some of the complexities of horse riding lessons as instructor, rider and horse are in constant communication between each other, simultaneously across multiple sensorial boundaries. Riding, learning to ride and teaching riding involve complex interplays of different sensorial stimuli including, but not limited to, visual cues, verbal instructions, body-to-body communication and abstract knowledge about specific movements and paces. This indicates that the riding lesson is a complex communicative process, but this is further complicated by the necessity to connect across species boundaries, as well as sensorial horizons.

Translation across species

Learning any physical skill or practice is a complex multi-sensorial experience, but riding is further complicated by the necessity to communicate, understand and perform across species boundaries as well. Potter (2008) argues that the dominant Western sensory lexicon is too heavily constrained by our allegiance to a five senses model – sight, sound, touch, taste, smell. She argues that these five senses are not sufficient for explaining complex physical and cultural practices and that other sensations are often equally if not more important, using the significance of heat as a sensation in understanding contemporary dance as an example. The five traditional senses are not sufficient for understanding the sensations and experiences of riding either. Although humans embedded in Western culture tend to focus predominantly on the five traditional senses in our descriptions of physical practices, this does not mean that we do not experience these practices in and through different sensorial channels. Importantly, horses are not constrained by western modes of thinking about sensation, and equine communication differs markedly from human forms (Keaveney 2008). Consequently, when thinking and talking about riding, and learning to ride, we need to move beyond a focus on the traditional five senses and consider riding experiences in ways that are more reflective of the combined sensory apparatus of both human and equine actors.

This is where the concept of 'feel,' introduced above, is informative. 'Feel' is very hard to define, but is something that all riders aspire to. It connotes a form of interspecies communication that defies words, and is experienced through two bodies, human and equine, as a sensation of mutual understanding and collaboration. To be a rider who has 'feel' suggests that one is proficient in interspecies communication and can 'speak' and 'listen' to the horse one is riding. This 'speaking' and 'listening' are not verbal, oral or aural processes. To be in harmony with the horse, to embody the concept of 'feel,' is an incredible sensation for the rider and probably also for the horse, who recognizes an attentive and sensitive human partner. Although feel is a sensation internal to the rider–horse dyad, the effects of achieving such moments can be seen by the instructor who witnesses a harmonious and balanced riding performance.

I frequently heard instructors say that 'feel' cannot be taught. It was presented in riding lesson situations as an almost mythical concept, a magical moment that defies words and explanation. However, I witnessed and experienced moments that captured the sensation of 'feel,' however transitory and fleeting. Jumping lessons often provided riders with moments that embodied this sense of oneness with the horse. When jumping, the rider has to 'go with' the horse over the fence in order to remain in balance. Very often the rider is not able to achieve this, as she misjudges when the horse will take off in front of the fence, or does not position the horse in the correct place from which to jump the fence smoothly. One lesson I observed involved a woman who had lost confidence jumping due to an earlier accident. The instructor told her that she was 'over riding;' the aids (messages) she was giving the horse were too strong and consequently the horse was approaching the fences too fast, taking off either far away or very close to the fence, resulting in an uncomfortable and unsettling sensation for the rider. As this happened the rider was getting more tense and worried, leading her to 'over ride' even more acutely, with the consequent effect that the horse was getting faster and beginning to panic. The instructor called the rider into the center of the ménage, told her to stop and take some deep breaths and try and calm down. "He knows his job," the instructor said of the horse. "He doesn't need you to manage every step. Just trust him." The rider set off to attempt the jumps again, following the instructor's advice to concentrate on counting the rhythm of the horse's canter strides in her head in order to calm herself down. I could hear her whisper "Canter, canter, canter" – marking the three-time rhythm of the pace. As she approached the fence she continued to count and this time she didn't panic and rush the horse, and he jumped the fence beautifully. The rider was calmer, and stayed in balance over the fence. When she landed she was grinning, overjoyed with herself and the sensation of jumping the fence in harmony with the horse. After that, she remained much calmer and her jumping technique improved noticeably. Talking to her afterwards she told me how the simple task of counting the rhythm of the pace allowed her to relax and let the horse jump the fence. Once she felt this happen effectively she was hooked – looking to recreate the fluid sensation of being at one with him as he tackled the fence.

In this example the rider's own anxieties were blocking her ability to communicate effectively with the horse. Horses are very sensitive creatures and pick up on tension in the rider's body, and in this case this was spiraling into disharmony. The instructor's decision to effectively call a 'time-out' was crucial as it enabled the rider to calm down physically and mentally, and the distraction of counting the canter rhythm stopped the rider from hassling the horse into the fence when they tried again. The instructor was an important facilitator here, intervening to redirect the rider's nervous energy away from the horse (albeit, the rider was not intentionally troubling the horse) and onto another activity (counting the rhythm). This enabled the horse to perform his task – jumping the fence – without the worry of the rider's anxious nagging. When this happened horse and rider were able to tackle the fence in harmony, communicating bodily beyond the confines of the rider's conscious thought but in a way that made sense to both parties.

However, the complexities of interspecies multi-sensorial communication are not always managed successfully within the confines of the lesson. Understanding learning through the lens of emplacement encourages a focus on the interplay between bodies, mind(s) and environment (Pink 2011) and the ways different species experience the same physical environment have consequences for how riding and learning develop. Much of the training of horses builds on equine temperaments and instinctual responses, and as horses become more attuned to their rider and the experience of being ridden their natural 'flight' response becomes less prevalent. Yet it is always possible, and all riders experience horses 'spooking' at scary stimuli, even though the source of the threat is not always apparent to the rider. In such moments, the complexities of communicating across species boundaries come to the fore.

One lesson I observed involved a relatively new horse–rider partnership. Still in the early stages of forging a working relationship, the horse and rider had not yet fully developed mutual trust and understanding. Throughout much of the lesson this was initially only apparent through an unwillingness of the horse to respond quickly to all of the rider's commands. However, breakdown in communication escalated when the horse began to respond quickly and almost violently to changes in the weather. Throughout the course of the lesson the wind picked up, and with this objects began to rattle and move. The horse, much to the alarm of the rider, began to spook at these movements, leaping sideways, spinning around and even rearing slightly. Thompson and Nesci (2013) suggest that riding always involves an element of fear and that the sensation of being in control and harmony with the horse always entails an appreciation of the real possibility of slipping over to lack of control and miscommunication. This is exactly what happened in this lesson situation. As the horse responded more erratically to changes in the external environment, the rider first became frustrated and then scared. This resulted in tension throughout her body which was communicated to the horse and raised his level of tension. The rider also began to reprimand the horse, again increasing tension in the partnership and exacerbating the problems. A particularly strong gust of wind upended a nearby bin, causing a loud crash to which the horse spooked violently. The rider responded by grabbing hold of the reins, tensing forward and shouting at the horse. Sensing panic in his rider's body the horse also panicked and reverted to his default response to a fearful situation – flight. He took off at a fast gallop around the ménage, with the rider hanging on stiffly and screaming. The instructor remained calm. She used her voice to soothe both horse and rider and managed to coax the horse back to trot and then to walk. Disaster was averted this time, but a breakdown in communication had occurred between horse and rider.

In this example, the different sensorial responses and apparatus of horse and human clashed. Rather than producing harmony, horse and rider miscommunicated, with the breakdown in understanding escalating as the event unfolded. The instructor was able to use her authoritative position in the context of the lesson to avert further disaster and calm down both parties. As mentioned above, horses often seem to recognize the authority of the instructor and respond to her verbal commands more quickly and decisively than they do to those of the rider. In this case, this was fortunate as it prevented further mishap. Speaking to the rider after the lesson she explained that fear overtook her and although she knew she needed to relax in order to calm the horse down, she could not make herself embody this sensation. Although this was a relatively severe case of miscommunication and one that could have resulted in injury to rider and/or horse, misunderstanding often occurs within riding. Horses respond differently to external cues than do humans, and pick up on their riders' feelings of fear and anxiety. Riding is thus a complex interplay between species, and the instructor can be an important mediator in trying to maximize understanding and effective communication between horse and rider.

Conclusion

The examples presented in this chapter illustrate some of the complexities of interspecies communication that occur when humans ride horses. Most horse riders have been asked by non-riders, "Why are you still having lessons? I thought you knew how to ride?" This is a frustrating question for the rider, as it belies the complexity and difficulty of riding, and riding well. However, the question is also revealing about two important elements of riding that are manifest within riding lessons.

Firstly, riding is a process and as such requires constant learning, refinement and training. West and de Bragança (2012) argue that riding takes a lifetime to learn, with no quick fixes, and that the journey, more than the end result, is the reason for engaging in the practice. As illustrated throughout this chapter, riding involves complex communication across species and sensorial boundaries, and these communicative processes are influenced by a variety of external factors, such as the environment, the demands of equestrian sport and disposition of horse and rider. Riding lessons are thus important for helping riders learn to communicate more effectively with the horse in a variety of contexts, for different purposes and at different stages of development in the career of both horse and rider. One is never 'done' with learning to ride. It is an evolving process that constantly challenges and surprises the rider with the necessity to adapt, improve or learn new skills. Indeed the need to be constantly learning is a key attraction of the activity for many riders.

Secondly, the naïve question of the non-rider highlights, paradoxically, the complexity of riding as a practice. To the external observer, it appears that the rider is doing very little and this appearance of stillness is more pronounced with more experienced and highly skilled riders. However, as argued throughout this chapter, the rider is *always* doing something. The uniquely intimate nature of body-to-body communication that occurs between horse and rider means that the two partners are constantly acting on and with each other, whether they intend to or not. The complexity of communicating across both species and sensorial boundaries makes riding – and riding well – an extremely difficult physical and mental practice that requires collaboration and negotiation between horse and rider and thus both partners require regular training and guidance from a knowledgeable instructor to improve communicative channels and interspecies understanding.

Riding is an embodied form of knowledge that is stored, communicated, learned and performed in and through distinct bodies. The instructor is important in helping to pass on some of this intricate equestrian heritage to both horse and rider, who have to work together to achieve harmony and partnership. Thinking of horse human relationships beyond the traditional dyadic form of horse and rider and including a third actor – the instructor in this case, but in other contexts, such as sporting competition, this third player could be a judge – draws attention to the complexities of interspecies communication and collaboration that underpin horse human relationships through riding.

References

Bäckström, Åsa. 2012. "Knowing and Teaching Kinesthetic Experience in Skateboarding: An Example of Sensory Emplacement." *Sport, Education and Society* 19(6): 1–21.

Birke, Lynda. 2007. "'Learning to Speak Horse': The Culture of Natural Horsemanship." *Society & Animals* 15(3): 217–239.

Birke, Lynda and Keri Brandt. 2009. "Mutual Corporeality: Gender and Human/Horse Relationships." *Women's Studies International Forum* 32(3): 189–197.

Birke, Lynda, Mette Bryld and Nina Lykke. 2004. "Animal Performances: An Exploration of Intersections between Feminist Science Studies and Studies of Human/Animal Relationships." *Feminist Theory* 5(2): 167–183.

Brandt, Keri. 2004. "A Language of Their Own: An Interactionist Approach to Human–Horse Communication." *Society & Animals* 12(4): 299–316.

Carter, Bob and Nickie Charles. 2013. "Animals, Agency and Resistance." *Journal for the Theory of Social Behavior* 43(3): 322–340.

Dashper, Katherine. 2012. "Together, yet Still Not Equal? Sex Integration in Equestrian Sport." *Asia-Pacific Journal of Health, Sport and Physical Education* 3(3): 213–225.

Dashper, Katherine. 2013. "Beyond the Binary: Gender Integration in Equestrian Sport," in *Gender and Equestrian Sport: Riding around the World*, edited by Miriam Adelman and Jorge Knijnik, 37–53. New York: Springer.

Dashper, Katherine. 2014. "Tools of the Trade or Part of the Family? Horses in Competitive Equestrian Sport." *Society & Animals* 22(4): 352–371.

Dashper, Katherine. 2015a. "Listening to Horses: Developing Attentive Interspecies Relationships through Sport and Leisure." *Society & Animals*. (In press)

Dashper, Katherine. 2015b. "Strong, Active Women: (Re)doing Femininity through Equestrian Sport and Leisure." *Ethnography*. (In press)

Downey, Greg. 2005. *Learning Capoeira: Lessons in Cunning from an Afro-Brazilian Art*. Oxford: Oxford University Press.

Ellsworth, Elizabeth. 2005. *Places of Learning: Media, Architecture, Pedagogy*. Abingdon: Routledge.

Evans, John, Brian Davies and Emma Rich. 2009. "The Body Made Flesh: Embodied Learning and the Corporeal Device." *British Journal of Sociology of Education* 30(4): 391–406.

FEI. "Definitions of Paces and Movement." [Internet] Available from www.s10.zetaboards.com/Judges_Notebook/topic/136573/1/. Accessed 26 November 2014.

Fors, Vaike, Åsa Bäckström and Sarah Pink. 2013. "Multisensory Emplaced Learning: Resituating Situated Learning in a Moving World." *Mind, Culture and Activity* 20(2): 170–183.

Fortin, Sylvie and Daryl Siedentop. 1995. "The Interplay of Knowledge and Practice in Dance Teaching: What We Can Learn from a Non-Traditional Dance Teacher." *Dance Research Journal* 27(2): 3–15.

Game, Ann. 2001. "Riding: Embodying the Centaur." *Body & Society* 7(4): 1–12.

Gilbert, Michelle and James Gillett. 2012. "Equine Athletes and Interspecies Sport." *International Review for the Sociology of Sport* 47(5): 632–643.

Haraway, Donna Jeanne. 2008. *When Species Meet*. Minneapolis: University of Minnesota Press.

Keaveney, Susan M. 2008. "Equines and Their Human Companions." *Journal of Business Research* 61(5): 444–454.

Kirksey, S. Eben and Stefan Helmreich. 2010. "The Emergence of Multispecies Ethnography." *Cultural Anthropology* 25(4): 545–576.

Latimer, Joanna and Lynda Birke. 2009. "Natural Relations: Horses, Knowledge, Technology." *The Sociological Review* 57(1): 1–27.

Lave, Jean and Etienne Wenger. 1991. *Situated Learning: Legitimate Peripheral Participation*. Cambridge: Cambridge University Press.

Maurstad, Anita, Dona Davis and Sarah Cowles. 2013. "Co-being and Intra-action in Horse–Human Relationships: A Multi-species Ethnography of Be(com)ing Human and Be(com)ing Horse." *Social Anthropology* 21(3): 322–335.

Oma, Kristin Armstrong. 2010. "Between Trust and Domination: Social Contracts between Humans and Animals." *World Archaeology* 42(2): 175–187.

Parviainen, Jaana. 2002. "Bodily Knowledge: Epistemological Reflections on Dance." *Dance Research Journal* 34(4): 11–26.

Pink, Sarah. 2011. "From Embodiment to Emplacement: Re-Thinking Competing Bodies, Senses and Spatialities." *Sport, Education and Society* 16(3): 343–355.

Potter, Caroline. 2008. "Sense of Motion, Senses of Self: Becoming a Dancer." *Ethnos* 73(4): 444–465.

Samudra, Jaida Kim. 2008. "Memory in Our Body: Thick Participation and the Translation of Kinesthetic Experience." *American Ethnologist* 35(4): 665–681.

Savvides, Nikki. 2012. "Communication as a Solution to Conflict: Fundamental Similarities in Divergent Methods of Horse Training." *Society & Animals* 20(1): 75–90.

Sklar, Deidre. 2000. "Reprise: On Dance Ethnography." *Dance Research Journal* 31(1): 70–77.

Thompson, Kirrilly and Chanel Nesci. 2013. "Over-Riding Concerns: Developing Safe Relations in the High-Risk Interspecies Sport of Eventing." *International Review for the Sociology of Sport*. doi 10.1177/1012690213266.

West, Daune and D. Francisco de Bragança. 2012. "A Systemic Approach to Eliciting and Gathering the Expertise of a 'Knowledge Guardian': An Application of the Appreciative Inquiry Method to the Study of Classical Dressage." *Systemic Practice and Action Research* 25(3): 241–260.

Wipper, Audrey. 2000. "The Partnership: The Horse–Rider Relationship in Eventing." *Symbolic Interaction* 23(1): 47–70.

Wuff, Helena. 2001. *Ballet across Borders: Career and Culture in the World of Dancers.* Oxford: Berg.

7 "Follow the Horse"

The Complexities of Collaboration between the Lasso-pole Horse (*uurgach mor'*) and his Rider among Mongolian Horse Herders

Charlotte Marchina

I was convinced during the first few days after arriving in the Mongolian capital of Ulaanbaatar in 2008 that my Mongolian driver and I would get into a car accident every time we drove through the city center. At every junction, drivers would often wait until the very last moment to brake and avoid another car coming sideways. Despite this, I was never involved in an accident or even saw one. Drivers always managed to keep a few centimeters' distance between their respective cars. When I returned to the capital, after spending six weeks of riding horses with Mongolian herders, this style of driving became clearer. This entails both driving a car and riding a horse as a kind of "joint project" (Argent 2012, 124), where in moments of uncertainty both car and horse act in an agentive fashion.

Mongolian herders love talking about their horses. Herders consider horses the most valuable of the "five muzzles" (horses, camels, cattle, sheep and goats) that they breed. They mainly express admiration for stallions, as proud mounts, protectors of the horse herds. Herders appreciate elegant and light racehorses and spirited riding horses. Observing herders at work, however, I noticed another type of horse that while rarely mentioned spontaneously, was highly valued for his precious and rare qualities: the lasso-pole horse. Herders pasture their animals on a fenceless steppe; when they need to capture them, they use a lasso-pole (*uurga*), a long wooden stick with a leather noose at the end.[1] The Mongol rides a lasso-pole horse (*uurgach mor'*) specially trained to assist the rider. The horse is supposed to identify which animal needs to be captured and helps his rider to catch and stop the animal. As an accomplished mount and rider, the lasso-pole horse and the herder exemplify a Mongolian conception of the human horse relationship. In this relationship the horse becomes a full and cooperative partner and is encouraged to take his own initiative in the context of daily pastoral tasks.

In what follows, I focus on partnership and collaboration in the human horse relationship among Mongolian herders. My analysis is inspired by Argent's (2012) literature on human horse partnerships. My goals include both expanding my ethnography on the meaning of horses among Mongolian people, and relating my research to the wider literature on horses and humans. Thus, I focus on how Mongolian rider and horse learn to collaborate and the processes that are involved. The relationship between the rider and the lasso-pole horse serves as a paradigm for the meaning of horses in Mongolia. My analysis addresses three key issues: what herders appreciate in horses, what they do with their horses and what working with horses means to them.

The horse in Inner Asia

Horse human relations remain marginally studied among the horse civilizations (Ferret 2009) in Inner Asia. Most works of Western, Russian and Mongolian researchers focus on the material and symbolic aspects of Mongolia's horse culture (Aubin 1986a, 1986b, 1999; Bianquis-Gasser 1999; Humphrey 1974, 1975; Lacaze 2010a, 2010b; Lipec 1984; Poppe 1962; Poucha 1969; Rintchen 1977; Serruys 1974; Veit 1985; Zhambaldorzh 1996). The work of French anthropologists and experienced riders such as Maj (2007) and especially Ferret (2006, 2009, 2010) marks a turning point in horse studies of Inner Asia, specifically in Siberia and Kazakhstan and provides a detailed study of horse riding and breeding techniques. More recent studies feature horse breeding (Fijn 2011) and techniques of the body (Lacaze 2012). They analyze how Mongolian herders use their horses as instruments to detect ghosts and other invisible entities (Delaplace 2010).

In this chapter, I propose a more dynamic approach by highlighting the capacity for agency of each individual horse and human with a focus on more pragmatic interactions that occur between men and horses in the practice of riding a lasso-pole horse. In contrast to research on human–reindeer interactions in Siberia that rather simplistically focuses on human–animal cooperation (Stépanoff 2012), my aim is to introduce a higher level of complexity to the examination of human–animal collaborations. I depict the horse as an animal that has developed complex social skills, and whose performance of cooperative activities is multifaceted. This study draws on fieldwork conducted from 2008 to 2013. During that period, I conducted open-ended interviews in central Mongolia (Arhangai province) and closely observed herders' and horses' interactions. Data and analysis provided here highlight how a finely tuned, observational multi-species ethnographic approach (Hamilton and Placas 2011; Haraway 2008; Kirksey and Helmreich 2010) to a triadic relationship consisting of two horses and one human can shed new insight into the complex entanglements that characterize human horse relations among Mongolian herders.

To call a horse a horse

Mongolian herders practice extensive breeding among multiple species. They keep herds of up to several dozen horses, who pasture freely when they are not needed. Almost all horses are used as mounts and provide the herders with food (meat and mare's milk) and other raw materials (hide and hair). Depending on his main function and current circumstances, what Westerners call "horse" may be designated in Mongolian by two distinct terms, depending on type and context of human horse engagements. Distinction is made between the horse as a member of a collective *aduu* that refers to a herd horse(s) or horse herd(s) and *mor'* that refers to an individual horse that is mounted or saddled at the moment it is discussed. This is an important distinction. Furthermore, among riding horses (*unaany mor'*) one distinguishes between several different categories. The main ones are the sheep horse (*honiny mor'*), used to drive the flocks, the racehorse (*hurdan mor'*, literally "fast horse") and the lasso-pole horse (*uurgach mor'*). Each category of horse relates to precise tasks.

While the herd horse (*aduu*) evokes an animal that provides products, the riding horse (*mor'*) is seen as a work companion. Nonetheless, *aduu* and *mor'* are not exclusive terms. In fact, a very large proportion of *aduu* horse herds are at least occasionally ridden. The herders usually use two or three riding horses to drive the herds and flocks during the day. A working horse is used for several consecutive days, during which it is allowed to graze only at night. After the horse has lost weight, it is released with the herd. Another horse of the herd is captured and serves as working horse for the next few days. The former passes from *mor'* to *aduu*, the latter from *aduu* to *mor'*. The transformation from riding horse to working horse occurs through capture.

Capturing a horse with a lasso-pole horse

In order to capture a horse, the rider proceeds in a succession of steps. These steps include tracking, capturing with the noose of the lasso-pole, immobilizing, and then leading the horse to the right place. These actions can follow each other very quickly and require attention, ability and speed from both the rider and his mount. The efforts of horse and rider are combined in a process of complex coordination. It is important that rider and mount maintain the same trajectory as the chased animal. This is a delicate task as the chased animal will take many sharp turns at a great speed. The pursuers risk breaking the lasso-pole and hurting themselves. While riding a lasso-pole horse, the rider may drop the reins partially or totally in order to focus on the handling of the pole. Thus, the horse is expected to track the chased horse on his own initiative. He does so by following the same trajectory at the same speed as the other horse. If the mount is not very experienced, however, his rider can give him indications through the pole. Apart from being an object connecting the herd horse and the rider, the lasso-pole also becomes a means of communication between the rider and the lasso-pole horse, and is used to indicate in which direction his mount should go. The rider can simply point with the pole in the direction of the tracked horse and ensure that his mount sees the end of the pole. As recent studies in animal behavior show (Maros et al. 2008), all horses understand pointing gestures as long as they are maintained, and this is the case with the pole. Although herders state that the horse just has to know which horse to follow, the rider, despite having dropped the reins, no doubt sends intentional indications concerning the speed by using his whip, his voice and his legs, and probably also unintentional indications concerning the direction by orienting his body and directing his gaze toward the target horse. As many Western riders and researchers point out, horses are "excellent muscle-readers" (Despret 2004, 114) and have developed capacities for moving in synchrony with humans and other horses (Argent 2012). This phase of the pursuit illustrates one of the most complex forms of coordination between a Mongolian rider's and horse's synchronized movements. This is what Hansen (2014, 255) refers to as "the micro-materiality of cross-species communication," to describe when horse and rider not only coordinate their movements between each other, but also in accordance with a third agent, the followed horse.

Once the noose is placed around the horse's neck, the rider twists the lasso-pole with one hand to tighten the noose and stop or at least slow the captured horse. If the trapped horse is relatively docile, he comes to a standstill. If he still seeks to escape, the rider has to alternate and repeatedly pull and release the lasso-pole so as not to give the horse the opportunity to lean on it. As soon as the noose is inserted around the other horse's head, the lasso-pole horse should brake, by "sitting" (*suuh*). He "sits" in stretching his forelegs, and bending his hind legs under his body. The horse's forehand moves up and his rump goes down. In this way the lasso-pole horse anchors himself to the ground. The rider, decreasing speed, can then easily use his saddle and the body of his horse as point of support. In doing so the rider generally uses the stirrups as lever points by sitting back even behind his saddle. According to the interviewed herders, a good lasso-pole horse should achieve this "sitting" on his own initiative once the rider has inserted the noose over the tracked horse's head. Usually, however, the herder gives an indication to his mount by pulling slightly on the reins, sitting back or behind his saddle or by giving a signal with his foot to ensure that the action is executed quickly. If the target horse stands still but refuses to follow the herder to the encampment, the herder tries to place the horse in front of him (herder) and then pulls the captured horse in the desired direction. In order to achieve this the rider continues to pull on the pole and leans in the direction in which he is pulling, using the whole body of his mount as a point of support. The rider will sometimes even hang on the side of his horse, with the stirrups tied together, to help keep the balance. Thus, while the sequence preceding the stopping of the captured horse provides a kind of fluid centaur performance, where two bodies become in sync with each other (Argent 2012), in the next phase a rider may be partially pulled off his saddle by the chased horse, or end up hanging on the side of his mount. Synchrony is abruptly broken as the rider stops the captured horse, replacing the centaur image by two individuals trying, in coordinated but disharmonious movements, not to fall and to get the captured animal to a standstill. Once the captured horse is in front of him and stands still, the rider can sit back in his saddle and lead the captured horse after him.

Without considering the positions of the lasso-pole horse and the captured horse in terms of an opposition between subject (the horse taking part in the capture) and object (the horse undergoing the capture) one can very clearly observe a difference of status between the lasso-pole horse, *mor'* and partner on one hand, and the captured horse, *aduu* and non-partner on the other. While the former collaborates, the latter clearly does not. Some captured horses are more cooperative than others. The observation and interview data gathered suggest that captured horses can further be classified into two categories, depending on their relationships with humans: the capricious ones (*aashtai*) and the docile ones (*nomhon*). It should be noted that belonging to one or another category depends on how advanced the breaking or training is. The most docile horses are often those who are ridden and frequently in contact with humans, while the most spirited horses are often untamed (*emneg*). These two subcategories reflect distinct behaviors and attitudes of a horse during the capture. Each category of horse requires a different technique.

Capturing a capricious or untamed horse is a strenuous physical exercise. It sometimes requires going so far as to exhaust and strangle the target animal, until the horse yields to being led. The strategy to exhaust the horse consists of alternately racing after the target horse then slowing down. Bayarsaikhan (2006) refers to a method consisting of forcing the horse to cross rivers. This not only wears him down, but also encourages him to drink, making him gain weight which in turn slows him down. There are many different techniques to approach an unyielding horse. One consists of the rider approaching him from the "correct side" (*zöv tal*) – the left side. This allows the rider to handle the pole more easily and freely. The best way to immobilize a horse seeking escape is to ensure that the noose's strap is placed on the throat, and not on the base of the neck. In fact, if the strap is located on the base of the neck, it has no effect on the horse and the rider cannot stop the horse by his arms' strength alone. Only a docile horse that is used to being captured stops when the strap is placed on the base of his neck. The only way for a rider to immobilize a horse that continuously struggles to escape is by strangling him. It is not unusual to see these animals abandon resistance only when they are deprived of air and collapsing to the ground. Whenever possible, herders try to pull heavily on the pole only when the galloping chased horse's forelegs are in the air, so that he has no point of support and loses momentum. A herder I interviewed minimized somewhat the role of the rider in stating that the lasso-pole horse was doing most of the work and that the only decisive action coming from the rider was choosing carefully where to place the noose: on the muzzle, on the throat, or on the base of the neck (for accustomed horses). Although it is certainly the most difficult movement of the three, inserting the noose over the muzzle has the advantage of immediately turning the captured horse's head and breaking the horse's forward momentum. Yet the most common technique is throttling by targeting the throat.

Horses that have become habituated to capture tend to become less laborious catches. Indeed, the majority of the Mongolian horses are familiar with the lasso-pole, since they are primarily used as riding horses. Most lasso-pole horses are used to being captured. All horses of the herd, including those who are not regularly captured, seem to be familiar with the use of the pole. It is worth noting that, while the herder, whether on horseback or on foot, causes considerable agitation among the herd until the target horse is captured, most of the horses stand still or at least calm down as soon as the target horse is caught. Herd horses seem to associate the capture of a horse with the fact that they do not risk being captured themselves and therefore do not need to seek to escape anymore. Some horses even stand still as soon as they are captured. Sometimes, it is even enough for the herder to pass a rope over the neck of the horse, who then stops and lets the human handle him easily.

Becoming a lasso-pole horse: Processes at work

Mongolian herders state that the lasso-pole horse knows his job. The lasso-pole horse knows what he has to do and when. Yet, an accomplished lasso-pole horse is a rare animal, the result of a long process that involves selection and training. Among the herders there is no conception of horse breeds. Instead there are types of horses to which herders give specific functions. In order to make good helpers of their riding horses, the herders seek to give them a function that matches their innate skills. These abilities manifest themselves by physical and mental predispositions. These "signs" (*shinzh*) are sometimes recognizable at an early age and are common knowledge among the herders. Current breeding manuals as well as manuscripts dating back to the 18th century identify characteristics or "signs of the horse" or *moriny shinzh* (Aubin 1999; Poucha 1969) that determine a good sheep horse, or an ideal pacer, race horse or lasso-pole horse (Gongor 2006). Although certain traits are desirable they do not, however, necessarily guarantee that the horse will perform or function well.

Mongolian herders underline the importance of combining several traits of a good lasso-pole horse. First, the horse has to be fast enough to pursue the tracked horse, but also sturdy enough to be subjected to the rider's destabilizing movements and strong enough to help the rider stop the capture horse that is running away. Paradoxically, the lasso-pole horse must be both sturdy and light enough to keep pace with the target horse. This paradoxical horse, "heavy enough, without sacrificing speed" (Legrand 1997, 306), should, according to the herders, have both fine and stubby legs. Beyond these morphological features, herders also emphasize the lasso-pole horse's movement. It is important that he has a fast gallop with fluid movements. The horse should be responsive, as measured by the "softness" (*zöölhön*) or sensitivity of his mouth. The horse should feel the slightest tensions of the reins and stop immediately. The herding manuals also stress features valued in a lasso-pole horse. These include good eyesight, quick starting speed, suppleness, strong and sensitive vertebrae and the ability to brake by "sitting" (Gongor 2006, 21).

These physical traits must be combined with cognitive skills. The qualities most mentioned by the herders I interviewed were intelligence (*uhaan*) and alertness (*sergelen*). These cognitive qualities enable coordination between both the rider's and the horse's intentions and movements. The most important quality sought in a lasso-pole horse is the ability of the horse to follow the direction in which the rider leans, otherwise the horse may fall. In addition, a lasso-pole horse is expected to understand which horse should be tracked and anticipate his rider's actions. It is striking that the cognitive skills conferred to the lasso-pole horse, intelligence and alertness, are terms commonly used when talking about humans. The similarity between humans and horses concerns not only the terms used to describe these "skills" (*chadvar; chadal*), but also their development process. For the Mongols, both human and horse, these skills reflect innate predispositions and capacities that exist in nascent form and can only be fully developed through learning and experience.

The development of a horse's potential is tested during moments of play and herder games or equestrian competitions. I observed a 16-year-old boy playing with his horse's balance by leaning heavily alternately on the right and left side of his mount, pretending to pick something up from the ground. He would lean over so far his hand would touch the ground. The rider could not refrain from smiling when the horse successfully, although with some difficulty, avoided falling. Playing with a young mount by testing his physical limits in order to know whether he might eventually become a good lasso-pole horse is a way of selecting the horse before a more advanced training. At an equine age of four, herders consider a horse's morphology mature enough to begin advanced training. The next step is learning to maintain a regular trajectory and speed despite the rider's unbalanced movements and the lack of indications or aids. These skills are tested during herder games called "*aduuchin*" (literally "horse breeders"). These are small local affairs. Contestants are young accomplished herders, around the age of twenty, who are eager to compete in the proceedings. Two competitions consist of picking up objects (a lasso-pole and anklebones) lying on the ground, while maintaining a straight trajectory at full gallop. This event requires consistency on a long distance (approximately 200 meters) and precision at the very moment of grasping the object. Competitions that reward the best herders include several events that place herder and horse alternately as partners and opponents or rivals. These include races; jumping from a horse to another (while horses are galloping side by side); riding untamed horses and capturing horses with a lasso or a lasso-pole. These highly physical trials require complete mastery of riding techniques and of handling of the lasso-pole and the lasso.

Falling because of uneven movements and drifting from the desired track are the two main failures the lasso-pole horse must first learn to avoid.

Once horses have passed through the selection process, horse and rider will need to learn to coordinate their movements. Today, the inexperienced rider is paired with the experienced horse and the inexperienced horse is paired with the experienced rider. [This matching of experienced rider and inexperienced horse or vice versa is common practice in riding sports such as showjumping in the West (Thompson and Birke 2014)]. The first skill a lasso-pole rider must learn is how to properly insert the noose over the horse's head without tangling it or hitting the horse's head with the pole (see Bayarsaikhan 2006). Initially, this exercise is undertaken with an experienced and docile horse who is accustomed to being captured. According to the herders, the young lasso-pole horses develop habits by repeating the same actions: for example by repeatedly hearing his rider yelling for him to go as fast as the chased horse, he will eventually quicken by himself to follow the other horse. Likewise, when the rider combines two actions such as sitting back in his saddle and pulling on the reins he expects the horse to learn to associate the two clues and to sit. Some riders may hold the pole with both hands, while also holding the reins in the left hand, and expect the ridden horse to halt and sit when the horse feels the tug of the captive horse on the pole (Nergüi et al. 2009, 371).

It must be emphasized, however, that an accomplished lasso-pole horse is a rare mount. For being a good lasso-pole horse entails having certain innate characteristics paired with an experienced rider and these are essential elements needed to carry out advanced training. Several herders who did not have a lasso-pole horse explained it by the absence of the characteristic "signs" among their horses, or their own lack of know-how regarding the lasso-pole. When they do not have a proper lasso-pole horse, herders can sometimes ride a horse that is accustomed to "chase" (*hööh*) and to "follow" (*dagah*) an animal that needs to be captured, although this type of mount is not able to "sit."

The more experienced the horse is, the more efficiently he achieves the task. An experienced lasso-pole horse "knows which movements should be done when and eventually carries them out by himself" (Ferret 2006, 595). Being a lasso-pole horse is not only a matter of advanced training coupled with innate morphological and cognitive skills, such as intelligence and alertness; a horse must also express agency. Herders expect that the experienced horse will take the initiative. Here again, parallels are striking with the British show jumping horse or American roping horse, who are relied upon to make their own decisions (Thompson and Birke 2014; Lawrence 1982). Nevertheless, what is remarkable in Mongolia is that even ordinary horses are very commonly encouraged to take initiatives in order to become autonomous agents.

The horse's agency in Mongolian horse riding

Mongolian horse riding practices encourage the horse to take an active part in the decisions as the horse–rider pair move together as partners. The main aids used in Mongolian horse riding are the rider's seat, the action of the hands through the reins, the iron bit, the voice and sometimes a whip. Mongolian riders rarely use leg aids. Indeed, they are seldom in direct contact with the horse, because of the long leather pieces of the typical Mongolian saddle. Generally, herders expect a good horse to take the initiative and start galloping by himself when leading his rider away from the encampment, or to slow down when approaching a yurt. On a steep path, the rider sometimes lets his mount choose the best way. Initiatives are also often expected when the rider enters a state of decreased consciousness. When a child is exhausted by the pastoral tasks of the day and almost falls asleep on horseback, his horse continues to do the job of driving the sheep flock back home. A man, so drunk that he is unable to give any indication to his horse, is brought safely back home by the skillful animal. Knowing the way, the horse carries his rider home, while paying attention to keeping his rider on his back. The horse does so by counterbalancing his uneven movements when walking. These situations result from a mutual learning. The rider learns to stay in place despite a decreased state of consciousness, and the horse learns to ensure that his rider does not fall. The horse continues to follow the right direction without any indication from his rider. These situations testify to the long-term cohabitation of human and horse and their intimate familiarity with each other.

As elsewhere in Inner Asia, herders seek a capacity for autonomy in a horse that will allow the horse to help them in their tasks. Although herders like to feel that they dominate their mounts, herders do not aim for total submission of the horse (Ferret 2006). On several occasions herders even told me how much they appreciate the spirited character of a horse that, far from being punished or suppressed, is a highly valued quality. By letting their horses alternate between the statuses of *aduu*, herd horse, and *mor'*, riding horse, the Mongolian herders act to make their horses more reactive and spirited mounts. In fact, passing from herd horse to riding horse can be challenging, as a herd horse may not have been ridden for several consecutive months. Hence, a horse freshly taken out of the herd may be reluctant, forcing his rider to update the breaking and training.

Human horse collaboration

This ethnographic study of human-horse interactions in Mongolia reveals a multiplicity of ways of considering different types of horses and different ways of being with them. Mongolian language and practices stress a kind of "multi-speciesness" of horses. Mongolian horses shift between categories rooted in and defined by their innate capacities, training, different tasks or functions and alternating periods of being tame or cooperating with humans and being wild or released to the herd. Among Mongolian horses, some individuals have privileged relationships with humans. The lasso-pole horse is in this regard more involved in cooperative actions than an ordinary horse. This type of horse has exceptional morphological, physiological and cognitive skills that allow the rider to rely on him and to delegate tasks to him. This very delegation of tasks is what makes the lasso-pole horse a real partner in a collaborative activity.

It is a principle of typical Inner Asian horse riding that, "the more a horse is trained, the less the rider has to act" (Ferret 2006, 595). According to the herders I interviewed, much of the learning lies in repeating the action – that is, creating "shared routines" (Sanders 2007, 326). By daily repeating the same tasks and activities, herders develop the autonomy of the horse, who learns over the time what is expected from him and acts to become an efficient collaborator.

The more Western oriented literature stresses the importance of horse human relationship as a partnership that does not involve "the generic 'horse,' but specific individuals" (Birke 2008, 115). As we have seen throughout this chapter, in Mongolia when it comes to human horse interactions, individuality on the part of the horse also matters (Maurstad et al. 2013). This is especially true in Mongolian human horse relationships. The herders' discourse emphasizes the role of the lasso-pole horse, while minimizing the rider's agency. The rider's qualities are only marginally mentioned, while the focus is primarily on the horse. According to Mönhzhargal, a herder I interviewed, the rider does nothing difficult, as the horse does almost "everything [...] going in this or that direction, galloping when necessary, and pulling." Herders expect the ideal lasso-pole horse to act on its own to stop a captured horse. Yet the initiatives taken by the horse must correspond with his rider's intentions. Here, collaboration relies on attributing reciprocal intentions. It is this "ability of attributing intentions to others, and even of understanding others as beings that attribute intentions to you," that represents a kind of reciprocity that exists between humans and all domesticated animals (Despret and Porcher 2007, 122) that is realized at a very sophisticated level in the case of the rider and the lasso-pole horse.

Rather than the centaur's "kind of unique alchemy" (Wipper 2000, 56) or state of harmony between two specific individuals who work most of the time together, the Mongolian human horse partnership comprises two individuals who are constantly adjusting to each other. They are two individuals collaborating together in order to achieve a "joint action" (Sanders 2007). By synchronizing their movements and using their capacity for autonomy, both rider and mount demonstrate a "joint attention" (Tomasello 2009, XIII). At its highest level, human horse cooperation in Mongolia requires thus a fine tuned coordination, joint attention and autonomy, all of which are recognized as necessary conditions to "effective partnership" (Thompson and Birke 2014, 75).

Beyond highlighting the complexities of the collaboration processes involved in riding a lasso-pole horse, this study is an invitation to follow the horse. By following the horse, I will focus on explaining how my Mongolian informants draw distinctions between what they identify as the human's and the horse's perspectives. Mongolian herders recognize agency in animals, who are engaged in a practice of "co-shaping" performance and partnership with humans (Maurstad et al. 2013, 324).

Note

1 Transliteration follows the rules of *Études Mongoles & Sibériennes, Centrasiatiques & Tibétaines*: http://emscat.revues.org/1752. All translations, whether from Mongolian or French, are mine. I would like to thank Charles Stépanoff for his insightful comments since the beginning of this work. I am very grateful to the editors, Dona Davis and Anita Maurstad, for their highly helpful suggestions and comments. I am also indebted to Jacques Legrand, Grégory Delaplace, Andrea-Luz Gutierrez Choquevilca, Raphaël Blanchier, Laurence Caillet, Alice Doublier, Clémence Jullien, Christilla Marteau d'Autry and Chloé Paberz for their comments. Fieldwork was conducted with financial support from INALCO and International Research Group (GDRI) "Nomadisme société et environnement en Asie centrale et septentrionale."

References

Argent, Gala. 2012. "Toward a Privileging of the Nonverbal. Communication, Corporeal Synchrony, and Transcendence in Humans and Horses." In *Experiencing Animal Minds. An Anthology of Animal–Human Encounters*, edited by Julie A. Smith and Robert W. Mitchell, 111–128. New York: Columbia University Press.

Aubin, Françoise. 1986a. "L'art du cheval en Mongolie." [The Art of Horses in Mongolia] *Production pastorale et société* [Pastoral Production and Society] 19: 129–149.

Aubin, Françoise. 1986b. "Le folklore comme mass media : L'exemple de la selle chez les Mongols." [Folklore as Mass Media: The Example of the Saddle among the Mongols] *L'Ethnographie* [Ethnography] 82(98–99): 119–144.

Aubin, Françoise. 1999. "Critères d'appréciation des chevaux dans la tradition des nomades mongols." [Appreciation Criteria of Horses in the Mongolian Nomads' Tradition] *Cahiers de la Société des études euro-asiatiques* [Papers of the Society for Euro-Asian Studies] 8: 65–86.

Bayarsaikhan, Bekhjargal. 2006. *Travelling by Mongolian Horse*. Ulaanbaatar: Interpress.

Bianquis-Gasser, Isabelle. 1999. "Le cheval dans la société mongole contemporaine. Pratiques quotidiennes et rites festifs." [The Horse in Contemporary Mongolian Society. Daily Practices and Festive Rituals] *Cahiers de la Société des études euro-asiatiques* [Papers of the Society for Euro-Asian Studies] 8: 87–101.

Birke, Lynda. 2008. "Talking about Horses: Control and Freedom in the World of 'Natural Horsemanship.'" *Society & Animals* 16(2): 107–126.

Delaplace, Grégory. 2010. "Le cheval magnétomètre. Dressage et « choses invisibles » en Mongolie contemporaine." [The Magnetometer Horse. Training and "Invisible Things" in Contemporary Mongolia] In *Miscellanea Asiatica. Mélanges en l'honneur de Françoise Aubin* [Miscellanea Asiatica. Collection in Honor of Françoise Aubin], 121–139. Sankt Augustin: Institut Monumenta Serica.

Despret, Vinciane. 2004. "The Body We Care for: Figures of Anthropo-Zoo-Genesis." *Body & Society* 10(2–3): 111–134.

Despret, Vinciane and Jocelyne Porcher. 2007. *Être bête* [Being a Beast]. Arles: Actes sud.

Ferret, Carole. 2006. *Techniques iakoutes aux confins de la civilisation altaïque du cheval. Contribution à une anthropologie de l'action* [Yakut Techniques on the Edge of the Altaic Horse Civilization. Contribution to an Anthropology of Action]. Paris: EHESS. (PhD Dissertation)

Ferret, Carole. 2009. *Une civilisation du cheval. Les usages de l'équidé de la steppe à la taïga* [A Horse Civilization. The Uses of Equidae from Steppe to Taiga]. Paris: Belin.

Ferret, Carole. 2010. "Éducation des enfants et dressage des chevaux. Dès analogies aux modes d'action." [Bringing Up Children and Training Horses. From Analogies to Modes of Action] In *Miscellanea Asiatica. Mélanges en l'honneur de Françoise Aubin* [Miscellanea Asiatica. Collection in Honor of Françoise Aubin], 141–172. Sankt Augustin: Institut Monumenta Serica.

Fijn, Natasha. 2011. *Living with Herds. Human–Animal Coexistence in Mongolia.* Cambridge: Cambridge University Press.

Gongor, D. 2006. *Mal tanih uhaan* [The Art of Knowing Livestock]. Ulaanbaatar.

Hamilton, Jennifer A. and Aimee J. Placas. 2011. "Anthropology Becoming … ? The 2010 Sociocultural Anthropology Year in Review." *American Anthropologist* 113(2): 246–261.

Hansen, Natalie Corinne. 2014. "Embodied Communication. The Poetics and Politics of Riding." In *Sport, Animals, and Society*, by James Gillett and Michelle Gilbert, 251–276. New York: Routledge.

Haraway, Donna Jeanne. 2008. *When Species Meet.* Minneapolis: University of Minnesota Press.

Humphrey, Caroline. 1974. "Horse Brands of the Mongolians: A System of Signs in a Nomadic Culture." *American Ethnologist* 1(3): 471–488.

Humphrey, Caroline. 1975. "Notes on Hair-Cutting and Castration in Mongolian Horse Herds." *Journal of Anglo-Mongolian Society* 2(1): 70–79.

Kirksey, S. Eben and Stefan Helmreich. 2010. "The Emergence of Multispecies Ethnography." *Cultural Anthropology* 25(4): 545–576.

Lacaze, Gaëlle. 2010a. "Domestication du poulain et dressage de l'enfant. Éduquer le corps chez les Mongols." [Domesticating a Foal and Bringing Up a Child. Educating the Body among Mongols] In *Miscellanea Asiatica. Mélanges en l'honneur de Françoise Aubin* [Miscellanea Asiatica. Collection in Honor of Françoise Aubin], 209–224. Sankt Augustin: Institut Monumenta Serica.

Lacaze, Gaëlle. 2010b. "Les parfaits coursiers du Naadam." [The Perfect Steeds of the Naadam] *Études Mongoles & Sibériennes, Centrasiatiques & Tibétaines* 41 [Mongolian, Siberian, Central Asian and Tibetan Studies]. http://emscat.revues.org/index1618.html.

Lacaze, Gaëlle. 2012. *Le corps mongol. Techniques et conceptions nomades du corps* [The Mongolian Body. Techniques and Nomadic Conceptions of the Body]. Paris: L'Harmattan.

Lawrence, Elizabeth. 1982. *Rodeo: An Anthropologist Looks at the Wild and the Tame.* Knovville: University of Tennessee Press.

Legrand, Jacques. 1997. *Parlons mongol* [Let's Speak Mongolian]. Paris: L'Harmattan.

Lipec, Rahil' Solomonovna. 1984. *Obrazy batyra i ego konia v tiurko-mongol'skom èpose* [Figures of the Hero and his Horse in Turco-Mongolian Epic Poetry]. Moscow: Nauka.

Maj, Emilie. 2007. *Le cheval chez les Iakoutes chasseurs et éleveurs. De la monture à l'emblème culturel* [The Horse among the Yakut Hunters and Herders. From Mount to Cultural Emblem]. Paris: EPHE. (PhD Dissertation)

Maros, Katalin, Márta Gácsi, and Ádám Miklósi. 2008. "Comprehension of Human Pointing Gestures in Horses (Equus Caballus)." *Animal Cognition* 11: 457–466.

Maurstad, Anita, Dona Davis, and Sarah Cowles. 2013. "Co-Being and Intra-Action in Horse–Human Relationships: A Multi-Species Ethnography of Be(com)ing Human and Be(com)ing Horse." *Social Anthropology* 21(3): 322–335.

Nergüi, D., N. Batsuur', and B. Bin'yee. 2009. *Mongol malchny sudar orshivai* [Treaty on Mongolian Husbandry]. Ulaanbaatar.

Poppe, Nikolaus. 1962. "Pferdenamen in der Geschichte und Sage der Nomaden Zentralasiens." [Horse names in the History and Tales of the Nomads of Central Asia] *Oriens Extremus* 9(2): 97–104.

Poucha, Pavel. 1969. "Über eine mongolische Hippologie. Bemerkungen zum mongolischen Text *Morin-u sinjil-ü sudur*." [About a Mongolian Hippology. Remarks on the Mongolian Text *Morin-u sinjil-ü sudur*] *Zeitschrift der Deutschen Morgenländischen Gesellschaft* [Journal of the German Oriental Society] 1(2): 738–741.

Rintchen, Yöngsiyebü. 1977. "Pourquoi on offre des chevaux et des moutons aux esprits chamaniques mongols." [Why Mongolian Shamanic Spirits Are Offered Horses and Sheep] *L'Ethnographie* [Ethnography] 74–75: 155–156.

Sanders, Clinton R. 2007. "Mind, Self, and Human–Animal Joint Action." *Sociological Focus* 40(3): 320–336.

Serruys, Henry, ed. 1974. *Kumiss Ceremonies and Horse Races: Three Mongolian Texts*. Wiesbaden: Otto Harrassowitz.

Stépanoff, Charles. 2012. "Human–Animal 'Joint Commitment' in a Reindeer Herding System." *HAU: Journal of Ethnographic Theory* 2(2): 287–312.

Thompson, Kirrilly and Lynda Birke. 2014. "'The Horse Has Got to Want to Help'. Human–Animal Habituses and Networks of Relationality in Amateur Show Jumping." In *Sport, Animals, and Society*, edited by James Gillett and Michelle Gilbert, 69–84. New York: Routledge.

Tomasello, Michael. 2009. *Why We Cooperate*. Boston: MIT Press.

Veit, Veronika. 1985. "Das Pferd – Alter Ego der Mongolen ?" [The Horse: Alter Ego of the Mongols?] In *Fragen der mongolischen Heldendichtung* [Issues on Mongolian Epic Poetry], edited by Walter Heissig, 3: 58–88. Wiesbaden: Otto Harrassowitz.

Wipper, Audrey. 2000. "The Partnership: The Horse–Rider Relationship in Eventing." *Symbolic Interaction* 23(1): 47–70.

Zhambaldorzh, S. 1996. *Morin erdene* [Treasure Horse]. Ulaanbaatar.

8 My Horse Is *Not* My Therapist

Embodied Communicative Practices and the Construction of Meaning in Dressage

Susan M. DiGiacomo

In a recently published article titled "'My Horse Is My Therapist': The Medicalization of Pleasure among Women Equestrians," Davis et al. (2015) identify three distinct types of narrative that emerged from interviews with women who are long-term and in many cases lifetime riders. First, the majority of their informants stated, simply and straightforwardly, that they ride for the pleasure of riding and being with horses. A second group described the pleasures they experience as "therapeutic." The authors' analysis of these narratives shows that pleasure, in order to be culturally legitimate, cannot exist only for itself, but has to be framed discursively and experienced in medicalized terms as therapy in order to justify significant investment of time and money in equine activities, and to deflect resentment of this investment by non-rider spouses, partners and family members, who often see horses as an "addiction." A small minority of informants, however, characterized riding and the time they spend in the company of horses as a form of therapy in a literal sense: as a kind of alternative medicine. Engaging the equine therapy literature to argue that in contrast to approaches (see Kruger and Serpell 2010) that overdraw the distinction between therapeutic and recreational riding as well as between popular and biomedical healing systems, the authors argue that the narratives they collected reveal the complexity, fluidity and ambiguity of the boundary between therapy and recreation, impairment and well-being.

This chapter raises serious issues. We live in a world in which the concept of addiction has expanded outward from chemical dependency to structure our understanding of a wide range of human behaviors and experiences. People are described as being addicted to their work, to exercise, to the Internet, to sex, to food, to fashion, to gambling; addiction has become one of those "metaphors we live by" (Lakoff and Johnson 1980). Metaphors of this kind not only affect the way we talk about what we do; they structure, systematically, how we go about these activities and experience them, and they are so deeply naturalized that they are invisible to us as metaphors. This is precisely what is 'cultural' about them. There is an inescapable cultural logic at work here. If normal, everyday horse human relationships and attachments are therapy, it is because normal, everyday experiences of grief, worry, distractibility, stress *and* pleasure have been pathologized, and not only by DSM-V. As Davis et al. (2015) point out, this process operates socially not only from the top down, but also from the bottom up; the notion that the pursuit of pleasurable activities amounts to "obsessions or self-indulgent behavioral addictions" is present in popular culture as well as in medical discourse.

Through an autoethnographic account of riding, in this chapter I want to challenge the notion that "my horse is my therapist." For years, I had kept my riding life separate from my professional life as a kind of preserve, although I had subjected other dimensions of my life to the anthropological gaze: initially, factory work (Mulcahy 1976, Mulcahy and Faulkner 1977), and later on, serious illness. Developing a life-threatening disease was what made me a medical anthropologist, and my early publications in this field were autoethnographic (DiGiacomo 1987, 1995). But perhaps because the only analytic strategies suggested by colleagues for the study of riding were Foucauldian disciplines-of-the-body approaches with their overtones of regimentation and coercion (see Hearne 1986), I resisted it. It wasn't until a few years ago in my graduate course in phenomenology, when I began, tentatively, to use what I do with horses to illustrate the related analytic concepts of embodiment (Csordas 1990) and what Csordas (1993) has called "somatic modes of attention," that I began seriously to entertain the possibility of writing anthropologically about my relationship with horses.

I am one of those people born with the "horse gene" (Davis et al. 2014, 2015), an attraction to horses that ontologically precedes reason or memory, though for long periods until the age of 31 I was a self-taught rider depending on books and irregular access to horses. From the age of 13, however, I knew what I wanted, and it was dressage: classical horsemanship. 'Dressage' is a French word that simply means 'training,' and its object is to transform the horse into the best possible version of himself. In 1964, the Spanish Riding School went on international tour for the first time, and I saw them perform in the Boston Garden. I was transfixed by the beauty and balletic quality of the spectacle, by the complete at-oneness of horse and rider. I wanted with every fiber of my being to do that, and was crushed to learn that the Spanish Riding School accepted only male students (in 2008 the school admitted its first two female students).

It was not until I was in graduate school that I finally had the opportunity to be trained as a rider, and in unusual circumstances. In 1980, near the end of my dissertation fieldwork in Barcelona and after months of steadily worsening ill health, a doctor diagnosed Hodgkin's lymphoma, a cancer of the immune system. When I finally emerged from the vortex of surgery and treatment six months later, I felt alarmingly old at age 29, with a body I could not use. Climbing a single flight of stairs left me gasping for breath, my legs trembling. Initially I tried alternating walking with jogging over short distances, always on a level surface. Eventually I was able to do this for half a mile, but it left me drained of energy and nauseated with fatigue, and I gave it up. Two years later, in 1982, I applied for and was awarded a university fellowship to support the writing of my dissertation, and attached to it was the privilege of being able to take any course I wanted without having to pay for the credits. So I signed up for a place in a riding class, and for two years my life was perfectly balanced between writing and riding. I was lucky to be trained by one of the best. In 1982 the director of riding at the University of Massachusetts at Amherst was Sue Blinks, who would later go on to help the US equestrian team win a bronze medal in dressage at the 2000 Olympic Games in Sydney. All my teachers were sensitive and tactful. I explained my medical history and its consequences, and they made it possible – remarkably, in classes of ten horses and riders – for me to participate normally, stopping to rest when I needed to.

Riding was the only physical activity I was so deeply committed to that I would keep at it despite pain, breathlessness and exhaustion, and it gave me back the use of a body badly damaged by radiotherapy, and restored my sense of being alive in the world of the living after having sojourned so long in the twilight world Susan Sontag (1978, 3) memorably called "the kingdom of the sick." When my cancer returned after a four-year remission, I found I was unable to go back there, to volunteer for the most horrible form of sickness I could imagine. I resisted diagnosis for almost five months because I could not give up the nearly normal life I had reclaimed at the cost of so much physical, emotional, and intellectual effort. Eventually my growing sense of dread made it impossible for me to lose myself in writing. This dread was not misplaced. I was facing major surgery to remove the tumor attached to my heart, followed by an extremely aggressive eight-drug chemotherapy protocol projected over 13 months. Riding, however, was the one thing I *could* do because it gave me the relief of true forgetfulness during those five months of self-imposed diagnostic delay. On a horse, I did not have cancer. I was simply a rider. Serious riding joins your whole body and your whole mind simultaneously in a paradoxical condition of unselfconscious self-awareness. Every perfect jump, every balanced transition, was the practical affirmation of life over death. More than thirty years after the fact, riding still retains this meaning for me (DiGiacomo 1995).

Given my medical history, it would be very easy for me to accept the my-horse-is-my-therapist approach to riding, and most readers would, I think, find this completely credible. Instead, in a move that will at first seem counter-intuitive, I will argue that my horse is *not* my therapist, and riding is *not* therapy. I am a medical anthropologist as well as a rider, and the anthropologist in me is all too aware of how medicalization invades forms of experience that are not self-evidently medical and transforms them into pathologies of body or mind. The condition of cancer survivor – independently of your actual disease – is one of these experiences, requiring psycho-oncologic therapeutic intervention to transform vulnerability into strength, and personality defects into character (DiGiacomo 1992; DiGiacomo and Sumalla 2012; Sumalla et al. 2009).

Shortly after my cancer was first diagnosed, a friend – also an anthropologist – remarked to me that having cancer is like being black: you are totally defined by a single characteristic. As Susan Sontag (1978) showed, the metaphoric freight cancer bears shapes how others see you, and the image – reflected in many best-selling self-help books for cancer patients (see, for example, Simonton et al. 1978; Siegel 1986) – is of the emotionally inert person struggling unsuccessfully with the burden of unresolved emotional conflicts and unmet emotional needs. A person, ultimately, who is complicit in her own misfortune, having allowed these emotional wounds to turn inward and fester, ultimately taking the form of a malignancy. A person in need of therapy in order to achieve the personal growth necessary to survive her illness. The diagnosis explains everything you need to know about this person (see DiGiacomo 1992 for a deconstruction of this discourse).

Cancer is not the only illness in which this occurs. Persons with serious mental illness also find themselves trapped in a similarly totalizing diagnosis. Correa-Urquiza et al. (2006, 55) analyze the way in which "interpretive circularities" operate in psychiatric care, and how – paradoxically, with the best of intentions – this ends by desocializing the experience of the mentally ill. If persons with a diagnosis of mental illness behave transgressively, or simply question social norms, this is typically attributed to their disorder. If they are passive and accepting of social norms, this is also interpreted as a consequence of their underlying pathology. And if everything a person with schizophrenia does or says – or does not say or do – is attributed to their diagnosis, it follows that all their activities should be therapeutic. The result is "absolute illness" (Correa-Urquiza 2009, 103) requiring total therapy: the re-creation of the total institution of the psychiatric asylum outside its walls, in the fabric of a society in which persons with a diagnosis of mental illness can never have any identity other than 'patient.' Correa-Urquiza (2009, 107; my translation) pauses momentarily to reflect on:

> [...] the growing number of social practices justified as "therapeutic" – those relative to dance, music, the plastic arts and the arts in general – that identify themselves in these terms and end up contributing, perhaps without intending it, to a tendency to pathologize everyday life. Should we not consider the possibility that, in some way, the label of "therapeutic" has a pathologizing effect, that it pathologizes identities and deprives individuals of the capacity to manage and define their own lives? I do not mean to say that it actually causes specific mental disorders, but that it locates what is existential in the domain of the pathological, and social processes in the domain of therapeutic utility, reducing the social world to two opposing categories: those who provide therapy, and those who receive it.

If we follow this line of thought to its logical conclusion, being required to live in a world in which everything you did had to have therapeutic value might be enough to drive a sane person crazy.

Surviving my illness was inseparable from two processes: finding my voice and my identity as an anthropologist, a process I've analyzed elsewhere (see DiGiacomo 2004), and becoming, at last, the rider I had always wanted to be. 'Therapy' is a "thin description" (Geertz 1973:7), a narrowly reductionistic reading of both. When I first began to write ethnographically about my illness, some people (both professional colleagues and others who were not) said that it must have been 'therapeutic' to do so, as if writing could be reduced to an instrumental activity. It was not 'therapeutic'; it was self-realization, and so was riding. I am a rider in the same way I am an anthropologist. There is something beyond pleasure in both: there is desire, understood not just as something to be fulfilled in a pleasurable way but as a form of work in the sense of a calling, a vocation whose fulfillment is self-realization. I ride because I need to ride, not because I need therapy. I ride because my horse and I create something together when we ride together. And this something – something that is close to art, or at least aims for it – matters to me in the same way anthropology matters to me.

Riding and writing are ways of being in the world, and perfect counterpoints to each other. The gratifications of writing are cerebral and often long deferred – it can take years to see your work in print – but those of riding are immediate and embodied. In serious illness, what the philosopher Havi Carel (2011, 37–38) calls the "intentional arc" – the motor intentionality, temporal structure, human setting, and existential situation that joins our embodied selves to the world – is shattered. Riding, and especially dressage, reconstructed it. Riding is the ultimate contact sport (Davis et al. 2014), and dressage is its highest manifestation. Dressage is both a sport and a performing art, both highly stylized and aestheticized *and* firmly grounded in the horse's natural gaits and movements (Xenophon 2006 [1893]; Podhajsky 1967), a fully naturalcultural practice that flows from culturally elaborated somatic modes of attention (Csordas 1993) in which both horses and riders attend both to their own bodies, and to each other's bodies with their own bodies. The goal in dressage is effortless movement that fuses horse and rider into a single being: a centaur (Game 2001).

The sociologist Ann Game (2001) has written movingly of how she, her horse KP, and their trainer overcame KP's medically unexplained sudden-onset paralysis by riding through it together. Riding, here, is not a mere physical exercise for the horse or a mechanical application of skills by the rider. It is what Game (2001, 4–5) calls an "enlivening process" embodied and inhabited by horse and rider together: a *relation*. She pauses in mid-article to reflect momentarily on a human counterpoint to KP's experience: riding for the disabled. I was, and to some extent still am, a disabled rider. My radiation-scarred lungs recovered, up to a certain point, during those two years of riding while I wrote my dissertation in the early 1980s. But I lost my sense of balance to a neurotoxic drug I took as part of the eight-drug chemotherapy protocol, and one of the long-term sequelae of my disease and its treatment is chronic fatigue, a structural weakness that interferes with both thought and movement. When my horse and I ride together, I am enlivened, like KP, by a relation in which my body 'forgets' that it lost its balance in the war, and recovers a bodily memory of balance that riding elicits through contact with my partner's body. This is the human analogue to the way in which KP's body retained a memory of cantering that was elicited when Game drew on the 'horse' in herself, cantering with her own body to support KP into movement. KP's story shows us what is implied in taking the image of the centaur seriously. It requires "a fearless capacity for otherness and difference" (Game 2001, 7).

What I first learned in my early riding classes was to feel the rhythm of the horse's gaits and follow it with my body so as not to interfere with the horse's balance and freedom of movement. We memorized and performed introductory and training level dressage tests, read assigned books, and took written as well as mounted examinations. Developing cognitive understandings of what we were learning to do was a necessary part of sedimenting that knowledge in our bodies.

In time, and at a different barn, I met the horse I would buy years later: CC, an appendix American Quarter Horse, part Thoroughbred and part Quarter Horse. This makes him somewhat taller than the average Quarter Horse, and lacking in the breed's characteristic downhill build. CC is his barn name, the initials of his first owner; his papers say something else. She donated him to the barn at age three, and he was five years old when my instructor paired me with him, thinking we might 'click,' and we did. With her talking me through it from the ground, I learned to communicate the beginnings of collection by sending energy with my legs from his hindquarters toward his forehand and using tiny half-halts to contain it, and he got it. He stepped farther under his body with his hind feet and flexed at the poll, his back rounded upward into my seat, and he reached into the contact. His trot was suddenly on a qualitatively different plane, light and cadenced, and I sensed his joy in it as well as mine.

CC was, however, a school horse, so I was not the only person to ride him. The barn served the nearby college's riding program and its riding team, which competed, often quite successfully, in regional, zone and national intercollegiate shows in the US and Canada. Riders compete in hunter seat equitation, on the flat and over fences, and are judged not only on the effectiveness of their communication with their horse, but on their appearance. Their position must be perfect and maintaining it must look effortless. This is harder than it sounds, because competitions are held at different schools and the team's horses are not transported to shows along with them, so competitors are almost always riding horses they have never been on before. And the horses must contend with unfamiliar riders whose levels of skill are variable. If what is most at stake is your appearance on a horse, what you want most of all is to be assigned a horse that will make you look good in front of the judges. CC never felt it was his responsibility to do that, and the noise and bustle of a competition day at the barn made him nervous and likely to shy at unexpected movements and sights. Even in regularly scheduled classes, he was not especially tolerant of rider mistakes; he expected his rider to do it right the first time, and did not appreciate people bouncing on his back at the sitting trot or canter, or leaning on the reins to keep their balance. He was taught to jump, but was not a talented jumper and did not particularly enjoy jumping. All of these traits were, of course, real liabilities in a school horse at a college barn, and with time, he came to dislike his job. As a result, most of the students did not want to ride him in lessons, and even less at shows.

In one especially bad period of anger and frustration, CC stopped responding even to me. There were days when I got on and closed my legs to ask him to go forward, and he backed up instead, then moved unwillingly into a short, vertical trot with his head up to avoid the bit and his back hollowed: the inverse of what I wanted him to do, and knew he was capable of from prior experience. And it was that prior experience that had led me to ask the owner of the barn to let me know first if it ever crossed her mind to sell him. In addition to riding him in lessons, I had leased CC for periods of a month at a time in the summers when I could ride almost every day, and developing a partnership with him was gratifying, for both of us. What he really wanted in life was to have his own person, and once he got that, he relaxed. The person he has most of the year is the man who free-leases him from me, a retired police officer who, like me, was born with the horse gene and simply needs a horse in his life. Tom boards him on a farm where he has plenty of outdoor time in his own paddock, from which he can see other horses in their paddocks, and a comfortable box stall in the barn, and they ride outdoors through the surrounding fields and woods: less technically demanding than the riding we do in the covered school when I am in the US and move him back to the barn, but it is pleasurable, and uphill work is good for strengthening the muscles in his hindquarters. Even on days he does not ride because of the weather, Tom often spends time with him.

In Catalonia, where I live and work most of the year, I found a barn, a schoolmaster horse, and a trainer to take me to a higher level. Flamingo is now over 20, a retired competition horse donated to the barn by his former owner, half Pure Spanish Horse and half something else, who has the pedagogical vocation CC lacks. With Flamingo I am the student, and with CC the teacher. I develop as a rider from learning to elicit what Flamingo knows, and he is generous: he does not hold mistakes against me or blame me for other riders' mistakes, so that with my trainer's help I can figure out what I did wrong, ask correctly, and get the response I want. CC can do basic things: walk, trot, canter, extend and shorten his stride, leg-yield (move both forward and sideways away from the pressure of my leg, bent slightly away from the direction in which he is traveling) and shoulder-in (a suppling exercise performed on three tracks, in which the horse's body bends around the rider's inside leg so that his inside hind leg and outside foreleg travel on the same line). What I can transfer to him in the time we have available – a month in the summer, a month in the winter – is not everything Flamingo knows, but what I have learned from him about communication in order to refine these basic abilities.

With Flamingo I have been able to move beyond this to more difficult exercises, including the half-pass, a forward-and-sideways movement in which the horse is bent in the direction in which he is traveling, the outside forelegs and hind legs crossing over the inside legs, body parallel to the arena wall, the forehand leading. When done well it looks effortless. This apparent effortlessness requires skill and athleticism from both horse and rider – the ability to use different parts of their own body separately from each other, but in synchrony with parts of the other's body – to keep the forward impulsion, balance, and the correct bend, and not lose rhythm. We have done this at both the trot and the canter, and at the trot we have been able to do something harder still: a change of rein at X in the center of the arena, so that we start a half-pass to the left and at X straighten, change the bend, and continue with half-pass to the right in a zig-zag. When this exercise flows, it transports both of us. As Vicki Hearne (1986, 110) observes, "The apotheosis of skill can take you to the threshold of art, but cannot take you over it." One thing is to ride a correct half-pass, while making minor adjustments to the horse's position and to your own to preserve impulsion, bend, balance and rhythm; another thing entirely is for the half-pass to produce itself through both the rider's and the horse's body simultaneously. Horse and rider produce it together as the result of something that is much more like a conversation (Hearne 1986) happening in fractions of seconds than it is like something so mechanical as "adjustment." As Maurstad et al. (2013, 324) write, these are those fleeting "intercorporeal moments of mutuality" in which horse and human engage, through somatic modes of attention (Csordas 1993), as subjects, agents, and self-aware partners, transforming each other in the process. Flamingo returns momentarily to the competition arena, rejoicing in his own beauty like Xenophon's parade horse, and I am suddenly close to that childhood dream of being a student rider in the Spanish Riding School, of being the momentary repository of a great tradition of horsemanship.

These moments are something like a state of grace, what Game (2001, 10) calls "rapture" or self-surrender. In self-carriage, Flamingo is neither held in a frame by me nor is he leaning on me to hold him up; he is experiencing what Vicki Hearne (1986, 135) describes as moments of "congruence and contact with [his] own splendor" while simultaneously attending to me, his ears swiveled back, 'listening' through the embodied language of contact and pressure. I feel what I think of, with apologies to Milan Kundera, as the unbearable lightness of being: simultaneously relaxed and focused, in that paradoxical state of unselfconscious self-awareness. The fusion of power and lightness that we co-create and co-inhabit in a *now* that is outside linear time is an intensely enlivening intimation of immortality.

Conclusion

In their analysis of Radio Nikosia, a weekly radio program and registered cultural association in Barcelona produced and broadcast entirely by a group of persons with a diagnosis of serious mental illness, in most cases schizophrenia, Correa-Urquiza et al. (2006; see also Correa-Urquiza 2009) argue that any therapeutic effects it has are secondary to its primary effect: the production of an alternative radiophonic space in which social issues of many kinds, including but not limited to mental illness, can be discussed from unconventional and even subversive perspectives. This analysis emerges from what the Nikosians (as they call themselves) say about their own work in radio. Without denying the reality of their illness and suffering, they refuse to subscribe to the meanings placed on it from outside, which they feel are reductionistic and fail to capture the complexity of their experience. They come to the Radio Contrabanda studio on Wednesday afternoons having prepared the program at a prior meeting, and they come to provide a public service, as citizens with something to say to other citizens, from inside a liminal space capable of generating new meanings and identities. If the radio program had been defined a priori as a therapeutic activity, this would have drained it of its social and political impact, neutralizing and delegitimizing it as a practice, reducing it to one more way of keeping mental patients busy. The Nikosians have enough therapy in other parts of their lives; what they want is work as social responsibility, as meaningful engagement, as purpose in life. A life of value; a life capable of creating value. They want the ability to work out for themselves what really matters, and live accordingly: moral agency, as Arthur Kleinman (2006) has conceptualized it.

Readers of the foregoing pages, perhaps especially non-riders, will notice that I have used a morally loaded language in discussing horses' characters and responses to people, both positive and negative. Horses may take pleasure, even pride and joy, in their work, or they may get angry and feel frustrated by a rider's clumsiness, inexperience or incompetence. They may be generous and forgiving, or intolerant. The vocabulary is extensive: horses may be kind or mean, honest or inveterate fakers, introverted or extroverted, sane or psychotic, have a good (or bad) work ethic. I am not the only rider to do this. Xenophon used the same kind of anthropomorphic language. So did Alois Podhajsky, who has left an indelible imprint on modern dressage, and so have all other great riders and trainers.

As Davis et al. (n.d.) observes, recreational riders and their teachers also blur interspecies boundaries, playfully and metaphorically characterizing horses as drivers of particular kinds of cars (a Lamborghini or a Mack truck), and as favorite cartoon characters (Bullwinkle) in order to pair horse and rider personalities more successfully in lessons. The authors argue that these practices are not rounded in naïveté or ignorance, but in intimate long-term engagements with horses, and that these relationships should be seen not as incomplete versions of relations between human beings, but as complete versions of relations between members of different animal species; a moral relation, because it is premised on and reaffirms the subjectivity and agency of each party to it.

The "my horse is my therapist" discourse furnishes another metaphor for talking about connection in horse human relationships, but it disturbs me because it so easily instrumentalizes the relationship in the service of self-help, which is often a mechanism for the production of socially acceptable selves. I heard this expressed more or less explicitly in a weekly radio program broadcast on Catalan national public radio on 14 September 2013, "*L'ofici de viure*" ("The craft of living", whose subtitle is "Tools for emotional well-being"). In equine therapy as 'coaching' to develop personal or professional goals, the horse is seen as an accepting presence that does not judge or force and has no prejudices, as an open psychological space in which the person can discover his or her strengths, weaknesses and points of stagnation. The horse's role is to teach the person confidence, self-control, patience, emotional intelligence and leadership qualities: not surprisingly, characteristics highly valorized in the capitalist marketplace. As one informant in a marketing study of people's experience with their horses phrased it, "Recently…working with the natural horsemanship has helped me understand how better to work with people. For example, don't keep nagging when they start to do what you've asked (it's kind of like the old adage don't keep selling beyond the sale)" (Keaveney 2008, 452).

In the introductory chapter of her book *Adam's Task: Calling Animals by Name*, Vicki Hearne (1986, 16) asserts that "the training relationship is a moral one," and then spends the rest of the book explaining what this means, through a careful dissection of her relationships with the many dogs and horses she has trained. Training, and serious riding, depend on the co-creation of an embodied nonlinguistic system of communication through which horse and rider become legible to each other, each open to understanding by the other. While it is true, as Maurstad et al. (2013, 326) point out, that "it is the human who has decided that the language shall be spoken in the first place and, second, the one who decides what signals and signs to speak with," it is also true that the horse brings something to this conversation. Xenophon (2006 [1893], 56, 60) notes, more than once, that the highly trained horse has been "induced by a man to assume all the airs and graces which he puts on of himself when he is showing off voluntarily…imitating exactly the airs that he puts on before other horses." Hearne (1986, 160) reiterates this observation and expands on it:

> The jump, like the complicated movements of dressage, is an imitation of nature, especially of various movements that horses perform for the sake of sexual display or in the course of exercising claim rights […]. But the movements of dressage and formal jumping, properly performed, don't mean [this]. They mean the natural movements themselves. This is why the language of analysis and criticism of riding at the highest levels is the language of art criticism.

Hearne argues, and I agree with her, that horses, at least some highly developed horses, possess a sense of artistry – even my horse CC can be fleetingly open to it – and she poses (Hearne 1986, 161–162) the crucial question: "If this is an art for the horse, then the horse must intend it, and what does the horse intend, what can the horse possibly mean by it? And does – can – the horse mean by it anything like what the rider means, or can mean?" When horse and rider together cross the boundary that separates skill from art, the true significance of the often-misunderstood concept of 'submission' or 'obedience' becomes clear. Non-riders often mistakenly assume that it means the horse has been coerced by the rider, instrumentalized for the sake of spectacle. Hearne (1986, 163) likens 'submission' at this level of artistry to "the intensely accurate responsiveness of a great performer to a good audience, another case of the collapse of command and obedience into a single supple relation." 'Relation' is the key word here, and the rider's part in it is not necessarily or always that of director. Echoing Podhajsky, Hearne (1986, 163) continues:

> It is [...] as though the rider thinks and the horse executes the thought, without mediation or any sort of cuing; but it is also the other way around on the back of a great horse – it is as though the horse thinks and the rider creates, or becomes, a space and direction for the execution of the horse's thoughts. The rider is the person who shoulders the burden of knowing [...] what the horse means.

These moments of total congruence stop linear time, situating – for the duration of the performance – the horse, the rider, and those in the audience who are sufficiently open to understanding what they are witnessing, in eternity. This is what my 13-year-old self saw in the performance of the Spanish Riding School, even from as far back as I was sitting in the stands at the Boston Garden, and what explains why my eyes filled with tears and a chill went up my spine. And it remains the source of the desire that brings me back to the barn as often as possible.

Hearne concludes by noting that some highly trained horses, if left to their own devices in a pasture, become not peaceful and lazy but depressed if their work ceases for some reason. This is not, of course, human depression, but as Hearne (1986, 164) points out, "it takes more than mere comfort for his or her spine to be restored to a feeling of congruence with the landscape." Horses, she says, have their own "grammar of time," one that lacks our detailed verb tenses for past, present and future, but this does not mean that they live in a never-ending present. Horses both remember and anticipate, and that gives them, Hearne (1986, 165) says, "some sensitivity to the knowledge of death, and it makes them nervous, just as it makes us nervous. That knowledge," she continues, "is what they are relieved of, just as their riders are, in the tremendous concentration of horsemanship at the highest levels." And then she arrives at the moral heart of the relation between horse and human: "nothing short of the tremendous artistic task of training them in such a fashion that they can be released from time could ever justify our interfering with their greater serenity, our imposing our stories and our deathly arithmetics on their coherent landscapes."

As I discovered, one may be released from time, relieved of the knowledge of death even at lower levels of horsemanship that nonetheless aspire to its highest artistic expression. Nothing that therapy can offer comes remotely close to this. What dressage gives me is much closer to what the Nikosians derive from their work in radio: not therapy, but meaningful engagement that gives them a space of release from illness and suffering and access to the meaning of their humanity in a world full of uncertainties and dangers (see Kleinman 2006). This is fundamentally a moral undertaking.

Let me close with a brief reflection on the anthropological study of horse human intra-action through the lens of embodiment. The criticism of phenomenology is that you cannot study experience because all experience is mediated by language, and therefore all you can study are *representations* of experience. Clifford Geertz (1983, 58), in his famous and much-reprinted essay "From the Native's Point of View", says, "The ethnographer does not, and, in my opinion largely cannot, perceive what his informants perceive. What he perceives…is what they perceive 'with' – or 'by means of', or 'through'…". We can reach some way, even quite a long way, into the shared experiential worlds of horses and riders by focusing on what they experience 'with,' 'by means of' or 'through': what Ann Game (2001, 5) calls "the riding," the natural-cultural communicative relation between horse and rider that is brought to life in dressage. Some of this experience "comes to, or is brought to language" (Csordas 1994: 11) in riders' talk, blurring and even erasing opposing categories of nature and culture, subject and object, self and other. Anthropologists who are also riders have experience to which they bring language that is at once evocative and analytic. And if we take seriously the idea that language is not just a system of representations but a modality of being-in-the-world, then dressage understood as a system of embodied communication has in common with language that it "not only represents…but 'discloses' our being-in-the-world" (Csordas 1994, 11).

References

Carel, Havi. 2011. "Phenomenology and Its Application in Medicine." *Theoretical Medicine and Bioethics* 32: 33–46.

Correa-Urquiza, Martín, T. Silva, M. Belloc and A. Martínez-Hernáez. 2006. "La evidencia social del sufrimiento. Salud mental, políticas globales y narrativas locales." ["The Social Evidence of Suffering: Mental Health, Global Politics and Local Narratives."] *Quaderns de l'Institut Català d'Antropologia* 22: 47–69.

Correa-Urquiza, Martín. 2009. *Radio Nikosia: La rebelión de los saberes profanos (Otras prácticas, otros territorios para la locura)*. [*Radio Nikosia: The Rebellion of Lay Knowledge (Other Practices and Other Territories for Madness.*] Unpublished doctoral dissertation, Departament d'Antropologia, Filosofia i Treball Social, Universitat Rovira i Virgili, Tarragona, Catalonia.

Csordas, Thomas J. 1990. "Embodiment as a Paradigm for Anthropology." *Ethos* 18(1): 5–47.

Csordas, Thomas J. 1993. "Somatic Modes of Attention." *Cultural Anthropology* 8: 135–156.

Csordas, Thomas J. 1994. "Introduction: The Body as Representation and Being-in-the-World." In *Embodiment and Experience: The Existential Ground of Culture and Self*, edited by Thomas J. Csordas, 1–24. New York: Cambridge University Press.

Davis, Dona L., Anita Maurstad and Sarah Dean. 2014. "'I'd Rather Wear Out than Rust Out': Autobiologies of Ageing Equestriennes." *Ageing & Society* 4 November, DOI: 10.1017/S0144686X14001172.

Davis, Dona L., Anita Maurstad and Sarah Dean. 2015. "'My Horse Is My Therapist': The Medicalization of Well-Being Among Women Equestrians." *Medical Anthropology*, 5 November.

Davis, Dona L., Anita Maurstad and Sarah Dean. n.d. "Barn Banter: An Exploration of Anthropomorphism and Equine-o-morphism as Agency." In *Equine Agency in Human Horse Relations*, edited by Gala Argent, (forthcoming). Pittsburgh: Pennsylvania State University Press.

DiGiacomo, Susan M. 1987. "Biomedicine as a Cultural System: An Anthropologist in the Kingdom of the Sick." In *Encounters with Biomedicine: Case Studies in Medical Anthropology*, edited by Hans A. Baer, 315–346. New York: Gordon and Breach Science Publishers.

DiGiacomo, Susan M. 1992. "Metaphor as Illness: Postmodern Dilemmas in the Representation of Body, Mind and Disorder." *Medical Anthropology* 14: 109–137. Special issue: The Application of Theory in Medical Anthropology, edited by Merrill Singer.

DiGiacomo, Susan M. 1995. "The Case: A Narrative Deconstruction of 'Diagnostic Delay'." *Second Opinion* 20(4): 21–35.

DiGiacomo, Susan M. 2004. "Autobiografia crítica i teoria antropològica. Reflexions a l'entorn de la identitat cultural i professional." ["Critical Autobiography and Anthropological Theory: Reflections on Cultural and Professional Identity."] *Revista d'Etnologia de Catalunya* 25: 124–134.

DiGiacomo, Susan M. and Enric C. Sumalla. 2012. "Del esencialismo biológico a la experiencia encarnada: el cáncer como aprendizaje." ["From Biological Essentialism to Embodied Experience: Cancer as Apprenticeship."] *Iglesia Viva* 252: 37–56.

Game, Ann. 2001. "Riding: Embodying the Centaur." *Body & Society* 7(4): 1–12.

Geertz, Clifford. 1973. *The Interpretation of Cultures*. New York: Basic Books.

Geertz, Clifford. 1983. *Local Knowledge: Further Essays in Interpretive Anthropology*. New York: Basic Books.

Hearne, Vicki. 1986. *Adam's Task: Calling Animals by Name*. New York: Alfred A. Knopf.

Keaveney, Susan M. 2008. "Equines and Their Human Companions." *Journal of Business Research* 61: 444–454.

Kleinman, Arthur. 2006. *What Really Matters: Living a Moral Life Amidst Uncertainty and Danger*. Oxford and New York: Oxford University Press.

Kruger, Katherine and James Serpell. 2010. "Animal-Assisted Interventions in Mental Health: Definitions and Theoretical Foundations." In *Handbook on Animal Assisted Therapy: Theoretical Foundations and Guidelines for Practice*, edited by Aubrey Fine, 33–48. Amsterdam: Elsevier.

Lakoff, George and Mark Johnson. 1980. *Metaphors We Live By*. Chicago: Chicago University Press.

Maurstad, Anita, Dona Davis and Sarah Cowles. 2013. "Co-Being and Intra-Action in Horse–Human Relationships: A Multi-Species Ethnography of Be(com)ing Human and Be(com)ing Horse." *Social Anthropology* 21(3): 322–335.

Mulcahy, Susan D. 1976. *Blue-Collar Women: Patterns of Work and Commitment in a Factory*. Unpublished MA thesis, Department of Anthropology, University of Massachusetts at Amherst.

Mulcahy, Susan D. and Robert R. Faulkner. 1977. "Work Individuation among Women Machine Operators." *Sociology of Work and Occupations* 4(3): 303–326.

Podhajsky, Alois. 1967. *The Complete Training of Horse and Rider in the Principles of Classical Horsemanship*. Col. V.D.S. Williams and Eva Podhajsky, translators. No. Hollywood, CA: Wilshire Book Company.

Siegel, Bernie S., MD. 1986. *Love, Medicine & Miracles: Lessons Learned about Self-Healing from a Surgeon's Experience with Exceptional Patients*. New York: Harper and Row.

Simonton, O. Carl, MD, Stephanie Mathews-Simonton, and James L. Creighton. 1978. *Getting Well Again: A Step-by-Step, Self-Help Guide to Overcoming Cancer for Patients and Their Families*. Los Angeles, CA: J.P. Tarcher.

Sontag, Susan. 1978. *Metaphor as Illness*. New York: Farrar, Straus and Giroux.

Sumalla, Enric C., C. Ochoa, and I. Blanco. 2009. "Posttraumatic Growth in Cancer: Reality or Illusion?" *Clinical Psychological Review* 29: 24–33.

Xenophon. 2006 [1893]. *The Art of Horsemanship*. Morris H. Morgan, translator and editor. Mineola, New York: Dover Publications, Inc.

9 The Human Horse Relationship Challenged by Pregnancy and Motherhood

Nora Schuurman and Maarit Sireni

In recent years, the significance of emotions, embodiment, and everyday practices in human animal relationships has attracted increasing interest. A number of studies devoted to human horse relations within contemporary equestrian culture have foregrounded encounters between horses and women (Butler and Charles 2012). These studies have directed attention to the widespread Western process of "feminization" in amateur equestrianism and to the challenges this development poses for research (Adelman and Knijnik 2013, 5). One of the questions concerns the ways in which horses figure in the everyday life of the people interacting with them and, in particular, how the human horse relationship remains a part of the lives of these women during times of major change in their personal life.

In this chapter, we subject one such case to scrutiny, namely the simultaneousness of the performances of the human horse relationship and motherhood. Our focus is both on how pregnancy and childbirth affect the relationship with the horse, and on how the human horse relationship shapes the experience of becoming a mother. We explore the ways in which the emotional and identity conflict resulting from two embodied states, being with the horse and pregnancy, is managed, as well as the impacts of the various experts involved in supporting the expectant mother. In the analysis, we concentrate on the aspect of embodiment and possible ways of coping with the emergent conflict. We also ask how the horse reacts to the newborn baby and how the birth of the child affects the relationship with the horse. Our aim is to pay attention to the significance of an emotionally close human animal relationship in everyday life as well as in identity building. We also aim to highlight the ways in which external authorities defining parenthood may contribute to problems in other, meaningful spheres of life such as keeping a horse.

The study derives from the recent discussions about embodiment and relationality in human animal studies (Barad 2003; Birke et al. 2004), especially the process of becoming with the significant (animal) other (Haraway 2008). We also utilize studies of pregnancy as a performative process (Longhurst 2000, 2008), gender in equestrianism (Butler and Charles 2012), and the position of animals as family members (Charles and Davies 2011). The impact of feminist studies upon theory-building within human animal studies is an issue that is frequently brought up, to highlight the common interest in deconstructing hierarchies and recognizing otherness. In human animal studies, this discussion has contributed to the concepts of animal subjectivity and agency, and also to recent emphasis on embodiment and performativity in the study on human animal relationships (Barad 2003; Birke et al. 2004; Haraway 2008). The purpose of this chapter is to utilize the research traditions involving both gender production and the social status and cultural meanings of companion animals.

The material used for this chapter consists of a blog kept by a horse owner and mother in Finland. In this blog, the author contemplates the ways in which her pregnancy and motherhood transform her relationship with her horse, and the cultural understandings and values concerning both motherhood and the practice of keeping horses. As in many other Western countries, in Finland riding is predominantly a female activity, as more than 90 percent of those who ride are women and girls (The Equestrian Federation of Finland 2014). This is reflected in the culture of keeping leisure horses. Tending horses is, however, not new to women, since in agrarian times women participated in the care of horses and bore considerable responsibility for their well-being (Leinonen 2013). In parallel with its increasing popularity since the 1970s, riding has attained its present gendered status. Suggested reasons for this development include the social environment of the stable yard and the increasing acceptance of expressing emotions towards animals (Ojanen 2012).

The embodied human horse relationship

We approach the human animal relationship and pregnancy as performances, focusing on embodiment, emotions, and identities in relation to other people and to animals. Relationships between humans and animals have recently been scrutinized as performative processes produced in interactions and practices (Barad 2003; Birke et al. 2004). According to Birke et al. (2004, 171), "the notion of performativity can serve a useful purpose in clarifying how human/animal relationships are constructed by discursive practices." The focus is on the material aspect of the relationship, including embodied communication with the animal and the agency of the animal (Despret 2004). In the "agential realism" presented by Karen Barad (2003, 810), material phenomena and practices are brought alongside linguistic discourses, and the embodied experience becomes part of the performance produced by both human and non-human actors. Thus, the animal is understood as an actor and as an agent participating in the construction of the human animal relationship (Birke et al. 2004).

According to Barad (2003) and Haraway (2008), a human animal relationship transforms both partners in a way that would not happen without their encounter. This is the basic idea in the concept "becoming with" another (Haraway 2008, 4). A relationship with an animal shapes the human and constructs for her an identity based on shared experiences with the animal, and vice versa (Despret 2004; Irvine 2004). Haraway (2008) illustrates this process by describing her relationship with her dog as a partnership that develops and deepens through shared activities in agility, based on embodied communication between the two. In such a process the boundary is blurred between human and animal, and culture and nature.

Like other relationships with companion animals, human horse encounters are not only instrumental but also emotional. Keeping a horse is experienced as a way of life that demands from the owner long-term commitment to and responsibility for the animal, provides companionship and mutual enjoyment, and contributes to identity building (Keaveney 2008). A relationship with a horse is typically based on interaction and shared experiences in daily life, and in contemporary society, the horse is increasingly perceived as a family member. When an animal has the status of a family member it is talked to, its feelings are interpreted, its viewpoint is considered and its death is mourned in a similar way to that of a human family member (Charles and Davies 2011). Contrary to previous thought, a companion animal does not act as a substitute for a missing human family member such as a child or sibling but gives to its owner something that another human cannot offer (Sarmicanic 2007). The status of animals as family members is so established in contemporary societies that a new concept of "a hybrid family," referring to families comprising both humans and animals, has been suggested (Franklin 2006, 142). The emergence of hybrid families also contributes to the dissipation of the hierarchical boundary between humans and other animals in Western thought (Charles and Davies 2011).

Human horse interactions are to a large extent based on embodied communication, culminating in riding, where the rider and the horse give messages and clues to each other that are often invisible to onlookers. The communication is not only technical but ultimately aims at a state of shared flow where rider and horse experience a feeling of togetherness in thinking, acting, feeling, and movement (Keaveney 2008), described in research literature as the mythical figure of a centaur (Thompson 2011). Due to this bodily closeness, an emotional bond is easily developed between horse and rider.

In equestrian culture embodiment is also gendered. The tradition of equestrian sports is strongly masculine, which is still reflected in the social world of riding as an idolization of physical work and power, similar to sports such as boxing or weightlifting (Brown 2006). Women who ride aspire to possessing a body that is perceived as strong, enduring injury, and capable of hard stable work (Butler and Charles 2012). In equestrian culture, such a body is considered physical capital, and thus riding does not require stereotypical femininity of women. According to Ojanen (2011), the culture of 'stable girls' tending horses at riding schools challenges the cultural conceptions of girlhood by extending the boundaries between genders. At the stable yard, girls are free of the expectations of femininity experienced elsewhere. The yard, however, also supports Protestant work ethics by reproducing the traditional ideal of a strong, agrarian woman (Ojanen 2011). The stable yard is a community where the relationship between human and horse is performed as ambivalent, both free and traditional, with regard to the production of femininity.

The performance of pregnancy

Judith Butler's theoretical constructions of gender and performativity have been utilized in the analysis of the constitution of various subjects in different places and at different times. According to Butler (1990, 33), we "do" gender through bodily acts. She understands gender to be "the repeated stylization of the body, a set of repeated acts within a highly rigid frame that congeal over time to produce the appearance of substance, of a natural sort of being" (Butler 1990, 33). Repeated performances of socially and culturally expected behaviors establish regulatory practices for acting out a feminine or masculine subject. By disrupting these normative expectations, individuals can cause 'gender trouble' and subvert hegemonic constructions of gender.

Drawing on Butler's notions of gender and performativity, Robyn Longhurst (2000) has examined how pregnancy is played out in public places and whether the behavior of individuals meets or challenges normative expectations surrounding the exposure of pregnant bodies in public. According to Longhurst, pregnancy can be understood as being socially constructed in the sense that there are normative expectations about 'doing' pregnancy in specific ways. These are closely linked with expectations related to gender and femininity in a specific geographical context (Holloway 1999). An expectant mother negotiates her way of doing pregnancy in interaction with the sociocultural context, drawing on prevailing cultural values. Pregnancy is performed in bodily acts, becoming normative and, when repeated frequently enough, taking on the appearance of being natural (Longhurst 2000). For example, pregnant women are assumed to act in a demure and modest manner when occupying public spaces, or to be more emotional and irrational, bursting into tears and behaving in unpredictable ways (Longhurst 2000). Although pregnant bodies cannot be considered as fixed and stable, they are often presented as 'natural.' In the natural sciences, pregnancy and childbirth are understood as the purpose of the female body (Longhurst 2000).

There are several actors involved in the definition of acceptable ways of being pregnant. Pregnant bodies, as well as citizens' desires, pleasures and sexuality, are regulated and controlled in societies through discursive power. In modern societies, expertise has penetrated into the private sphere (Giddens 1990). Doctors, midwives and other medical experts play a key role in regulating and controlling pregnant women through medical discourses on pregnancy, thus defining proper ways of being pregnant. In Finland, for instance, expectant mothers are eligible for maternity benefits only if they contact a maternity clinic in the early stage of a pregnancy and continue to follow the health care program intended for them. First of all, pregnant women are advised to lead a healthy life that will be good for the baby; they are expected to avoid alcohol and other intoxicants; and they are advised to eat proper food, do some physical exercise, and rest sufficiently. Medical experts are also in the position to use discursive power in controlling other than purely medical aspects of pregnancy, as the empirical material of this chapter will show.

Interpretations of how to do pregnancy in public and private places vary; for example, only a few decades ago in Western societies pregnant bodies were not permitted to be shown in public, as their appearance was seen as improper. For the same reason, it was presumed that pregnant bodies would be hidden beneath loose clothing (Longhurst 2008). Women were expected to behave in a modest and restrained way that would indicate that they were concentrating on their sacred role as becoming mothers. Any other appearance would indicate that a mother was not prepared to put her child first. Wearing a bikini in public would be an example of such a performance, disrupting normative expectations and causing "pregnancy trouble" in contemporary Western societies (Longhurst 2000, 456).

There is no doubt that understandings and interpretations of what is proper and improper have changed. Pregnant women can occupy jobs in the public sphere and take part in social life outside the home. In Finland, combining pregnancy and paid work has been interpreted as normal since the 1970s, as there is a long tradition of the dual-income family model, supported and promoted by the welfare state (Ellingsæter et al. 2006). Thus, in the Finnish context the presence of pregnant women in the labor market does not receive much attention. What is striking is that pregnant women have also come out of the closet in many other spheres of life: they run marathons, participate in beauty contests – and wear sexy and revealing clothes rather than loose maternity clothing (Longhurst 2008). This transformation does not, however, indicate the disappearance of regulatory practices shaping and defining pregnant bodies (Longhurst 2000). Instead, old expectations have been replaced by new ones. One evidently new requirement is for pregnant women to be active consumers who construct their identities through material culture. In the sphere of personal style, there are many options available to pregnant women.

'Looking gorgeous' even when the pregnancy is evident is one of the dominant expectations related to pregnant bodies in contemporary Western societies. It presumes a healthy lifestyle and regular physical exercise, not to mention clothes, haircut, and make-up of the right style. The gorgeous pregnant body can make itself visible at work, night-clubs, cafes, gyms, and other public places. It seems that in Western societies women have abandoned or contested the old interpretation of pregnant bodies as modest and private (Longhurst 2008).

The study

With the rise of the social media, the popularity of blogs has increased substantially in the past few years. In the social sciences an interest has emerged in studying virtual communities or the "blogosphere" (Hookway 2008, 93). Blogs, defined by Hookway (2008) as public diaries or self-narratives, are useful data for research. They are publicly available, naturalistic data in textual form, and they enable easy access to populations otherwise difficult to reach, providing insight into everyday life. Their archived nature also provides an opportunity to study social processes across both space and time.

The blog under scrutiny was sampled for a larger study focusing on the everyday life of horse owners, based on the analysis of fifteen blogs. The blog used for this study is titled *Ruuhkavuosiratsastaja* (*Riding in the Hectic Years*). The blogger, named *Anniina* in the blog, is a woman aged between 29 and 32 while blogging, is married, and becomes pregnant shortly after purchasing her first horse. In her blog she recounts the experiences of a horse owner becoming a mother. Her background as a horse enthusiast is at the riding school that she returned to after a break of several years during her early adulthood. It is at the riding school that she finds her horse, gradually moving into the world of commercial livery yards, where she constructs her identity as a horse owner. She also develops an ambition to participate in equestrian sports and sets out to train and eventually compete in eventing, until physical restrictions due to the horse's old age limit the achievement of her aims. Anniina has two children during the period of her blogging, and her role as a mother is thus foregrounded in the blog. Motherhood affects her horse-keeping significantly, while her relationship with her horse and the horse itself participate in the construction of her identity as a mother.

The blog starts in September 2009. The material used for the analysis consists of the posts published up to May 2013, a total of 270 posts consisting of over 6,700 words. From this body of material we compiled data for this chapter consisting of forty-four excerpts of various lengths. This material was thematized according to five themes: the impact of pregnancy on everyday life with the horse; the role of experts in reproducing the conceptions of pregnancy; the experiences of pregnancy as influenced by the human horse relationship; reconstructing the human horse relationship after childbirth; and the relationship between the child and the horse. The themes were further developed to illustrate (i) the impact of pregnancy on the human horse relationship and vice versa; (ii) the role of experts and the guilt experienced by the author; and (iii) the experiences of reconstructing the relationship between the author, the horse, and the child. In the remainder of this chapter, we present the results of this thematic analysis.

The human horse dyad challenged

Anniina's pregnancy and the ways in which it transforms her relationship with her mare, Tintti, do not emerge in a void but interfere with the ongoing relationship between the author and her horse. In this relationship, the horse has agency, her actions have meaning for the animal itself. The horse also has gender, a notable issue contributing to the relationship. In equestrian culture, mares carry a negative reputation outside actual breeding practices, as their hormonal cycle is claimed to interfere with riding activities and make the horses uncooperative. In the case of Anniina's horse, this phenomenon is recognized but easily overcome: "Usually any negative aspects of being a mare disappear from Tintti in riding as she is a nice and hard-working girl who tries to please and to do right, and she wants praise."

The excerpt also demonstrates that it is the act of riding that represents the mutual enjoyment in shared practices for both human and horse and thus appears as the core of their relationship. When the author is pregnant, achieving this aim becomes difficult. Contrary to many other fields of action, riding as an embodied state is considered to be exclusionary of pregnancy. One of the strongest themes in the blog is the author's increasing distress occasioned by not being able to ride or to do things together with her horse. Gradually, she has to give up riding as the pregnancy progresses:

> In week 24 I had a few anticipatory contractions and at the same time, Tintti started circling around when I tried to mount, so I decided to give up riding. [...] It did not feel good to me either. We did, however, take long walks on the lead until the final weeks. Tintti always waited for me nicely when I had to breathe a little in the uphill stretches.

At this stage of her pregnancy, the bodily restrictions of riding are felt by both the author and the horse, and she then acts to change the embodied nature of the relationship from riding to walking together. The agency of the horse becomes clear when it communicates to the author its unwillingness to be ridden. The author then interprets the change felt by the horse, as the alteration in the rider's balance and increase in weight make it uncomfortable for the horse to carry her. The author identifies with the horse, nor does she feel good about riding her horse any longer. Riding is replaced by other activity, with the horse accommodating to the author's clumsy movements. The transformation in shared practices illustrates the process of becoming with the significant other (Haraway 2008; Birke et al. 2004). The relationship is flexible and there is a search for new manifestations when the old ones are found to be inaccessible.

Later in her pregnancy, the author feels the loss of riding more severely. The following excerpt describes a position where the feelings about pregnancy according to expectations are challenged by her separation from the horse and riding. The author refuses to acknowledge the naturalized interpretation that the female body exists primarily for childbirth, and that fulfilling this task is both natural and can only provide happiness and satisfaction (Longhurst 2000):

> I crave for riding. Instead, I can hardly pull Pinke [the elder daughter] to the kindergarten on the sledge without a feeling of strain around my belly. It makes me feel the strain around my head too. [...] Excuse me, but I think that the whole glow of motherhood is only a way to assure people who feel like humpback whales that it is going to be all right.

Pregnancy is an embodied state with concrete consequences for daily life. Instead of being natural, it is performed as an illness, an anomaly that prevents normal life, including riding. Pregnancy also keeps the author literally away from the world of the horse. Gradually, the relationship changes from one based on embodied encounters to a more distant one characterized by longing. In addition, during her pregnancy Anniina finds it increasingly difficult to fulfil her duties of caring for the animal:

> But you know, in this state the feeling of being useless is multiplied tenfold! You are away and relying on the phone. On top of this, you cannot move without huffing and puffing. [...] If somebody were to dare to come and say, enjoy, I might become violent, at least verbally.

The experience of being distanced and therefore useless illustrates the difficulty of fitting together the embodied experiences of motherhood and a human horse relationship with the related practices and responsibilities, leading to a crisis in both. It is not only a question of denying the performance of pregnancy as natural but of worry and longing caused by separation from the horse. The desire to be with the emotionally close animal is fulfilled only in her dreams:

> With a waistline of 108 centimeters, you can only dream about riding. Last night I dreamed that I was eventing. In the competition, I had to ride the same cross-country course twice. I doubted whether Tintti could gallop the same long straight again but she said she could if she was allowed to trot part of the long journey. We agreed on this and finished the course. At the finish, we toasted our achievement together. Tintti promised to go to competitions with me as soon as Little Brother was born.

This excerpt illustrates the importance of riding in Anniina's relationship with her horse. The experience of separation is ultimately overcome in the competition, in a shared endeavor where mutual communication is seamless, and both human and horse enjoy the activity. Competing in riding is also the activity that is obviously impossible to carry out during pregnancy. At this stage, the author's pregnancy has altered her human horse relationship in a profound way. As Haraway (2008) notes, the process of becoming with is a messy one and does not only consist of positive experiences.

Experts and guilt

Expert authorities such as the maternity clinic nurse and the doctor have a central position in monitoring the author's pregnancy and childbirth. Their role is evident in their recommendations to reduce riding during pregnancy. Their main concerns are for the health and safety of the unborn child, and the risk of miscarriage in the case of a fall, although there are no exact rules for this based on science. That is nevertheless why the health care professionals interfere with Anniina's riding activity and thereby her relationship with her horse. In expert speech, the author's pregnancy excludes riding, the central part of her relationship with her horse: "The nurse at the maternity clinic asked again and again if I had given up riding. I rode less but I couldn't stop before I had to. This happened a little after the middle of my pregnancy."

The external power of the experts is rarely challenged but is internalized as self-discipline. As Wynne (1996) notes, trust in experts is often misinterpreted in research. In cases where there are no alternatives, people sometimes act as if they trust the experts they depend on. In Finland, nurses at public maternity clinics have a lot of influence on expectant mothers, and challenging them would leave the mother without the support she needs. The various experts involved in the author's pregnancy, however, present contradictory advice:

> The doctor gave me instructions to ride as long as it felt good. [...] The maternity clinic nurses, in contrast, only see the risk in my hobby of a fall, and when I mention my hobby I feel more or less like a criminal. I wonder when they will call up the child welfare authorities.

In such a situation the author, a layperson, is left alone with contradictory advice and with the consequent feelings of guilt if the advice is not followed. It is notable that no discussion takes place with the experts about alternative ways of spending time with the horse. The influence of the experts is also so powerful that it can only be questioned by other experts. In the blog, this is done by an encouraging midwife at the maternity hospital whose expert status is supported by her own experience of horses and riding: "During my pregnancy everybody made me believe that riders had more sections than other people. My midwife had four horses herself and at least she thought these beliefs were just myths."

After the birth of the child, Anniina is eventually able to return to riding. At first, the aim is to regain her former relationship with the horse, consisting solely of herself and the horse: "It is actually very liberating to be on horseback on my own and not pregnant." Things are, however, more complicated. Firstly, there is guilt. The former conflict between pregnancy and the human horse relationship has now been transformed in a way that the author has not expected. She either feels guilt about neglecting the child when she is with the horse or about neglecting the horse when tending the child. She describes her guilt as something she 'instinctively' took with her from the maternity hospital:

> At home, I felt a great enthusiasm to get to the stables and guilt for not taking care of my horse. At the yard, I felt guilty about not being at home, enjoying the time with the baby, which is always depicted as being so short. [...] I also felt guilty about buying a horse but letting other people take care of it. And always there would be someone unsuspecting who added to my anguish by saying, "how could you leave your child", or by asking, "who is riding your horse now?"

Although the situation is different than before, the guilt felt by the author can be understood as a continuation of the performative crisis between pregnancy and the human animal relation into motherhood. Being a good mother and a good horse owner are difficult to combine, and the author tries to cope with the commentary from her social environment cognitively, explaining to herself that motherhood and horse ownership do not exclude each other. She realizes that "it was not a question of knowledge or will but of feeling. Guilt was somewhere deeper. I had given birth to it myself." The control exercised by the experts, now internalized by the author, is repeated in the new situation.

With time, practical solutions are found. Things improve when the baby takes to sleeping at the yard, while the mother gets the chance to ride: "I really started to enjoy my maternity leave." Even then, she expects people to find fault with her action. Finally, she gets a chance to ride "in the night shift" when the baby is sleeping at home, with the father looking after it: "For the first time after she was born I did not feel guilty when riding."

Coping strategies and a transformed relationship

During her pregnancy, the strategies used by the author to cope with the incompatibility of her two bodily states are twofold: waiting for the reunion with the horse after childbirth, and a parody of the pregnant body. In the parody, the horse is replaced by a chair resembling a saddle that the author calls "Salli the Motherhood Mount." Salli is a commercial brand of chair that resembles a real saddle and on Salli it is possible for Anniina, the "Casual Cowboy" to sit and even move a little, as if on horseback:

> I am not allowed to sit on my Kieffer [a brand of saddle] anymore. I spend the days on my new Salli. [...] I cannot ride for the whole day, it tires my back. Luckily the chair has a spring feature for impatient children so I can move around sufficiently.

In the blog, the author has attached humorous photographs of herself, big-bellied and sway-backed and in an old T-shirt, sitting in the saddle chair. The photographs also represent a parody of the performance of 'looking great,' enforced by the use of commercial chair and saddle brands. The casual cowboy rejects the demands of being sexy and feminine, but the expression also refers to the masculine femininity of the world of sport where the female body is strong and tough (Butler and Charles 2012). Her difficulty in holding on to the flexible gender identity created at the yard epitomizes the gender ambivalence within equestrian culture. The tragedy of the parody is in the inevitable distance to the very animal contributing to the construction of her identity, and in the consequent emotional crisis in the human animal relationship.

The ultimate aim for the author is to get away from the state of pregnancy as quickly and with as little injury as possible. She is not only waiting for the baby to be born but, after the childbirth, the renewal of her relationship with her horse. She demonstrates this by taking an inspiring book with her to the maternity hospital. The book compensates for the missing horse when the separation is total – albeit a temporary one:

> I have started dreaming of the summer and stared at Mark Todd videos on YouTube and dreamt of a better eventing seat. I'm waiting for Mark's biography from Amazon. I hope it comes before we go to the hospital. I want it with me. Watching some videos made me cry, I wanted to be in the saddle so much.

The birth of the child as such is not enough to bring back the lost relationship with the horse. When returning to riding, the author will have to rebuild the embodied connection, a challenge for a body that is still recovering from childbirth. She contemplates the challenge well before her due date: "I think with horror about the size I will be when I get back into the saddle again. When all the muscles of my middle part have been blown into atoms and I have to start building up my condition again from the beginning."

Afterwards, she reports on her return to riding, with the conflict apparently resolved: "I had promised myself a proper recovery but was back in the saddle three weeks after giving birth. I had a feeling I was my own self again." A human animal relationship is, however, always in a state of becoming, and a return to the past as it was is not possible. In the relationship between the author and her horse, there is also a third party, the newborn baby. When the mother rides, the baby sleeps in the pram beside the arena so that the mother can stop by the pram to rock it when needed. During the stops, the horse "rests her hind leg and closes her eyes." Before long, the horse is accustomed to this interruption in the riding exercise: "Tintti is already fully used to the pram and comes nicely beside it so that the mother can rock the pram from horseback. On the other hand, Tintti also knows that she can easily try to stop by the red buggy for no reason, just to get a break."

The horse interprets the situation from its own viewpoint, as a chance for a rest, and acts in order to achieve this goal, thus displaying agency. The horse's action, however, affects the shared activity of riding, and the author has to take subsequent action to achieve her own goal, which is to concentrate on her riding: "Nowadays I put Pinke to sleep in the canopy so that the pram is not within view and Tintti does not have a too big temptation to try and turn into a nanny even when the child does not need it."

When the second child is born, the pram reappears at the yard. The horse immediately takes on its previous action: "It goes without saying that Tintti remembered right away what you were supposed to do by the pram: stand still and be on maternity leave, that is, avoid working." When the child grows, the interaction between horse and child develops in unexpected ways, and the horse acknowledges the child's position as an individual actor. In the following excerpt, the child is to give the horse an apple but this is not actually what happens:

> When the stable door was opened I told Pinke to give the apple [to Tintti]. Tintti approached her little friend ears pricked. And then: pang! Pinke threw the apple at Tintti and it hit her in the muzzle, right in the middle of the nose. For some strange reason the horse did not (true to its habits) snort but calmly turned her head away, looked at us for a moment and approached Pinke again. […] Tintti did not show any signs of being angry at her little friend but approached her as hopefully as always.

The author concludes that if anyone else had treated the horse like this, the horse would not have reacted in the same way. The horse's action is not solely related to the violent act but to the person committing it and to the relationship between the animal and the child. During the pregnancy and as a small baby, the child was an object, not an active agent in the human horse relationship but rather a source of conflict. In the incident described above it is evident, however, that the composition has changed. Not only has the child acquired agency but this also transforms the agency of the horse in an emerging relationship based on embodied communication. Further, the child–horse encounter transforms the role of the child by including her in the old human horse relationship and thus providing a solution to the conflict experienced by the author.

Instead of the previous human horse relationship, there is now a triad of relationships, each one different from the other, as is seen in the author's amazed reactions to the interactions between the child and the horse. For her, the event took place "for some strange reason." In another example, the child enjoys riding on the horse, led by the mother on the ground: "I told her how we rode together when she was in my belly. Pinke was proud of riding on her own now. Tintti was suddenly her horse." The human horse dyad developing into a triad illustrates the process of becoming with the significant other, or others, in ways that are sometimes unexpected. In the case described, the development also leads to a firmer establishment of the horse as a family member, thereby dissolving the guilt between the need to tend the horse and also to tend the baby.

Conclusion

In this chapter, we have demonstrated how pregnancy and a human horse relationship may be incompatible embodied states, leading to a temporary crisis in the relationship with the horse, and ultimately to its transformation. Because of her relationship with her horse affecting her identity, the author does not take part in the performance of looking great suggested by Longhurst (2008). Neither is it possible for her to perform the human animal relationship, including encounters and spending time with the horse, caring for it, and sharing success in competitions. Attempts at managing the mutually exclusive embodied states finally lead to what Gregson and Rose (2000, 441) term "performative instability," where a performance is disrupted by contextually variable and frequently unexpected occurrences. In this case, the instability is due to the incompatibility of the bodily states central to the performances. As they derive from material processes they cannot be changed according to situation. The author aims at controlling the instability with coping strategies concentrating on parody and planning for the future, and in this way succeeds in controlling the performance and maintaining her identity as a horse owner.

The role of experts in producing the conflict is evident. In particular, the ambivalent attitude of the maternity nurses towards the human horse relationship of the expectant mother concentrates on the medical risks, not on finding a solution to the problems experienced within the relationship. The definitions of pregnancy in society highlight the one-sidedness of the expectant mother's identity and life situation. A human horse relationship, however, includes the responsibility of the owner to care for her horse and its welfare. The case analyzed illustrates the situation in contemporary society where individual lives include different commitments that cannot simply be dissolved but have to be taken into account during pregnancy. The failure of those who have as their task to support expectant mothers in conflict situations leads not only to practical problems but also to feelings of guilt.

The conflict and related feelings of guilt are still present after the child is born, but are manifested in a different way. The expectations in society concerning the mother of a new-born baby are felt in much the same way as during the pregnancy, with the difference that the conflict is no longer primarily embodied but is epitomized in the competing needs of commitment of time and energy to the baby and the horse. The pressures from the social environment result in a need to find coping strategies to preserve both identities, that of a mother and that of a horse owner. A solution finally emerges in the inclusion of the child in the human horse relationship, a process in which the agency of the horse plays a significant role. For the horse, the child carries specific meanings, first in shaping the practices of riding, and later in creating a personal companionship that does not require or exclude the previous relationship between the author and the horse but adds to it. As a result, the horse is increasingly felt to be part of the family.

The process of becoming with the significant other involves mutual change, as according to Barad (2003) and Haraway (2008) the partners do not pre-exist their relationship. Without her identity as a horse owner, the author's experience of becoming a mother would have been very different, and she would probably have produced a different interpretation of pregnancy and motherhood, and gender in general. At the same time, her embodied state of being pregnant has temporarily endangered her relationship with her horse but has eventually transformed it to include the child. The study demonstrates that both gender and human animal relationships are produced in embodied practices where the agency of the animal can play a role (Barad 2003; Birke et al. 2004). This also applies to situations where the animal is not present. As Charles and Davies (2011) note, human animal relationships are interwoven in individual life stories and not always without conflict.

References

Adelman, Miriam and Jorge Knijnik. 2013. *Gender and Equestrian Sport: Riding around the World*. New York, Springer.

Barad, Karen. 2003. "Posthumanist Performativity: Toward an Understanding of How Matter Comes to Matter." *Signs: Journal of Women in Culture and Society* 28(3): 801–831.

Birke, Lynda, Mette Bryld and Nina Lykke. 2004. "Animal Performances. An Exploration of Intersections between Feminist Science Studies and Studies of Human/Animal Relationships." *Feminist Theory* 5(2): 167–183.

Brown, David. 2006. "Pierre Bourdieu's 'Masculine Domination' Thesis and the Gendered Body in Sport and Physical Culture." *Sociology of Sport Journal* 23: 162–188.

Butler, Deborah and Nickie Charles. 2012. "Exaggerated Femininity and Tortured Masculinity: Embodying Gender in the Horseracing Industry." *The Sociological Review* 60(4): 676–695.

Butler, Judith. 1990. *Gender Trouble: Feminism and the Subversion of Identity*. London and New York: Routledge.

Charles, Nickie and Charlotte Aull Davies. 2011. "My Family and Other Animals: Pets as Kin." In *Human and Other Animals: Critical Perspectives*, edited by Bob Carter and Nickie Charles, 69–92. Basingstoke and New York: Palgrave Macmillan.

Despret, Vinciane. 2004. "The Body We Care for: Figures of Anthropo-zoo-genesis." *Body & Society* 10(2/3): 111–134.

Ellingsæter, Anne Lise and Arnlaug Leira, 2006. *Politicising Parenthood in Scandinavia: Gender Relations in the Welfare State*. Bristol: The Policy Press.

Franklin, Adrian. 2006. "'Be(a)ware of the Dog': A Post-humanist Approach to Housing." *Housing, Theory and Society* 23(3): 137–156.

Giddens, Anthony. 1990. *The Consequences of Modernity*. Cambridge: Polity Press.

Gregson, Nicky and Gillian Rose. 2000. "Taking Butler Elsewhere: Performativities, Spatialities and Subjectivities." *Environment and Planning D: Society & Space* 18: 433–452.

Haraway, Donna. 2008. *When Species Meet*. Minneapolis: University of Minnesota Press.

Holloway, Sarah. 1999. "Reproducing Motherhood." In *Geographies of New Femininities*, edited by Nina Laurie, Claire Dwyer, Sarah Holloway and Fiona Smith, 91–112. Edinburgh Gate: Longman.

Hookway, Nicholas. 2008. "'Entering the Blogosphere': Some Strategies for Using Blogs in Social Research." *Qualitative Research* 8(1): 91–113.

Irvine, Leslie. 2004. *If You Tame Me: Understanding Our Connection with Animals*. Philadelphia: Temple University Press.

Keaveney, Susan M. 2008. "Equines and Their Human Companions." *Journal of Business Research* 61(5): 444–454.

Leinonen, Riitta-Marja. 2013. *Palvelijasta terapeutiksi: ihmisen ja hevosen suhteen muuttuvat kulttuuriset mallit Suomessa*. [From Servant to Therapist. The Changing Cultural Models of Human Horse Relationship in Finland]. Oulu, Finland: University of Oulu.

Longhurst, Robyn. 2000. "Corporeographies of Pregnancy: 'Bikini Babes'." *Environment and Planning D: Society and Space* 18: 453–472.

Longhurst, Robyn. 2008. *Maternities: Gender, Bodies and Space*. New York: Routledge.

Ojanen, Karoliina. 2011. *Tyttöjen toinen koti. Etnografinen tutkimus tyttökulttuurista ratsastustalleilla*. [Another Home for Girls. An Ethnographic Study on the Girl Culture at the Horseback Riding Stables]. Helsinki: Suomalaisen Kirjallisuuden Seura.

Ojanen, Karoliina. 2012. "You Became Someone: Social Hierarchies in Girls' Communities at Riding Stables." *Young* 20(2): 137–156.

Sarmicanic, Lisa. 2007. "Companion Animals." In *Encyclopedia of Human–Animal Relationships: A Global Exploration of Our Connections with Animals*, edited by Marc Bekoff, 163–174. Westport, CT: Greenwood Press.

The Equestrian Federation of Finland. 2014. "Facts and Figures: Equestrianism in Finland." Accessed 3 November, http://www.ratsastus.fi/.

Thompson, Kirrilly. 2011. "Theorizing Rider–Horse Relations: An Ethnographic Illustration of the Centaur Metaphor in the Spanish Bullfight." In *Theorizing Animals. Rethinking Humanimal Relations*, edited by Nik Taylor and Tania Signal, 221–253. Leiden: Brill.

Wynne, Brian. 1996. "May the Sheep Safely Graze? A Reflexive View of the Expert– Lay Knowledge Divide." In *Risk, Environment and Modernity: Towards a New Ecology*, edited by Scott Lash, Bronislaw Szerszynski and Brian Wynne, 44–83. London: Sage.

Part III

Performance, Practice and Presentation

10 An Introduction to Contemporary Native American Horse Culture

Notes from the Northwest Plateau

Amelia-Roisin Seifert

The coming of the equine species to indigenous North Americans was nothing short of a cultural revolution. Horses were a profoundly culturally enriching invasive species, unique among the species that make up native life-worlds in their ability to extend the agency of human beings. The following chapter is an illustration of the meaningfulness of horses today to three Northwest American tribes. While horses are no longer central to the socio-economic life of native people, they remain a contemporary keystone of ethnic identity and tribal traditions.

Though the image of the mounted 'Indian Brave' is ubiquitous in popular representations of Native Americans, very little research exists that addresses contemporary native horse culture. All too often, representations of indigenous people are mired in the ethnographic present.[1] The research on which the following 'notes from the field' are based is a long overdue follow-up study that bridges the gap in the literature between reservationizing and today. The following chapter is an ethnographically illustrated homage to the diverse manifestations and cultural survival of a powerful inter-species bond.

Horses are unique in their ability to afford to humans an entirely new way of being in the world, what Barclay (1980, xi) aptly refers to as "the centaur complex." The centaur is the phenomenological sum of the intertwined capabilities and intentions of horseperson and horse (Game 2001). Through equestrianism, humans gain an entirely new set of abilities, most notably amplified strength and speed, while horses, in turn, become socialized into human culture. Equestrian culture is dependent on the mutual intertwining of the lives and societies of both species, human and equine.

The paradigm of 'cultural keystone species' is particularly illustrative in the case of Native American equestrianism. Developed specifically to describe the centrality of certain plant and animal species to indigenous cultures, this term is applicable to any life-form upon which the life-ways of a culture are dependent. Though the term was developed to highlight the salience of species that provided food or material products that underpinned a way of life, it is developed below to include the centrality of a species to cultural identity, even when it is no longer materially relied upon.

This chapter presents an introduction to the shifting but consistently vital role of horses in native culture. After situating this research in the literature and ethnographic context, three distinct but related illustrative cases will be offered: the Nez Perce horse breed as a cultural keystone species (Garibaldi and Turner 2004) and a symbol of tribal sovereignty; horses as partners in the traditional and more recently instituted public displays of parading and relay racing (respectively); and range horses as changing and contested units of value on the reservation. These issues will bring to light the perpetual interplay between historical precedent, tradition, cultural change and identity in the context of a multi-species relationship.

Background

Substantial publications addressing native horse culture are few and far between. A horse culture baseline is to be found in the wave of ethnological works that emerged in the early twentieth century. These works consisted entirely of reconstructed ethnographies. Typical of this style of salvage ethnography are Ewers (1955) and Roe (1955), the two major scholars of Indian horse culture, who, though researching fifty years after final reservation settlement, were interested only in the pre-contact past rather than the current role of the horse in post-reservation Indian life. These monographs sought to explain the diffusion of horses amongst the tribes (Haines 1938a, 1938b; Turney-High 1935), and the impact that the adaption of the horse had on previously hunter-gatherer socio-economic structures, material culture and religion (Ewers 1955; Haines 1960; Roe 1955; Wissler 1914, 1927; Wilson 1924). The work of Lawrence (1985) is the only contemporaneously focused material available, but it falls short on participant observation, and essentially reiterates the historical findings of earlier scholars, while noting the persistence of rodeo and parade based horsemanship on plains reservations.

These scholars agree that the horse percolated upwards from south to north through trade networks. As Mullin (1999) notes, human animal relationships reflect humans' relationships with other humans. In the case of domesticated species, these interactions are often from their outset mediated by historical forces. This sense of contingency is communicated by a tribal historian and senior elder of the Nez Perce tribe in this historical account:

> There are stories of us going south [...] we knew who the Spanish people were, so there are stories like this that verify that we went to these different places. So if we went there, we would have seen a horse, and we would have asked questions about it [...]. What is this animal? What do you use it for? Is it useful like the dog? So we would have acquired horses that way, either trade or through stealing, either way. So that's why I say it was probably around 1700, and the pueblo revolt was

> around 1680, and that freed up a lot of horses [...] I say that the horse we got was probably around 1700.
>
> (Author interview, November 2013)

The horse was not just appropriated: it was adopted, like a long lost relative, into the life-world of the indigenous people. Prior to the coming of the horse, the only domesticated animal in this culture was the dog. Though Ewers (1955) suggests that the impact of the horse on social life increased stratification by creating substantial wealth differences, Wissler (1914) and my informants reiterate that horses impacted the quality, but not the essential structure of indigenous life-ways. As a newly adopted keystone species, horses did not provide food or material animal products, but instead extended the agency of their human keepers.

Equestrian cultural forms are emergent from the relationship between landscape, animals, humans and historical constraints. Horses enabled the development of equestrian culture – an inter-species cultural form, albeit one in which one species is dominant. Horse husbandry, equestrian techniques and practices were creolized and synthesized with creative indigenous improvisation. The ethno-hippology and equestrianism that developed with such great alacrity reflected, and continues to reflect, the values, priorities, understandings and life-worlds of those native Americans who became horse peoples.

Methodology

I draw from 14 months of fieldwork living and riding with native people in the plateau culture area of the Northwestern States of the US. Fieldwork was conducted from July 2013 to October 2014. My search for horse people took me, via the kinship networks of my informants, to several reservations. I orbited primarily between families in three different reservations and tagged along with them to dozens of events featuring horses across several states. All three are very rural, medium sized tribes, who traditionally followed a semi-nomadic yearly round based on salmon fishing, edible root digging and hunting deer and elk. Each reservation has a different (though overlapping and not exclusive) focus to their equestrianism. The Nez Perce Reservation in Idaho, official home of the Nez Perce people, is unusual in its relationship to a specific breed of horse. The Confederated Umatilla Indian Reservation (hereafter Umatilla), home to the Cayuse, Umatilla and Walla Walla tribes (as well as some Nez Perce), has a strong history of horse parading and rearing large semi-wild herds. The Colville Indian Reservation (hereafter Colville), home to nine bands that make up the Confederated Colville Tribes, is nationally famous amongst native people for its success in racing.

Despite conducting over 100 interviews, my most useful data came from "deep hanging out" (Geertz 1998, 69) across three states. This includes leaning on pasture gates, riding shotgun on long drives, swilling Coors on truck beds at rodeos, going on trial rides with friends' uncles and loitering in the backstretch at race meets and the like, where these plateau tribes circulate to meet and compete with one another. Aware of the understandably fraught historical relationship between Native Americans and anthropologists, I came to 'Indian country'[2] primarily as an equestrian seeking to learn about the lives of other equestrians, and secondarily as an anthropologist.

As well as being a prerequisite for observing the finer details of human horse interaction, 'knowing horses' was the common ground that I shared with my informants. Little by little, month by month, my elders (that is, anyone older, and therefore automatically senior) observed that I had an adequate understanding of horses' behavior and needs that incrementally let me engage more directly with their mounts, until I was able to help start Nez Perce horse youngsters, ride to honor family in parades, hot walk race horses and generally get casually involved in the yearly round of equestrian activity.

The academic stance, that based on my experiences living on the 'Rez' seemed the only obvious way of anthropologically engaging with a dynamic group of people living in a contested modernity, is what Clifford (2013, 13) calls anthropological "realism." In his seminal volume on the 'new' indigenous anthropology, he emphasizes the precarious positioning of the ethically engaged researcher of indigenous culture: "for a non-native anthropologist to take seriously the current resurgence of native, tribal or aboriginal societies we need to avoid both romantic celebration and knowing critique" (Clifford 2013, 13). The post-colonial anthropologist must avoid both reductive stereotyping and arrogant skepticism of indigenous knowledge and tradition in an attempt to relate the complex cultural realities of indigenous people. To this end, I borrow from Clifford's analytical tool kit the concepts of *performance* and *articulation* of culture and tradition. In order to avoid writing reductively about social change, terms of process that do not lend themselves to systematization are usefully employed. The following notes from the field gesture toward a wider project that fruitfully engages contemporary expressions of native equestrian culture contextualized against a backdrop of complex and ongoing historical processes.

The Nez Perce horse: Reclamation of a cultural keystone species

The powerful symbolic role of the horse in contemporary Nez Perce life is highlighted by a passage from my field notes below. Linking the past with the present, this is just one of about half a dozen annual memorial 'empty saddle' ceremonies instituted as a form of cultural restitution by the tribe in the 1990s, in parallel with the foundation of a tribal horse breeding program. These memorials take place at various locations of loss relating to the Nez Perce war and flight from the US army in 1877. The Redheart memorial, outlined below, commemorates the eight-month incarceration of thirty-three members of the Redheart band during the Nez Perce War. The memorial was founded by the great-great granddaughter of the military man Erskine Scott Wood, who had become friends with the famous Nez Perce Chief Joseph just before the war started. It is an acknowledgement and reconciliation:

> I arrived at Fort Vancouver Historical Park around 9. [Tribal horse program manager] was there with four horses tied to the tribe's stock trailer. They were three recently broke five-year-olds from the tribes' breeding program and an old-timer. I helped him saddle them, and the eldest Redheart and relatives affixed their family trappings to the horses. The oldest Redheart son mounted Red Sky, the older horse and led the horse procession around the crowd. He was followed by his brother, cousin and the tribe's official wrangler, each leading a horse. I was later told by a Redheart that the ridden horse represented all the men who had passed in the war. The second horse, carrying an 'empty' traditional Indian women's saddle and dressed in trappings, represented the loss of the women and their crafting skills. The last horse, bearing empty saddle, laden with fluffy child's blankets represented the captive toddler who had died while being held at Fort Vancouver. The child's blankets carried by the horse were given to a toddler of equivalent age in the crowd. After they circled the traditional three times they were extensively photographed by local media, then the horses were put back on the tribes' trailer [...] the ceremony, attended by the town mayor, and about three hundred native and white people, continued with honour songs, a small giveaway, honouring of veterans and speeches of recognition and reconciliation, followed by a salmon feast.
>
> (Author's fieldnotes, 19 April 2014)

As this narrative shows, the horse is salient to contemporary Nez Perce culture on three levels. On the immediate phenomenological level, individual Nez Perce people experience horses not just as non-human personalities and tools of movement, but as living artefacts or embodiments of a cultural continuity from the pre-reservation past. On a social level, as culture bearers and ritual actors, horses continue their role as a cultural keystone species for the tribe. Lastly, this tribe has taken their relationship with horses a step further, propelling them firmly into the political realm, with the creation of an official, national breed. The formal establishment of 'national' animal breeds is a biopolitical statement that almost ubiquitously accompanies the rise of a nation state.

The Nez Perce are known through the horse world as the originators of the famous Appaloosa – the spotted 'Indian pony' that is now one of the largest breed registries in America. Nez Perce horses and the Nez Perce (*Nimipuu* – 'the people' – as they call themselves) mutually developed one another. After initially acquiring horses, which they named *s'ik'em*, in the late 17th century, they were one of the first tribes to practice selective breeding through Spanish style castration. By the time of first contact with the explorers Lewis and Clark in 1806, the Nez Perce were mentioned in Lewis's diary for their fine horses. The horses were noted with what we would today identify as a strain of Appaloosa coloring: "They appear to be of an excellent race [...] many of them appear like fine English coursers; some of them are pied with large spots of white, irregularly scattered, and intermixed with a dark brown bey [sic]" (Clark et al. 2002, 333).

Unfortunately, this first contact was followed by escalating encroachment into native homelands by Anglo people. In 1877, things came to a head between the Nimipuu and the United States. The 'non-treaty' Nimipuu, those who would not accept Christianity and refused to ratify the reservation created in the 1855 treaty, were forced into flight. In a famous display of stamina, around 800 men, women and children, taking with them around 2,000 horses, outpaced the US army for 1,170 miles in four months, over what is now known as the Nez Perce Trail. They were tragically defeated within sight of safe haven across the Canadian border.

After their surrender, the Nez Perce were systematically unhorsed. Their herds were taken from them and distributed among local whites or methodically slaughtered by the army.[3] On the reservations, equestrianism was actively restricted, with some missionaries even seeking to ban 'colorful ponies' (along with traditional dress, language and lifestyles). This traumatic rupture of the intertwined lives of the Nimipuu and their horses is still a raw trauma for informants four or five generations beyond living memory.

By unhorsing these people, the 'centaur' basis of their equestrian culture was interrupted. However, the narrative of their horses continued independently. Local whites took interest in the unique spotted strain (*ma'min* in the Nimipuu tongue), and in 1938 founded the Appaloosa Horse Club. The breed was thus named after the Palouse River area near the reservation where remnants of the scattered Nimipuu herds were popular. The exotically colored and hardy Appaloosa is now a substantial official breed that has registered over half a million horses worldwide.

Horses once more became an active feature of the Nimipuu tribal narrative in the early 1990s, when one of the progenitors of the Appaloosa Horse Club set up a charitable foundation on the reservation with the intention of breeding old-line Appaloosas for the use of the Nez Perce. At the time, the tribe only had one family who were substantially active as horse producers. However, there are some tensions in the Nimipuu community around the Appaloosa horse breed's association with *soyapos*, white people. Catalysed by this *soyapo* intervention, the tribe itself also started a horse program based around the creation of a Nez Perce horse breed and registry. Some felt that the Appaloosa, developed by whites, was no longer true to the physical type of the horses that their equestrian ancestors rode, so the Nez Perce horse breed was created to physically resemble horses from the pre-contact past, based on historical descriptions and photographs. The breed is a formalized biocultural bricolage (Lévi-Strauss 1966) based on crossing of old-line Appaloosas and

Akle-tekes, a distinctively long and lean endurance horse from the Eurasian steppes. Interestingly, Appaloosa coloring is desirable but not requisite for this new breed, that focuses instead on a general phenotype.

The foundation of this breed marked a renaissance of tribal equestrian practices. Youth programs were formed to reintroduce young people to their equestrian heritage. The primary activities of these (three) groups is to take young people to travel by horseback over historical landscapes, most notably joining with the (non-native) Appaloosa Club's annual 'Chief Joseph Ride' ride that follows sections of the Nez Perce trail. Riderless horse memorials were instituted at historically traumatic battle sites, in which the tribe's horses were deployed to bring honor to the fallen and give the people a focus for their historical grief. The annual cycle of memorials has continued since their institution in the 1990s.

The (re)creation by the tribe of an authentic Nez Perce horse was a powerful act. Throughout the twentieth century, there has been an observable rise in formally constituted animal 'breeds.' As Lawrence (1985, x) notes, this has included a "theme of the transformation of the horse by different groups of people into a form that communicates their particular values and expresses a truth about their society that is not easily expressed through other means." The Nez Perce horse is not a large scale or commercialized breed, with only about 300 registered to date, and about 60 currently owned by the tribe. Regardless, the breed is a potent contemporary biopolitical symbol through which ideas of sovereign national identity, authenticity and history are expressed through equine blood and breeding (c.f., Ritvo 1987; Cassidy 2002, 2009).

How does one account for the powerful symbolic value invested in horses by native people, even in this instance where the horse population is small, and equestrianism is no longer subject to wide participation? *S'ik'em* are best understood in the contemporary Nimipuu ethnosphere as a cultural keystone species. Cultural keystone species is a concept developed recently by Garibaldi and Turner (2004, 4) as a metaphorical parallel with ecological keystone species. They posit that: "Just as certain species of plants or animals appear to exhibit a particularly large influence on the ecosystem they inhabit, the same is true in social systems. We have termed these organisms *cultural keystone species* and define them as the culturally salient species that shape in a major way the cultural identity of a people."

The continuing role of the horses as a symbolic though no longer instrumental aspect of Nez Perce life is articulated in the revival of a 'Nez Perce' horse, and the ubiquity of the image of the *ma'min* in contemporary Nimipuu art, business signage and any educational materials about the tribe. Contrary to those who see the Nez Perce horse as a tragic icon of a vanished world, I propose that the continued salience of horses to rituals, cultural displays and public identity discourses is evidence that horses retain their status as a cultural keystone species.

This case study is uniquely powerful as it is the only known case of the establishment of an official tribal breed, the equine equivalent of an ethnic group that reflects the values of the people who have, through selective breeding, created it (Ritvo 1987). We see here how Nimipuu horses remain dynamic, positive symbols of a 21st century people, evolving from a socio-ecological keystone role to a polyvalent symbol of bittersweet sovereign identity. This is a singular example of the trajectory of the horse as a cultural keystone species, but the concept applies just as saliently to all equestrian Native American tribes. While horses are always symbols of pride and cultural strength, they are also often much more than symbols, and are integrated in a diversity of ways into the social fabric of native life.

Contemporary Native American equestrian performance

While the horse remains a symbolic keystone species, the articulation and performance of equestrianism takes many forms. In many places, equestrian practices and skilled horsemanship are still very much in evidence. Rodeo is in fact the most prevalent horse based sporting culture across Indian country, and, despite only accounting for about one percent of the American population, native people are disproportionately successful at the top levels. However, for the sake of brevity this section is limited to expressions of horse cultural practices that are exclusive to native people. In this section, I present two cases from my fieldwork, one in which we see the historical continuity of a 'traditional' native practice and attendant material culture in native horse parading on the Umatilla Reservation, and another that highlights the cultural dynamism that allows for the development of a 'new' native horse-sport, in the case of Indian relay racing at the Colville Reservation. Each highlights how underlying human horse cultural values are reiterated and transmuted in two present-day articulations of equestrian heritage.

Horse parades

The Confederated Tribes of the Umatilla Indian Reservation (hereafter CTUIR) have an unusually complete retention of very old regalia and horse trappings partially because the tribe has always been a part of the nationally famous Pendleton Round-up, that has taken place in the town adjacent to the reservation annually since 1910. Its popularity with the rodeo-going public and other Indian visitors has been attributed to the extensive involvement of the tribe with the rodeo. This involvement includes tribal members riding in two public parades through the town; a mounted Indian ladies' beauty pageant that is judged mostly on the quality of the traditional trappings and regalia worn by the girls and their horses; pow-wow dancing competitions; a daily horse parade, and Indian dancing performance in the arena during the rodeo competition. During 'Round-up,' there is a tepee encampment of several hundred lodges where many tribal members spend the week in their family's traditional 'spot.' The main 'Indian' event of Pendleton Round-up is the Happy Canyon Night Show, in which 500 local tribal and Anglo people perform the story of their two peoples' meeting in the form of a 'Wild West' show. Each year two young native women are selected to spend the year as 'Happy Canyon Princesses.' These girls ride in over a dozen parades and rodeos for hundreds of miles around to draw attention to the rodeo and night show. This role was invented as a promotional tool for the 'Happy Canyon' show, but is highly valued and sought after by the CTUIR community. In the words of a recent princess: "it's a big accomplishment [for the princesses] [...] it's not just promoting happy canyon, it's promoting who WE are, as Indian people, our tradition, out outfits, our horse regalia and all that" (Author interview, July 2014).

A prerequisite for competing in beauty pageants or auditioning for a princess role is having access to extensive heirloom trappings and regalia. This has meant that these beautiful items have often been retained by families, or more recently, made by families, for their girls. Consequently, Pendleton Round-up and the Umatilla Reservation are one of the best places to see full horse trappings and regalia.

Horse regalia is usually based on brain tanned buckskin and decorated with traditional beading. Beading entered the canon of native crafting as a staple style of decoration after contact with whites. The tiny glass beads used were appropriated through trade and integrated into beautiful articulations of an evolving native traditional aesthetic. A full set of horse regalia includes, but is not limited to: a martingale, forehead roseate and a 'back drape' – either a crupper or hanging attached to the back of the saddle. In addition, horses can sport decorative headstalls, reins, cuffs around the pastern and bells attached to any of the above to accentuate movement. If one is available, ladies ride in a traditional decorated Indian women's saddle, with a pommel and cantle about a foot high made of wood and covered in buckskin. Men sometimes ride bareback. However, stock saddles are the standard for both genders. Horses in this cultural area are *not* painted,[4] but sometimes sport feathers in mane or tail.

Full regalia for the rider of a horse thus dressed is usually highly decorated buckskin clothing, beaded ankle and wrist cuffs and moccasins. For women, traditional regalia includes a headband with feather (one for single women, two for married), or a basket hat, otter skin hair wraps around the classic two braids, and jewelry. Women can also wear the simpler wing-dress, elk tooth or shells dress. A woollen Pendleton blanket is worn draped over the legs. Standard accessories to women's regalia are decorative beaded 'handbags' hung from the pommel, and 'bonnet cases' – tubes of rawhide in which a woman would traditionally have carried her man's war bonnet. Men also wear buckskin, ranging from full leggings and shirt to a simple breech-clout, and a war bonnet or roach, with bone jewelry. Long hair is usually worn in a single braid. If full regalia is not available, both men and women can wear western jeans, boots and a 'ribbon shirt' – a western style shirt accentuated with hanging ribbon decorations, a translation of western aesthetics into a native vernacular style.

Even in public displays, presenting the 'centaur' unit of horse and rider in this way is never dressing-up, and regalia is certainly not costume. Rather, it is the most formal way that a native person can dress. Horses are dressed similarly to their people, showing how they are considered a 'centaur' unit, not aesthetically separate from their rider, and part of tribal culture in everything including dress style.

The value of regalia inheres in its relation to those who made it or wore it through the generations. It is a material embodiment of family history. More recently-made pieces are no less valuable. They represent a material embodiment of familial love and effort, and the articulation of the historical continuity of ethnic crafting skills. An ex-Happy Canyon princess I interviewed told the story of her full matching set of horse and rider regalia: "my mom came up with that on her own, no patterns or anything, she just started beading and that's what came to her, and you know, that's part of what makes it so special, as well, is 'cuz its made by love, by my mother."

All parading by Indian people is always done for someone other than the rider, either to honor or memorialize. Sometimes this is a general riding in honor of tribal ancestors, or one's family, but it can be very specific. While the Pendleton round-up parading and similar public parades and pageants are the most visible form of Indian horse parade, arguably the most 'authentic' and culturally specific, are the rides that are part of tribal or personal celebrations or memorials. Horses and regalia are both costly and in limited supply, so someone in possession of either is called upon to ride or loan their horses or regalia for ceremonial occasions as a duty to their family or tribal ancestors.

Ceremonial horse parades had declined from the beginning of the twentieth century, but experienced a resurgence in the 1990s, around the same time as the Nez Perce tribe founded their horse program. The occasions that feature ceremonial horse parades for the Umatilla tribes include the 'July grounds' (on the Fourth of July, when native people could historically get away with having a large celebration because their authorities could dismiss it as an outburst of patriotism), Treaty Day and Veterans' Day. Horse parades are also a feature of celebrations that honor recent victories, like the regaining of a traditional tribal homeland. As we have seen with the Nez Perce, horses are often part of the social grieving rituals at battle sites or graveside memorials where an 'empty' horse honors those who have passed. Turning is a traditional form of prayer, and these ceremonial rides always circle three times.

The period around 1990 saw the resurgence of a variety of culturally specific equestrian forms. The Nez Perce horse program, Umatilla Reservation ceremonial parades and, as we shall detail below, the cross-tribal development of Indian relay racing all (re)-emerged around this time. While the sociocultural circumstances behind this resurgence are beyond the scope of this chapter, this congruency highlights the historically contingent nature of human animal cultural forms.

Indian relay racing

The rise of Indian relay racing, leading to the recent (2013) founding of the Professional Indian Horse Racing Association (hereafter PIHRA), is a wonderful example of a contemporary articulation and strengthening of a uniquely native sport. While the origins of Indian relay are blurred by time, and several tribes claim to have originated the sport independently of one another (PIHRA 2014), it rose to prominence at pow-wows and county fairs during the 1980s. In some places it was originally open to all comers, was called 'pony express' and was practiced with saddles, using regular saddle horses. As it has grown in popularity, it has become exclusive to enrolled Indian people and racing practices have been standardized. The PIHRA now sanctions most of the races and puts on an annual championship that in 2014 was attended by a record-breaking 30 teams, competing for $75,000 in prize money in front of a crowd of 15,000 people (PIHRA 2014).

Relay is a team extreme sport, and success derives from a well-practiced, smoothly functioning team and a little bit of luck. Indian relay is run on half-mile oval tracks. A team consists of three horses, a jockey, a mugger, and two holders. There are definitely human and equine "bodies for the job" (Bourdieu 1984, 191). Competitive teams use specially (re)trained racing breed thoroughbred or quarter horses. It is often the horse's second career after being purchased or claimed off big professional flat racing tracks. The jockey must be big and athletic enough (usually around 6 foot and mid-20s) to leap onto tall racehorses, and is always male. The holders and muggers must be strong and tough enough to catch and hold excited racehorses. It is a powerfully male sport, and women are usually only present in a supportive family capacity. Those few who are actively involved in the scene tend to be 'sugar-grandmas' who may own the horses and sometimes act as trainer for the team.

There are usually heats of about three to six teams, and a winning team may compete up to four times in a weekend to become champions at that event. The jockey and team wear matching outfits that combine athletic wear and traditional regalia. The horses wear mild bridles and no saddle. Many teams paint symbols with various meanings on their horses and have a personal pre-race team ritual. Races go like this: jockeys on or standing next to their first horse line up at the start (different events can choose between standing or 'running' starts), while the other two horses are held in the team's assigned change-over area, by the start line. A gun fires, the riders take off at around 30 miles per hour, and less than a minute later come careening into their change-over areas. It is the mugger's job to wave down and catch the incoming thousand-pound animal, while the rider leaps off and in a few steps vaults onto the waiting number two horse and takes off again, ideally avoiding colliding with the up to six other teams, who are all doing the same things in tight proximity. This is repeated for the third and final horse and in a matter of minutes, the race is over. Relay races are a tremendous spectacle and often the most popular spectator event at rodeos and fairs that feature them.

The reward for success in this sport is prestige, with a little money on the side, though there is a move to include bigger purses as the sport aims to become more professional. Participants form a sporting subcultural 'community of practice' (Lave 1991) based around a modern day 'warrior' ethos of masculine bravado, skill and competition, anchored by a love of horses. Relay has been described by some informants as an arena in which to duke out old tribal differences, but the majority of socializing behind the scenes is friendly, bordering on bacchanalian, with children looked after and even fed by friends and relatives within the clique of racing people. Jockeys are revered by all as local heroes, and provide role models of modern warriors for the youngest generation. As one Colville trainer I interviewed explains: "These young kids want heroes, they need heroes, and that's part of our generation, our Indianness, it's to be like the warriors of the past." The cultural capital (Bourdieu 1986) that goes with successful membership of a team is a huge influence in keeping articulations of the intergenerational and interspecies equestrian sporting tradition alive on the reservation.

Kinship is paramount in the reproduction of native equestrian practices. The family, rather than the individual, is the fundamental unit of native society. Family can extend out to the third or fourth remove, and includes in-laws and those referred to as 'family' through their close association and shared lives. Racing runs in families, as does parading on the Umatilla Reservation and horse breeding on the Nez Perce Reservation. Native horsemanship skills are reproduced inter-generationally, rather than through institutions, apprenticeships or sporting societies. Subsequently, one of the main concerns in keeping equestrian skills current lies in intergenerational transmission problems. The historic unresolved trauma of cultural colonializing, and the challenges of 'rez life' have interrupted many of the basic structures of cultural reproduction. However, despite these challenges, the cultural capital that can be acquired through participation in racing – as well as parading, beauty pageants, breeding horses and indeed any successful cultivation of horsemanship – helps ensure the continuation of these unique articulations of interspecies connectedness.

The very recent institution of a pan-tribal Indian Relay sporting body is testament not only to cultural survival, but to a contemporary articulation of native independence and dynamism in sport. Relay weaves together the old (war paint on horses, riding bareback, etc.) with appropriations of elements from the non-native horse-culture milieu, including the acquisition of assistive technologies such as trailers, horse-walking machines, performance enhancing medication and feed, therapeutic techniques such as chiropractor practices and leg wrapping and even horse bloodlines. In a powerful example of ongoing cultural innovation, this plurality of equicultural techniques and practices are repurposed to enable emergent expressions of native horsemanship. The continuing rise of this sport is in firm opposition to those who presume that native culture is static and that authenticity, and indeed equestrian heroism, are things that are now a tragic bygone.

Feral horses on 'the rez'

Horses, in the generalized abstract, are most certainly cultural keystone species for entire Native American horse-tribes. However, on the level of the individual human equine relationship, horses can be considered anything from close kin, to an expensive road hazard. How is this range of relationships possible?

Ever since Levi-Strauss pointed out that animals provide a conceptual resource, they have been variously interpreted as 'windows' or 'mirrors' (Mullin 1999) of human relationships and culturally specific ways of understanding the world. Horses are somewhat uniquely positioned in their relationship with humans as an extension of human agency rather than as wildlife, or livestock kept for sustenance. Subsequently, the humans' relationship to the equine species particularly has been one of the most dramatically subject to human social change (Barclay 1980).

Amongst the tribes I lived with, there are many stories about the natural world and the animal people who were there before humans, but horses, as something that came long after the time before human people, only feature in legends and stories about the more recent past, rather than myths. That is not to lessen their import. I was told more than once that "getting the horse was like finding a long lost relative." Horse owners frequently conceptualize horses as sharing in human kinship networks. However much a part of the family individual horses may be, horses are categorically awkwardly liminal, neither entirely established as part of the human world nor integrated into the natural biosphere.

It is this liminality that creates great debate about the future of horses in native life. Discussion of the feral horse 'issue' on reservations (as in American society at large) is where thinking about horses' place in a changing world becomes very explicit, and raises many conflicting emotions. I followed this debate most closely on the Umatilla Reservation, where the remnants of the 'cayuse' horse herds are at issue. The November issue of the tribe's newspaper reports that during the combined gathers of 2013 and 2014, the feral horse population had been reduced from 502 to around 50 (Phinney 2014). Fifty head is the number that the range management programs argue is sustainable, based on a new tribal feral horse policy. They argue that horses' grazing and trampling of water holes puts pressure on wild game animals and cattle. That *any* of these horses were left shows how the policy makers do acquiesce to the cultural value these herds represent for some of the people.

The lives of native people and their horses have adapted to significant changes in their social environments over the years. Before the reservation range was parceled up under the Allotment Act of 1887, the preferred method of horse-keeping was to allow horses to live as independent herds on the range, dormant resources to be rounded up and rapidly removed from the society of other equines, when needed, and abruptly 'broken into' a life that revolved around human society. With reservationizing, the extent to which people were able to retain their herds depended on their access to range land that varied by reservation and family. The Indians on the Umatilla Reservation successfully retained much of their vast herds after being put on the reservation, insisting that their treaty of 1855 include provision for collective grazing of horses and cattle. For some time, it was the leading livestock producing reservation in America, with upwards of 10,000 (Walker 1998) head of horses on the range that is now home to 50.

However, demand for horses dropped dramatically with the dawn of motorized transport. Annual round-ups of the range horses, once a point of pride and a cultural resource, finally petered out in the 1950s. The wild horse population at the Umatilla Reservation was at its lowest right before the major recession of 2007–2009, when it started to rise again, due to people who could no longer afford to hay their horses turning them loose for lack of alternatives.

The tribe, like many others in similar positions, was faced with a very divisive dilemma centering on the appropriate articulations of human (feral) horse relationships, with many uncomfortably in the middle. Active horse people themselves are divided over this – many refer to the feral horses as 'shitters,' as that is all they do, and feel that a horse that has not been raised to a role in human life, and is not a managed natural resource, is no longer of any value. This may seem counter-intuitive, as these are often the people who are highly skilled equestrians themselves, and treat their own horses with great care and compassion. Also on the side which feels that there is no place for feral horses are cattle-owning ranchers (usually white) who see them as unproductive livestock eating their cattle's forage. On the other hand, the tribe's identity literally rides on their equestrian heritage. Horses were the pride of the tribes and afforded generations of native people the opportunity to live and move on the land as centaurs, their lives improved materially and spiritually by these animals. The fate of the leftover feral horses, some feel, is in parallel with the tribe's: "They were untamed, like us," one of my informants lamented. The ongoing debate highlights the continuum on which horses are valued. Their value as symbols is universally positive for native people, but what the hairy, flighty, living horses out on the range represent to individuals varies dramatically.

Conclusion

This has been intended to be a step away from the popularly held notion that native people live in an allochronic world (Fabian 1983), and are of another time, their culture slowly fading away and being cheapened by cultural exchange. Instead, this has been a celebration of culturally specific meaningfulness and innovation. This focus highlights the utility of Clifford's (2004) call for an enlarged conversation about tradition that dissolves the binary opposition between modernity and tradition. He points to Phillips's (2004, 25) argument that "only when we stop defining tradition as resistance to modernity does the term become again a means of raising essential questions about the ways in which we pass on the life of cultures – questions that necessarily include issues of authenticity as well as innovation, practice as well as interpretation."

By focusing on the ever-evolving story of these native people and their horses, we can come to appreciate the fluidity with which a population can adapt to rapidly changing cultural landscapes while retaining, in new forms, core relationships with the non-human world. This chapter has gestured towards the goal of multi-species ethnography to "consider humans' relationship with other species in relation to a specific cultural and historical context and the way in which such relationships are influenced by humans' relationships with other humans" (Mullin 1999, 219). This case shows, with particular relevance to indigenous people, that these shared inter-species heritages continue to be keystones of the 21st century cultural identity that can strengthen claims to modern notions of sovereignty in which traditional human animal values are still articulated.

This is a summary introduction to the vital and on-going story of horse culture in the Native American Northwest. The themes emergent herein beg further analysis along a variety of lines. A focus on practices and issues surrounding cultural keystone species, as ethnographic portals into wider socio-cultural issues, could offer fruitful lines of investigation in any culture in this time of rapid social change. We almost owe it to the non-human world to write the (non-human) animals back into the story of life on this planet. An examination of the developing fates of species upon which entire cultures have been dependent seems like a good place to start.

Notes

1 'The ethnographic present' is a writing style historically used by anthropologists to describe a (usually indigenous) culture in an ahistoric time period, ignoring processes of cultural change in order to describe a culture as if it were historically stable and homogenous.
2 The term used by native people themselves to refer to the inter-connected Fourth World network of reservations across America.
3 This horse slaughter at the last battle site is still painfully present in the collective folk memory. It is difficult to find documentation that ratifies this exact event, but similar incidents are recorded. Examples can be found in Trafzer and Scheuerman (1986, 36); Ruby and Brown (1972, 258).
4 This is traditionally a plains cultural practice, though it is being taken up by native riders in other cultural areas.

References

Barclay, Harold. 1980. *The Role of the Horse in Man's Culture*. London: J. Allan.
Bourdieu, Pierre. 1984. *Distinction: A Social Critique of the Judgment of Taste*. Cambridge: Harvard University Press.

Bourdieu, Pierre. 1986. "The Forms of Capital." In *Handbook of Theory and Research for the Sociology of Education*, edited by J. Richardson, 241–258. New York: Greenwood.

Cassidy, Rebecca. 2002. *The Sport of Kings: Kinship, Class and Thoroughbred Breeding in Newmarket*. Cambridge: Cambridge University Press.

Cassidy, Rebecca. 2009. "The Horse, the Kyrgyz Horse and the 'Kyrgyz Horse'." *Anthropology Today* 25(1): 12–15.

Clark, William, Meriwether Lewis and Gary E. Moulton. 2002. *The Definitive Journals of Lewis & Clark: From the Ohio to the Vermillion*. Lincoln: University of Nebraska Press.

Clifford, James. 2004. "Traditional Futures." In *Questions of Tradition*, edited by Mark Phillips and Gordon Schochet, 152–168. Toronto: University of Toronto Press.

Clifford, James. 2013. *Returns*. Cambridge: Harvard University Press.

Ewers, John. 1955. *The Horse in Blackfoot Indian Culture – with Comparative Materials from Other Western Tribes*. Washington, DC: Smithsonian Institution Press.

Fabian, Johannes. 1983. *Time and the Other: How Anthropology Makes It Object*. New York: Columbia University Press.

Game, Ann. 2001. "Riding: Embodying the Centaur." *Body & Society* 7(4): 1–12.

Garibaldi, Ann and Nancy Turner. 2004. "Cultural Keystone Species: Implications for Ecological Conservation and Restoration." *Ecology and Society* 9(3): 1–13.

Geertz, Clifford. 1998. "Deep Hanging Out." *The New York Review of Books* 45(16): 69–72.

Haines, Francis. 1938a. "Where Did the Plains Indians Get Their Horses?" *American Anthropologist* 40(1): 112–117.

Haines, Francis. 1938b. "The Northward Spread of Horses among the Plains Indians." *American Anthropologist* 40(3): 429–437.

Haines, Francis. 1960. "Nez Perce Horses: How They Changed the Indian Way of Life." *Idaho Yesterday* 4(1): 8–11.

Lave, Jean. 1991. "Situating Learning in Communities of Practice." *Perspectives on Socially Shared Cognition* 2: 63–82.

Lawrence, Elizabeth Atwood. 1985. *Hoofbeats and Society: Studies of Human Horse Interactions*. Bloomington: Indiana University Press.

Lévi-Strauss, Claude. 1966. *Levi-Strauss/Weightman: Savage Mind*. Portsmouth: Heinemann Educational Publishers.

Mullin, Molly H. 1999. "Mirrors and Windows: Sociocultural Studies of Human–Animal Relationships." *Annual Review of Anthropology* 28: 201–224.

Phillips, Mark Salber. 2004. "What Is Tradition When It Is Not 'Invented'? A Historiographical Introduction." In *Questions of Tradition*, edited by Mark Phillips and Gordon Schochet, 3–29. Toronto: University of Toronto Press.

Phinney, Will. 2014. "Nearly 300 Horses Removed from Hills." *Confederated Umatilla Journal*, November 2014, 11.

PIHRA (Professional Indian Horse Racing Association). 2014. "Indian Relay – America's First Extreme Sport", last modified 2014, accessed 21 December 2014, http://professionalindianhorseracingassociation.com/about-pihra/about-indian-relay/.

PIHRA (Professional Indian Horse Racing Association). "All Nations Indian Relay Championships a Huge Success," last modified 13 October 2014, accessed 21 December 2014, http://professionalindianhorseracingassociation.com/all-nations-indian-relay-championships-a-huge-success/.

Ritvo, Harriet. 1987. *The Animal Estate: The English and Other Creatures in the Victorian Age*. Cambridge: Harvard University Press.

Roe, Frank Gilbert. 1955. *The Indian and the Horse*. Vol. 41. Norman: University of Oklahoma Press.

Ruby, Robert H. and John A. Brown. 1972. "The Cayuse Indians–Imperial Tribesmen of Old Oregon." *American Anthropologist* 76: 587–588.

Trafzer, Clifford E. and Richard D. Scheuerman. 1986. *Renegade Tribe: The Palouse Indians and the Invasion of the Inland Pacific Northwest*. Pullman: Washington State University Press.

Turney-High, Harry. 1935. "200. The Diffusion of the Horse to the Flatheads." *Man* 35: 183–185.

Walker, Deward E. 1998. *Handbook of North American Indians, Volume 12: Plateau*. Washington, DC: Smithsonian Institute.

Wilson, Gilbert Livingstone. 1924. "Hidatsa Horse and Dog Culture." *Anthropological Papers of the American Museum of Natural History* 15: 153–154.

Wissler, Clark. 1914. "The Influence of the Horse in the Development of Plains Culture." *American Anthropologist* 16(1): 1–25.

Wissler, Clark. 1927. "The Culture-Area Concept in Social Anthropology." *American Journal of Sociology* 32: 881–891.

11 *Escaramuzas Charras*

Paradoxes of Performance in a Mexican Women's Equestrian Sport

Ana C. Ramírez

The term *charreada* (or *charro*, competition) refers to the ensemble of events included in a traditional form of Mexican rodeo. One of those events is the *escaramuza* or skirmish. The *escaramuza* can be performed as either a non-competitive exhibition or a highly-regulated competitive event. As competitive sport, *escaramuza* consists of an eight member, all female precision riding team. They perform *puntas* [sliding stops] and displays or specific, coordinated movements at a full gallop. This is a highly valued, colorful and dramatic spectacle that involves great difficulty and risk of high-speed collisions. The women or young girls individually and collectively execute the movements while riding sidesaddle. They are garbed in colorful, voluminous dresses (*ranchera* or *Adelita* style) or wear the female version of *charro* (Mexican cowboy) attire.

The team, rather than individual riders, is judged in each and every detail. Competitive teams vie to qualify for a place in the National *Charro* Championship, an event that is considered to be the party of the year. Although many teams never make it to the championship, about 80 *escaramuza* teams (at least 560 female riders from Mexico and the US) compete at the championship. The first place prize may consist of a pick-up truck equipped with a trailer for eight horses, and a trophy or medals may also be awarded.

The *escaramuza* is a sport of growing complexity. The rulebook has increased from a 9-page pamphlet in 1991 to a tome with over 100 pages today. Judging *escaramuzas* has evolved from a secret score sheet known only to judges, to a multi-situated, videotaped, publicly-announced scoring system that must be explained to the teams' captains at the end of the competition. Both team movements and dress are judged. Like synchronized swimming, the sport is scored subjectively. Judges score twelve exercises or movements that range in difficulty from 16 to 28 points, depending on how many riders simultaneously make a cross or spin, and how short the distance is between them. Riders are penalized each time a horse loses his/her pace and trots instead of canters (Federación Mexicana de Charrería 2012). Judges' scores often provoke controversy.

How the sport's participants *escaramuceras* and *charro* queens are dressed is a major concern in *charrería*. The goal is to dazzle judges and observers. *Escaramuceras*' attire is a matter of negotiation among mothers and daughters with each group having their own ideas of 'looking good.' Mothers and daughters must also work with their trainers, who are obliged to read the most recent rulebook to learn what attire is acceptable or forbidden. Seamstresses and those who pay for the costumes also have their say. There was a time in the *escaramuza* competitions when one could dress and do one's hair as one liked, but with the movement to formalize these events, clothing and hair were subjected to more restrictive rules in order to preserve the newly-invented image of the Mexican woman. Now, a woman's/girl's hair must *always* be worn pulled back and clasped with a bow; the neckline must always be high. *Escaramuceras* should always wear pants (if following *charra* custom, of the same color or material as the skirt) or 'whites' (i.e., fitted, ankle-length pantaloons of white material that tuck into calf-length boots, as in the 'Adelita' style). Also, sleeves must always be below the elbow; because modesty is the required norm, no underarms will ever be seen. The rules also forbid adding any metallic fabric to the dresses, and ribbons, *rebozos* [shawls] with glitter or other eye-catching adornments. Despite this fascination with costume, teams risk being disqualified if a new hair bow has 'too many flowers or glitter' and a female judge announces it as 'untraditional.'

Explicitly designed to foster patriotism and national unity and to promote Mexican customs and traditions, the *charreada* is also associated with an intense cult of virility. This cult of virility helps to reproduce the patriarchal, male-dominated social order of the family, the hacienda and the nation (Nájera-Ramírez 2002). With its blatantly sexist policies, why, year after year, do so many women seek to participate in this sport? From my perspective as an 'outside-insider,'[1] I will consider the *escaramuza* team performance in terms of women's massive participation in rodeo as a male-dominated sport. Special attention is paid to a combination of three elements. The first addresses the practice of riding *charra* fashion while sitting on a Mexican sidesaddle (which I call *albarda Lepe*). During competitions riders ride their horses at high speeds through a series of complex movements, all the while firmly attached to their sidesaddles. This limited mobility on the saddle is potentially dangerous to *escaramuza* team members. Moreover, they must perform these dangerous, high-speed maneuvers while heavily dressed and still looking good and feminine in costumes that are hardly adapted for riding. This leads to my second point, that this is a unique sport very much focused on sequences of photographic moments (evidencing synchrony, symmetry, and the uniformity of all team members, right down to their riding tackle). It does, however, give little attention to the equestrian skills or the very act of riding. Finally, the competitive nature of these competitions encourages riders to do what it takes to meet at designated crossing points and to turn or spin the horse around at high speeds. All this must be done while avoiding collisions.[2]

Paradox and logic

The discussion identifies two paradoxical aspects of this sport. First, although *escaramuza* does require a degree of horsemanship or riding ability on the part of the participants, the craft of horsemanship or act of riding itself, and the embodied mutualities of horse human relationship are of limited note or relevance. Instead, emphasis is placed on costume, equipment and photographic moments. The central concern is with looking good. All the team members are attired in matching elaborate dresses while performing in synchrony with each other. Much of the horse is actually hidden under the voluminous skirts the women wear. Furthermore, in the sidesaddle the rider sits above the horse and does not come into contact with the horse's back. For many of these young women their horses have become a performing tool that must be sold when it starts to refuse to obey. Yet, within the *escaramuza* community there is certainly a minority counter narrative that calls to women involved in *charrería* to turn their gaze upon their horses, to look under their skirt and find the horse, the companion they choose to become with, in the first place. A second paradox stems from the fact that the *escaramuza* is becoming a growing and successful contemporary 'sport' that continues to exist in a more traditionally defined and persistently sex segregated, male-dominated *charro* society. Yet, the intersections of gender and this sport are neither as straightforward nor unambiguous as one may assume given the patriarchal nature of traditional, Mexican rodeo culture. In what follows I argue, following Nájera-Ramírez's (2002) ethnographic study of Mexico's national *escaramuza* movement (Movimiento Nacional de Escaramuzas) from an insider's perspective, that there are paradoxes that characterize this cultural practice called *charrería*, despite the 'cultural logic' that Nájera-Ramírez (2002, 207) finds in it.

Women in *charrería*

Gender discrimination in the *charrería* is a complex issue. While the Mexican Charrería Federation presents itself as committed to democratic processes, as indeed the Mexican Constitution has prohibited sexual discrimination since 1974, women in *charrería* are not the equals of men. Despite the fact that they pay the same membership dues, they can neither be voting members nor qualify for election to a National Board of directors for the Charro Federation. With certainty, the conversion of the *escaramuza* into a sport has effectively established a broad pretext for discrediting women who wish to participate in the *charrería* on a par with men. References to women often include terms that allude to their refusal to be submissive. Referring to a woman who was practicing *charro* events, a *charro* said to me: "She looks like a *mamarracho* [complete mess]. They've got their place so why don't they just dress up like little ladies [*mujercitas*] and do the *escaramuza*?" Such statements also discredit those men who would like to join in the *escaramuza*, as a complement to the *charreada*, on a par with women. These men are called derogatory names like queer or faggot. Yet, the intersections of gender and performance in traditional Mexican rodeo are more complex than the issue of voting rights and gender stereotyping would make them appear.

Two influential studies (Sands 1993; Nájera-Ramírez 2002) address the complexities of gender in terms of the position of women in the *escaramuza charrería*. Sands (1993, 176) depicts the sport as "a cultural fantasy about capable, strong women cloaked in gentility and beauty." According to Sands, women accept and value their role of making the *charreada* festive and colorful. They take pride in their performance, the thrills of riding and competition for titles. They both revel in and glorify the tradition. In doing so, however, "they rarely ponder the significance of their role in the gender iconography of Mexican culture" (Sands 1993, 185). Sands reasons that this is probably because women's roles in *charrería* harmonize with their role expectations in larger society. In contrast, Nájera-Ramírez (2002, 208) argues that women in *charrería* "do indeed engage in critical reflection on gender roles and relations." Some women do show a heightened awareness of their subordinate roles within the *charreada*. Nájera-Ramírez describes the case of a group of women in California, who in the late 1980s organized their own competition where they performed the *charro suertes* (riding and roping events) and rebelliously rode astride (i.e., not sidesaddle). However, when this sport's international[3] authority, the Federación Mexicana de Charrería (2008) found out about this event, they not only refused to sanction it but even threatened to ban the participants from the Federation if they continued that activity (Nájera-Ramírez 2002).

Through the studies of Sands (1993) and Nájera-Ramírez (2002) we see three kinds of responses to women's roles in traditional Mexican rodeo sporting culture. First, there are those who do not question their roles; second, there are those who rebel against their 'traditional' roles; and third, there are those who enjoy the sport despite its restrictions. Yet, we see in Nájera-Ramírez's (2002) account (if not so much in Sand's) that confronting traditional sexism and patriarchy within *charrería* is a sensitive matter that requires a great deal of courage, skill, cultural knowledge, persistence, and a bit of tact or diplomacy. This challenge to sexist practices and ideologies constitutes a kind of nuanced insider's mediation or cultural logic that demands a great deal of hard work, seriousness, commitment and clarity. It also requires a kind of discourse that forbids the use of such words as equality, justice and feminism. Instead, the logic employs terms like family values, unity, tradition, motherhood, as well as (since the 1990s) the use of Catholic emblems (like rosaries, devoted virgins and crucifixes). This logic, rather than the politics of confrontation, holds the promise of bringing about the miracle of being heard even when the ears of others are not open. Indeed, this is exactly how female competition sports in *charrería* began to grow during the 1980s.

My own experiences with the *escaramuceras* illustrate the complexities of gender in this sport and within the traditional rodeo overall. *Escaramuceras* are not a homogeneous group. On the one hand, why do we not simply leave and go somewhere else, some place where gender relations are marked by equality and respect? Some of us who stay on have found something there that made it worthwhile in spite of all the derision imaginable. Others eventually came to feel that it was no longer worth it and left. Still there were others who simply never felt the urge to enter. *Charro* authorities know well that the presence of women would bring children to *charro* arenas. With children there is a chance to continue this sport and tradition through the generations. Sometimes the same authorities wish to control women, to limit us to a supporting role of taking care of things, while restricting our roles in rodeo sports performance or within the wider organizational structures. Yet, relegated to the margins of traditional Mexican rodeo, women continue to work hard to be one of the few of hundreds of teams to compete in the *Escaramuza Nacional* championships. Only non-*charro* feminists express a hope to 'civilize,' through our feminine presence, a space marked by patriarchal, masculine barbarism. I would argue that changing the system from within calls for a more nuanced approach to understanding the gender roles played by both men and women in *charrería*.

Enter the father

Gendered ambiguity is evidenced when it comes to how a girl enters the sport. When a daughter expresses a wish to ride, it is so often the fathers, and not the mothers, who provide support and accompany them in their activities with the horses. In my interviews with *charras* (2000–2003 fieldwork; see Ramírez 2005), I soon realized that, while not absent from their comments, mothers were rarely mentioned. While mothers do participate actively in the sport, their participation centers on the looking good aspects of performance. Mothers share their daughters' worries and frustrations with fabric stores and seamstresses, etc. When it comes to the actual space around the horse, however, fathers become dominant. What benefits may arise from this father–daughter bond that revolves around animals? The animals bring the interest of father and daughter together. This introduces a different dynamic or dimension to the feminine/masculine axis than those discussed by Sands (1993) and Nájera-Ramírez (2002). In acceding to her wish to become an *escaramucera*, a girl's father supports his daughter and accompanies her in the *lienzo* (arena where the sport takes place). This is an area where mothers rarely enter. While it is, of course, true that father–daughter desires may overlap and mirror each other, it is also true that it is not really the daughter's wish to ride but a dream of the father that he attempts to realize through her. This hybridization of interests is more the rule than the exception. For example, one of my informants told me how her father (who was unable to ride because of injuries suffered in a train accident) decided to form an *escaramuza india* [Indian style, explained below] with his daughters. He was tough on them. Some of them could not take it, but others did and, in the end, the effort brought satisfaction for all. She said: "To put it simply: we performed the *escaramuza* [every weekend]. For years, we didn't spend a weekend at home. We traveled a lot, were invited to parties, made a lot of friends and had a lot of fun!" Another interviewee felt no direct or immediate attraction to riding, but as she came to conquer her initial fear she found that it brought her closer to her father, and to the opportunities he was opening up for her. With time, it brought them both meaningful rewards. Tere Cano, another *escaramucera*, lost her mother when she was four, but it was not her father, David, who introduced her to horses and urged her to practice riding, for he was not particularly interested in the *charrería*. Rather, it was her uncle, Filogonio:

> [...] I was sad, I didn't want to study and didn't know what to do. My uncle asked me: "Why don't you come to the *lienzo* to ride"? Blessed remedy! I loved it! I'd hurry to do my chores and go at the crack of dawn, help bathe the horses, take them over to the hills at Santa María to work them out with the kids. We'd take sandwiches or tacos and water. I felt great out there, I knew it was my thing.
>
> (Teresa Cano, interview, Morelia, 19 June 2003)

Accounts like these show that it is a mistake to divide the world into two orders (masculine and feminine) and to restrict their possible modes of interrelating to uni-dimensional factors such as: imitation (women who harbor male desires) or negation (men who dismiss the value, voice and existence of women). This leads us to the second paradox. To the observer *escaramuza* is clearly an equestrian activity but participants have little to say about their horses or about the art or practice of riding with them. Yet when horses do enter the picture they not only invite further thinking about intersections of naturalized differences and their relation to systems of domination that may arise as the relationship between father and daughter becomes mediated by horses, but also provide an interesting counterpoint to discussions concerning the mutuality in the horse human relationship (Maurstad et al. 2013).

Rider, horse and saddle

In the early 1980s, before *escaramuza* became a competitive sport, two styles of riding co-existed in *charrería*. The first was the *escaramuza charra*, where women rode sidesaddle in the traditional *Adelita* or *charra* costume. The second, or so-called 'Indian' style performance, consisted of women mounted astride and bareback, wearing different styles of dress that mostly evoked native Mexican and North American outfits. Called *Rarámuri* after the Chihuahua Indians, costumes consisted of cotton pants, feathers, *Huichol*-style embroidered blouses or *chinaco* suits (this last inspired by nineteenth-century Mexican liberal warriors). Indian style, although performed as a kind of spectacle in official *charreadas*, has been banned from official *charro* programs since 1991. A few *escaramuzas* still perform both styles, according to the occasion. For the most part, however, riding sidesaddle defines the sport. Albeit riding astride in a sidesaddle is very uncomfortable, women may choose to do so when warming up or cooling down their horses and while working out and rehearsing a routine. Riding astride is an option in cases of emergency such as slipping saddle, broken horn or missing stirrup but is punished with a loss of points in competition.

The type of saddle used by *escaramuceras* affects the nature of their embodied relationship with the horse. The *albarda Lepe* (or Lepe sidesaddle) is named after Filemón Lepe. Lepe was a *charro* who in 1927 modified a 'normal' *charro* saddle to make a proper sidesaddle for his daughter, Guadalupe (Lupe), who was to ride in a patriotic parade (see Rodríguez's unpublished manuscript 1988, 208; Ramírez 2005).[4] Unlike the 'modern' sidesaddle of the English hunter-style mount (late 19th to first half of the 20th century, with its flat seat and two pommels) the *albarda Lepe* is just the 'normal' *charro* saddle with three horns. The rider's legs are fixed on the left side of the horse, using the three horns. The seat is high off the horse as is the rider's right leg. Useless as it is, the right stirrup is kept, maybe as a reminiscence of the 'normal' saddle and in case the rider wishes to use it.

The *albarda Lepe* uses the same saddle-tree as the 'normal' *charro* saddle, but without the top, central horn, which is made specifically for roping cattle. Up in the fork, the saddle-maker inserts two iron pieces as 'cow horns' and, on the left side, a third horn or 'leaping head.' These iron horns are then padded with foam rubber and covered with leather and suede. The rider's legs are hooked around the upper horn, against the leaping head. If the rider needs, or wants, to clinch in order to feel more secure (since she must stay in the saddle at all costs throughout the event), then she must pull her left leg up to where the saddle-maker placed the leaping head. She chooses a point where the saddle-tree is thick, usually high off the horse's back. For this reason, the leather strap that holds the left stirrup has to be shortened to a point that leaves the left leg and left spur useless, for they cannot transmit any messages to the horse's body. Many *escaramuceras* attach their left stirrup directly to the cinch, thus fixing their left foot and stabilizing the foot even more. The seat of the *albarda Lepe* has suede covering over the 'normal' seat that stretches from the cantle to the pommel (i.e., covering the entire saddle bow). The remaining 7–9 inches of empty space are padded with leather or foam rubber.

The *albarda Lepe* is a powerful and still active element of *charra* gear; indeed, it was largely responsible for the massive participation of women in *charrería* for the following reasons: first, it is very common and costs about the same as the 'normal' *charro* saddle (when new, perhaps $300 USD) and making an *albarda Lepe* is not a particularly complex task for Mexican saddle-makers. Second, it can be lavishly adorned to 'upgrade' or enhance prestige according to the established *charro* categories (from the *faena* or working level to the *gala* or elaborate costume level). Third, dresses look spectacular on it. Fourth, and most importantly, it is easy for an inexperienced rider to use as it allows even poor riders to stay on their horses, no matter what.

Of course, this is not to suggest that all *escaramuceras* are bad horsewomen. They must, however, ride with no feel of the horse's back and an inability to use leg aids. The truth is that there are many excellent riders, even among those who learned in the *albarda* and hate to ride astride. However, as I can state based on my own experience, *escaramuceras* can perform, compete, and even win contests and prizes although they know next to nothing about riding well. This is because the *albarda Lepe* disguises poor horsewomanship. Lawrence is wrong when she observes that "women in *charrería* are expert riders" (1994: 705). Because the *albarda Lepe* attaches the rider to the saddle, it enables even girls or women with very little interest in riding to stay on a galloping (or bucking) horse. Many *escaramuceras* just want to look attractive, have fun, and meet dashing *charros*. Recently, an experienced trainer told me that he works out and rehearses the routine with a double hope: that the horses will learn it, and that the *escaramuceras* will not impede the horse's efforts. There are even urban legends that come straight from the horse's mouth – so to speak– about *escaramuceras* who fell while performing, but their horses just went right on galloping without them to complete the routine. Thus, the *escaramuza* competition proves that horses loyally understand, forgive, and correct the misguided directions of voluntarily handicapped riders.

There are further questions about what seems to be another kind of co-being with horses, apart from the one-to-one somatic attunement that prevails in other equestrian activities (Maurstad et al. 2013). Bodies of different species and conditions get tuned individually and collectively in this way of riding perched above the horse's back and unable to use effective leg aids. I remember well the first time I sat on my new *albarda Lepe*, when I was a teenager. It was a foam rubber *albarda*, made in my hometown, Morelia, by a fine saddlemaker. Though I only vaguely recall that he took some measurements before setting to work (of my right leg while sitting as if I was on the *albarda*), none of those measurements were used in any significant way since he had to choose between two or three standard saddle-trees. My father and I put my new *albarda* on a mare who had never used one before. He was worried that her shoulder blade could be damaged from riding with it for too many hours. It only took me a second to climb up on it, balance myself in the saddle using both stirrups, and then swing my right leg over the saddle between the horns. I was sitting 7 inches above the horse's back. The new seat was cushy, but tight as a drum, and I bumped along on it with every stride. Soon it obtained the memory of my body: my gluteal bones about 5 inches from the horse's back, but my right leg still placed atop the pommel, between the horns, 8 inches high.

Before becoming an *escaramucera*, I used to mount my horse astride, usually bareback, but when I used the *albarda* for the first time, I soon learned that riding *a mujeriegas* [in a 'womanly' manner] was all about being firmly attached to that saddle with both legs. In sum, in the *albarda*, the rider sits high above the horse's back, is securely fixed into the saddle and leg aids are difficult to use. It is a type of riding that largely fails to realize a great deal of embodied mutuality between horse and rider. Rider and horse do not feel each other as in more conventional types of riding sport. Commands are limited to using the *freno* (the bit, literally 'brakes') and pulling the reins (which are joined in one). The transmission of aids to the horse through body language is rather imprecise because of the position of one's legs and the height of the seat. However, it does not matter exactly how you ride, you and your horse must gallop and perform all the maneuvers that your team has agreed to do. When we eventually hired a trainer of the 'old school' he had nothing to say about *how* we were riding in our *albardas*. All he was concerned with was galloping fast, reaching the crossing points on time, and trying not to crash into one another. Surely, it was hell for our horses.

What about you and your horse?

The *albarda Lepe* is undesirable not only because it disguises poor horsewomanship but because it allows the rider to don lavish, glamorous clothes that can be attractively spread out over the saddle, thus shifting the focus to looking good. Horses may be crushed in collisions with each other, their bodies and mouths maimed or lacerated with spurs and harsh bits, and their minds deeply damaged. Yet, all this suffering means little, or nothing, to officials of the *Charro* federation, trainers or owners, as long as the horse gives no trouble while performing the required routines. Indeed, when a horse becomes difficult, the trainer or other *charros* may suggest using a more severe bit, many times complemented with *bajador*, a tie-down strip or standing martingale. This last is used to prevent the horse from raising its head thus avoiding the pressure or pain caused by the bit. The *bajador* did not exist in *charrería* before the late 1980s. But if the trouble persists, the trainer can ask for a new horse. Horses become disposable for their riders and coaches. Yet there is certainly room for improved horsemanship and indications that not all riders see their horses as a kind of performance machine.

During fieldwork in 2000–2003 and in seminars held in 2014, I have over the years insisted on emphasizing the importance of horsewomanship over and above the billowing skirts and embroidered attire. In my own case, the exposure to ideas that were already present in a marginal *charrería* but reinforced in finding out about what Pat Parelli called "natural horsemanship"[5] allowed some of us to loosen the stabilized attachment of our legs, lower the right stirrup, forget about the leaping horn, and focus on how we could best handle our horses. In September 1991, the escaramuza charra Las Gaviotas, from Playa Azul, Michoacán, was invited by the President of the National Charro Federation, Carlos Pascual, to the lienzo charro El Pedregal (one of the most prestigious arenas in Mexico) to exhibit their riding skills *a mujeriegas* (using the *albarda Lepe*). We performed the full routine with our right foot outside the stirrup, changing leads, jumping, and doing the *punta* [sliding stop] with no bridle. We did not question the use of the *albarda Lepe* (or our attire, or the politics involved). We simply showed that we could stop abusing our horses' mouths but continue to be well-balanced riders.

Additionally some riders do become attached to and care about their horses. Ana, an *escaramucera* from Veracruz, told me that she had a beloved, but not particularly attractive, horse. Her *escaramuza* trainer insisted that she replace him with a *de línea* horse (i.e., a bred quarter horse). Though she eventually saved enough money to buy a beautiful and expensive horse from a famous breeder in Texas, her old horse continues to perform much better (interview with Ana, Naucalpan, 20 December 2014). Another story comes from Sarah Cárdenas Clements (now 22) who tells me about her rescue mare. Born in Ensenada, Baja California, she has spent all her life on horses. She is a member of the *escaramuza charra* in Ensenada, Baja California, who in 2008 traveled to train in Tijuana's *lienzo charro*. She rode a beautiful seal-brown colored [*retinto*] horse though she was not particularly happy with him: "He bucks, not while doing the routine, and [...] see [...] we just don't get along very well." While practicing before a *charreada*, Sarah met a mare that she called Princess:

> She looked at me and walked right towards me. I was moved by her gesture. I saw a kind of sadness in her eyes, but also a light. She was so skinny you could see all her bones. I thought "she won't last two weeks over there," [so] I talked with the *charros* who were running the herd, asking who owned that mare. The owner was there and he identified me by my *retinto* horse, which he liked a lot and could use in *colas*. So I said, "I'll trade my horse for your mare." He couldn't believe it! He asked me if I also wanted money and I said "No, just the mare." The way she looked at me was [...] simply in disbelief.
>
> (interview with Sarah Cárdenas Clements, *Aeropuerto Benito Juárez*, Mexico City, 28 October 2014)

That supposedly wild mare let Sarah touch her, put a halter over her head, load her into Sarah's trailer, and take her all the way back to Ensenada. Sarah's mother was furious about what she considered an unfair trade. Princess had to be fed and cared for during months before Sarah could try to ride her. But when she did, she found a sweet and fine saddle horse that has gained admiration while performing *escaramuza*. That mare executed a gorgeous *punta* for the first time in 2009; one that was videotaped and shared on Youtube![6]

Thus the paradox here is that in my research on and participation in *escaramuza* competitions, I found people who are deeply engaged in horse-womanship and who sincerely care about their horses. The beauty and synchrony of *escaramuza* performance, however, comes at a cost. Alongside a focus on the *escaramuza* competition as based on the 'photographic sequence' of eight elaborately costumed riders galloping a routine, is the fact that the performances are often cruel to the horses that themselves are seen as disposable. Nor do the performances require a degree of accomplished horsewomanship, or a felt, embodied sense of co-being between horse and rider.[7] Moreover the Lepe saddle itself contributes to back pain, cramps, sprains, bruises and scoliosis for the riders.[7] This to me seems hardly fair to either horse or rider and certainly open to challenge and change. For example, the Federación Nacional de Charrería may require evaluations of horses' health and settle this as a condition in order to compete. Julieta Gordoa, one of the founders of the Movimiento Nacional de Escaramuzas in the 1980s and now *escaramuza* judge, has been working designing a sidesaddle that rides lower on the horse than the *Lepe* saddle. Other *escaramuceras* may decide to fight for the right to ride astride.

Sands (1993) and Nájera-Ramírez (2002) have shown that *escaramuza* is a feminine cultural practice embedded in engendered structures that have complex roots within a larger society. Nájera-Ramírez (2002, 220) states that "[It is] only by understanding the cultural logic of a tradition that one can become an effective participant in changing the power and politics of that tradition." In this chapter, I have highlighted perspectives that remain unseen and untold, but which are crucial to this cultural logic, setting out from the presence-and-absence of horses. On the one hand, I underscore the complexities of the kind of 'beloved' patriarchy that helps to feminize women and allows them to mount horses and pursue their own desires. On the other hand, I take a closer look at the *albarda Lepe* that connects women to the sport but at the same time places them apart from their horses. Any attempt to challenge the sexism and animal exploitation involved in this sport must take into account the complex, positioned and paradoxical qualities that underlie it (Ramírez 2014, 141–142).[8]

Notes

1 From 1982 to 1997, I was a member of *escaramuzas charras* (La Guadalupana de Regionales Valladolid, Morelia; Las Gaviotas de Emiliano Zapata, Playa Azul; La Señorial, Valle de Guayangareo, Morelia), belonged to *charro* associations, and judged *escaramuza* competitions. In 2013, I was invited to discuss the origins, development and trends related to the *escaramuza* at seminars for *escaramuza* trainers. I thank María Eugenia (Maru) García de Silvestre for the opportunity to meet so many great riders and people engaged with this singular sport. Of course, I am especially grateful for this opportunity to speak freely about my research findings and thoughts – feminist and animalist. This chapter is based on narrative data and observation during fieldwork conducted in 2003 (for my Ph.D. dissertation) and between 2013 and 2014 at *Congreso Nacional Infantil* and at three seminars for *escaramuza* trainers. In this last fieldwork, I interviewed 9 *escaramuza* trainers, 3 sidesaddle sellers and 4 stableboys in open-ended format about specific questions. For example, how do they choose how long (restrictive) a martingale should be on an *escaramuza* horse and what do they do if a horse gets hurt or refuses to

perform? At 2014 seminars I made more general and reflexive questions, such as how do you feel about riding sidesaddle?; do you or your horse have health issues that you can relate to riding that way?; why do you use the martingale?; how are the horses responding to performance demands?; what makes a good *escaramuza* horse nowadays? At the seminars, I collected data from 12 *escaramuza* trainers and 15 riders. Unless I stated to the contrary, I used people's real names in quotations. I focus on the sidesaddle and the martingale because these are technologies that can disguise the rider's hands' abusive movements and poor riding skills during the four minutes when eight galloping horses perform.

2 The documentary *Escaramuza: Riding from the Heart* (Yahraus and Rosenthal 2012) shows the challenges and the hard work that a competitive team (Azaleas, from California) needs to overcome in order to be at the National *Charro* Championship. It also shows how horses are excluded from the narrative.

3 Since the 1960s *charro* associations officially federated in Mexico have grown across the United States. Today there are 14 *charro* associations competing in Illinois, many more in Arizona, Nuevo Mexico, Texas, and Colorado, Nevada and California, among others. The growth of *charro* clubs in the USA was promoted by Ronald Reagan as a way to undermine Cesar Chavez and the United Farm Workers movement, see Ramírez 2014.

4 In reality, *albarda* is not a good name for this kind of saddle because it is derived from an Arab word meaning pack-saddle. As far as I know, the only author who used the term *albarda* as it is understood today was Captain José Ignacio Lepe (Filemón's son, Lupe and Rosita's brother), in his dictionary: "*Albarda* [...] saddle used by women to ride with both legs to the left" (Lepe 1972). It is illustrated with a modern English hunter sidesaddle.

5 Guided by Alfonso Aguilar, a former *charro* fellow at *Regionales Valladolid*, Pat Parelli visited Playa Azul, Michoacán, with his family on a leisure tour while giving talks and exhibitions to people "who had troubles with their horses," and were open to new ways of handling them. Certainly we were. With financial support from my family, I traveled to Parelli's ranch in Clements, CA, and took his first 3-week international Natural Horsemanship course. After that, I shared the experience with the members of the *Gaviotas*. My brother Marcelino, our trainer, went even further by establishing the Manejo Natural del Caballo (MNC).

6 Eder1401, "Escaramuza charra de Ensenada" https://www.youtube.com/watch?v=Br-OwkWGQOU&index=2&list=FLa2K-FDMufwENnTJqn8AvDg (Accessed 20/12/2014).

7 All of the *escaramuceras* (26) who attended the December 2014 seminar in Naucalpan said that they suffered from backaches, cramps, sprains, bruises, muscular pain, scoliosis… which they attributed to riding sidesaddle.

8 I am grateful to my daughter, Ana Zacil Vieyra, and Paul Kersey for questions, comments and correcting English versions of this text.

References

Federación Mexicana de Charrería. 2008. *Estatuto de la federación Mexicana de Charrería* [Statute of the Mexican Federation of Charreria]. http://www.fmcharreria.com/federacion/estatutos (Accessed 20 December 2014).

Federación Mexicana de Charrería. 2012. *Reglamento de escaramuzas y damas charras* [Regulation of Skirmishes in Lady Charras]. Mexico: Federación Mexicana de Charrería, Secretaría del Deporte, http://www.vozcharra.com/formatosfmch/Reglamento%20de%20Escaramuzas%20FMCH%202012.pdf (Accessed 20 December 2014).

Lawrence, Elizabeth Atwood. 1994. "Ranch Women and Men on Both Sides of the Border." *American Anthropologist* 96(3): 703–705.

Lepe, José Ignacio. 1972 [1951]. *Diccionario de asuntos hípicos y ecuestres* [Dictionary of Equine and Equestrian Matters]. México: Editorial Porrúa.

Maurstad, Anita, Dona Davis and Sarah Cowles. 2013. "Co-being and Intra-Action in Horse–Human Relationships: A Multi-Species Ethnography of Be(com)ing Human and Be(com)ing Horse." *Social Anthropology* 21(3): 322–336.

Nájera-Ramírez, Olga. 2002. "Mounting Traditions: The Origin and Evolution of la escaramuza charra." In *Chicana Traditions: Continuity and Change*, edited by N. E. Cantú and O. Nájera-Ramírez, 207–223. Urbana: University of Illinois Press.

Ramírez Barreto, Ana Cristina. 2005. *El juego del valor. Varones, mujeres y bestias en la charrería en Morelia, 1923–2003* [The Brave Game: Males, Females and Beasts in the Charrería in Morelia]. Doctoral dissertation in social anthropology, Center for Anthropological Studies, *El Colegio de Michoacán*, Zamora, Mexico.

Ramírez Barreto, Ana Cristina. 2014. "Diversidad cultural en condiciones polémicas" [Cultural Diversity during Polemical Conditions]. In *Memorias del Diplomado en Desarrollo Cultural y Políticas Públicas* [Memory of the Cultural and Public Politics of Development in Diplomacy], edited by M. R. García H. Pimentel, 130–142. Morelia: Secretaría de Cultura.

Rodríguez Cervantes, Ignacio. 1988–1991. *Historia de la charrería*. [History of Charreria]. 2 vols. (Unpublished manuscript), Mexico.

Sands, Kathleen M. 1993. *Charrería Mexicana: An Equestrian Folk Tradition*. Tucson: University of Arizona Press.

Yahraus, Bill and Robin Rosenthal. 2012. *Escaramuza: Riding from the Heart*. Littlerock, CA: Pony Highway Productions.

12 Horse Things

Objects, Practices and Meanings on Display

Anita Maurstad, Dona Lee Davis, and Sarah Dean

Peppermints, husbands, saddles, bits and reins: this diverse collection of objects has one thing in common. They are objects that riders identify as illustrative of their relationships to horses. As part of a multispecies ethnographic study on horse human relationships among riders in North Norway and Midwest US, we asked riders, "One of us (Anita) works in a museum, and if we were to make an exhibition of horse human relationships using objects, what object would you pick as representative of your relationship with your horse?" Many riders, like Emerita, responded with hesitancy and confusion, asking, "Gee, what a question! An object! What do you mean?" Yet, as informants attempted to grapple with the question and rephrase it in terms meaningful to them and their own experiences, patterns were revealed. Taken together the narrated items from the 60 interviewed riders make up a multifaceted collection of objects that both resonate with typical notions of the materiality of museum collections, but are also associated with less material attributes, meanings and functions.

Museum work can be divided into three broad categories: documentation, collection and exhibition. Our study speaks first and foremost to documentation and collection. We analyze how informants' narratives about horse-associated objects illustrate the meaning of horses. We explore how responses to the museum question express more subjective and experiential relations among humans and horses and illustrate the complex entanglements that constitute humans and horses as individuals and as pairs. Most traditional museum displays of the horse human relationship would split materiality and animality, displaying the horse in a natural science section, and any objects connected to horsemanship in ethnographic sections. Saddles, bits and reins would easily find a place in the latter department. Peppermints and husbands, however, would not. So too would be the fate of other objects in our rider collection – Lara's footstool and Urdur's horse smell. The latter objects bear witness to a connection between animal, human and object that is far too little understood. The new and emergent field of multi-species ethnography (MSE) offers perspectives that shed light on these connections (Kirksey and Helmreich 2010). In a pointedly dynamic take on MSE, Pálsson (2013, 28) describes human animal relations as "ensembles of biosocial relations." In a similar vein, Ingold (2013, 8–9) speaks of species beings as "biosocial becomings." Life unfolds as "a tapestry of mutually conditioning relations," he maintains, "never complete, never finished. It is always work in progress."

Such processual perspectives on becoming are also the focus of recent material culture studies, as well as in other disciplines focusing on materiality. We become in engagements with things (Miller 2005, 2010), and materiality matters and is enacted (Barad 2007). Actor Network Theory has a focus on relational materialities: "entities achieve their form as a consequence of the relations in which they are located" (Law 1999, 4). Objects have their own dynamics as agentive, active and interactive. Neither objects nor subjects are sovereign as actors. Mutual agencies are in place, but things are not without significance. According to Preda (1999, 356) artifacts can be seen as "materialized skills and knowledge and [they] require from human actors complementary skills and knowledge." Damsholt and Gert Simonsen (2009, 15) focus on these agentive processes using the concept "materializing," drawing attention to the fact that materiality is a result of activities, of doings, "an active verb," as they phrase it. It is in materializing processes that the real is established and stabilized.

While these materiality scholars discuss humans and artifacts we add one more non-human component to the equation, the horse. We ask how defined objects enlist horse and human in certain activities, activities that also define identities and relationships. Our refined research questions are thus how objects can express the subtleness of relations between humans and horses, as well as what objects do in these relations. How do objects contribute to and define various social actors, themselves included? How do things contribute to drawing boundaries, making horse and human as distinct creatures, and as a relational pair? As we will illustrate, the narrated horse things reveal a kind of interspecies communication that ontologically informs the personalities and identities of both species. We close the analysis discussing exhibiting narrated horse things that matter at the museum.

Narrated horse things

Our analysis of horse things is based on narrative data collected in sixty open-ended interviews with US Midwestern and north Norwegian horse people who participate in different equestrian sports and ride within a variety of local settings.[1] Anticipating that our data would bubble from the ground up and reflect "culture in talk" (Quinn 2005, 2), we asked the same general questions about why people ride and what it means to them.[2] We used an open-ended interview format, grounding riders' own reflections of how they relationally portray and enact themselves and horses. The majority of riders participate in a range of equestrian activities: endurance, eventing, dressage, and gaited horse riding. There are 52 women and 8 men in our sample, aged 20 to 70. The authors of this chapter are all experienced horsewomen, affording us an insider knowledge and familiarity with the field (Brandt 2004). The local environments and sport communities that riders belong to are small. In order to not jeopardize anonymity, we have chosen to leave out contextual information about who the interviewees are. Riders chose their own fictional names, which are utilized within quotes.

The museum question was posed towards the end of each interview when riders often had talked for an hour about their relationships to horses. A typical reply to the museum question would include objects belonging to different material categories but replies would also frequently include less tangible or immaterial elements. For example, Red and Daisy's responses are fairly straightforward. Red mentions saddle and pasture as objects associated with his horse relationship. For Daisy, it is saddles, stethoscope and treats. Treats for Daisy connote not only the treats but also the feeling of pleasure that is shared between Daisy and her horse when she offers him treats. Many informants mention the smell of the horse or barn setting. Smell is less tangible but certainly one can relate to what is being said. Like the treat, smell evokes a multitude of feelings, but also relates to being there in the presence of horses. Judy's reply, husbands, is less straightforward. It needs further explanation and context. Judy goes on to explain that she chose husbands, first, because various stages of her riding career were associated with different time periods, thus different husbands; second, because putting the husbands in a museum would get them out of her life, therefore, allowing her to do her horse thing.

Our analysis of such positioned and personalized objects, however, needs structure or a way of weaving the commonplace, the material, the immaterial and the idiosyncratic together. We do so by granting objects agency. Rather than see the objects as static or inert we, like our informants, instill them with a dynamic, active or interactive quality that goes well beyond the simple notion of representing or representation. In the body of this chapter, we will address objects that are agentive with respect to *being on* the horse, and objects relating to *being with* them. In addition we make a point about *being there*. This latter, more esoteric category encapsulates the emplaced aspects of horse human relationships. Howes (2005) notes that while *embodiment* refers to integration of mind and body, the concept *emplacement* allows for a consideration of the larger environment. Here we broaden the idea of environment to include animals. Following Howes (2005) we focus activities in environments where social, physical as well as sensorial characteristics shape perception, and where the boundaries between material and immaterial and more sensory and subjective aspects are blurred.

Being-on-the-horse things

Horse and human bodies communicate through a set of cues and signs. Emplaced on the horse, the rider's use of bodily weight, balance, and breath are various means through which the rider communicates with the horse.

The signals are based on ethological ideas about what is natural to the horse, but they need to be learned by horse and rider; they are new material-semiotic practices (Birke et al. 2004). Saddles and bridles are common elements in this communication. These are also objects that many riders mention as important. Ajay says:

> What object? Saddles of course, bridles, my boots, my helmet, I guess [...] I guess I'm kind of hyper sensitive about how my saddle feels on my horse. How it fits him and if he's comfortable in it. The same with the bridle. You know all that equipment has evolved over time. But it still remains very much the same for the most part. At least we are becoming more and more aware that it's got to be comfortable for them to do their job right.

Saddles are well-known museum items. Some riders responded, "saddles" because they think that typical museum objects are what we are after. Like Pixie, who says: "Saddle? Is that what she (Anita) is getting at?" Responding to such questions from our informants we say that anything goes – pick the first object that crosses your mind. Pixie then goes on to choose her objects as treats, an item that we will comment on later. The reports of saddles in our narrated collection are many, however. Riders want a saddle that fits the horse, a well-fitting saddle. The explanations provide these objects with more qualities than the obvious functions of holding the rider positioned, as well as being a traditional museum piece. The narratives enable seeing the communicative aspects of this item. Halla picks saddle and bridle because "that connects you immediately to that horse." Thus: well-fitting is not only about form. Well-fitting is about communication. Gear needs to fit for the horse to be willing. Second, there is an interesting agentive component here. What saddles are is dependent on human perception and handling. The human must first assess which saddle fits, how this item works in the relationship between horse and rider. Furthermore, human handling becomes essential. Susanna, in describing the use of another typical piece of horse gear, the reins, explains this aspect of use in more detail. She says reins are the most important tool for communicating with horses. The reins are there more or less constantly, and it is through the reins that you 'talk' (uses her fingers to illustrate quotation marks) with the horses. She explains that there are various grips or rein aids, like leading reins, half halts, or you can shorten your reins and collect your horse or ride with loose reins. And asked whether the reins are a soft or a hard instrument, Susanna replies that it depends on the person using them. Here is an interesting aspect of materializing processes taking place. It depends on the sensations of the rider: "That rider feel. One can be very hard in hand, and very soft, almost like riding with a sewing thread, the horse being so sensitive for it, or for the communication between you," she says.

The reins are a good example of Preda's (1999) point about artifacts being materialized skills and knowledge, requiring complementary skills and knowledge from humans. Or as Law (1999) holds, that materialities are performed in relations. They are objects, pieces of leather, or synthetic materials, but crucial in their agencies with humans and horses. They claim certain uses, are open to multiple uses, and following from use arise versions of horses and humans: hard mouths or soft mouths, hard riders or soft riders. That use of horse things matters to persons is also something Ola describes. His object is the shoe, and he explains:

> I think that shoeing is so much. Imagine you take an animal and put on a shoe, nail it tight and adapt it, and the animal shall walk with this shoe, that you are allowed to do that, from an animal that is 4–500 kilos of muscles, and you can just lift the foot and nail and hammer and cut into this, that is an amazingly great vote of confidence, really, from that animal.

In summary, many riders pick functional, well-known gear as their horse things, and the narratives situate these rather clearly defined material objects as having as clear relational qualities. They are, on the one hand, stabilizing devices in the human horse relationship. They enable riding; the saddle helps to balance on the horse, the shoes help the horse to move on certain surfaces. Different riders may use the horse things differently, and one and the same rider may over time attend to horse and object in different ways. The objects are open to human choices, choices that are not always visible. And the choices matter, ontologically (Mol 1999). From practice comes different versions of horse and human, as well as the objects themselves. The activities invite and propose different versions of the elements of the network. As such they are agentive, part of communicative practices, not passive devices. They enable various embodied and emplaced communicative practices that enable and stabilize the relationship between the parties. With the narratives, the practices with objects reveal details on how object, horse and human together constitute each other. The horse is constituted as a creature to have respect for, but also one that must accept human choices of gear and use of gear. The human is constituted in special roles vis à vis horse and object, deciding for instance, that a bit, an iron bar, as Ernst describes it, shall be a communicative device. There follows a human identity of being decisive about horse handling. And the metal bar comes in different agentive versions – as a rough metal gadget, or a softer, more gentle version. There are indeed a number of versions of object, horse and human here.

Being-with-the-horse things

The human horse relationship is also involving situations where human and horse have the same footing. In the stall, at the field, in the paddock – there are many sites where humans are being with their horses, and the narratives of riders reveal that the horse human relationships exhibit very sensuous materialities intra-acting. Among the objects that we will categorize or place as illustrative and agentive in these being-with situations, is the brush. Henriette explains why she picks the brush: "has to do with – first of all, closeness, the closeness to the animal, touch, feel it. When I brush I always keep one hand on the horse, and use the other to brush." And Rebecca says that "just brushing them, it's relaxing for the horse, it's relaxing for me." Also Sky maintains that the horses like this. She chooses brushes as her objects because: "they all love to be brushed, and each horse has a certain spot they love to have brushed. And some horses like a hard brush because they like you to rub them down and give them a massage, some horses want a soft brush, and some horses love face brushes because they like a face massage."

These few quotes speak to sensory elements of the horse human relationship. Brushes certainly have practical values but are also associated with touch. Touch has agentive powers. As Henriette witnesses – it establishes contact between the two. It enlists the parties in a bond. It stabilizes the bond, humans figure places where the horse likes to be rubbed, and the horse can expect his or her needs to be met by the human. It is a sensory experience, a different kind of body contact than being on the horse. Brushes then, work with human and horse agency interactively. The parties are enlisted, given tasks and roles in the relationships.

So too do other objects. Becca chooses the lead line as her object and speaks of it as a communicative device. As a rider you can feel and understand the horse, plus what kind of relation you have to this particular horse by watching the lead line:

> You can ask the horse, you can tell his state of mind if he's pulling back on it and not releasing, so that there is slack in the line. You know that there is something going wrong because he should be yielding to you. You instantly know where you are with him, if there is a battle or if he's willing to yield and say okay we're partners in this, by the way you move it left or right, or jiggle it to let him know he needs to back up, there is so much communication with that lead line.

A nice intra-relationship between object, human and horse is expressed here, and it is also visible to other spectators. One can look at the lead line and it speaks, it reveals what kind of relationship the horse and human have.

Sophia has a different experience with the lead rope. This is one of the objects that she picks as a museum object because it is telling of who her horse is: "You know, give him that lead rope, that'd have to go in there [to the museum collection] because he sees that and he's at the end of the pasture." Her horse is sometimes hard to catch at the pasture, she says, and she carries treats. However, they too often fail to do their job: "I carry peppermints in my pocket and he knows that there are peppermints there – doesn't mean that you are gonna catch him, but he'll get close enough to get one and run." We could say that treats as object do not always perform as we wish.

Treats are an object mentioned also by other riders. There are many peppermints, cookies, carrots and even Dr. Pepper in our narrated museum collection. And treats are agentive. Some expert horse people say that one should not give treats to horses. They might start biting or nibbling. Others say horses deserve treats as a token of appreciation (Ofstad 2014). So treats definitely do things. Treats may enact a version of the horse that some do not want, or other versions, that are wanted. To Daisy they are domesticating devices, creating horses that are interested in people: "Ever since they were little they would come in and stick their head in [the barn door] and be interested in what we're doing, and we would hand them treats and that's our training tool so that we don't have to go catch them."

Summing up, the things mentioned in this section have quite obvious qualities concerning biosocial becomings (Ingold and Pálsson 2013). Horses are trained to do what humans want, be with people. They have to learn how to communicate with this other species – they should not bite or kick their human counterparts. As such the things riders choose are quite common horse equipment. What the narratives do is highlight the things that are actually there, important to the very practices of becoming horse and human. Objects are part of relationships, and here they contribute to actions. In the act of brushing horses, human, brush and horse are involved in doing body-mind-environment interrelated work of importance for their relationship and – we add – their materialities – who they become, as horses and humans.

Being-there things

Material objects such as those presented so far are mentioned by approximately half of our informants, yet a large group of the objects identified are less representative and hardly present in museum displays. Thus they are more difficult to categorize. They are objects where boundaries between material and immaterial, or more sensory and subjective aspects are blurred. However, if we look for what they do, we find that they reveal important aspects of the horse human relationship, and they are agentive, enabling and doing things in the network. As such they are important objects in our collection. We name them 'being-there things.'

A first object is the footstool of Lara. Lara often sits down and listens to the horses chew their hay. She also enjoys watching them eat: "that little plastic footstool that I'm sitting on when the horses are chewing their hay [...] it's the situation of sitting there [...] related to hanging around which is sort of a great part of being together with the horses."

The footstool is a commodity of emplacement enabling Lara, as holds Howes (2005, 7): "to reposition ourselves in relationship to the sensuous materiality of the world." Ethnographic exhibitions may well include footstools and chairs, but the sensuous qualities mentioned by Lara are rarely expressed. Yet sensations are concepts important to both human animal relations and material relations. Our question about what objects riders associate with their horses allows them to express practices with horses involving objects and senses. Being with horses invokes many senses – listening, watching, smelling – sensing being there. Like Lara, Urdur also speaks of how she enjoys listening to the horses chewing and explains it as soothing. She also speaks of smell: "difficult, [to pick an object] well now it has become a part of the daily routine that the smell of horse, I wear it always, but I remember that when I was a child and had it not in the daily routine, because I had it only when I was in the stable or at the farm, and just that smell of horse was fantastic."

Emma and Barbara refer to other sensations. Emma looks out the window. "I don't know if this is an object, the first thing that popped into my mind when you said that is that I picture myself sitting in a room and there is a window and I get to look out the window." There is not necessarily a horse there to look at, but for Emma: "the window is a path to something else. And horses represent freedom for people. I think originally it meant mobility and movement [...] moving towards a goal, maybe you have a goal in mind but also moving away from where you are stuck at now." And Barbara says: "It's that happy feeling. It's like Peter Pan at my house thinking happy thoughts. Running across the prairie, it's just even watching the horse run. When [named horse] runs, it's just power and muscle and hair and wind; that's what I think of."

Summing up our being-there categorization enlists many immaterial objects, as well as immaterial aspects of material objects. Although immaterial, they have many of the same functions as the material objects referred to in this chapter. They reveal communicative and sensory qualities in the horse–human–object relation and are agentive in enlisting human actions versus horses. As such, immaterialities are also processually enacting certain types of horses and humans.

This section provides a glimpse into the joy that riders experience from being with horses. It is a joy, an emplaced joy that involves many senses and materialities. Urdur wears the smell and thrives with it. It is a part of her material body, her sensations of who she is, and what she is. Barbara has Peter Pan moments. Other riders enjoy the beauty of their horses. These joyous situations have agentive powers. Lara's practice of sitting on the footstool is part of her biosocial becoming. It affects both her and the horses. Lara says that she sometimes uses the stool in situations where the horses in her outdoor stall are stressed because of bad weather and heavy winds. Being there, she soothes the horses with her presence, calming them as herd leader, as she is not afraid of the winds (see Brandt 2006). The stool is also therapeutic. It soothes Lara to sit down after stall work and enjoy.

Horse things and the museum

Starting out with a question of how objects can express the more subtle aspects of relationships between horses and humans, and what objects do in these relationships, we now possess a sampling of narrated horse things that illustrate the meaning of horses to humans. Many of the items in our collection are easy to display at the museum in the sense that an audience would recognize them as things belonging to a horsey world. They are also easy to set up, as they exist as clear and bounded materialities. As a contribution to museum studies however, we have shown that without the backgrounding context of the narratives, the meanings of the things are obscured. No spectator sees that the saddle is about communication. No spectator sees that there are many ways to use the bit, each way invoking certain exemplars of horses. Narratives on use are necessary. Materialities are never just things, with no social attachment or story. They are, as argued by Law and Mol (1995), both social and material, and they are unstable. Reins as a piece of leather, used to stop the horse, are only minor parts of the story. That reins are delicate communicative devices, with varying identities, is a story not to be seen unless you add the perspective of relational materialities (Law 1999).

Other lessons to museum studies are that many items are not material. We have dealt with immaterial horse objects earlier in the text. The next example of Laura's "light rays," however, needs additional context. Asked to explain light rays as her chosen object, Laura says:

> I wrote a piece when I was an English major for my final portfolio about horses and riding, and trying to put things to words for my professors who did not have any experience with horses. I just remember that there are some mornings when you get to the barn early enough. I like to ride in the morning when it is cool. If the sun is hitting just right through the windows then you have those really beautiful golden sunrises. It comes through the window and makes everything seem like a dream. It's not something that you see all the time. It's just golden and streaking through and lighting the arena.

Not only does Laura choose an immaterial thing that speaks to joy and meaning, she has also tried to use this thing in a text in order to describe the meaning of horse to an audience. It is an eloquent example of things that matter, including Laura's conscious presence in the setting. It also exemplifies the positioned and personalized choices of things that riders bring forth. In sum, however, the range of more and less material responses speaks to the same issues, that of meaning of horses and how human, horse and object become in agentive practices. We want to underline that it is everyday practices that riders talk about, and in these common activities, through handling little ordinary things as for instance the object treats, different versions of the elements of the network are shaped.

As museum work, our study is first and foremost a documentation of horse human relations with a focus on what things can reveal about relations. In asking riders to choose potential museum objects, we inadvertently set them in dialogue with museum audiences and curators. It is interesting that our sample of riders did not pick objects that necessarily accord with what audiences stereotypically expect to see or experience in a museum. Only two riders picked objects with typical museum properties such as age and memory. These were Katla's antique halter and Niki's saddle, which she was given as a present from her father. Riders were perfectly willing to let their everyday objects go to the museum. Yet their ideas of relevant things, like peppermints and smells, may not find accord with museum professionals. Urdur might smell of horse, but experts would probably not have identified that as her object. An important point is, however, that neither would Urdur, if it had not been for Anita's museum question. As a museum expert, Anita posed this question and took the lead in analyzing the findings. It is the combined effort between experts and non-experts that has created this collection of horse things.

As such, our study is also illustrative for what museums can be and do with respect to contemporary issues like the relationships between humans and other animals. Our goal is to offer and propose new dialogues in human animal studies. Interspecies communication and relationships are not new to the genre (Wipper 2000; Game 2001; Despret 2004; Birke 2009, Birke, Bryld and Lykke 2004; Brandt 2004, 2006; Birke and Brandt 2009; Argent 2012; Davis et al. 2013; Maurstad et al. 2013), but the fact that things contribute in ontologically informing the personalities and identities of both species is. The narrated horse things reveal interesting aspects of how the meaning of horses is multifold to humans, who have long-term and intimate daily relations with horses.

If exhibited at the museum these perspectives will reach a wider audience. Johansen (2002) discusses how museums compete with new media on the knowledge scene. People get more spectacular views of lions and polar bears on the National Geographic Channel, than by seeing them stuffed in the museum. Our study of horse things illustrates the importance of seeing animals in new ways, as more than species to be observed, be it stuffed or explained in films or zoos or other media. Museums are venues for dialogues about these complexities. Museums also need to engage themselves. The perspective that we are biosocial becomings (Ingold and Pálsson 2013), our culture and nature becoming in everyday and changing practices, challenges traditional museum presentations of culture and nature. Most university museums have natural science or natural history sections that display animals as specimens. Dodd et al. (2013) show that there are ideological, cultural and pragmatic dimensions that lay behind museum collections and displays of animals. Knowledge about animals is established as a combination of scientific and cultural practices. This cultural perspective on knowledge production of nature is important, as our perceptions of animals are closely correlated with ways of displaying them and our perceptions guide our actions in relationship to animals.

In a future exhibition design process, key concerns are how to exhibit relational materialities and immaterialities. We believe it can be done. But objects cannot do it alone. They need to be contextualized. The things we have collected are contextual in several ways. They both witness and they make relationships between humans and horses. They are also telling of relationships between the riders and us as interviewers. It is here, in the interview context, that the narrated objects get identities. Moreover, as grounded in narratives that arise in contexts, they do not always have a clear boundary, like Emma's window, which is "a path to something else." Left alone at the museum, this window, as well as the other items, will enter new contexts. Narratives need to follow the objects into the museum. Thus any design effort into exhibition making would need to strongly link the three museum fields of work: documentation, collection and exhibition. Our study has first and foremost presented the background knowledge for beginning the design process.

The road from research and documentation of human horse relations to museum collections and exhibitions has its cobblestones. There are limits to displaying relational materialities. But the theme is important. Animals matter to human becoming, things matter, and paraphrasing Preda (1999, 364), we think that re-conceptualizing our relationships to things and animals will help us see the social world anew and move us toward a better understanding of how our relationship to things and animals changes us. Museums are good places for working at these re-conceptualizations.

Notes

1 Interviewees were recruited at competition events and clinics, in riders' homes, and at local barns and riding facilities. All interviews were recorded and later transcribed. Transcribed interviews ranged from 10 to 28 double spaced pages. Data were collected summer 2011 to spring 2012.

2 They are: 1) Why do you ride? 2) Tell me about your life as a rider. 3) How does this relate to the kind of person you are? 4) How does riding relate to other aspects of your life? 5) How is your experience the same or different from the experiences of other people?

References

Argent, Gala. 2012. "Toward a Privileging of the Nonverbal: Communication, Corporeal Synchrony, and Transcendence in Humans and Horses." In *Experiencing Animal Minds: An Anthology of Animal–Human Encounters*, edited by Julie A. Smith and Robert W. Mitchell, 111–128. New York: Colombia University Press.

Barad, Karen. 2007. *Meeting the Universe Halfway. Quantum Physics and the Entanglement of Matter and Meaning*. Durham and London: Duke University Press.

Birke, Lynda. 2009. "Interwoven Lives: Understanding Human/Animal Connections." In *Investigating Human/Animal Relations in Science, Culture and Work*, edited by Tora Holmberg, 18–33. Uppsala Universitet: Centrum för genusvetenskap.

Birke, Lynda and Keri Brandt. 2009. "Mutual Corporeality: Gender and Horse/Human Relationships." *Women's Studies International Forum*, 32: 189–197.

Birke, Lynda, Mette Bryld and Nina Lykke. 2004. "Animal Performances. An Exploration of Intersections between Feminist Science Studies and Studies of Human/Animal Relationships." *Feminist Theory* 5: 167–183.

Brandt, Keri. 2004. "A Language of Their Own: An Interactionist Approach to Human–Horse Communication." *Society & Animals* 12(4): 299–316.

Brandt, Keri. 2006. "Intelligent Bodies: Embodied Subjectivity in Human-Horse Communication." In *Body/Embodiment. Symbolic Interaction and the Sociology of the Body*, edited by Dennis Waskul and Philip Vannini, 141–153. Hampshire: Ashgate.

Damsholt, Tine and Dorthe Gert Simonsen. 2009. "Materialiseringer. Processer, relationer og performativitet" [Materializations, Processes, Relations and Performance], In *Materialiseringer. Nye Perspektiver på Materialitet og Kulturanalyse* [Materializations, New Perspectives on Materiality and Cultural Analysis], edited by Tine Damsholt, Dorthe Gert Simonsen and Camilla Mordhorst, 9–39. Aarhus: Aarhus Universitetsforlag.

Davis, Dona, Anita Maurstad and Sarah Cowles. 2013. "'Riding up Forested Mountain Sides, in Wide Open Spaces, and with Walls': Developing an Ecology of Horse–Human Relationships." *Humanimalia* 4(2): 54–83.

Despret, Vinciane. 2004. "The Body We Care For: Figures of Anthropo-zoo-genesis." *Body & Society* 10(2–3): 111–134.

Dodd, Adam, Karen A. Rader and Liv Emma Thorsen. 2013. "Introduction." In *Animals on Display: The Creaturely in Museums, Zoos, and Natural History*, edited by Liv Emma Thorsen, Karen A. Rader and Adam Dodd, 1–11. Pennsylvania State University Press.

Game, Ann. 2001. "Riding: Embodying the Centaur." *Body & Society* 7(4): 1–12.

Howes, David. 2005. "Introduction: Empires of the Senses." In *Empire of the Senses*, edited by David Howes, 1–17. Oxford, New York: Berg.

Ingold, Tim. 2013. "Prospect." In *Biosocial Becomings: Integrating Social and Biological Anthropology*, edited by Tim Ingold and Gisli Pálsson, 1–22. Cambridge: Cambridge University Press.

Ingold, Tim and Gisli Pálsson. 2013. *Biosocial Becomings: Integrating Social and Biological Anthropology*. Cambridge: Cambridge University Press.

Johansen, Anders. 2002. "Museet i Dagens Mediesituasjon" [The Museum in Today's Media Situation]. In *Tingenes Tale. Innspill til Museologi* [Object's Talk, Input to Museology], edited by Anders Johansen, Kari Gaarder Losnedahl and Hans-Jakob Ågotnes, 192–209. Universitetet i Bergen: Bergen Museums Skrifter.

Kirksey, S. Eben and Stefan Helmreich. 2010. "The Emergence of Multispecies Ethnography." *Cultural Anthropology* 25(4): 545–576.

Law, John. 1999. "After ANT: Complexity, Naming and Topology." In *Actor Network Theory and After*, edited by John Law and John Hassard, 1–15. Oxford: Blackwell Publishers/The Sociological Review.

Law, John, and Annemarie Mol. 1995. "Notes on Materiality and Sociality." *The Sociological Review* 43: 274–294.

Maurstad, Anita, Dona Davis and Sarah Cowles. 2013. "Co-being and Intra-action in Horse–Human Relationships: A Multi-species Ethnography of Be(com)ing Human and Be(com)ing Horse." *Social Anthropology* 21(3): 322–355.

Miller, Daniel. 2005. *Materiality*. Durham and London: Duke University Press.

Miller, Daniel. 2010. *Stuff*. Cambridge: Polity Press.

Mol, Annemarie. 1999. "Ontological Politics. A Word and Some Questions." In *Actor Network Theory and After*, edited by John Law and John Hassard, 74–90. Oxford: Blackwell Publishers/The Sociological Review.

Ofstad, Ellen. 2014. "Kommunikasjon og Motivasjon: Godbiter fra Ellen Ofstad" [Communication and Motivation: Treats from Ellen Ofstad]. *Islandshest, Medlemsblad for Norsk Islandshestforening*. [Icelandic Horse Society Magazine] 2: 16–19. Lindesnes: Arena Media as.

Pálsson, Gisli. 2013. "Ensembles of Biosocial Relations." In *Integrating Social and Biological Anthropology*, edited by Tim Ingold and Gisli Pálsson, 22–42. Cambridge: Cambridge University Press.

Preda, Alex. 1999. "The Turn to Things: Arguments for a Sociological Theory of Things." *Sociological Quarterly* 20(2): 347–366.

Quinn, Naomi. 2005. "Introduction." In *Finding Culture in Talk: A Collection of Methods*, edited by Naomi Quinn, 1–34. New York: Palgrave.

Wipper, Audrey. 2000. "The Partnership: The Horse–Rider Relationship in Eventing." *Symbolic Interaction* 23(1): 47–70.

13 Biosocial Encounters and the Meaning of Horses

Anita Maurstad and Dona Lee Davis

Multispecies ethnographers seek to explore and understand the complex kinds of relationships that humans form with other animals. The aim is not to characterize humans in contrast to other living beings (Hamilton and Placas 2011), but to bring other species back into anthropology (Kirksey and Helmreich 2010). The concept of multispecies ethnography arises in a time when a wide variety of disciplines are questioning the nature–culture split and challenging the division of labor between the natural and social sciences. The philosopher and quantum physicist Barad (2007, 139) develops the idea of "intra-action," as a way of crossing boundaries between nature and culture, nonhumans and humans, and the social and natural sciences. She employs the term "inter-acting" to describe a process where persons, objects and instruments of observation meet but part unchanged. In contrast, "intra-acting" entails a kind of engagement or entanglement that changes the participants. Referring to these participants or entities as "relata", Barad states "relata do not preexist relations; rather, relata-within-phenomena emerge through specific intra-actions" (Barad 2007, 140). Haraway (2008, 17) applies this thinking to human animal relations, stating that "The partners do not precede their relating; all that is, is the fruit of becoming with: those are the mantras of companion species." An intra-actionist approach is also foundational for those involved in Actor-Network-Theory. In a review of the discipline's status in 1999, Law (1999, 4) discusses "relational materiality" as a concept that covers how entities (or things) achieve their form "as a consequence of the relations in which they are located."

Within this new theoretical language for understanding human society and its relations to nature "biosocial becomings" (Ingold 2013, 9) is a newcomer. 'Biosocial' is not a new concept. It was for instance used in 1969 with the new *Journal of Biosocial Science* (Pálsson 2009). In its former meanings, the goal was to forge a common ground between biology and sociology. Today, as used in their recently edited volume, Ingold and Pálsson (2013) apply the concept to similar processes as those discussed by Barad (2007), Haraway (2008), and Law (1999), but embed it in new frames and frameworks. As such it supports and expands perspectives on intra-actions and relational materialities. More specifically, Ingold (2013) discusses evolution as a life process and maintains that we give primacy to processes of ontogenesis. Ontogenesis entails how individual organisms grow, not as bounded entities, but within a greatly expanded field of relations. Environment, in this sense, can best be understood as "a zone of interpenetration [...] [where] organisms grow to take on the forms they do, incorporating into themselves the lifelines of other organisms as they do so" (Ingold 2013, 11). Furthermore, a theory on biosocial becomings entails that we "think of humans, and indeed all creatures of all other kinds, in terms not of what they *are*, but of what they *do*" (Ingold 2013, 8, original emphasis). In this line of thought, with the focus set on performance, humans are not to be seen "as species beings, but as biosocial becomings" (Ingold 2013, 9).

The present volume is unique in that it is the first multispecies ethnography volume on horses. It employs a cross-cultural perspective to engage what is variable and what is universal in horse human relationships. With the aid of a multispecies ethnographic lens, the chapters explore new ways of seeing how horse and human lives can be intertwined in everyday life, through time, as well as across a range of activities and transactions. In this last chapter of the book, we revisit the contributors' chapters with special emphasis on practices that matter to horse and human as biosocial becomings. What distinguishes the idea of biosocial becomings from more bioculturally oriented concepts (e.g., Goodman, 2013) is an emphasis on sociality and the social constitution of being (Pálsson 2013). Here, we will sharpen the focus and look at how the ethnographies explicate the dynamic and multiple practices by which humans become with horses in more detail. First, we focus on horses and humans and the various ways they are co-involved in the processes of biosocial becoming. Next, we address horses as agentive partners in human engagements. Third, we take a closer look at encounter values as forms of practice but also as realms of meaning – how we deal with animals influences how we see them (to paraphrase Dodd et al. 2013). In the final section of the chapter we engage those who have been critical of multispecies ethnography and argue the need for research that focuses on practices, relations and processes in order to increase understanding about how humans and horses grow as biosocial becomings.

Biosocial becomings

Human entanglement with horses has a long history. It goes back at least 6,000 years (see Chapter 1). Oma (Chapter 2) takes us back 1,000 to 1,500 years as she explores the ontological statuses of horses in two different historical situations. In pagan, Iron Age, tribal Scandinavia horses were engaged in multiple intra-activities with humans. Horses had symbolic roles in transgressing borders between life and death and were the primary sacrificial animal both in collective bog sacrifices and in more private contexts. Religious practices included feasting on horseflesh in honor of the pagan gods Thor and Odin. Horses were also understood to share cognitive capacities with humans. They could, for instance, grieve with humans.

With the new state formation that accompanied the introduction of Christianity, horses' roles in human lives changed. The ontological status of horses as holding dominion over the cosmological landscape, traversing boundaries between spheres of life and death, threatened the Church and undermined the foundation of the new state and its Christian laws. Horses had to give way for Jesus. To eradicate the Iron Age cult and its religious practices the earliest Christian laws forbade the consumption of horseflesh. Failure to follow the new laws was punished with loss of property or even being banished from the country. Oma finds, however, that the symbolic role of horses lived on in secret, at least to early medieval times. Since then humans as biosocial becomings have changed. Today, unlike the people of the Iron Age described by Oma, very few Scandinavians enjoy the bodily sensation of eating horseflesh.

Yet, horses and humans also become together in modern societies although the relationship may be enacted in a number of different ways. The volume adds insights into how horses are implicated in the formation of national, cultural and regional identities from a range of countries including Egypt, Mexico, Mongolia, Finland, Western Ireland, and indigenous peoples in the American West. Horses and humans also intra-act as individuals as seen in chapters on individual becomings from Norway, Great Britain, Spain and Midwest US. Interestingly however, practices with horses reveal similar stories within this range of environments. In a biosocial perspective, there is something about what humans and horses do together. Their combined activities create, effect, and affect the worlds (however defined: horse human, individual or collective, material or symbolic) that they share together.

In Ireland, for example, people in the Connemara district have for a long time intertwined their lives with the pony (Brown, Chapter 5). Complex symbolic and material processes shape these practices. Connemara ponies are sold at markets as breeding stock and as potential competitors or athletes. At markets the ponies are subjected to the buyers' gaze. Observers discuss what they see, and more importantly, what they want to see. Conformation is critically evaluated. The breeding for new or improved characteristics is noted and debated. When elements of this discourse are materialized in official protocols, they set guidelines or standards for evaluating beauty and performance. As they come to define the distinctiveness of the breed, the protocols become regimens of what the horse should be. These descriptions travel well beyond regional and national boundaries as the ponies are marketed globally. Discussions and protocols are elements that also shape humans. Brown describes how people see the horse as a symbol of themselves and transformations in horse are likened to transformation in human identities. The ponies have come to symbolize economic oppression and the hardship and suffering of the past. Like their ponies the Connemara people have had the strength to persevere through times of adversity.

How human identities are intrinsically linked to horses among the Native Americans is the topic of Seifert's ethnography (Chapter 10). Horses embody a cultural continuity with the past and there is a deeply felt mutual ontogenetic relationship, or a series of becomings, between horses and the Nez Perce. The Nez Perce practiced selective breeding in the late 17th century and were noted for their fine horses. However, the US army took away their horses in the 19th century as punishment for refusal to ratify a treaty with the United States. This historic event is still a raw, painful trauma for the Nez Perce. Contemporary Nez Perce identify their past lives as intertwined with horses, and they seek to pursue, reestablish and reinvent former practices. The Nez Perce have begun to breed horses again, trying to refine and improve the physical type that their ancestors rode. They are, however, not only breeding for the horses' biological attributes but also their horses' social attributes. Former tribal equestrian social practices are sought and brought to life with new social activities, such as taking young people to travel over historical landscapes, thus introducing young people to their equestrian heritage.

The breeding of Arab horses by humans in Egypt is also done for purposes of identity and tradition. In addition, Lange (Chapter 3) finds that the mainstream establishment of the global Arabian horse world breeds for conformation and aesthetics. When trained, horses are not ridden. Rather, they are trained to present themselves as good looking. With reference to concepts in performance art, Lange sees these breeding activities as a process of composing living sculptures. A sophisticated and discerning human knowledge of horse beauty confers human memberships in the exclusive communities of these breeders. At the same time, Tahawi Bedouins breed for a different set of horse meanings in which riding qualities matter more. Despite these differences, there is a parallel between the two Egyptian practices of breeding and the cases that Brown and Seifert describe: humans see themselves and acquire their identities, not only from being with horses, but also from transforming horses in accordance with ideas about who humans are. Breeding is often thought of as a strictly biological phenomenon. After all, it is about creating or as breeders would say, enhancing a species. What these chapters show, however, is how socially and culturally rooted breeding is. Breeding creates a horse type that, according to Gilbert and Gillett (2012, 633) becomes "a material and cultural artifact." There are certain cultural ideals about what the horses should look like, and they differ among the Connemara, Arab and Nez Perce horses. What is same and similar are the human debates over attributes preferred. Ideals are debated and become materialized in protocols and studbooks, where they have profound effects on horses as symbol and soma-form through time and space. These breeding standards, protocols and ideals of beauty, performance, and function also affect the humans who breed horses. Breeding speaks, in these cases, to who people want to be, to individual and collective identities. They engender not only how a people identify with a past but how they renegotiate the past into the present and the future. As such, these contributions are relevant examples of how both society and individual identities are structured through intra-actions with animals. These breeding standards and practices describe how culturally specific knowledge systems, marked by distinctive styles and practices of horsemanship, serve to link peoples or societies with their past, distinguish them from others, and place them within intersections of local, national and global economies.

The volume also addresses one-on-one intra-actions between horses and humans, in this case a pregnant blogger (Chapter 9). At first glance becoming pregnant by itself does not seem to be a kind of intra-activity, at least not between human and horse. But as the woman's material body changes she describes how it affects her relationship to the horse. Through a detailed focus on social activities and thoughts, the authors reveal how the pregnant woman, this new biosocial becoming, engages in new activities with the horse, and these are activities that change the horse. As the pregnancy progresses, the woman walks the horse instead of riding her. The horse transforms from being a riding partner to becoming a walking companion. This also transforms the woman. From having a body fit for riding before pregnancy, she feels as if her muscles are "blown into atoms" when starting to ride after the birth of her child.

Schuurman and Sireni (Chapter 9) also provide insight into more psychological and material dimensions of the relationship, and actions that follow. The affective relationship the woman has with the horse changes into one also consisting of guilt, while pregnant, for not spending enough time with the horse. When the baby arrives, the woman feels guilty about not spending enough time with the baby. As the baby grows older, she brings the child along to the riding premises in a pram, and pauses at the pram during rides to look to the child. The horse picks up on this activity and begins to initiate such pauses at the pram herself. The pram becomes visible as a material element in the environment that has effects. In fact, it becomes included in the ontogenesis of the horse human relationship that itself develops as a part of an expanding field of relations. Focusing also on non-horse people's part in the horse human relation: here, they are the experts that state that riding is dangerous during pregnancy, we see more zones of penetration (Ingold 2013). In the blogger's narrative horse and human, together, become linked to other life-lines in the environment. Looking at pregnancy in this biosocial perspective thus places the biological and the social within one or the same domain (Ingold 2013).

Affective and biosocial dimensions of the human horse relationship are also of concern in Maurstad, Davis and Dean's Chapter 12. Here, the authors identify and describe the sensuous, emotional and material effects and affects of horse human communication and collaboration. Through the authors' focus on how objects contribute to social activities with horses, this chapter sheds light on the fact that humans and horses also become in engagements with things. Objects like brushes, well-fitting saddles, bits and reins attached to the bits are hardly static entities. They are agentive and transformative in the relationship. The authors' point is that activities matter. Use of reins, saddles and brushes enacts versions of both horses and humans. The human's use of reins enacts humans as either delicate, giving riders (soft on the mouth) or rough, restricting riders (hard on the mouth). Likewise, horses become either soft and giving on the mouth or hard and unyielding on the mouth. The analysis also reveals the intra-connections between the biological and the social. The very smell of the horse is something noted by one of the informants, who says she "wears it always." Horse human relationships and becomings are about much more than sitting on the horse, sensing two bodies intra-acting. It is about seeing that there are intra-connections between and within a range of materialities and immaterialities as they come to matter in some more or less predictable but also, as the case of Judy's husbands illustrates, in idiosyncratic and surprising ways.

This point of a specific situational or wider encompassing context is further elaborated when Dashper (Chapter 6) writes about riding in an arena with a trainer. Dashper recognizes arenas as environments where all sorts of intra-actions take place. These can include strong winds that cause buckets to fly and horses to spook. Certainly flying buckets influence the way a horse and human communicate, but Dashper is more interested in the triadic kinds of communication that occur among the trainer, horse and rider. All three parties are engaged in the activity of communicating a rider's intentions to a horse and instructing the horse to perform certain actions. The trainer becomes part of the rider as she is the 'eyes on the ground.' She observes performances and translates what she sees. The instructor constantly evaluates and gives feedback based on how horse and rider actions meet with her expectations. Usually she verbalizes what social actions are needed, in order for the two bodies or intra-actors to change and improve what they are doing. But she can also sit herself on the horse, making imprints that last. Emplaced on the horse, the instructor correctly and effectively signals the right bodily actions, what Dashper calls kinesthetic empathy. The more novice rider remounts afterwards and makes use of the new imprints that have been established in the physical and mental body of the horse.

Dashper's approach is highly reflective and incorporates analysis of her own experiences as a rider taking a lesson. We, the readers, ride with her as in her narrative she masters the medium trot. Engagements with horses, she argues, add a new sense to the human repertoire, that of feel. Rider feel is a specific encounter value that many have written about as a highly sought sensation (Game 2001; Maurstad et al. 2013). The biosocial perspective allows for a more nuanced or detailed understanding of this process of feeling. As Dashper demonstrates, horses are not constrained by Western modes of thinking about sensation. The illiterate horse does not know that humans have labeled only five senses. Riding horses activates a combined sensory apparatus of humans and horses. Activities transform humans as biosocial becomings, providing them with new senses. In addition, Dashper's chapter points to the fact that it takes lifetimes to know how to do things better with horses. Engagements with horses are lifelong social activities with effects on both horse and human bodies.

Processual effects on intra-acting bodies are also the focus of DiGiacomo (Chapter 8). She analyzes the equestrian sport of dressage as on-going conversations between horse and human minds and bodies. As a young woman recovering from cancer treatment, DiGiacomo began two life processes simultaneously. She started training for anthropology as well as riding. She experiences how, at that time in her life, riding joined her body and mind in what she calls 'a paradoxical condition of unselfconscious self-awareness.' Her point is that riding and writing at these life stages was not therapeutic. Instead these practices were about becoming as an individual; it was a kind of strongly felt self-realization. In focusing on the personalities of, and practices with, the two horses she rides, CC and Flamingo, she also demonstrates that the meaning of horses is multiple. The horses are agentive in their relationships with DiGiacomo in different ways. Coming to dislike his job as a riding school horse, CC stopped responding to human wishes after a while. When sold to DiGiacomo, he relaxed and she can now teach him various dressage exercises. He is not, however, as skilled as a highly schooled horse she also rides. Flamingo has a 'pedagogical vocation,' she says, and in this relationship it is the horse that is the teacher.

Applying a biosocial perspective to various ethnographies of horse human entanglements in varied geographical and cultural contexts, we have focused upon how horse and human intra-activities come to effect the growth of the two parties as organisms. With the exception of Maurstad, Davis and Dean, the different contributors to this volume do not use the concept of biosocial becomings in their analysis. Yet, their enriched and detailed accounts of a variety of social practices and engagements with horses fit well with a perspective that frames activities as intra-actions and biosocial becomings. As partners that intra-act, both horse and human change by engaging with each other. The narratives specifically point to how, as mutuality or affinity develops, biology and sociality is one and same domain (Ingold 2013).

Agency

Throughout the ethnographies in this volume, horses are awarded agency. The author that most explicitly presents agentive practices is Marchina (Chapter 7), who writes about the Mongolian practices of capturing horses from fenceless pastures or the wide-open steppes. The process involves a rider, a horse and the material object of a lasso-pole. The rider selects a horse to be captured and chases the horse together with the lasso-pole horse and the lasso-pole. The ideal is to put the noose of the lasso-pole around the horse's neck, bringing him or her to a standstill. If the captured horse is familiar with this procedure, the horse often settles when captured. If not, more of a struggle is involved. The ridden horse is taught to sit back on his or her haunches in order to anchor the rider, the horse and the lasso-pole against the captured horse. Horses who show promise are selected and trained to work as lasso-pole horses. When knowing what to do, it is expected that a good horse will make his or her own decisions, and run in the right direction with minimal aids or interference from the rider. A good horse also shows initiative when he or she, without aids from the rider, takes off at a gallop when moving away from an encampment and slows down when approaching a yurt. Not all horses do this, but those who do are treasured. Mongolians appreciate the specific skills of a horse but they also value other equine attributes such as spiritual character, intelligence and alertness in their horses.

Mongolians speak of horses that think and make their own choices in horse human activities. Conceptualizing agentive practices in a relational perspective, we also focus on more subtle agentive practices, such as how horses stimulate human activities and are part of human growth processes. We apply Barad's (2007, 141) dynamic look at agency: "Agency is not an attribute but the ongoing reconfigurings of the world." Thus, agency is not a static or passive state of being; instead, agency involves intra-acting partners. In using a relational framework that perceives parties as intra-acting with or affecting each other, we pay particular attention to the very practices that horses initiate with humans. Mongolians appreciate horses that think and make their own choices, but they also express how practices matter to horse and human becoming. Repeated actions, shared collaborative routines and training are the basis for creating a successful team. Moreover, horses structure Mongolian society. It is men who deal with horses, and kids start early on to practice riding in the ways needed for being good at capturing horses later on. As part of their growing up as Mongolians on the steppes, or their ontogenesis from a biosocial perspective, kids both train their own riding skills, as well as explore the potentials a horse might have as lasso-pole horse by exercising the necessary maneuvers at full gallop. Kids' play as learning to work in this culture is thus crucial for both humans and horses as biosocial becomings. As with human identities, horse identities are fluid rather than fixed. They move in and out of the category lasso-pole horse as they shift between being herd horses, horses at work and horses as playmates.

In Leinonen's chapter on changing cultural models of the Finnhorse (Chapter 4), people's narratives show that horses have had different agentive roles over time. The workhorses of pre-industrial Finland are seen as hard-working and trusting, enjoying their work with humans. Yet these connections to human lived lives and ideas about horses come to expand, change and multiply through time. As warhorses they are heroes, attributed with a real willingness to go to war with humans, and fight with their fellow Finns. Today roles for horses are more versatile. Horses are still viewed as servants but have now entered the service industry and perform psychological services (therapy) for humans. Horses might not reflect on these changes themselves, but in a relational perspective horses as agents engage humans as farmer/logger peasants, warriors and clients, respectively. They are different biosocial becomings in the different time periods that inform Leinonen's chapter. Like Seifert, she also makes the point that the past persists in the present. But Leinonen's past is the lifetimes of her informants as she makes the point that perspectives of an older type of horse persist in the minds, memories and bodies of her informants. Among the Finnish people, individually and collectively, childhood experiences, their early encounters with horses, have made lasting imprints on human minds and bodies.

Also writing about modern versions of traditional practices, Ramírez (Chapter 11) presents a type of riding that fails to recognize the embodied mutuality between horse and rider. This ethnography may be taken to indicate that horses viewed as dispensable or exchangeable objects are not awarded agency. However, in the Mexican rodeos, horses are agentive in the sense that they are needed for the female equestrian drill teams, the *escaramuzas charras*. They enable the cultural presentation of gender. They also inspire Ramírez to take action. Ramírez is critical of practices harmful to both the body and mind of the horses used in this sport. These include use of harsh bits and spurs, as well as saddles designed to benefit the presentation of the rider, but which prohibit the rider from feeling the horse's back. In an intra-actionist approach, however, she leads a movement for more humane performances, even going so far as to assemble a team who ride well and perform complex maneuvers without bridles.

Discussing things' participation in human actions, Latour (2005, 72) maintains that: "In addition to 'determining' and serving as a 'backdrop for human action' things might authorize, allow, afford, encourage, permit, suggest, influence, block, render possible, forbid and so on." Atkinson and Gibson (2014, 287) apply Latour's perspectives to the study of humans and animals and maintain that such studies must "recognize how interaction with animals 'might authorize, allow, afford [... and so on]' our own actions as well as those of animals." While we certainly stress that the agencies of elements with personalities, horses, are different from those of things, this section has shown that horses do 'allow, encourage, influence and render possible' a set of human actions. In intra-activities, horses are, indeed, embodied and influential partners. Although the agency of the horse is certainly shaped, contained or constrained by horse human intra-actions, humans do see horses as agentive partners. Seeing agency as an intrinsic aspect of practices in which horse with human stimulate and initiate certain activities, the contributors have addressed both historic and present day situations where horse agencies become visible. It should also be noted that this section has focused on three chapters in particular, but horse agencies run through all the narratives in this volume.

So far we have commented on agentive qualities that horses reveal in relational activities with humans. Another relational quality is that of "encounter value," a term Haraway (2008, 46) uses to addresses commercial, as well as non-commercial, relations that embed dogs in society and culture.

While Haraway discusses value-added dogs, we will attend to aspects of horses' encounter value in the next section.

Encounter values

Gilbert and Gillett (2012) refer to Haraway's (2008, 46) concept of "encounter value" in analyzing values pertaining to the commercial breeding, marketing and sale of sport ponies. They point to an interesting relationship between encounter values and monetary values. A high encounter value from training may be reflected in the price when the horse is sold. A horse that has been entangling with humans is also different in more respects than one who does not have these experiences. For example, if a rider has bonded with the horse, and/or if the parents of the children who ride the ponies have bonded with the horse, the price may rise even higher. The encounter value may exceed that of the pony's monetary value. As such, encounter values are interesting economic variables. They can be accounted for and measured as the above example suggests. Encounter values may also be viewed in terms of embodied sensations that underlay processes of biosocial becomings on the human's part. These need not always be positive. For example a person may need to sell a horse for a variety of reasons, including economic and social reasons, and find it very painful to part from a horse partner. Encounter values in and between horse and human can explain such pain. Growing together over years, the human may feel that she is selling a part of herself. A number of Sarah Dean's trail riding informants, like Judy and her husbands (Chapter 12), privileged the encounter value of their horses over those of their partners or husbands.

Encounter values then, are of monetary and non-monetary kinds. We find both reflected in the chapters of this volume. In Part I, which focuses on commodification and identity, Oma elaborates on encounter values of the religious and symbolic kind. Horses were well emplaced in the Iron Age economy. Lange and Brown describe horses as internationally marketed commodities. Horses are contested units of value and represent both traditional and modern identities. This is also reflected in Leinonen's chapter as she presents several horse types; workmates and healers are extremes at a continuum spanning a hundred years. What is same and similar in this section of the volume is a focus on how horses are embedded as capital in parts of larger economic systems.

In Part II on communication and relation, the more non-monetary values come to the fore. Dashper and DiGiacomo elaborate on horse human encounters in performance and sport. These authors shed light on a different set of encounter values, those particular to a particular partnership between horse and human. Partnership is also explored in Schuurman and Sireni's chapter, where the horse is part of the household pregnancy. Intimacy and close bonds characterize these relationships. The horse is friend, household member and part of the extended family. On the Mongolian steppes horse encounters are part of larger systems. As Marchina writes, they move in and out of one-on-one human encounters dependent on this pastoralist culture's needs.

In Part III on performance, practice and presentation, the focus shifts to more generic and collective types of encounter values. Seifert and Ramírez write about horses as valuable cultural bearers, while Maurstad, Davis and Dean focus on encounters that include a wide variety of material, as well as less material elements such as the more sensual, less palpable experiences of horse human relationships.

Encounter values are varied in that they may be particular to a specific partnership, but also generic. To a particular pair of horse and human, there are effects and affects from mutually growing together, a sense of co-being arising with everyday practices that engage horse and human (Maurstad et al. 2013). Horses also shift roles through time, and across cultures, and they are meaningful on local and national levels, to personal as well as collective identities. Meanings of horses are hardly constant or static, but variously and broadly defined. The chapters in this volume document how various forms of horse human engagements or entanglement intra-act to configure individual and collective identities and boundaries among horse human, self and other. Identities in this sense are not fixed as they develop and take shape through encounters. In sum, horse human encounters are meshworks; complex interwoven series of mutualities, webs of action, intra-action and meaning that shape horse human engagements. The next section, which is our concluding section, will focus on the need for more research into these meshworks.

Studying animals

Ways we study animals influence what we see, and what we see influences ways we study. In an edited volume on scientific practices with animals (Dodd et al. 2013), the different contributors show how ideas about animals arise as a combination of scientific and cultural practices. Discussing the practices behind displaying the famous Saint Bernard named Barry, Thorsen (2013) illustrates this point with reference to how Barry is displayed in two different time periods. Barry lived in a group of hospice dogs that were known for rescuing people that got lost on the snowy paths of the Swiss Alps. Originally displayed at the Natural History Museum of Bern in 1815, one year after his death, he was presented as the servant of his time. His body was mounted to signal a humble attitude and his head was lowered. Portrayals of the heroic Barry in the second half of the nineteenth century did impact the shaping of the breed Saint Bernard. Being mounted anew in 1923, however, he was presented with ideas of the new time. The small humble dog did not serve the new ideas right. Now he holds his head upright, standing high and alert. Thorsen makes the point that in fact he is too tall according to the biology of a dog: "the mount from 1923 is about ten centimeters taller than Barry had been, making the dog nearly as tall as he is long, proportions that are absent in all dog breeds" (Thorsen 2013, 144). Thorsen's work frames Barry as an interesting biosocial becoming, one where the social has had a clear impact on dog's biology.

We bring in this example to illustrate that scientific as well as cultural ideas about animals often have a direct effect on their reality. Scientific research on human animal intra-actions may reveal such processes through which ideas shape ontologies. Theoretically and empirically, multispecies research can lead to new insights into the co-constitution of humans and animals as biosocial becomings. Multispecies ethnography is not a radical break with former perspectives. It is more of a difference in emphasis: as we refocus here, from interaction to intra-action, and from being to doing. There are, however, some critical voices as to how multispecies ethnography research should be conducted. Atkinson and Gibson (2014, 270) critique the work of Haraway (2008) for "replicating a very human exemptionalist perspective of animals as objects of use." These scholars could also criticize the contributors in the present volume for speaking of horses as objects for human use. In some situations they are objects. Ramírez's ethnography illustrates a cultural neglect of important animal sensations and a lack of sensory feedback between horse and rider. The multispecies ethnographic perspective, however, also in Ramírez's account, focuses on practices, on how intra-activities shape both humans and horses, and this presupposes a subject interest in the horses. Moreover, the intra-activities that are described in this volume show that humans see the horses with whom they engage as subjects. They see personalities; talent, intellects, spiritual and alert characters – that is, a range of subject qualities in terms of the diversity that exists in being a horse. In the daily encounters with horses humans cannot avoid seeing horses as personalities. Some charm humans, others are detestable; there is a range of horse personalities to be perceived (Davis et al. n.d.).

Another critical concern of Atkinson and Gibson (2014), and also Kemmerer (2011), is that studies of animals should recognize the unequal power balance between humans and animals. Kemmerer (2011) actually warns against theorizing about animals, as these very theories may be developed to serve the interests of humans. While we certainly agree that these are fair concerns, we disagree with taking a stance not to study humans and animals, because any attempt to do so is contaminated or compromised by what would inevitably be a human-centered approach. The intra-action perspective we draw upon in this chapter to revisit and analyze the contributors' descriptions of various horse human encounters reveals a range of practices that shed light on horses and humans as biosocial becomings in ways that go beyond merely the serving of human interests. As employed by the contributors, the multispecies perspective actually centers horses in description and analysis. Taken together and individually by situating horse human in a variety of topics, times and places the contributors make horses more visible. Individually and together, the authors create necessary insights and identify a nuanced series of junctures for exploring the balance of power among humans and horses. Again, we refer to Ramírez, who writes about the human sport of *charreada* and how the sport is embedded in human culture. She expresses concerns over treatment of the horse in these activities but she also offers solutions or strategies for a more humane sport. It is possible to ride a horse with less harmful gear, while still performing well in the *charreada*. Likewise, contributors are sensitive to power issues, both presenting them and subjecting them to critical analysis. Leinonen, in discussing how horses are talked about during the different eras of the last century, touches upon power issues as she points to different models of human horse partnerships, that of friend and that of leader. These, as well as the other chapters in this volume, provide rich ethnographic narratives on horse human encounters that contribute to a greater understanding of how horse human practices, as intra-active processes, shape ontologies and meanings.

In conclusion, this volume's research on horse human encounters presents ethnographic tales from a number of situations where biosocial becomings grow relationally. The chapters contribute to biosocial theory "highlighting a move from states of being and discrete things with given essences and identities to movement, relations and processes" (Pálsson 2013, 244). This final chapter has sought to establish how the concept "biosocial becoming" (Ingold 2013, 9) expands and enriches former concepts in the theoretical language for understanding human society and its relations to nature. Scholars in various disciplines have focused human becoming with other entities or 'relata' through concepts like "become with" each other (Haraway 2008, 17), as "relational materialities" (Law 1999, 4), as "relata-within-phenomena [that] emerge through specific intra-actions" (Barad 2007, 140). In accordance with Pálsson (2013, 243), who maintains that "the pragmatics of purpose and becoming need to be reintroduced into accounts of the unfolding of life," we have used biosocial becoming, this newcomer to the theoretical field, to view these more mundane aspects of social practice. The contributors to the volume focus on everyday practices between horses and humans, as individuals and collectivities, and show how horses act upon humans in "surprising and nuanced ways," an outcome that multispecies ethnographer Hayward (2010, 584) advocates as a benefit of the discipline. It is our contention that multispecies ethnography and biosocial theory bring animals, literally, together with humans in ways that open up new frameworks for anthropological analysis and understanding that move beyond reductionist or essentialist dichotomies of nature and culture and human and animal.

References

Atkinson, Michael and Kass Gibson. 2014. "Communion without Collision: Animals, Sport, and Interspecies Co-presence." In *Sport, Animals, and Society*, edited by James Gillett and Michelle Gilbert, 268–289. New York: Routledge.

Barad, Karen. 2007. *Meeting the Universe Halfway. Quantum Physics and the Entanglement of Matter and Meaning*. Durham and London: Duke University Press.

Davis, Dona, Anita Maurstad and Sarah Dean. n.d. "Barn Banter: An Exploration of Anthropomorphism and Equine-o-morphism as Agency." In *Equine Agency in Human Horse Relations*, edited by Gala Argent, (forthcoming). Pittsburgh: Pennsylvania State University Press.

Dodd, Adam, Karen A. Rader, and Liv Emma Thorsen. 2013. "Introduction." In *Animals on Display: The Creaturely in Museums, Zoos, and Natural History*, edited by Liv Emma Thorsen, Karen A. Rader and Adam Dodd, 1–11. Philadelphia, PA: Pennsylvania State University Press.

Game, Ann. 2001. "Riding: Embodying the Centaur." *Body & Society* 7(4): 1–12.

Gilbert, Michelle and James Gillett. 2012. "Equine Athletes and Interspecies Sport." *International Review for the Sociology of Sport* 47(5): 632–643.

Goodman, Alan. 2013. "Bringing Culture into Human Biology and Biology Back into Anthropology." *American Anthropologist* 115(3): 359–373.

Hamilton, Jennifer A. and Aimee J. Placas. 2011. "Anthropology Becoming...? The Sociocultural Year in Review." *American Anthropologist* 113(2): 246–261.

Haraway, Donna. 2008. *When Species Meet*. Minneapolis: University of Minnesota Press.

Hayward, S. Eva. 2010. "Fingereyes: Impressions of Cup Corals." *Cultural Anthropology* 25(4): 577–599.

Ingold, Tim. 2013. "Prospect." In *Biosocial Becomings: Integrating Social and Biological Anthropology*, edited by Tim Ingold and Gisli Pálsson, 1–22. Cambridge: Cambridge University Press.

Ingold, Tim and Gisli Pálsson. 2013. *Biosocial Becomings: Integrating Social and Biological Anthropology*. Cambridge: Cambridge University Press.

Kemmerer, Lisa. 2011. "Theorizing 'Other'." In *Theorizing Animals. Re-thinking Humanimal Relations*, edited by Nik Taylor and Tania Signal, 59–85. Leiden: Brill.

Kirksey, S. Eben and Stefan Helmreich. 2010. "The Emergence of Multispecies Ethnography." *Cultural Anthropology* 25(4): 545–576.

Latour, Bruno. 2005. *Reassembling the Social. An Introduction to Actor-Network-Theory*. Oxford: Oxford University Press.

Law, John. 1999. "After ANT: Complexity, Naming and Topology." In *Actor Network Theory and After*, edited by John Law and John Hassard, 1–15. Oxford: Blackwell Publishers/The Sociological Review.

Maurstad, Anita, Dona Davis and Sarah Cowles. 2013. "Co-being and Intra-action in Horse–Human Relationships: A Multispecies Ethnography of Be(com)ing Human and Be(com)ing Horse." *Social Anthropology* 21(3): 322–355.

Pálsson, Gisli. 2009. "Biosocial Relations of Production." *Comparative Studies in Society and History* 51(2): 288–313.

Pálsson, Gisli. 2013. "Retrospect." In *Integrating Social and Biological Anthropology*, edited by Tim Ingold and Gisli Pálsson, 229–249. Cambridge: Cambridge University Press.

Thorsen, Liv Emma. 2013. "A Dog of Myth and Matter: Barry the Saint Bernard in Bern." In *Animals on Display: The Creaturely in Museums, Zoos, and Natural History*, edited by Liv Emma Thorsen, Karen A. Rader and Adam Dodd, 128–153. University Park: Pennsylvania State University Press.

Index

Note: Page numbers followed by an 'n' refer to notes.

Collins

AQA A-level Physics

Peter Edmunds

Organise and Retrieve your Knowledge

Acknowledgements

The author and publisher are grateful to the copyright holders for permission to use quoted materials and images.

P27: Electron diffraction pattern, © Science Photo Library

P136: View of VLA radio telescope, © Science Photo Library

Every effort has been made to trace copyright holders and obtain their permission for the use of copyright material. The author and publisher will gladly receive information enabling them to rectify any error or omission in subsequent editions.

All facts are correct at time of going to press.

Published by Collins
An imprint of HarperCollins*Publishers* Limited
1 London Bridge Street
London SE1 9GF

HarperCollins*Publishers*
Macken House
39/40 Mayor Street Upper
Dublin 1
D01 C9W8
Ireland

ISBN 978-0-00-876038-0

10 9 8 7 6 5 4 3 2 1

First published 2025

British Library Cataloguing in Publication Data.

A CIP record of this book is available from the British Library.

Author: Peter Edmunds
Practice papers adapted from content written by Carol Tear
Publisher: Clare Souza
Commissioning and editorial: Richard Toms
Inside concept design: Ian Wrigley
Layout and artwork creation: Six Red Marbles, India
Cover design: Sarah Duxbury
Production: Bethany Brohm
Printed in the United Kingdom by Martins the Printers

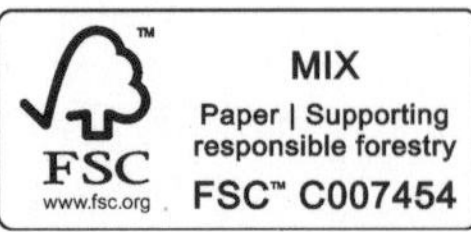

This book contains FSC™ certified paper and other controlled sources to ensure responsible forest management.

For more information visit: www.harpercollins.co.uk/green

How to use this book

Each topic is presented on a two-page spread

Use the QR code to access a support video for the topic

Topics exclusive to A-level are labelled

Make your own list of key words for the topic

Answer the key questions to ensure you understand fundamental ideas

Organise your knowledge with concise explanations and examples

Make your own summary notes using words or sketches

Embed your knowledge with retrieval questions for each topic (use separate sheets of paper if you need more space for workings)

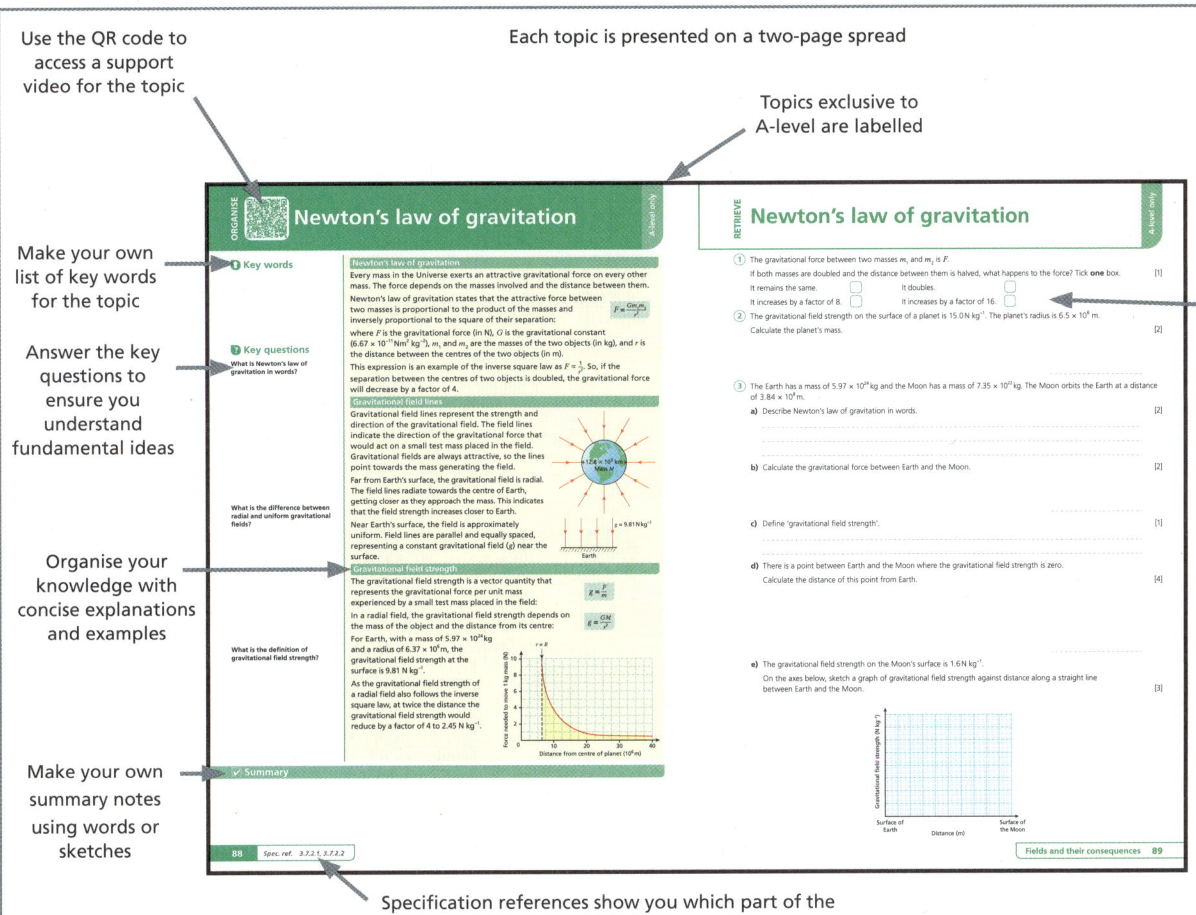

Specification references show you which part of the AQA course is being covered

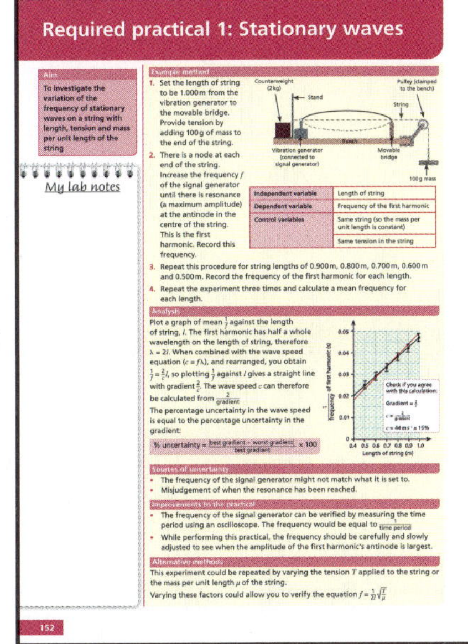

Explore each required practical and make your own supporting notes

Section B

Each of questions 7 to 31 is followed by four responses, A, B, C and D. For each question select the best response.

Only **one** answer per question is allowed.

For each answer completely fill in the circle alongside the appropriate answer.

CORRECT METHOD WRONG METHODS

If you want to change your answer, you must cross out your original answer as shown.

If you wish to return to an answer previously crossed out, ring the answer you now wish to select as shown.

0 7 A nucleus of $^{204}_{82}$Pb absorbs an alpha particle and emits a positron.

What is the product nucleus?

[1 mark]

A $^{206}_{85}$At

B $^{208}_{85}$At

C $^{208}_{83}$Bi

D $^{207}_{84}$Po

0 8 The drag force F on a spherical object of radius r falling with terminal velocity v is given by:

$F = 6\pi\eta rv$

What are the units of η?

[1 mark]

A kg m^{-1}

B kg m^{-1} s^{-1}

C kg m^{2} s^{-1}

D m s^{-2} kg^{-1}

174

Try the practice papers to help prepare for the exams

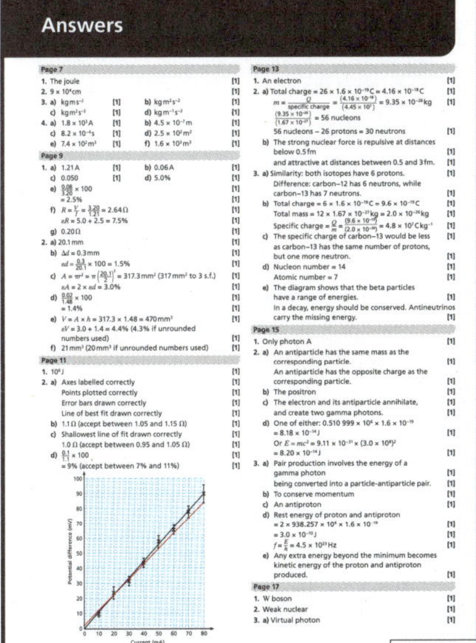

Answers are provided at the back of the book (excluding for the key questions, which aim to encourage self-study)

To access the ebook, visit **collinshub.co.uk/ebooks** and follow the step-by-step instructions.

Contents

Contents

ORGANISE

SI units and prefixes

Key words

Key questions

What are the seven SI base units?

What are the most commonly used prefixes in physics?

How can you convert from cm^2 to m^2?

SI units

Physicists use standardised units to measure and describe quantities accurately. The International System of Units (SI) gives a foundation of seven SI base units.

Every measurable quantity in physics can be expressed in terms of these SI base units.

Quantity	SI base unit	Symbol
Length	metre	m
Mass	kilogram	kg
Time	second	s
Electric current	ampere	A
Temperature	kelvin	K
Amount of substance	mole	mol
Luminous intensity	candela	cd

For example, the newton (N) is the most commonly unit used for a force. The newton can be represented in terms of SI base units as:

$$\text{newton (N)} = \text{kg m s}^{-2}$$

This can be shown from the equation $F = ma$, which is part of Newton's second law. Since acceleration is measured in m s^{-2}, multiplying this by the mass in kg gives kg m s^{-2} as the unit for force.

Prefixes

Prefixes are commonly used to represent very large or very small quantities efficiently. Some examples are:

- If a power station is creating a power of 1 500 000 000 W (or 1.5×10^9 W), this can be represented as 1.5 GW.
- If the wavelength of light is 5.20×10^{-7} m, this can be given as 520 nm.
- If the radius of a nucleus is 2.0×10^{-15} m, this can be represented as 2.0 fm.

Prefix	Symbol	Factor
Tera	T	$\times 10^{12}$
Giga	G	$\times 10^{9}$
Mega	M	$\times 10^{6}$
Kilo	k	$\times 10^{3}$
Deci	d	$\times 10^{-1}$
Centi	c	$\times 10^{-2}$
Milli	m	$\times 10^{-3}$
Micro	μ	$\times 10^{-6}$
Nano	n	$\times 10^{-9}$
Pico	p	$\times 10^{-12}$
Femto	f	$\times 10^{-15}$

Often, a quantity given with a prefix will need to be converted before it is used in an equation. For example, if you want to calculate the speed of a car in m s^{-1} and you are told that it travels 2.4 km in a time of 2.0 minutes, then you would need to convert 2.4 km into metres by multiplying by 10^3. You would also need to convert 2.0 minutes into seconds by multiplying by 60. The calculation would then be:

$$\text{speed} = \frac{\text{distance}}{\text{time}} = \frac{2.4\,\text{km}}{2.0\,\text{minutes}} = \frac{2.4 \times 10^3\,\text{m}}{2.0 \times 60\,\text{s}} = 20\text{ m s}^{-1}$$

Another example of a unit conversion is changing from cm^2 to m^2. Imagine a square of side length 1 m × 1 m: its area is 1 m^2. As there are 100 cm in 1 metre, the square will also have side length 100 cm × 100 cm. Therefore, 10 000 cm^2 are equal to 1 m^2.

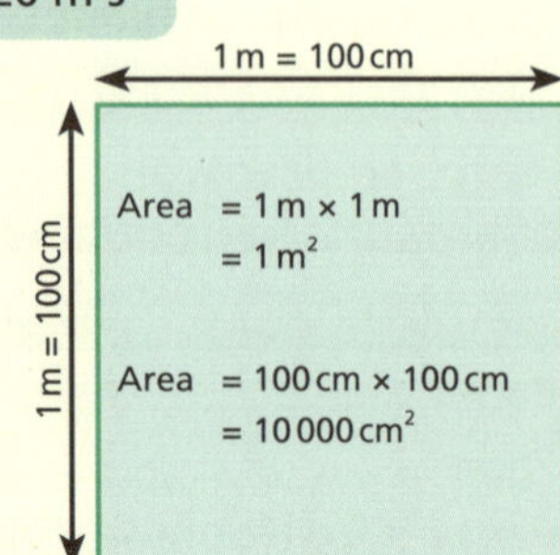

Similarly, for a cube of side length 1 m × 1 m × 1 m, you would find that there are 1 000 000 cm^3 in 1 m^3.

Summary

RETRIEVE

SI units and prefixes

1) Which of these is **not** an SI base unit? Tick **one** box. [1]

The kilogram (kg) ☐ The joule (J) ☐ The mole (mol) ☐ The metre (m) ☐

2) Which of these distances is the longest? Tick **one** box. [1]

800 m ☐ 0.2 km ☐ 9×10^4 cm ☐ 5×10^2 m ☐

3) In this question, you will need to rewrite units in SI base units.

a) Using the equation $F = ma$, write the newton in SI base units. [1]

....

b) Using the equation $W = Fs$, write the joule in SI base units. [1]

....

c) Using the equation $P = W \div t$, write the watt in SI base units. [1]

....

d) Using the equation stress = $F \div A$, write the pascal in SI base units. [1]

....

4) Write each of the following quantities in terms of the base units without prefixes. Give your answers in standard form.

a) Convert 1.8 kA into A. [1]

....

b) Convert 450 nm into m. [1]

....

c) Convert 820 μs into s. [1]

....

d) Convert 2 500 000 cm^2 into m^2. [1]

....

e) Convert 7.4×10^8 cm^3 into m^3. [1]

....

f) Convert 1.6×10^{12} mm^3 into m^3. [1]

....

ORGANISE

Uncertainties

Key words

Key questions

How do you calculate absolute and percentage uncertainties?

How do you calculate the absolute uncertainty if you add or subtract two values with uncertainty?

How do you calculate the percentage uncertainty if you multiply or divide two values with uncertainty?

How do you calculate the percentage uncertainty if a quantity with uncertainty is raised by a power?

Absolute, fractional and percentage uncertainties

Measurements in physics always come with a degree of uncertainty. Understanding and calculating this uncertainty helps us to gauge the reliability of experimental results.

To reduce the chance of random error, an experiment would typically be repeated multiple times. In this case, the absolute uncertainty (Δa) of measurement a can be calculated by taking the range of results divided by 2:

$$\text{absolute uncertainty} = \Delta a = \frac{\text{range}}{2}$$

For example, imagine that you have measured the potential difference across a component three times: 6.0 V, 6.3 V and 5.7 V. You would write the average result as the mean value ± absolute uncertainty. In this case, V ± ΔV would be 6.0 ± 0.3 V (where the 0.3 V has been calculated from half the range).

Another way of expressing uncertainties is as a fractional uncertainty. This is the ratio of the absolute uncertainty to the mean value:

$$\text{fractional uncertainty} = \frac{\Delta a}{a} = \frac{\text{absolute uncertainty}}{\text{mean value}}$$

This can be turned into a percentage uncertainty (εa) by multiplying by 100:

$$\text{percentage uncertainty} = \varepsilon a = \frac{\Delta a}{a} \times 100 = \frac{\text{absolute uncertainty}}{\text{mean value}} \times 100$$

Returning to the example above, the percentage uncertainty in the potential difference would be $\frac{0.3}{6.0} \times 100 = 5\%$, so you could also write the potential difference as 6.0 V ± 5%.

Combining uncertainties

There are three rules to remember when combining uncertainties:

1. When adding or subtracting two values, the absolute uncertainties are added to find the combined absolute uncertainty.
2. When multiplying or dividing two values, the percentage uncertainties are added to find the combined percentage uncertainty.
3. When a quantity with uncertainty is raised to a power, the percentage uncertainty is multiplied by the power. This gives the percentage uncertainty of the calculated value.

Rule	Measured value calculation		Uncertainty calculation
Addition and subtraction rule	If $a = b + c$	or $a = b - c$	$\Delta a = \Delta b + \Delta c$
Multiplication and division rule	If $a = bc$	or $a = b \div c$	$\varepsilon a = \varepsilon b + \varepsilon c$
Power rule	If $a = b^c$		$\varepsilon a = c \times \varepsilon b$

For example, again imagine that you have a potential difference of 6.0 V ± 5% across a component. If the current flowing through the component was measured to be 1.2 ± 10%, the resistance could be calculated using $R = \frac{V}{I}$. The percentage uncertainty in the resistance could be found by adding the percentage uncertainties. This would lead to a resistance of 5.0 Ω ± 15%.

Summary

RETRIEVE

Uncertainties

1. The current flowing through a resistor is measured five times to be:

   1.24 A 1.16 A 1.28 A 1.18 A 1.19 A

   a) Calculate the mean value of the current. [1]

   b) Calculate the absolute uncertainty of the current. [1]

   c) Calculate the fractional uncertainty of the current. [1]

   d) Calculate the percentage uncertainty of the current. [1]

   The potential difference across the resistor is measured to be 3.20 ± 0.08 V.

   e) Calculate the percentage uncertainty in the potential difference. [2]

   f) Calculate the resistance of the component, including the percentage uncertainty. [2]

   g) Calculate the absolute uncertainty of the resistance of the component. [1]

2. The diameter of a coin is measured three times to be:

   19.8 mm 20.4 mm 20.1 mm

   a) Calculate the mean diameter of the coin. [1]

   b) Calculate the percentage uncertainty in the diameter of the coin. [2]

   c) Calculate the cross-sectional area of the coin, including the percentage uncertainty. [2]

   The width of the coin is measured to be 1.48 ± 0.02 mm.

   d) Calculate the percentage uncertainty of the width of the coin. [2]

   e) Calculate the volume of the coin, including the percentage uncertainty. [2]

   f) Calculate the absolute uncertainty of the volume of the coin. [1]

ORGANISE

Graphs and estimation

Key words

Key questions

How do you calculate the percentage uncertainty in a gradient?

How do you calculate a percentage uncertainty in a y-intercept?

Why is estimation useful?

Graphs

When plotting experimental data on a graph, error bars are included to visually represent the absolute uncertainty in each measurement.

Typically, error bars are drawn as vertical or horizontal lines that extend from each data point. Error bars extend by the absolute uncertainty above and below the mean value.

When data points are linear, the uncertainty in the gradient can be estimated by using a line of best fit and one of either a steepest or shallowest line of fit. The gradients of both lines can be found by using $m = \frac{\Delta y}{\Delta x}$

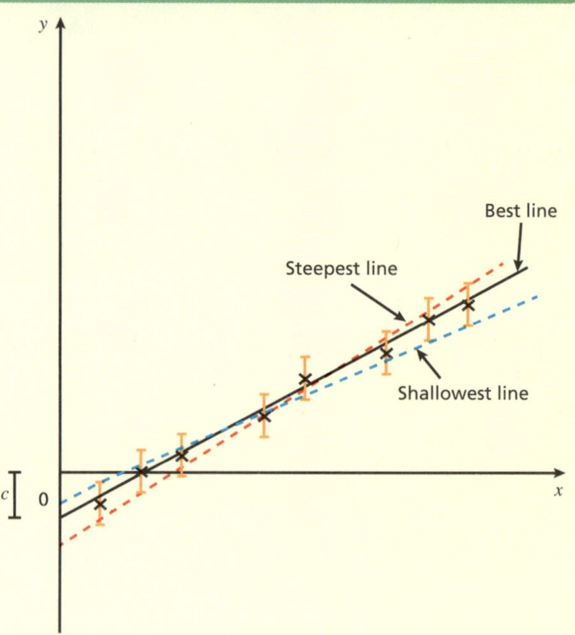

These gradients can then be used to calculate the uncertainty in the gradient:

$$\text{percentage uncertainty in gradient} = \frac{|\text{best gradient} - \text{worst gradient}|}{\text{best gradient}} \times 100$$

The percentage uncertainty will always be a positive value due to the modulus bars. Note that by going from the best gradient to one of the worst gradients, that is already a rough measure of half the range (and therefore the absolute uncertainty in the gradient). This equation is therefore the same as how you would calculate the percentage uncertainty in a range of different results.

Similarly, the percentage uncertainty in the y-intercept can also be found:

$$y\text{-intercept} = \frac{|\text{best } y\text{-intercept} - \text{worst } y\text{-intercept}|}{\text{best } y\text{-intercept}} \times 100$$

Estimation

Physicists often need to estimate physical quantities to check if their values are reasonable. Estimation involves making an informed guess based on typical values and everyday knowledge. This can be used to confirm results or to make approximations where precise values are not necessary.

For example, if you were asked to estimate the gravitational potential of a book on a table then you could estimate the mass of the book to be 1 kg and the height of the table to be 1 m. Using $E_p = mgh$, the gravitational potential energy would then be approximately 100 J.

Summary

RETRIEVE

Graphs and estimation

1. A car is travelling at a speed of 60 mph.

   What is the best estimate for the kinetic energy of the car? Tick **one** box. [1]

   10^{10} J ☐ 10^{8} J ☐ 10^{6} J ☐ 10^{4} J ☐

2. The potential difference across a component is measured at different currents. The data is shown in the table.

Potential difference (mV)	Current (mA)
10 ± 2	10
24 ± 4	20
32 ± 3	30
44 ± 4	40
58 ± 4	50
66 ± 3	60
78 ± 4	70
90 ± 6	80

a) Using the graph paper below, plot a graph of potential difference against current. Draw error bars to represent the uncertainty in the potential difference and draw a line of best fit. [4]

b) The resistance of the component is calculated from the gradient of the line of best fit.

Calculate the gradient of your line of best fit. [1]

c) Draw the shallowest line of fit and calculate its gradient. [2]

d) Calculate the percentage uncertainty of the resistance. [2]

ORGANISE

Atoms and nuclei

Key words

Key questions

What are isotopes?

What is 'specific charge'?

Describe the range of the strong nuclear force.

What are the general equations for alpha and beta-minus decay?

The atom

The atom consists of a nucleus and electrons that orbit the nucleus. The nucleus consists of protons and neutrons (which are collectively referred to as **nucleons**).

Particle	Location	Charge (C)	Mass (kg)
Electron	Orbiting the nucleus	-1.6×10^{-19}	9.11×10^{-31}
Neutron	In the nucleus	0	1.675×10^{-27}
Proton	In the nucleus	$+1.6 \times 10^{-19}$	1.673×10^{-27}

To show how many protons and neutrons are in an atom or nucleus, the nuclide notation ${}^{A}_{Z}X$ is used. X is the chemical symbol for the element, Z is the atomic number (which gives the number of protons) and A is the nucleon number (the total number of protons and neutrons).

Isotopes are atoms with the same atomic number (Z), but different nucleon numbers (A).

Specific charge

The specific charge of a particle is its charge to mass ratio:

$$\text{specific charge} = \frac{\text{charge}}{\text{mass}} = \frac{Q}{m}$$

The units of specific charge are therefore C kg^{-1}. For example, you could calculate the specific charge of the proton. This would be $\frac{1.60 \times 10^{-19}}{1.673 \times 10^{-27}} = 9.56 \times 10^{7}$ C kg^{-1}.

The specific charge of an electron is much higher at 1.76×10^{11} C kg^{-1} due to its lower mass. You can also calculate the specific charge of nuclei and ions.

The strong nuclear force

Protons inside a nucleus electrostatically repel each other. The strong nuclear force binds together protons and neutrons in the nucleus and is needed for nuclear stability. The strong nuclear force is repulsive at distances below 0.5 fm, but is strongly attractive between 0.5 and 3 fm. Beyond 3 fm there is zero force.

Unstable nuclei

Unstable nuclei undergo radioactive decay. Here are two examples of this.

Alpha (α) decay occurs when a nucleus emits an alpha particle. An alpha particle consists of two protons and two neutrons. Therefore, the general equation for alpha decay is:

$${}^{A}_{Z}X \rightarrow {}^{A-4}_{Z-2}Y + {}^{4}_{2}\alpha$$

Beta-minus (β⁻) decay occurs when a neutron is converted into a proton, an electron (which can also be referred to as a β^- particle) and an electron antineutrino ($\bar{\nu}_e$). The general equation for beta-minus decay is:

$${}^{A}_{Z}X \rightarrow {}^{A}_{Z+1}W + {}^{0}_{-1}\beta + \bar{\nu}_e$$

The electron antineutrino was discovered as early experiments on beta-minus decay showed that the energy of the emitted electron was variable, which suggested missing energy. To account for this discrepancy, Wolfgang Pauli hypothesised that the antineutrino was responsible. Neutrinos (or antineutrinos) are neutral, nearly massless particles. Their presence in beta decay conserves both energy and momentum.

Summary

RETRIEVE

Atoms and nuclei

1 Which of these particles has the largest magnitude of specific charge? Tick **one** box. [1]

An electron ☐ A proton ☐ A neutron ☐ An alpha particle ☐

2 The nucleus of an isotope of iron has a specific charge 4.45×10^{7} C kg^{-1}. The atomic number of iron is 26.

a) Calculate how many neutrons are in the isotope of iron. Assume that the mass of a proton and neutron are identical at 1.67×10^{-27} kg. [3]

....

b) The strong nuclear force keeps the nucleons bound together in the iron nucleus.

Describe how the strong nuclear force varies with nucleon separation. [2]

....

....

3 Carbon has two stable isotopes, carbon-12 ($^{12}_{6}C$) and carbon-13 ($^{13}_{6}C$).

a) Describe one similarity and one difference between carbon-12 and carbon-13. [2]

....

....

....

b) Calculate the specific charge of a carbon-12 nucleus. Assume that the mass of a proton and neutron are identical at 1.67×10^{-27} kg. [3]

....

c) State and explain, without calculation, how the specific charge of carbon-13 would compare to that of carbon-12. [2]

....

....

....

d) Nuclei of carbon-14 are unstable and undergo beta-minus decay to form an isotope of nitrogen:

$$^{14}_{6}C \rightarrow \, ^{A}_{Z}N + \, ^{0}_{-1}\beta + \bar{\nu}_e$$

State the nucleon and atomic numbers of the nitrogen isotope. [2]

....

....

e) The energies of the beta particles produced in the above decay are measured.

Describe how the diagram shown provides evidence for the electron antineutrino. [2]

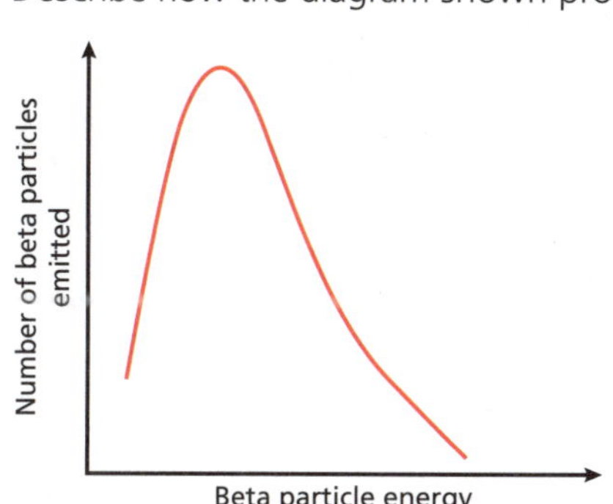

....

....

....

....

ORGANISE

Particles and antiparticles

Key words

Key questions

What is an antiparticle?

How can you calculate the energy of a photon?

What happens if a particle meets an antiparticle?

What is 'pair production'?

Particles and antiparticles

For every particle, there is a corresponding antiparticle. Antiparticles have the same mass as their particle counterparts but the opposite charge. Some examples of particles and antiparticles are shown in the table.

Particle	Mass (kg)	Rest energy (MeV)	Charge (C)
Electron	9.11×10^{-31}	0.510999	-1.6×10^{-19}
Positron	9.11×10^{-31}	0.510999	$+1.6 \times 10^{-19}$
Proton	1.673×10^{-27}	938.257	$+1.6 \times 10^{-19}$
Antiproton	1.673×10^{-27}	938.257	-1.6×10^{-19}
Neutron	1.675×10^{-27}	939.551	0
Antineutron	1.675×10^{-27}	939.551	0

The rest energy of a particle (in joules, J) can be calculated using $E = mc^2$, where m is the rest mass and c is the speed of light ($3.0 \times 10^8\,\text{m s}^{-1}$). Particles and antiparticles typically have small masses and so the unit the MeV is more commonly used than the joule. 1 eV is equal to 1.6×10^{-19} J.

Photons

Electromagnetic radiation can be described as both a wave (with frequency and wavelength) and as a stream of particles (photons). This is known as **wave–particle duality**. Each photon carries energy proportional to the frequency of the radiation: the higher the frequency (or the shorter the wavelength), the greater the photon's energy.

The energy E of a photon (in joules) is given by the formula $E = hf$ where h is the Planck constant (equal to 6.63×10^{-34} J s) and f is the frequency of the photon (in hertz). This expression can also be rewritten as $E = \frac{hc}{\lambda}$ by using the wave speed equation. Here, λ is the wavelength of a photon (measured in metres).

Annihilation and pair production

If a particle (such as an electron) and its antiparticle (a positron) were to ever meet while at rest, they would annihilate and convert their masses into energy in the form of two gamma photons. In this case, the energy of each photon is equal to the rest energy of the particle, which for an electron or positron is 0.510999 MeV.

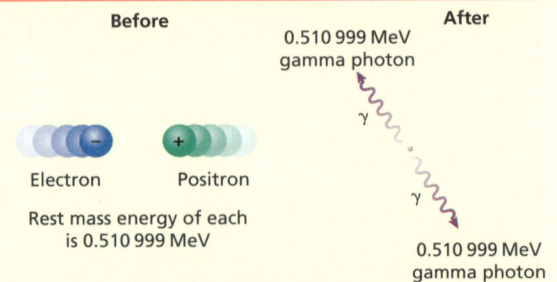

However, if the electron and positron possess kinetic energy before they annihilate then each gamma photon produced in annihilation will carry more energy. This is because it will include a portion of the kinetic energy from the colliding particles. The total energy of the two photons can be calculated as:

total photon energy = 2 × rest energy + total kinetic energy

If a photon with enough energy passes near a nucleus, it can be converted into a particle–antiparticle pair (like an electron and a positron). The nucleus is needed as it recoils to conserve momentum. This process is called **pair production**.

Pair production requires the photon's energy to be at least equal to the rest energy of the electron and positron combined (so 2 × 0.510999 MeV). Any extra energy becomes kinetic energy of the particle and antiparticle produced.

Summary

RETRIEVE

Particles and antiparticles

1 Gamma photon A has an energy of 1.20 MeV.

Gamma photon B has an energy of 9.60×10^{-14} J.

Which of the photons have sufficient energy to cause pair production of an electron and a positron? Tick **one** box. [1]

Both photons A and B ☐ Only photon A ☐

Only photon B ☐ Neither photon A nor B ☐

2 An electron meets its antiparticle.

a) Describe what an antiparticle is. [2]

b) State the antiparticle of an electron. [1]

c) Describe what happens when the electron meets its antiparticle. [2]

d) Show that the rest energy of the antiparticle of an electron is 8.2×10^{-14} J. [1]

3 A gamma photon has sufficient energy to cause pair production of a proton and another particle X.

a) Describe what pair production is. [2]

b) State why pair production can only happen if a gamma photon passes near a nucleus. [1]

c) State the name of particle X. [1]

d) Calculate the minimum frequency the gamma photon needs to cause pair production of the proton and particle X. The rest energy of a proton is 938.257 MeV. [3]

e) The gamma photon causes pair production of the proton and particle X, but has more energy than the minimum energy required.

State what happens to the excess energy of the photon. [1]

ORGANISE

Particle interactions

Key words

Key questions

What are the four fundamental forces?

What is an exchange particle?

What are four examples of particle decay through the weak interaction?

Fundamental forces and exchange particles

All interactions between particles are governed by four fundamental forces, each mediated by exchange particles (also called gauge bosons). During an interaction, these exchange particles transfer force, energy, charge and momentum from one particle to another. Below, the fundamental forces are tabulated from strongest to weakest.

Fundamental force	Particles that experience the force	Exchange particle	Range
Strong nuclear / Strong interaction	Hadrons and quarks	Pions between hadrons; gluons between quarks	~ 3×10^{-15} m (3 fm)
Electromagnetic	Charged particles	Virtual photon	Long (follows inverse square law)
Weak nuclear	All particles	W^+/W^- boson	Short (~ 10^{-18} m)
Gravitational	Particles with mass	Graviton (not yet experimentally confirmed)	Long (follows inverse square law)

The weak interaction is responsible for particle decay

You need to know four specific examples of the weak interaction:

Name of particle interaction	Equation	Exchange particle
Beta-minus decay	$n \rightarrow p + e^- + \bar{v}_e$	W^- boson
Beta-plus decay	$p \rightarrow n + e^+ + v_e$	W^+ boson
Electron capture	$p + e^- \rightarrow n + v_e$	W^+ boson
Electron-proton collision	$p + e^- \rightarrow n + v_e$	W^- boson

In **beta-minus decay**, a neutron decays into a proton and an electron (to conserve charge). During this interaction, the beta particle (an electron) was observed to have a range of energies. An electron antineutrino is responsible for this 'missing' energy (and is also needed to conserve lepton number). **Beta-plus decay** is almost the opposite process with a proton transforming into a neutron, a positron and an electron neutrino.

Electron capture and electron-proton collisions have the same equation but are subtly different processes. **Electron capture** involves a proton-rich nucleus absorbing an electron that is orbiting the nucleus. The proton and electron transform into a neutron and an electron neutrino. An **electron-proton collision** is similar but happens when a high-energy electron collides with a proton.

Feynman diagrams to represent particle interactions

This Feynman diagram represents beta-minus decay. Typically, axes aren't drawn, but you can think of the y-axis as being time and the x-axis being space. The diagram shows that over time the neutron decays into a proton, electron and electron antineutrino.

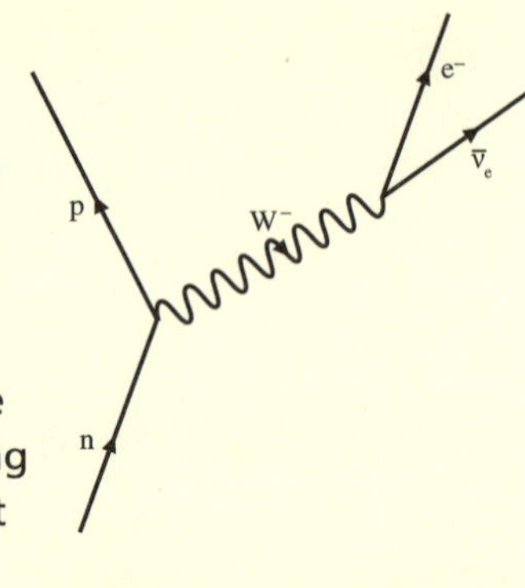

Particles and antiparticles are represented with straight lines, while exchange particles are shown by wavy lines. The point where particles interact is called a **vertex**. The charge going into a vertex must equal the charge coming out of the vertex; this is why the exchange particle must be the W^- boson in this example.

Summary

RETRIEVE

Particle interactions

1. Which exchange particle is responsible for the decay of a neutron into a proton? Tick **one** box. [1]

   W boson ☐ Pion ☐ Gluon ☐ Virtual photon ☐

2. Electron capture is an example of which fundamental force? Tick **one** box. [1]

   Gravitational ☐ Weak nuclear ☐ Electromagnetic ☐ Strong nuclear ☐

3. A nucleus contains protons and neutrons. The protons inside a nucleus repel each other through the electromagnetic force.

   a) Name the exchange particle of the electromagnetic force. [1]

   ....

   b) Explain what is meant by an exchange particle. [2]

   ....

   ....

   ....

   c) Another force acts on the protons and neutrons inside a nucleus.

   State the name of this force and compare it to the electromagnetic force. [3]

   ....

   ....

   ....

   ....

4. Beta-plus decay is one example of the weak interaction.

   a) Write the equation for beta-plus decay. [1]

   ....

   b) State another interaction that is due to the weak interaction. Include an equation for the process. [2]

   ....

   ....

   c) In the space below, draw a Feynman diagram that shows beta-plus decay. [3]

ORGANISE

Quarks and hadrons

Key words

Key questions

What do a hadron, a baryon and a meson consist of?

What are the quark compositions of a proton and a neutron?

What are the quark compositions of kaons and muons?

Quarks

Quarks are fundamental particles. This means that they cannot be broken down into anything smaller. You need to know about three types of quark 'flavour': up, down and strange.

Quarks also cannot exist by themselves, which is called quark confinement.

Quark	Charge	Baryon number	Strangeness
Up (u)	$+\frac{2}{3}$	$+\frac{1}{3}$	0
Down (d)	$-\frac{1}{3}$	$+\frac{1}{3}$	0
Strange (s)	$-\frac{1}{3}$	$+\frac{1}{3}$	–1

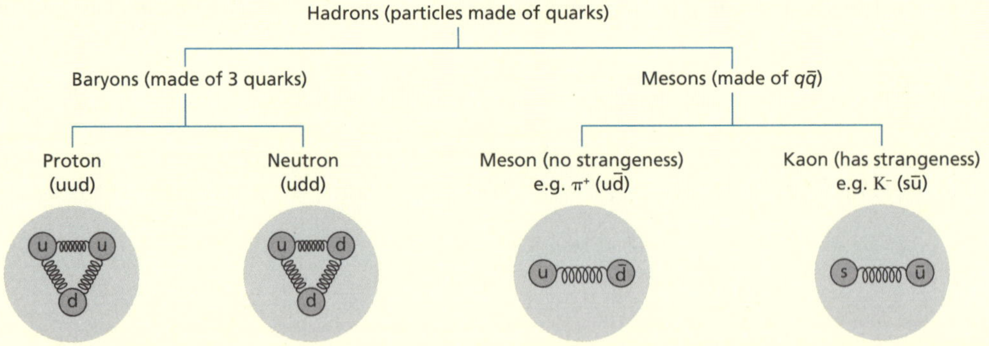

Hadrons (particles made of quarks)

Baryons (made of 3 quarks)

Mesons (made of $q\bar{q}$)

Proton (uud)

Neutron (udd)

Meson (no strangeness) e.g. π^+ ($u\bar{d}$)

Kaon (has strangeness) e.g. K^- ($s\bar{u}$)

The two types of hadron: baryons and mesons

Baryons are made from three quarks, which is why individual quarks have a baryon number of $+\frac{1}{3}$ (as baryons have a baryon number of +1). Two examples of baryons are protons and neutrons, which are only made of up and down quarks.

Mesons are made from a quark and an antiquark (and therefore have a baryon number of 0). The kaon is a meson that has strangeness. This means that a kaon must contain either a strange quark or a strange antiquark. A strange quark has a strangeness of –1, while a strange antiquark has a strangeness of +1. Another type of meson is the pion. Pions have no strangeness and so only consist of up and down quarks and antiquarks.

Particle	Charge	Baryon number	Strangeness	Quark composition
Proton	+1	+1	0	uud
Neutron	0	+1	0	udd
K^- meson	–1	0	–1	$s\bar{u}$
K^+ meson	+1	0	+1	$u\bar{s}$
K^0 meson	0	0	+1	$d\bar{s}$
π^- meson	–1	0	0	$d\bar{u}$
π^+ meson	+1	0	0	$u\bar{d}$
π^0 meson	0	0	0	$u\bar{u}$ or $d\bar{d}$

An antibaryon has three antiquarks and so has a baryon number of –1.

Summary

RETRIEVE

Quarks and hadrons

1. Which statement below is **incorrect**? Tick **one** box. [1]

   A π^+ meson has a baryon number of 0 ☐

   A proton has a baryon number of +1 ☐

   A strange quark has a strangeness of –1 ☐

   An antineutron has a baryon number of +1 ☐

2. A meson has one down quark and a strange antiquark ($d\bar{s}$).

   a) Determine the strangeness and charge of the meson. [2]

   b) State the name of the meson. [1]

3. A positive kaon decays into a positive pion and a neutral pion: $K^+ \rightarrow \pi^+ + \pi^0$

   a) Kaons and pions are both mesons.

   Describe what is meant by a meson. [1]

   b) State the quark composition of the positive kaon. [1]

   c) State the quark composition of the positive pion. [1]

   d) State the quark composition of the neutral pion. [1]

4. A negative delta baryon decays into a proton and a neutral pion: $\Delta^- \rightarrow n + \pi^-$

   a) Describe what is meant by a baryon. [1]

   b) State the quark composition of the neutron and the negative pion. [2]

   c) The negative delta baryon has a strangeness of 0.

   Determine its quark composition. [1]

   d) All the particles in this interaction are hadrons.

   Describe what is meant by a hadron. [1]

Leptons and conservation laws

Key words

Key questions

Why does strangeness not have to be conserved in weak interactions?

What three quantities always need to be conserved in a particle interaction?

What does a negatively charged muon decay into?

What does a positively charged kaon decay into?

Leptons are fundamental particles

Two 'flavours' of lepton are the electron and the muon. The muon is significantly heavier than the electron and is therefore unstable, decaying into the electron via the weak interaction.

Lepton	Lepton number	Charge
Electron (e^-)	$L_e = +1$	–1
Muon (μ^-)	$L_\mu = +1$	–1
Electron neutrino (v_e)	$L_e = +1$	0
Muon neutrino (v_μ)	$L_\mu = +1$	0

Electrons and muons each have associated neutrinos: the electron neutrino (v_e) and the muon neutrino (v_μ). Neutrinos are very difficult to detect: they travel at very close to the speed of light, have tiny masses (almost zero) and carry no electric charge.

For a particle interaction to occur, it must obey four conservation laws

1. Conservation of charge (Q). The total electric charge before and after the interaction must be the same.
2. Conservation of baryon number (B). Baryons (e.g. protons and neutrons) have B = +1; antibaryons have B = –1. Particles that aren't baryons or antibaryons have B = 0.
3. Conversation of lepton number (L). Each lepton flavour has its own lepton number (L_e and L_τ), e.g. an electron and its associated neutrino each have $L_e = +1$. The muon and its associated neutrino each have $L_\mu = +1$.
4. Conservation of strangeness (S). Strangeness is conserved in strong interactions but can change by ±1 in weak interactions. This is because the weak interaction can cause a change in quark character (e.g. a strange quark can transform into an up quark).

Examples of particle interactions

1. **Beta-minus decay.** The proton is the only stable baryon as it has a lower mass than other baryons. During beta-minus decay, a neutron decays into a proton. This conserves baryon number, but an electron is needed to conserve charge. As an electron is produced, an electron antineutrino is required to conserve lepton number. To transform a neutron into a proton, a down quark transforms into an up quark. This is an example of the weak interaction, as there is a change in quark character.

	n	→	p	+	e^-	+	$\bar{v}_e$
Q	0	→	+1	–	1	+	0
B	+1	→	+1	+	0	+	0
L	0	→	0	+	1	–	1

2. **Muon decay.** The muon is heavier than the electron and so decays into the electron. This conserves charge and baryon number but violates electron lepton number and muon lepton number. Therefore, an electron antineutrino and a muon neutrino are required. This is another example of the weak interaction.

	μ^-	→	e^-	+	$\bar{v}_e$	+	v_μ
Q	–1	→	–1	+	0	+	0
B	0	→	0	+	0	+	0
L_μ	+1	→	0	+	0	+	1
L_e	0	→	+1	–	1	+	0

3. **Production of particles with strangeness.** Strange particles are produced by the strong interaction. Strangeness is conserved so particles are made in pairs with opposite strangeness.

	p	+	p	→	p	+	p	+	K^+	+	K^-
Q	+1	+	1	→	+1	+	1	+	1	+	–1
B	+1	+	1	→	+1	+	1	+	0	+	0
L	0	+	0	→	0	+	0	+	0	+	0
S	0	+	0	→	0	+	0	+	1	–	1

4. **Kaon decay.** Strange particles decay via the weak interaction, and kaons decay into pions through this process. Strangeness can therefore change by ±1 in this interaction. The weak interaction is responsible for a change in quark character.

	K^+	→	π^+	+	π^0
Q	+1	→	+1	+	0
B	0	→	0	+	0
S	+1	→	0	+	0

Summary

RETRIEVE

Leptons and conservation laws

1. A proton-rich nucleus undergoes beta-plus decay.

   a) Write an equation that describes beta-plus decay. [1]

   b) State and explain which interaction is responsible for beta-plus decay. [2]

2. The Σ^- baryon has strangeness of –1 and undergoes decay into a neutron and particle X. Particle X has a strangeness of 0.

   $\Sigma^- \rightarrow n + X$

   a) State and explain which interaction is responsible for the decay of the Σ^- baryon. [2]

   b) Determine the quark composition of the Σ^- baryon. [1]

   c) Using conservation laws, determine the identity of particle X. [4]

3. A student proposes that the Λ baryon is produced in the following interaction:

   $p + n \rightarrow \pi^+ + \pi^- + \pi^0 + \Lambda$

   The quark composition of the Λ baryon is uds.

   a) Determine the charge of the Λ baryon. [1]

   b) The Λ baryon has strangeness of –1.

   State the interaction that is responsible for producing strange particles. [1]

   c) Using conservation laws, determine whether the interaction is possible. [4]

   A separate student proposes that the Λ baryon then undergoes the following decay:

   $\Lambda \rightarrow p + \pi^-$

   d) Using conservation laws, determine whether the interaction is possible. [4]

ORGANISE

The photoelectric effect

Key words

Key questions

What were the main findings of the photoelectric effect experiment?

What is meant by the 'threshold frequency'?

What is meant by the work function of a material?

Why are some photoelectrons released with more kinetic energy than others?

Wave theory of light

The wave theory of light predicted the behaviour of light interacting with matter based on its wave-like properties. If light was shone onto a metal surface, the light waves were thought to transfer energy gradually to electrons on the surface. This would mean that low frequency light could eventually eject electrons if it illuminated the surface for long enough. It was also thought that increasing light intensity would eject more electrons from a metal surface and increase their kinetic energy.

The photoelectric effect

Predictions from the wave theory were inconsistent with experimental results. When light was shone onto a metal surface, it was found that:

1. Electrons were only emitted from a metal surface if the light frequency was above a critical value. This value is now called the **threshold frequency** and it is specific to the metal. Below this frequency, no electrons were emitted, regardless of the light intensity.
2. Electrons were ejected immediately when the light frequency was above the threshold frequency. There was no time delay.
3. The maximum kinetic energy (E_k) of the electrons increased with the light frequency, not its intensity. Increasing the intensity only increased the number of electrons emitted, not their energy.

Albert Einstein explained the above results by introducing the photon model of light. Here, light is composed of discrete packets of energy called **photons**. Each photon has an energy E equal to $E = hf$ (see page 14).

When a photon strikes the metal surface, its energy is transferred to a single electron. The emitted electrons are called **photoelectrons** and this process of releasing photoelectrons from a metal surface is called the **photoelectric effect**.

The work function and threshold frequency

As there is a minimum photon frequency (f_0) needed to release a photoelectron from a metal surface, there is also a minimum photon energy. This is called the **work function** (ϕ). The threshold frequency is linked to the work function by $\phi = hf_0$.

If the photon energy is less than the work function, no photoelectrons are released from the metal surface. For example, potassium has a work function of 2.3 eV. If red light (of photon energy 1.8 eV) is incident onto a potassium surface, no photoelectrons are released. However, green light of photon energy 2.5 eV and blue light of photon energy 3.1 eV do release electrons as they have a higher photon energy than the work function.

Any excess photon energy above the work function becomes the kinetic energy of the emitted photoelectrons, so that $hf = \phi + E_{k(max)}$. Here ϕ is the work function (in joules) and $E_{k(max)}$ is the maximum kinetic energy of emitted photoelectrons. This is a maximum kinetic energy as any electrons deeper in the metal surface need more energy to escape.

To measure the kinetic energy of the photoelectrons, a stopping potential (V_s) can be applied to the metal surface. At this potential, $eV_s = E_k$ (where e is the charge of the electron) and electrons are attracted back to the metal surface to prevent escape.

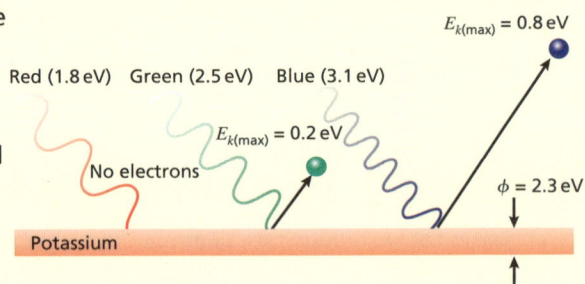

Summary

RETRIEVE

The photoelectric effect

1 A gold leaf electroscope can be used to demonstrate the photoelectric effect.

A zinc plate is negatively charged and attached to a metal rod. A gold leaf is in contact with the metal rod.

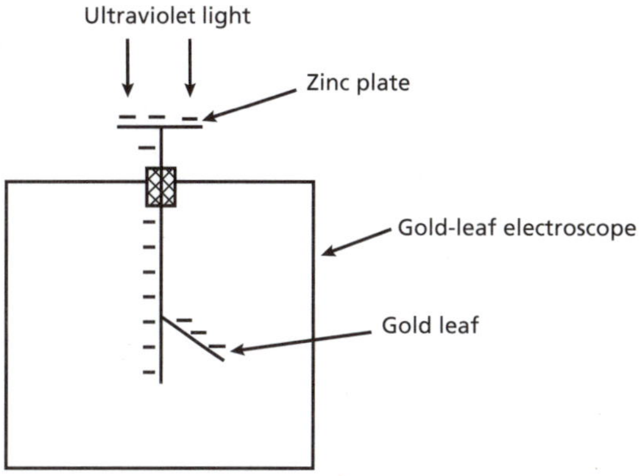

a) Explain why the gold leaf is repelled by the metal rod. [1]

b) Describe what is meant by the 'photoelectric effect'. [2]

c) When ultraviolet light is shone onto the zinc plate, the gold leaf is observed to fall. When the ultraviolet light is replaced with a white light, the gold leaf remains in its original position.

Explain these observations. [2]

2 The diagram shows a photocell which is used to demonstrate the photoelectric effect.

Photons of frequency 1.3×10^{15} Hz are incident onto an aluminium surface of work function 4.2 eV. Some photoelectrons are released from the aluminium surface. The resulting current can be measured on an ammeter.

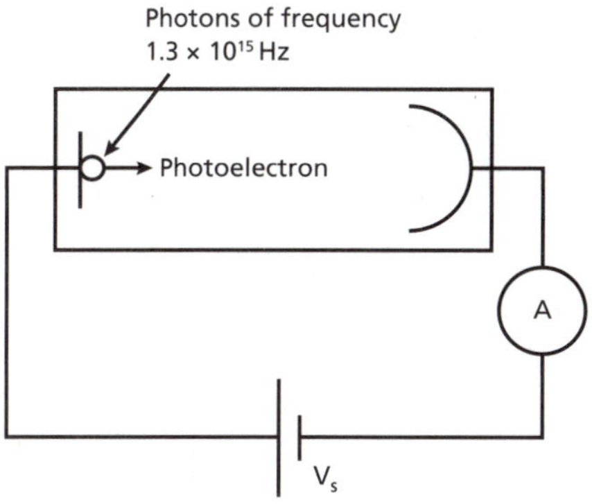

a) Explain what is meant by the phrase 'work function'. [2]

b) Calculate the threshold frequency for aluminium. [2]

c) Calculate the maximum kinetic energy of the emitted photoelectrons when there is no potential applied to the aluminium surface. [2]

d) A potential is now applied to the aluminium surface.

Calculate the minimum potential needed to stop a current being detected in the circuit. [2]

ORGANISE

Energy levels

Key words

Key questions

How can an electron become excited?

What is de-excitation?

How does a fluorescent lamp work?

How is an emission spectrum made?

How is an absorption spectrum made?

Energy levels and excitation

Electrons in atoms exist in discrete energy levels. A photon can excite an electron to a higher energy level but only if its energy exactly matches the energy difference between two levels. The photon needs this exact energy as it is absorbed during this process. An excited electron will de-excite into a lower energy level, emitting a photon. The photon has energy equal to the energy difference between levels.

Electrons colliding with an atom can also transfer energy, exciting electrons within the atom to a higher energy level. The electron loses kinetic energy equal to the energy difference between energy levels. Therefore, the electron needs to possess a minimum kinetic energy (rather than an exact energy).

If an electron within an atom is given enough energy to escape the atom entirely, then **ionisation** occurs. The ionisation energy is the energy required to remove an electron from the atom when it is in the lowest energy state (the ground state).

An energy level diagram for hydrogen is shown in question 2 on page 25. Note how the energy levels are negative, which is because an electron is defined to have a potential energy of zero when it is not bound to a nucleus (at infinity). If an electron is electrostatically bound to a nucleus, energy must be transferred to ionise it. Therefore, the energy of each energy level is less than zero (and so negative).

De-excitation and line spectra

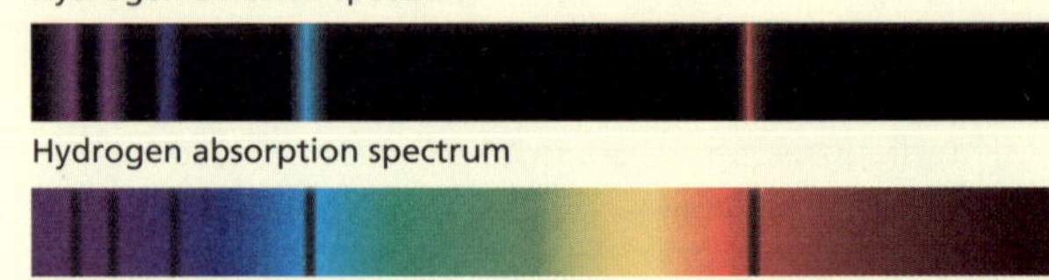

An emission spectrum is formed when electrons de-excite from a higher energy level (E_2) to a lower energy level (E_1). This process emits a photon with energy equal to the energy difference between energy levels: $hf = E_2 - E_1$

Here, h is the Planck constant (6.63×10^{-34} J s) and f is the photon frequency.

An absorption spectrum is formed when a continuous spectrum passes through atoms. The atoms absorb photons of specific energies, exciting the electrons from lower to higher energy levels. These photons are removed from the continuous spectrum, creating dark lines against a bright background. These dark lines occur at the same wavelengths as the bright lines in the emission spectrum.

Fluorescent lamps

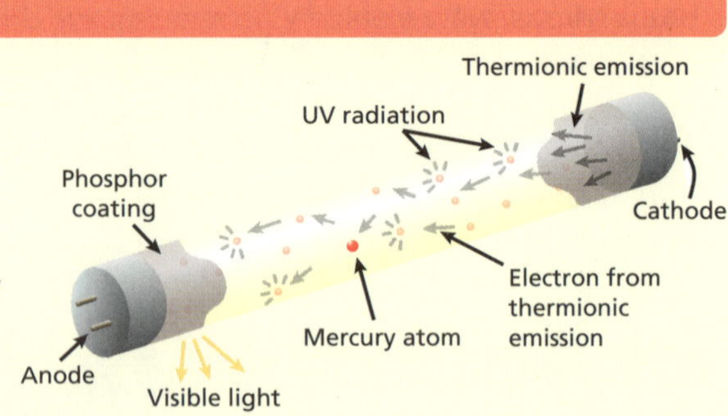

A fluorescent lamp works through excitation and de-excitation of electrons in mercury atoms:

1. Thermionic emission releases electrons.
2. The electrons collide with mercury atoms and excite electrons within the mercury atoms.
3. When the excited electrons in mercury de-excite, they emit ultraviolet (UV) photons.
4. The tube of a fluorescent lamp has a phosphor coating. This phosphor absorbs the UV photons and becomes excited.
5. When the phosphor de-excites, it re-emits lower frequency visible photons.

Summary

RETRIEVE

Energy levels

1 An atom has energy levels E_1 = −6.0 eV and E_2 = −1.5 eV.

a) Determine the energy required to excite the atom from E_1 to E_2. [1]

b) A photon is responsible for this excitation.

Calculate the frequency of the photon. [2]

c) Explain why the energies of the energy levels are negative. [2]

2 The diagram shows the energy levels of hydrogen.

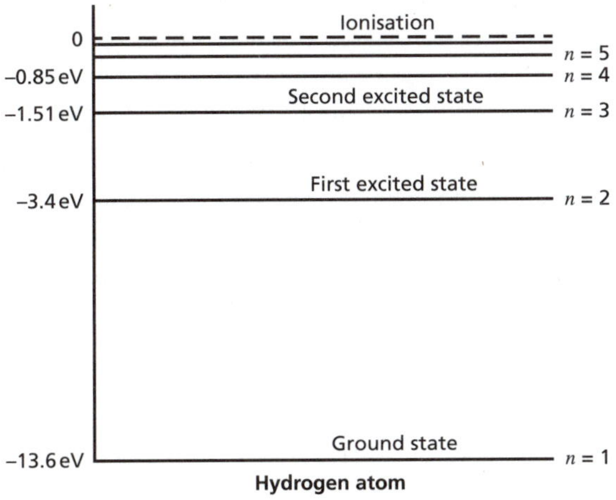

a) A photon of energy 12.5 eV cannot excite an electron from the ground state to the second excited state, but an electron of kinetic energy 12.5 eV can. Explain why. [3]

b) Calculate the longest wavelength of photon that could be emitted from de-excitation from the second excited state to the ground state. [3]

c) A hydrogen discharge lamp can be used to form an emission spectrum. The photon wavelengths in this emission spectrum can be compared to absorption spectra and used to show that the Sun contains hydrogen.

Describe the difference between emission and absorption spectra. [3]

d) Explain how line spectra provide evidence for discrete energy levels in atoms. [2]

3 Describe how a fluorescent lamp emits visible photons. [6]

ORGANISE

Wave–particle duality

Key words

Key questions

What is 'wave–particle duality'?

What is the evidence for electrons behaving as a wave?

What is the evidence for light behaving as particles?

What is peer review?

Electron diffraction: demonstrating the wave-like properties of particles

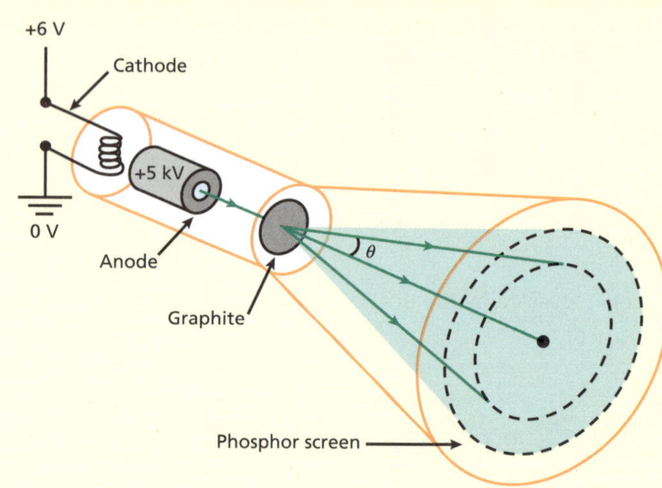

Electrons are released from a cathode by thermionic emission. The electrons are then accelerated across a potential difference (p.d.) towards an anode. The kinetic energy of electrons after acceleration across a p.d., V, is E_k = eV (where e is the charge on an electron). So, if an electron is accelerated across a p.d. of 1 kV, it gains 1 keV of kinetic energy (where 1 eV is equal to 1.6×10^{-19} J; the same number as the charge on an electron).

These electrons are then directed towards a thin graphite or metal target. They diffract and strike a phosphor screen. The phosphor fluoresces where electrons collide with it. Concentric rings appear on the phosphor screen, similar to the diffraction pattern observed with electromagnetic waves. Maxima are formed when electrons arrive in phase and constructively interfere. Minima are formed when electrons arrive out of phase and destructively interfere.

The de Broglie wavelength

Electrons behaving in the way described above shows that they act as waves. As they also show particle-like properties (such as having discrete mass and charge), you can say that electrons demonstrate **wave–particle duality.** In other words, the electron behaves as both a wave and a particle simultaneously.

This was explained by Louis de Broglie, who proposed that particles made of matter (like electrons) can have a wavelength (λ) associated with their motion:

$$\lambda = \frac{h}{mv}$$

where h is the Planck constant (6.63×10^{-34} J s), m is the mass of the particle and v is the particle's velocity.

This explains why the spacing of the diffraction pattern depends on the particle velocity. Diffraction is maximised when the particle's wavelength is similar to the gap that it is travelling through. In the electron diffraction example above, the smaller the accelerating potential difference, the more spread out the diffraction pattern is. This is because the electron's wavelength reduces and is closer to the spacing of nuclei in the graphite target (which is of the order of 10^{-10} m).

Development of wave–particle duality over time

Originally, as light was observed to diffract and interfere, it was considered to be purely a wave. Experiments such as the photoelectric effect led to the concept of photons (particles of light) and wave–particle duality for light.

Similarly, electrons were once considered purely particles until electron diffraction revealed their wave nature. The acceptance of wave–particle duality required rigorous experimental evidence and **peer review**.

Summary

RETRIEVE

Wave–particle duality

1. Electrons are accelerated through a potential difference of 5.0 kV and targeted towards a thin graphite sheet.

   The photo shows the resulting electron pattern on a phosphor screen, which is used as evidence for the wave–particle duality of electrons.

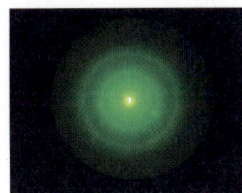

   a) Explain what is meant by electrons demonstrating 'wave–particle duality'. [1]

   b) Explain why the pattern on the phosphor screen is evidence that electrons behave as waves. Include a description of what causes the bright rings. [2]

   c) Describe why the phosphor fluoresces when an electron collides with it. [2]

   d) Show that the velocity of electrons after they have been accelerated is approximately 4×10^{7} m s^{-1}. The mass of an electron is 9.11×10^{-31} kg. [2]

   e) Calculate the de Broglie wavelength of these electrons. [1]

   f) Describe what would happen to the pattern if the accelerating potential difference was decreased. [3]

   g) Light also demonstrates wave–particle duality.

   State **one** piece of evidence for light behaving as a stream of particles. [1]

2. Interference effects have been observed for molecules that contain 2000 atoms.

   a) Describe why molecules can undergo interference. [2]

   b) The molecule had a mass of 4.2×10^{-23} kg.

   Calculate the de Broglie wavelength of one of these molecules travelling at 150 m s^{-1}. [1]

   c) Give **one** reason why it might be more difficult to observe interference for particularly large molecules. [1]

Progressive waves

Key words

Key questions

What is a progressive wave?

What is a transverse wave?

What is a longitudinal wave?

How many degrees/radians are there in one complete wave cycle?

Progressive waves

A progressive wave transfers energy from one place to another, without transferring matter. In these waves, the particles of the medium oscillate around a fixed position, passing the wave's energy along.

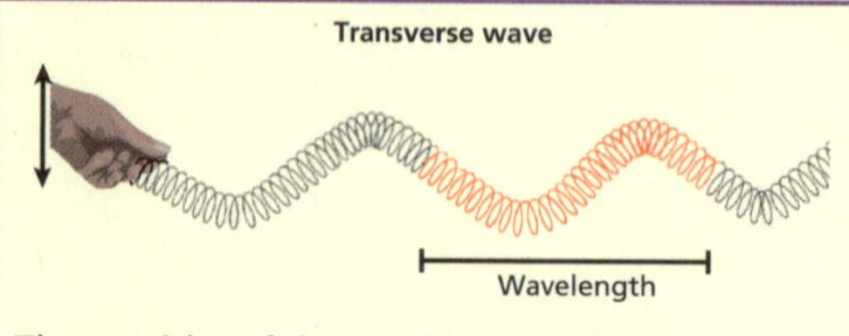

The particles of the medium oscillate perpendicular to the direction of energy transfer. Examples include electromagnetic waves and waves on a string. Electromagnetic waves have electric and magnetic field components, which oscillate at right angles to each other. They also travel at the speed of light (3.0×10^8 m s^{-1}) and can travel through a vacuum.

Longitudinal wave

Compression Rarefaction

Wavelength

The particles of the medium oscillate parallel to the direction of energy transfer. Sound is one example of a longitudinal wave. Longitudinal waves consist of compressions (regions of high pressure and density) and rarefactions (regions of low pressure and density).

For both transverse and longitudinal waves, the displacement from the equilibrium position can be shown to vary with distance or time. The maximum displacement from the equilibrium position is known as the **amplitude**.

Other key wave quantities are:

- **Wavelength** (λ), measured in m, is the distance between two successive points in phase in a wave.
- **Frequency** (f), measured in Hz, is the number of waves passing a point every second.
- **Time period** (T), measured in s, is the time for one complete oscillation, given by $T = \frac{1}{f}$
- **Wave speed** (c), measured in m s^{-1}, can be calculated using $c = f\lambda$.

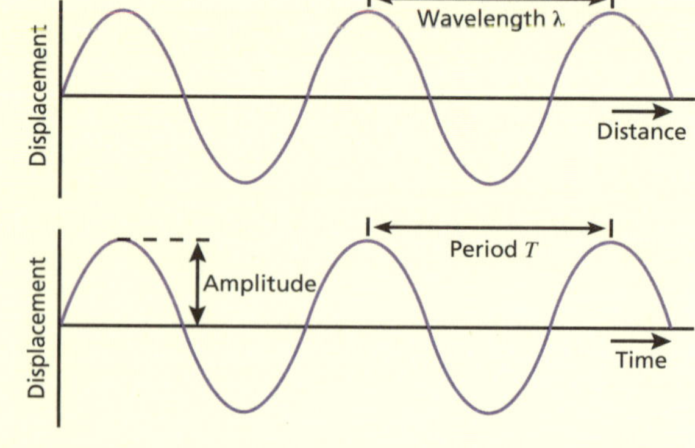

Phase and phase difference

Phase describes the position of a point on a wave within a complete cycle, relative to the start of the cycle. It tells you how far along the wave has progressed through its oscillation. Phase is measured in angles, either in degrees or radians. There are 360° or 2π radians in one complete wave cycle.

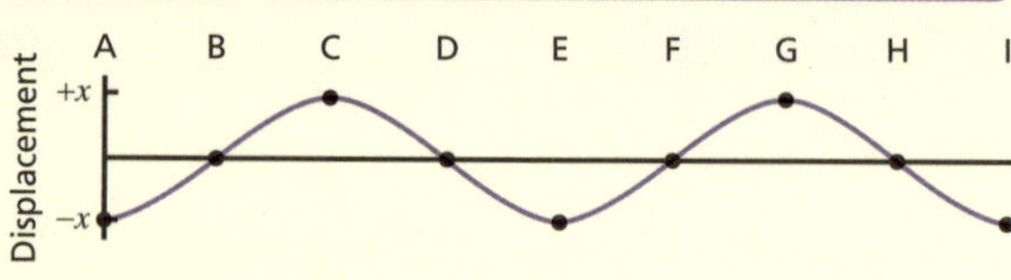

	B	C	D	E	F	G	H	I
Phase difference from A (degrees)	90	180	270	360	450	540	630	720
Phase difference from A (radians)	$\frac{\pi}{2}$	π	$\frac{3\pi}{2}$	2π	$\frac{5\pi}{2}$	3π	$\frac{7\pi}{2}$	4π

Summary

Progressive waves

1 The diagram shows three points on a wave.

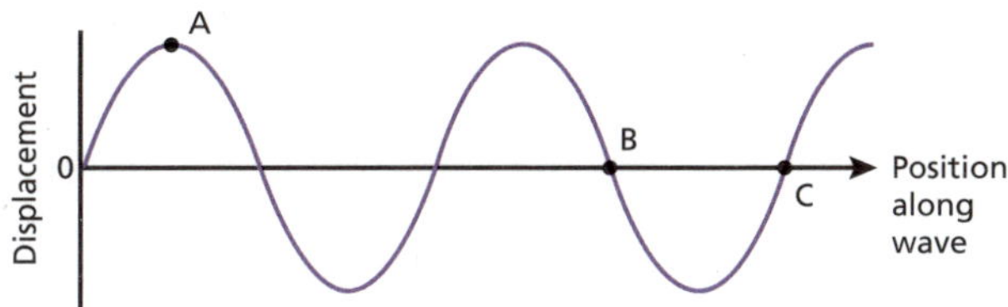

a) State the phase difference between A and B. Give your answer in degrees and radians. [1]

b) State the phase difference between A and C. Give your answer in degrees and radians. [1]

c) State the phase difference between B and C. Give your answer in degrees and radians. [1]

d) The distance between B and C is 0.45 m.

Calculate the wavelength of the wave. [1]

2 Visible light is part of the electromagnetic spectrum. Green light has a wavelength of 532 nm.

a) Describe the properties of an electromagnetic wave. [3]

b) Calculate the frequency, in THz, of green light. [2]

c) Calculate the minimum distance between two points in the green light that have a phase difference of $\frac{\pi}{2}$ radians. [2]

3 A sound wave has a time period of 2.5 ms. Sound is a longitudinal wave.

a) Describe what is meant by a 'longitudinal wave'. [2]

b) Calculate the frequency of the sound wave. [2]

c) The speed of sound in air is 340 m s^{-1}.

Calculate the wavelength of the sound wave. [1]

d) Calculate the minimum distance between two points in the sound wave that have a phase difference of 180°. [1]

ORGANISE

Polarisation

Key words

Key questions

What is meant by 'unpolarised light'?

What is meant by 'polarised light'?

What happens when you pass unpolarised light through a polarising filter?

What are some applications of polarising filters?

Unpolarised and polarised waves

Transverse waves can either be unpolarised or polarised.

In **unpolarised** waves, oscillations occur in multiple planes perpendicular to the direction of wave travel. Light from sources such as the Sun or a lamp is unpolarised, meaning its electric field oscillates in all directions perpendicular to the wave's travel.

A **polarised** wave has its oscillations restricted to a single plane, perpendicular to the direction of wave travel. Longitudinal waves, such as sound, cannot be polarised because their oscillations occur in the same direction as the wave's propagation.

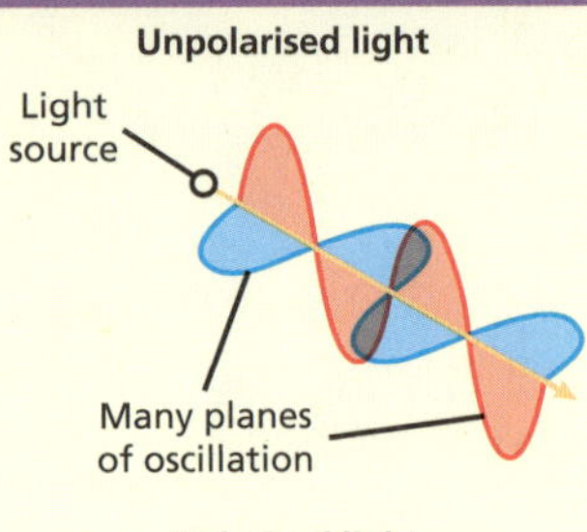

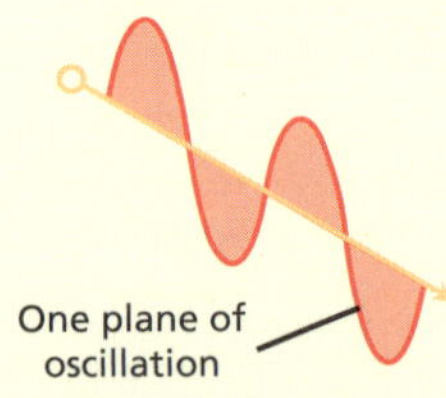

Polarising filters

A polarising filter allows only oscillations in a specific plane to pass through, blocking all others. When unpolarised light passes through a polarising filter, only the component of the light oscillating in the filter's transmission axis is transmitted. For example, if unpolarised light passes through a vertical polarising filter, only vertically polarised light is transmitted.

If polarised light then passes through a second filter, called an **analyser**, the intensity of the transmitted light depends on the relative angle between the transmission axes of the polarising filter and the analyser:

- If the axes are aligned, all polarised light passes through the analyser.
- As the analyser is rotated, the transmitted intensity decreases gradually.
- If the axes are perpendicular, no light passes through.

This experiment was proof that light is transverse as only transverse waves can be polarised.

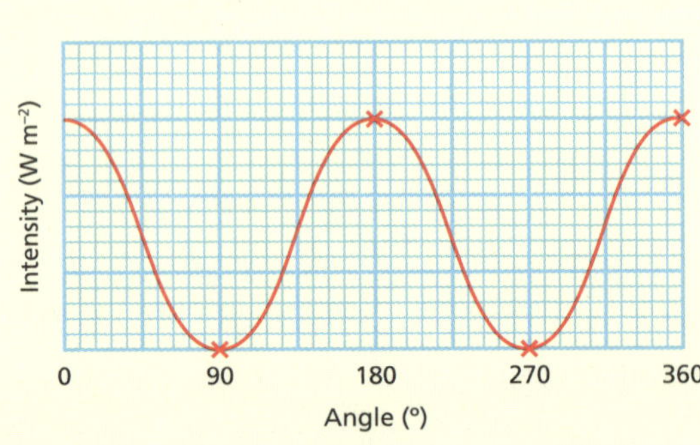

Applications of polarising filters

When light reflects off surfaces like water or glass, it becomes partially polarised. Polaroid sunglasses use polarising filters to block this partially polarised light. This reduces glare and improves visibility.

Radio and TV signals are often polarised. For optimal reception, the receiving aerial must align with the plane of polarisation of the transmitted signal. For example, if the transmission is vertically polarised, the receiving aerial must also be vertically orientated.

Summary

RETRIEVE

Polarisation

1. Which of these waves **cannot** be polarised? Tick **one** box. [1]

   Ultraviolet light ☐ Microwaves ☐

   Sound ☐ Visible light ☐

2. What is the angle of an analyser relative to a polarising filter when no light is transmitted? Tick **one** box. [1]

   0° ☐ 45° ☐

   90° ☐ 180° ☐

3. Describe an experiment to demonstrate that light is a transverse wave using polarising filters. Include a clear method, expected observations and how the results support the conclusion. [6]

4. A photographer wants to take a photo of some fish under the surface of a lake, but there is too much glare from reflections from the water. The photographer decides to attach a polarising filter to the front of their camera to help reduce these reflections.

   a) Describe what is meant by 'polarised light'. [2]

   b) Describe how using the polarising filter can be used to reduce the glare from reflections. [2]

   c) State **one** other application of polarising filters. [1]

5. Unpolarised microwaves pass through two polarising filters. The first filter has its transmission axis vertically aligned, while the second filter is rotated through 360°. [2]

   In the space below, sketch a graph showing how the intensity of microwaves emerging from the second filter varies with its angle of rotation. Assume that the transmission axis of the second filter is initially horizontally aligned. [2]

ORGANISE

Superposition and stationary waves

Key words

Key questions

What is the principle of superposition?

How is a stationary wave formed?

What is a 'node'?

What is an 'antinode'?

Formation of stationary waves

The principle of **superposition** states that when two or more waves overlap, the resultant displacement is the vector sum of the individual displacements.

A stationary wave is formed when two waves of the same frequency, wavelength and amplitude overlap while travelling in opposite directions. The waves superpose and interfere, creating nodes (where there is zero displacement) and antinodes (where there is maximum displacement).

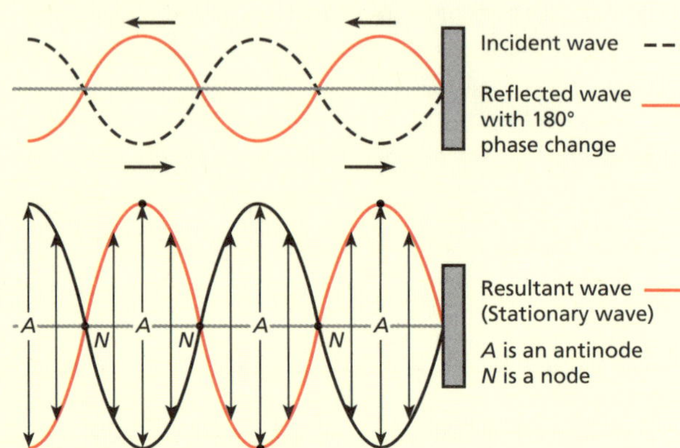

Stationary waves are often caused by reflections. If a wave is reflected by a boundary, it has a 180° phase change. A stationary wave will form as the reflected wave will have the same frequency, wavelength and amplitude as the incident wave.

Waves on a string

A string fixed at both ends can form stationary waves at specific frequencies. These are called the **harmonics** of the string:

- The first harmonic has one antinode in the middle and nodes at both ends.
- Higher harmonics (second harmonic, third harmonic, etc.) have additional nodes and antinodes.

The frequency, f, of the first harmonic of a stationary wave on a string is given by:

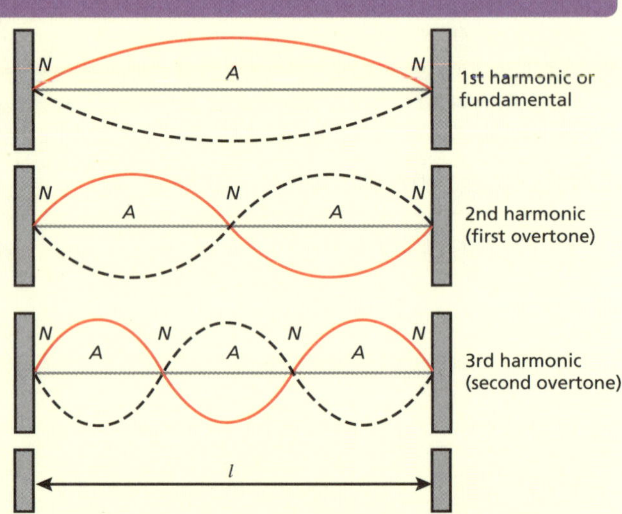

$$f = \frac{1}{2l}\sqrt{\frac{T}{\mu}}$$

where l is the length of the string (in m), T is the tension applied to the string (in N) and μ is the mass per unit length of the string (in $kg\,m^{-1}$). This frequency should be multiplied by n for the nth harmonic.

Stationary waves in other contexts

Stationary waves can form when microwaves reflect off a metal plate. Nodes (no signal) and antinodes (maximum signal) can be detected using a microwave detector. Stationary sound waves can form in pipes or tubes. Nodes form at closed ends, while antinodes form at an open end of a tube.

Summary

RETRIEVE

Superposition and stationary waves

1) The distance between two adjacent nodes on a string vibrating in its second harmonic is 0.60 m.

What is the wavelength of the wave? Tick **one** box. [1]

0.30 m ☐ 0.60 m ☐ 1.20 m ☐ 1.80 m ☐

2) The frequency of the first harmonic on a string is 40 Hz. The string is replaced with one of half the mass per unit length and the tension applied to the string is doubled.

What is the new frequency of the first harmonic? Tick **one** box. [1]

40 Hz ☐ 57 Hz ☐ 80 Hz ☐ 160 Hz ☐

3) A microwave emitter directs microwaves towards a metal plate. A microwave detector is moved along the direction of microwave travel and a stationary wave is established.

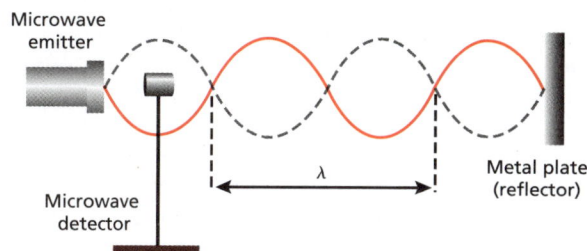

a) Describe how a stationary wave is formed in this experiment. [3]

b) The microwaves have a frequency of 2.45 GHz and the distance between two consecutive nodes is measured to be 6.1 cm.

Show that the speed of light is approximately $3.0 \times 10^8\,\mathrm{m\,s^{-1}}$. [3]

4) A string of length 0.80 m driven at a frequency of 36 Hz vibrates in its third harmonic.

a) In the space below, sketch a diagram of the third harmonic. Label any nodes with an N and antinodes with an A. [3]

b) Describe how nodes and antinodes are formed. [2]

c) The string has a mass per unit length of $1.8\,\mathrm{g\,m^{-1}}$.

Calculate the tension applied to the string. [2]

ORGANISE

Two-source interference

Key words

Key questions

What is meant if two waves are said to be 'coherent'?

Why are maxima and minima formed in Young's double-slit experiment?

What safety precautions should be taken when using lasers?

What does the interference patten look like if white light is directed onto a double slit?

Coherence and path difference

Interference occurs when two or more waves overlap and superpose, producing regions of constructive and destructive interference. For a clear interference pattern to form, the waves must be **coherent**. Coherent waves have the same frequency and wavelength, and a constant phase difference.

The **path difference** is the difference in the distance travelled by two waves to a specific point. Constructive interference occurs when the path difference is $n\lambda$ (where n is an integer, and λ is the wavelength) as this is when the waves arrive in phase with each other. Destructive interference occurs when two waves arrive completely out of phase with each other, when the path difference is $(n + 0.5)\lambda$.

Young's double-slit experiment and laser safety

An interference pattern is formed when light from a monochromatic source, such as a laser, is passed through two closely spaced slits and directed onto a screen. These slits act as two coherent sources emitting light waves. At certain points on the screen, the waves from both slits arrive in phase. They constructively interfere, producing bright fringes (maxima).

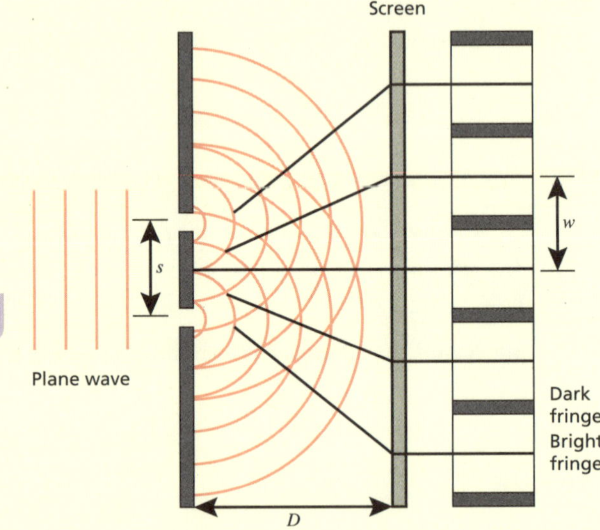

At other points, the waves from the slits arrive out of phase. They destructively interfere, producing dark fringes (minima).

The pattern consists of alternating bright and dark fringes.

The spacing w between adjacent bright (or dark) fringes is given by:

$$w = \frac{\lambda D}{s}$$

where D is the distance to the screen and s is the slit separation.

Lasers produce intense and collimated beams of light that can cause serious eye damage. Laser safety goggles can be worn to reduce the risk, but lasers should still never be directed at anyone and should be kept at waist height.

The double-slit experiment can also be carried out with other waves, such as microwaves or sound waves.

Interference with white light

An interference pattern is also observed if white light is directed onto a double slit. White light consists of multiple wavelengths, whereas laser light is monochromatic. When white light is directed onto a double slit, the central maximum is white. This occurs because, for the path difference of zero (in the middle of the screen), all wavelengths of light arrive in phase and constructively interfere.

Away from the central maximum, the conditions for constructive interference differ for each wavelength. Within white light, red has the longest wavelength and violet has the shortest. The result is that, for maxima other than the central maximum, a spectrum is formed (with red on the outer edge and violet on the inner edge).

Summary

RETRIEVE

Two-source interference

(1) Which of the following will **not** decrease the fringe spacing in a double-slit experiment? Tick **one** box. [1]

Increasing the distance between the slits ☐

Decreasing the distance from the slits to the screen ☐

Decreasing the wavelength of the light ☐

Decreasing the width of the slits, keeping the slit separation the same ☐

(2) Two sound waves of frequency 170 Hz emerge from a double slit. One of the sound waves travels 4.0 m to a microphone, while the other travels 5.0 m. The speed of sound is 340 m s^{-1}.

Which of the following is the correct description of what the microphone will detect? Tick **one** box. [1]

Maxima as the phase difference is 180° ☐

Maxima as the phase difference is 360° ☐

Minima as the phase difference is 180° ☐

Minima as the phase difference is 360° ☐

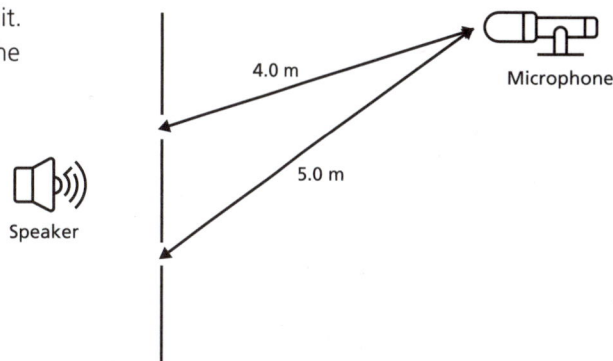

(3) Green laser light of wavelength 532 nm is directed onto a double slit of slit spacing 500 μm. The resulting interference pattern is viewed on a screen at a distance of 1.50 m from the double slit.

a) Calculate the fringe spacing between maxima. [2]

b) Explain why bright and dark fringes are formed on the screen. [3]

c) The green laser is replaced with a red one.

Describe and explain how the interference pattern is different. [2]

(4) A Young's double-slit experiment is set up using microwaves at a frequency of 10.0 GHz. The slits are separated by 5.0 cm, and a microwave detector is positioned 1.5 m from the slits. The detector is used to locate points of constructive and destructive interference.

a) The detector is moved to a position 45 cm away from the central maximum.

Determine whether constructive or destructive interference will occur at the detector's position. [5]

b) The microwaves emerging through each of the double slits are coherent.

Explain what is meant if two microwaves are coherent. [2]

ORGANISE

Diffraction

Key words

Key questions

When is diffraction maximised?

What does the interference pattern from a single slit look like?

What is the path difference for the *n*th order maxima of a diffraction grating?

How do you convert from lines/metre to slit spacing?

Diffraction

Diffraction is the spreading out of waves as they pass through a gap or around an obstacle. It occurs for all types of waves, including sound, light and water waves.

When the size of the gap or obstacle is similar to the wavelength of the wave, diffraction is maximised. If the gap is much larger than the wavelength, the wave passes through with little diffraction.

Diffraction through a single slit

When monochromatic light passes through a single slit:

- a central maximum is produced that is very bright and twice as wide as other fringes
- secondary maxima (to either side) are dimmer, with decreasing brightness away from the centre.

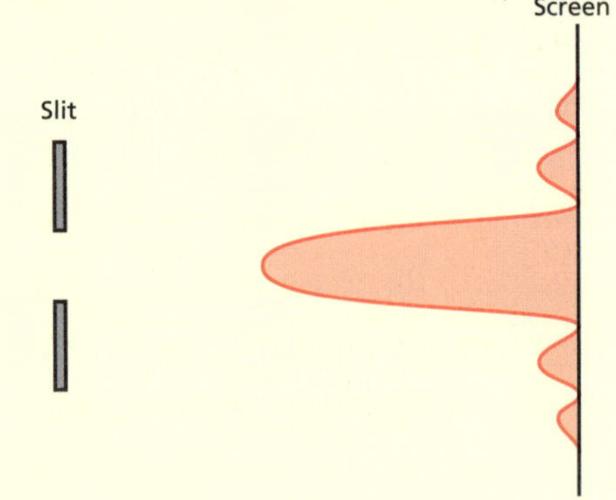

This pattern arises due to the interference of waves emerging from different parts of the slit.

When white light passes through a single slit, the central maximum is white as all wavelengths constructively interfere. The fringes around the central maximum are split into spectra, with red fringes being wider and more spread out than blue fringes due to the longer wavelength of red light.

Diffraction gratings

A diffraction grating consists of many closely spaced slits (or lines), producing sharp and bright maxima due to the interference of waves.

For light passing through a grating, maxima occur when waves from adjacent slits arrive at a screen in phase. This happens when the path difference between adjacent slits is equal to $n\lambda$ (where n is the order of the maxima and λ is the wavelength).

Path difference $= x_2 - x_1 = n\lambda$

$\sin\theta = \frac{O}{H}$

$\sin\theta = \frac{n\lambda}{d}$

$d\sin\theta = n\lambda$

From trigonometry, it can be shown that the path difference from adjacent slits is also equal to $d\sin\theta$ (where d is the slit spacing and θ is the angle of the maximum from the central axis).

Therefore, combining these gives: $d\sin\theta = n\lambda$

Diffraction gratings are usually labelled as having a certain number of lines/metre (N). This is related to the slit spacing by the equation $d = \frac{1}{N}$

Maximum diffraction order

It is not possible for the angle of the maximum from the central axis, θ, to be more than 90°. This means that there is a maximum diffraction order (n_{max}) that can be viewed on the screen:

$$n_{max} = \frac{d\sin 90}{\lambda} = \frac{d}{\lambda}$$

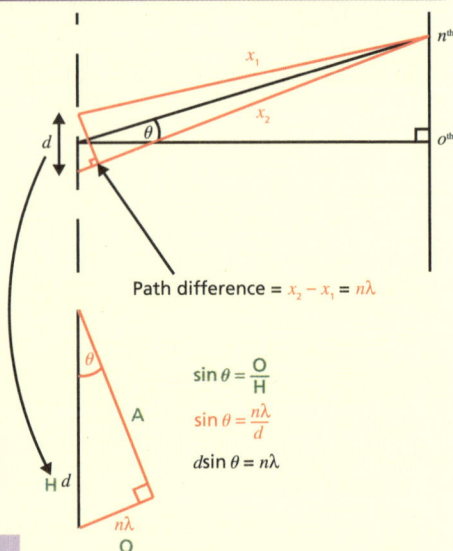

Summary

RETRIEVE

Diffraction

1) A diffraction grating is illuminated with light of two different wavelengths (500 nm and 600 nm).

Which of the following statements is correct? Tick **one** box. [1]

- The maxima for 600 nm are closer to the central maximum. ☐
- The spacing between the maxima is identical for both wavelengths. ☐
- The maxima for 500 nm are closer to the central maximum. ☐
- The maxima for both wavelengths coincide. ☐

2) When white light passes through a single slit, which of the following statements is correct? Tick **one** box. [1]

- All wavelengths diffract equally, forming a single bright central maximum. ☐
- Longer wavelengths diffract more, causing the central maximum to appear white and other maxima to form spectra. ☐
- Shorter wavelengths diffract more, creating a broad spectrum for the central maximum. ☐
- Diffraction does not occur for white light. ☐

3) Red laser light of wavelength 650 nm is incident onto a diffraction grating that is labelled as having '500 lines/mm'.

a) Calculate the slit spacing in metres. [2]

b) Calculate the angle between the two second order maxima. [3]

c) Determine the maximum order that is viewed on a screen. [2]

d) The diffraction grating is replaced with a single slit.

Describe the interference pattern that is formed by single-slit diffraction. [2]

4) One application of diffraction is to measure the wavelengths of light from lasers or light emitted by stars. A device called a spectrometer can be used to do this.

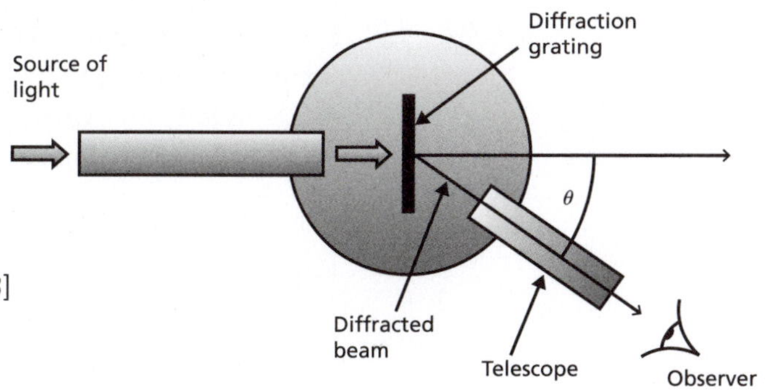

a) Monochromatic light is directed towards a diffraction grating that has 1000 lines/mm. The first order maximum is detected at an angle of 22°.

Calculate the wavelength of the light. [3]

b) Another application of diffraction is to measure atomic spacing using X-rays. This is a technique called X-ray crystallography.

State **one** similarity and **one** difference between X-rays and visible light. [2]

ORGANISE

Refraction and reflection

Key words

Key questions

What is refraction?

What is Snell's law?

What are the conditions for total internal reflection?

Refractive index

Refraction is the change in direction of a wave as it passes from one medium to another. This occurs because the wave's speed changes when it enters a medium with a different refractive index.

The refractive index, n, measures how much a medium reduces the speed of light relative to its speed in a vacuum, so that:

$$n = \frac{c}{c_s}$$

where c is the speed of light in a vacuum (equal to 3.00×10^8 m s^{-1}) and c_s is the speed of light in a substance.

The refractive index of air is approximately equal to 1.

Snell's law of refraction

Snell's law relates the angles of incidence (θ_1) and refraction (θ_2) at a boundary between two materials:

$$n_1 \sin\theta_1 = n_2 \sin\theta_2$$

where n_1 is the refractive index of the first medium and n_2 is the refractive index of the second medium.

Note that the angles of incidence and refraction are measured from the normal (which is perpendicular to the boundary).

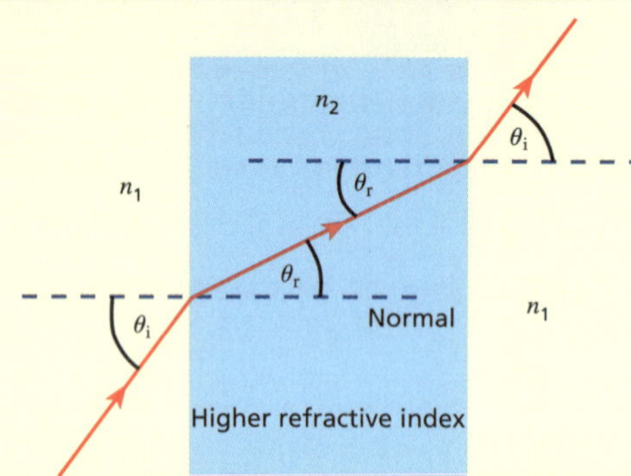

When light enters a medium with a higher refractive index ($n_2 > n_1$), such as from air to water, the light slows down and refracts towards the normal ($\theta_2 < \theta_1$).

When light enters a medium with a lower refractive index ($n_2 < n_1$), the light speeds up and refracts away from the normal ($\theta_2 > \theta_1$). An example is light exiting water into air.

Total internal reflection

Total internal reflection occurs when:

- light travels from a medium with a higher refractive index (n_1) to a medium with a lower refractive index (n_2)
- the angle of incidence exceeds the critical angle (θ_c).

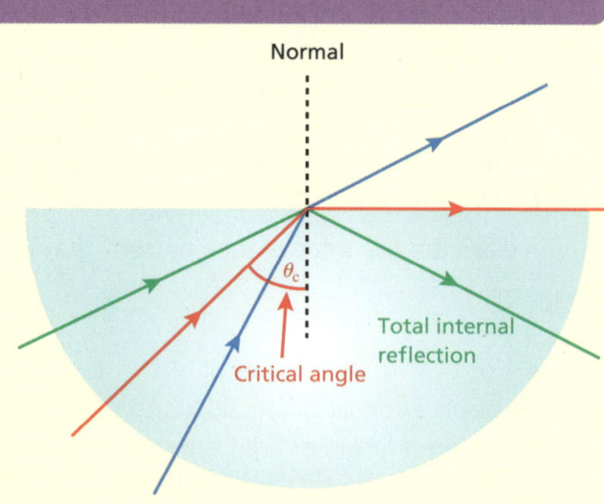

The critical angle is the angle of incidence at which the angle of refraction becomes 90°. If 90° is substituted into the equation for Snell's law, an expression for the critical angle (θ_c) is obtained: $n_1 \sin\theta_c = n_2 \sin 90$

This leads to: $$\sin\theta_c = \frac{n_2}{n_1}$$

When $\theta_1 < \theta_c$, light is partially refracted and partially reflected.
When $\theta_1 = \theta_c$, the refracted ray travels along the boundary.
When $\theta_1 > \theta_c$, all the light is reflected back into the higher refractive index medium.

Summary

RETRIEVE

Refraction and reflection

1. When light travels from air into a different medium, its speed decreases by 30%.

   Which is the correct refractive index of the medium? Tick **one** box. [1]

   0.7 ☐ 1.3 ☐ 1.4 ☐ 1.7 ☐

2. a) State the **two** conditions required for total internal reflection to occur. [2]

   b) A light ray is incident onto the boundary between diamond (n = 2.42) and air.

   Calculate the critical angle. [2]

3. A ray of light strikes the surface of water in a fish tank, with an angle of incidence of 50°. Water has a refractive index of 1.33

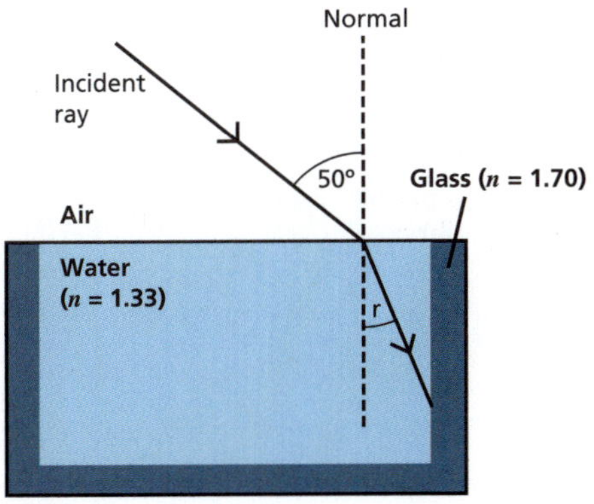

   Normal
   Incident ray
   50°
   Glass (n = 1.70)
   Air
   Water (n = 1.33)
   r

   a) Calculate the speed of light in water. [2]

   b) The ray of light refracts into the water.

   Calculate its angle of refraction. [2]

   c) The ray of light continues until it strikes the vertical glass surface of the fish tank. Glass has a refractive index of 1.70

   Determine what next happens to the ray of light. [3]

4. Describe an experiment that a student could undertake to measure the refractive index of a glass block. Include a description of a graph that could be plotted to obtain the refractive index. [4]

ORGANISE

Optical fibres

Key words

Key questions

What is the structure of an optical fibre?

Why are repeaters used in long-distance fibres?

What causes material dispersion?

What causes modal dispersion?

Structure of an optical fibre

An optical fibre is a thin, flexible strand of glass or plastic that can transmit light over long distances by the process of total internal reflection. An optical fibre consists of a core surrounded by cladding:

- The core is the central region of the fibre where light is transmitted. It has a higher refractive index than the surrounding cladding.
- The cladding is a layer surrounding the core with a lower refractive index. It prevents light from escaping the core by ensuring that total internal reflection occurs. The cladding also protects the core from damage and signal loss due to contact with external substances.

In a step-index optical fibre, the core has a uniform refractive index and there is a sharp boundary between the core and the cladding.

Signal degradation in optical fibres

There are three main causes of signal degradation in optical fibres:

1. **Absorption** occurs when some light is absorbed by the material of the core, converting it into thermal energy. This reduces the signal's amplitude and limits the distance it can travel. To combat absorption, optical fibres are made from materials with very high transparency and repeaters are used in long-distance fibres. Repeaters amplify and regenerate the signal, compensating for losses due to absorption.
2. **Material dispersion** occurs because the refractive index of the fibre material depends on the wavelength for light. Different wavelengths travel at different speeds in the core, causing them to take different times to travel through the optical fibre. Shorter wavelengths (e.g. violet light) travel slower than longer wavelengths as violet experiences a higher refractive index. Material dispersion is minimised by using monochromatic light from a laser. This ensures that only a single wavelength is used so that all parts of the light travel at the same speed through the fibre.

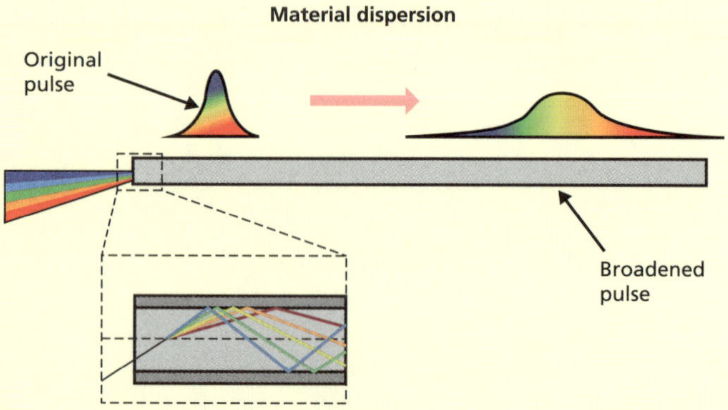

3. **Modal dispersion** occurs in multimode fibres, where different light rays travel along different paths (modes) in the fibre core. Rays that take longer paths arrive later than those that take shorter and more direct paths. This leads to a spreading out of pulses over time.

   Modal dispersion is reduced by single-mode fibres that contain a narrow core. The refractive index of the cladding is also chosen to be very close to that of the core (meaning that the critical angle is close to 90°). These factors minimise the angles that light can take while travelling through the core.

Both material and modal dispersion are examples of **pulse broadening**. This refers to the spreading out of light pulses as they travel through the fibre.

Summary

RETRIEVE

Optical fibres

1. Which property of cladding ensures total internal reflection in an optical fibre? Tick **one** box. [1]

   Higher refractive index than the core ☐ Lower refractive index than the core ☐

   The same refractive index as the core ☐ A reflective coating ☐

2. Optical fibres suffer from pulse broadening.

   Explain what causes pulse broadening and how an optical fibre can be designed to minimise pulse broadening. [6]

3. A red ray of light travels through air and strikes the core of an optical fibre with an angle of incidence of 15.5°. It refracts into the core with an angle of refraction of 10.5°. The refractive index of the cladding is 1.4

   a) State the purpose of the cladding in an optical fibre. [1]

   b) Calculate the critical angle for the core-cladding boundary. [4]

   c) The optical fibre is 5.5 km long.

   Calculate the time it takes for the red ray of light to pass through the optical fibre. Assume that the optical fibre is straight and horizontal. [3]

   d) A violet ray of light is now incident on the core of the optical fibre at a larger angle of incidence.

   Describe how the time for the violet ray of light to pass through the fibre compares with the red ray. [3]

   e) For both rays, the amplitude of light exiting the fibre is significantly lower than the amplitude that entered the fibre.

   Explain why this happens and what can be done to reduce this reduction in amplitude. [3]

Scalars and vectors

Key words

Key questions

What is the difference between a scalar and a vector?

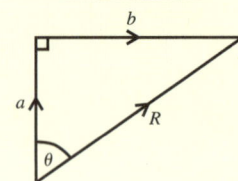

How can you find the resultant magnitude and direction of two vectors at right angles to each other?

What is the vertical component of a vector, *u*, at an angle of θ to the horizontal?

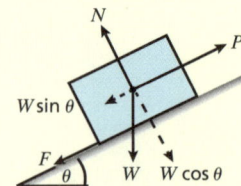

What is the horizontal component of a vector, *u*, at an angle of θ to the horizontal?

Scalars and vectors

A **scalar** is a quantity that has a magnitude only, without direction. A **vector** is a quantity that has both a magnitude and a direction.

Vectors are represented using arrows. The length of the arrow represents the magnitude of the vector, while the direction of the arrow shows the vector's direction.

Scalar quantities	Vector quantities
Speed	Velocity
Mass	Force
Time	Acceleration
Distance	Displacement
Energy	Momentum
Power	Moment

Vector addition and subtraction

If two vectors are at right angles to each other, Pythagoras' theorem is used to find the resultant magnitude: $R = \sqrt{a^2 + b^2}$

Trigonometry is used to find the angle (θ) of the resultant vector: $\theta = \tan^{-1}\left(\frac{b}{a}\right)$
where a and b are the magnitudes of the two vectors.

Scale diagrams can also be drawn to determine the magnitude and direction of a resultant vector:

1. Draw the first vector to scale, using a ruler and protractor.
2. From the tip of the first vector, draw the second vector to scale.
3. Connect the tail of the first vector to the tip of the second vector to form the resultant.
4. Measure the length and angle of the resultant to determine its magnitude and direction.

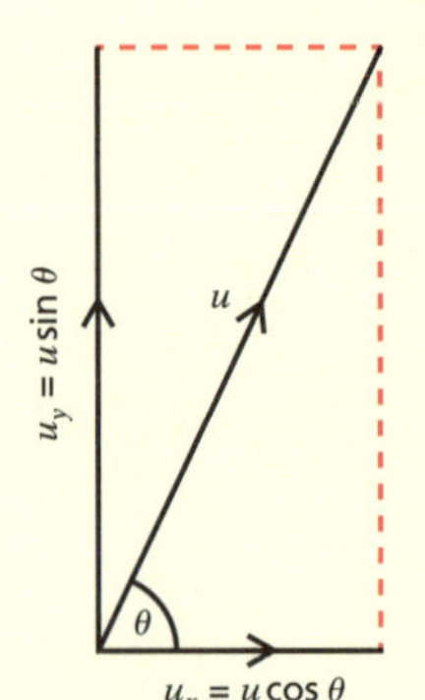

Vectors can also be resolved into perpendicular components. The horizontal component of a vector, u, at an angle of θ to the horizontal is $u_x = u\cos\theta$. The vertical component is $u_y = u\sin\theta$.

Sometimes it can be more convenient to resolve a vector parallel to and perpendicular to a slope.

Equilibrium

An object can only be in equilibrium if the resultant force acting on the object is zero. In other words, the vector sum of the forces must form a closed loop.

To solve equilibrium problems, forces can be resolved horizontally and vertically. The forces in each direction must be balanced.

Alternatively, components of forces can be resolved parallel and perpendicular to an inclined slope. An example of this is shown in the diagram, which shows a free body force diagram of an object in equilibrium on a slope.

The weight (W) is shown acting downwards, while the normal reaction force N acts at 90° to the slope. A pushing force (P) is applied to the object to keep it in equilibrium.

In equilibrium, the forces perpendicular to the slope are balanced: $N = W\cos\theta$

Similarly, the forces parallel to the slope are balanced, which leads to: $P = W\sin\theta$

Summary

RETRIEVE

Scalars and vectors

1 A force of 45 N is applied to an object at an angle of 30° to the horizontal.

Calculate the horizontal and vertical components of this force. [2]

2 An object has two forces applied to it: a vertical force of 5.0 N and a force of 4.0 N at an angle of 20° above the horizontal.

Draw a scale diagram and use it to determine the resultant force acting on the object. [4]

3 A 5.0 kg mass rests on a slope inclined at an angle of 30° above the horizontal. A frictional force prevents the mass from sliding down the slope and keeps it in equilibrium.

a) Calculate the component of the block's weight parallel to the slope. [2]

b) If the mass is in equilibrium, state the value of the frictional force. [1]

c) Calculate the normal contact force exerted by the slope on the block. [2]

4 Two cables support an object of weight 9.5 N. One cable has a tension T_1 at an angle of 50° above the horizontal. The other cable has a tension T_2 at an angle of 40° above the horizontal. The object is in equilibrium and the diagram is not to scale.

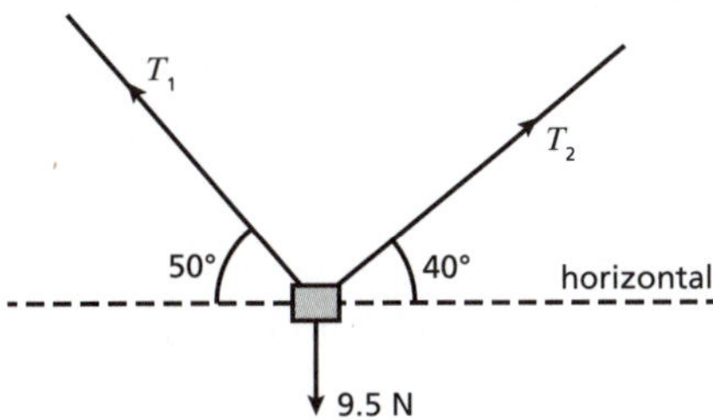

Calculate the values of T_1 and T_2. [4]

T_1 = ... T_2 = ...

Moments

Key words

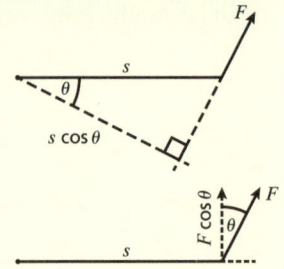

Key questions

What is the principle of moments?

When does an object topple over?

What is a 'couple'?

Moments

The moment of a force is the turning effect of a force about a pivot:

> moment = force × perpendicular distance from the pivot to the line of action of the force

The unit of a moment is the Newton-metre (Nm).

The diagram shows an example of a force that is not acting perpendicularly to a pivot.

In this situation, you have two options:

1. Find the perpendicular distance from the force to the pivot. In this case it is $s\cos\theta$. Therefore, the moment would equal $Fs\cos\theta$.
2. Find the component of the force that is perpendicular to the pivot ($F\cos\theta$). Multiplying this by s also gives a moment equal to $Fs\cos\theta$.

Principle of moments

For an object to be in equilibrium, the sum of the clockwise moments about any point must equal the sum of the anticlockwise moments. This is known as the principle of moments.

In the diagram, a uniform beam is pivoted at its centre of mass. The centre of mass of an object is the point at which its entire weight appears to act. For a uniform and regular solid, the centre of mass is at its centre. If the beam is in equilibrium, then the anticlockwise moment (= W_1d_1) is equal to the clockwise moment (= W_2d_2).

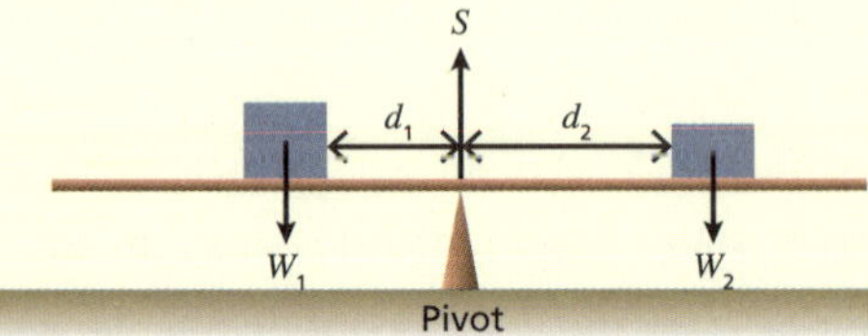

Stability and toppling

The position of the centre of mass greatly affects the stability of an object. An object topples over when the line of action of its weight falls outside its base.

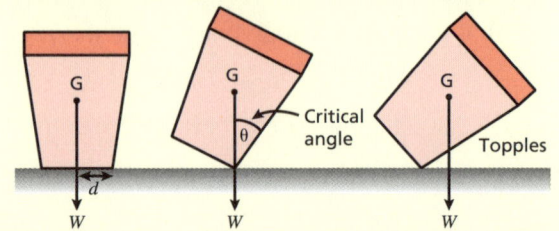

For example, sports cars have a low centre of mass and a wide base. This increases stability and reduces the risk of the car toppling over during sharp turns.

Couples

A couple is a pair of equal and opposite coplanar forces that act at different points. This produces a turning effect but no resultant linear force.

> moment of a couple = force × perpendicular distance between the lines of action of the forces

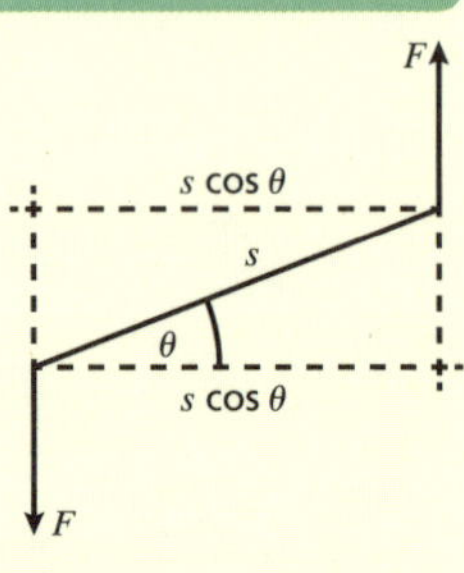

In the example shown in the diagram, you need to calculate the perpendicular distance between the two forces. This is $s\cos\theta$ and so the moment of a couple = $Fs\cos\theta$.

Summary

RETRIEVE

Moments

1 A steering wheel has a radius of 0.30 m and has a moment of a couple of 18 Nm applied to it.

What is the magnitude of the forces that act tangentially on opposite sides of the wheel? Tick **one** box. [1]

30 N ☐ 60 N ☐ 90 N ☐ 120 N ☐

2 A uniform horizontal beam has a pivot at its centre and has a 60 N weight hung 0.50 m from the pivot.

What force must be applied 1.5 m from the pivot to balance the beam? Tick **one** box. [1]

20 N ☐ 60 N ☐ 90 N ☐ 180 N ☐

3 A uniform beam of length 4.0 m and weight 120 N is supported at its two ends, A and B.
A weight of 25 N is placed 1.5 m from end B and the beam is in equilibrium.

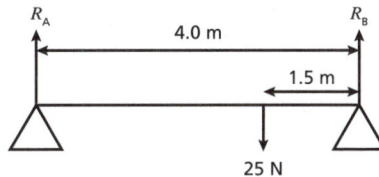

a) Calculate the reaction force from support A. [4]

....

b) Calculate the reaction force from support B. [2]

....

4 A uniform rectangular box, 2.0 m tall and 0.80 m wide, is placed on a flat surface so that its centre of mass is 1.0 m above the ground.

Determine whether the box will topple if it is tilted so that its edge makes an angle of 30° with the ground. [2]

....

....

....

5 A uniform beam of length 0.60 m is pivoted at one end to a wall. The other end of the beam has a downwards force of 75 N applied to it and is supported by a cable at an angle of 30° above the horizontal. The beam has a weight of 85 N and is in equilibrium. The diagram is not drawn to scale.

Calculate the tension, T, in the cable. [4]

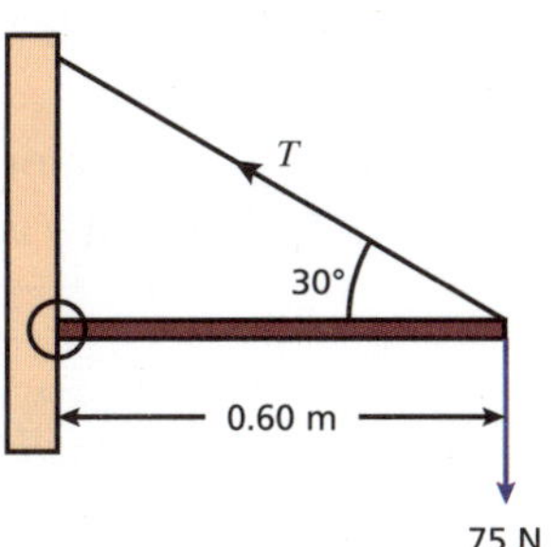

....

ORGANISE

Motion graphs

Key words

Key questions

What is the difference between speed and velocity?

What is the difference between average and instantaneous velocity?

How do you obtain the instantaneous velocity from a curved displacement–time graph?

How do you obtain the displacement from a curved velocity–time graph?

Definitions

Quantity	Definition
Displacement, s	The direct distance moved in a specific direction from a reference point. Displacement is a vector quantity.
Speed	The rate of change of distance. Speed is a scalar quantity.
Velocity, v	The rate of change of displacement. Velocity is a vector quantity, given by $v = \frac{\Delta s}{\Delta t}$
Acceleration, a	The rate of change of velocity. Acceleration is a vector quantity, given by $a = \frac{\Delta v}{\Delta t}$
Average velocity	The total displacement divided by the total time.
Instantaneous velocity	The velocity of an object at a specific moment in time.

Motion graphs

The motion of an object can be represented on displacement–time, velocity–time and acceleration–time graphs.

Type of graph	Description of what the graph can be used for
Displacement–time	The gradient is used to calculate the velocity of an object.
Velocity–time	The gradient represents the acceleration of an object.
	The area under the graph gives the displacement of an object.
Acceleration–time	The area under the graph represents the change in velocity.

The graph shows a velocity–time graph where there is non-uniform acceleration. Initially, the acceleration is increasing as the gradient of the velocity–time graph is increasing. After a time, the acceleration decreases (as the gradient decreases).

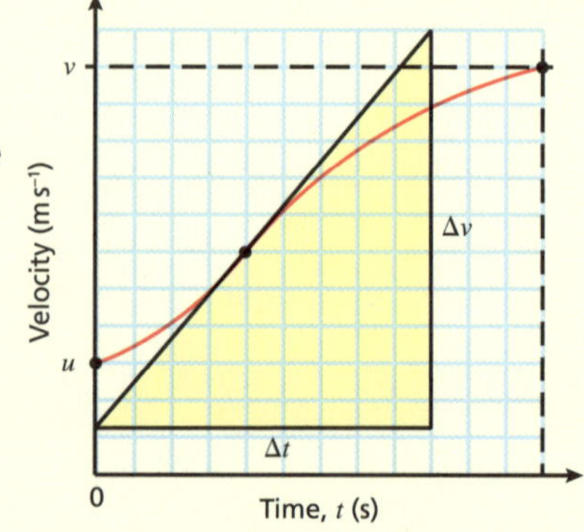

To calculate the instantaneous acceleration, you can draw a tangent to the curve. The gradient of the tangent will give the instantaneous acceleration. Similar can be done when obtaining the instantaneous velocity from a curved displacement–time graph.

To estimate the distance travelled under a curved velocity–time graph, you can approximate the area under the curve by dividing it into small sections such as rectangles or trapeziums. For a rough estimate, count the squares below the curve on graph paper, accounting for partial squares when necessary. For more precision, divide the area into trapeziums by drawing vertical lines at equal time intervals. The area of a trapezium can be calculated by $A = \frac{a+b}{2}h$, where a and b are the velocities at the start and end of the interval, and h is the time interval. Summing these areas gives an approximation of the total distance travelled. Smaller intervals improve the accuracy.

Summary

RETRIEVE

Motion graphs

1. A displacement–time graph has a decreasing gradient. What does this signify about the motion? Tick **one** box. [1]

   The object is accelerating. ☐ The object is decelerating. ☐

   The object is moving at a constant velocity. ☐ The object is stationary. ☐

2. An object is dropped from rest and falls freely under gravity for 5.0 seconds.

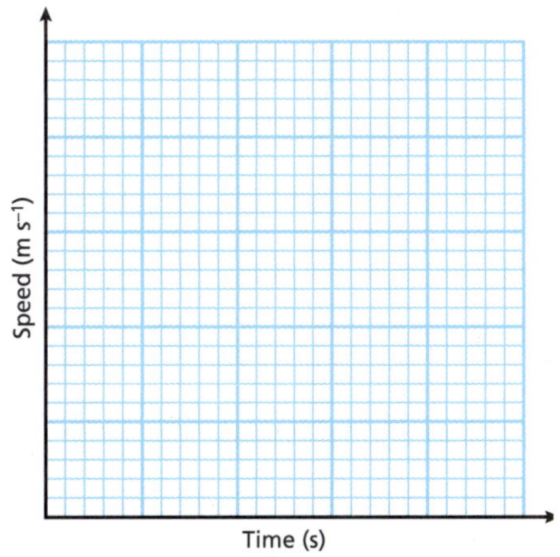

   Speed ($m\ s^{-1}$)

   Time (s)

   a) Using the axes given, sketch the speed–time graph for this motion. Assume that air resistance is negligible. [2]

   b) Using your sketch, determine the distance fallen. [2]

   ....

   c) Using the same axes, sketch a modified speed–time graph if air resistance is **not** negligible. [2]

3. A ball is thrown upwards with an initial velocity of $3.1\ m\ s^{-1}$. The graph shows how the velocity of the ball changes with time.

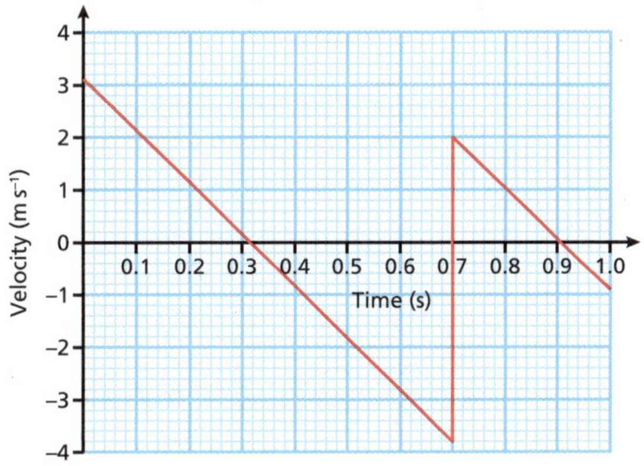

   Velocity ($m\ s^{-1}$): 4, 3, 2, 1, 0, −1, −2, −3, −4

   Time (s): 0.1, 0.2, 0.3, 0.4, 0.5, 0.6, 0.7, 0.8, 0.9, 1.0

   a) Using the graph, calculate the acceleration due to gravity. [2]

   ....

   b) Using the graph, calculate the maximum displacement that the ball reaches from its starting position. [2]

   ....

   c) After a time of 0.70 s, the ball hits the ground.

   Calculate the height above the ground from which the ball was originally thrown. [2]

   ....

   d) The ball rebounds from the ground, but at a lower velocity than when it hit the ground. Explain why. [1]

   ....

   ....

ORGANISE

Equations of motion

Key words

Key questions

What does it mean if an object is said to be 'at rest'?

If an object is moving upwards at a positive velocity, what is its acceleration due to gravity?

Which equation of motion should be used if you want to find acceleration from displacement, time and initial velocity?

Equations of motion

When an object's acceleration remains constant, its motion can be described using the equations of motion. These equations relate displacement (s), initial velocity (u), final velocity (v), acceleration (a) and time (t). The four equations of motion are:

1. $v = u + at$
2. $s = \frac{(u + v)}{2}t$
3. $s = ut + \frac{1}{2}at^2$
4. $v^2 = u^2 + 2as$

When solving a question, it is important to lay your working out clearly. You can do this by writing each of the variables under each other in the order '*suvat*':

s –
u –
v –
a –
t –

This makes it easy to identify what variables you have and which equation you should use.

A ball is thrown upwards with an initial velocity of 8.0 m s^{-1}. Calculate the maximum height that the ball reaches.

At the ball's maximum height, it will have an instantaneous velocity of 0 m s^{-1}. First, complete the variables that are known.

s – s
u – 8.0 m s^{-1}
v – 0 m s^{-1}
a – −9.81 m s^{-2}
t –

Note that the acceleration has been filled out as −9.81 m s^{-2}. This is because the ball is accelerating due to gravity and the direction of acceleration is opposite to that of the initial velocity. As you don't have any information about the time (and don't need to calculate the time), you need to use the equation of motion that does not include t. This is $v^2 = u^2 + 2as$. Therefore $0^2 = 8.0^2 + 2 \times (-9.81)s$, which leads to $s = \frac{64}{19.62} = 3.3$ m.

An object, initially at rest, is dropped from a height of 25 m. Calculate the time it takes for the object to reach the ground.

If the object is initially at rest, its velocity is 0 m s^{-1}. The following variables are therefore known.

s – 25 m
u – 0 m s^{-1}
v –
a – 9.81 m s^{-2}
t – t

The equation of motion used to solve this question should be $s = ut + \frac{1}{2}at^2$ as you do not have any information about the final velocity. Therefore, $25 = 0 + \frac{1}{2} \times 9.81t^2$, which leads to a time of 2.3 s.

It is important to note that these equations assume uniform acceleration. This often means that you need to consider the air resistance as negligible. In reality, air resistance increases the faster an object is moving.

Summary

RETRIEVE

Equations of motion

1. A stone is dropped from rest from a 45-metre high cliff.

   In the questions below, assume that the air resistance is negligible.

   a) Calculate the time taken for the stone to reach the ground. [2]

   b) Calculate the velocity of the stone just before it reaches the ground. [2]

2. A ball is thrown vertically upwards with a speed of $12.5\,\mathrm{m\,s^{-1}}$ and experiences negligible air resistance.

   a) Calculate the maximum height reached by the ball. [2]

   b) Find the total time for the ball to return to its starting point. [2]

3. A cyclist starts from rest and accelerates uniformly at $0.50\,\mathrm{m\,s^{-2}}$ for a time of 10 seconds.

   a) Calculate the velocity of the cyclist after 10 seconds. [2]

   b) After 10 seconds, the cyclist then travels at a constant velocity for 2.0 minutes.

   Calculate the total distance travelled by the cyclist. [3]

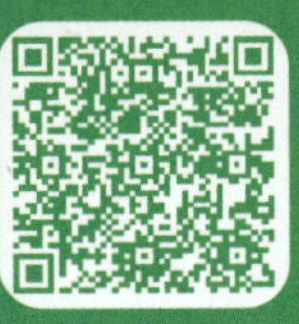

ORGANISE

Projectile motion

Key words

Key questions

While an object is undergoing projectile motion, what happens to the horizontal velocity?

An object is launched with a velocity of $40\,m\,s^{-1}$ at an angle of 20° above the horizontal. What are the initial horizontal and vertical velocities?

What happens to the range of a projectile if air resistance is not negligible?

Projectile motion

Projectile motion involves the motion of an object under the influence of gravity, with no other external forces acting on it. Air resistance is considered to be negligible. Therefore, the horizontal velocity of the object is constant (as no horizontal forces act on it). The vertical velocity experiences constant acceleration due to gravity. Treat the horizontal and vertical velocities independently.

Projectile launched horizontally	
Initial horizontal velocity	u
Horizontal velocity at time t	u
Initial vertical velocity	0
Vertical velocity at time t	$-gt$

Projectile launched at angle θ	
Initial horizontal velocity	$u\cos\theta$
Horizontal velocity at time t	$u\cos\theta$
Initial vertical velocity	$u\sin\theta$
Vertical velocity at time t	$u\sin\theta - gt$

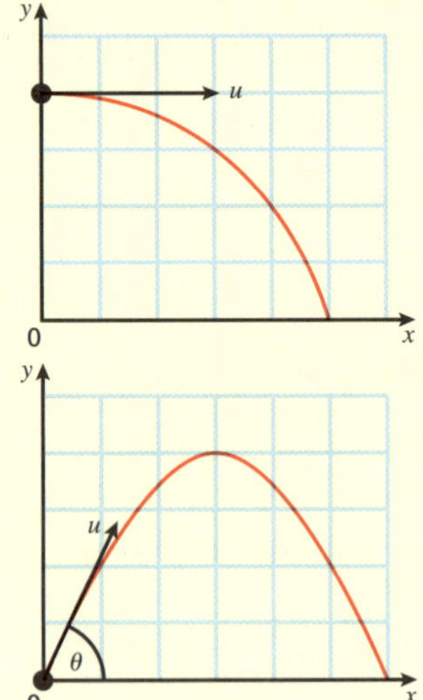

A football is kicked at a velocity of $12\,m\,s^{-1}$ at an angle of 30° above the horizontal. Calculate the horizontal distance the football travels before it hits the ground. Assume that air resistance is negligible.

Initial horizontal velocity = 12cos 30 = $10.4\,m\,s^{-1}$

Initial vertical velocity = 12sin 30 = $6.0\,m\,s^{-1}$

The first step is to calculate the initial horizontal and vertical velocities.

s – 0 m

u – $6.0\,m\,s^{-1}$

v –

a – $-9.81\,m\,s^{-2}$

t – t

The next step is to calculate the time it takes for the football to reach the ground. This is done by only considering the vertical velocity and using an equation of motion. Writing each of the known variables under each other in the order '*suvat*' will help you select which equation of motion to use.

In this case, the equation $s = ut + \frac{1}{2}at^2$ should be used.

Therefore, $0 = 6.0t + \frac{1}{2} \times (-9.81)t^2$, which leads to a time of 1.22 s.

The horizontal distance can then be calculated by using the horizontal velocity in the equation $s = vt$ so that $s = (12\cos 30) \times 1.22 = 12.7\,m$

Drag forces

The range of a projectile decreases if you consider drag forces such as friction and air resistance. This is primarily because the horizontal velocity will decrease over time.

As the speed of an object increases, so does friction and air resistance. If an object is accelerating due to gravity, the acceleration will decrease over time as the resultant force downwards will decrease. When the weight is equal to the drag forces, a maximum **terminal velocity** is reached. This is because there is no resultant force downwards and therefore no acceleration.

Terminal velocity is also reached for vehicles such as cars. A car has a maximum possible driving force forwards. If the drag forces are equal to this driving force, the forces are balanced and there is no acceleration.

Summary

RETRIEVE

Projectile motion

1. A projectile is launched horizontally from a height of 15 m.

   If the initial horizontal speed is $3.0\,m\,s^{-1}$, how far does it travel horizontally before hitting the ground? Tick **one** box. [1]

   3.2 m ☐ 5.2 m ☐ 7.2 m ☐ 9.2 m ☐

2. A tennis player serves a ball from a height of 2.3 m, at a distance 12 m away from the net. The tennis ball is served at an initial velocity of $25\,m\,s^{-1}$ at an angle of 5.0° below the horizontal. Assume that air resistance is negligible and that the diagram is not drawn to scale.

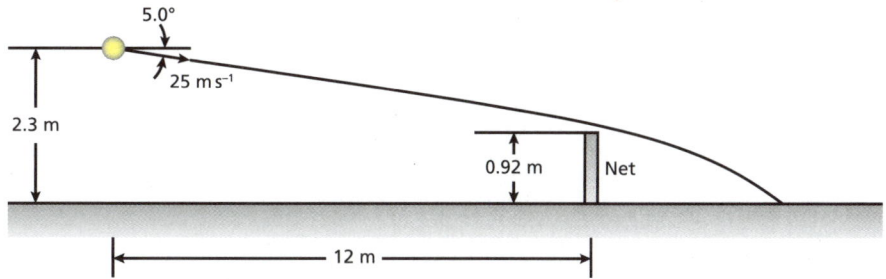

   a) Calculate the horizontal and vertical components of the initial velocity. [2]

   Horizontal velocity = ..., Vertical velocity = ...

   b) Calculate the time it takes for the ball to reach the net. [2]

   ....

   c) The net is at a height of 0.92 m above the ground. Determine whether the ball clears the net. [3]

   ....

   ....

   ....

   ....

3. A projectile is launched from a cliff of height 85 m at a velocity of $45\,m\,s^{-1}$ and an angle of 20° above the horizontal.

   a) Calculate the time taken to reach the ground. [2]

   ....

   b) Calculate the horizontal distance travelled before the projectile reaches the ground. [2]

   ....

   c) Calculate the resultant velocity of the projectile just before it reaches the ground. [4]

   ....

Newton's laws of motion

Key words

Key questions

What happens to an aeroplane if it is travelling with no resultant force acting on it?

What is Newton's second law?

Why are the normal contact force and weight not a Newton's third law pair?

Newton's first law of motion

Newton's first law of motion is that an object will remain at rest or continue to move at a constant velocity unless acted upon by an external resultant force. This law explains the concept of inertia – the resistance of an object to changes in its motion.

An object at rest stays at rest

An object acted upon by a balanced force stays at rest

An object acted upon by an unbalanced force changes speed and direction

An object at rest stays at rest

An object acted upon by an unbalanced force changes speed and direction

An object in motion stays in motion

An object acted upon by an unbalanced force changes speed and direction

A stationary object stays stationary unless a resultant force is applied.

A moving object maintains its speed and direction in the absence of a resultant force.

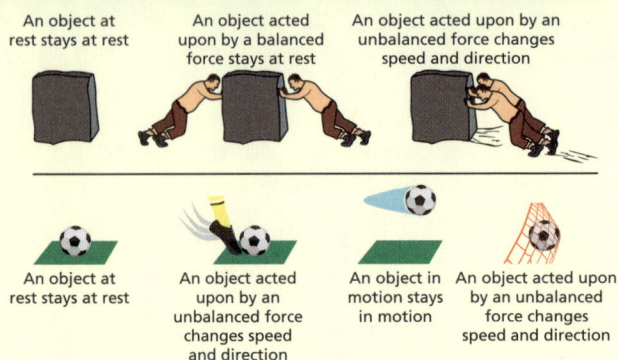

Newton's second law of motion

The acceleration of an object is directly proportional to the resultant force acting on it and inversely proportional to its mass.

$F = ma$ where F is the resultant force acting on the object (in newtons, N), m is the mass of the object (in kilograms, kg) and a is the acceleration of the object (in m s^{-2}).

- The greater the resultant force, the greater the acceleration for the same mass.
- For a constant force, an object with a larger mass experiences smaller acceleration.

Newton's second law can also be expressed in terms of momentum.

This can be shown by substituting $a = \frac{\Delta v}{\Delta t}$ into $F = ma$ to obtain: $F = m\frac{\Delta v}{\Delta t}$

In words, the resultant force acting on an object is equal to the rate of change of momentum of the object.

Newton's third law of motion

When an object exerts a force on a second object, the second object exerts an equal force in the opposite direction. The forces always need to be of the same type. Examples of this include:

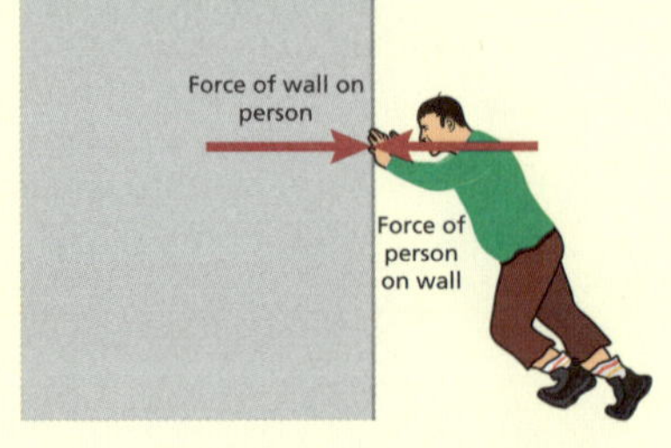

- When you push against a wall with your hand, the wall exerts an equal and opposite force back on your hand.
- When you walk, your foot exerts a force backwards on the ground and the ground exerts a force forward onto you.

A common misconception is that weight and the normal reaction force are Newton's third law pairs. This is not the case as they are different types of force (weight is gravitational and reaction force is contact). The true Newton's third law pair for weight is the gravitational force that the object exerts on the Earth.

Summary

RETRIEVE

Newton's laws of motion

1. Which of the following is **not** an example of Newton's first law? Tick **one** box. [1]

   A passenger lurching forward when a car stops suddenly ☐

   A stationary book remaining at rest on a table ☐

   A rocket accelerating upwards after its engines fire ☐

   An aeroplane continuing at the same velocity with no resultant force acting on it ☐

2. Two ice-skaters, one heavier than the other, push against each other on an ice rink.

   Which statement is correct? Tick **one** box. [1]

   The lighter skater exerts a greater force on the heavier skater. ☐

   The heavier skater exerts a greater force on the lighter skater. ☐

   Both skaters exert equal and opposite forces on each other. ☐

   Both skaters experience an equal acceleration. ☐

3. A car of mass 1200 kg is towing a trailer of mass 600 kg. The driving force is 4000 N, and the resistive forces on the car and trailer are 800 N and 400 N respectively.

   a) Calculate the acceleration of the car. [2]

   ....

   b) Calculate the tension in the connection between the car and the trailer. [2]

   ....

4. A 12 kg box is being pushed up a ramp with a 150 N force parallel to the incline. The ramp is at an angle of 20° above the horizontal and the box is experiencing a frictional force of 10 N.

   Calculate the acceleration of the box. [2]

   ....

5. Explain how a helicopter can remain hovering in place using Newton's laws of motion. [5]

   ....

   ....

   ....

   ....

   ....

   ....

ORGANISE

Momentum

Key words

Key questions

What is the principle of conversation of momentum?

What is the difference between an elastic and an inelastic collision?

What does the area under a force–time graph represent?

Give three features of cars that keep passengers safe.

Principle of conservation of linear momentum

Momentum (p) is the product of an object's mass (m) and its velocity (v): $p = mv$

Momentum is a vector quantity and is measured in units of kg m s^{-1}.

The total momentum of a system of objects remains constant, provided no external forces act on the system. This is called the **principle of conservation of momentum.**

In a collision between two or more objects, the total momentum before the collision is the same as it is after the collision.

For two colliding objects of masses m_1 and m_2:

$$m_1u_1 + m_2u_2 = m_1v_1 + m_2v_2$$

where u is the initial velocity and v is the final velocity of the objects.

Elastic and inelastic collisions

In an **elastic collision,** both momentum and kinetic energy are conserved.

In an **inelastic collision**, momentum is still conserved but kinetic energy is not. The principle of conservation of energy is not violated, though, as kinetic energy is transferred into other energy stores (e.g. thermal energy).

Impulse and force–time graphs

Impulse is the change in momentum (Δp) of an object when a force (F) is applied over a period of time (Δt): impulse $= F\Delta t = \Delta p = m\Delta v$

This equation is derived from Newton's second law. The resultant force acting on an object is equal to the rate of change of momentum of the object:

$$F = ma = m\frac{\Delta v}{\Delta t}$$

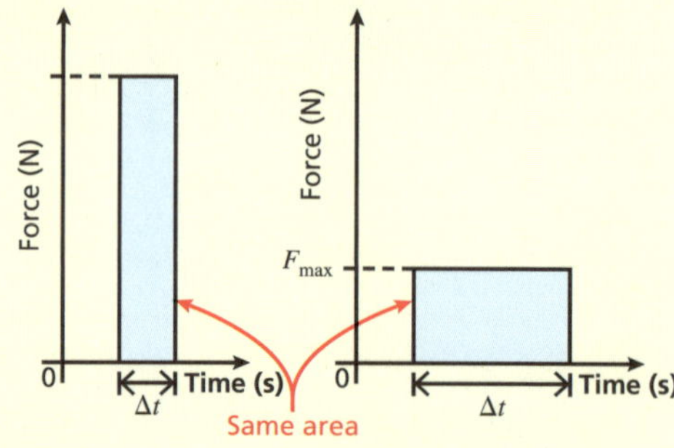

The area under a force–time graph represents the impulse. For a given impulse, a shorter contact time increases the impact force. To deliver a greater impulse and increase the speed of an object, it is beneficial to increase the force and/or the contact time (e.g. by following through when kicking a football).

Ethical transport design

It is important that vehicles are designed to be as safe as possible for both pedestrians and passengers. Crumple zones, air bags and seat belts all increase the time that it takes for a passenger to come to a stop. This reduces their rate of change of momentum and therefore the force that they experience.

Some more modern cars have pop-up bonnets to protect pedestrians in the event of an accident.

Summary

RETRIEVE

Momentum

1. Two objects collide elastically. Which of the following is conserved? Tick **one** box. [1]

   Kinetic energy only ☐ Momentum only ☐

   Both momentum and kinetic energy ☐ Neither momentum nor kinetic energy ☐

2. A 10 kg object moving at 6.0 m s^{-1} collides and sticks to a stationary 2.0 kg object.

   What is the final velocity of the combined mass? Tick **one** box. [1]

   3.0 m s^{-1} ☐ 4.0 m s^{-1} ☐ 5.0 m s^{-1} ☐ 6.0 m s^{-1} ☐

3. A football of mass 450 g is initially stationary on the ground. A player kicks the ball, applying a force that varies with time. The force–time graph experienced by the football is shown.

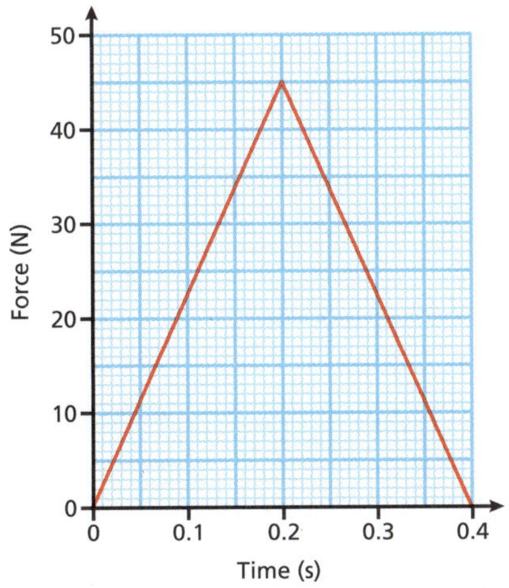

   a) Using the graph, calculate the total impulse delivered to the ball during the kick. [2]

   ....

   b) Calculate the ball's velocity immediately after the kick. [2]

   ....

4. Two balls collide on a horizontal surface. Ball A has a mass of 2.0 kg and is moving to the right with a velocity of 5.0 m s^{-1}. Ball B has a mass of 3.0 kg and is moving to the left with a velocity of 2.0 m s^{-1}. After the collision, ball A rebounds with a velocity of 1.0 m s^{-1} to the left.

   a) Calculate the velocity of ball B after the collision. [3]

   ....

   b) Determine whether this is an elastic collision. [3]

   ....

   ....

   ....

   c) The collision lasted for 0.10 s.

   Calculate the average force exerted by ball B on ball A. [2]

   ....

5. A 1500 kg car moving east at 20 m s^{-1} collides with a 1000 kg car moving north at 15 m s^{-1}. After the collision, the two cars stick together.

   Calculate the magnitude and direction of the velocity of the combined mass after the collision. [6]

   ....

ORGANISE

Energy and power

Key words

Key questions

What does the area under a force–displacement graph represent?

What is the definition of power?

What is the principle of conservation of energy?

Work done and power

Work done (W) is the product of a force and the displacement moved (s) in the direction of the force:

$$W = Fs\cos\theta$$

where θ is the angle between the force and displacement.

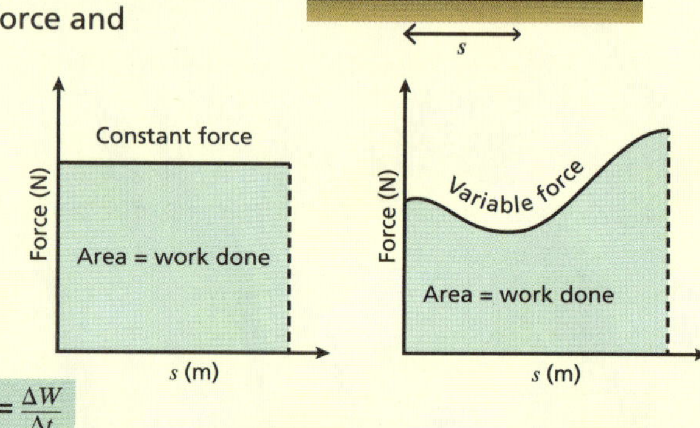

The area under a force–displacement graph represents the work done. For constant forces, the area is a rectangle. For variable forces, the area may need to be approximated using trapeziums.

Power (P) is the rate of doing work or transferring energy:

$$P = \frac{\Delta W}{\Delta t}$$

Power is measured in units of watts (W), while work done and energy are measured in units of joules (J).

By combining the equations for work done and power, power can also be expressed in terms of the product of force and velocity (v):

$$P = \frac{F\Delta s}{\Delta t} = Fv$$

The principle of conservation of energy

Energy cannot be created or destroyed; it can only be transferred from one energy store to another. The total energy in a closed system remains constant. This is called the principle of conservation of energy.

Two energy stores include gravitational potential energy (the energy store due to an object's height) and kinetic energy (the energy store of an object's motion). The change in gravitational potential energy (ΔE_p) of a mass (m) being raised a height (Δh) can be calculated by $\Delta E_p = mg\Delta h$. The kinetic energy (E_k) of a mass moving at a velocity (v) can be calculated by $E_k = \frac{1}{2}mv^2$.

If a ball is thrown upwards into the air, the initial kinetic energy store is transferred into the gravitational potential energy store. At its maximum height, it has zero energy in its kinetic energy store (as the ball is not moving) and a maximum in its gravitational potential energy store.

As the ball then falls, the reverse happens. Its gravitational potential energy store is transferred into the kinetic energy store again.

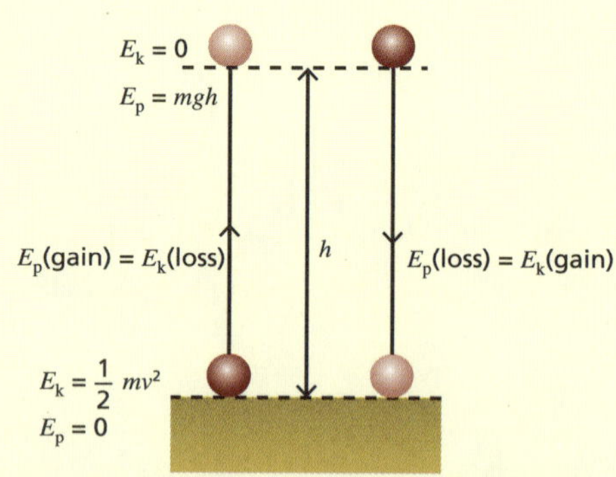

Efficiency

Efficiency is a measure of how effectively energy is transferred between one energy store and another.

$$\text{efficiency} = \frac{\text{useful output power}}{\text{input power}}$$

Energy and power losses are unavoidable and often involve the loss of energy into the thermal energy store of the surroundings.

Summary

RETRIEVE

Energy and power

1 A cyclist of mass 70 kg is travelling up a hill inclined at 20° above the horizontal. The cyclist applies a force of 250 N parallel to the slope to travel 500 m along the hill in 100 s.

a) Calculate the gravitational potential energy gained by the cyclist. [2]

b) Calculate the work done by the cyclist. [1]

c) Explain why the work done by the cyclist is larger than the gravitational potential energy gained by the cyclist. [2]

2 A van's engine provides 120 kW of power while it is travelling at a constant velocity of 24 m s^{-1}. The van has a mass of 4200 kg.

a) Calculate the resistive force that is opposing the motion of the van. [1]

b) The van now travels up a hill inclined at 2.5° above the horizontal.

Calculate the component of the weight parallel to the hill. [2]

c) The van increases the power of the engine to continue travelling at a velocity of 24 m s^{-1}.

Calculate the new power of the van's engine. [2]

3 A beach ball is dropped from the top of a cliff. While falling to the ground, the ball reaches terminal velocity and loses 120 J from its gravitational potential energy store. The ball reaches the ground with a speed of 18 m s^{-1} and a kinetic energy of 22 J.

a) Calculate the mass of the beach ball. [2]

b) Calculate the height of the cliff. [2]

c) Calculate the average resistive force experienced by the ball as it falls. [2]

ORGANISE

Hooke's law

Key words

Key questions

What is Hooke's law?

What is the definition of the spring constant?

What is elastic deformation?

What is plastic deformation?

Hooke's law

The extension of an elastic object, such as a spring, is directly proportional to the force applied. This is known as Hooke's law.

The equation that describes this is: $F = k\Delta L$

where F is the force applied to the object (in newtons, N), k is the spring constant (in Nm^{-1}) and ΔL is the extension of the object (in m).

The **spring constant** is sometimes referred to as the stiffness of a spring. It is defined as the force required to extend or compress a spring by 1 metre.

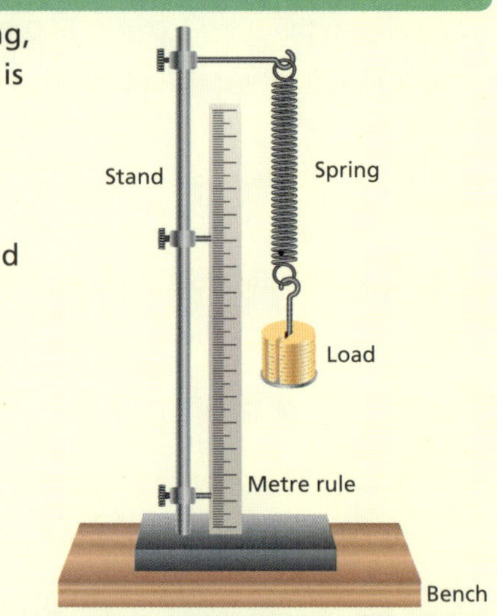

Force–extension graphs

A force–extension graph can be used to study the behaviour of a spring or other materials. The graph has various sections:

- **Elastic region:** the region where the object behaves elastically. This means the material returns to its original shape when the force is removed.
- **Limit of proportionality:** the point where the force and extension stop being directly proportional. Beyond this point, Hooke's law no longer applies.
- **Plastic region:** here, the material undergoes permanent deformation. When the force is removed, the material does not return to its original shape because it has been stretched beyond its elastic limit.
- **Fracture point:** where the material can no longer withstand the applied force and breaks or fractures.

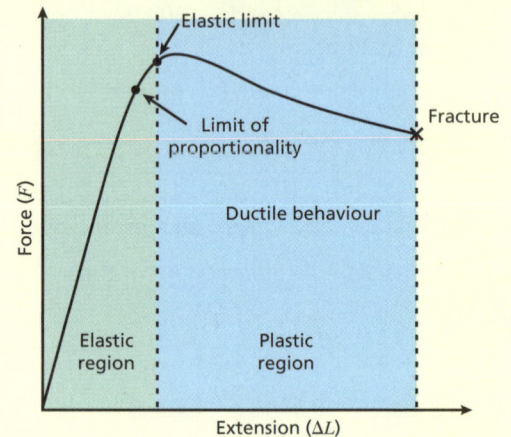

Elastic limit
Limit of proportionality
Fracture
Ductile behaviour
Force (F)
Elastic region
Plastic region
Extension (ΔL)

When a force is applied to a spring and it extends, elastic strain energy is stored in the spring. This energy is represented by the area under the force–extension graph.

For a spring obeying Hooke's law:

$$\text{elastic strain energy} = \frac{1}{2} F\Delta L$$

If you substitute $F = k\Delta L$ into this equation, you obtain:

$$\text{elastic strain energy} = \frac{1}{2} k(\Delta L)^2$$

The elastic strain energy is the potential energy stored in the spring, which can be transferred into the kinetic or gravitational potential energy stores in certain situations. For example, if someone jumps and extends a trampoline, the stored elastic potential energy in the springs will transfer into the kinetic energy store of the person. As the person rises, their kinetic energy store will then be transferred into their gravitational potential energy store.

Summary

RETRIEVE

Hooke's law

1. Spring A of spring constant k has extension ΔL when a force F is applied to it. Spring B has double the spring constant, but half the force applied to it.

   Which is the correct extension of spring B? Tick **one** box. [1]

   $\frac{\Delta\Delta L}{4}$ ☐ $\frac{\Delta\Delta L}{2}$ ☐

   $\Delta\Delta L$ ☐ $4\Delta L$ ☐

2. A spring is used to launch a toy car horizontally. The spring constant is 200 Nm^{-1} and the spring is compressed by 15 cm.

   a) Calculate the elastic strain energy stored in the spring. [1]

   ....

   b) Assuming no energy losses, calculate the velocity of a 500 g toy car as it leaves the spring. [2]

   ....

3. A bungee jumper of mass 75 kg is attached to a bungee cord with a spring constant of 150 Nm^{-1}.

   a) Calculate the extension of the bungee cord if the bungee jumper is suspended by it in equilibrium. [2]

   ....

   b) The bungee jumper now falls a total distance of 45 m.

   Calculate the extension of the bungee cord when the jumper first comes to rest. [3]

   ....

4. Describe an experiment to determine the spring constant and limit of proportionality of a spring. Include the equipment required, a method and how you would analyse the data. [6]

ORGANISE

Bulk properties of solids

Key words

Key questions

What is the definition of density?

Why does tensile strain have no units?

How does the stress–strain graph of a brittle material differ to that of a ductile material?

Density

Density (ρ) is a measure of the mass of an object per unit volume.

It is calculated using: $\rho = \frac{m}{V}$

where m is the mass of an object (in kg) and V is the volume of the object (in m^3).

Density has units of kg m^{-3}.

Tensile stress and tensile strain

When materials are stretched, they experience tensile stress and strain.

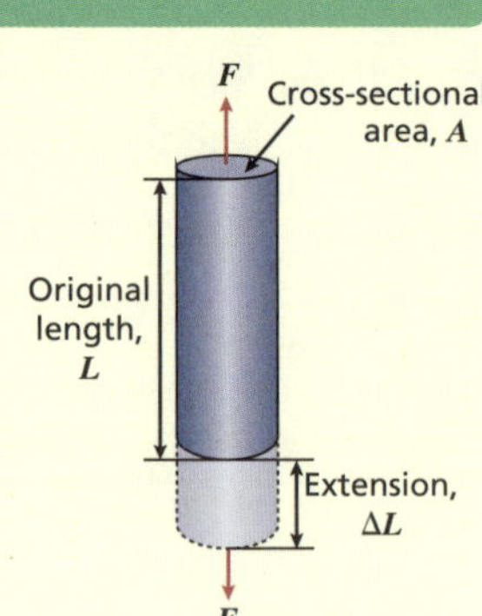

Tensile stress is the force applied per unit cross-sectional area: $\text{tensile stress} = \frac{F}{A}$

Due to this equation, tensile stress can be represented in units of Nm^{-2} or pascals (Pa). 1 Nm^{-2} is equal to 1 pascal.

Tensile strain is the fractional extension of a material: $\text{tensile strain} = \frac{\Delta L}{L}$

where ΔL is the extension of a material and L is the unstretched length of the material.

As tensile strain is a ratio, it is a unitless quantity.

Stress–strain graphs

Stress–strain graphs provide insights into how materials behave under tensile forces. In a similar way to a force–extension graph, there is an initial elastic section and a plastic section.

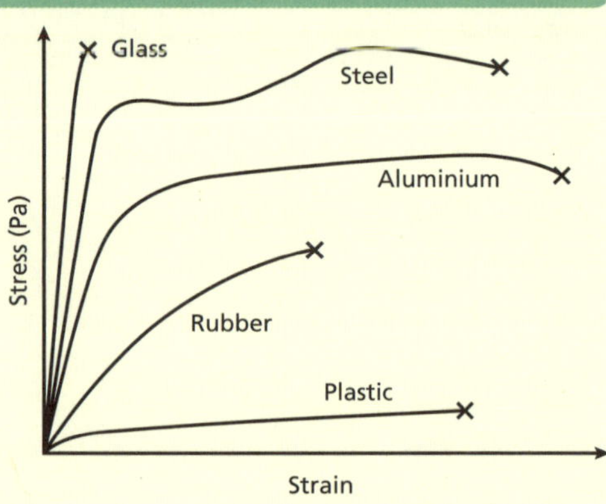

Different types of materials include:

- Brittle materials break with little or no plastic deformation. The stress–strain graph of a brittle material (such as glass) is characterised by a steep, almost straight line followed by a sudden failure.
- Stiff materials (e.g. steel) resist deformation and therefore have a steep gradient in the elastic section.
- Ductile materials undergo significant plastic deformation before breaking. Aluminium and copper are two ductile materials, and this makes it easy to draw the materials out into long wires.
- Flexible materials (such as rubber and plastic) show large extensions with relatively low forces.

Every material has a breaking stress. This is the maximum stress that a material can handle without breaking.

Summary

RETRIEVE

Bulk properties of solids

1. Which word best describes a material that undergoes significant plastic deformation before breaking? Tick **one** box. [1]

   Brittle ☐ Ductile ☐ Elastic ☐ Stiff ☐

2. A sphere of radius 5.0 cm is made from a brass alloy that contains 70% copper and 30% tin by volume. The density of copper is 8900 kg m^{-3} and the density of tin is 7300 kg m^{-3}.

   Calculate the mass of the sphere. [4]

3. A cylindrical rod is made from a material with a density of 7800 kg m^{-3}. The rod has a length of 2.5 m and a radius of 1.5 cm. A tensile force of 1200 N is applied to the rod, causing it to stretch elastically.

   a) Calculate the mass of the rod. [2]

   b) Calculate the tensile stress on the rod due to the applied force. [2]

   c) The rod experiences a strain of 3.5×10^{-4}

   Calculate the extension of the rod. [1]

   d) The rod is now subjected to a force greater than its elastic limit.

   Describe the difference between elastic and plastic deformation. [2]

   e) The material of the rod has a breaking stress of 600 MPa.

   Calculate the maximum tensile force that can be applied to the rod before it breaks. [2]

ORGANISE

The Young modulus

Key words

Key questions

What is the definition of the Young modulus?

What does the gradient of a stress–strain graph represent?

What is the difference between elastic and plastic deformation?

What does the area under a stress–strain graph represent?

The Young modulus: a measure of how stiff a material is

The Young modulus is defined as the ratio of tensile stress to tensile strain, provided the material is behaving elastically:

$$\text{Young modulus} = \frac{\text{tensile stress}}{\text{tensile strain}}$$

As tensile stress has units of Pa (or Nm^{-2}) and tensile strain is unitless, the Young modulus therefore also has units of Pa (or Nm^{-2}).

If you substitute the formulae for tensile stress and tensile strain into the expression for the Young modulus, you obtain:

$$\text{Young modulus} = \frac{\frac{F}{A}}{\frac{\Delta L}{L}} = \frac{FL}{A\Delta L}$$

This is particularly useful when the original length L, cross-sectional area A, force F and extension ΔL are known.

Stress–strain graphs

Sections of a stress–strain graph:

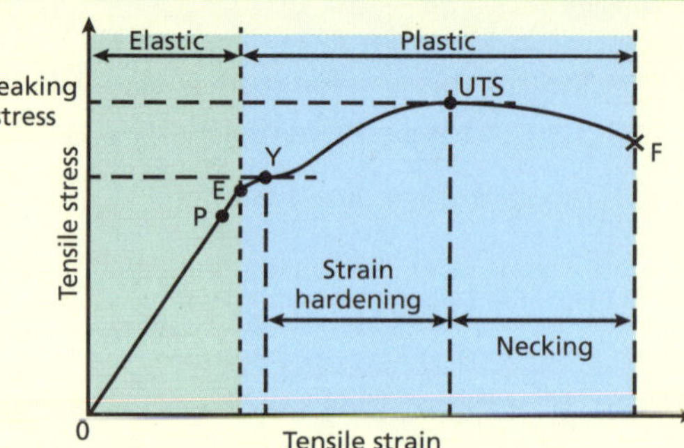

1. **Limit of proportionality (P).** Up until this point, stress is directly proportional to strain. The Young modulus can be calculated from the gradient of the linear region.
2. **Elastic limit (E).** This is the maximum point in the elastic region where the material can still return to its original shape. Beyond the elastic limit, plastic deformation takes place.
3. **Yield point (Y).** Beyond the yield point, small increases in stress can result in significant increases in strain.
4. **Ultimate tensile stress (UTS).** This is the maximum stress that the material can withstand. Beyond this point, the material undergoes 'necking'. This is where the cross-sectional area reduces at its weakest point, leading to fracture (F).

The area under a stress–strain curve gives the strain energy per unit volume stored in the material.

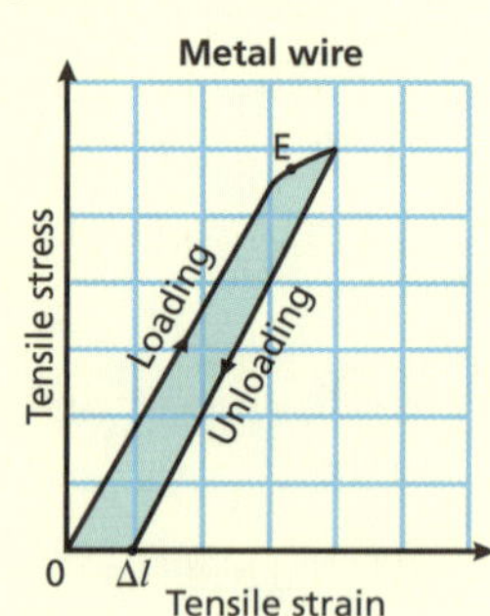

If a metal wire is loaded beyond its elastic limit, it becomes permanently deformed. Therefore, once unloaded, it does not go back to its original length. The area between the loading and unloading curves represents the energy per unit volume required for permanent deformation. The wire therefore becomes longer.

When rubber is loaded and unloaded within its elastic limit, the unloading curve does not match up with its loading curve. This is called **hysteresis**. The area within the hysteresis loop represents the elastic strain energy that is converted into internal energy, causing the rubber to warm up during stretching and relaxation.

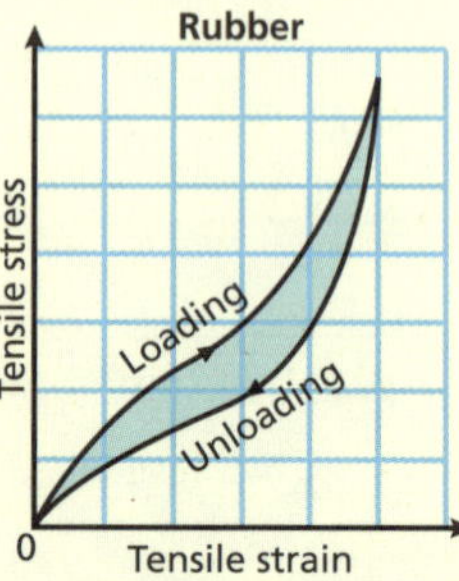

Force–extension graphs can also show loading and unloading behaviours in materials, in a similar way.

Summary

RETRIEVE

The Young modulus

1. A wire with a cross-sectional area of 1.5×10^{-6} m^2 and a length of 2.0 m extends by 1.5 mm under a load of 200 N.

   What is the Young modulus of the wire? Tick **one** box. [1]

   1.0×10^{11} Pa ☐ 1.5×10^{11} Pa ☐

   1.8×10^{11} Pa ☐ 2.0×10^{11} Pa ☐

2. A uniform beam of length 0.50 m is pivoted at one of its ends to a wall. The other end of the beam has a downwards force of 105 N applied to it and is supported by a steel cable at an angle of 30° above the horizontal. The beam has a weight of 65 N and is in equilibrium.

   The steel cable has a cross-sectional area of 1.5×10^{-6} m^2 and a Young modulus of 2.0×10^{11} Pa.

   Calculate the extension of the cable due to the tension (T) in the cable. The uniform beam is held so that it is horizontal. The diagram is not drawn to scale. [6]

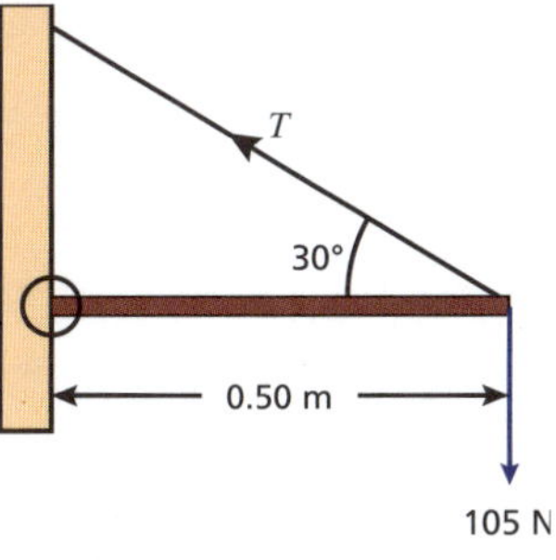

3. A stress–strain graph for a metal wire is shown.

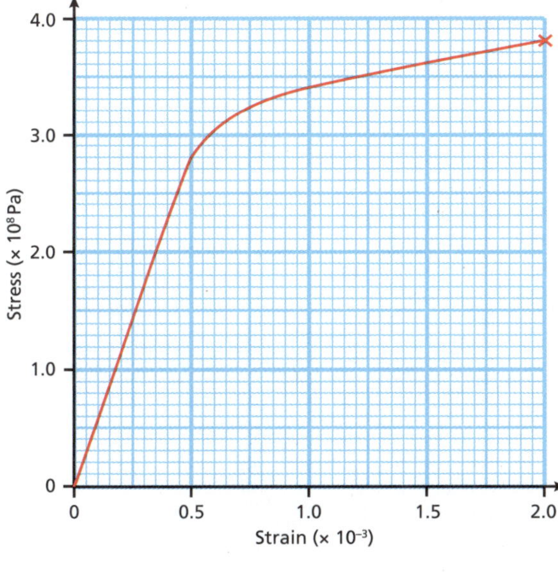

   a) Using the graph, calculate the Young modulus of the metal wire. [2]

   b) The elastic limit of the metal is reached at a stress of 3.1×10^8 Pa.

   Calculate the elastic strain energy per unit volume at this stress. [2]

   c) The metal wire is now loaded beyond its elastic limit to a stress of 3.4×10^8 Pa.

   On the graph above, sketch what the unloading curve would look like. [1]

   d) State what the area between the loading and unloading curves represents. [1]

   e) The metal wire can be described as being ductile.

   Describe how the stress–strain graph for a ductile material differs to that of a brittle material. [2]

ORGANISE

Current, potential difference and resistance

Key words

Key questions

What are the definitions of current, potential difference and resistance?

What do the I–V graphs look like for an ohmic conductor, a filament lamp and a semiconductor diode?

How is the current changed in a circuit to measure the I–V characteristics of different components?

Why does the resistance of a filament lamp increase with current?

Definitions

Current is the rate of flow of electric charge: where I is the current in amperes (A), Q is the charge in coulombs (C) and t is the time in seconds (s).

$$I = \frac{\Delta Q}{\Delta t}$$

Potential difference (p.d.) is the work done per unit charge to move charge between two points in a circuit: where V is the p.d. in volts (V) and W is the work done in joules (J).

$$V = \frac{W}{Q}$$

Resistance (R) is a measure of the opposition to the flow of current in a circuit and is defined as the ratio of the p.d. across a component to the current flowing through it: where R is the resistance of the component in ohms (Ω).

$$R = \frac{V}{I}$$

Current–potential difference (I–V) characteristics

A variable resistor is connected in series with the component to control the current in the circuit. An ammeter (ideal, with negligible resistance) is placed in series to measure the current. A voltmeter (ideal, with infinite resistance) is connected in parallel with the component to measure the p.d. across it.

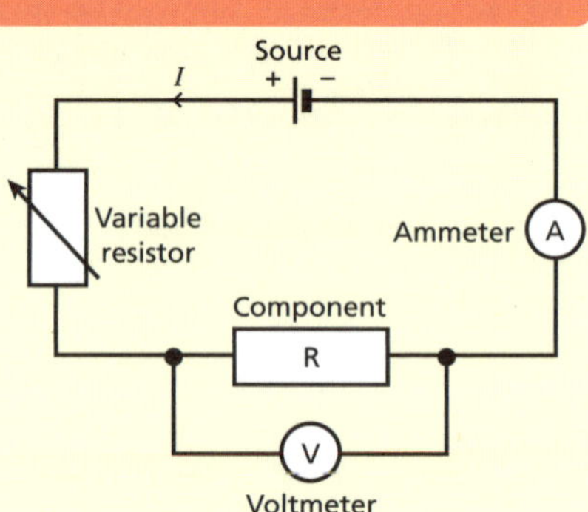

An ohmic conductor

For a component of constant resistance, the p.d. across a component is directly proportional to the current flowing through it. This is known as Ohm's law, and any component that obeys Ohm's law is referred to as an 'ohmic conductor'. The I–V graph for an ohmic conductor is a straight line through the origin, with the gradient representing $\frac{1}{R}$. A resistor acts as an ohmic conductor, as long as the temperature of the resistor remains constant.

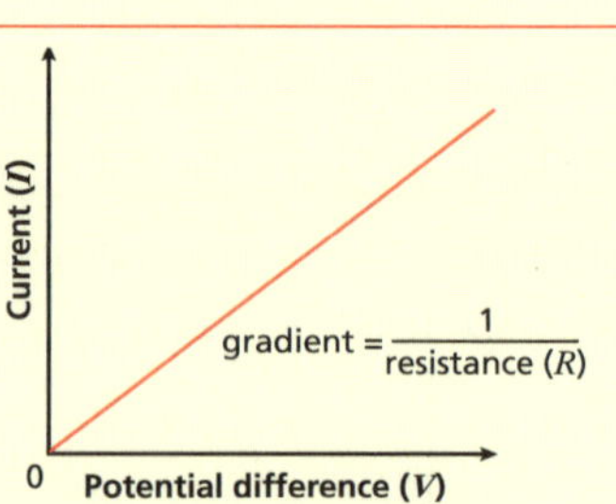

A filament lamp

As the current increases, the filament's temperature rises. This increase in temperature causes the resistance to increase because the ions in the filament vibrate more, leading to more frequent collisions between electrons and the ions. This impedes the flow of electrons and increases the resistance. The I–V graph is a curve that decreases in gradient at higher currents, showing increasing resistance.

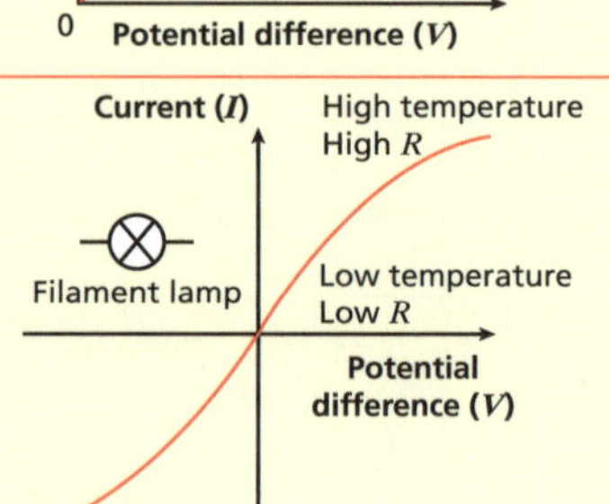

A semiconductor diode

A diode allows current to follow primarily in one direction. In forward bias, significant current begins to flow only after a threshold p.d. In reverse bias, the current is negligible until breakdown occurs at a high p.d.

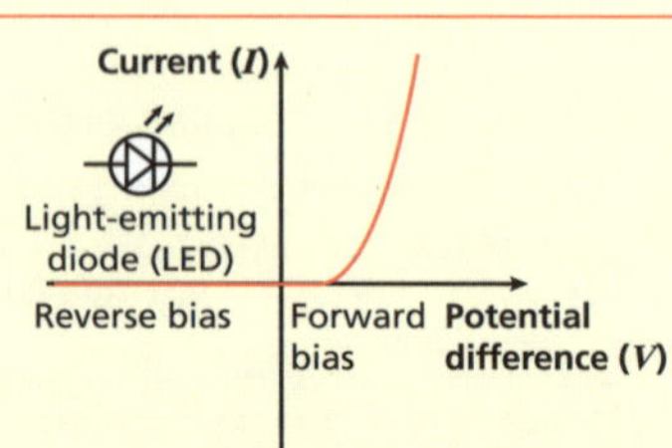

Summary

RETRIEVE

Current, potential difference and resistance

1 Which row shows the correct combination of resistances for an ideal ammeter and an ideal voltmeter? Tick **one** box. [1]

	Ideal ammeter resistance (Ω)	Ideal voltmeter resistance (Ω)
A	Zero	Zero
B	Zero	Infinite
C	Infinite	Zero
D	Infinite	Infinite

A ☐ B ☐ C ☐ D ☐

2 The I–V characteristics of a filament lamp are measured. The filament lamp is rated at 15 V, 1.0 A and has a resistance of 5.0 Ω at small currents.

a) Using the axes below, sketch the current–potential difference curve for this lamp. Label this curve L. [4]

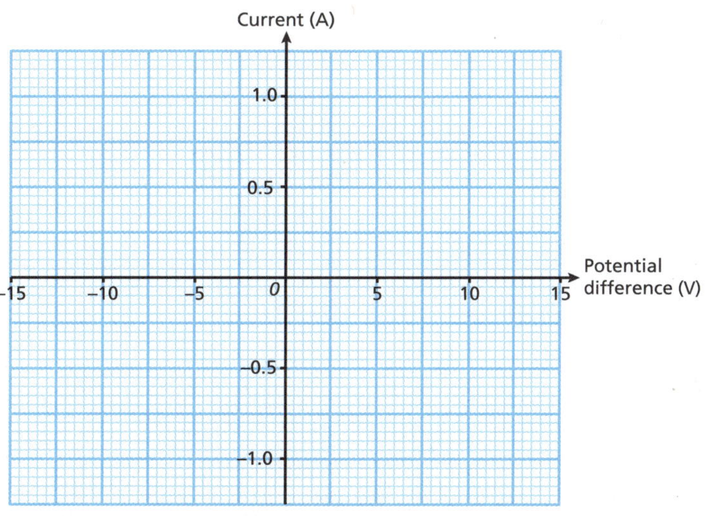

b) On the same axes, sketch the current–potential difference characteristic of an ohmic conductor of 15 Ω resistance. Label this O. [2]

c) In the space below, draw a circuit that could be used to determine the I–V characteristics of the filament lamp. [2]

d) Explain the difference between the I–V characteristics of a filament lamp and an ohmic conductor. [3]

ORGANISE

Resistivity

Key words

Key questions

What factors affect the resistance of a material?

How does temperature affect the resistance of a NTC thermistor?

What is a superconductor?

What are the common applications of superconductors?

Resistivity

The resistance (R) of a material depends on three main factors:

1. Length (L). Resistance is directly proportional to the length of the conductor. A longer wire offers more resistance to the flow of current.
2. Cross-sectional area (A). Resistance is inversely proportional to the cross-sectional area. A thicker wire provides less resistance.
3. Material properties. Resistance depends on the material's ability to conduct electricity, which is described by its resistivity (ρ).

These factors combine to give an equation for resistance: $R = \frac{\rho L}{A}$

where R is the resistance of the material (in Ω), ρ is the resistivity (in Ω m), L is the length (in m) and A is the cross-sectional area (in m^2).

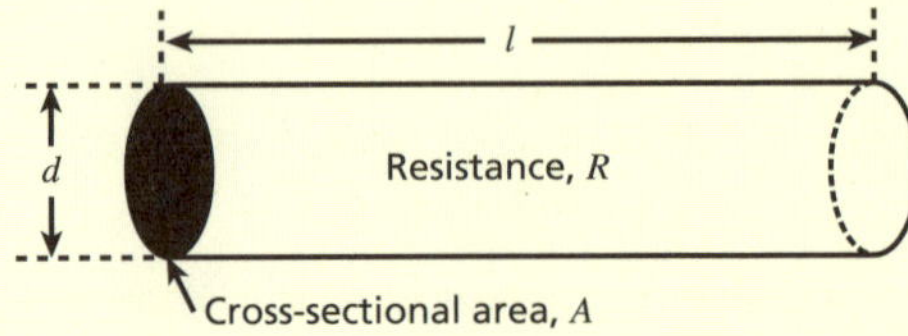

Rearranging this equation gives an expression for the resistivity: $\rho = \frac{RA}{L}$

Resistivity is constant for a given material at a specific temperature.

Effect of temperature on resistance

For a metallic conductor, resistance increases with temperature. At higher temperatures, metal ions vibrate more. This increases their collisions with free electrons and impedes current flow.

For negative temperature coefficient (NTC) thermistors, heating releases more charge carriers. This increases conductivity and so resistance decreases as temperature increases. Thermistors are commonly used as temperature sensors.

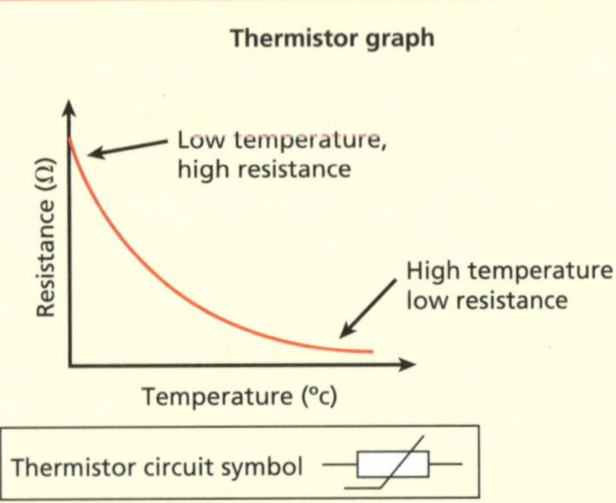

Superconductors

Superconductors have zero resistivity below a certain temperature, known as the critical temperature (T_c). As the material has no resistivity, it also has no resistance. This means that there are no energy losses due to heating. This property makes superconductors useful in applications where high currents are required.

Common applications of superconductors include MRI scanners, magnetic levitation (maglev) trains and particle accelerators.

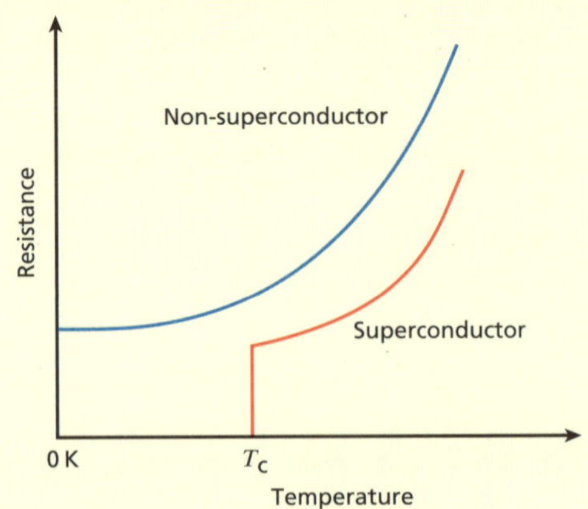

These applications require powerful magnetic fields, generated by large currents. Superconductors generally require cooling to extremely low temperatures, often using liquid helium or nitrogen, to reach their critical temperature.

Summary

RETRIEVE

Resistivity

1 If the length of a wire is doubled and its radius is doubled, what happens to its resistance? Tick **one** box. [1]

Halved ☐ Doubled ☐ Quadrupled ☐ Stays the same ☐

2 A transmission cable is made of copper, which has a resistivity of $1.7 \times 10^{-8}\ \Omega\,m$. The cable is 5.0 km long and has a diameter of 2.0 mm.

a) Calculate the resistance of the copper cable. [3]

The copper cable is replaced with a superconductor.

b) Explain why replacing the copper cable with a superconductor improves the efficiency of transmission. [2]

c) State **one** other application of superconductors and explain why they are advantageous for this application. [2]

The critical temperature of the superconductor used is 90 K.

d) In the space below, sketch a graph of resistance against temperature for the superconductor. [2]

e) Describe the challenges involved in maintaining superconductors at temperatures below their critical temperature. [2]

3 State and explain how temperature affects the resistance of a metal and a negative temperature coefficient (NTC) thermistor. [4]

ORGANISE

Circuits

Key words

Key questions

How do you calculate the total resistance of resistors in series and parallel?

What is Kirchhoff's first law?

What is Kirchhoff's second law?

Resistance in series and parallel

When resistors are connected in **series**, the total resistance is the sum of the individual resistances: $R_T = R_1 + R_2 + R_3 + \ldots$

In series, the same current flows through all components and the total potential difference (p.d.) across the circuit is shared between the components.

When resistors are connected in **parallel**, the total resistance is given by: $\frac{1}{R_T} = \frac{1}{R_1} + \frac{1}{R_2} + \frac{1}{R_3} + \ldots$

In parallel, the p.d. across each branch is the same and the total current is the sum of the currents flowing through each branch.

Energy and power in circuits

The energy transferred (E) in an electrical circuit is the work done by the circuit to move charge (Q) through a potential difference (V) so that $E = Q \times V$

This expression, combined with $Q = I \times t$, leads to: $E = I \times V \times t$

Power (P) is the rate at which energy is transferred or work is done in the circuit ($P = \frac{E}{t}$). Substituting $E = I \times V \times t$ into this expression gives: $P = I \times V$

Finally, substituting $V = I \times R$ and $I = \frac{V}{R}$ into $P = I \times V$ gives: $P = I^2 \times R = \frac{V^2}{R}$

Kirchhoff's laws

The total current entering a junction in a circuit is equal to the total current leaving the junction. This is known as **Kirchhoff's first law** and is a result of conservation of charge.

For a parallel circuit with three paths, the total current (I) is equal to the sum of the currents flowing through each of the three paths: $I = I_1 + I_2 + I_3$

In any closed loop of a circuit, the total energy supplied by a source (like a battery or power supply) is equal to the total energy dissipated across the components in the circuit.

The **electromotive force (emf)** is the total energy supplied by a source per unit charge. Each component in a circuit has a p.d. drop across it. This is the energy per unit charge dissipated across each component.

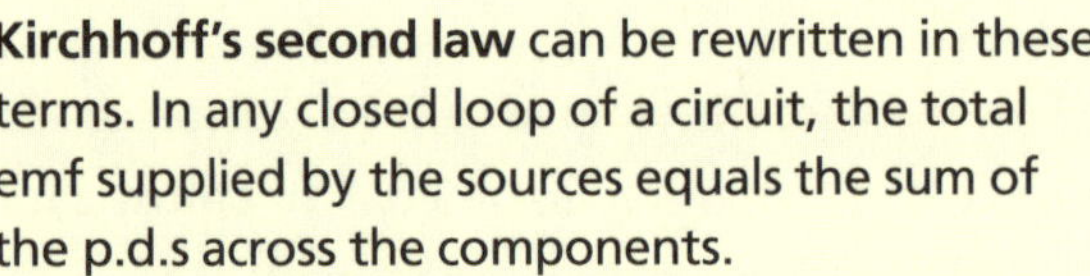

Kirchhoff's second law can be rewritten in these terms. In any closed loop of a circuit, the total emf supplied by the sources equals the sum of the p.d.s across the components.

For a circuit with three resistors, the emf (ε) is equal to the sum of the p.d. drops across each component: $\varepsilon = V_1 + V_2 + V_3$

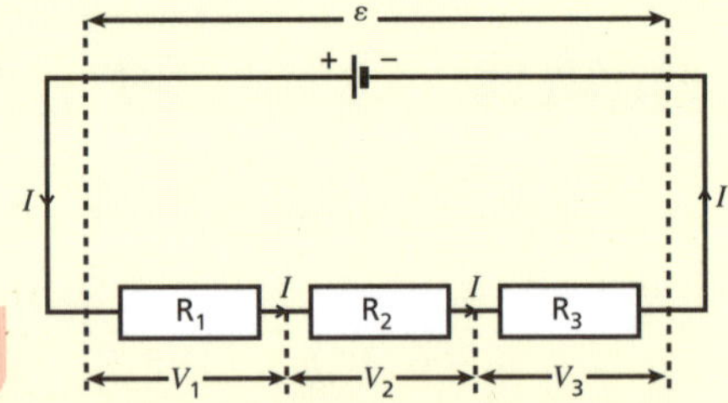

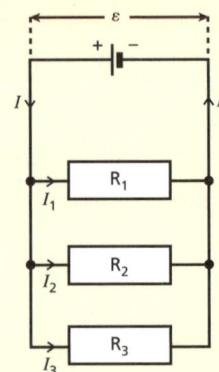

Cells in series and parallel

The total emf of cells in series is the sum of their individual emfs, provided they are connected with the same polarity.

For cells in parallel, the total emf is equal to the emf of a single cell.

Summary

RETRIEVE

Circuits

1 Calculate the total resistance between points A and B in the circuit shown. Tick **one** box. [1]

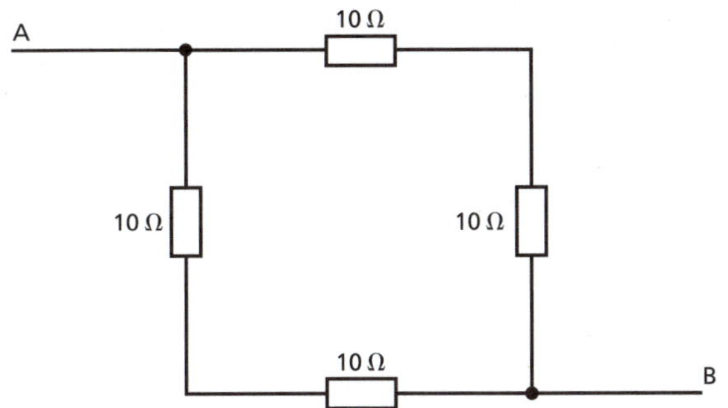

- 2.5 Ω ☐
- 10 Ω ☐
- 20 Ω ☐
- 40 Ω ☐

2 A power cable is made of aluminium strands with resistivity $\rho = 2.7 \times 10^{-8}$ Ωm. Each strand has a length of 50 m and a diameter of 1.0 mm.

a) Calculate the resistance of a single strand. [3]

....

b) A current of 200 A flows through a single strand.

Calculate the power lost due to heating, in kW. [2]

....

c) The entire cable is made from 100 strands connected in parallel.

Calculate the total resistance of the entire cable. [2]

....

d) A current of 200 A now passes through the entire cable. State and explain an advantage of transmitting power through the entire strand instead of through a single strand. [2]

....

....

....

3 A circuit diagram is shown. Calculate the resistance of R_1 and R_2, as well as the missing readings on the voltmeter and ammeter. [6]

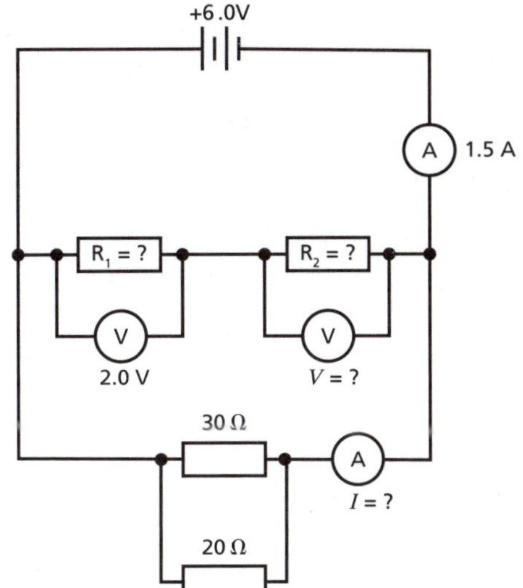

R_1 = ...

R_2 = ...

V = ...

I = ...

ORGANISE

Potential dividers

Key words

Key questions

What is a potential divider?

What is a potentiometer?

What are two applications of potential dividers?

Potential dividers

A potential divider is a circuit designed to divide an input potential difference (V_{in}) into smaller output potential differences. This is achieved by using resistors in series. In series, the same current flows through all components. Therefore, the potential difference (p.d.) is split in the ratio of the resistances. By varying the ratio of the resistors, the output p.d. can be controlled.

If two resistors R_1 and R_2 are connected in series to a battery or power supply, the ratio of the resistances can be used to find the ratio of p.d.s across the two resistors:

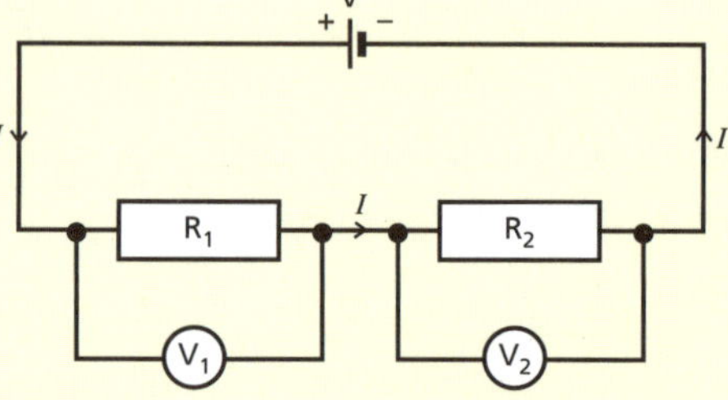

$$\frac{V_1}{V_2} = \frac{R_1}{R_2}$$

where V_1 is the p.d. across R_1 and V_2 is the p.d. across R_2.

As the total resistance in this circuit is equal to $R_1 + R_2$, the p.d. across R_1 is given by:

$$V_1 = \left(\frac{R_1}{R_1 + R_2}\right) V_{in}$$

Similarly, the p.d. across R_2 is given by:

$$V_2 = \left(\frac{R_2}{R_1 + R_2}\right) V_{in}$$

If one of the resistors is a variable resistor, then the output voltage can be varied.

Potentiometers

A potentiometer is a type of potential divider that allows you to vary the output p.d. manually. It consists of a single variable resistor with a sliding contact that divides the resistor into two parts. By moving the sliding contact, the resistance of each part changes. This adjusts how the input p.d. is split between the two sections.

Potentiometers are commonly used in headphones and speakers to adjust the loudness of sound and to control the brightness of lights or screens.

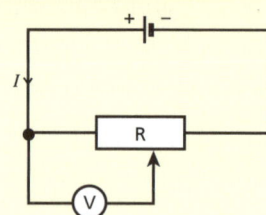

Applications of potential dividers

In potential divider circuits, LDRs or thermistors are placed in series with a fixed resistor to vary the output p.d. based on light intensity or temperature.

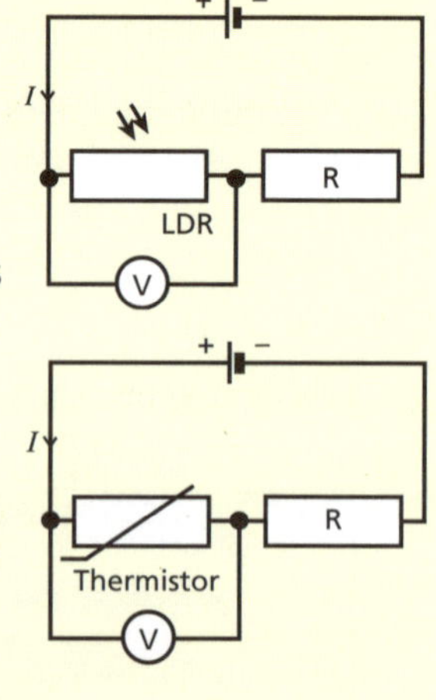

The resistance of an LDR decreases in bright light and increases in darkness. An LDR can be used to turn on lights automatically in the dark as the p.d. across the LDR increases when the LDR's resistance increases. A relay can activate the lights when the p.d. across the LDR reaches a certain threshold.

The resistance of a thermistor decreases as temperature rises and increases as temperature falls. Therefore, in a similar way to the LDR, a thermistor can be used in heating circuits to activate heaters. When the p.d. across a thermistor increases in response to lower temperature, a relay switches the heating on.

Summary

RETRIEVE

Potential dividers

1 The circuit shown in the diagram consists of a 12 V battery with negligible internal resistance connected in series with a 2.0 Ω fixed resistor and a 0 Ω to 10 Ω variable resistor.

An ideal ammeter is placed in series with the circuit and an ideal voltmeter is connected in parallel across the variable resistor.

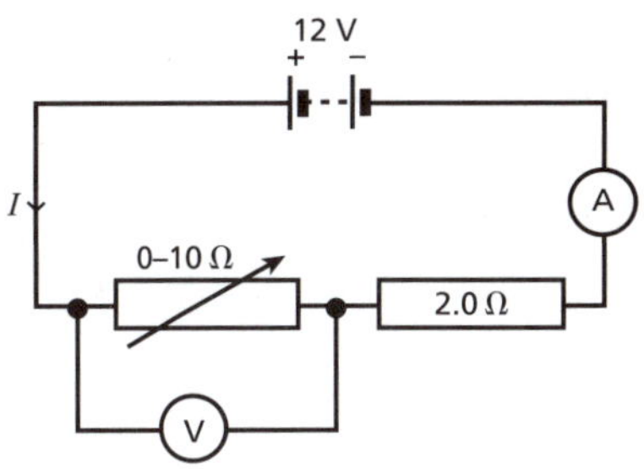

a) Calculate the maximum possible reading of the voltmeter. [3]

b) The variable resistor is adjusted so that the voltmeter reads 8.0 V.

Calculate the resistance of the variable resistor. [2]

2 A temperature-sensing circuit is powered by a 6.0 V battery in series with an ideal ammeter, a fixed resistor (R_1) and a thermistor. At a temperature of 20°C, the resistance of the thermistor is 1.8 kΩ. An ideal voltmeter placed across R_1 measures a potential difference of 4.5 V. The battery has negligible internal resistance.

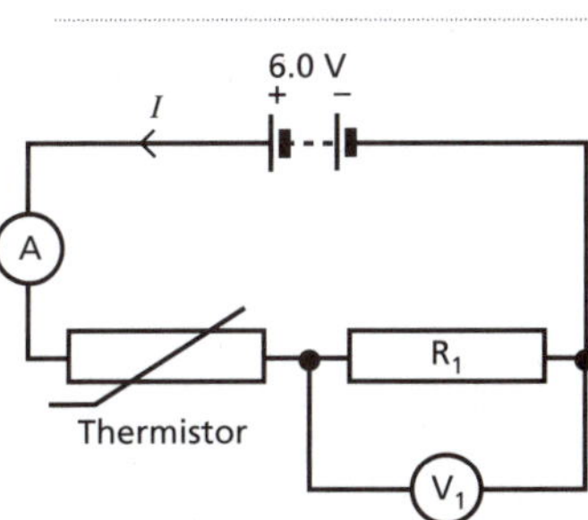

a) Calculate the total current flowing through the circuit. [2]

b) Calculate the resistance of R_1. [2]

c) The temperature rises, which increases the potential difference across R_1 to 5.0 V.

Calculate the new resistance of the thermistor. [2]

d) The temperature remains at the higher value as in part c) and the voltmeter is swapped for a non-ideal voltmeter of resistance 0.90 kΩ.

Calculate the new reading on the non-ideal voltmeter. [4]

ORGANISE

Electromotive force and internal resistance

Key words

Key questions

What is the definition of emf?

Why is the terminal potential difference less than the emf?

What is the terminal potential difference equal to when there is no current flowing?

What does the gradient of a graph of terminal potential difference against current represent?

Electromotive force (emf)

The emf is the energy provided per unit charge by a power source (such as a battery or cell):

$$\varepsilon = \frac{E}{Q}$$

where ε is the electromotive force (measured in volts, V), E is the energy supplied by the source (in joules, J) and Q is the charge (in coulombs, C).

For a battery, the emf is the amount of chemical energy converted to electrical energy for each coulomb of charge.

Internal resistance

All power sources, such as batteries, have some internal resistance (r) due to the materials that they are made from. This internal resistance causes some energy to be dissipated as heat within the source itself when a current flows.

Due to the internal resistance, not all the emf is available to an external circuit. This is because there is a potential difference drop across the internal resistance. This is commonly referred to as 'lost volts'. The terminal potential difference (V) is the energy per unit charge available to the external circuit.

Using Kirchhoff's second law, the total emf supplied by the source equals the sum of the potential differences across the internal resistance and the external resistance of the circuit:

$$\varepsilon = V + Ir$$

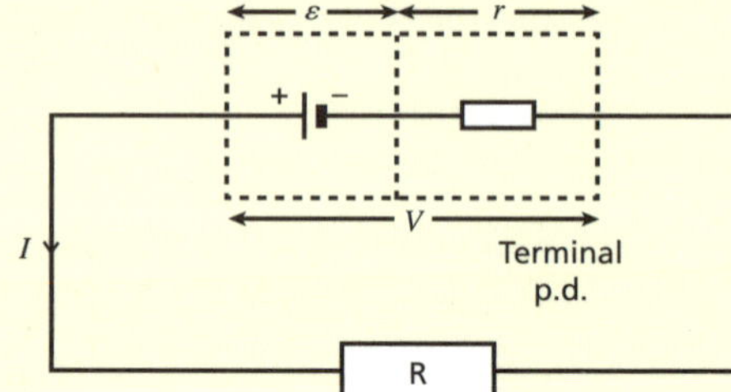

The term Ir represents the potential difference drop across the internal resistance.

The terminal potential difference is also equal to IR, where R is the external load resistance of the circuit.

Therefore, the emf can be expressed as:

$$\varepsilon = I(R + r)$$

Graph of terminal potential difference against current

The terminal potential difference can also be expressed in terms of the emf:

$$V = \varepsilon - Ir$$

This formula highlights that as the current (I) increases, the terminal potential difference decreases because more energy is dissipated within the power source.

If a graph of terminal potential difference is plotted against current, the y-intercept represents the emf of the power source when no current flows. The gradient of the line is negative and equal to the internal resistance ($-r$). A steeper gradient indicates a higher internal resistance.

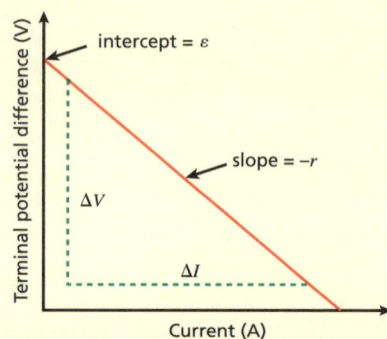

Terminal potential difference (V)
intercept = ε
slope = $-r$
ΔV
ΔI
Current (A)

Summary

RETRIEVE

Electromotive force and internal resistance

1 A terminal potential difference of 6.0 V is measured across a battery with an emf of 9.0 V and 1.5 Ω internal resistance.

What is the current in the circuit? Tick **one** box. [1]

1.0 A ☐ 1.5 A ☐

2.0 A ☐ 3.0 A ☐

2 A power supply with an emf of 15.0 V supplies a current of 3.0 A to an external circuit. The terminal potential difference is 13.5 V.

a) Calculate the internal resistance of the power supply. [2]

....

b) Calculate the resistance of the external circuit. [2]

....

c) Calculate the power dissipated in the internal resistance. [2]

....

3 A battery has an emf of 12.0 V and an internal resistance of 0.40 Ω. It is connected to a load resistance of 5.0 Ω.

a) Calculate the total current in the circuit. [2]

....

b) Calculate the terminal potential difference across the battery. [2]

....

c) Calculate the percentage of the total power supplied by the battery that is dissipated as heat in the internal resistance. [3]

....

4 A cell with an emf of 6.0 V and an internal resistance of 0.20 Ω is connected to two resistors, R_1 = 4.0 Ω and R_2 = 6.0 Ω, that are connected in parallel to each other.

Calculate the terminal potential difference of the cell. [4]

....

ORGANISE

Circular motion

A-level only

Key words

Key questions

How many radians are there in a circle?

In what direction does a centripetal force act?

Why does a banked corner reduce the friction required for turning?

Circular motion

If an object moves in a circle at constant speed, it is still accelerating because the direction of its velocity is constantly changing. This acceleration is called **centripetal acceleration** and it always acts towards the centre of the circle. To sustain this motion, a centripetal force is required. This also acts towards the centre of the circle.

Radians and angular speed

A **radian** is a measure of an angle. One radian is the angle subtended at the centre of a circle when the length of the arc is equal to the radius of the circle. As the circumference of a circle is $2\pi r$, there are 2π radians in a complete circle.

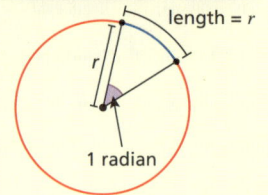

Angular speed (ω) is defined as the angle travelled per second, measured in radians per second (rad s^{-1}). Angular speed is related to the linear speed by:

$$\omega = \frac{v}{r}$$

where v is the linear speed (in m s^{-1}) and r is the radius of the circle that the object is travelling around.

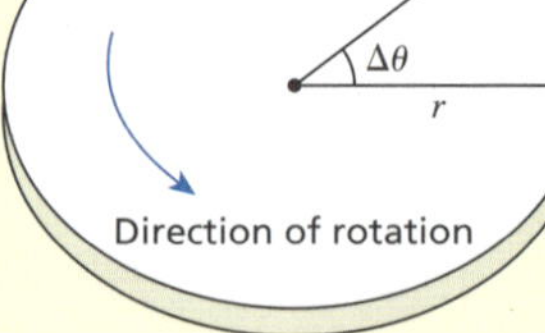

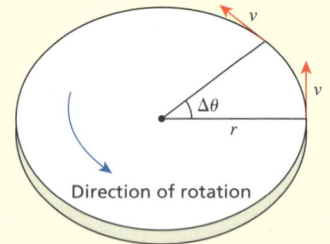

Angular speed can also be expressed in terms of the frequency of rotation:

$$\omega = 2\pi f$$

Centripetal acceleration and force

In circular motion, the centripetal acceleration is directed towards the centre of the circle. Centripetal acceleration is given by:

$$a = \frac{v^2}{r} = \omega^2 r$$

If these expressions are substituted into the expression for Newton's second law ($F = ma$), new expressions for the centripetal force are obtained:

$$F = m\frac{v^2}{r} = m\omega^2 r$$

Examples of circular motion

Circular motion can be observed in real-world situations. Here are a few examples:

1. A car cornering. When a car turns on a flat road, the force of friction between the tyres and the road provides the centripetal force required for circular motion.

   On a banked corner, the road is tilted at an angle to help with turning. In this case, the normal reaction force from the surface and friction has horizontal components that contribute to the centripetal force.

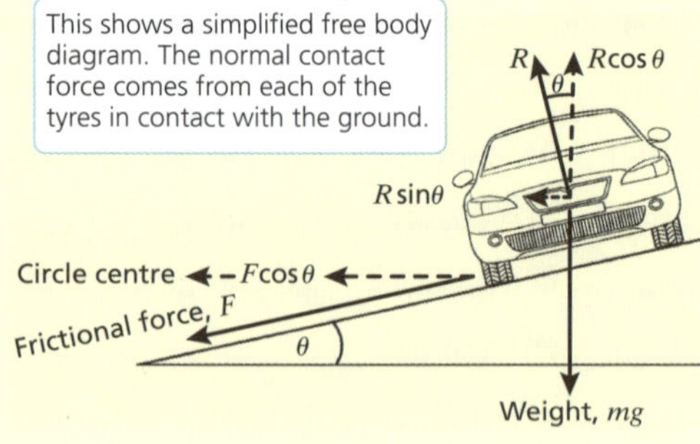

2. An object swung on a string. When an object is swung in a horizontal circle on a string, the tension in the string provides the centripetal force. The faster the object moves or the smaller the radius of the circle, the greater the tension needed to maintain the motion.
3. Planets orbiting a star. The gravitational attraction between a planet and a star acts as the centripetal force, keeping the planet in its orbit.

Summary

RETRIEVE

Circular motion

A-level only

(1) A wheel rotates at 120 revolutions per minute.

What is its angular speed in radians per second? Tick **one** box. [1]

6.3 rad s^{-1} ☐ 12.6 rad s^{-1} ☐ 720 rad s^{-1} ☐ 750 rad s^{-1} ☐

(2) A child on a swing moves in a circular arc of radius 1.5 m. At the lowest point of the swing, the speed is 4.0 m s^{-1}.

What is the tension in the rope if the child has a mass of 30 kg? Tick **one** box. [1]

294 N ☐ 320 N ☐ 614 N ☐ 730 N ☐

(3) A 0.50 kg mass is attached to a string and swung in a circular path of radius 1.2 m.

a) Calculate the tension in the string when the object moves with a speed of 6.0 m s^{-1} in a horizontal circle. Assume the string remains taut and level throughout. [2]

b) The mass is now swung in a vertical circle of the same radius.

Calculate the tension in the string when the object is at the highest point of the circle. The mass is moving at the same speed of 6.0 m s^{-1}. [2]

c) The mass is now swung while the string makes an angle of 50° above the horizontal. The mass moves in a horizontal circle, as shown in the diagram.

Calculate the angular speed of the mass. [4]

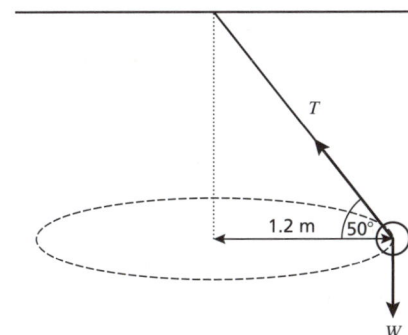

(4) A car of mass 1000 kg travels around a banked circular curve of radius 45 m at a speed of 20 m s^{-1}.

The curve is banked at an angle of 5.0° above the horizontal.

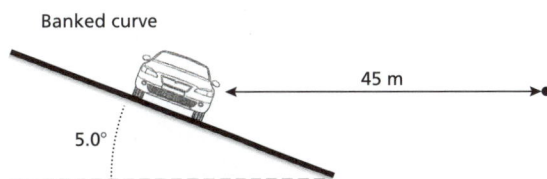

a) Calculate the centripetal force acting on the car. [2]

b) Calculate the value of the frictional force that is acting on the car parallel to and down the slope. [4]

ORGANISE

Simple harmonic motion

A-level only

Key words

Key questions

What conditions that are required for an object to undergo SHM?

What would be an expression for the displacement of an object undergoing SHM if it were to start at the equilibrium position at time $t = 0$?

What do the gradients of displacement–time and velocity–time graphs represent?

Conditions for simple harmonic motion

For an object to exhibit simple harmonic motion (SHM), its acceleration a must be directly proportional to its displacement x from the equilibrium position and must act towards the equilibrium position. This is expressed as:

$$a \propto -x$$

where the negative sign indicates that the acceleration acts in the opposite direction to the displacement.

Acceleration can also be expressed in terms of the angular speed ω as:

$$a = -\omega^2 x$$

Formulae that describe simple harmonic motion

The displacement x of an object in SHM at time t can be expressed as:

$$x = A\cos(\omega t)$$

where A is the amplitude (maximum displacement from the equilibrium position).

To use this equation, make sure your calculator is set to radians.

The choice of a cosine function assumes that the object starts at maximum displacement at time $t = 0$. A sine function could also be used if the object was at the equilibrium position at $t = 0$.

The velocity, v, of the object depends on both the angular speed and the displacement:

$$v = \pm\omega\sqrt{A^2 - x^2}$$

This expression shows that the velocity is greatest at the equilibrium position ($x = 0$) and decreases as the displacement increases. The maximum velocity is therefore:

$$v_{max} = \omega A$$

Similarly, the maximum acceleration occurs at the maximum displacement ($x_{max} = \pm A$) so that:

$$a_{max} = \omega^2 A$$

Simple harmonic motion graphs

A displacement–time graph for an object starting at maximum displacement A at time $t = 0$ is shown.

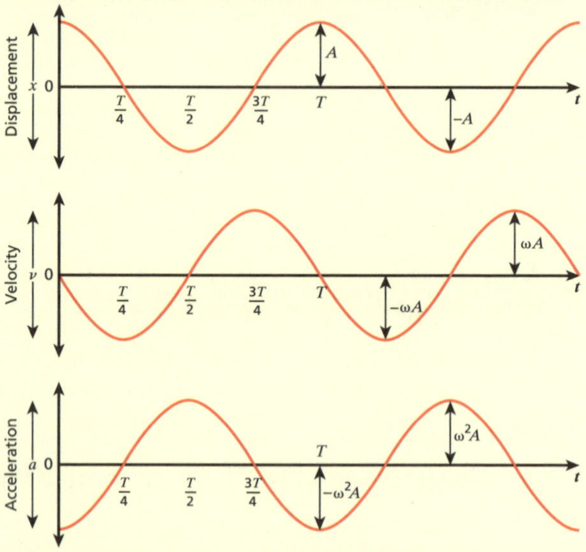

The gradient of the displacement–time graph represents the velocity of the object. Due to this, velocity–time and displacement–time graphs are out of phase by 90° (or $\frac{\pi}{2}$ radians). Note that the maximum amplitude of the velocity–time graph is equal to ωA.

In a similar way, the gradient of the velocity–time graph represents the acceleration of the object. An acceleration–time graph is 90° ($\frac{\pi}{2}$ radians) out of phase with the velocity–time graph. This means that the acceleration–time graph is 180° (π radians) out of phase with the displacement–time graph. The maximum amplitude of the acceleration–time graph is equal to $\omega^2 A$.

Summary

RETRIEVE

Simple harmonic motion

A-level only

(1) The displacement of an object undergoing simple harmonic motion is given by $x = 0.1\cos(5t)$.

What is the maximum acceleration of the object? Tick **one** box. [1]

$0.5\,m\,s^{-2}$ ☐ $1.25\,m\,s^{-2}$ ☐ $2.5\,m\,s^{-2}$ ☐ $5.0\,m\,s^{-2}$ ☐

(2) Which statement correctly describes the acceleration of an object undergoing simple harmonic motion? Tick **one** box. [1]

The acceleration is always directed towards equilibrium and is proportional to the displacement. ☐

The acceleration is independent of displacement. ☐

The acceleration is constant in magnitude and direction. ☐

The acceleration is always directed away from equilibrium and is proportional to the displacement. ☐

(3) A particle undergoes simple harmonic motion and oscillates with an amplitude of 0.30 m and a frequency of 5.0 Hz. The particle is released from its maximum displacement at a time of $t = 0$ s.

a) Calculate the maximum velocity of the particle. [2]

....

b) Calculate the time taken for the particle to move from its equilibrium position to a displacement of –0.20 m. [3]

....

c) Calculate the velocity of the particle at a time of 25 ms. [3]

....

d) Using the axes below, sketch the velocity–time curve for the particle's motion. [3]

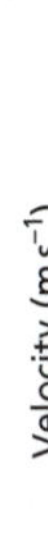

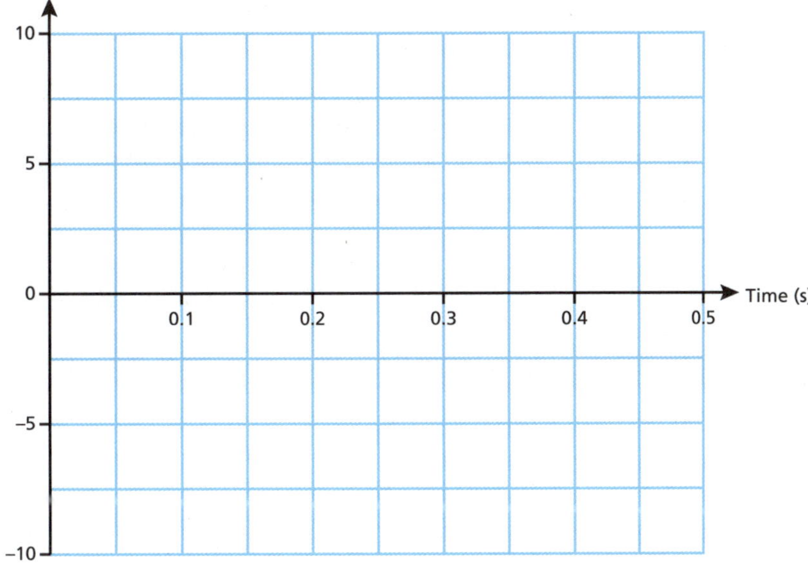

Simple harmonic systems

Key words

Key questions

What causes the restoring forces of a mass-spring system and a simple pendulum?

What effect does increasing the mass of a simple pendulum have on its time period?

If a pendulum is released from maximum displacement, what happens to its energy stores over time?

Mass-spring systems

A mass m attached to a spring oscillates with simple harmonic motion (SHM) when displaced from its equilibrium position and released.

A restoring force of $F = -\mathrm{k}x$ leads to an oscillation of time period:

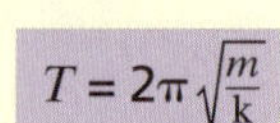

$$T = 2\pi\sqrt{\frac{m}{\mathrm{k}}}$$

where k is the spring constant of the spring (in $\mathrm{N\,m^{-1}}$).

This expression shows that a stiffer spring results in a shorter time period and that heavier masses oscillate with a longer time period. However, the time period does not depend on the amplitude of oscillation, A.

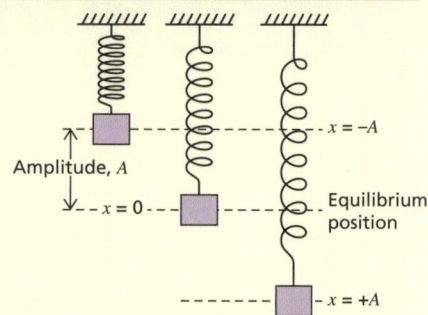

Simple pendulum

A simple pendulum consists of a mass (bob) attached to a string of length l.

When displaced, a restoring force of $F = -mg\sin\theta$ leads to SHM of time period:

$$T = 2\pi\sqrt{\frac{l}{g}}$$

The time period depends only on the length of the string and gravitational field strength, not on the mass of the bob. The derivation of this equation relies on the small angle approximation and so can only be used for small angles of displacement.

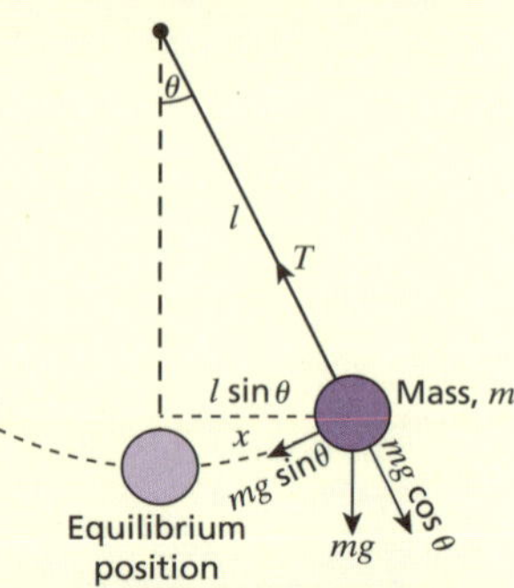

Energy in simple harmonic motion

In SHM, energy oscillates between the kinetic energy (E_k) and potential energy (E_p) stores. Due to the principle of conservation of energy, the total energy remains constant.

For both mass-spring systems and a simple pendulum, kinetic energy is maximum at equilibrium and can be calculated by:

$$E_k = \frac{1}{2}mv^2$$

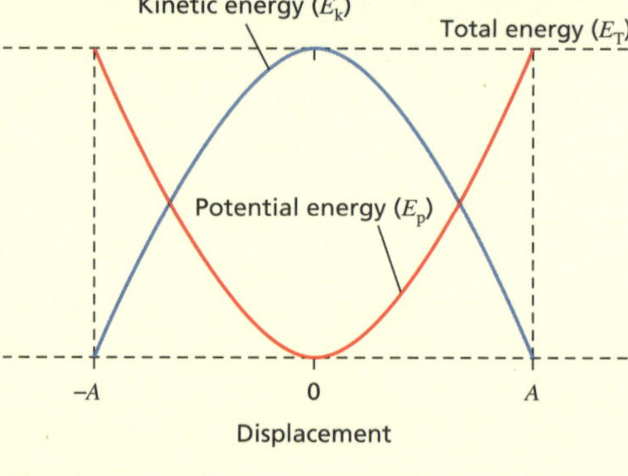

If the expression for velocity of an object undergoing SHM ($v = \pm\omega\sqrt{A^2 - x^2}$) is substituted into this formula, the kinetic energy can be calculated by:

$$E_k = \frac{1}{2}m\omega^2(A^2 - x^2)$$

At a displacement of $x = 0$, the maximum kinetic energy is therefore equal to $\frac{1}{2}m\omega^2A^2$. If the kinetic energy is less than this then this energy has been transferred to the potential energy store so that:

$$E_p = \frac{1}{2}m\omega^2x^2$$

For a horizontal mass-spring system, the potential energy would be elastic potential. For a pendulum, the potential energy would be gravitational potential.

The total energy E_T remains constant at:

$$E_T = E_k + E_p = \frac{1}{2}m\omega^2A^2$$

Summary

Simple harmonic systems

1 In a mass-spring system, the initial time period of oscillation is 2.0 s.

What will be the new time period if the mass is increased by a factor of 4 and the spring constant is decreased by a factor of 4? Tick **one** box. [1]

1.0 s ☐ 2.0 s ☐ 8.0 s ☐ 16.0 s ☐

2 A pendulum completes 20 oscillations in a time of 30.0 s.

a) Calculate the length of the pendulum. [3]

b) Describe and explain what effect, if any, increasing the mass of the pendulum bob would have on the time period of the pendulum. [2]

3 A horizontal mass-spring system consists of a mass of 0.20 kg attached to a spring of spring constant 150 $N m^{-1}$. The mass-spring system is undergoing simple harmonic oscillation.

a) Calculate the time period of oscillation. [2]

b) The amplitude of the oscillation is 0.15 m.

Calculate the maximum kinetic energy of the mass. [3]

c) Calculate the displacement for which the kinetic energy of mass is equal to its elastic potential energy. [3]

4 The graph shows how the kinetic energy of a particle undergoing simple harmonic motion varies with displacement.

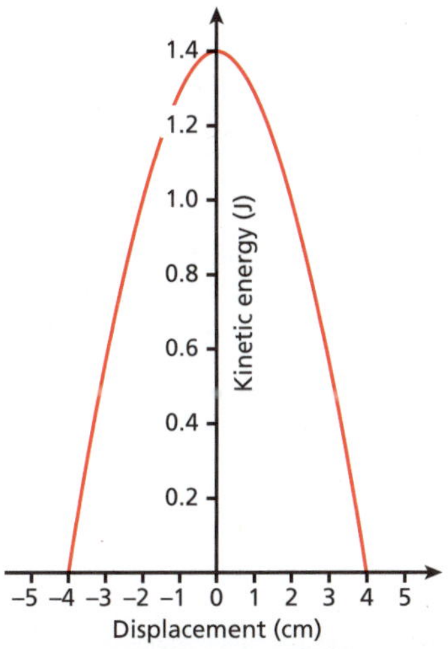

a) On the graph, sketch how the potential energy of the particle varies with displacement. [1]

b) The particle has a mass of 0.50 kg.

Using the graph, calculate the time period of oscillation. [3]

ORGANISE

Forced vibrations and resonance

A-level only

Key words

Key questions

What is meant by an object's natural frequency?

What happens if an object is driven at a frequency equal to its natural frequency?

What is the difference between light damping and critical damping?

Free and forced vibrations

Free vibrations occur when a system is displaced from its equilibrium position and allowed to oscillate without any external force acting on it. In this case, the system vibrates at its natural frequency. For example, if you displace a pendulum and let it go, it will oscillate freely at its natural frequency.

Forced vibrations occur when an external driving force is applied. The system oscillates at the frequency of the applied force rather than at its natural frequency.

Resonance and damping

Resonance occurs when the frequency of the external driving force (referred to as the driving frequency) matches the natural frequency of the system. At resonance, energy transfer from the driving force to the system is maximised. This results in a maximum amplitude of oscillation.

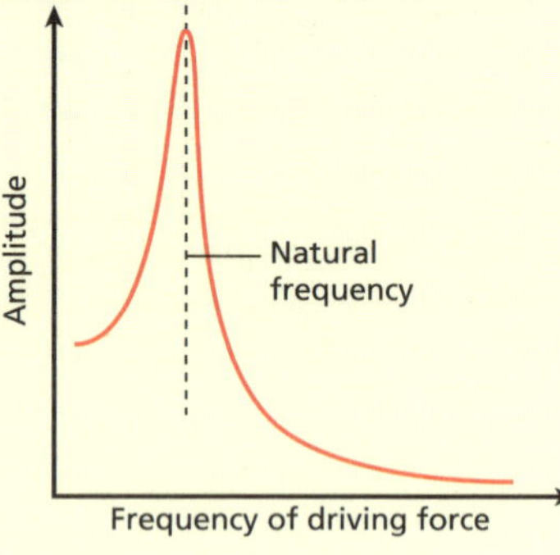

Large oscillations at resonance can lead to the failure of structures, e.g. the Tacoma Narrows Bridge (Washington, USA) collapsed in 1940 due to resonance caused by wind. To avoid this, oscillations can be damped.

Damping refers to the process by which energy is transferred from an oscillating system due to resistive forces.

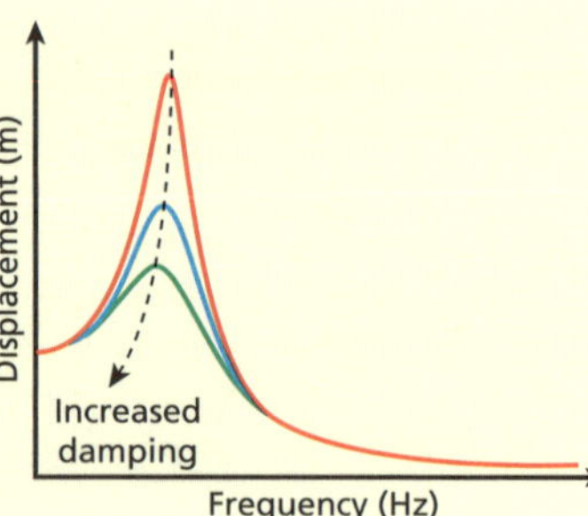

As damping increases:

- the maximum amplitude of oscillation is reduced
- the sharpness of resonance decreases
- the resonance peak shifts to a lower frequency.

Damping reduces the amplitude of oscillations over time, eventually bringing the system to rest if no external force is applied.

There are four types of damping:

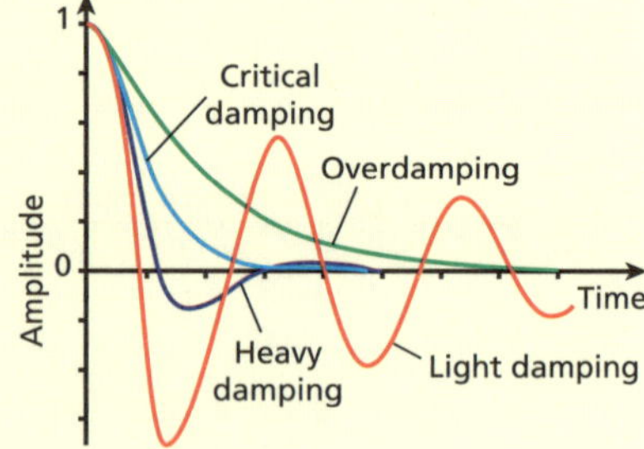

- **Light damping**. Oscillations continue, but the amplitude gradually decreases over time.
- **Heavy damping**. The amplitude of oscillations is reduced in a much shorter time.
- **Critical damping**. The system returns to equilibrium in the shortest possible time without oscillating.
- **Overdamping**. Equilibrium is reached without oscillations, but more slowly than in the critically damped case.

Examples of resonance and damping
Musical instruments – for example, a guitar string resonates at its natural frequency to form stationary waves.
Radios – tuning to a specific frequency creates resonance with incoming electromagnetic waves.
Buildings – earthquake-resistant buildings are damped to avoid resonating at seismic frequencies.
Vehicles – shock absorbers in cars use damping to reduce vibrations.

Summary

Forced vibrations and resonance

1. The diagram shows Barton's pendulum experiment. It consists of a driving pendulum and several other pendulums of varying lengths hanging beside it.

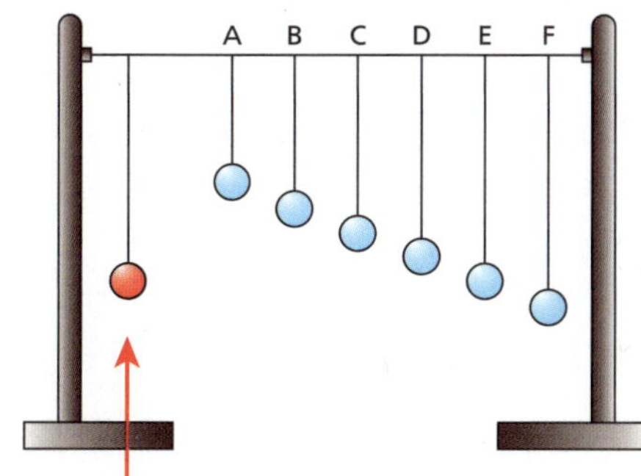

a) The driving pendulum has a length of 1.0 m.

Calculate the natural frequency of the driving pendulum. [3]

b) The driving pendulum sends vibrations along a taut string to the other pendulums, labelled A–F.

State and explain which of these pendulums will oscillate with the largest amplitude. [3]

c) The driving pendulum undergoes free vibrations, while pendulums A–F undergo forced vibrations.

Describe the difference between free and forced vibrations. [2]

d) The air provides light damping to the driving pendulum.

Explain what is meant by light damping and what will happen to the amplitude of the driving pendulum oscillations over time. [2]

2. Soldiers are often instructed to break step when crossing a bridge to avoid resonance effects.

a) Explain what is meant by resonance and describe the potential consequences of resonances in this situation. [3]

b) Describe how damping could reduce the risk of resonance in a bridge. [2]

c) Explain why breaking step reduces the chance of resonance occurring. [3]

ORGANISE

Thermal energy transfer

A-level only

Key words

Key questions

What does internal energy consist of?

What is the definition of specific heat capacity?

What is the definition of the latent heat of vaporisation?

How can the specific heat capacity of a liquid be measured?

Internal energy

Internal energy is the total energy of particles within a system, consisting of kinetic energy and potential energy. The kinetic energy is due to the motion of the particles, while the potential energy arises from the forces between particles. For example, in solids, particles are closely packed with strong intermolecular forces. In gases, particles are far apart with negligible interactions.

The internal energy of a system can increase in two ways:

1. Heating – energy is transferred to particles, increasing their kinetic energy.
2. Doing work – when work is done on a system, such as by compressing a gas, the internal energy increases.

During a change of state, the internal energy of the system changes because the potential energy of particles is altered. However, the kinetic energy (and therefore the temperature) remains constant during this process.

Specific and latent heat

The **specific heat capacity** (c) of a substance is the amount of energy required to raise the temperature of 1 kg of a substance by a temperature of 1 K (or 1°C).

When a substance is heated or cooled without changing state, the energy transfer is calculated using:

$$Q = mc\Delta\theta$$

where Q is the energy transferred (in J), m is the mass of the substance (in kg), c is the specific heat capacity (in J kg^{-1} K^{-1}) and $\Delta\theta$ is the temperature change (in K or °C).

The **specific latent heat of fusion** (or vaporisation) is the energy required to change 1 kg of a substance from solid to liquid (or liquid to gas) without a temperature change.

The energy transferred Q can be calculated using:

$$Q = ml$$

where l is the specific latent heat of fusion or vaporisation (in J kg^{-1}).

Continuous flow calorimetry to determine the specific heat capacity of a liquid

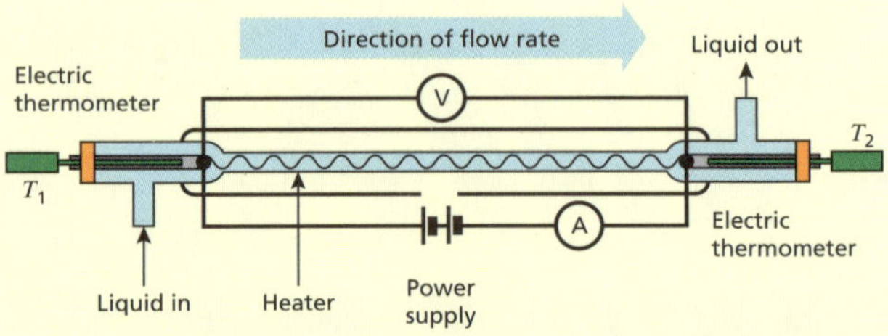

1. Liquid flows through the apparatus at a steady rate. The temperature difference $\Delta\theta$ between the inlet and outlet should be constant.
2. Record the flow rate, so that the mass (m_1) flowing through the calorimeter within a certain time (t_1) is known. Also record the potential difference across the heater (V_1) and the current through the heater (I_1) to calculate the energy supplied by the heater $Q_1 = I_1V_1t_1$. The energy supplied heats the liquid so that $Q_1 = m_1c\Delta\theta + H$, where H is the heat loss to the surroundings.
3. Adjust the flow rate and power supply for another set of readings (at the same inlet and outlet temperatures) so that $Q_2 = I_2V_2t_2 = m_2c\Delta\theta + H$
4. Since H is the same for each set of readings (as the inlet and outlet temperatures are the same), the two expressions can be subtracted from one another to eliminate H. This gives: $$Q_2 - Q_1 = (m_2 - m_1)c\Delta\theta$$ Rearranging this for the specific heat capacity leads to: $$c = \frac{Q_2 - Q_1}{(m_2 - m_1)\Delta\theta}$$

Summary

RETRIEVE

Thermal energy transfer

A-level only

1 Which of the following statements is true during a change of state? Tick **one** box. [1]

The kinetic energy of the particles changes. ☐

The potential energy of the particles remains constant. ☐

Both the kinetic and potential energies of the particles remain constant. ☐

The temperature of the substance remains constant. ☐

2 A 1.2 kg block of ice is initially at a temperature of –30°C. It is heated using a heater of power 400 W until it becomes water at 25°C.

Calculate how long this will take. You may need to use the following values:

- Specific heat capacity of ice = 2100 J kg^{-1} K^{-1}
- Latent heat of fusion of ice = 334 000 J kg^{-1}
- Specific heat capacity of water = 4200 J kg^{-1} K^{-1} [5]

3 A 0.50 kg block of metal at an initial temperature of 150°C is dropped into 2.0 kg of water at 20°C. The specific heat capacities of the metal and water are 900 J kg^{-1} K^{-1} and 4200 J kg^{-1} K^{-1} respectively.

Calculate the final equilibrium temperature, assuming no thermal energy loss. [4]

4 In a continuous flow calorimetry experiment, ethanol flows through a heater coil at a steady rate. The inlet temperature is 15°C and the outlet temperature is 25°C. Two sets of readings are taken using the equipment.

First set: Potential difference across coil = 12 V; current in coil = 2.5 A; time = 180 s; mass of liquid flowing past coil = 0.45 kg

Second set: Potential difference across coil = 14 V; current in coil = 3.0 A; time = 180 s; mass of liquid flowing past coil = 0.54 kg

The thermal energy lost to the surroundings is the same for each set of readings.

Calculate the specific heat capacity of ethanol. [5]

Ideal gases

Key words

Key questions

Why does the pressure of a gas increase if its volume is decreased?

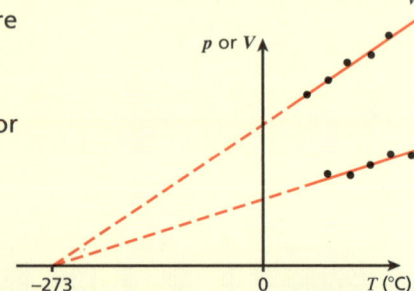

Why does the pressure of a gas reduce if its temperature is decreased?

How do you convert between degrees Celsius and kelvin?

What does the area under a pressure–volume graph represent?

Gas laws and absolute zero

An ideal gas is one that obeys the gas laws, which describe relationships between pressure (p), volume (V) and temperature (T).

Name of law	Description of gas law	Formula for gas law
Boyle's law	For a fixed mass of gas at constant temperature, the pressure of the gas is inversely proportional to its volume.	pV = constant
Charles's law	At constant pressure, the volume of a gas is directly proportional to its absolute temperature.	$\frac{V}{T}$ = constant
Pressure law	For a fixed mass of gas at constant volume, the pressure is directly proportional to its temperature.	$\frac{P}{T}$ = constant

The graph (right) shows how pressure varies with volume due to Boyle's law. When the volume of a gas decreases, the particles undergo more frequent collisions with the walls of the container each second. Each collision transfers momentum, so more collisions per second lead to a greater rate of change of momentum and therefore a higher force and pressure.

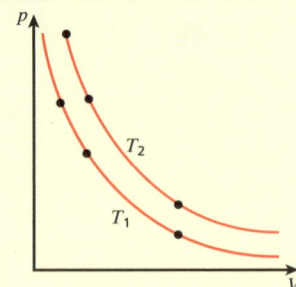

The next graph (below right) shows how pressure and volume vary with temperature due to the pressure law and Charles's law. The graph continues until a temperature of absolute zero. Absolute zero is the theoretical temperature where the pressure or volume of ideal gas would become zero. This corresponds to –273°C and is the basis of the Kelvin scale.

In the Kelvin scale: $T(K) = T(°C) + 273$

The ideal gas equation

The ideal gas equation combines the gas laws into a single expression: $pV = nRT$

where p is the pressure of the gas (in Pa), V is the volume of the gas (in m^3), n is the number of moles of gas, R is the molar gas constant (equal to 8.31 J K^{-1} mol^{-1}) and T is the temperature of the gas (in K).

The Avogadro constant (N_A = 6.02 × 10^{23} mol^{-1}) is the number of molecules (N) in one mole, so that $n = \frac{N}{N_A}$. This can be substituted into the ideal gas equation to obtain: $pV = \frac{N}{N_A}RT = NkT$

where k is the Boltzmann constant (equal to 1.38 × 10^{-23} J K^{-1}), where $k = \frac{R}{N_A}$

When a gas expands or is compressed, it does work on its surroundings. The **work done** by a gas is given by: $W = p\Delta V$ where ΔV is the change in volume.

Work done can also be calculated from the area under a pressure–volume graph.

Converting between mass and number of moles

The molar mass of a substance is the mass of one mole of its particles, usually expressed in grams per mole (g mol^{-1}) and is equal to its relative molecular mass (the sum of the relative atomic masses of its atoms). The number of moles, n, of a gas can be calculated from its mass m and molar mass M using: $n = \frac{m}{M}$

Summary

RETRIEVE

Ideal gases

A-level only

1 Which change will double the pressure of an ideal gas? Tick **one** box. [1]

The volume is halved at constant temperature. ☐

The temperature is halved at constant volume. ☐

The number of particles is halved at constant temperature and volume. ☐

The volume and temperature are doubled. ☐

2 A container holds 3.0 mol of a gas at a temperature of 27°C and a pressure of 450 kPa.

Calculate the volume of the gas. [3]

....

3 A gas, initially at a pressure of 100 kPa and a volume of $0.15\,m^3$, is compressed at a constant temperature to a volume of $0.12\,m^3$.

a) Calculate the pressure after the gas has been compressed. [2]

....

b) There are 5.0 moles of the gas.

Calculate the temperature of the gas. [2]

....

4 Explain why the pressure inside a car tyre increases when the temperature of the gas inside it rises. Assume that the volume of the tyre remains constant. [3]

....

....

....

....

5 A sample of argon gas expands from $0.030\,m^3$ to $0.080\,m^3$ at a constant pressure of 250 kPa.

a) Calculate the work done by the gas. [2]

....

b) The sample has a mass of 60 g and the molar mass of argon is $40\,g\,mol^{-1}$.

Calculate the temperature change as the gas expands. [4]

....

ORGANISE

Kinetic theory

A-level only

Key words

Key questions

How was the kinetic theory model developed?

What are the assumptions of kinetic theory?

Why does the internal energy of an ideal gas only depend on its kinetic energy?

Development of the kinetic theory model

The gas laws were derived empirically, meaning they were based on experimental observations. These laws describe the relationships between pressure, volume and the temperature of gases but do not explain the reasons behind them.

Kinetic theory later provided a theoretical framework to explain the gas laws, describing gases as collections of particles in constant random motion that collide with each other and the walls of their container.

Kinetic theory

The key assumptions of kinetic theory are:

1. The gas consists of a large number of identical particles.
2. The particles travel in straight lines and are in constant, random motion.
3. Collisions between particles and with container walls are perfectly elastic.
4. The time of collisions is negligible compared to the time between collisions.
5. No intermolecular forces act except during collisions.

To derive an expression for gas pressure in one dimension, consider a single gas molecule of mass m and velocity u colliding elastically with a wall of its container. It experiences a momentum change equal to $\Delta p = mu - (-mu) = 2mu$.

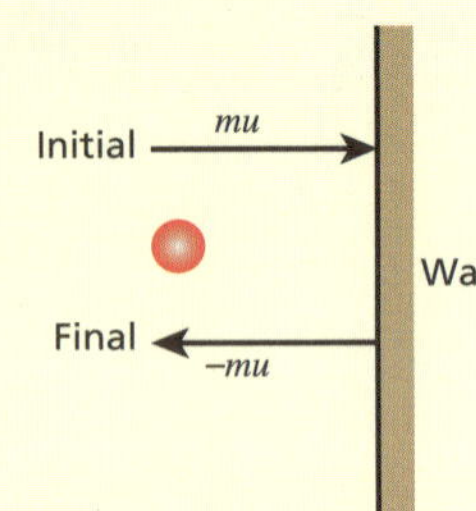

The time between successive collisions with the wall is $t = \frac{2L}{u}$, where L is the distance between the walls. The force acting on the wall is equal to the rate of change of momentum, so that $F = \frac{\Delta p}{t} = \frac{2mu}{\frac{2L}{u}} = \frac{mu^2}{L}$

If there are N molecules travelling at different speeds, $F = \frac{m(u_1^2 + u_2^2 + u_3^2 + ...u_N^2)}{L}$

The mean square speed of the N molecules is defined so that

$\overline{u^2} = \frac{(u_1^2 + u_2^2 + u_3^2 + ...u_N^2)}{N}$

Combining this with the earlier expression for the force gives $F = \frac{Nm\overline{u^2}}{L}$

This gives an expression for the pressure in one dimension to be:

$$p = \frac{F}{A} = \frac{\frac{Nm\overline{u^2}}{L}}{L^2} = \frac{Nm\overline{u^2}}{L^3} = \frac{Nm\overline{u^2}}{V}$$

where V is the volume of the cubic container.

To extend this derivation to three dimensions, consider particles of velocity v and w in the two perpendicular directions to u. The overall mean square speed can be shown to be $\overline{c^2} = \overline{u^2} + \overline{v^2} + \overline{w^2}$ by using Pythagoras' theorem. As the particles are moving in random directions, $\overline{u^2} = \overline{v^2} = \overline{w^2}$ so that $\overline{c^2} = 3\overline{u^2}$.

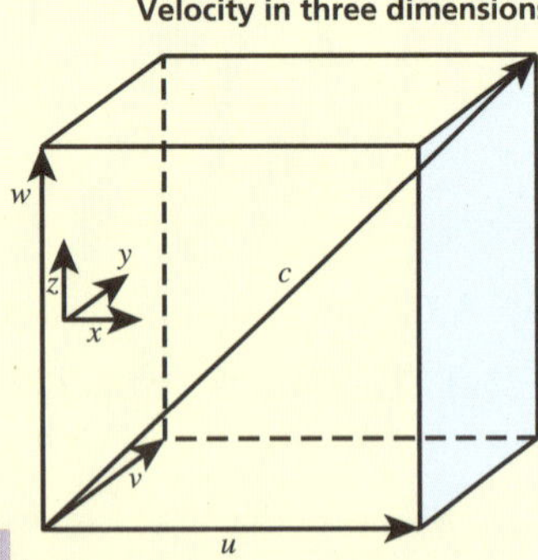

This gives an expression for pressure in three dimensions to be $p = \frac{Nm\overline{c^2}}{3V}$ and therefore $pV = \frac{1}{3}Nm\overline{c^2}$. Finally, this can be expressed in terms of the root mean square speed ($c_{rms} = \sqrt{\overline{c^2}}$) to give:

$$pV = \frac{1}{3}Nm(c_{rms})^2$$

Internal energy of an ideal gas

For an ideal gas, the internal energy arises solely from the kinetic energy of its particles as there are no intermolecular forces.

$$\text{kinetic energy of a gas molecule} = \frac{1}{2}m(c_{rms})^2 = \frac{3}{2}kT = \frac{3RT}{2N_A}$$

Summary

RETRIEVE

Kinetic theory

A-level only

1. Which assumption is **not** part of the kinetic theory of gases? Tick **one** box. [1]

   Gas particles are in constant, random motion. ☐

   Collisions between gas particles are perfectly inelastic. ☐

   The time of collisions is negligible compared to the time between collisions. ☐

   Intermolecular forces are negligible. ☐

2. A gas is stored in a container with a pressure of 200 kPa and a volume of $0.050\,m^3$. The gas contains molecules with a molecular mass of 4.0×10^{-26} kg and a root mean square speed of $2500\,m\,s^{-1}$.

   Calculate the number of molecules in the gas. [2]

   ....

3. A sample of oxygen gas (O_2) is at a temperature of 300 K. The molar mass of oxygen is $32\,g\,mol^{-1}$.

   Calculate the root mean squared speed of the oxygen molecules. [3]

   ....

4. This question is about the kinetic theory equation.

   a) State **two** assumptions made in kinetic theory. [2]

   ....

   ....

   ....

   b) Derive the expression $pV = \frac{1}{3}Nm(c_{rms})^2$, starting with momentum. [6]

   c) The initial pressure of a gas that consists of 2.5×10^{23} molecules is 250 kPa. The gas is stored in a sealed container of volume $0.020\,m^3$ and has a molar mass of $40\,g\,mol^{-1}$.

   Calculate the root mean square speed of the gas molecules. [3]

   ....

ORGANISE

Newton's law of gravitation

A-level only

Key words

Key questions

What is Newton's law of gravitation in words?

What is the difference between radial and uniform gravitational fields?

What is the definition of gravitational field strength?

Newton's law of gravitation

Every mass in the Universe exerts an attractive gravitational force on every other mass. The force depends on the masses involved and the distance between them.

Newton's law of gravitation states that the attractive force between two masses is proportional to the product of the masses and inversely proportional to the square of their separation:

$$F = \frac{Gm_1m_2}{r^2}$$

where F is the gravitational force (in N), G is the gravitational constant ($6.67 \times 10^{-11}\,\text{N}\,\text{m}^2\,\text{kg}^{-2}$), m_1 and m_2 are the masses of the two objects (in kg), and r is the distance between the centres of the two objects (in m).

This expression is an example of the inverse square law as $F \propto \frac{1}{r^2}$. So, if the separation between the centres of two objects is doubled, the gravitational force will decrease by a factor of 4.

Gravitational field lines

Gravitational field lines represent the strength and direction of the gravitational field. The field lines indicate the direction of the gravitational force that would act on a small test mass placed in the field. Gravitational fields are always attractive, so the lines point towards the mass generating the field.

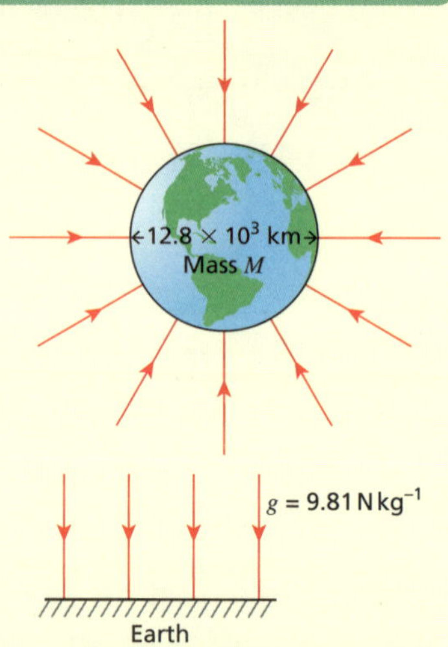

Far from Earth's surface, the gravitational field is radial. The field lines radiate towards the centre of Earth, getting closer as they approach the mass. This indicates that the field strength increases closer to Earth.

Near Earth's surface, the field is approximately uniform. Field lines are parallel and equally spaced, representing a constant gravitational field (g) near the surface.

$g = 9.81\,\text{N}\,\text{kg}^{-1}$

Earth

Gravitational field strength

The gravitational field strength is a vector quantity that represents the gravitational force per unit mass experienced by a small test mass placed in the field:

$$g = \frac{F}{m}$$

In a radial field, the gravitational field strength depends on the mass of the object and the distance from its centre:

$$g = \frac{GM}{r^2}$$

For Earth, with a mass of 5.97×10^{24} kg and a radius of 6.37×10^6 m, the gravitational field strength at the surface is $9.81\ \text{N}\,\text{kg}^{-1}$.

As the gravitational field strength of a radial field also follows the inverse square law, at twice the distance the gravitational field strength would reduce by a factor of 4 to $2.45\ \text{N}\,\text{kg}^{-1}$.

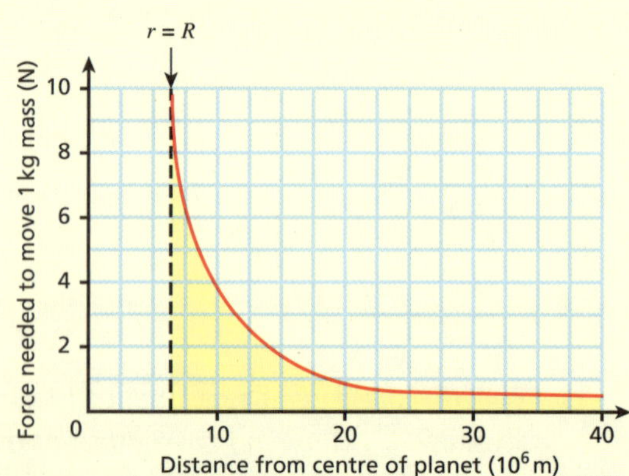

Summary

RETRIEVE

Newton's law of gravitation

A-level only

1. The gravitational force between two masses m_1 and m_2 is F.

   If both masses are doubled and the distance between them is halved, what happens to the force? Tick **one** box. [1]

   It remains the same. ☐ It doubles. ☐

   It increases by a factor of 8. ☐ It increases by a factor of 16. ☐

2. The gravitational field strength on the surface of a planet is 15.0 N kg^{-1}. The planet's radius is 6.5×10^6 m.

   Calculate the planet's mass. [2]

3. The Earth has a mass of 5.97×10^{24} kg and the Moon has a mass of 7.35×10^{22} kg. The Moon orbits the Earth at a distance of 3.84×10^8 m.

   a) Describe Newton's law of gravitation in words. [2]

   b) Calculate the gravitational force between Earth and the Moon. [2]

   c) Define 'gravitational field strength'. [1]

   d) There is a point between Earth and the Moon where the gravitational field strength is zero.

   Calculate the distance of this point from Earth. [4]

   e) The gravitational field strength on the Moon's surface is 1.6 N kg^{-1}.

   On the axes below, sketch a graph of gravitational field strength against distance along a straight line between Earth and the Moon. [3]

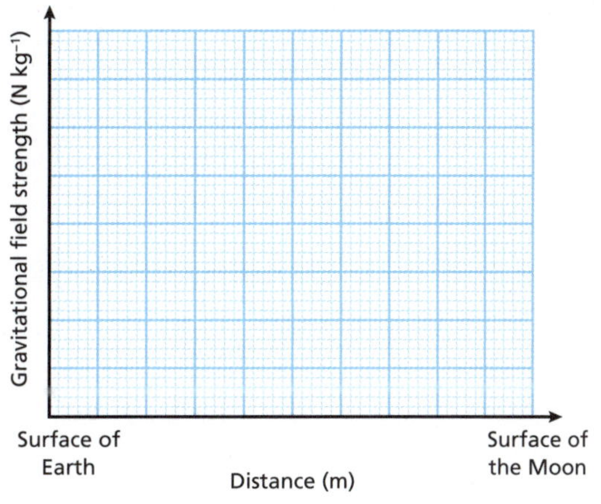

Gravitational potential

Key words

Key questions

What is the definition of gravitational potential?

How much work is done when moving along an equipotential?

What does the gradient of a V–r graph represent?

How do you calculate the gravitational potential if there is more than one mass?

Gravitational potential

Gravitational potential is defined as the work done per unit mass to move an object from infinity to that point in the field. At infinity, gravitational potential is defined to be zero. Gravitational potential is negative because work must be done against a gravitational field to move the object to infinity.

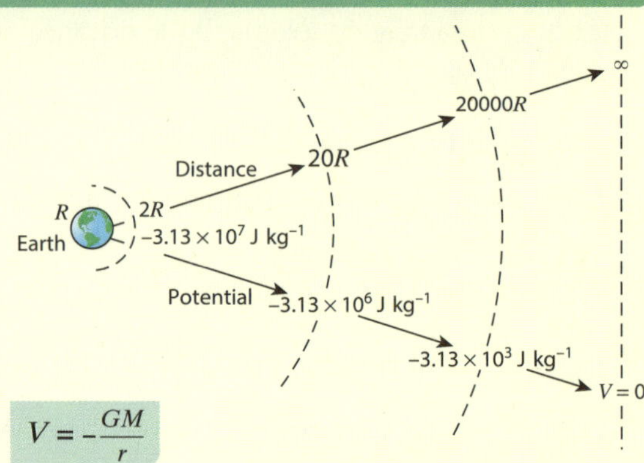

In a radial field, gravitational potential can be calculated by using:

$$V = -\frac{GM}{r}$$

where V is the gravitational potential (in J kg^{-1}), G is the gravitational constant (6.67×10^{-11} Nm^2 kg^{-2}), M is the mass of the object that creates the potential (in kg), and r is the distance to the centre of the mass.

Gravitational potential difference and equipotential surfaces

The **gravitational potential difference** (ΔV) between two points is the change in potential when moving between them. The work done to move a mass m across ΔV is:

$$\Delta W = m\,\Delta V = (V_2 - V_1)$$

For example, a rocket escaping from Earth's gravitational field experiences a change in potential from $V = -\frac{GM}{r}$ (Earth's radius r) to $V = 0$ at infinity.

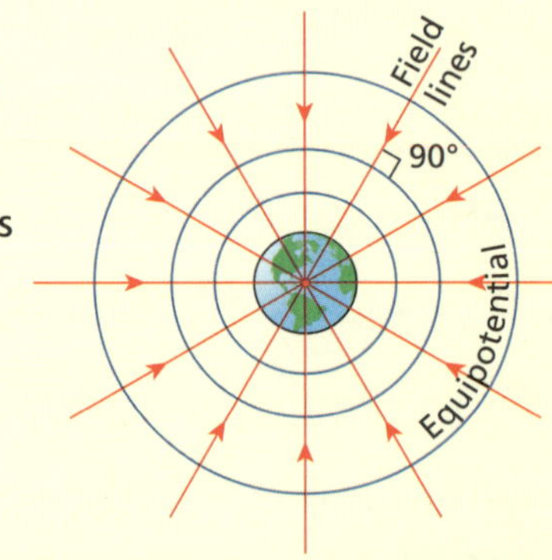

Equipotential surfaces are regions where all points have the same gravitational potential. No work is done when moving along an equipotential.

Equipotential surfaces are drawn as concentric circles around a point mass, as shown. Note that they are always perpendicular to gravitational field lines.

Graphs of gravitational potential and gravitational field strength

The gravitational field strength (g) is related to the potential gradient: $g = -\frac{\Delta V}{\Delta r}$

The negative sign shows that the gravitational field is in the direction of decreasing potential.

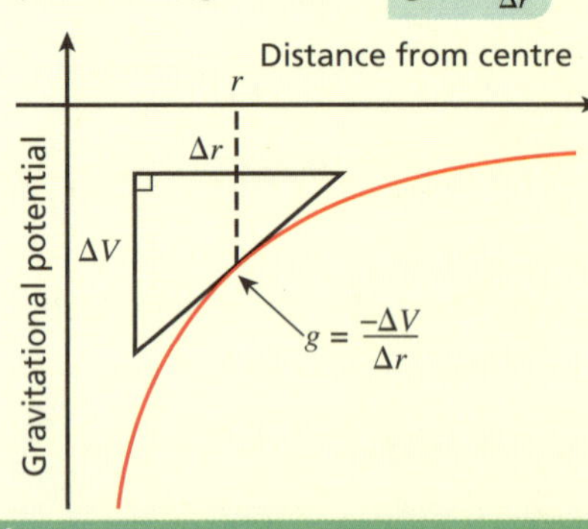

Due to this relationship, gravitational field strength is the negative of the gradient of a V–r graph. This can be determined by drawing a tangent to the graph and calculating the gradient of that tangent. The area under a g–r graph between two points gives the gravitational potential difference (ΔV) between those points.

Calculating gravitational potential due to multiple masses

Unlike gravitational field strength, gravitational potential is a scalar.

This means that, to find the total gravitational potential at a point influenced by multiple masses, the potentials due to each mass are added:

$$V_{total} = V_1 + V_2 = -\frac{GM_1}{r_1} - \frac{GM_2}{r_2}$$

Summary

RETRIEVE

Gravitational potential

A-level only

1. Which is the correct expression for the gravitational potential midway between two objects of mass M that are separated by a distance of $2R$? Tick **one** box. [1]

   $-\frac{GM}{R}$ ☐ $-\frac{2GM}{R}$ ☐ $-\frac{2GM}{2R}$ ☐ Zero ☐

2. At a distance R from a mass M, the gravitational potential is -10 MJ kg^{-1}.

   If the mass is doubled and the distance is halved, what is the new potential? Tick **one** box. [1]

   -10 MJ kg^{-1} ☐ -20 MJ kg^{-1} ☐ -40 MJ kg^{-1} ☐ -80 MJ kg^{-1} ☐

3. The International Space Station (ISS) has a mass of 450 000 kg and orbits at a height of 400 km above the Earth's surface.

   a) Define 'gravitational potential'. [2]

   b) Calculate the gravitational potential at the height of the ISS due to Earth's gravitational field. The radius of Earth is 6.37×10^{6} m and the mass of Earth is 5.97×10^{24} kg. [2]

   c) Explain, if the ISS were to experience no drag forces, why it requires no work to stay in orbit. [2]

   d) Calculate the energy required for the ISS to completely escape Earth's gravitational field from its current orbit. [2]

4. A spacecraft of mass 12 000 kg is exploring a binary star system. The two stars, A and B, are separated by a distance of 2.0×10^{11} m. Star A has a mass of 2.2×10^{30} kg and star B has a mass of 1.5×10^{30} kg. The spacecraft is located at a point 5.0×10^{10} m from star A and 1.5×10^{11} m from star B.

   a) Explain why gravitational potential is always negative. [2]

   b) Calculate the gravitational potential at the spacecraft's position due to star A. [2]

   c) Calculate the total energy required for the spacecraft to completely escape the gravitational field of both stars. [3]

ORGANISE

Orbits of planets and satellites

A-level only

Key words

Key questions

How can you derive an expression for orbital velocity?

How can you derive Kepler's third law?

What is an expression for the total energy of a satellite?

How can you derive an expression for escape velocity?

What is the time period of a geostationary satellite?

Orbital speed and Kepler's third law

For a planet or satellite of mass m in a circular orbit around a much larger mass M, the gravitational force provides the necessary centripetal force for circular motion. Therefore, the force from Newton's law of gravitation is equal to the expression for centripetal force: $\frac{GMm}{r^2} = \frac{mv_{orb}^2}{r}$

Rearranging this expression for the orbital speed (v_{orb}) gives: $v_{orb} = \sqrt{\frac{GM}{r}}$

Johannes Kepler noted that planets further from the Sun had longer orbits. To derive the link between the time period (T) of an orbit and its orbital radius (r), the orbital speed can also be expressed as: $v_{orb} = \frac{2\pi r}{T}$

where $2\pi r$ is the circumference of a circular object.

Therefore, $\frac{2\pi r}{T} = \sqrt{\frac{GM}{r}}$ and $\frac{4\pi^2 r^2}{T^2} = \frac{GM}{r}$

Finally, the expression can be written in terms of r^3: $T^2 = \left(\frac{4\pi^2}{GM}\right) r^3$

This is known as **Kepler's third law** and shows that $T^2 \propto r^3$ as the term $\frac{4\pi^2}{GM}$ is constant for a given central mass.

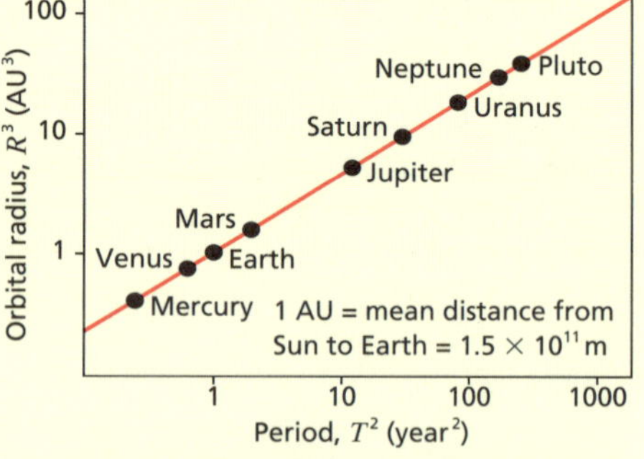

Energy in orbits

An orbiting satellite has kinetic energy equal to: $E_k = \frac{1}{2}mv_{orb}^2 = \frac{GMm}{2r}$

It also has gravitational potential energy equal to: $E_p = m\Delta V = -\frac{GMm}{r}$

The total energy is therefore equal to: $E_T = \frac{GMm}{2r} - \frac{GMm}{r} = -\frac{GMm}{2r}$

This total energy is negative, indicating a bound orbit.

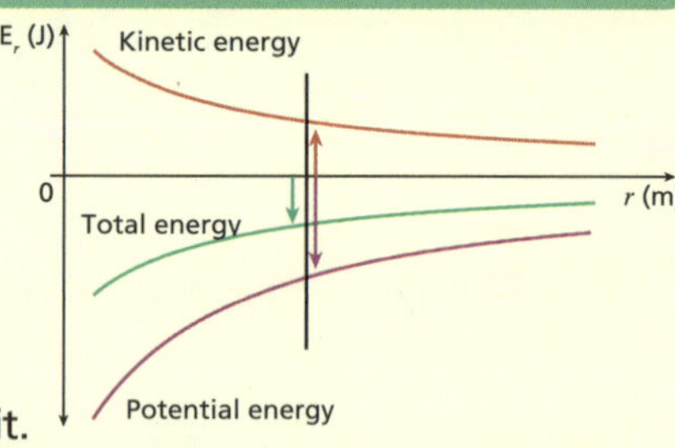

Escape velocity

Escape velocity (v_{esc}) is the minimum velocity an object needs to completely escape an object's gravitational field.

For an object to escape, its kinetic energy needs to be more than or equal to the work needed to go to infinity: $\frac{1}{2}mv_{esc}^2 \geqslant m\Delta V$ which leads to $\frac{1}{2}mv_{esc}^2 \geqslant m\frac{GM}{r}$

Rearranging for v_{esc} results in: $v_{esc} \geqslant \sqrt{\frac{2GM}{r}}$

Types of orbit

A geosynchronous orbit around Earth has a time period of 24 hours. A geostationary orbit is a special case of a geosynchronous orbit where the satellite remains fixed above the same point above the Earth's equator.

Satellites in low Earth orbits (LEO) have altitudes between 160 and 2000 km and have much shorter orbital periods. LEO satellites are used for Earth observations and communications.

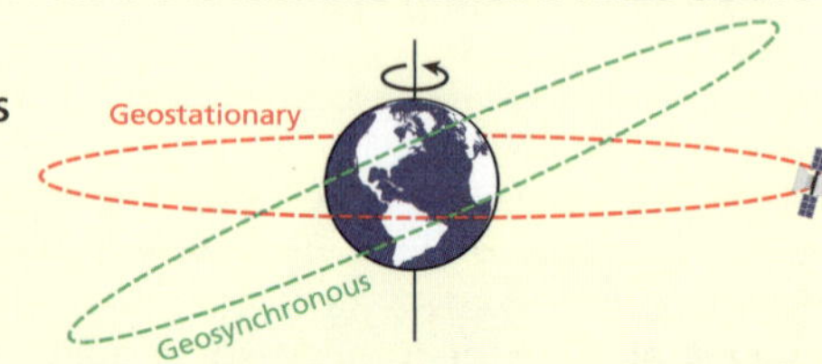

Summary

RETRIEVE

Orbits of planets and satellites

A-level only

1 Which expression correctly represents the escape velocity from a planet of mass M and radius R? Tick **one** box. [1]

$v_{esc} \geqslant \sqrt{\frac{GM}{2r}}$ ☐ $v_{esc} \geqslant \sqrt{\frac{GM}{r}}$ ☐ $v_{esc} \geqslant \sqrt{\frac{2GM}{r}}$ ☐ $v_{esc} \geqslant \sqrt{\frac{GM}{r^2}}$ ☐

2 A geostationary satellite has a time period of 24 hours and remains above the same point on the Earth's surface above the equator.

a) Derive Kepler's third law to show that $T^2 \propto r^3$. [5]

b) Show that the height of a geostationary satellite above the Earth's surface is approximately 36 000 km. The mass of Earth is 5.97×10^{24} kg and the radius of Earth is 6.37×10^6 m. [3]

c) Calculate the orbital velocity of a geostationary satellite orbiting Earth. [2]

d) Another type of satellite is a low Earth orbit (LEO) satellite.

State and explain **one** use each for LEO and geostationary satellites. [2]

3 A rocket of mass 1200 kg is launched from the surface of Earth to completely escape its gravitational field.

a) Calculate the escape velocity from Earth. [2]

b) Calculate the minimum kinetic energy the rocket requires to completely escape Earth's gravitational field. [2]

4 Show that the total energy of a satellite is equal to half of its gravitational potential energy. [3]

ORGANISE

Coulomb's law

A-level only

Key words

Key questions

What is Coulomb's law in words?

How are gravitational and electrostatic forces similar?

How are gravitational and electrostatic forces different?

Coulomb's law

Coulomb's law states that the force between two point charges is proportional to the product of the charges and inversely proportional to the square of the distance between them.

The magnitude of the force (F) is given by: $F = \frac{1}{4\pi\varepsilon_0}\frac{Q_1 Q_2}{r^2}$

where Q_1 and Q_2 are the magnitude of the charges (in C), r is the distance between the charges (in m) and ε_0 is the permittivity of free space (with a value of 8.85×10^{-12} F m^{-1}).

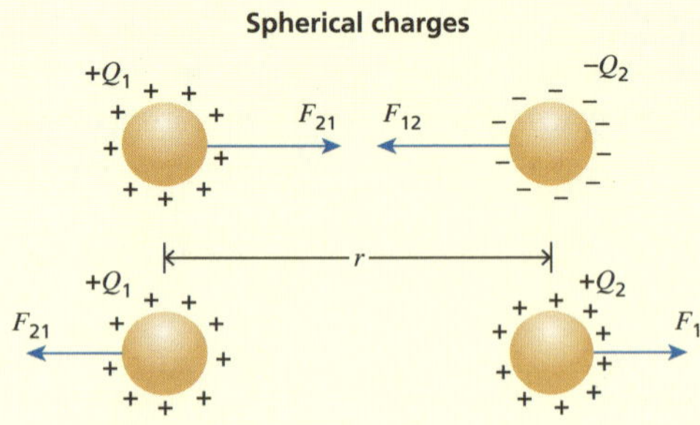

This law applies in a vacuum, but air can be approximated as a vacuum because its permittivity is close to that of free space.

The force between two charges is attractive when the charges have opposite signs (e.g. $Q_1 > 0$ and $Q_2 < 0$) and is repulsive when the charges have the same sign (e.g. $Q_1 > 0$ and $Q_2 > 0$).

For a charged sphere, the charge can be treated as if it is concentrated at the centre of the sphere, provided the charge is distributed uniformly.

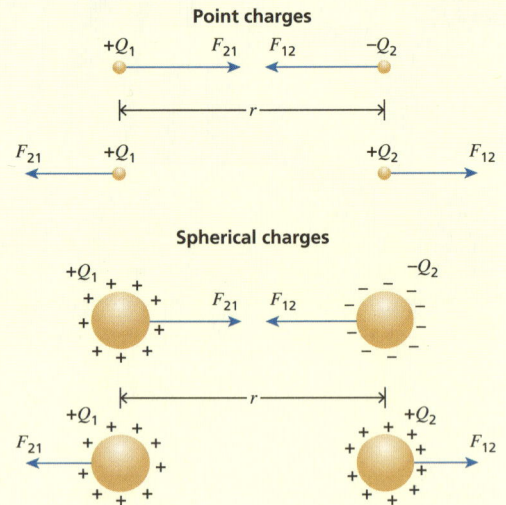

Comparison of gravitational and electrostatic forces

Coulomb's law and Newton's law of gravitation both describe forces that follow the inverse square law. However, they differ in magnitude and can differ in direction. Gravitational forces are always attractive, but electrostatic forces can also be repulsive.

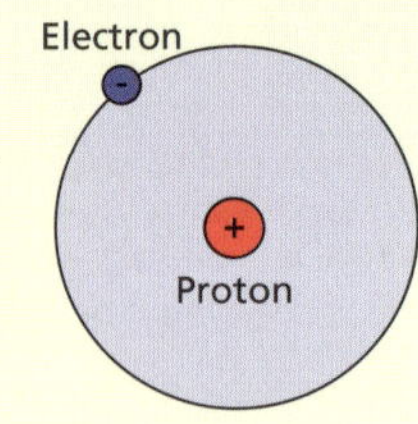

Let's look at the example of the gravitational force and electrostatic forces between an electron orbiting a proton at a distance of 5.3×10^{-11} m.

Using Newton's law of gravitation, the gravitational force is equal to:

$$F_g = \frac{G m_p m_e}{r^2} = \frac{(6.67 \times 10^{-11}) \times (1.673 \times 10^{-27}) \times (9.11 \times 10^{-31})}{(5.3 \times 10^{-11})^2} = 3.6 \times 10^{-47}\,\text{N}$$

Using Coulomb's law, the magnitude of the electrostatic force is equal to:

$$F_e = \frac{1}{4\pi\varepsilon_0}\frac{e^2}{r^2} = \frac{1}{4\pi \times (8.85 \times 10^{-12})} \times \frac{(1.6 \times 10^{-19})^2}{(5.3 \times 10^{-11})^2} = 8.2 \times 10^{-8}\,\text{N}$$

This means that, in this example, the electrostatic force is approximately 2.3×10^{39} times stronger than the gravitational force.

Summary

Coulomb's law

1. Two protons in a nucleus are separated by a distance of 1.5 fm.

   a) Calculate the gravitational force between the protons. [2]

   b) Calculate the electrostatic force between the protons. [2]

   c) Calculate the ratio of the electrostatic to gravitational force. [1]

   d) State the name of the force that keeps protons bound in the nucleus. [1]

2. Three charges each have a charge of +5.0 μC.

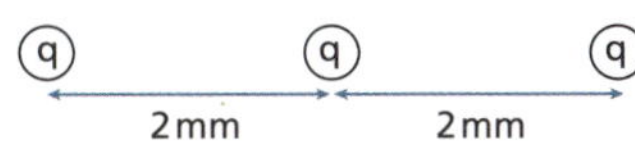

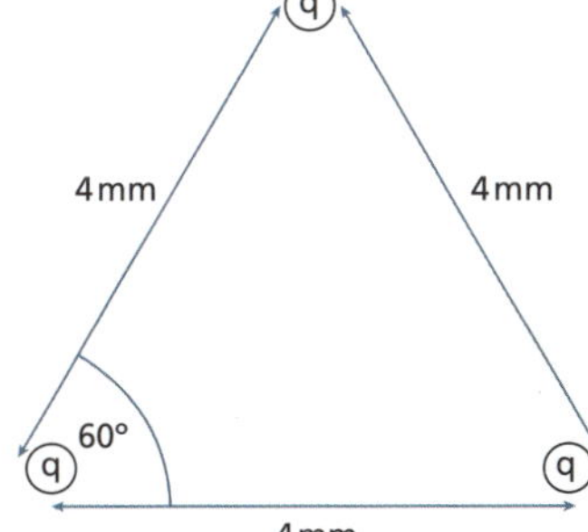

   a) The charges are initially arranged in a straight line, with the separation between adjacent charges being 2 mm.

   State the resultant force acting on the central charge and explain your reasoning. [2]

   b) The central charge is moved to form an equilateral triangle with the other two charges, where the side lengths of the triangle are 4 mm.

   Calculate the resultant force acting on the central charge. [3]

3. Two identical metal spheres of mass 50 g are suspended from a common point by massless insulating threads. The metal spheres each have a positive charge of q. The threads make an angle of θ = 10° to the vertical due to the electrostatic repulsion between the charges.

   Calculate the charge on each sphere if the separation between their centres is 35 cm. [5]

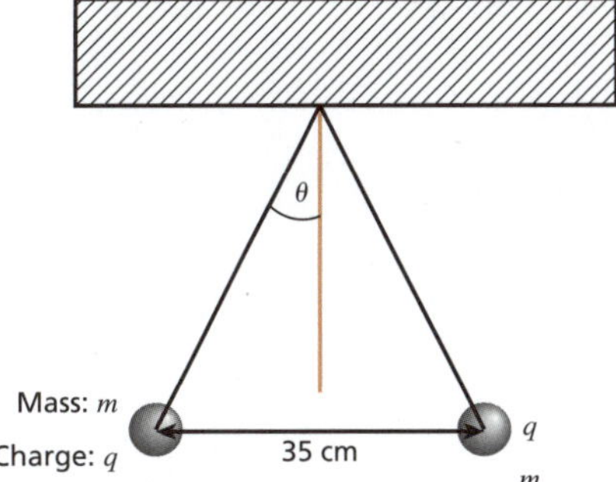

ORGANISE

Electric field strength

A-level only

Key words

Key questions

What is the definition of electric field strength?

How can you derive an expression for the electric field strength between two parallel plates?

What are two possible units for electric field strength?

What is an expression for the force acting on a charged particle between two parallel plates?

Electric fields are regions where charged particles experience a force

Electric fields are visualised using electric field lines, which indicate the direction and strength of the field. Point charges create radial fields, where field lines radiate outward from positive charges and inward towards negative charges.

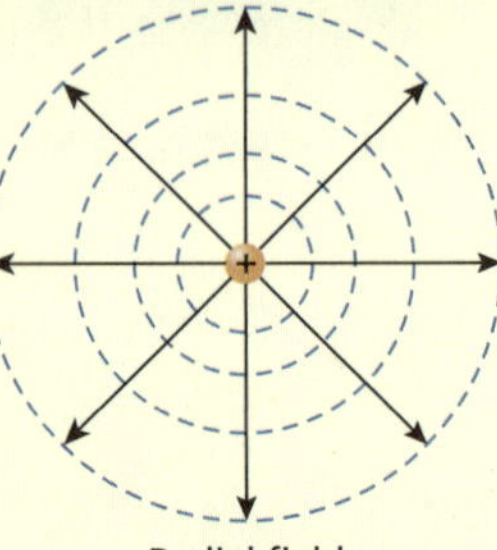

Radial field

Electric field strength, E, is a vector quantity and is defined as the force experienced per unit positive charge in an electric field:

$$E = \frac{F}{Q}$$

where the units of electric field strength are therefore $\mathrm{N\,C^{-1}}$.

Uniform electric fields

A uniform electric field is created between two parallel plates that have a potential difference (V) across them. The field lines between the plates are straight, parallel and equally spaced. This indicates that the electric field strength is constant between the plates. Near the edges of the plates, the field becomes slightly non-uniform.

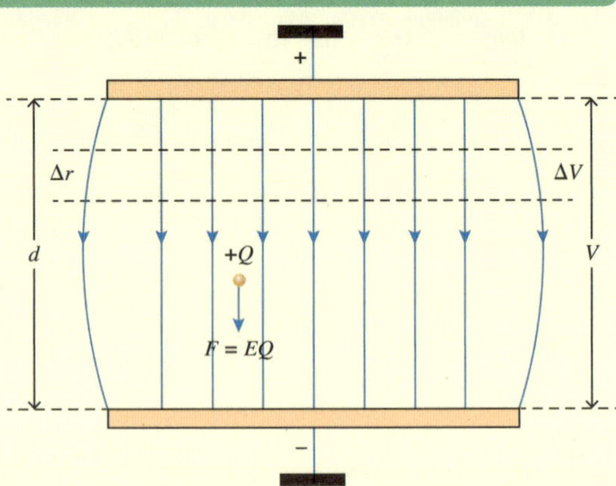

The electric field strength between two parallel plates is given by:

$$E = \frac{V}{d}$$

where V is the potential difference between the plates (in V) and d is the separation of the plates (in m). From this, you can see that an alternative unit for electric field strength is $\mathrm{V\,m^{-1}}$.

To derive this, the work done (W) moving a charge Q across a potential difference ΔV is given by:

$$W = Fd = Q\Delta V$$

As $E = \frac{F}{Q}$, this expression can be written as:

$$E = \frac{F}{Q} = \frac{\Delta V}{d}$$

Particles in uniform electric fields

When a charged particle enters a uniform electric field at right angles to the field lines, it experiences a constant force perpendicular to its initial velocity.

This force is equal to:

$$F = EQ = \frac{V}{d}Q$$

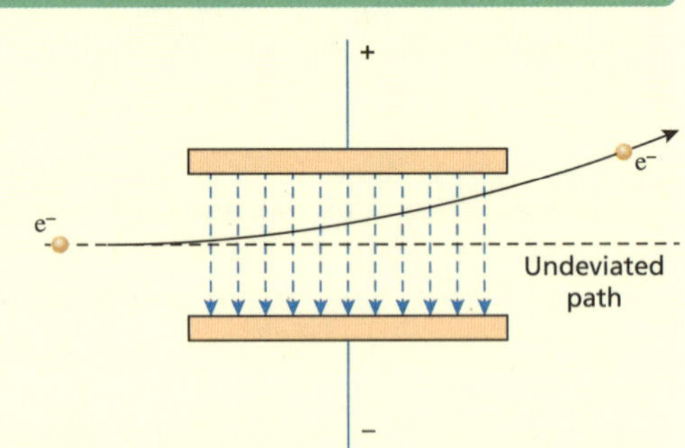

As shown, the particle follows a parabolic trajectory, similar to projectile motion. This is because it experiences a uniform acceleration in the field's direction while maintaining a constant velocity perpendicular to it.

Radial electric fields

A radial electric field is created by a point charge Q.
The electric field strength at a distance r from the charge is given by:

$$E = \frac{1}{4\pi\varepsilon_0}\frac{Q}{r^2}$$

This equation is derived from combining Coulomb's law and $E = \frac{F}{Q}$

Summary

RETRIEVE

Electric field strength

A-level only

1 Two point charges, +2.0 μC and –1.0 μC, are placed 0.50 m apart.

What is the net electric field strength at a point midway between the charges? Tick **one** box. [1]

- 1.4×10^5 N C^{-1} directed towards the –1.0 μC charge ☐
- 1.4×10^5 N C^{-1} directed towards the +2.0 μC charge ☐
- 4.3×10^5 N C^{-1} directed towards the –1.0 μC charge ☐
- 4.3×10^5 N C^{-1} directed towards the +2.0 μC charge ☐

2 A point charge creates a radial electric field in a vacuum. The electric field strength is 450 N C^{-1} at a distance of 0.30 m from the charge.

a) Define electric field strength. [2]

....

....

....

b) Calculate the magnitude of the charge creating this field. [2]

....

c) A second charge of +2.0 nC is placed 0.30 m from the original charge.

Calculate the magnitude of the force experienced by the second charge due to the electric field of the first charge. [2]

....

d) Calculate the distance from the +2.0 nC charge where the net electric field strength is zero. [4]

....

3 Two parallel plates are separated by 50 mm, with a potential difference of 1200 V applied across them. An electron enters the region between the plates horizontally with a velocity of 1.0×10^6 m s^{-1}.

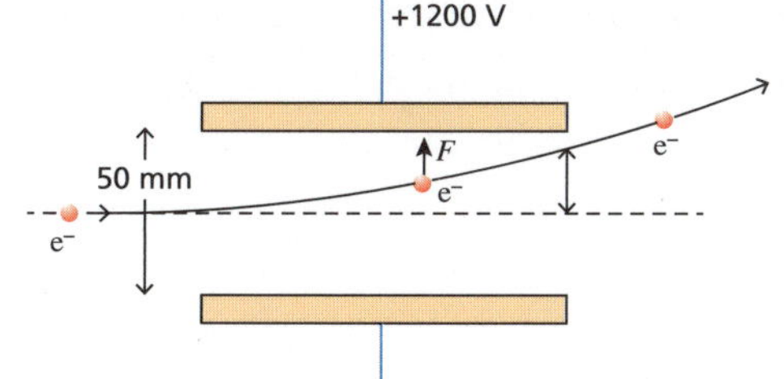

a) On the diagram, draw the electric field lines between the plates. [2]

b) Calculate the force on the electron while it is between the parallel plates. [3]

....

c) Determine the minimum length of the plates required for the electron to collide with one of them. [4]

....

ORGANISE

Electric potential

A-level only

Key words

Key questions

What is the definition of electric potential?

What is an equipotential surface?

What does the gradient of a V–r graph represent?

What does the area under an E–r graph represent?

Electric potential and equipotential surfaces

Electric potential, V, at a point in an electric field is defined as the work done per unit positive charge to bring a small positive test charge from infinity to that point. At infinity, the electric potential is defined to be zero.

Electric potential is a scalar quantity. Unlike vector quantities such as electric field strength, potentials from multiple charges are simply summed together.

The potential difference (p.d.) between two points is defined as the work done per unit charge to move a positive charge between those points.

The work done in moving a charge Q through a p.d. ΔV is therefore: $\Delta W = Q\Delta V$ where the units of p.d. (and potential) are volts (V).

Equipotential surfaces are regions where the electric potential is the same at every point. Due to this, no work is done in moving a charge along an equipotential surface.

Equipotential surfaces are perpendicular to electric field lines. In a radial field (around a point charge), the equipotential surfaces are concentric spheres.

In a uniform field (between parallel plates), the equipotential surfaces are equally spaced parallel planes.

This is due to the fact that electric field strength is equal to the potential gradient:

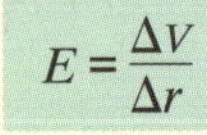

$$E = \frac{\Delta V}{\Delta r}$$

Electric field lines and equipotentials

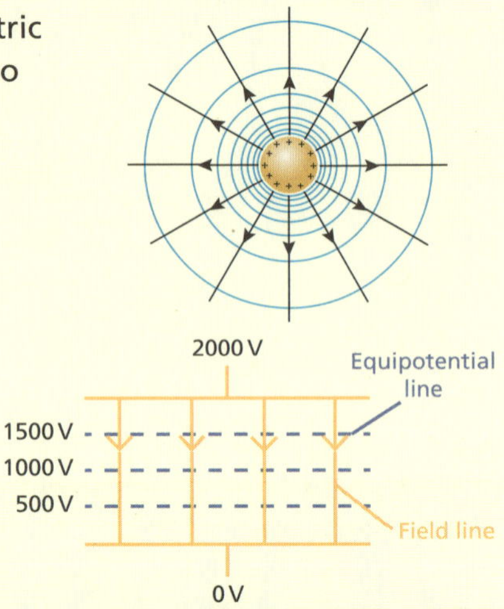

Electric potential of a radial field

The electric potential due to a point charge Q at a distance r from the graph is given by:

$$V = \frac{1}{4\pi\varepsilon_0}\frac{Q}{r}$$

A sketch of electric potential against distance is shown (for both a positive charge and a negative charge). The gradient of a V–r graph gives the electric field strength at that point. To determine this, a tangent to the curve would need to be drawn and the gradient of that tangent found.

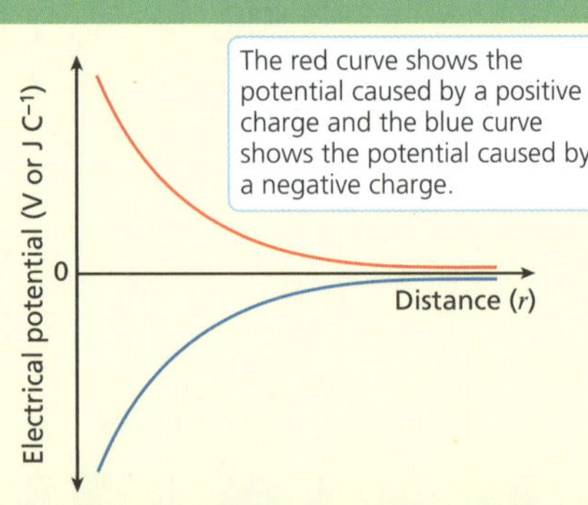

The red curve shows the potential caused by a positive charge and the blue curve shows the potential caused by a negative charge.

Finding electric potential from E–r graphs

The p.d. ΔV between two points can be determined from the area under a graph of electric field strength against distance. The total area under the graph gives the work done per unit charge to move between the points.

A sketch of electric field strength against distance is shown (for both a positive charge and a negative charge). You can approximate the area under a curve by dividing it into trapeziums.

The red curve shows the electric field strength caused by a positive charge and the blue curve shows the electric field strength caused by a negative charge.

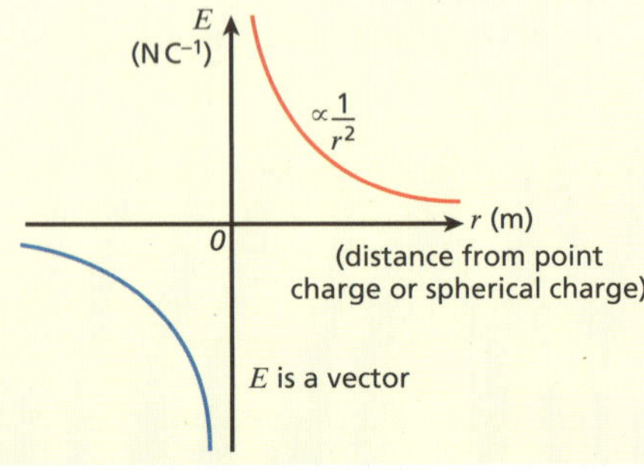

Summary

RETRIEVE

Electric potential

A-level only

1. Which of the following statements is true about electric potential? Tick **one** box. [1]

   It is a vector quantity. ☐ It is always positive. ☐

   It is zero at infinity. ☐ It is independent of charge. ☐

2. Which of the following statements is true for equipotential surfaces? Tick **one** box. [1]

   They are parallel to electric field lines. ☐ They are perpendicular to electric field lines. ☐

   Work is done moving a charge along them. ☐ They only exist in uniform fields. ☐

3. A point charge of +3.0 μC creates a potential of 4500 V at a distance *r* away from the charge.

   a) Define 'electric potential'. [2]

   b) Calculate the distance *r* from the point charge. [2]

4. Two point charges of +2.0 μC and −1.0 μC are placed 30 cm apart.

   a) Calculate the electric potential at a point midway between the two charges. [3]

   b) Calculate the work done to move a +1.0 nC charge from infinity to this point. [2]

5. An alpha particle is initially at rest and is then accelerated between two parallel plates with a potential difference of 1.5 kV across them. After being accelerated, the alpha particle is directed towards a stationary gold nucleus.

   a) Calculate the velocity of the alpha particle after it has been accelerated through the potential difference. [3]

   b) Calculate the distance of closest approach between the alpha particle and the gold nucleus before the alpha particle comes to rest due to electrostatic repulsion. Assume that the gold nucleus remains stationary. The atomic number of gold is 79. [3]

ORGANISE

A-level only

Comparing gravitational and electric fields

Key words

Key questions

What is a force field?

What are two similarities between gravitational and electric fields?

What is a difference between gravitational and electric fields?

Force fields are regions where bodies experience a non-contact force

Force fields are represented as vectors:

- In a gravitational field, the field lines point towards the mass creating it.
- In an electric field, the field lines point away from positive charges and towards negative charges.

	Gravitational fields	Electric fields
Cause of field	Mass	Charge
Force between two masses/charges	Newton's law of gravitation: The attractive gravitational force between two masses is proportional to the product of the masses and inversely proportional to the square of the separation between them: $F = \frac{Gm_1 m_2}{r^2}$	Coulomb's law: The force between two charges is proportional to the product of the charges and inversely proportional to the square of the separation between them: $F = \frac{1}{4\pi\varepsilon_0}\frac{Q_1 Q_2}{r^2}$
	Similarity: Both forces follow the inverse square law.	
Constant of proportionality	$G = 6.67 \times 10^{-11}\,\mathrm{Nm^2\,kg^{-2}}$	$\frac{1}{4\pi\varepsilon_0} = \frac{1}{4\pi\left(8.85 \times 10^{-12}\right)} = 8.99 \times 10^9\,\mathrm{Nm^2\,C^{-2}}$
	Difference: Gravitational forces are much weaker than electrostatic forces.	
Direction of force	Always attractive between masses.	Attractive between charges of opposite signs. Repulsive between charges of the same sign.
	Difference: Gravitational forces are always attractive, while electrostatic forces can be attractive or repulsive.	
Field strength	The force per unit mass: $g = \frac{F}{m}$	The force per unit positive charge: $E = \frac{F}{Q}$
	Similarity: Both fields can be represented by field strengths and field lines.	
Definition of potential	The work done per unit mass in bringing an object from infinity to that point in the field.	The work done per unit charge in bringing a test positive charge from infinity to that point in the field.
Potential of a radial field	Potential is defined to be zero at infinity. $V = -\frac{GM}{r}$	Potential is defined to be zero at infinity. $V = \frac{1}{4\pi\varepsilon_0}\frac{Q}{r}$
	Similarity: Both gravitational and electrostatic fields have potentials. The potential of both fields is defined to be zero at infinity.	
Work done moving between potentials	$\Delta W = m\Delta V$	$\Delta W = Q\Delta V$
	Similarity: Both fields have equipotential surfaces. No work is done in moving a mass/charge along an equipotential surface.	
Field strength from potential gradient	$g = -\frac{\Delta V}{\Delta r}$	$E = \frac{\Delta V}{\Delta r}$

Summary

RETRIEVE

Comparing gravitational and electric fields

A-level only

1. Two identical spheres, each of mass M and charge Q, are placed at a distance r away from each other in a vacuum. The spheres are stationary, with their electrostatic repulsion balancing the gravitational attraction between them.

   a) Describe any similarities and differences between gravitational and electrostatic forces in radial fields. [2]

   b) Show that the ratio $\frac{M}{Q}$ is equal to $\sqrt{\frac{1}{4\pi\varepsilon_0 G}}$ [3]

   c) The charge on each sphere is 6.4×10^{-11} C.

   Calculate the mass of each sphere. [2]

2. The electric field strength near Earth's surface varies depending on the weather conditions. Under fair-weather conditions, it is approximately equal to 100 V m^{-1} directed downwards.

   A small particle, with mass 1.0 g and charge −20.0 μC, is released from rest near Earth's surface.

   a) State the direction of the electrostatic force on the particle. [1]

   b) State the definition of electric field strength. [2]

   c) Calculate the net force acting on the particle, including both the magnitude and direction. [3]

   d) The particle falls a distance of 50 m in the fields.

   Calculate the total work done on the particle, assuming that the gravitational and electric fields are uniform. [5]

ORGANISE

Capacitance

A-level only

Key words

Key questions

How does a capacitor store electrostatic potential energy?

What is the definition of capacitance?

How does a dielectric increase the capacitance of a parallel plate capacitor?

Capacitance

A capacitor is an electronic component that stores electric charge and electrostatic potential energy. It consists of two conductive plates separated by a **dielectric**.

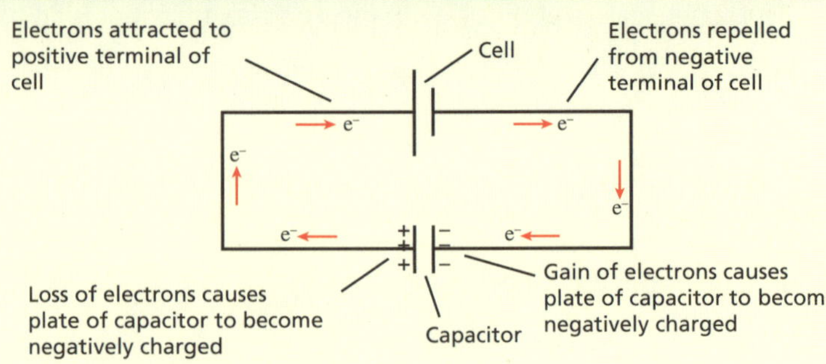

Electrons attracted to positive terminal of cell
Cell
Electrons repelled from negative terminal of cell
e⁻
Loss of electrons causes plate of capacitor to become negatively charged
Capacitor
Gain of electrons causes plate of capacitor to become negatively charged

The capacitance of a capacitor is defined as the charge stored per unit potential difference:

$$C = \frac{Q}{V}$$

where C is the capacitance measured in farads (F), Q is the charge stored in coulombs (C) and V is the potential difference (p.d.) across the plates in volts (V).

Parallel plate capacitors

If a capacitor is made from two parallel plates, its capacitance is given by:

$$C = \frac{A\varepsilon_r\varepsilon_0}{d}$$

where A is the area of overlap of the plates in m^2, d is the separation between the plates in metres (m), ε_0 is the permittivity of free space (with a value of 8.85×10^{-12} F m^{-1}) and ε_r is the relative permittivity of the dielectric.

Relative permittivity is the ratio of a material's permittivity to the permittivity of free space (ε_0) and is unitless.

Dielectrics

A dielectric is an insulating material placed between the plates of a capacitor. Its presence increases the capacitance, meaning that the capacitor can store more charge per unit p.d.

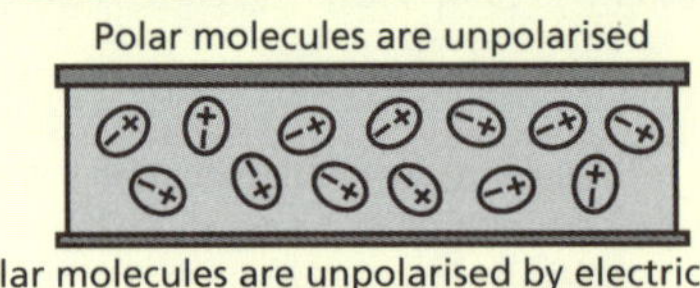

Polar molecules are unpolarised
Polar molecules are unpolarised by electric field

Dielectrics consist of polar molecules that have a positively charged end and a negatively charged end. In the absence of an electric field, these molecules are randomly aligned. When an electric field is applied, the molecules rotate so that their negative ends are attracted to the positive plate and their positive ends to the negative plate. This creates an electric field in the opposite direction to that produced by the parallel plates.

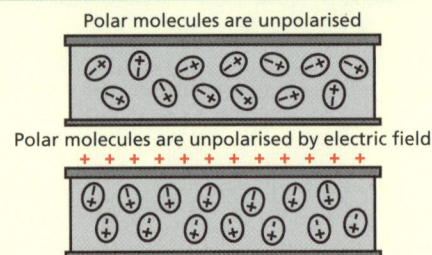

The alignment of the polar molecules allows more charge to be stored on the plates for the same applied p.d. This is because the positive ends of the molecules attract additional electrons to the negatively charged plate (and the negative ends repel more electrons from the positively charged plate).

Cylindrical capacitors

To fit into small electronic devices, parallel plate capacitors are often rolled into cylindrical shapes. This compact design maintains the same capacitance while significantly reducing their physical size, making them ideal for use in smartphones, laptops and other compact electronics.

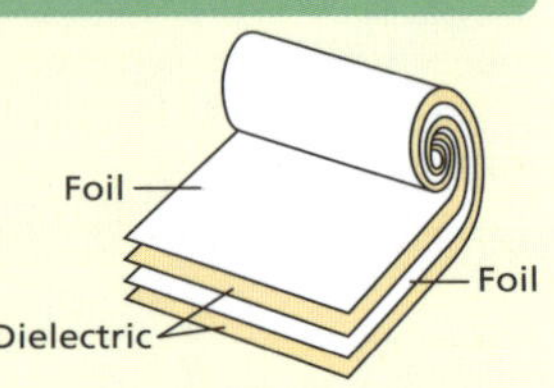

Foil
Foil
Dielectric

Summary

RETRIEVE

Capacitance

A-level only

(1) A capacitor has a capacitance C when the plates are separated by a vacuum.

The plate separation is halved and a dielectric with relative permittivity $\varepsilon_r = 4$ is inserted.

What is the new capacitance? Tick **one** box. [1]

- $0.5C$ ☐
- $2C$ ☐
- $4C$ ☐
- $8C$ ☐

(2) A square parallel plate capacitor has a side length of 5.0 cm and a capacitance of 10.0 pF. The plates are initially separated by air.

a) State what is meant by a capacitance of 10.0 pF. [2]

b) Calculate the separation between the plates. [3]

c) A potential difference of 2.5 kV is applied across the capacitor.

Calculate the amount of charge stored by the capacitor. [1]

d) A dielectric is inserted between the plates, increasing the capacitance to 25.0 pF.

Describe how a dielectric increases the capacitance. [4]

e) Calculate the relative permittivity (ε_r) of the dielectric. [1]

f) State **two** other ways of increasing the capacitance of the capacitor. [2]

ORGANISE

Charging a capacitor

A-level only

Key words

Key questions

How can you rearrange the formula $V = V_0\left(1 - e^{-\frac{t}{RC}}\right)$ to give an expression for the capacitance?

What is meant by the 'time constant'?

What does the area under a V–Q graph for a capacitor represent?

Charging a capacitor

When a capacitor is connected to a power supply or a battery through a resistor, it begins to charge. Initially the potential difference (p.d.) across the capacitor is zero so the entire supply p.d. (V_0) is across the resistor, driving a large initial current.

As electrons accumulate on one plate of the capacitor and leave the other, a p.d. builds up across the plates. This reduces the current through the circuit. Eventually, the capacitor becomes fully charged when its p.d. is equal to the supply p.d. ($V = V_0$). At this point, no current flows.

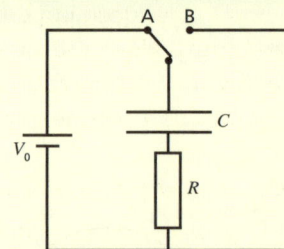

Capacitor charging graphs and equations

When a capacitor charges, the p.d. across the capacitor (V), the charge stored by the capacitor (Q) and the current in the charging circuit (I) change over time (t):

- The p.d. across the capacitor is given by the expression: $V = V_0\left(1 - e^{-\frac{t}{RC}}\right)$
- As $Q = CV$, the charge stored by the capacitor is given by: $Q = Q_0\left(1 - e^{-\frac{t}{RC}}\right)$
- Finally, the current flowing through the charging circuit is represented by: $I = I_0 e^{-\frac{t}{RC}}$

In these equations, R is the resistance in the charging circuit and C is the capacitance of the capacitor.

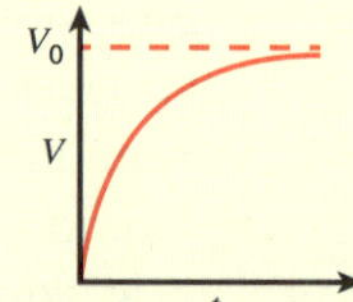

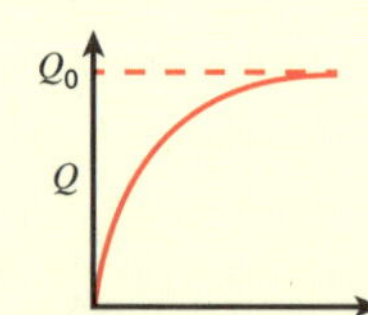

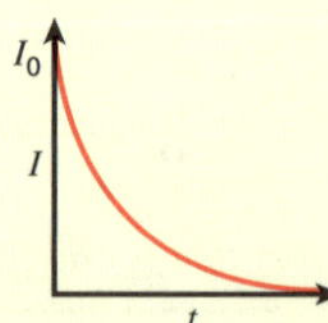

Time constant

The time constant (τ) determines the rate at which the capacitor charges or discharges and is given by the equation: $\tau = RC$

After a time equal to τ, the p.d. and charge reach approximately 63% of their maximum values during charging. The current in the circuit decreases to approximately 37% of its initial value after τ.

Energy stored by a capacitor

The energy stored by a capacitor can be calculated from the area under a graph of p.d. across the capacitor vs. charge stored by the capacitor:

area under V–Q graph $= \frac{1}{2} Q \times V$

Using $Q = CV$, the energy stored by a capacitor can be expressed in two other ways:

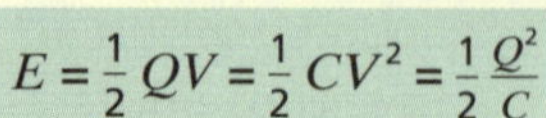

While charging a capacitor, the total energy transferred by the power source is equal to $E = QV$. Therefore, only half of the energy supplied is stored in the capacitor. The other half is lost in heating any resistance in the circuit.

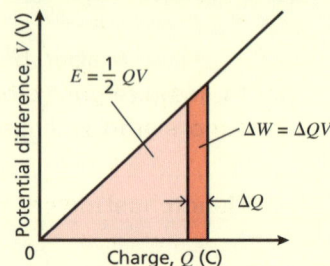

Summary

RETRIEVE

Charging a capacitor

A-level only

1 A capacitor of capacitance 5.0 μF is charged by a 12.0 V battery through a 10 kΩ resistor.

a) Calculate the time constant for this circuit. [2]

b) Calculate the potential difference across the capacitor after a time of 0.020 s. [2]

c) Calculate the energy stored in the capacitor after it is fully charged by the circuit. [2]

d) State and explain why your answer to part c) is only half of the total energy transferred by the battery. [2]

2 A 20.0 μF capacitor is charged through a resistor. The current in the circuit decreases to 20% of its initial value after a time of 1.5 s.

Calculate the resistance of the resistor. [3]

3 A capacitor is charged by a battery through a 2.0 kΩ resistor. It is observed that it takes a time of 4.0 s for the potential difference across the capacitor to increase to 3.0 V and that the initial current in the circuit is 5.0 mA.

Calculate the capacitance of the capacitor. [4]

ORGANISE

Discharging a capacitor

A-level only

Key words

Key questions

How can you rearrange the formula $Q = Q_0 e^{-\frac{t}{RC}}$ to give an expression for the resistance?

What does the gradient of a Q–t graph represent?

What does the area under an I–t graph represent?

How can you show that $T_{\frac{1}{2}} = 0.69RC$?

Discharging a capacitor

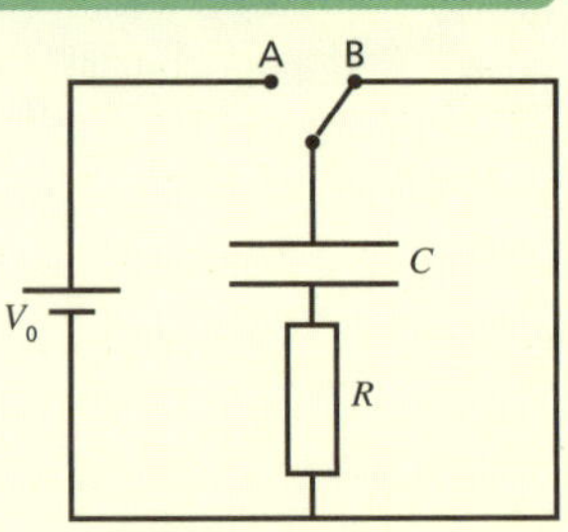

The circuit shown contains a capacitor, a resistor and a two-position switch connected to a cell. When the switch is in position A, the capacitor charges.

When the switch is moved to position B, the capacitor is disconnected from the power source and is connected to the resistor. The stored charge begins to flow through the resistor, causing the charge on the capacitor to decrease. As the charge decreases, so does the potential difference across the capacitor and the current flowing through the circuit. The rate of discharge is determined by the resistance (R) and the capacitance (C) of the circuit.

Capacitor discharging graphs and equations

When a capacitor discharges through a resistor, the charge stored by the capacitor (Q), the potential difference across the capacitor (V) and the current in the discharging circuit (I) decrease exponentially over time.

- The potential difference across the capacitor is given by: $V = V_0 e^{-\frac{t}{RC}}$
- As $Q = CV$, the charge stored by the capacitor also decreases exponentially as: $Q = Q_0 e^{-\frac{t}{RC}}$

  The gradient of a Q–t graph represents the magnitude of the current flowing in the discharging current as: $I = \frac{\Delta Q}{\Delta t}$
- The current itself in the discharging circuit is represented by: $I = I_0 e^{-\frac{t}{RC}}$

  The area under an I–t graph gives the total charge transferred from the capacitor while it is discharging.

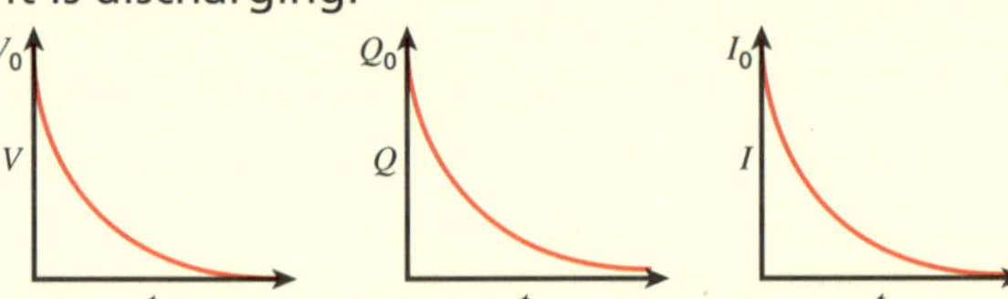

Time constant and time to halve

While discharging, the time constant ($\tau = RC$) is the time it takes for the p.d. across a capacitor, the charge stored by the capacitor or the current in the discharging circuit to fall to $\frac{1}{e} \approx 37\%$ of its initial value.

Another useful quantity is the time to halve ($T_{\frac{1}{2}}$), which is the time it takes for those quantities to reduce to 50% of their initial value.

It can be shown that $T_{\frac{1}{2}} = 0.69RC$ by starting with an expression for the exponential decay of potential difference across the plates of a capacitor: $0.5V_0 = V_0 e^{-\frac{T_{1/2}}{RC}}$

Cancelling V_0 on each side of the equation and taking natural logarithms leads to: $\ln 0.5 = -\frac{T_{1/2}}{RC}$

Rearranging this expression finally gives: $T_{\frac{1}{2}} = -RC \ln 0.5 \approx 0.69RC$

Summary

RETRIEVE

Discharging a capacitor

1. A capacitor with an initial charge of 50 μC discharges through a 1.5 kΩ resistor. After a time of 5.0 ms, the charge stored by the capacitor has reduced to 30 μC.

   What is the capacitance of the capacitor? Tick **one** box. [1]

   0.65 μF ☐ 5.0 μF ☐
   6.5 μF ☐ 15.0 μF ☐

2. A 47 μF capacitor discharges through a 1.2 kΩ resistor.

   What is the time taken for the charge to reduce to 25% of its initial value? Tick **one** box. [1]

   30 ms ☐ 78 ms ☐
   140 ms ☐ 170 ms ☐

3. A defibrillator uses a 100 μF capacitor charged to a potential difference of 5.0 kV. The capacitor charges through a patient's body, modelled as a 50 Ω resistor.

   a) Calculate the time constant of the circuit. [2]

   ....

   b) Calculate the time taken for the potential difference across the capacitor to drop to 1.0 kV. [3]

   ....

   c) Calculate the amount of energy that is delivered to the patient in the first 2.0 ms. [4]

   ....

4. A capacitor in a camera flash circuit has a capacitance of 330 μF. The capacitor has a potential difference of 300 V across it before the flash discharges.

   a) Calculate the energy stored in the capacitor before discharge. [1]

   ....

   b) The flash discharges 90% of its energy in a time of 5.0 ms.

   Calculate the resistance of the circuit. [5]

   ....

Magnetic flux density

ORGANISE

A-level only

Key words

Key questions

What does the direction of the thumb and fingers represent in the right-hand rule?

What does the direction of the thumb and fingers represent in Fleming's left-hand rule?

What is the definition of magnetic flux density?

Magnetic field lines (flux lines)

A magnetic field is a region in which magnetic forces act on moving charges or magnetic materials. Magnetic field lines represent the direction and strength of a magnetic field:

- Field lines always travel from a North pole to a South pole.
- The closer the lines, the stronger the magnetic field.

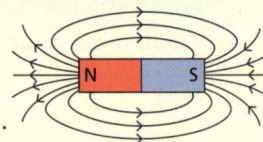

A uniform magnetic field has field lines that are equally spaced and parallel. This can be created by placing two opposite poles of bar magnets together with a small gap.

When a current flows through a wire, it generates a magnetic field around the wire. The direction of this field can be determined using the **right-hand rule**. Your thumb goes in the direction of the current. The direction that your fingers curl around the wire represents the direction of the magnetic field lines.

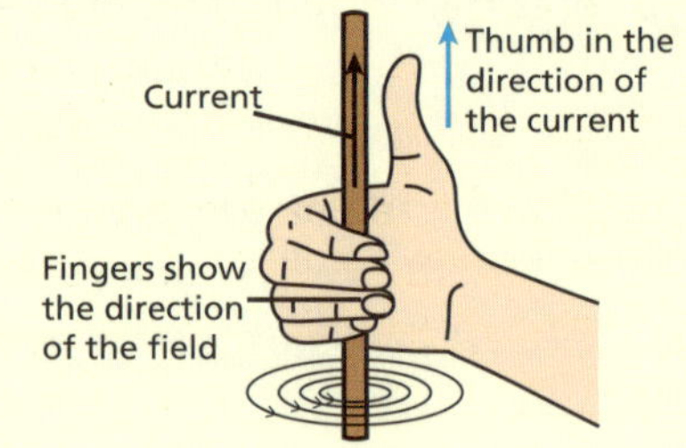

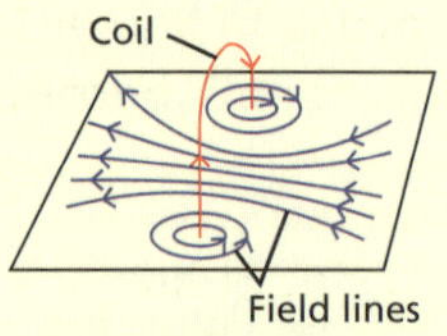

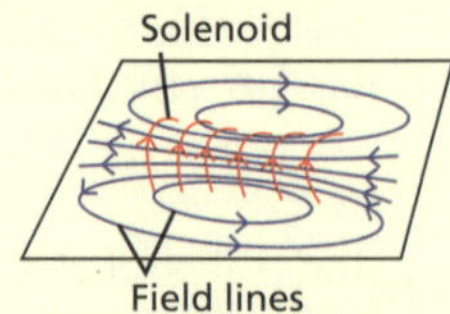

The right-hand rule can also help you to visualise the field lines around a single loop of wire, or a solenoid. A solenoid has a magnetic field pattern similar to that of a bar magnet.

Force on a current-carrying wire

When a wire carrying a current is placed in a magnetic field, it experiences a force (F) due to the interaction between the permanent magnetic field and the electromagnetic field created by the current (I).

The magnitude of the force is given by: $F = BIl \sin \theta$

where B is the magnetic flux density (in tesla, T), l is the length of the wire in the field (in m) and θ is the angle between the current and the magnetic field.

If the field is perpendicular to the wire, then: $F = BIl$

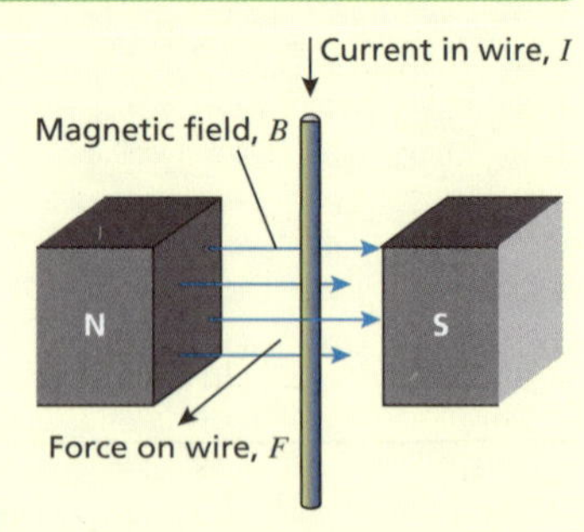

Fleming's left-hand rule

The direction of the force on a current-carrying wire in a magnetic field can be found using Fleming's left-hand rule. Hold your left hand with the thumb, first finger and second finger at right angles to each other and they respectively indicate the direction of the force (motion), the direction of the magnetic field and the direction of the current.

For charged particles, the current is in the same direction as the motion of a positive charge. For electrons, the current is in the opposite direction to their motion.

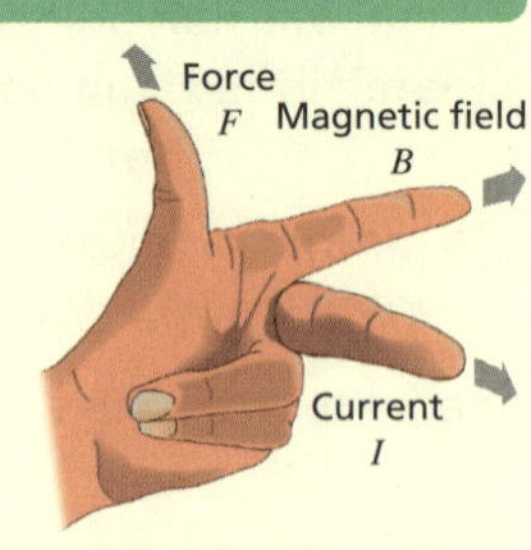

Magnetic flux density

The magnetic flux density (B) is defined as the force per unit current per unit length of wire when the field is perpendicular to the current:

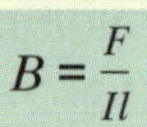

$$B = \frac{F}{Il}$$

Summary

RETRIEVE

Magnetic flux density

A-level only

1. An electron is travelling from left to right in a uniform magnetic field directed into the page.

× × ×
× e × ×
× × ×
× × ×

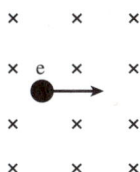

What is the direction of the force acting on the electron? Tick **one** box. [1]

Up ☐ Down ☐ Left ☐ Right ☐

2. A wire of length 0.40 m is perpendicular to a uniform magnetic field and carries a current of 5.0 A. The wire floats in equilibrium and has a mass of 120 g.

What is the magnetic flux density of the field? Tick **one** box. [1]

0.32 T ☐
0.59 T ☐
1.1 T ☐
1.4 T ☐

3. A straight wire of length l initially carries a current I and is placed in a magnetic field with a magnetic flux density B. The wire is initially perpendicular to the magnetic field and the force on the wire is F.

The current is increased to $2I$, the magnetic flux density is increased to $2B$ and the wire is rotated to make an angle of 30° to the field.

What is the new force on the wire in terms of F? Tick **one** box. [1]

$\frac{F}{2}$ ☐
F ☐
$2F$ ☐
$4F$ ☐

4. A wire of length 0.50 m carrying a current of 3.5 A is placed in a magnetic field with a magnetic flux density of 0.25 T. The angle between the wire and the magnetic field is 60°.

a) Explain what is meant by a magnetic flux density of 0.25 T. [2]

b) Calculate the magnetic force on the wire. [2]

c) The wire is slowly rotated until it is parallel to the field lines.

State and explain what happens to the magnitude of the force on the wire. [2]

d) Other than changing the angle of the wire, suggest another way of reducing the force on the wire. [1]

ORGANISE

Moving charges in a magnetic field

A-level only

Key words

Key questions

How can you derive an expression for the radius of the circular motion of a charged particle moving in a magnetic field?

Why does a velocity selector only let particles of a certain velocity pass through it?

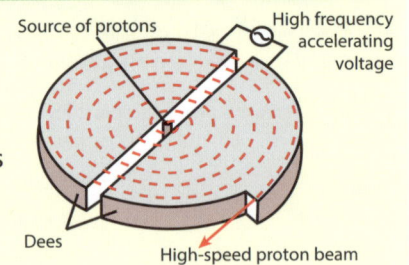

How can you derive an expression for the cyclotron frequency?

Motion of a charged particle in a magnetic field

When a charged particle moves with velocity v perpendicular to a magnetic field of flux density B, it experiences a force equal to: $F = BQv$

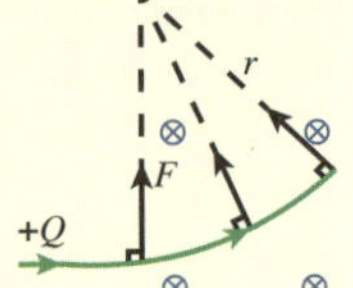

A charged particle moving perpendicular to a magnetic field follows a circular path as the magnetic force acts as a centripetal force: $F = BQv = \frac{mv^2}{r}$

where m is the particle's mass and r is the radius of the circular path.

Rearranging this expression for r leads to: $r = \frac{mv}{BQ}$

The direction of force can be determined using Fleming's left-hand rule. Remember that the direction of current is the same as the direction of motion of a positive charge. For electrons, the current is in the opposite direction to its motion.

The velocity selector

A velocity selector uses electric and magnetic fields to filter particles based on their velocity. The diagram shows a positively charged particle that is experiencing an upwards magnetic force and a downwards electrostatic force.

The magnetic force is equal to $F_B = BQv$, while the electrostatic force is equal to $F_E = \frac{V}{d}Q$. The magnetic force is velocity dependent, while the electrostatic force is not. Only particles for which $F_B = F_E$ exit the velocity selector.

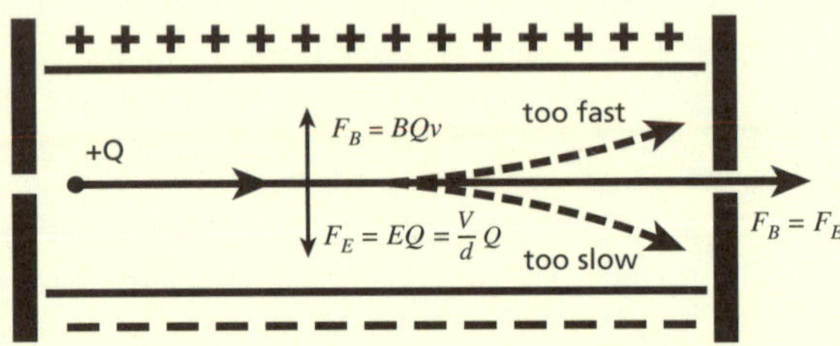

Particles that are travelling too quickly are deflected upwards (and particles that are travelling slowly are deflected downwards).

The cyclotron

A cyclotron is a device used to accelerate charged particles. Two hollow semi-circular electrodes called **dees** are placed in a uniform magnetic field. The magnetic field forces the particles into circular paths within the dees. A gap between the dees has an alternating electric field, which accelerates the particles.

Source of protons
High frequency accelerating voltage
Dees
High-speed proton beam

The frequency of the alternating electric field can be derived from the time it takes for a particle to complete a circular path within a dee: $T = \frac{2\pi r}{v}$

Substituting $r = \frac{mv}{BQ}$ into this expression gives: $T = \frac{2\pi m}{BQ}$

In turn, this leads to: $f = \frac{BQ}{2\pi m}$

This frequency is called the **cyclotron frequency** and it is independent of the radius and velocity of the particle.

Summary

RETRIEVE

Moving charges in a magnetic field

A-level only

1. A mass spectrometer is used to measure the specific charge of positive ions. The ions are accelerated through a potential difference of 5.0 kV and then pass through a velocity selector. They then enter a region with a uniform magnetic field, where the radius of their circular orbit is measured.

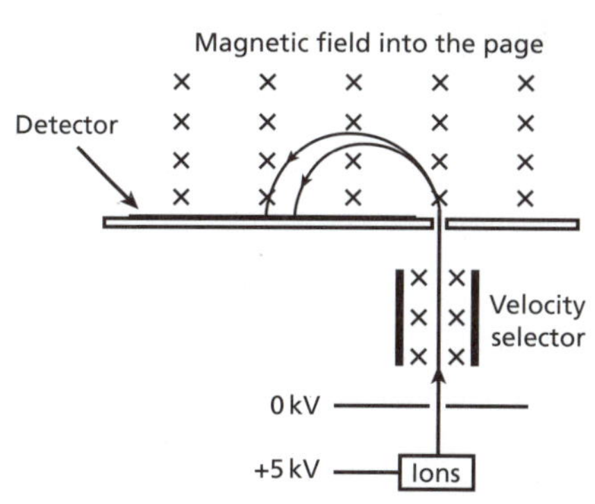

a) The ions are initially at rest and have a charge of $+3.2 \times 10^{-19}$ C and a mass of 3.3×10^{-26} kg.

Calculate the velocity of the ion after it has been accelerated through the potential difference of 5.0 kV. [3]

b) Explain how the velocity selector ensures only ions with a specific velocity pass through undeflected. [3]

c) Derive an expression for the radius of the circular orbit of the ions once they enter the region with a uniform magnetic field. [2]

d) In the region with a uniform magnetic field, the radius of the ion's circular orbit is measured to be 0.20 m.

Calculate the magnetic flux density of the magnetic field. [2]

2. **a)** Describe how a cyclotron accelerates charged particles, mentioning the roles of the magnetic field and the alternating electric field. [3]

b) Show that the frequency of the alternating electric field in a cyclotron is independent of both the radius of the circular path and the velocity of the particle. [4]

Magnetic flux and flux linkage

Key words

Key questions

What are the units of magnetic flux and magnetic flux linkage?

What is the difference between magnetic flux and magnetic flux linkage?

What happens to the magnetic flux through a coil as the coil is rotated in a magnetic field?

Magnetic flux

Magnetic flux (Φ) is the product of the magnetic flux density (B) and the area of the surface (A) it passes through perpendicularly:

$$\Phi = BA$$

If the magnetic field is not perpendicular to the surface, only the perpendicular component contributes to the flux:

$$\Phi = BA\cos\theta$$

where θ is the angle between the magnetic flux density and the normal to the surface.

The unit of magnetic flux is the weber (Wb), where 1 Wb = 1 T m^2

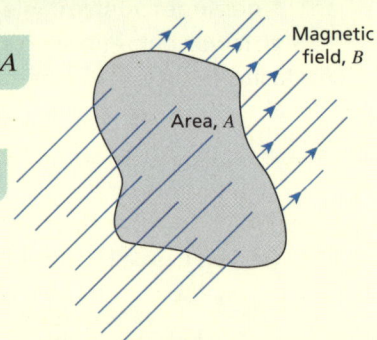

Magnetic field, B

Area, A

Magnetic flux linkage

Magnetic flux linkage is the total magnetic flux passing through a coil multiplied by the number of turns (N):

$$\text{magnetic flux linkage} = N\Phi = BAN$$

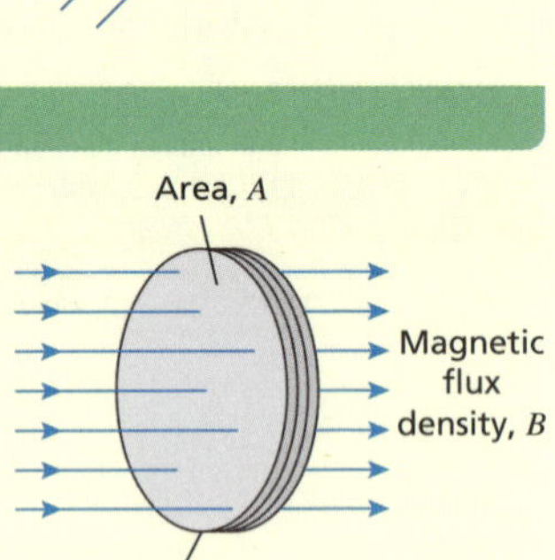

As the number of turns is unitless, the unit of magnetic flux linkage is also the weber (Wb). To distinguish flux linkage from flux, the unit of magnetic flux linkage is sometimes expressed as weber-turns.

In a similar way to magnetic flux, if the magnetic flux density is at an angle θ to the normal of the coil, the flux linkage becomes:

$$N\Phi\cos\theta = BAN\cos\theta$$

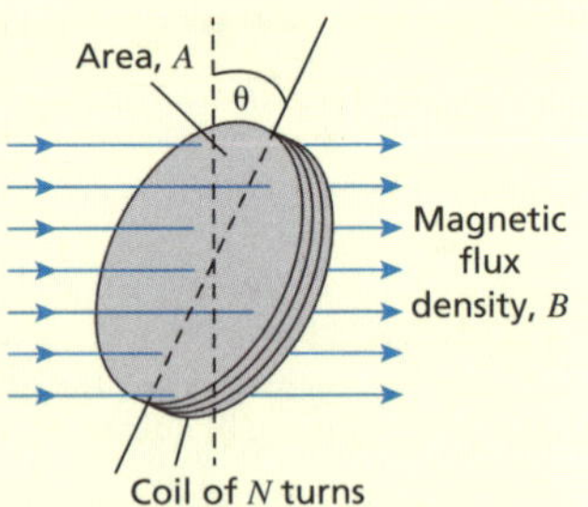

Flux linkage in a rotating coil

When a coil with N turns and area A rotates in a magnetic field, the flux linkage changes as the angle θ between the normal to the coil and the magnetic flux density varies:

- At $\theta = 0°$ (coil perpendicular to the field), flux linkage is a maximum: $N\Phi_{max} = BAN$
- At $\theta = 90°$ (coil parallel to the field), the flux linkage is zero: $N\Phi = 0$

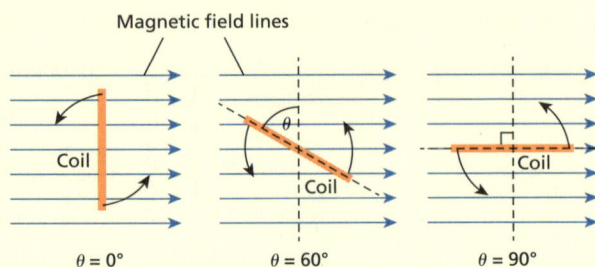

Magnetic field lines

Coil

$\theta = 0°$ $\theta = 60°$ $\theta = 90°$

If the coil is rotated with an angular speed ω, the magnetic flux linkage at a time t can be expressed as:

$$N\Phi\cos\omega t = BAN\cos\omega t$$

where $\omega = \frac{\theta}{t}$ and therefore $\theta = \omega t$.

Note that the above expression relies on the coil having a maximum flux linkage at time $t = 0$ (and therefore must be perpendicular to the magnetic field at time $t = 0$).

Summary

RETRIEVE

Magnetic flux and flux linkage

A-level only

1. A coil with 200 turns and an area of $0.050\,m^2$ is placed in a magnetic flux density of 0.30T.

   If the normal to the coil is at an angle of 30° to the magnetic flux density, what is the flux linkage? Tick **one** box. [1]

   0.6 Wb ☐

   0.9 Wb ☐

   1.5 Wb ☐

   2.6 Wb ☐

2. When is the magnetic flux linkage through a coil zero? Tick **one** box. [1]

   The magnetic flux density is perpendicular to the coil. ☐

   The magnetic flux density is parallel to the coil. ☐

   The magnetic flux density is 45° to the coil. ☐

   The magnetic flux linkage through a coil can never be zero. ☐

3. A square coil with 50 turns and a side length of 20 cm is initially placed at right angles to a magnetic flux density of 0.25T.

   a) Calculate the magnetic flux passing through the coil. [2]

   ....

   b) Calculate the magnetic flux linkage in the coil. [1]

   ....

   c) The coil is slowly rotated through 180°.

   Describe what happens to the magnetic flux linkage as the coil rotates. [4]

   ....

   ....

   ....

   ....

   ....

4. A circular coil with 500 turns and a radius of 0.15 m is placed in a uniform magnetic flux density of 0.40T. The coil is rotated at an angular speed of $2.0\,rad\,s^{-1}$. Initially, the normal to the coil is perpendicular to the magnetic field.

   a) Calculate the maximum flux linkage in the coil. [3]

   ....

   b) Calculate the flux linkage at a time of 1.0 s. [2]

   ....

ORGANISE

Electromagnetic induction

A-level only

Key words

Key questions

What is Faraday's law of induction?

What is Lenz's law?

How does an alternator generate an alternating current?

What are three ways of increasing the emf induced in an alternator?

Laws of induction

Electromagnetic induction is the process of generating an electromotive force (emf) in a conductor when there is a change in magnetic flux linkage. **Faraday's law** states that the induced emf (ε) is proportional to the rate of change of magnetic flux linkage: $\varepsilon = -N\frac{\Delta\Phi}{\Delta t}$

The negative sign indicates the direction of the induced emf, as explained by **Lenz's law**.

Lenz's law states that the direction of the induced emf is such that it opposes the change in magnetic flux that causes it. This law ensures conservation of energy.

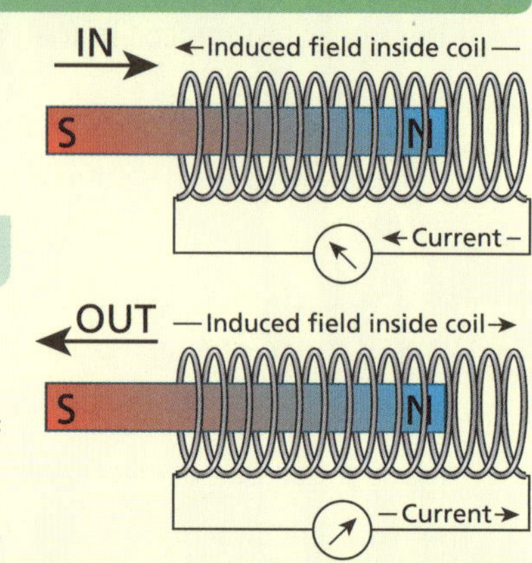

Induced emf in a moving conductor

When a straight conductor of length l moves at velocity v perpendicular to a magnetic field of flux density B, an emf is induced: $\varepsilon = Blv$

Coil rotating in a magnetic field

An alternator consists of a coil of wire inside a uniform magnetic field. When the coil rotates in the field, the flux linkage in the coil changes over time:

$$\text{magnetic flux linkage} = BAN\cos\omega t$$

where B is magnetic flux density, A is the area of the coil, N is the number of turns in the coil and ω is the angular speed of rotation.

When the coil is perpendicular to the magnetic field, the flux linkage is a maximum. When the coil is parallel to the field, the flux linkage is zero.

The induced emf is equal to the rate of change of flux linkage and so is equal to:

$$\varepsilon = -N\frac{\Delta\Phi}{\Delta t} = BAN\omega\sin\omega t$$

The emf also varies sinusoidally with time, with a maximum value of $BAN\omega$.

The emf is the negative gradient of a Φ–t graph. Its maximum value is when the flux linkage is changing most rapidly (when the coil is parallel to the magnetic field).

The emf is zero when the gradient of the Φ–t graph is zero. This occurs when the coil is perpendicular to the magnetic field.

An alternator

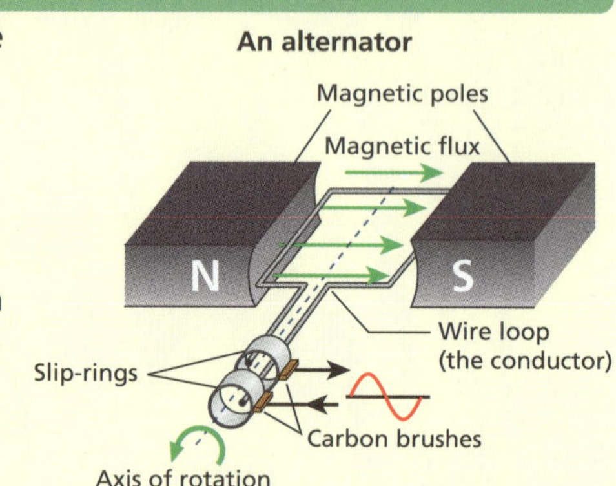

Graphs of magnetic flux and emf against time for a coil rotating in a magnetic field

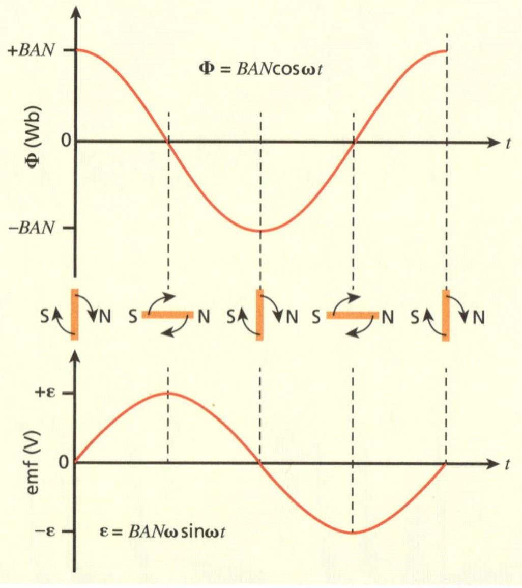

Summary

RETRIEVE

Electromagnetic induction

1 A straight conductor of length 1.5 m moves at 10 m s^{-1} through a magnetic flux density of 0.20 T.

What is the emf induced across its ends? Tick **one** box. [1]

0.03 V ☐ 0.3 V ☐ 3.0 V ☐ 30.0 V ☐

2 A non-magnetic cylinder and a strong magnet of the same size are dropped through a vertical copper pipe.

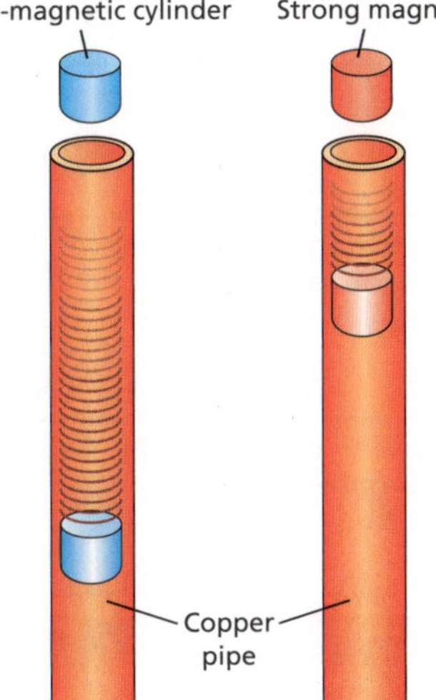

a) Using Faraday's and Lenz's laws, explain why the strong magnet takes longer to fall through the pipe. [5]

b) State and explain how the time it takes for the strong magnet to fall through the pipe would be affected if it was made of a material with a higher resistivity. [3]

c) State and explain how the time it takes for the strong magnet to fall through the pipe would be affected if it had a cut along its length. [3]

3 A square coil of side length 0.10 m and 200 turns is placed in a magnetic field with a magnetic flux density of 0.020 T.

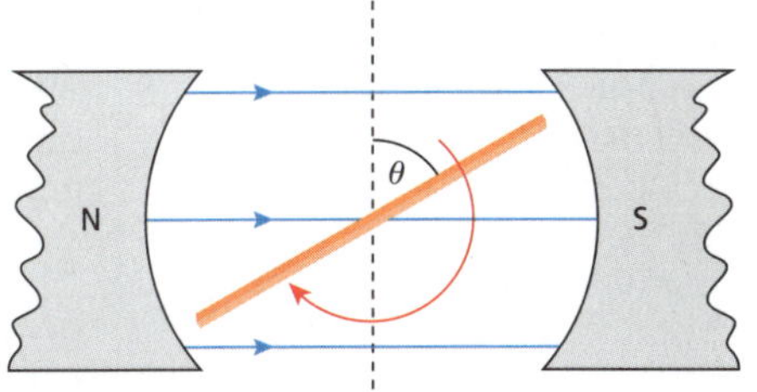

The coil is rotated with a time period of 0.10 s. On the axes provided, sketch the graphs of flux linkage and induced electromotive force against time. The coil's initial position is perpendicular to the direction of the magnetic field. [5]

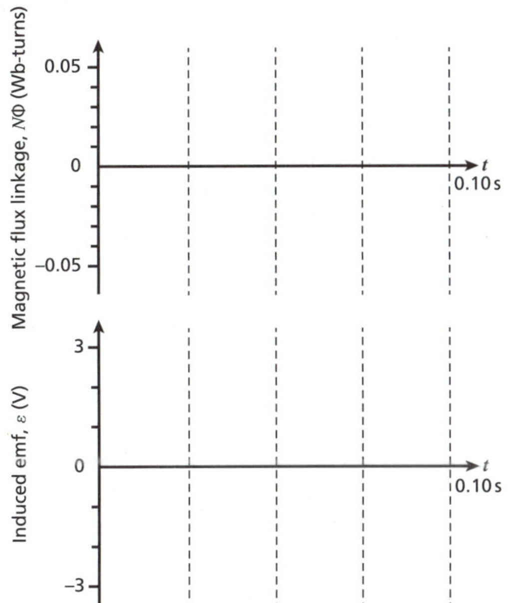

Alternating currents

Key words

Key questions

What are two sources of direct current?

What is meant by a root mean square potential difference?

How can the peak-to-peak potential difference of an a.c. signal be measured using an oscilloscope?

How can the frequency of an a.c. signal be measured using an oscilloscope?

Direct current (d.c.) and alternating current (a.c.)

Direct currents flow in one direction only and are produced by batteries and d.c. generators (such as the dynamo). **Alternating currents** continuously change direction in a sinusoidal manner and are produced by a.c. generators (such as the alternator) and used in household mains electricity.

Definitions

Quantity	Definition	
Peak current (I_0) and peak potential difference (V_0)	The maximum values of current or potential difference in a sinusoidal a.c. waveform.	
Root mean square (rms) current (I_{rms}) and potential difference (V_{rms})	The value of alternating current or potential difference that produces the same power as a d.c. value of that amount.	$I_{rms} = \frac{I_0}{\sqrt{2}}$ $V_{rms} = \frac{V_0}{\sqrt{2}}$
Peak-to-peak current (I_{pp}) and potential difference (V_{pp})	The total difference between the maximum positive and maximum negative values of current or potential difference.	$I_{pp} = 2I_0$ $V_{pp} = 2V_0$

Mains electricity

The rms value of the mains potential difference is 230 V. The peak voltage (V_0) can therefore be calculated:

$$V_0 = \sqrt{2}V_{rms} = \sqrt{2} \times 230 = 325\text{ V}$$

The peak-to-peak potential difference is therefore 650 V. The frequency of mains electricity is 50 Hz.

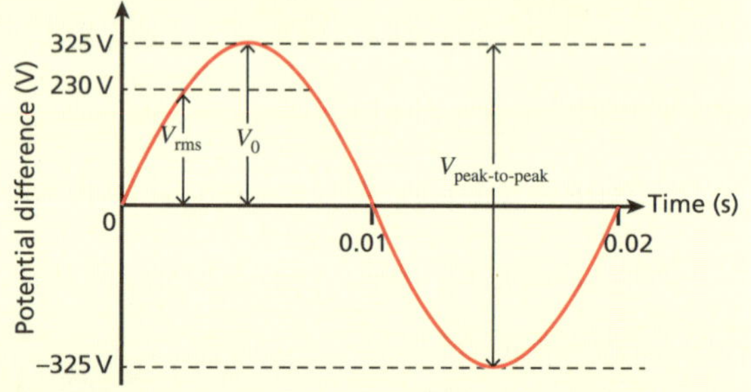

Oscilloscopes

An oscilloscope is used to visualise d.c. and a.c. signals. The time base control adjusts the horizontal scale, determining the time interval displayed per division. The volts per division control sets the vertical scale.

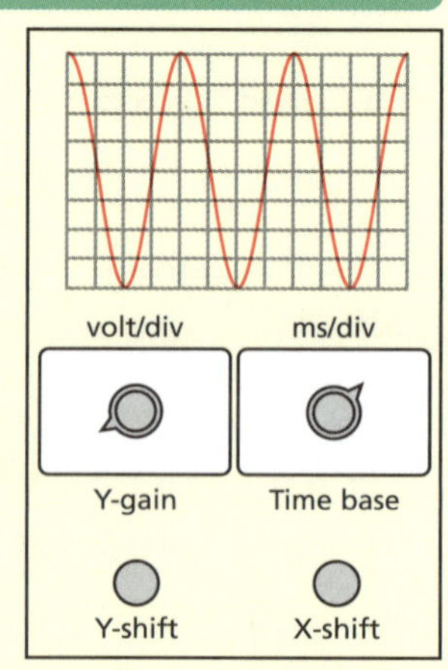

An oscilloscope can be used to measure peak-to-peak potential difference. Adjust the vertical gain so that the signal takes up as much of the oscilloscope screen as possible. Count the vertical divisions between the maximum and minimum points of the wave and multiply by the volts per division setting. To make this easier, the time base can be switched off (so that the signal just moves up and down).

The oscilloscope can also be used to measure the time period and frequency of a signal. Set the time base so that at least one full wave (or more) is clearly displayed on the screen. Measure the time for one complete time period (T) by counting the horizontal divisions and multiplying by the time base setting. Calculate the frequency of the signal using: $f = \frac{1}{T}$

Summary

RETRIEVE

Alternating currents

1 What is the rms current of a sinusoidal a.c. signal with a peak-to-peak value of 10.0 A?

Tick **one** box. [1]

3.5 A ☐ 5.0 A ☐ 7.1 A ☐ 10.0 A ☐

2 On an oscilloscope, the time base is set to 5 ms/div and a sinusoidal signal spans 4 divisions for one complete cycle.

What is the frequency of the signal?

Tick **one** box. [1]

50 Hz ☐ 60 Hz ☐ 100 Hz ☐ 200 Hz ☐

3 The vertical gain of an oscilloscope is set to 2.5 V/div.

If the peak-to-peak potential difference displayed spans 8 divisions, what is the rms potential difference?

Tick **one** box. [1]

1.8 V ☐ 7.1 V ☐ 14 V ☐ 20 V ☐

4 A coil with 400 turns rotates with a constant angular speed in a magnetic field with a flux density of 0.12 T. The induced emf is analysed using an oscilloscope. The oscilloscope trace shows a sinusoidal potential difference and the time base is set to 0.2 s/division.

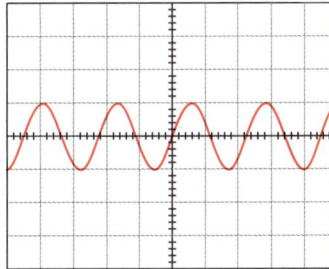

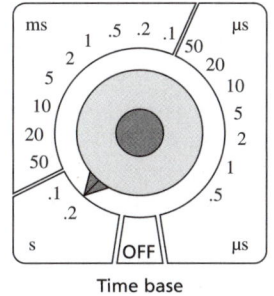

ms 1 .5 .2 .1 50 20 10 5 2 1 .5 μs 2 5 10 20 50 .1 .2 s OFF μs

Time base

a) Using the trace on the oscilloscope screen, calculate the frequency of rotation of the coil. [3]

....

b) Describe how to use the oscilloscope to accurately measure the peak emf. [3]

....

....

....

....

c) The peak emf of the coil is measured to be 4.0 V.

Calculate the area of the coil in the magnetic field. [2]

....

d) The coil is now rotated at a much faster angular velocity.

State and explain what changes might need to be made to the oscilloscope settings. [4]

....

....

....

....

....

Transformers

Key words

Key questions

What is a transformer made of?

How does a step-up transformer increase a potential difference?

Why are transformers not 100% efficient?

Why are step-up transformers used before transmitting electrical power over long distances?

Transformers

Transformers change the magnitude of alternating currents and potential differences.

When an alternating current flows through the primary coil, it creates a changing magnetic flux in the core. According to Faraday's law, the electromotive force (emf) induced in the secondary coil is equal to the rate of change of magnetic flux linkage:

$$\varepsilon = -N\frac{\Delta\Phi}{\Delta t}$$

A transformer consists of two coils of wire wound around a laminated iron core

Primary coil
Secondary coil
I_p
I_s
V_p
N_p
N_s
V_s
Soft iron core
Magnetic flux Φ

Transformers rely on alternating currents because only a changing magnetic flux can induce an emf. Direct current does not vary with time, so it does not produce the changing flux necessary to induce an emf in the secondary coil.

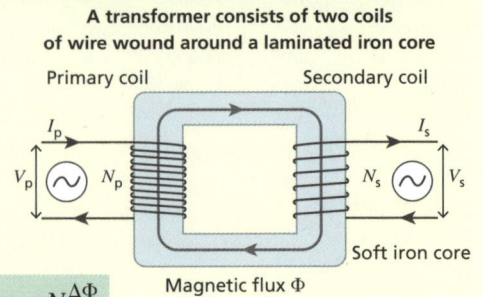

Step-up and step-down transformers

A **step-up transformer** has more turns in the secondary coil (N_s) than in the primary coil (N_p). This greater number of turns increases the flux linkage in the secondary coil, inducing a higher emf. The potential difference across the secondary coil (V_s) is higher than the potential difference across the primary coil (V_p). A **step-down transformer** works in the opposite way.

The relationship between the number of turns and the potential differences in the two coils is given by the transformer formula:

$$\frac{N_s}{N_p} = \frac{V_s}{V_p}$$

Transformer efficiency

The efficiency of a transformer can be calculated through the ratio of the output power to the input power:

$$\text{efficiency} = \frac{I_s V_s}{I_p V_p}$$

where I_p is the current in the primary coil and I_s is the current in the secondary coil. Multiply the result by 100 to convert the efficiency to a percentage.

While ideal transformers are 100% efficient, real ones experience losses:

1. Eddy currents are induced in the iron core due to the changing magnetic flux. These currents produce heat and waste energy. Laminating the core reduces eddy currents by limiting the paths available for current flow.

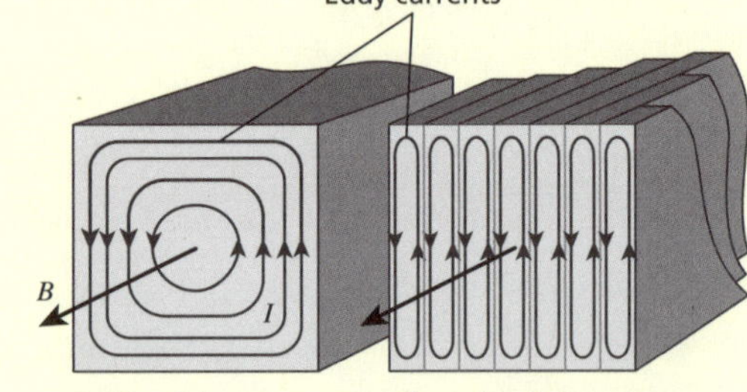

2. Resistance in the wires also causes heat loss. Using low resistance materials like copper minimises this energy loss.
3. Not all the magnetic flux produced by the primary coil links with the secondary coil.

Transmission of electrical power

To minimise energy losses over long distances, low currents are used. The power loss in transmission lines is given by:

$$P = I^2 R$$

By increasing the potential difference with step-up transformers, the current is reduced. This therefore reduces any power loss due to heating.

Summary

RETRIEVE

Transformers

A-level only

1. A power station produces an alternating current, which is passed into a step-up transformer before being transmitted over long distances.

   a) Explain why a step-up transformer is typically used before transmitting electrical power over long distances. [2]

   b) The step-up transformer increases the rms potential difference from 25 kV to 275 kV with an efficiency of 95%. The rms current in the primary coil is 800 A.

   Calculate the rms current in the secondary coil. [2]

2. The core of a transformer is made from thin laminated sheets of iron.

   a) Explain why laminating the iron core increases the efficiency of the transformer. [2]

   b) The transformer has 5000 turns on its primary coil and 200 turns on its secondary coil. The primary coil is connected to a mains power supply with an rms potential difference of 230 V.

   Calculate the rms potential difference across the secondary coil. [2]

   c) Describe how a transformer works and explain why your answer to part b) is less than the potential difference across the primary coil. [3]

   d) The transformer is 90% efficient and the rms current in the secondary coil is 8.0 A.

   Calculate the rms current in the primary coil. [2]

   e) Explain why a transformer cannot be used to vary the potential differences of a d.c. power supply. [2]

Rutherford scattering

Key words

Key questions

What is the plum pudding model?

What were the main observations of Rutherford's gold foil scattering experiment?

What were the main conclusions of Rutherford's gold foil scattering experiment?

Evolution of atomic models

The concept of atoms dates back to Ancient Greece, where the philosopher Democritus proposed that all matter was made of indivisible particles called 'atomos'. This idea remained speculative until John Dalton, in the early 19th century, provided evidence for the existence of atoms. Dalton suggested that matter consisted of tiny, solid spheres that were each unique to a chemical element.

In 1897, J.J. Thomson discovered the electron, proving that atoms were not indivisible but contained smaller subatomic particles. Thomson proposed the plum pudding model of the atom, where negatively charged electrons were embedded in a ball of positive charge. While this model was ground-breaking, Ernest Rutherford's gold foil scattering experiment showed it to be inaccurate.

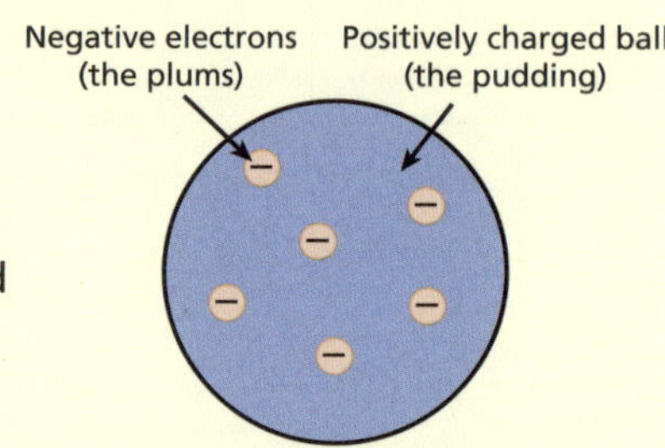

According to the plum pudding model, alpha particles (helium nuclei) passing through a thin gold foil should experience little to no deflection. As the charge was thought to be spread out throughout the atom, it was thought that most alpha particles would pass straight through. However, when the experiment was performed, the results did not match these predictions and this led to the rejection of the plum pudding model.

Rutherford's experiment

In 1909, Hans Geiger and Ernest Marsden conducted an experiment under Rutherford's direction to investigate the structure of the atom. A thin gold foil was bombarded with a beam of alpha particles and the scattering pattern was observed on a fluorescent screen:

- Most alpha particles passed straight through the gold foil, indicating that atoms are mostly empty space.
- Some alpha particles were deflected through small angles, suggesting the presence of a positively charged nucleus.
- A very small number of alpha particles were deflected by angles greater than 90°, showing that the positive charge and most of the mass of the atom are concentrated in a small central nucleus.

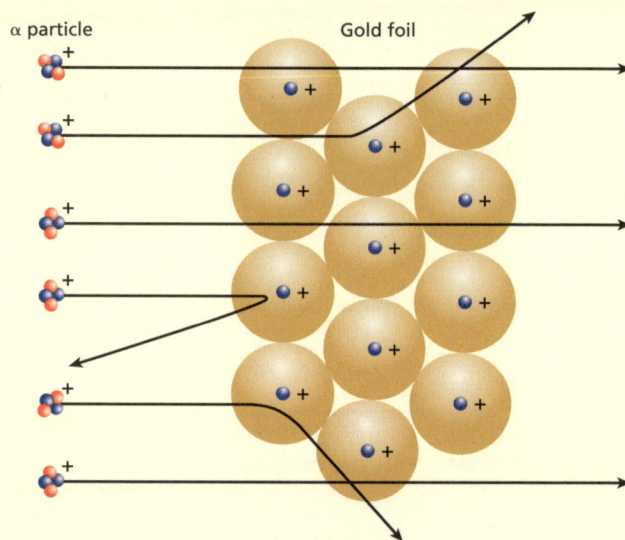

The results of this experiment led to the development of the **nuclear model**.

The nuclear model proposes that:

- atoms consist of a small and dense, positively charged nucleus
- negatively charged electrons orbit the nucleus
- the nucleus contains most of the atom's mass.

Summary

RETRIEVE

Rutherford scattering

A-level only

1. According to the plum pudding model, what would happen to alpha particles directed at a thin sheet of gold foil? Tick **one** box. [1]

   All alpha particles would be absorbed by the gold foil. ☐
   Due to electrostatic repulsion, the alpha particles would reflect backwards towards the alpha source. ☐
   Some alpha particles would be deflected through large angles. ☐
   All alpha particles would pass straight through with little deflection. ☐

2. In Rutherford's gold foil scattering experiment, most of the alpha particles travelled straight through the gold foil.
   What is the correct conclusion that can be drawn from this observation? Tick **one** box. [1]

   There is a positively charged nucleus. ☐
   Most of the mass is in the nucleus. ☐
   Most of the atom is empty space. ☐
   Electrons are negatively charged. ☐

3. Describe Rutherford's gold foil scattering experiment. Include a description of the observations of the experiment and the conclusions that those observations led to. [6]

4. Prior to the nuclear model of the atom, the plum pudding model was the accepted model of the atom.

   a) Describe the difference between the nuclear model of the atom and the plum pudding model. [4]

   b) Describe how scientific models evolve over time. [2]

ORGANISE

Alpha, beta and gamma radiation

A-level only

Key words

Key questions

What objects absorb α, β and γ radiation?

Which type of radiation is most ionising?

What are some sources of background radiation?

What are the dangers of radiation?

Properties of alpha, beta and gamma radiation

Radiation is emitted from unstable nuclei in three main forms: alpha (α), beta (β^-) and gamma (γ). Their properties can be experimentally identified using simple absorption experiments. Radiation is detected using a Geiger–Müller detector.

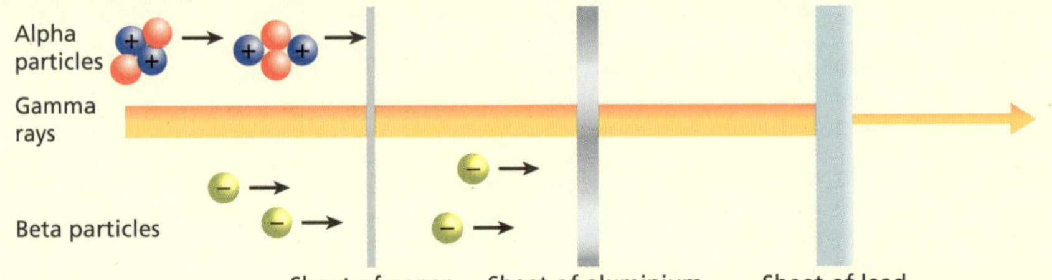

Type of radiation	Constituents	Penetrating power	Ionising power	Deflected by electric (E) and magnetic (B) fields?
Alpha (α)	Helium nucleus (two protons and two neutrons)	Absorbed by a few centimetres of air or a sheet of paper	Very weakly ionising	Has a charge of +2 and so is deflected by E and B fields
Beta (β^-)	High energy electron	Passes through paper but is absorbed by a few millimetres of aluminium	Weakly ionising	Has a charge of −1 and so is deflected by E and B fields
Gamma (γ)	Electromagnetic wave (photons)	Can penetrate paper and thin aluminium but is absorbed by several centimetres of lead or metres of concrete	Strongly ionising	Has no charge and so is not deflected by E or B fields

The inverse-square law for gamma radiation

Gamma radiation consists of electromagnetic waves that travel outward in all directions from a source. As they spread out, their intensity decreases according to the inverse-square law:

$$I = \frac{k}{x^2}$$

where I is the intensity, k is a constant and x is the distance from the source.

Background radiation

Radiation is present naturally in the environment and from human-made sources.

Natural sources include cosmic rays (high energy particles from space), radon gas (which is released from certain rocks and soil) and certain foods that contain naturally occurring radioactive isotopes such as potassium-40.

Human-made sources include radiation from medical sources and fallout from nuclear weapons testing or nuclear waste.

When measuring the activity of a radioactive source, it is important to subtract background radiation from any measurements.

Radiation in medicine

Radiation poses dangers including cell damage, mutation and an increased risk of cancer. However, it is widely used in medicine for diagnosis and treatment.

Medical tracers involve introducing a radioactive substance into the body to track its movement and locate abnormalities. These tracers must have a half-life long enough to complete measurements (e.g. a few hours) but short enough to minimise excessive exposure. Gamma radiation is used as it is penetrating enough to be detected outside of the body (and is less ionising than alpha and beta radiation).

Summary

RETRIEVE

Alpha, beta and gamma radiation

A-level only

1. A student is measuring the count rate at different distances from a radioactive source. Before starting, the student measures the background radiation and records it as 1140 counts/hour.

a) State the name of the detector used to measure radioactive count rates. [1]

b) Name **two** sources of background radiation. [2]

c) At a distance of 20 cm from the radioactive source, the detector measures a count rate of 1550 counts/minute.

Calculate the count rate that would be measured at a distance of 1.0 m from the radioactive source. [4]

2. A radioactive isotope is being considered for use as a medical tracer.

a) State the primary risk associated with exposure to radiation. [1]

b) Four isotopes, shown in the table, are available for consideration.

Isotope	Type of radiation emitted	Half-life
A	Alpha	2 days
B	Beta	6 hours
C	Gamma	3 hours
D	Gamma	2 weeks

From the table, state and explain which isotope is most suitable to use as a medical tracer. [3]

3. This question is on alpha, beta and gamma radiation.

a) Radon gas is an alpha emitter. Alpha particles are blocked by skin and yet radon gas still poses a risk.

Explain why. [1]

b) One application of beta radiation is in monitoring the thickness of aluminium foil.

Explain why beta radiation is suitable for this application and not alpha or gamma radiation. [3]

ORGANISE

Radioactive decay

A-level only

Key words

Key questions

What is the definition of the decay constant?

What is the definition of the becquerel?

What are two definitions of half-life?

What does the gradient of a $\ln(N)$–t graph represent?

The decay constant

Radioactive decay is a random process. It is impossible to predict exactly when a single nucleus will decay but, for a large number of nuclei, radioactive decay follows a predictable pattern.

Each radioactive isotope has a decay constant (λ), which represents the probability of a nucleus decaying per unit time. The units of the decay constant are therefore s^{-1}. The rate of decay of a radioactive sample is proportional to the number of undecayed nuclei remaining (N):

$$\frac{\Delta N}{\Delta t} = -\lambda N$$

The minus sign in this equation indicates that the number of nuclei decreases over time. As N becomes smaller, the rate of decay also decreases.

Exponential decay

The number of undecayed nuclei at any time (t) can be expressed as:

$$N = N_0 e^{-\lambda t}$$

where N_0 is the number of undecayed nuclei at time $t = 0$.

The activity (A) is the number of decays per second in the sample and is directly proportional to N:

$$A = \lambda N$$

The unit of activity is the becquerel (Bq), where 1 Bq = 1 decay per second. Due to $A = \lambda N$, the activity also undergoes exponential decay:

$$A = A_0 e^{-\lambda t}$$

Radioactive half-life

The half-life ($T_{\frac{1}{2}}$) is the time taken for half the nuclei in a sample to decay. Due to this, it can also be defined as the time taken for the activity to decrease by half. You can derive an expression for the half-life by substituting $t = T_{\frac{1}{2}}$ and $N = \frac{N_0}{2}$ into $N = N_0 e^{-\lambda t}$.

This results in: $T_{\frac{1}{2}} = \frac{\ln 2}{\lambda}$

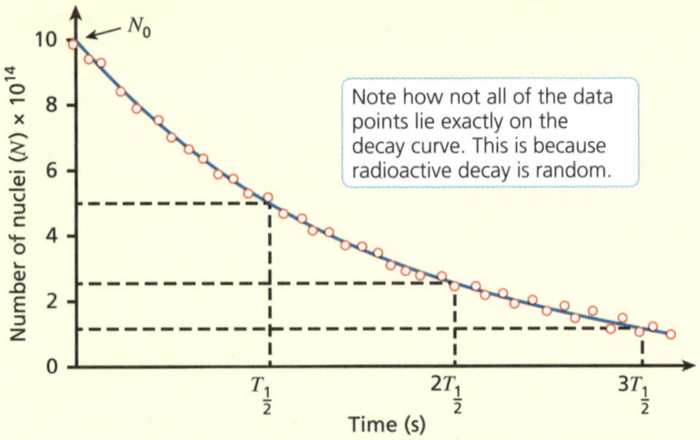

Half-life can be determined experimentally by the following:

- Plotting decay curves of N or A against t. The half-life is the time taken for the number of nuclei or the activity to halve. If you try to determine half-life in this way, it is important to measure the half-life two or three times at different positions on the curve. An average half-life can then be calculated.
- Plotting a logarithmic graph of $\ln(N)$ against t. If you take the natural logarithm of both sides of the exponential decay equation, you obtain: $\ln(N) = \ln(N_0) - \lambda t$

  Therefore, a plot of $\ln(N)$ against t gives a straight line with a gradient of $-\lambda$ and a y-intercept of $\ln(N_0)$.

Applications of radioactive decay

Carbon-14 dating is used to date organic remains. Living organisms maintain a constant ratio of carbon-14 to carbon-12. However, after death, carbon-14 decays. Measuring the remaining proportion of carbon-14 allows the age of the sample to be calculated. Half-life also needs to be considered with radioactive waste management. Long-lived isotopes require safe storage over thousands of years to reduce risks.

Summary

RETRIEVE

Radioactive decay

A-level only

1 The decay constant of a radioactive isotope is 4.0×10^{-4} s^{-1}.

What fraction of the original nuclei remains after a time of 30 minutes? Tick **one** box. [1]

0.24 ☐

0.49 ☐

0.65 ☐

0.99 ☐

2 Carbon-14 is a radioactive isotope with a half-life of 5730 years. The amount of carbon-14 in an organism decreases over time after death due to radioactive decay. A fossilised bone is found and scientists determine that 18% of the original carbon-14 remains.

a) State what is meant by a half-life of 5730 years. [1]

b) Calculate the decay constant of carbon-14 in units of s^{-1}. [2]

c) Calculate the age of the bone. [3]

d) Explain why carbon dating is not suitable for determining the age of a bone that is around 100 years old. [1]

3 A radioactive sample has a mass of 5.0 mg, a molar mass of 230 g mol^{-1} and a decay constant of 2.0×10^{-3} s^{-1}.

a) State what is meant by a decay constant of 2.0×10^{-3} s^{-1}. [1]

b) Calculate the initial number of radioactive nuclei in the sample. [2]

c) Calculate the activity of the sample after a time of 2.0 minutes. [3]

Nuclear instability

Key words

Key questions

What are the two forces that act on nucleons inside a nucleus?

Why does a large stable nucleus have more neutrons than protons?

Why is technetium-99m ideal for use in medical imaging?

Graph of N against Z for stable nuclei

On a graph of neutron number (N) against proton number (Z), stable nuclei form a curve known as the 'line of stability':

- For light nuclei ($Z < 20$), the stability line closely follows the $N = Z$ line.
- For heavier nuclei ($Z > 20$), the stability line curves above the $N = Z$ line. When $Z = 80$, $N = 120$.

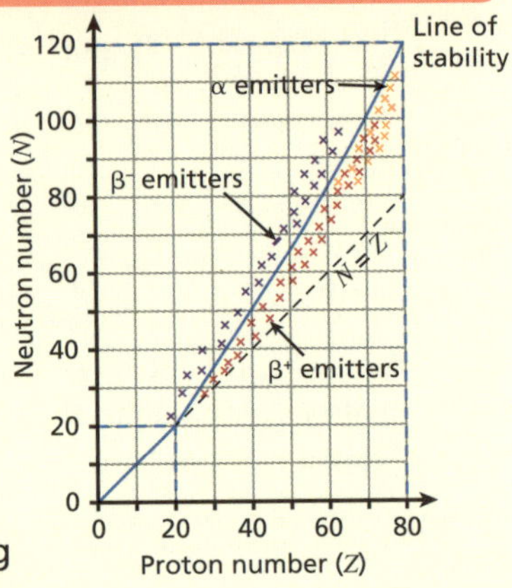

The strong nuclear force is responsible for holding protons and neutrons together in the nucleus. The strong nuclear force is attractive but has a maximum range of only 3 fm. Due to this short range, the strong nuclear force becomes less effective at counteracting the long-range electrostatic repulsion between protons in large nuclei. As neutrons do not experience electrostatic repulsion, more neutrons are needed for stability.

Modes of radioactive decay

1. **Alpha (α) decay** in heavy nuclei. The nucleus emits an alpha particle ($^4_2$He), decreasing N by 2 and Z by 2. Therefore, alpha decay only happens to nuclei below the stability line (otherwise the nucleus would go further from the stability line and become less stable). One example is: $^{238}_{92}\text{U} \rightarrow {}^{234}_{90}\text{Th} + {}^{4}_{2}\text{He}$	2. **Beta-minus (β⁻) decay** occurs in neutron-rich nuclei above the stability line. A neutron converts into a proton, emitting an electron (e^-) and an electron antineutrino. Therefore, N decreases by 1 and Z increases by 1. One example is: $^{14}_{6}\text{C} \rightarrow {}^{14}_{7}\text{N} + {}^{0}_{-1}\text{e}^- + {}^{0}_{0}\bar{\upsilon}_e$	3. **Beta-plus (β+) decay** occurs in proton-rich nuclei below the stability line. A proton converts into a neutron, emitting a positron (e^+) and an electron neutrino. Therefore, N increases by 1 and Z decreases by 1. One example is: $^{11}_{6}\text{C} \rightarrow {}^{11}_{5}\text{N} + {}^{0}_{1}\text{e}^+ + {}^{0}_{0}\upsilon_e$

Nuclear excited states

Nuclei have discrete energy levels. When a nucleus undergoes radioactive decay, the resulting daughter nucleus is often left in an excited energy state. These excited nuclei can then release energy by transitioning to a lower energy state, emitting high-energy gamma photons in the process.

Caesium-137 decays by beta-minus emission

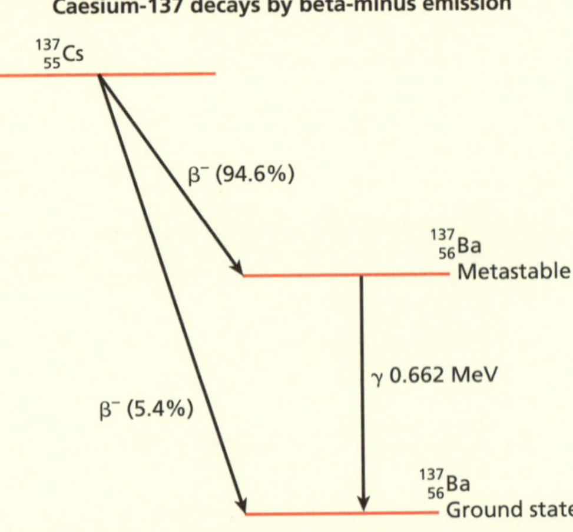

An important application of nuclear excited states is the use of technetium-99m in medical imaging. The 'm' stands for metastable, which means that the nucleus is in an excited state for a long period of time before de-exciting and emitting gamma photons. Technetium-99m is ideal for medical imaging as it is a pure gamma emitter and has a half-life of 6 hours. Gamma radiation is penetrating enough to be detected outside of the body and, as technetium-99m is a pure gamma emitter, there is no unnecessary ionisation and cell damage caused by alpha or beta radiation.

Summary

RETRIEVE

Nuclear instability

1 **a)** In the space below, sketch a graph of neutron number against atomic number for stable nuclei and indicate where alpha, beta-minus and beta-plus emitters are located. [5]

b) Explain the shape of the graph you have drawn above in terms of the strong nuclear force and electrostatic repulsion. [4]

2 In a hospital, a technetium generator is used to provide technetium-99m for medical imaging. The generator produces technetium by the beta-minus decay of molybdenum-99.

a) Complete the nuclear equation for the beta-minus decay of molybdenum-99. [1]

$^{99}_{42}Mo \rightarrow$

b) After the beta-minus decay, technetium-99m is produced in an excited nuclear state. The difference between the energy levels of the excited state and the ground state is 140 keV.

Calculate the frequency of the gamma photons emitted as the nucleus de-excites. [3]

c) Explain why technetium-99m is particularly well-suited for medical imaging. [2]

d) Molybdenum-99 has a half-life of 66 hours. If a generator initially contains 5.0 g of molybdenum-99, calculate the remaining mass of molybdenum-99 after a time of one week. [3]

e) The hospital needs to minimise exposure to medical staff and patients.

Describe **two** safety precautions that should be implemented when handling radioactive materials like molybdenum and technetium. [2]

ORGANISE

Nuclear radius

A-level only

Key words

Key questions

Why does the closest approach of alpha particles give an upper bound estimate for the nuclear radius?

How can you derive an expression for the closest approach of an alpha particle to a nucleus?

How can the nuclear radius can be measured by electron diffraction?

How can you derive that nuclear density is constant?

Closest approach of alpha particles

Alpha particles are positively charged and experience electrostatic repulsion as they approach a positively charged nucleus. If an alpha particle is directed towards a nucleus and repelled backwards, the distance of closest approach can be calculated.

At the distance of closest approach, the initial kinetic energy of the alpha particle is converted into electrostatic potential energy:

$$E_K = \frac{1}{2}mv^2 = Q_\alpha \Delta V = \frac{1}{4\pi\varepsilon_0}\frac{Q_\alpha Q_{\text{nucleus}}}{r}$$

where, m is the mass of the alpha particle, v is the velocity of the alpha particle, Q_α and Q_{nucleus} are the charges of the alpha particle and the nucleus respectively, and r is the distance of closest approach.

Rearranging this expression for r leads to:

$$r = \frac{1}{2\pi\varepsilon_0}\frac{Q_\alpha Q_{\text{nucleus}}}{mv^2}$$

This method provides an upper bound estimate of the nuclear radius as the alpha particle does not come into contact with the nucleus.

Electron diffraction

Electron diffraction is a measurement and so offers a more accurate value of the nuclear radius. A beam of electrons is directed towards a thin metal or graphite target. The electrons diffract through nuclei and a diffraction pattern is measured, showing intensity versus scattering angle.

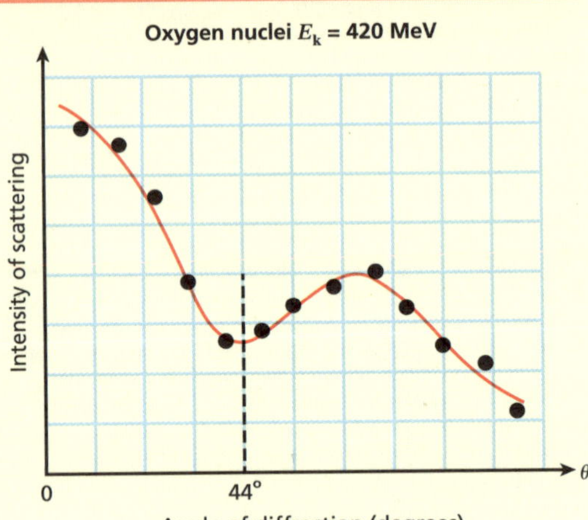

From the diffraction graph (e.g. for oxygen), the position of the first minimum allows the nuclear radius to be determined using $\sin\theta_{\text{min}} = 0.61\frac{\lambda}{R}$. λ is the de Broglie wavelength of the electrons and R is the nuclear radius.

Nuclear radius and density

Experimental data shows that the nuclear radius (R) depends on the cube root of the nucleon number (A):

$$R = R_0 A^{\frac{1}{3}}$$

where R_0 is the radius of a single nucleon (approximately equal to 1.2 fm).

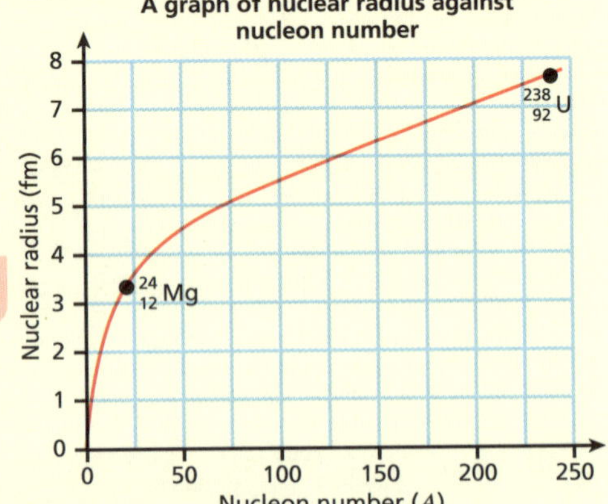

The density of a nucleus can be calculated by:

$$\rho = \frac{\text{mass of nucleus}}{\text{volume of nucleus}}$$

The mass of the nucleus is Am, where A is the nucleon number and m is the mass of a single nucleon. The volume of the nucleus is $\frac{4}{3}\pi R^3$.

Substituting this and $R = R_0 A^{\frac{1}{3}}$ into the expression for density gives:

$$\rho = \frac{Am}{\frac{4}{3}\pi\left(R_0 A^{\frac{1}{3}}\right)^3} = \frac{m}{\frac{4}{3}\pi R_0^3}$$

This expression shows that nuclear density is constant as all the terms are constants. Substituting in $R_0 = 1.2 \times 10^{-15}$ m and $m = 1.67 \times 10^{-27}$ kg gives a density of 2.3×10^{17} kg m^{-3}.

Summary

RETRIEVE

Nuclear radius

A-level only

1. An alpha particle is accelerated to a kinetic energy of 5.0 MeV and directed towards a gold nucleus. Gold has an atomic number of 79.

   a) Calculate the distance of closest approach between the alpha particle and the gold nucleus. [3]

   b) Without calculation, describe how this distance of closest approach would differ if a nucleus with a smaller atomic number (but the same mass number) was used instead of gold. [2]

   c) In a separate experiment, electrons are diffracted through a thin gold foil, producing a diffraction pattern.

   Explain why the nuclear radius from this experiment will be lower than that calculated in the experiment in part b). [2]

   d) In the space below, sketch a graph of electron intensity against diffraction angle. [2]

2. It can be shown that all nuclei have the same approximate density, regardless of size.

   a) The mass number of aluminium is 27.

   Calculate the volume of an aluminium nucleus. Assume that the radius of a single nucleon is 1.2 fm. [3]

   b) Show that the nuclear density of aluminium is approximately 2.3×10^{17} kg m^{-3}. [2]

   c) Show that all nuclei have the same approximate density. [2]

ORGANISE

Mass and energy

A-level only

Key words

Key questions

Why is the mass of a nucleus less than the sum of the masses of the individual nucleons?

What is the definition of binding energy?

What is nuclear fission?

Which is the most stable element?

Mass defect and binding energy

Einstein's equation, $E = mc^2$, shows the equivalence of mass and energy. In nuclear reactions, small changes in mass result in significant energy changes.

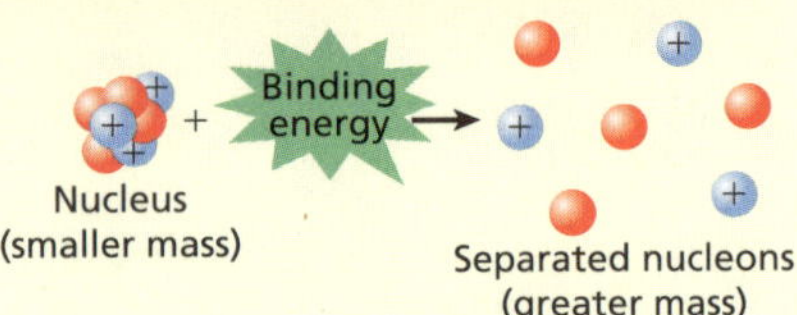

The mass of a nucleus is less than the sum of the masses of its individual nucleons. This difference, known as the **mass defect**, is due to something called **binding energy**. The binding energy is defined as the energy needed to separate a nucleus into its constituent protons and neutrons. This energy is needed to overcome the strong nuclear force.

The binding energy (E_b) is given by: $E_b = \Delta mc^2$

where Δm is the mass defect (in kilograms) and c is the speed of light.

The binding energy gives an indication of the stability of a nucleus. A higher binding energy per nucleon means greater stability.

The atomic mass unit (u) is defined as $\frac{1}{12}$ the mass of a carbon-12 atom and is equal to 1.661×10^{-27} kg. In terms of energy, 1 atomic mass unit can also be expressed as 931.5 MeV.

	Rest mass in kg	Rest mass in u	Rest energy in MeV
Atomic mass unit	1.661×10^{-27}	1	931.5
Proton	1.673×10^{-27}	1.00728	938.257
Neutron	1.675×10^{-27}	1.00867	939.551
Electron	9.11×10^{-31}	5.5×10^{-4}	0.510 999

Fission and fusion

Fission is the splitting of a large nucleus into two smaller nuclei, accompanied by the release of energy and additional neutrons.

For example: ${}^{235}_{92}U + {}^{1}_{0}n \rightarrow {}^{92}_{36}Kr + {}^{141}_{56}Ba + 3{}^{1}_{0}n$

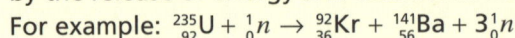

In fission, the total mass of the products is less than the original mass.

Fusion involves combining two small nuclei to form a larger nucleus, releasing energy in the process. One example of nuclear fusion is: ${}^{2}_{1}H + {}^{3}_{1}H \rightarrow {}^{4}_{2}He + {}^{1}_{0}n$

Fusion releases significantly more energy per kilogram of fuel than fission as the mass difference between the reactants and products is larger (and there is a larger change in binding energy per nucleon). The energy released in fission and fusion reactions can be calculated by: $E = \Delta mc^2$

Graph of binding energy per nucleon

The graph of average binding energy per nucleon against nucleon number increases until iron-56. This shows that iron-56 is the most stable element, with a binding energy of around 8.8 MeV/nucleon.

Elements with a lower nucleon number than iron-56 can release energy through nuclear fusion. Elements with a higher nucleon number than iron-56 release energy through nuclear fission.

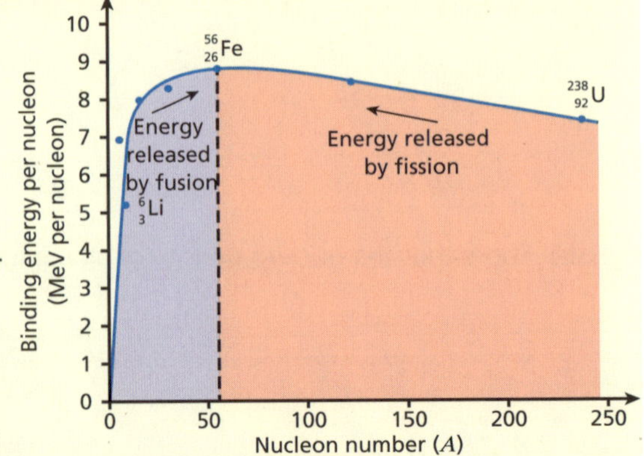

Summary

RETRIEVE

Mass and energy

A-level only

1 The binding energy per nucleon for iron-56 is 8.8 MeV, while for uranium-235 it is 7.6 MeV.

a) Calculate the total binding energy of an iron-56 nucleus. [1]

b) If a uranium nucleus undergoes fission, explain why the products are more stable than the original nucleus. [1]

c) In the space below, sketch a graph of binding energy per nucleon against nucleon number. Indicate regions where nuclear fusion and nuclear fission are possible. [3]

2 Uranium-235 undergoes induced fission when its nucleus absorbs a neutron:

$$^{235}_{92}\text{U} + ^{1}_{0}n \rightarrow ^{92}_{36}\text{Kr} + ^{141}_{56}\text{Ba} + 3^{1}_{0}n$$

Calculate the energy released during a single fission event. The masses of $^{235}_{92}\text{U}$, $^{92}_{36}\text{Kr}$ and $^{141}_{56}\text{Ba}$ are 235.0439 u, 140.9144 u and 91.9263 u respectively. [4]

3 In a fusion reaction, deuterium $\left(^{2}_{1}\text{H}\right)$ and tritium $\left(^{3}_{1}\text{H}\right)$ nuclei combine to form a helium $\left(^{4}_{2}\text{He}\right)$ nucleus:

$$^{2}_{1}\text{H} + ^{3}_{1}\text{H} \rightarrow ^{4}_{2}\text{He} + ^{1}_{0}n$$

a) The mass of the $^{4}_{2}\text{He}$ nucleus is 4.0015 u.

Calculate the binding energy per nucleon of $^{4}_{2}\text{He}$. [3]

b) Calculate the energy released per fusion event in MeV. The masses of $^{2}_{1}\text{H}$ and $^{3}_{1}\text{H}$ nuclei are 2.0136 u and 3.0155 u respectively. [4]

ORGANISE

Induced fission

A-level only

Key words

Key questions

What is induced fission?

What is the role of the moderator?

What is the role of the control rods?

How is high-level radioactive waste handled?

Nuclear fission and chain reactions

Nuclear fission is the process in which a large nucleus splits into two smaller nuclei, releasing energy. **Induced fission** occurs when a thermal (slow-moving) neutron is absorbed by a fissile nucleus, such as uranium-235 or plutonium-239. The nucleus becomes unstable and splits into two daughter nuclei and several fast-moving neutrons, releasing energy in the form of the kinetic energy of the products.

A typical fission reaction of uranium-235 is: ${}^{235}_{92}\text{U} + {}^{1}_{0}n \rightarrow {}^{92}_{36}\text{Kr} + {}^{141}_{56}\text{Ba} + 3{}^{1}_{0}n$

The neutrons produced can go on to cause further fission reactions, leading to a chain reaction. If each fission event produces at least one neutron that induces further fission, the reaction is self-sustaining. This is how a nuclear reactor operates. If too many neutrons escape without causing fission, the reaction will die out. The critical mass is the minimum amount of fissile material needed to maintain a chain reaction.

Components of a nuclear reactor

A nuclear reactor is designed to maintain a controlled chain reaction. This is achieved using a moderator, control rods and coolant.

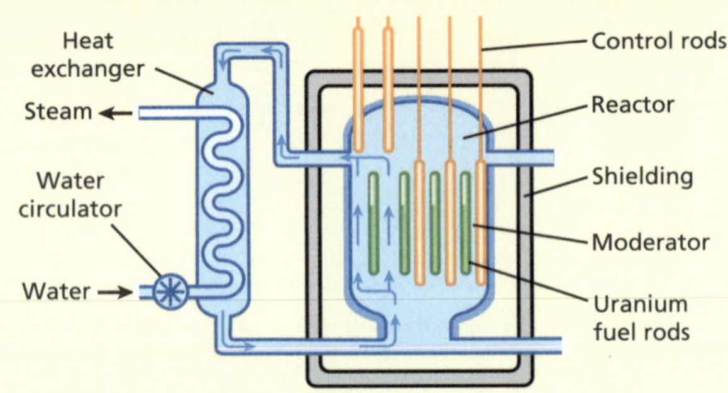

The moderator slows down neutrons so they become thermal and are more likely to be absorbed by a uranium-235 nucleus. Neutrons collide elastically with moderator nuclei, transferring some of their energy and reducing their speed. To maximise energy transfer in elastic collisions, the material that the moderator is made from should have a low atomic mass. Usually, water or graphite is used as the moderator.

Control rods absorb neutrons to regulate the chain reaction. To slow down the reaction, control rods are inserted further into the reactor core. Boron or cadmium is usually used as the control rod material. The coolant removes heat produced in the reactor and transfers it to generate electricity. Water is the most common coolant.

Safety aspects of nuclear reactors

As nuclear fuel is highly radioactive, fuel rods are remotely handled using robotic arms. The reactor is also surrounded by thick concrete shielding to absorb radiation and protect workers. In the event of an emergency, the reactor must be shut down immediately to stop the chain reaction. Control rods are fully inserted into the core to absorb all neutrons and stop fission.

Spent fuel rods and fission products are the main source of high-level radioactive waste. This waste is stored in cooling ponds for several years before being vitrified (sealed in molten glass), encased in steel containers and buried deep underground in a stable geological location for thousands of years.

There are risks to nuclear power, as seen with meltdowns in Chernobyl (1986) and Fukushima (2011). It is therefore important to balance the risk and benefits. While nuclear waste is difficult to handle and accidents are possible, there are many benefits to nuclear power. These include low carbon dioxide emissions (helping to combat global warming); high energy density (the energy released per kilogram of fuel far exceeds coal or gas); and nuclear power being a reliable source of energy.

Summary

RETRIEVE

Induced fission

1 Which material is commonly used as a control rod in nuclear reactors? Tick **one** box. [1]

Boron ☐ Water ☐ Graphite ☐ Sodium ☐

2 A nuclear reactor contains fuel rods, a moderator, control rods and coolant.

a) Explain the function of each of these components in the reactor. [4]

b) Suggest a suitable material for the moderator and explain why it is effective. [2]

c) State the main cause of high-level radioactive waste. [1]

d) Describe how high-level radioactive waste is disposed of. [3]

e) State **one** advantage of nuclear power. [1]

3 A nuclear reactor relies on a controlled chain reaction to sustain energy production.

a) Explain what is meant by a chain reaction in the context of nuclear fission. [2]

b) The critical mass of uranium-235 is approximately 50 kg.

Explain why a mass below this value will not sustain a chain reaction. [1]

c) Describe **two** safety features of a nuclear reactor. [2]

Telescopes

Key words

Key questions

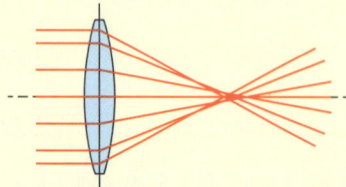

What is 'chromatic aberration'?

What is 'spherical aberration'?

What are advantages of using reflecting telescopes?

What is a disadvantage of using a reflecting telescope?

Refracting telescopes have two converging lenses

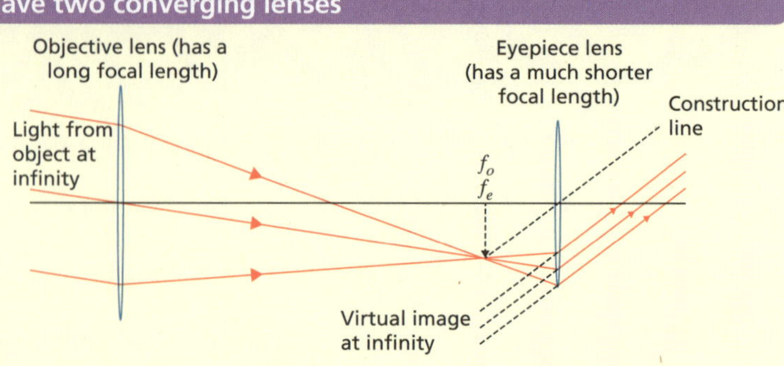

In a refracting telescope, the **objective lens** refracts incoming parallel rays so that they converge to a focal point.

The **eyepiece lens** is its focal length away from the focus created by the objective lens. This causes the light rays emerging from the eyepiece to become parallel to each other and an image is formed at infinity (known as **normal adjustment**). Rays emerging from the eyepiece lens are parallel to the construction line (drawn from the focal point through the centre of the eyepiece lens without a change in direction).

Angular magnification in normal adjustment

The angular magnification, M, of a telescope is defined as:

$$M = \frac{\text{angle subtended by image at eye}}{\text{angle subtended by object at unaided eye}}$$

The magnification is also equal to the ratio of the focal lengths of the objective lens (f_o) and the eyepiece lens (f_e):

$$M = \frac{f_o}{f_e}$$

The total length of a refracting telescope is given by $f_o + f_e$.

Reflecting telescopes use mirrors rather than lenses

Light enters the telescope and is reflected from a large concave primary mirror, bringing the light towards a focus. However, before reaching this focal point, the light reaches a smaller convex secondary mirror. As the light reflects back on itself, the size of a Cassegrain telescope is more compact than a refracting telescope. However, the secondary mirror blocks some of the incoming light.

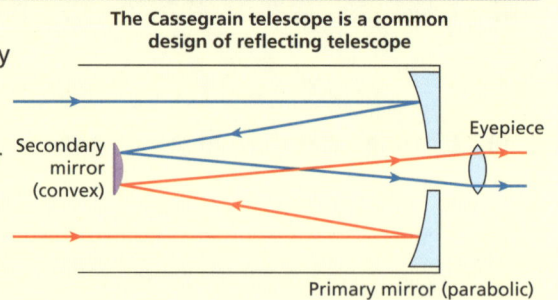

The Cassegrain telescope is a common design of reflecting telescope

Secondary mirror (convex)

Eyepiece

Primary mirror (parabolic)

Spherical and chromatic aberration

Spherical aberration	Chromatic aberration
Occurs when a lens or mirror does not bring all incoming rays to the same focal point. This results in a blurred image. Refracting telescopes suffer from more spherical aberration than reflecting telescopes. In a reflecting telescope, spherical aberration can be corrected using parabolic mirrors.	Arises because lenses refract different wavelengths of light by different amounts. Shorter wavelengths (such as violet and blue light) are refracted more than longer wavelengths (such as red light). This results in a blurred image with coloured fringes around the object. Reflecting telescopes do not suffer from chromatic aberration. 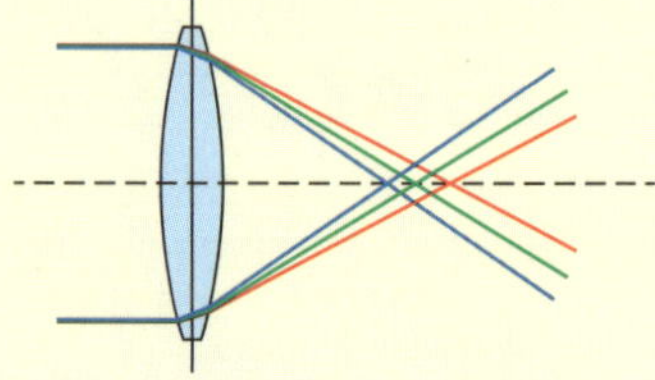

Summary

RETRIEVE

Telescopes

A-level only

(1) A comet of diameter 15 km is 1.0×10^9 m from Earth. A refracting telescope with an objective lens of focal length 2.0 m and an eyepiece lens of focal length 5.0 cm is used to observe the comet.

a) Calculate the angle subtended by the image of the comet when viewed through the telescope. [3]

b) In the space below, draw a fully labelled ray diagram for a refracting telescope in normal adjustment. [4]

c) Explain why refracting telescopes suffer from chromatic aberration. [1]

(2) A Cassegrain reflecting telescope consists of a parabolic concave primary mirror and a convex secondary mirror, which directs light through a hole in the primary mirror to the eyepiece lens.

a) In the space below, draw a fully labelled ray diagram for a Cassegrain reflecting telescope in normal adjustment. [3]

b) A choice must be made between using a refracting or a reflecting telescope for an observatory.

Discuss the advantages and disadvantages of choosing a reflecting telescope. [4]

Comparing telescopes

Key words

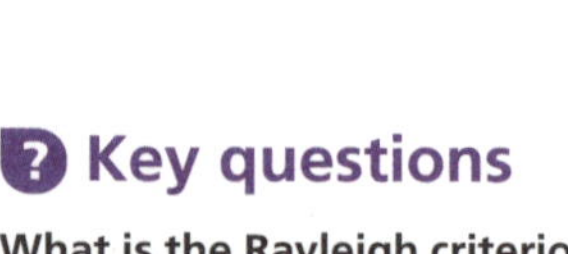

Key questions

What is the Rayleigh criterion?

Why is it beneficial for radio telescopes to have a large diameter?

Why are infrared, ultraviolet and X-ray telescopes based in space?

What is 'quantum efficiency'?

Rayleigh criterion and collecting power

The **Rayleigh criterion** states that two objects can just be resolved when the central maximum of the diffraction pattern (Airy disc) from one object overlaps with the first diffraction minimum of the other.

The **minimum angular resolution** of a telescope (θ, in radians) is given by: $\theta \approx \frac{\lambda}{D}$

where λ is the wavelength of the observed radiation and D is the diameter of the telescope's aperture.

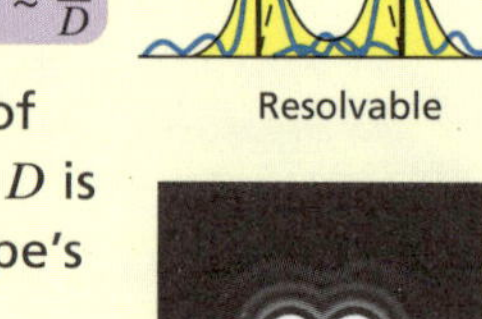

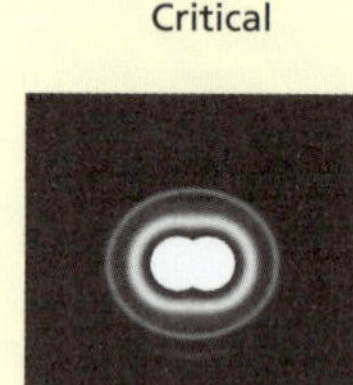

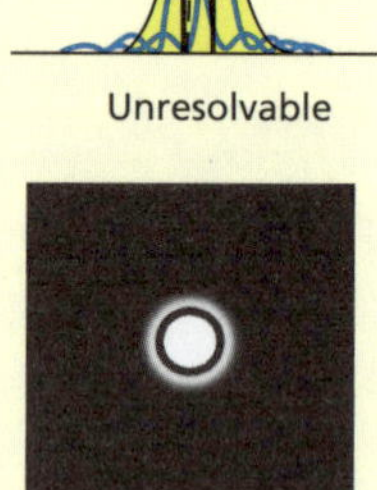

The **collecting power** determines how much light or radiation a telescope gathers: collecting power ∝ diameter^2

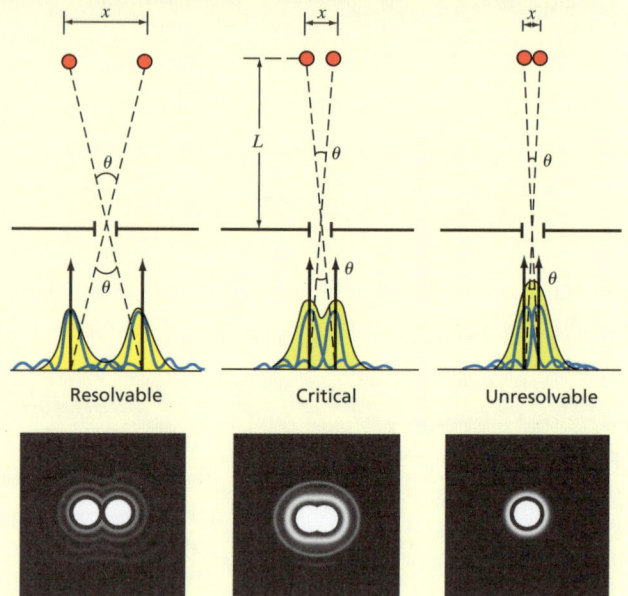

Radio telescopes

A radio telescope has a large parabolic dish that reflects radio waves to a receiver at the focal point. The dish can be hundreds of metres across to compensate for the poor angular resolution caused by long wavelengths. Some radio telescopes link multiple dishes together in an array.

Since radio waves can pass through the atmosphere, radio telescopes can operate on Earth's surface. However, they are often located in remote areas to avoid interference from human-made signals.

Infrared, ultraviolet and X-ray telescopes

These telescopes are placed in space to detect wavelengths that are mostly blocked by Earth's atmosphere. Infrared telescopes are useful for observing cool objects like dust clouds and exoplanets. They must be cooled to avoid interference from their own thermal radiation.

Glass absorbs ultraviolet and X-rays, so lenses cannot be used. Instead, mirrors focus these wavelengths, with grazing incidence mirrors required for X-rays.

Comparing the eye and charge-coupled devices (CCDs) as detectors

CCDs have a higher quantum efficiency (around 80%) than the human eye (4–5%).

Quantum efficiency is the percentage of incident photons that are detected:

$$\text{quantum efficiency} = \frac{\text{number of photons detected}}{\text{number of photons incident}} \times 100$$

CCDs also allow images to be stored, processed and analysed digitally.

Summary

RETRIEVE

Comparing telescopes

A-level only

1. An optical telescope observes visible light at a wavelength of 500 nm using a 2.5 m diameter mirror. A radio telescope of diameter 100 m observes at a wavelength of 21 cm.

   a) State **one** similarity and **one** difference between the construction of a radio telescope and an optical telescope. [2]

   b) Compare the collecting powers of the two telescopes. [2]

   c) Compare the minimum resolvable angles of the two telescopes. [2]

   d) Describe the best locations for placing optical and radio telescopes and explain why these locations are suitable. [2]

2. One of the aims of the James Webb Space Telescope (JWST) is to try to observe distant exoplanets.

   a) Explain why the JWST must be placed in space to observe infrared radiation effectively. [1]

   b) The JWST is trying to observe an exoplanet 5.0×10^{17} m away with a diameter of 1.5×10^{7} m. The telescope has a 6.5 m primary mirror and observes at a wavelength of 4.5 μm.

   Determine whether the exoplanet can be resolved. [3]

   c) The JWST is now used to observe a binary star system.

   Describe the conditions under which the two stars can be resolved as separate objects. [2]

   d) The detector on the JWST has a quantum efficiency of 80%. Explain what is meant by this. [1]

ORGANISE

Apparent and absolute magnitude

A-level only

Key words

Key questions

What is 'apparent magnitude'?

What is an arcsecond in degrees?

What is the definition of a parsec?

What is 'absolute magnitude'?

Apparent magnitude of a star

The apparent magnitude (m) is a measure of how bright a star appears from Earth. The apparent magnitude scale, first introduced by the Greek astronomer Hipparchus, classifies stars from 1 (brightest) to 6 (dimmest visible to the naked eye).

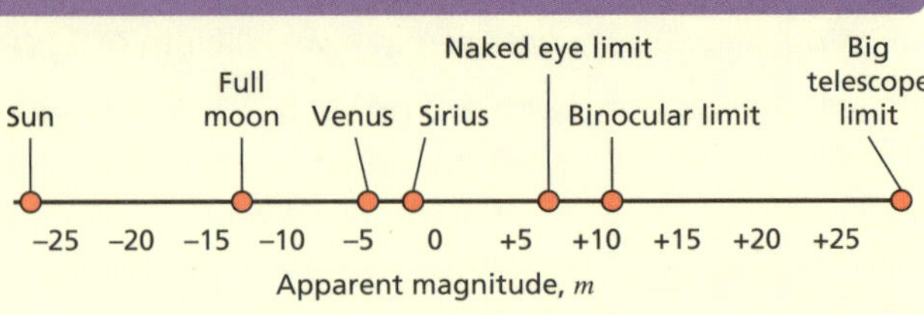

The scale was later refined into a logarithmic system, where a star with $m = 1$ is 100 times brighter than a star with $m = 6$. Therefore, a difference of 1 on the apparent magnitude scale corresponds to a change in brightness by a factor of 2.51 ($\sqrt[5]{100}$).

The relationship between the brightness (B) and apparent magnitude (m) of two stars is given by: $\frac{B_1}{B_2} = 2.51^{(m_2 - m_1)}$

where B_1 and B_2 are the brightness values of the two stars and m_1 and m_2 are their apparent magnitudes.

The smaller or more negative the apparent magnitude, the brighter the star in the night sky.

Astronomical distances

The astronomical unit (AU), parsec (pc) and light year (ly) are all units of astronomical distance.

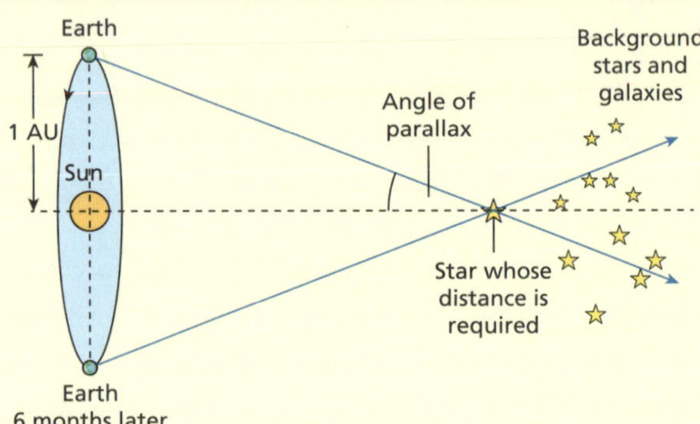

An **astronomical unit** is equal to 1.50×10^{11} m, which is the average Earth-to-Sun distance. A **parsec** is the distance at which an object would have a parallax angle of 1 arcsecond $\left(= \frac{1}{3600}^{\circ}\right)$ when viewed from Earth. The parallax angle is due to Earth orbiting the Sun at a distance of 1 AU.

Using trigonometry, it can be shown that 1 parsec is equal to 3.06×10^{16} m.

A **light year** is the distance that light travels in one year and is equal to 9.45×10^{15} m.

Absolute magnitude

The apparent magnitude of a star depends on the luminosity of the star and how far away it is from Earth. To make it easier to compare stars, astronomers use absolute magnitude (M). This is the brightness of a star at a distance of 10 parsecs. The relationship between apparent magnitude (m), absolute magnitude (M) and distance (d) in parsecs is given by: $m - M = 5\log\left(\frac{d}{10}\right)$

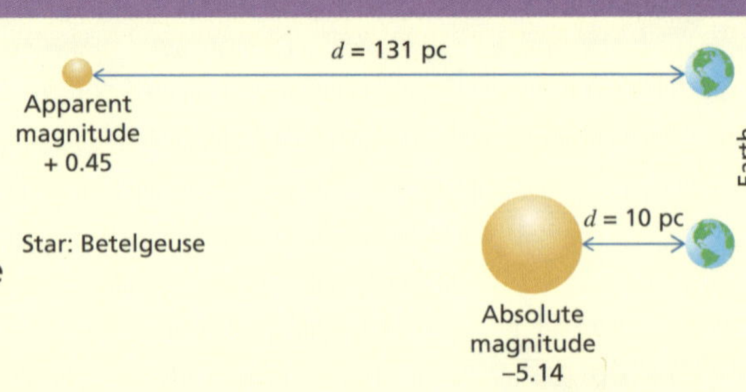

If a star is further away than 10 parsecs, its apparent magnitude will be less bright than its absolute magnitude.

Summary

RETRIEVE

Apparent and absolute magnitude

A-level only

1. The apparent magnitude of the star Sirius is −1.46 and the apparent magnitude of the star Vega is 0.03

   a) Explain what is meant by the term 'apparent magnitude'. [2]

   b) Calculate how many times brighter Sirius appears compared to Vega. [2]

2. A star has an apparent magnitude of +2.3 and is located 50 parsecs away from Earth.

   a) Define absolute magnitude and explain how it differs from apparent magnitude. [2]

   b) Calculate the absolute magnitude of the star. [2]

3. Two stars are observed to determine their distance from Earth in parsecs.

   a) Define the parsec. [2]

   b) When viewed from Earth, a star has a parallax angle of 0.05 arcseconds.

   Calculate its distance from Earth in parsecs. [1]

   c) Another star has an apparent magnitude of +5.2 and an absolute magnitude of +1.8

   Calculate its distance from Earth in parsecs. [3]

ORGANISE

Star classification by temperature

A-level only

Key words

Key questions

What is Wien's displacement law?

How does the luminosity of a star relate to its surface area and surface temperature?

Why does the brightness of a star decrease with distance away from the star?

Black body radiation

Stars emit radiation across the electromagnetic spectrum, but their intensity varies with wavelength. To classify stars by temperature, they are modelled as **black bodies** – idealised objects that absorb and emit all wavelengths of radiation perfectly.

A black body curve represents the intensity of radiation emitted by an object at different wavelengths. As temperature increases:

- the peak wavelength (λ_{max}) shifts to shorter wavelengths
- the total power emitted increases.

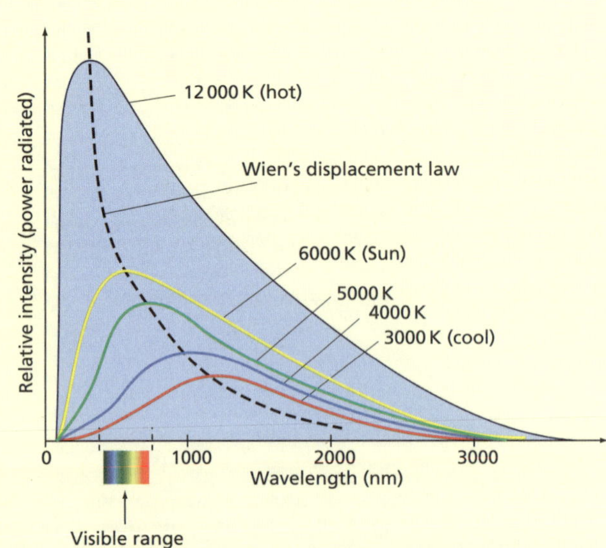

These properties allow scientists to estimate the temperature of a star by analysing its spectrum.

Wien's displacement law states that the peak wavelength of a black body spectrum is inversely proportional to its temperature:

$$\lambda_{max} T = 2.9 \times 10^{-3} \text{ m K}$$

where λ_{max} is the wavelength at which emission is strongest and T is the surface temperature of the black body in kelvin (K).

Stefan's law (the Stefan–Boltzmann law)

Stefan's law relates the luminosity (total power output) of a star to its temperature and surface area:

$$P = \sigma A T^4$$

where P is the luminosity of the star (in W), $\sigma = 5.67 \times 10^{-8}$ W m^{-2} K^{-4} (the Stefan–Boltzmann constant), $A = 4\pi R^2$ is the surface area of the star (in m^2) and T is the surface temperature of the star (in K).

The inverse square law

The brightness of a star (its apparent intensity) depends on the luminosity of the star and its distance from the observer. The inverse square law states that:

$$I = \frac{P}{4\pi r^2}$$

where I is the observed intensity (in W m^{-2}) and r is the distance to the star (in m).

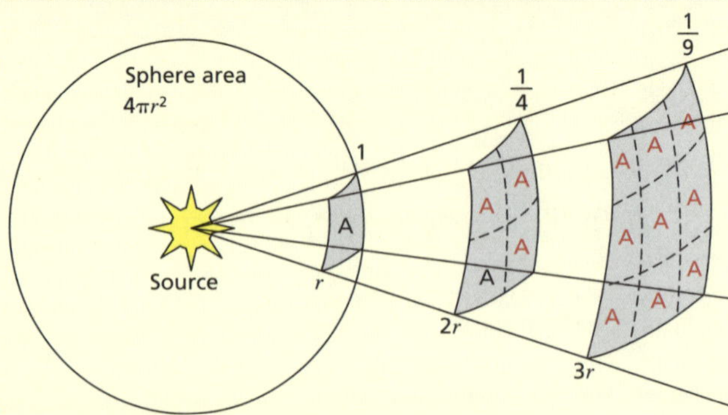

The inverse square law assumes that:

- the star emits radiation equally in all directions
- there is no absorption or scattering by interstellar material.

Summary

RETRIEVE

Star classification by temperature

A-level only

1. A star is observed to emit a peak wavelength of 450 nm.

   a) State, in words, Wien's displacement law. [1]

   b) Calculate the surface temperature of the star. [2]

   c) The star has a radius of 7.0×10^{8} m.

   Calculate its total power output. [3]

   d) The star is a distance of 1.5×10^{17} m from Earth.

   Calculate its intensity when observed from Earth. [2]

2. Star A is 150 parsecs from Earth. It is observed to emit a peak wavelength of 600 nm and the intensity of the star is measured to be 3.0×10^{-9} W m^{-2}.

   a) Calculate the radius of the star. [5]

   b) Sketch a graph of intensity against wavelength for star A. On the same axes, sketch a similar curve for another star, B, which has a surface temperature of 10 000 K. Label the curves A and B. [3]

ORGANISE

Stellar spectral classes

A-level only

Key words

Key questions

What is the order of the spectral classes of stars from hottest to coolest?

Which class of star has the strongest Balmer absorption lines?

What causes an absorption line?

Spectral classification of stars

Stars are classified into seven main spectral types (O, B, A, F, G, K, M), arranged in order of decreasing temperature and in categories of prominent absorption lines.

Spectral class	Intrinsic colour	Temperature (K)	Prominent absorption lines
O	Blue	25000–50000	Ionised helium (He^+), neutral helium (He), weak hydrogen (H) lines
B	Blue	11000–25000	Neutral helium, strong hydrogen lines
A	Blue-white	7500–11000	Strongest hydrogen Balmer lines, some ionised metals
F	White	6000–7500	Ionised metals
G	Yellow-white	5000–6000	Ionised and neutral metals (e.g. calcium, iron)
K	Orange	3500–5000	Neutral metals (e.g. iron, calcium, sodium)
M	Red	< 3500	Neutral atoms, strong molecular bands (e.g. titanium oxide, TiO)

Absorption lines

Stars emit light across a broad range of wavelengths, producing a continuous spectrum. However, when this light passes through the star's cooler outer layers, certain wavelengths are absorbed by elements in the star's atmosphere. These absorbed wavelengths appear as dark absorption lines in the spectrum.

The Balmer series refers to a set of hydrogen absorption lines seen in the visible spectrum. These occur when electrons in hydrogen atoms absorb energy and transition from the n = 2 energy level to higher energy levels.

The strength of Balmer lines varies with temperature because it depends on how many hydrogen atoms have electrons in the n = 2 state:

- Most hydrogen atoms are ionised in hot O stars (above 25 000 K), meaning they have lost their electrons. As a result, very few electrons are available to absorb light in the Balmer series, making hydrogen absorption lines weak.
- In cool K- and M-type stars, most hydrogen electrons remain in the n = 1 ground state. They require ultraviolet light (not visible light) to transition to higher levels so Balmer absorption lines are also weak.
- A-type stars have the strongest Balmer lines because many hydrogen atoms have electrons in the n = 2 state, allowing for maximum absorption of visible light.

Sketch of the Balmer absorption lines on the continuous spectrum of a class A star

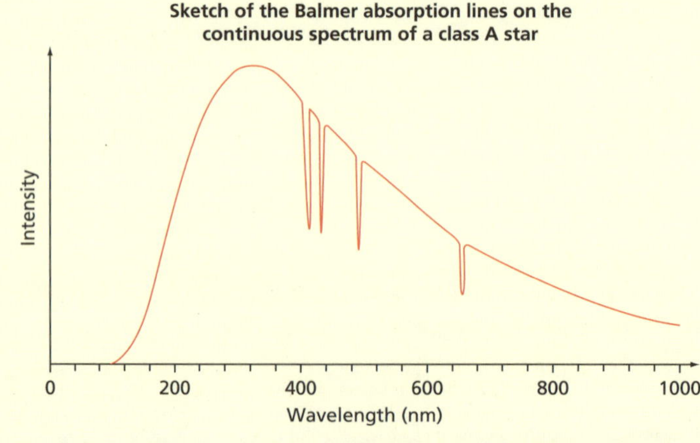

Summary

RETRIEVE

Stellar spectral classes

A-level only

(1) Two stars, X and Y, are observed. Their peak wavelengths are measured as 320 nm and 680 nm, respectively.

a) Calculate the surface temperature of each star. [3]

X = ..., Y = ...

b) Determine the spectral class of each star. [2]

c) Explain which of the two stars is likely to have the strongest hydrogen Balmer absorption lines. [2]

d) Describe how hydrogen Balmer absorption lines are formed in a star's spectrum. [3]

(2) Two stars, one in spectral class B and the other in class M, have the same apparent magnitude in the night sky.

a) State which of the stars will look blue in colour. [1]

b) The stars are similar in size to each other.

State and explain which star is likely to be further away. [3]

(3) The Sun is a star in spectral class G.

Describe the properties of a star in this spectral class. [4]

The Hertzsprung–Russell diagram

Key words

Key questions

What is the range of absolute magnitudes and temperatures on an HR diagram?

How does a Sun-like star evolve over time?

How does a protostar form?

The Hertzsprung–Russell (HR) diagram and its main regions

The HR diagram classifies stars based on their absolute magnitude and surface temperature (or spectral class). It can provide a visual representation of stellar evolution and how stars change over time.

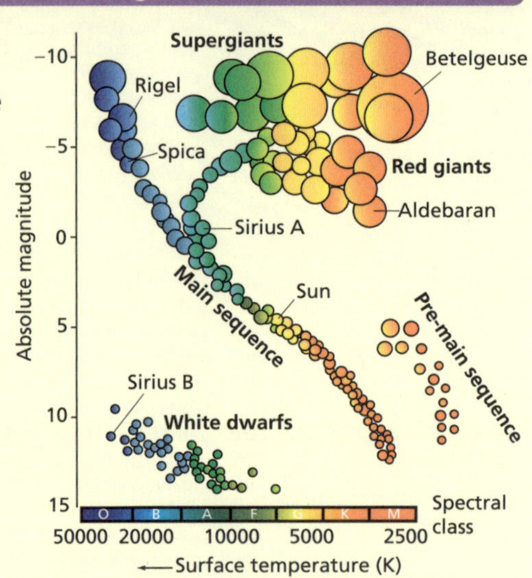

The HR diagram has:

- surface temperature (in K) or spectral class on the x-axis – temperature decreases from left to right (e.g. hot O-type stars on the left; cool M-type stars on the right).
- absolute magnitude on the y-axis – remember that the smaller or more negative the absolute magnitude, the brighter the star.

The **main regions** of the HR diagram are described in the table.

1. Main sequence	2. Giants and supergiants	3. White dwarfs
Stars spend most of their lifetime here, fusing hydrogen into helium. More massive stars are hotter, brighter and located towards the upper left of the HR diagram. The Sun is a main sequence star.	Stars that have left the main sequence expand and cool, becoming red giants or supergiants. Found above the main sequence, they typically have lower temperatures but higher luminosities.	The final stage for stars like the Sun. They are extremely hot, but small and faint, so they are located in the lower left part of the HR diagram. White dwarfs slowly cool over time.

Evolution of a Sun-like star

The evolution of a Sun-like star can be shown on an HR diagram (as shown) and consists of four stages:

1. Formation A protostar forms from a collapsing cloud of gas and dust (a nebula). It heats up until nuclear fusion of hydrogen begins.
2. Main sequence Once a star is on the main sequence, it remains stable for billions of years. The inwards gravitational forces are balanced by the outwards pressure from nuclear fusion.
3. Red giant phase When hydrogen in the core runs out, fusion stops and the core contracts. The helium core then heats up until fusion of helium begins. The outer layers expand and cool.
4. White dwarf Eventually the outer layers are shed, forming a planetary nebula. The core remains as a white dwarf, which cools over time and fades.

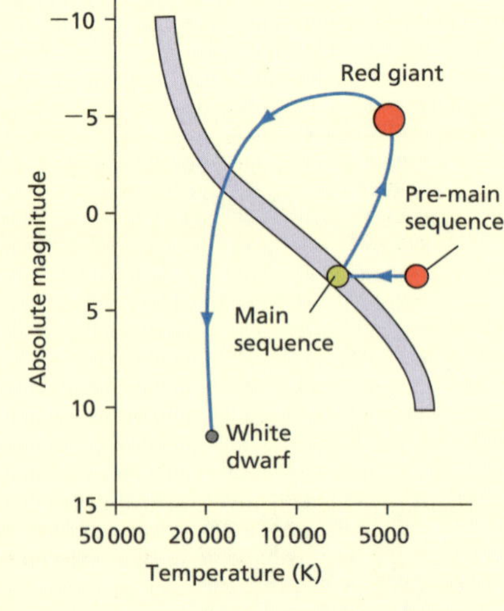

Summary

RETRIEVE

The Hertzsprung–Russell diagram

A-level only

1 a) Using the axes below, sketch a Hertzsprung–Russell diagram. Include values on the scales of each axis and label the position of main sequence, giant and white dwarf stars. [5]

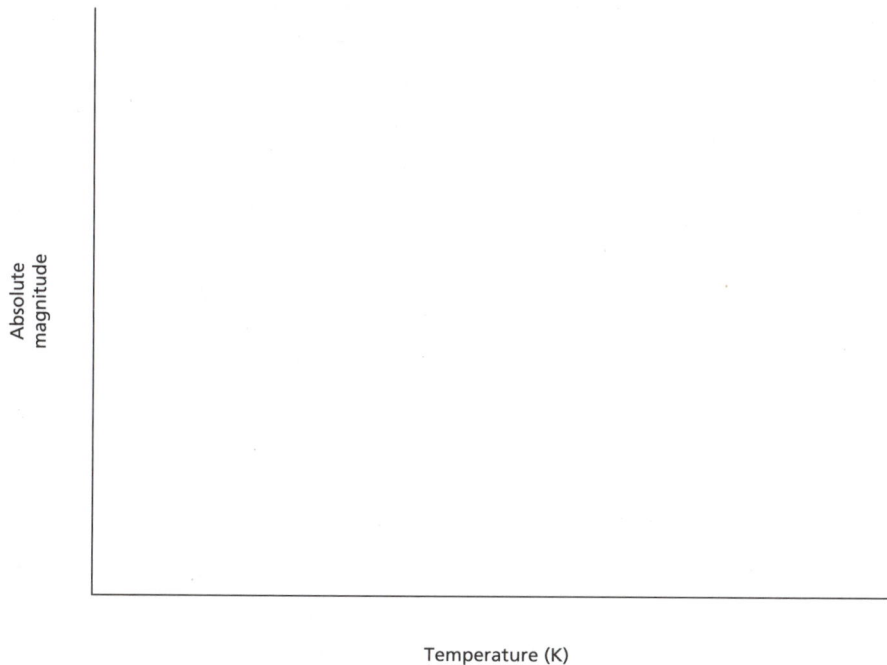

Absolute magnitude

Temperature (K)

b) Describe the evolution of a star similar to the Sun. [3]

2 The table provides data for three different stars.

Star	Absolute magnitude	Surface temperature (K)
Star A	−3.0	4500
Star B	+12.5	10 000
Star C	+4.5	6000

a) State and explain which star is a white dwarf. [2]

b) State and explain which star is a red giant. [2]

c) State and explain which star is a main sequence star. [2]

ORGANISE

Supernovae, neutron stars and black holes

A-level only

Key words

Key questions

How does a star between 1.4 and 3 solar masses evolve?

How does a star above 3 solar masses evolve?

Why are type 1a supernovae used as standard candles?

What is the defining property of a black hole?

Evolution of massive stars

Stars of greater than 1.4 solar masses evolve differently to stars of lower mass. Instead of forming white dwarfs, they go through an explosive end-of-life process:

- Stars of 1.4–3 solar masses expand into red giants, undergo a supernova explosion, and finally leave behind a neutron star.
- Stars > 3 solar masses become red supergiants, undergo a supernova, and collapse to form a black hole.

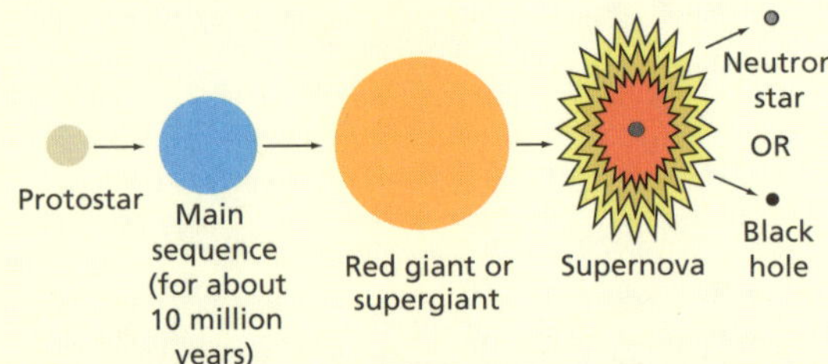

A supernova causes a rapid increase in absolute magnitude

The energy released by a supernova can outshine an entire galaxy and is roughly equal to the energy the Sun will release in its lifetime of 10 billion years. There are two main types of supernovae:

- **Type 1a supernovae** occur in binary systems (see page 148) where a white dwarf accumulates mass from its companion star. These have a consistent, peak absolute magnitude of –19.3, allowing them to be used as standard candles to measure distances.
- **Type II supernovae** occur when a single massive star collapses under its own gravity, triggering a violent explosion that leaves behind a neutron star or black hole.

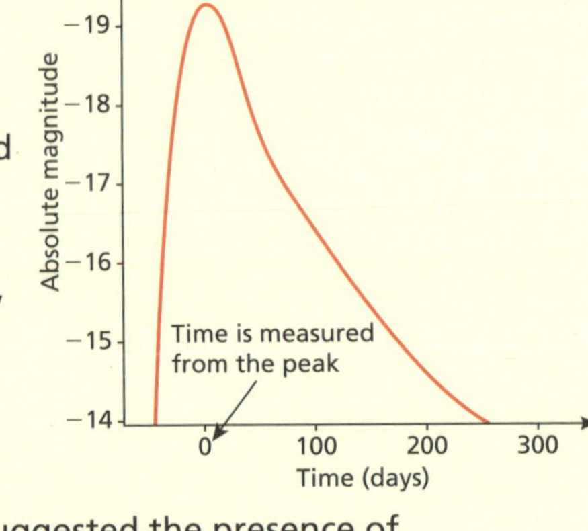

Observations of type 1a supernovae in distant galaxies led to the unexpected discovery that the Universe's expansion is accelerating. This suggested the presence of **dark energy**, an unknown force driving this acceleration.

Neutron stars and black holes

If the core left after a supernova is of 1.4 to 3 solar masses, it forms a **neutron star**. Neutron stars are incredibly dense objects around 20 km in diameter but with a mass greater than the Sun. Immense gravitational forces cause electrons and protons to form neutrons. The density of a neutron star is similar to that of a nucleus ($10^{17}\,kg\,m^{-3}$).

If the collapsing core of a supernova is greater than 3 solar masses, it forms a **black hole**. The defining property of a black hole is that its escape velocity exceeds the speed of light, meaning that nothing can escape from within its event horizon.

The Schwarzschild radius (R_s) gives the size of this event horizon: $R_s = \frac{2GM}{c^2}$
where G is the gravitational constant ($6.67 \times 10^{-11}\,Nm^2\,kg^{-2}$),
M is the black hole's mass and c is the speed of light ($3.0 \times 10^8\,m\,s^{-1}$).

Supermassive black holes exist at the centres of galaxies and can be millions to billions of solar masses.

Gamma-ray bursts (GRB)

GRB are extremely energetic explosions, often linked to the collapse of supergiant stars. They can also result from the merger of two neutron stars. A typical GRB releases more energy in seconds than the Sun will emit in its entire lifetime.

Summary

RETRIEVE

Supernovae, neutron stars and black holes

A-level only

1. Astronomers observe a type 1a supernova in a distant galaxy and use it to estimate the galaxy's distance from Earth.

   a) Explain why a type 1a supernova is suitable for use as standard candles. [1]

   b) The type 1a supernova has an absolute magnitude of −19.3 and an apparent magnitude of +10.0
   Calculate the distance to the supernova. [3]

   c) Describe why type 1a supernovae observations provide evidence for dark energy. [2]

   d) Sketch a graph showing the change in absolute magnitude over time for a type 1a supernova. [2]

2. A massive star with an initial mass of 30 solar masses evolves over time, eventually forming a black hole.

   a) Describe the evolution of this star from its formation to the point where it becomes a black hole. [3]

   b) Explain what is meant by the Schwarzschild radius. [1]

   c) The black hole that forms has a mass of 10 solar masses.
   Calculate its Schwarzschild radius. One solar mass is equal to 2.0×10^{30} kg. [2]

ORGANISE

The Doppler effect and Hubble's law

A-level only

Key words

Key questions

What is the Doppler effect?

In what two ways can scientists detect a binary star system?

What is Hubble's law in words?

What are three pieces of evidence for the Big Bang?

The Doppler effect

The Doppler effect occurs when a wave source moves relative to an observer, causing a shift in the observed wavelength and frequency. For $v << c$, the fractional change in frequency and wavelength is given by: $\frac{\Delta f}{f} = \frac{v}{c}$ $z = \frac{\Delta\lambda}{\lambda} = -\frac{v}{c}$

where Δf is the change in observed frequency; f is the emitted frequency; $\Delta\lambda$ is the change in observed wavelength; λ is the emitted wavelength; v is the relative velocity of the source (negative for recession, positive for approach); c is the speed of light; and z is the red-shift.

If $z > 0$, the object is red-shifted. If $z < 0$, the object is blue-shifted.

Binary star systems consist of two stars orbiting around their common centre of mass

If a binary star system is viewed head-on, one star moves towards us (is blue-shifted) while the other moves away (is red-shifted). Over time, the spectral lines of the stars oscillate between red-shift and blue-shift.

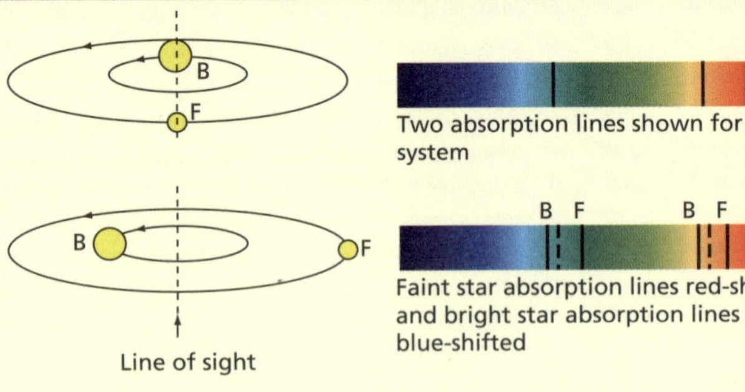

Two absorption lines shown for whole system

Faint star absorption lines red-shifted and bright star absorption lines blue-shifted

If one star passes in front of the other, there is a dip in the observed intensity. When the cooler star passes in front of the hotter star, there is a deeper dip in intensity.

Hubble's law and the Big Bang

Hubble discovered a relationship between the recessional velocity of galaxies and their distance from Earth: $v = H_0 d$

where v is the recessional velocity of the galaxy (in km s^{-1}), H_0 is the Hubble constant (approximately equal to 70 km s^{-1} Mpc^{-1}) and d is the distance to the galaxy (in Mpc).

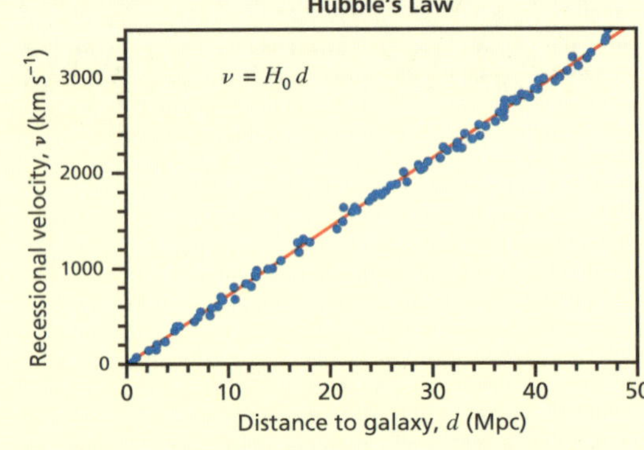

The age of the Universe can be estimated as: $t = \frac{1}{H_0}$

Using $H_0 = 70$ km s^{-1} Mpc^{-1}, this gives an approximate age of 14 billion years. Hubble's law supports the **Big Bang Theory**, which suggests that the Universe began from an extremely hot and dense singularity and has been expanding ever since.

Other evidence for the Big Bang includes cosmic microwave background radiation and the relative abundance of hydrogen and helium. The early Universe was filled with high energy gamma rays. As the Universe expanded, the wavelengths stretched due to red-shift, lowering their energy. Today, this radiation is observed as microwaves with a uniform temperature of 2.7 K, detected in all directions.

In the early Universe, hydrogen and helium were the first elements to be made. High initial temperatures caused hydrogen to fuse into helium. There is an observed 3 : 1 ratio of hydrogen to helium. If the Universe had expanded more slowly, there would be a higher fraction of helium.

Summary

RETRIEVE

The Doppler effect and Hubble's law

(1) A galaxy produces an absorption line at a wavelength of 600 nm, but it is observed at 618 nm on Earth.

a) Show that the red-shift z of the galaxy is 0.03 [2]

b) Calculate the velocity of the galaxy relative to Earth. [2]

c) Assuming that the Hubble constant is 70 km s^{-1} Mpc^{-1}, calculate the galaxy's distance from Earth in megaparsecs. [2]

d) Explain why red-shift measurements of galaxies provide evidence for the Big Bang. [2]

e) State **two** other pieces of evidence for the Big Bang. [2]

(2) In 2024, the James Webb Space Telescope measured the Hubble constant to be 72.6 km s^{-1} Mpc^{-1}.

a) Using this value of the Hubble constant, calculate the age of the Universe in years. [4]

b) The James Webb Space Telescope has also detected binary star systems.

Describe **two** ways in which a binary star system can be detected. [4]

ORGANISE

Quasars and exoplanets

A-level only

Key words

Key questions

How is a quasar formed?

Why can't exoplanets be detected directly?

What is the radial velocity method of detecting exoplanets?

What is the transit method of detecting exoplanet?

Quasars

The term 'quasar' originally stood for 'quasi-stellar radio source' because they were initially detected as star-like objects that emitted unusually strong radio waves. Later, optical spectra revealed that quasars had extremely large red-shifts. This meant that they were very distant and moving away at high speeds.

Quasars are now understood to be formed by an active galactic nucleus. Quasars form when gas and dust fall into a supermassive black hole. As material falls into the black hole, enormous amounts of electromagnetic radiation is emitted across the spectrum.

Quasars are very bright due to their large power output. Due to this, quasars are among the most distant measurable objects in the Universe.

Detection of exoplanets

An exoplanet is a planet that orbits a star other than the Sun. Exoplanets are difficult to detect directly because:

- they are much dimmer than their parent stars
- they are small and distant, making them hard to resolve with telescopes.

Instead of direct observation, astronomers use indirect methods to detect exoplanets. One of these methods is known as the **radial velocity method**.

A star and its planet orbit their common centre of mass. This causes a star to 'wobble' over time. If this causes the star to move more towards Earth then its spectra will be blue-shifted. If the star's motion is away from Earth then its spectra will be red-shifted.

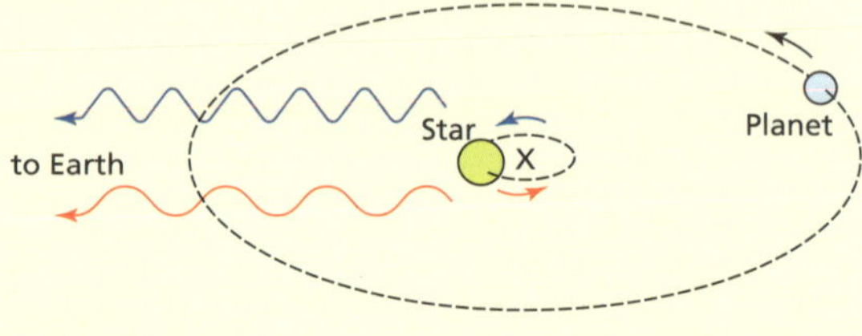

The amplitude of the shifts provides information about the exoplanet's mass and orbital period. This method is most effective for massive planets orbiting close to their stars. A small star will only slightly change the orbital motion of a much larger star and so will be much harder to detect.

A second method to detect exoplanets is known as the **transit method**. If an exoplanet's orbit is aligned such that it passes in front of its star (relative to Earth), it causes a temporary dip in brightness. The depth of the dip reveals the size of the exoplanet, while the time between transits gives the orbital period.

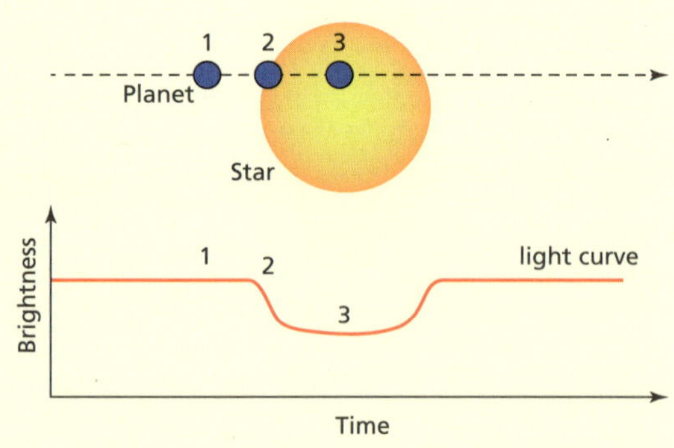

As this method relies on the planet passing in front of the star, it works best for planets with short orbital periods.

Summary

Quasars and exoplanets

1. The detection of exoplanets is a major challenge for astronomers. Despite this, thousands of exoplanets have been discovered using indirect detection methods.

   a) Explain why it is difficult to directly observe exoplanets. [2]

   b) State **two** indirect detection methods of exoplanets and explain how they work. [6]

   c) Describe the challenges of using indirect detection methods in discovering an Earth-sized exoplanet. [3]

2. A quasar is observed with an apparent magnitude of +9.0 and a red-shift value of 0.11

   a) State how a quasar forms. [1]

   b) Calculate the distance to the quasar in megaparsecs. Assume the Hubble constant is equal to 70 km $s^{-1}Mpc^{-1}$. [2]

   c) Calculate the absolute magnitude of the quasar. [3]

   d) The Sun has an absolute magnitude of +4.8

   Calculate how many times brighter the quasar is compared to the Sun. [2]

Required practical 1: Stationary waves

Aim

To investigate the variation of the frequency of stationary waves on a string with length, tension and mass per unit length of the string

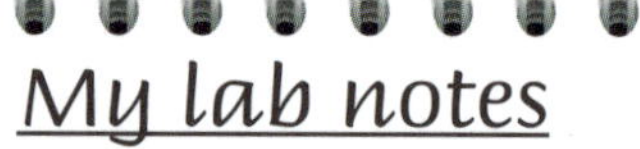

My lab notes

Example method

1. Set the length of string to be 1.000 m from the vibration generator to the movable bridge. Provide tension by adding 100 g of mass to the end of the string.
2. There is a node at each end of the string. Increase the frequency f of the signal generator until there is resonance (a maximum amplitude) at the antinode in the centre of the string. This is the first harmonic. Record this frequency.

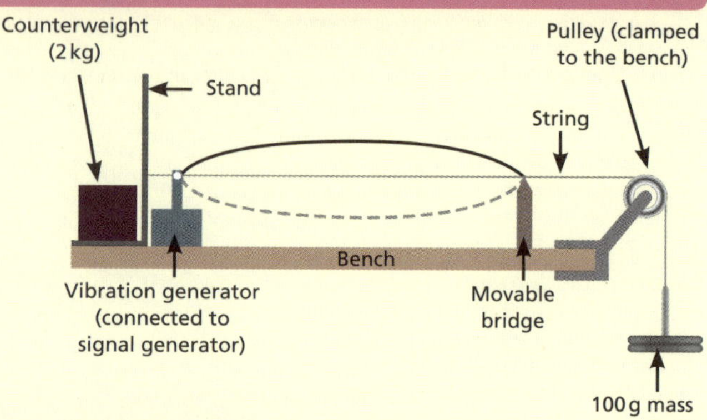

Independent variable	Length of string
Dependent variable	Frequency of the first harmonic
Control variables	Same string (so the mass per unit length is constant)
	Same tension in the string

3. Repeat this procedure for string lengths of 0.900 m, 0.800 m, 0.700 m, 0.600 m and 0.500 m. Record the frequency of the first harmonic for each length.
4. Repeat the experiment three times and calculate a mean frequency for each length.

Analysis

Plot a graph of mean $\frac{1}{f}$ against the length of string, l. The first harmonic has half a whole wavelength on the length of string, therefore $\lambda = 2l$. When combined with the wave speed equation ($c = f\lambda$), and rearranged, you obtain $\frac{1}{f} = \frac{2}{c}l$, so plotting $\frac{1}{f}$ against l gives a straight line with gradient $\frac{2}{c}$. The wave speed c can therefore be calculated from $\frac{2}{\text{gradient}}$

The percentage uncertainty in the wave speed is equal to the percentage uncertainty in the gradient:

$$\%\ \text{uncertainty} = \frac{|\text{best gradient} - \text{worst gradient}|}{\text{best gradient}} \times 100$$

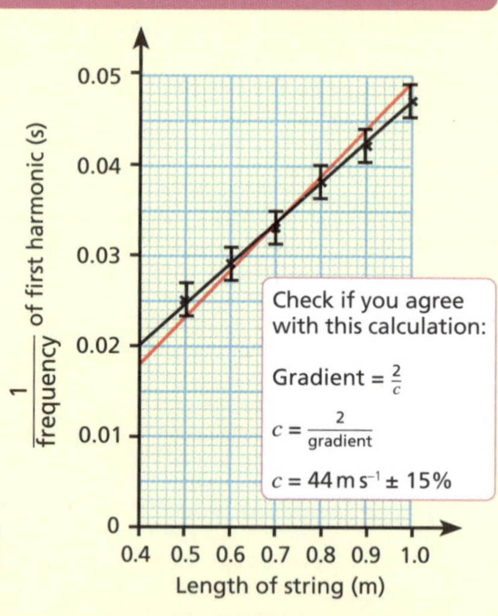

Sources of uncertainty

- The frequency of the signal generator might not match what it is set to.
- Misjudgement of when the resonance has been reached.

Improvements to the practical

- The frequency of the signal generator can be verified by measuring the time period using an oscilloscope. The frequency would be equal to $\frac{1}{\text{time period}}$
- While performing this practical, the frequency should be carefully and slowly adjusted to see when the amplitude of the first harmonic's antinode is largest.

Alternative methods

This experiment could be repeated by varying the tension T applied to the string or the mass per unit length μ of the string.

Varying these factors could allow you to verify the equation $f = \frac{1}{2l}\sqrt{\frac{T}{\mu}}$

Required practical 2: Interference

Aim

To measure the wavelength of light using Young's double-slit experiment and a diffraction grating

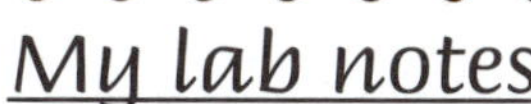

My lab notes

Method 1: Double slit

1. In a partially darkened room, position a laser so that it illuminates a double slit of known slit spacing. Ensure that the double slit is perpendicular to the laser beam.

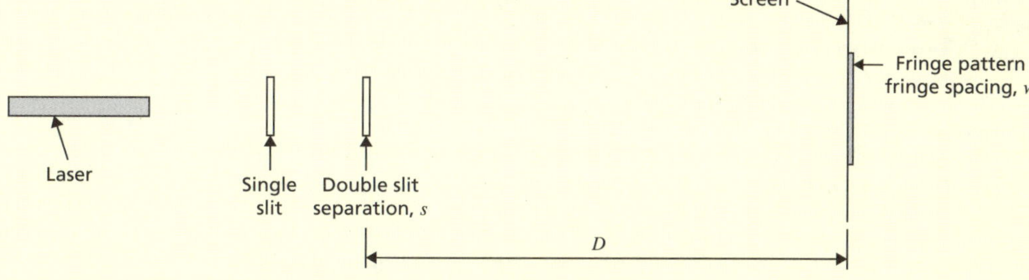

2. Place a white screen at a distance D (initially around 1 m) from the double slit.
3. Using vernier callipers, measure the fringe spacing w by taking measurements across multiple fringes. To reduce the percentage uncertainty, measure the distance across several fringes and divide by the number of fringes.
4. Repeat this procedure for distances of 0.900 m, 0.800 m, 0.700 m, 0.600 m and 0.500 m to the screen. Record the fringe spacing for each distance.
5. Repeat the experiment three times and calculate a mean fringe spacing for each length.

Independent variable	The distance from the double slit to the screen, D
Dependent variable	Fringe spacing, w
Control variables	Laser wavelength
	Slit separation

Analysis

Plot a graph of fringe spacing w against distance to the screen D. The gradient of this graph is equal to $\frac{\lambda}{s}$. Therefore, the wavelength can be determined from gradient × s.

The percentage uncertainty in the wavelength is equal to the percentage uncertainty in the gradient added to the percentage uncertainty in the slit spacing. This is due to the rules for combining uncertainties.

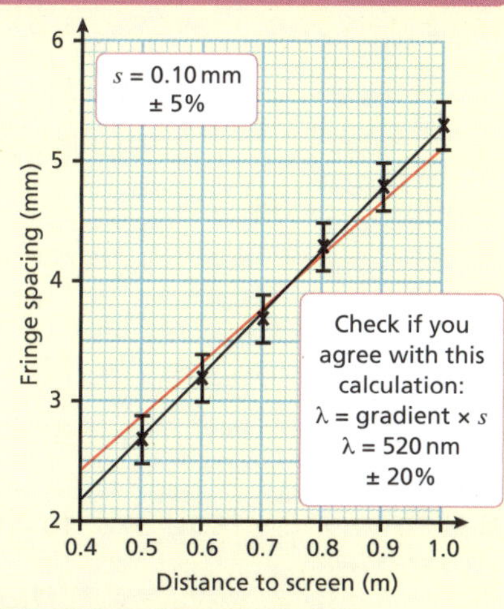

Rule	Measured value calculation	Uncertainty calculation
Multiplication rule	If $a = bc$	$\varepsilon a = \varepsilon b + \varepsilon c$

Method 2: Diffraction grating

1. Replace the double slit with a diffraction grating, with slit spacing d.
2. Position the grating so that it is perpendicular to the laser beam.
3. Observe the diffraction pattern formed on the screen. Identify the orders of diffraction.
4. Measure the angles θ of the first and second order diffraction maxima using a metre rule to measure the distance to the screen and the displacement from the central maxima. Use trigonometry to calculate θ.
5. Use the diffraction equation $d\sin\theta = n\lambda$ to determine the wavelength of the laser.
6. Repeat for multiple orders and calculate an average wavelength.

Required practical 3: Measuring g by free-fall

Aim

To measure the acceleration due to gravity by using a free-fall method

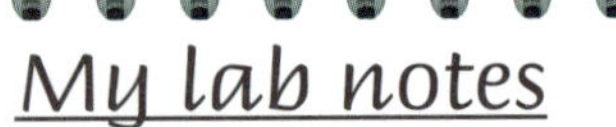

My lab notes

Example method

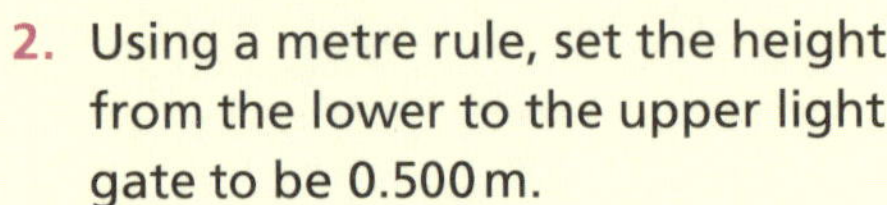

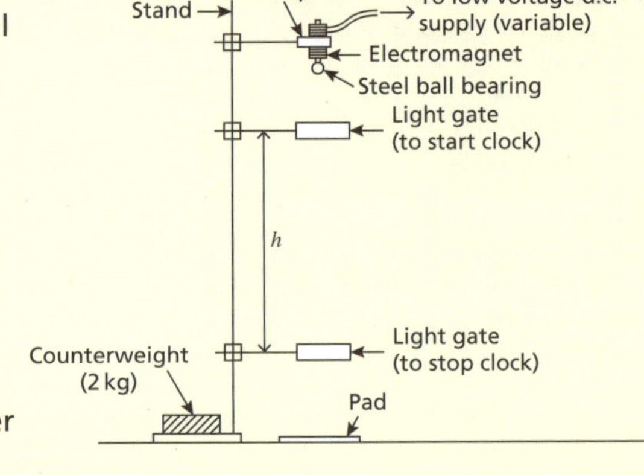

1. Attach an electromagnet to a stand, ensuring it holds a steel ball bearing directly above two vertically-aligned light gates. Secure the stand with a 2 kg counterweight or a G-clamp.
2. Using a metre rule, set the height from the lower to the upper light gate to be 0.500 m.
3. Switch off the electromagnet to release the ball bearing. The upper light gate starts a timer when the ball passes through and the lower gate stops it when the ball reaches it.
4. Take multiple readings of the time t for the ball to fall between different heights. Decrease the height h in 0.050 m intervals by moving the lower gate upwards.
5. Repeat the experiment three times and calculate a mean time for each distance.

Independent variable	The distance between the two light gates, h
Dependent variable	The time taken for the ball to fall between the two light gates, t
Control variables	Use the same ball to ensure constant mass and shape
	Keep the same release mechanism to ensure minimal variation in initial velocity

Analysis

The equation of motion $s = ut + \frac{1}{2}at^2$ can be used to analyse the results. For this experiment, $s = h$ and $a = g$.

Therefore $h = ut + \frac{1}{2}gt^2$

Rearranging this gives $\frac{2h}{t} = gt + 2u$

Therefore, if a graph of $\frac{2h}{t}$ against t is plotted, the gradient will be equal to g (the acceleration due to gravity).

The percentage uncertainty in the acceleration due to gravity is equal to the percentage uncertainty in the gradient:

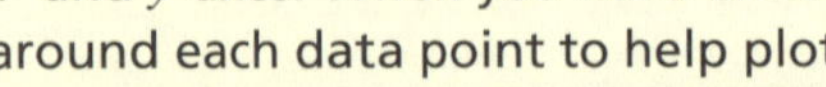

$$\% \text{ uncertainty} = \frac{|\text{best gradient} - \text{worst gradient}|}{\text{best gradient}} \times 100$$

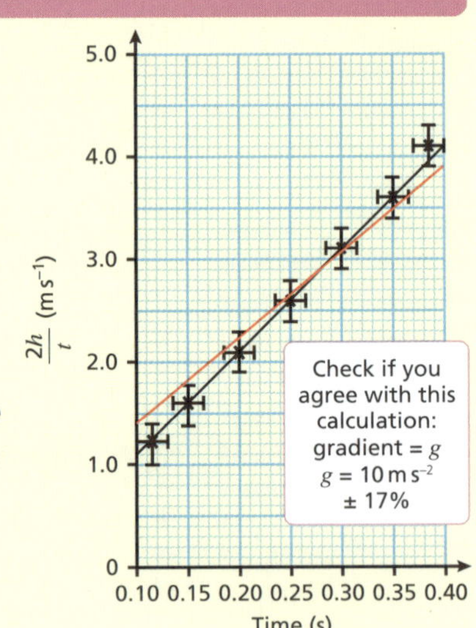

Note how the graph has error bars on both the x- and y-axes. When you have error bars on both axes, try to imagine a 'box' around each data point to help plot the line of worst acceptable fit.

Sources of uncertainty

- If the distance of falling is too great, air resistance will decrease the acceleration that the ball bearing experiences.
- Not ensuring the metre rule is vertical when measuring the distance between the light gates.

Alternative methods

This practical can be done without gates, with timing done with a stopwatch. However, doing the practical in this way will introduce large uncertainties due to human reaction time.

Required practical 4: Measuring the Young modulus

Aim

To measure the Young modulus of a material by measuring the extension of a wire under different loads

Example method

1. Suspend two wires (a test wire and a comparison wire of the same material and length) vertically from a rigid support.
2. Attach a metre rule to the comparison wire and a vernier scale to the test wire to measure extension. Add a small initial load to both wires to remove any slack.
3. Measure the original length of the test wire L using the metre rule.
4. Measure the diameter of the test wire in at least three different places using a micrometer screw gauge. Calculate the mean diameter and determine the cross-sectional area, $A = \frac{\pi d^2}{4}$
5. Add mass to the test wire and record the new position on the vernier scale.
6. Calculate the extension by subtracting the initial scale reading from the new scale reading.
7. Repeat the process, increasing the load in equal increments up to a suitable maximum mass.
8. Unload the wire step by step, taking extension readings during unloading to ensure that plastic deformation has not taken place.

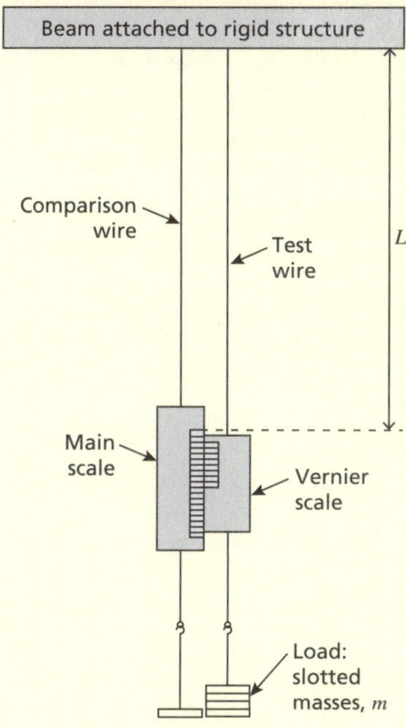

Independent variable	Force applied to the wire. This is the load (weight) added.
Dependent variable	Extension of the wire
Control variables	Same material, initial length and diameter of wire
	Same temperature to avoid thermal expansion

Analysis

Plot a graph of applied force ($F = mg$) against extension ΔL.

The Young modulus E is given by:

$$E = \frac{\text{tensile stress}}{\text{tensile strain}} = \frac{\frac{F}{A}}{\frac{\Delta L}{L}} = \frac{FL}{\Delta L A}$$

The Young modulus can therefore be calculated by:

$$E = \frac{L}{A} \times \text{gradient}$$

$L = 1.800$ m
$d = 0.27$ mm

Applied force (N)

Extension (mm)

Check if you agree with this calculation:
$E = \frac{L}{A} \times$ gradient
$E = 116$ GPa

Sources of uncertainty

- If the elastic limit is exceeded, the force versus extension graph will not be linear.
- Parallax error when reading the vernier scale.
- The wire should be free of kinks before starting the experiment.

Safety considerations

- If too much load is added, the wire may snap suddenly, so use safety goggles.
- Keep a padded surface below the masses, in case the wire fails and the masses fall.

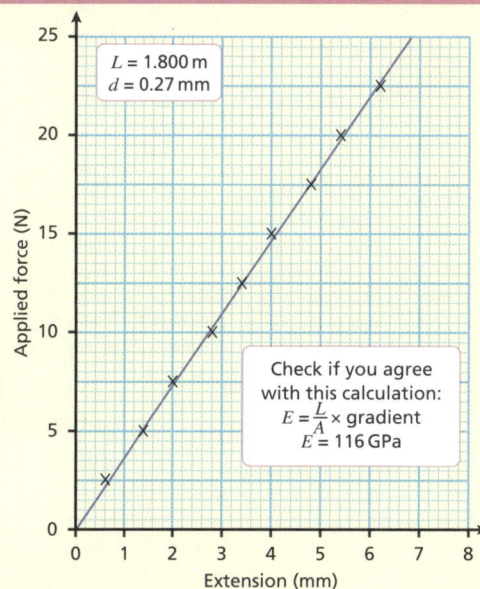

Required practical 5: Measuring the resistivity of a wire

Aim

To measure the resistivity of a wire by measuring its resistance, length and cross-sectional area

My lab notes

Example method

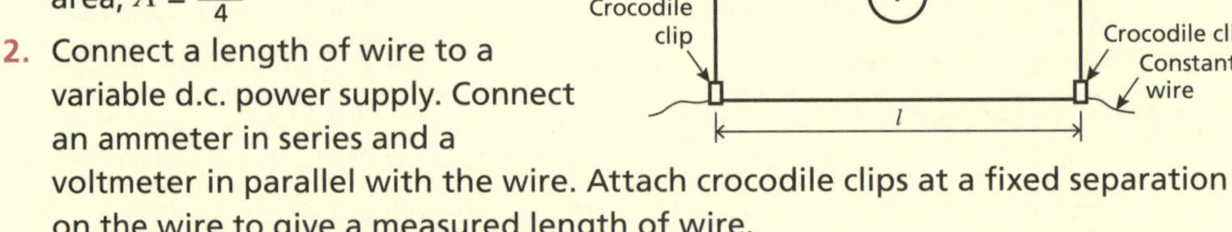

1. Measure the diameter of the wire in at least three different places using a micrometer screw gauge. Calculate the mean diameter and determine the cross-sectional area, $A = \frac{\pi d^2}{4}$
2. Connect a length of wire to a variable d.c. power supply. Connect an ammeter in series and a voltmeter in parallel with the wire. Attach crocodile clips at a fixed separation on the wire to give a measured length of wire.
3. Starting with a wire length of $l = 0.100\,\text{m}$, apply a small potential difference (e.g. 1.0 V) and record the current (I) and the potential difference (V) across the wire.
4. Calculate the resistance using $R = \frac{V}{I}$
5. Repeat for increasing wire lengths (e.g. 0.200 m, 0.300 m, etc.), ensuring that the wire does not heat up significantly.
6. Repeat the experiment three times and calculate a mean resistance for each length of wire.

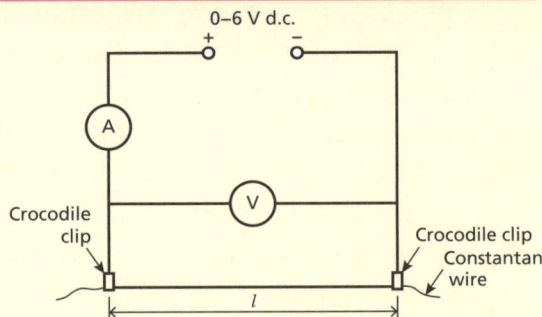

Independent variable	Length of wire
Dependent variable	Resistance of wire (calculated by measuring the potential difference across the wire and the current flowing through the wire)
Control variables	Wire material and diameter
	Temperature (kept constant by using small currents and switching the circuit off in-between readings)

Analysis

Plot a graph of the resistance R against the length of wire l.

The resistivity is given by: $\rho = \frac{RA}{l}$

The gradient of the graph is $\frac{R}{l} = \frac{\rho}{A}$, so the resistivity ρ = gradient × A

The percentage uncertainty in the resistivity is equal to the percentage uncertainty in the gradient added to the percentage uncertainty in the cross-sectional area of the wire.

The percentage uncertainty in the cross-sectional area of the wire is equal to twice the percentage uncertainty in the diameter of the wire. This is due to the rules for combining uncertainties.

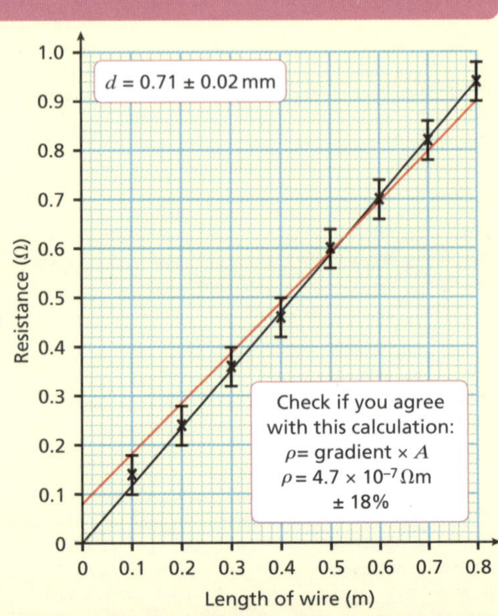

Rule	Measured value calculation	Uncertainty calculation
Multiplication rule	If $a = bc$	$\varepsilon a = \varepsilon b + \varepsilon c$
Power rule	If $a = b^c$	$\varepsilon a = c \times \varepsilon b$

Improvements to the practical

Use a jockey instead of crocodile clips as it makes a finer contact point with the wire (therefore improving the resolution of the measurement of the length of wire).

Safety considerations

If the current becomes too high, the wire will heat up. This will not only increase the measured resistivity but will also become a burn hazard.

Required practical 6: Measuring the emf and internal resistance of a cell

Aim

To investigate the electromotive force (emf) and internal resistance of an electric cell by measuring how the terminal potential difference of the cell varies with the current in the circuit

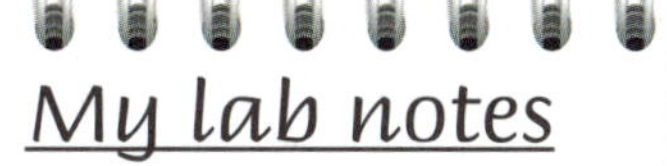

My lab notes

Example method

1. Set up the circuit with a cell, a variable resistor, an ammeter in series and a voltmeter in parallel across the cell.
2. With the switch open, record the reading on the voltmeter. This gives the emf of the cell (ε).
3. Close the switch and adjust the variable resistor to obtain pairs of readings of V and I over a wide range of values.
4. Open the switch between readings to prevent unnecessary discharge of the cell and heating of the circuit.
5. Repeat each measurement three times and take an average to reduce the effect of random errors.

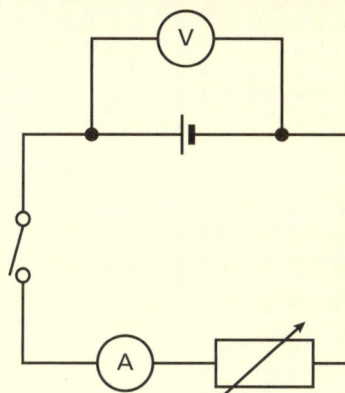

Independent variable	Current in the cell (I)
Dependent variable	Terminal potential difference across the cell (V)
Control variables	Use of the same cell/battery throughout

Analysis

The emf and internal resistance of the cell are related by: $\varepsilon = V + Ir$

Plot a graph of V against I. As $V = -rI + \varepsilon$, the y-intercept gives the emf (ε) of the cell and the gradient gives $-r$.

The internal resistance of the cell can therefore be found by: $r = -\text{gradient}$

The percentage uncertainty in the internal resistance is therefore equal to the percentage uncertainty in the gradient:

$$\%\ \text{uncertainty} = \frac{|\text{best gradient} - \text{worst gradient}|}{\text{best gradient}} \times 100$$

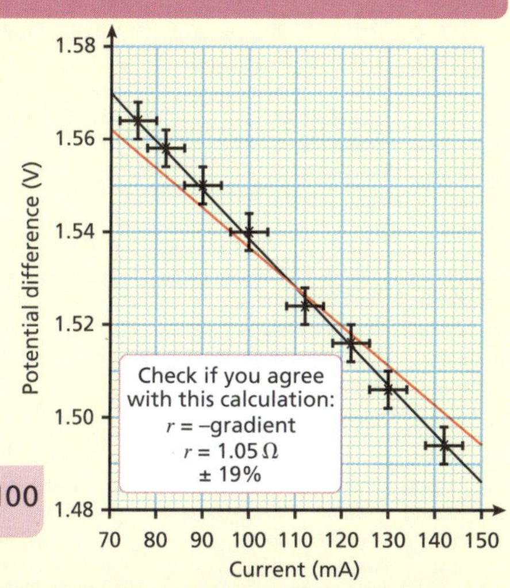

Sources of uncertainty

- If readings are not taken quickly, the battery could discharge during the experiment.
- If the temperature of the cell increases, this will increase the internal resistance and other resistances in the circuit.

Improvements to the practical

- A fresh cell can be used to ensure that the emf does not decrease over time.
- The circuit should only be closed for short periods of time, to ensure that the temperature of the circuit does not increase.

Safety considerations

If the current becomes too high, the cell and components in the circuit will heat up. This could become a burn hazard.

Required practical 7: Simple harmonic motion

A-level only

Aim

To investigate the simple harmonic motion of a mass-spring system and a simple pendulum by measuring the time period and exploring its dependence on mass (for the mass-spring system) and length (for the pendulum)

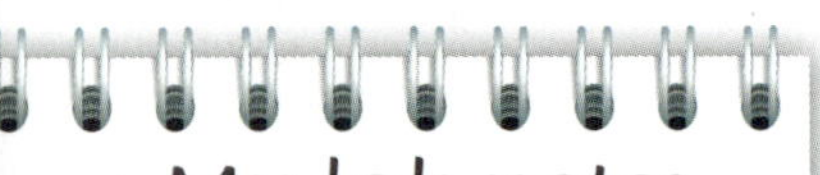

Example method (mass-spring system)

1. Attach a spring vertically from a clamp stand and hang a 100 g mass hanger from the spring.
2. Use a pin and Blu Tack® as a fiducial marker placed at the equilibrium position of the mass.

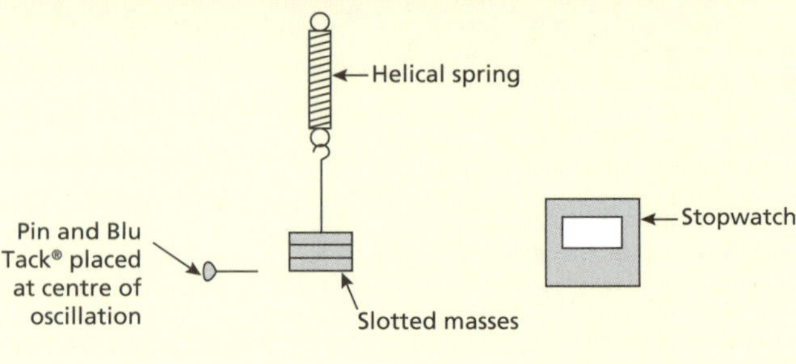

3. Displace the mass slightly downwards and release it so that it oscillates vertically with a small amplitude.
4. Use a stopwatch to measure the time for 10 complete oscillations and record the time.
5. Repeat this measurement three times and calculate the mean time period for 10 oscillations and the time period for a single oscillation by dividing by 10.
6. Add an additional 100 g mass to the mass hanger and repeat the measurements.
7. Repeat for a range of different masses.

Independent variable	Mass m attached to the spring
Dependent variable	Time period T of the oscillations
Control variables	Amplitude of oscillations (kept small)

Analysis

The time period T of a mass-spring system undergoing simple harmonic motion is given by:

$$T = 2\pi\sqrt{\frac{m}{k}}$$

where k is the spring constant of the spring.

Plotting T^2 against m will give a straight-line graph with a gradient of $\frac{4\pi^2}{k}$

Therefore, k can be calculated from $k = \frac{4\pi^2}{\text{gradient}}$ and the percentage uncertainty in k will be equal to the percentage uncertainty in the gradient.

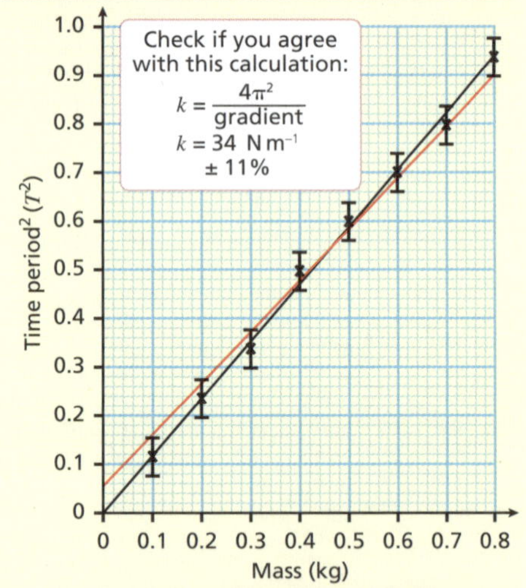

Sources of uncertainty

- Reaction time when using a stopwatch.
- Difficulty of judging the exact moment to start and stop timing. This is why a fiducial marker is used, with timing starting and stopping when the equilibrium position is reached.

Improvements to the practical

- Use of light gates instead of a stopwatch for more accurate timing.
- Use of a data logger and motion sensor to measure oscillation periods.

Example method (simple pendulum)

A similar practical can be performed with a simple pendulum. The time taken for 10 oscillations can be measured and the experiment repeated for different lengths of string. As the time period of a simple pendulum is given by $T = 2\pi\sqrt{\frac{l}{g}}$, plotting T^2 against l will give a straight-line graph with a gradient of $\frac{4\pi^2}{g}$

Required practical 8: Investigation of Boyle's law and Charles's law

A-level only

Aim

To investigate Boyle's law (the relationship between pressure and volume for a fixed mass of gas at constant temperature) and Charles's law (the relationship between volume and temperature for a fixed mass of gas at constant pressure)

Example methods

Boyle's law

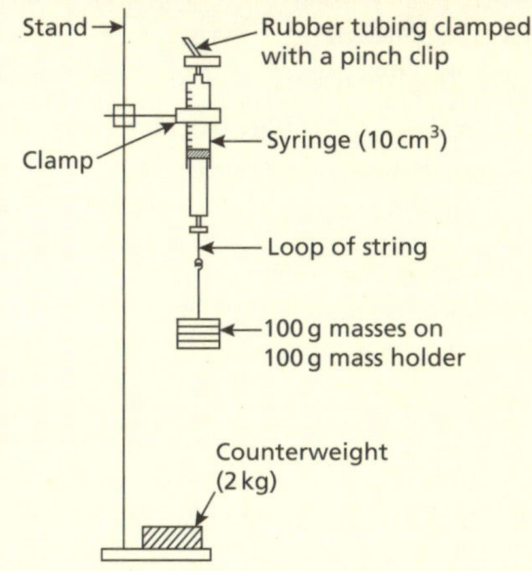

1. Remove the plunger from a 10 cm^3 syringe and measure the diameter of the rubber seal using a micrometer screw gauge.
2. Reinsert the plunger and draw 4.0 cm^3 of air into the syringe.
3. Attach a rubber tube to the nozzle of the syringe, then fold and clamp it securely to create an airtight seal.
4. Secure the syringe vertically in a clamp stand and suspend a 100 g mass hanger to the plunger of the syringe with string.
5. Measure and record the new volume of trapped air.
6. Increase the mass in 100 g increments, recording the volume at each stage.

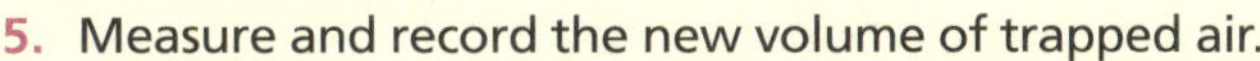

Charles's law

1. Use a glass capillary tube sealed at one end. A drop of coloured concentrated sulfuric acid acts as an indicator of air volume.
2. Secure the capillary tube vertically next to a 30 cm ruler using elastic bands.
3. Immerse the lower end of the tube into a beaker of water, initially at around 90°C.
4. Stir the water continuously to ensure uniform temperature and record the length of the trapped air column.
5. Allow the water to cool in 5°C intervals, stirring before each reading.
6. Record the new air column length and temperature for each interval until the water reaches room temperature.

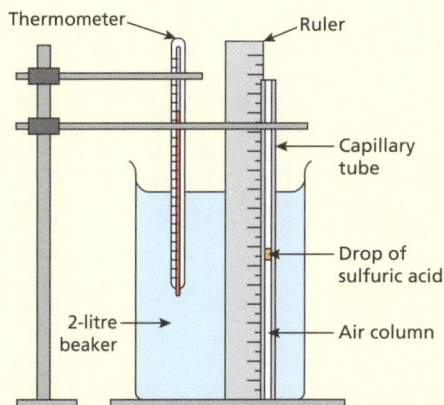

Thermometer
Ruler
Capillary tube
Drop of sulfuric acid
2-litre beaker
Air column

	Boyle's law	Charles's law
Independent variable	Applied force	Temperature
Dependent variable	Volume of air	Length of air column
Control variables	Temperature	Constant pressure

Analysis

Boyle's law

Calculate pressure using: $P = P_{atm} - \frac{mg}{A}$

where P_{atm} is the atmospheric pressure (101 kPa), m is the applied mass, $g = 9.81\ \text{N kg}^{-1}$ and A is the cross-sectional area of the plunger, $A = \frac{\pi d^2}{4}$

Plot a graph of $\frac{1}{V}$ (y-axis) against pressure (x-axis). It should result in a straight line through the origin (verifying $P \propto \frac{1}{V}$).

Charles's law

Plot a graph of length (which is proportional to volume as the cross-sectional area is constant) against temperature. The extrapolated x-intercept gives an estimate of absolute zero (= −273°C).

Improvements to the practical

Data loggers could be used to measure the pressure and temperature. For the Boyle's law practical, a sealed container with a varying volume could be used.

Required practical 9: Capacitor charge and discharge

A-level only

Aim

To investigate the charge and discharge of a capacitor in an electrical circuit and to determine the time constant by analysing the exponential behaviour of potential difference over time

Example method (capacitor discharging)

1. Set up the circuit with a capacitor, resistor, voltmeter and two-position switch.
2. Charge the capacitor by putting the switch in position A so that it is connected across the cell/power supply.

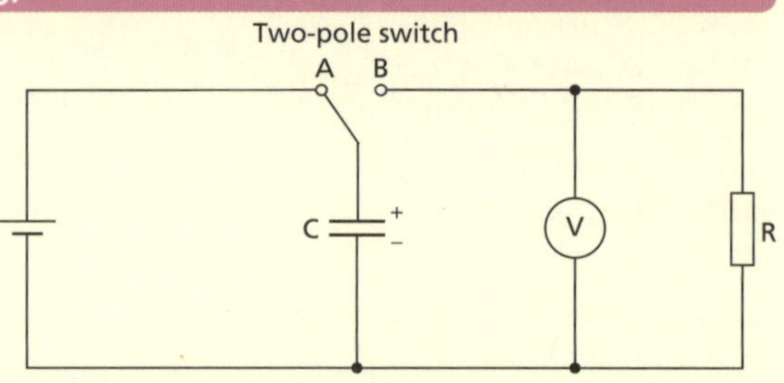

3. Record the potential difference across the capacitor at time $t = 0$.
4. Discharge the capacitor by moving the switch to position B, allowing it to discharge through a known resistance.
5. Continue recording readings at fixed time intervals (e.g. every 10 seconds) until the capacitor is almost fully discharged.

Independent variable	Time (t)
Dependent variable	Potential difference across the capacitor (V)
Control variables	Capacitance (C), resistance (R) and initial potential difference across the capacitor

Analysis

The potential difference across a discharging capacitance follows this equation: $V = V_0 e^{-\frac{t}{RC}}$

Plotting a graph of $\ln(V)$ (on the y-axis) against time (on the x-axis) will give a straight line of gradient $-\frac{1}{RC}$

Therefore, the time constant can be calculated from: $\tau = RC = -\frac{1}{\text{gradient}}$

Therefore, the percentage uncertainty in the time constant τ will be equal to the percentage uncertainty in the gradient.

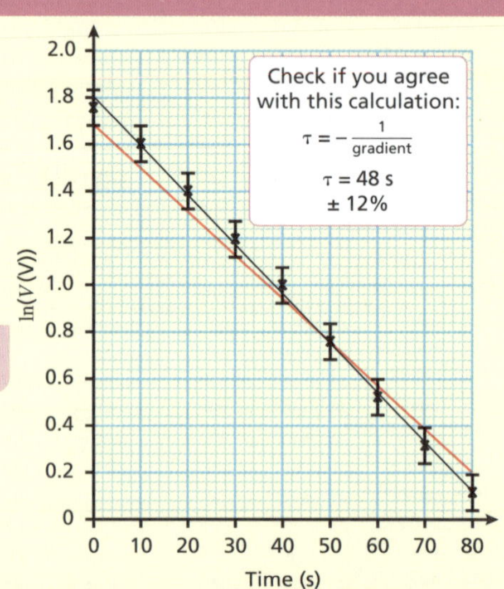

Improvements to the practical

It is difficult to monitor the stopwatch and the voltmeter at the same time, therefore using a data logger to automatically record the potential difference would be preferable. If data loggers aren't available, a video of the voltmeter and stopwatch next to each other can be recorded. Watching the video back allows for it to be paused, to more easily record the potential difference and time simultaneously.

Example method (capacitor charging)

A similar practical can be undertaken for capacitor charge. Connect a power source, a resistor and a capacitor in series (and a voltmeter in parallel across the capacitor). A graph of V against t shows an exponential increase in voltage as $V = V_0\left(1 - e^{-\frac{t}{RC}}\right)$.

The current can also be measured for capacitor charging or discharging.

Required practical 10: Force on a current-carrying wire in a magnetic field

A-level only

Aim

To investigate how the force on a current-carrying wire in a magnetic field varies with current and to measure the magnetic flux density of a uniform magnetic field

My lab notes

Example method

1. Position two magnets in a support on an electronic balance. Place a copper wire so that it is perpendicular to the magnetic field between the two magnets. Using crocodile clips, attach a thick copper wire to a series circuit that includes a power supply, a variable resistor and an ammeter. Support the copper wire using clamp stands.

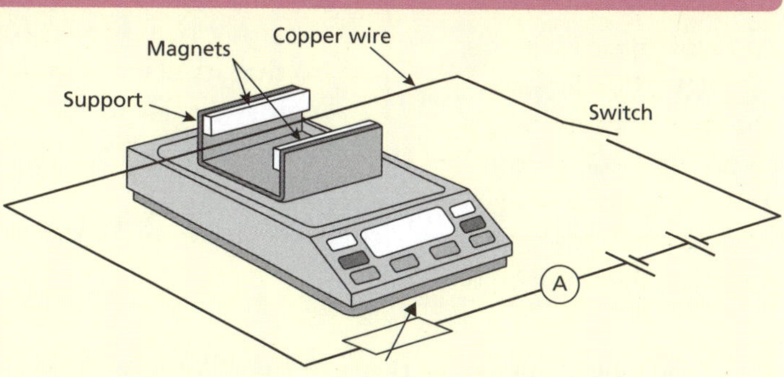

2. Measure the length of wire within the magnetic field using a ruler.
3. Set the electronic balance to zero before switching on the circuit.
4. Adjust the position of the variable resistor to vary the current in the circuit.
5. Record the mass read by the balance for different currents in the wire.

Independent variable	Current (I)
Dependent variable	Force acting on the wire (F)
Control variables	Length of the wire in the magnetic field (l), magnetic flux density (B) and ensuring that the wire remains perpendicular to the magnetic field

Analysis

The force acting on the wire due to the magnetic field is given by $F = BIl$ and there is an equal and opposite force acting on the balance. The force acting on the balance is also equal to the measured mass multiplied by the gravitational field strength (mg), so that: $BIl = mg$

Therefore, plotting a graph of the measured mass m (on the y-axis) against the current I (on the x-axis) gives a straight line with a gradient equal to $\frac{Bl}{g}$

As the length l and the gravitational field strength g are known, the magnetic flux density of the magnetic field can be determined by:

$$B = \text{gradient} \times \frac{g}{l}$$

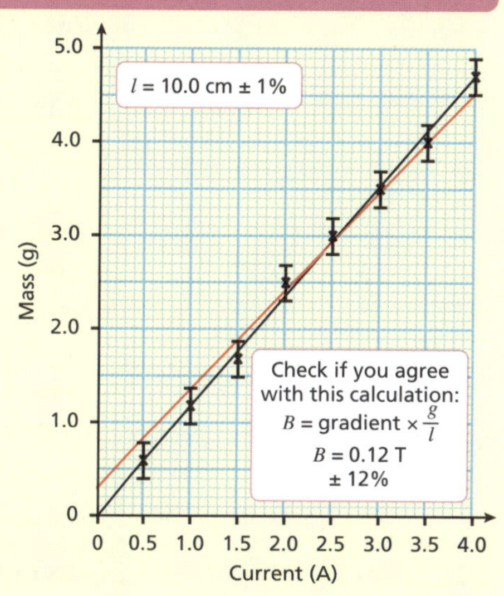

The percentage uncertainty in g is negligible. Therefore, the percentage uncertainty in B is equal to the percentage uncertainty in the gradient added to the percentage uncertainty in the length of the wire in the field, l.

Sources of uncertainty

- If the wire is not parallel to the magnetic field, the balance will record a lower-than-expected reading.
- As the balance is recording small values, errors can occur if it is not zeroed in-between readings.

Safety considerations

This practical is generally undertaken with strong magnets. There is a risk of them snapping together and pinching fingers between them. Care should be taken when handling the magnets.

Required practical 11: Investigating magnetic flux linkage

A-level only

Aim

To investigate how the magnetic flux linkage changes with the angle between a search coil and a magnetic field, using an oscilloscope to measure the induced emf

My lab notes

Example method

1. A large circular coil is connected to an a.c. supply. A search coil is clamped so that its plane is initially parallel to the circular coil's plane, meaning it is perpendicular to the magnetic field lines.

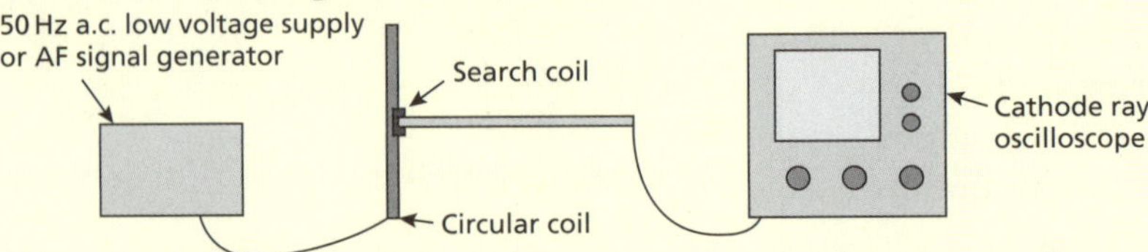

2. The search coil is connected to an oscilloscope. Measure and record the peak-to-peak potential difference (p.d.) displayed on the oscilloscope. To do this, count the vertical divisions between the maximum and minimum points of the signal and multiply by the volts per division setting. Divide this by 2 to find the maximum magnitude of the induced emf.
3. Use a protractor to measure the angle between the search coil and the plane of the circular coil. Change the angle of the search coil systematically in increments of 10°, measuring the induced emf at each step.

Independent variable	Angle between the search coil and the plane of the circular coil
Dependent variable	Induced emf (ε)
Control variables	Frequency of the a.c. power supply; Dimensions of the search coil

Analysis

The induced emf is equal to the rate of change of flux linkage.

As magnetic flux linkage = BAN cos θ, because the frequency of the a.c. supply is constant, the induced emf is proportional to BAN cos θ.

Therefore, if a graph of induced emf (on the y-axis) is plotted against cos θ (on the x-axis), a straight-line relationship should be observed.

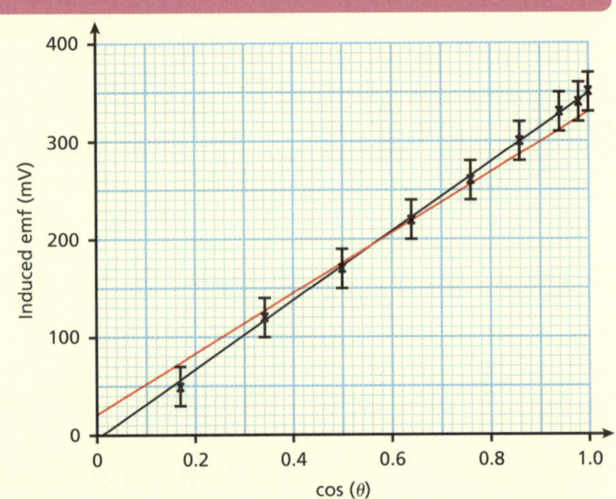

Sources of uncertainty

To reduce uncertainty in the induced emf, readings of the peak-to-peak p.d. should be taken and then halved. To help with this, the time base of the oscilloscope can be turned off (so that the signal just moves up and down). The vertical gain of the oscilloscope should be set so that the signal takes up as much of the oscilloscope screen as possible (without cutting off the peaks).

Improvements to the practical

If the induced emf is not large enough to easily read on an oscilloscope, the a.c. supply can be replaced with a signal generator. If the frequency of the signal from the signal generator is increased to a higher constant value, it will increase the induced emf.

Alternative methods

Instead of using a search coil and oscilloscope, a Hall probe and voltmeter could be used. This method allows for the investigation of static magnetic fields, unlike the search coil method (which requires a changing magnetic flux linkage to induce an emf). The Hall probe can be rotated at different angles in a permanent magnetic field, with the corresponding p.d. recorded. The Hall p.d. is proportional to the magnetic flux linkage passing through the Hall probe.

Required practical 12: Investigation of the inverse square law for gamma radiation

A-level only

Aim

To investigate how the intensity of gamma radiation varies with distance from a radioactive source

My lab notes

Example method

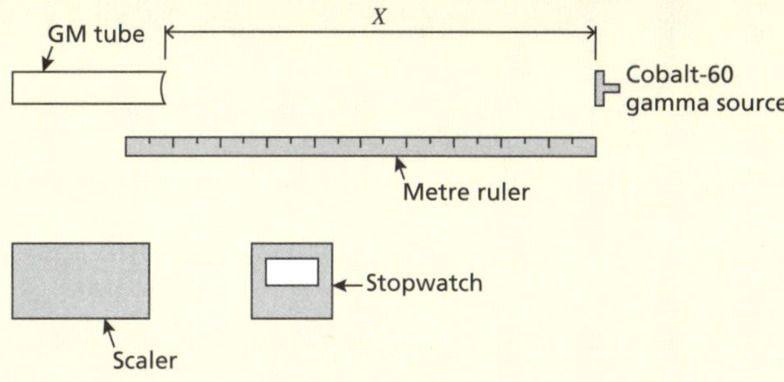

1. Measure the background radiation by switching on the Geiger–Müller (GM) tube without the gamma source present. Record the background count rate over a long period of time (e.g. 30 minutes).
2. Position the sealed cobalt-60 gamma source at a fixed distance (e.g. 5 cm) from the GM tube.
3. Record the count rate over a fixed time period (e.g. 2 minutes). Subtract the background count rate to obtain a corrected count rate (C').
4. Repeat for increasing distances at 5 cm intervals. Maintain the same time interval for all readings.

Independent variable	Distance from the gamma source to the detector (d)
Dependent variable	Corrected count rate, C' (proportional to intensity I)
Control variables	Same gamma source
	Same time interval for each measurement
	Same GM tube

Analysis

The inverse square law states that radiation intensity is inversely proportional to the square of the distance from the source:

$$I = \frac{k}{d^2}$$

If a graph of $\frac{1}{\sqrt{C'}}$ on the y-axis is plotted against d on the x-axis, the graph should be a straight line passing through the origin.

However, the exact position of the gamma source within the sealed source is unknown. There will therefore be a systematic error.

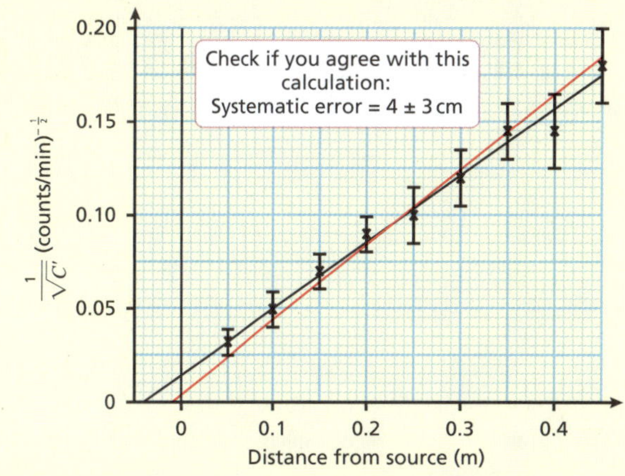

Sources of uncertainty

- Radioactive decay is random so there will be random fluctuations in count rate. The percentage uncertainty can be reduced by taking readings over a longer period of time, or by repeating and taking averages.
- The radioactive source is set back a small distance within its container. Therefore, the graph shows a systematic error.
- The radioactive source might not be a pure gamma emitter. If you wanted to ensure only gamma radiation was being detected, you could put thin aluminium between the radioactive source and the GM tube.

Safety considerations

- To minimise exposure time, plan the experiment in advance to reduce the time spent handling the radioactive source. Only have the source out of its storage container when necessary.
- To increase your distance from the source, hold it at arm's length using long tongs.
- Never point the radioactive source at yourself or others.

THIS PAGE HAS DELIBERATELY BEEN LEFT BLANK

Collins

A-level

Physics

Practice paper for AQA

Paper 1

Time allowed: 2 hours

Materials

For this paper you must have:

- a pencil
- a ruler
- a calculator
- a data and formulae booklet (see pages 229–232).

Instructions

- Answer **all** questions.
- Show **all** your working.

Information

- The maximum mark for this paper is 85.

Name: ....

Section A

Answer **all** questions in this section.

---

0 1 A strange particle, the K^- kaon, interacts with a proton and forms a particle X and a K^+ kaon.

0 1 · 1 Write an equation for this particle interaction.

[1 mark]

....

0 1 · 2 Show that the charge of particle X is –1.

[1 mark]

....

....

0 1 · 3 Deduce the baryon number and strangeness of particle X.

[2 marks]

baryon number ....

strangeness ....

0 1 · 4 Determine the quark structure of particle X.

[3 marks]

quark structure ....

0 2 · 1 A student wants to find the resistance of component X, shown in **Figure 1**. There is no ohmmeter, but other electrical equipment is available.

Complete this circuit diagram to show how you would measure the resistance of X.

[2 marks]

Figure 1

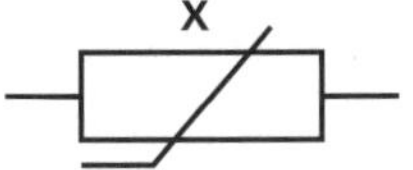

The student sets up the circuit in **Figure 2**, which contains component X.

Figure 2

3 V

X

A

Y = 200 Ω

B

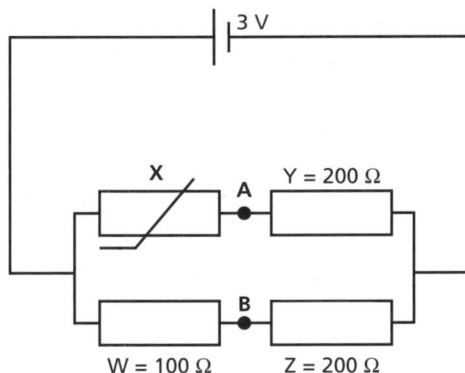

W = 100 Ω

Z = 200 Ω

The resistance of X is 100 Ω.

0 2 · 2 Calculate the total resistance of the circuit and the current drawn by the cell. The cell has negligible internal resistance.

[4 marks]

resistance .... Ω

current .... mA

0 2 · 3 An ammeter is connected between points A and B.

State and explain the current recorded by the ammeter.

[2 marks]

....

....

0 2 · 4 The resistance of component X decreases to 50 Ω.

Explain why the resistance decreased.

[2 marks]

....

....

....

0 2 · 5 State and explain the effect of this change on the current between A and B.

[3 marks]

....

....

....

....

0 3 Gliders move along a horizontal linear air track with negligible friction supported by a cushion of air.

0 3 . 1 A glider of mass 0.40 kg is moving with an initial velocity of 0.30 m s^{-1} towards a stationary glider of mass 0.25 kg. The gliders collide and stick together.

Show that their final velocity is about 0.2 m s^{-1}.

[3 marks]

0 3 . 2 The gliders reach the end of the track and rebound from a fixed barrier, travelling back at the same speed.

Determine the change in momentum when the gliders rebound.

[1 mark]

momentum .... kg m s^{-1}

0 3 . 3 In the next experiment two gliders C and D each of mass 0.20 kg are travelling towards each other and make an elastic collision.

State a difference and a similarity between elastic and inelastic collisions.

[2 marks]

....

....

0 3 . 4 The velocity of C is 0.30 m s^{-1} and of D is –0.20 m s^{-1}. After collision the final velocity of D is 0.30 m s^{-1}.

Calculate the final velocity of C and show whether the collision is elastic.

[5 marks]

final velocity of C .... m s^{-1}

elastic or inelastic? ....

0 4 A spring is suspended vertically and extends by 0.14 m when a mass of 0.31 kg is hung on its lower end.

0 4 · 1 Show that the spring constant of the spring is about 20 N m^{-1}.

[2 marks]

0 4 · 2 The spring is pulled down slightly and released so that it oscillates with simple harmonic motion about the equilibrium position with an amplitude of 0.025 m.

Calculate the period of the oscillation.

[1 mark]

period .... s

0 4 · 3 Explain at what point in the oscillation the tension in the spring will be at maximum value and calculate this maximum tension.

[3 marks]

....

....

maximum tension .... N

0 4 · 4 The mass and spring are taken to the Moon. Vertical oscillations with the same amplitude are set up in exactly the same way.

Without further calculation, comment on the changes, if any, that you would expect to the period of oscillation and the maximum tension.

[3 marks]

....

....

....

0 5 A marble of mass 6.0 g is rolled down the plastic track shown in **Figure 3**. Z is 0.10 m higher than Y. The path through Z is part of a circle of radius 0.75 m. Assume that friction is negligible.

Figure 3

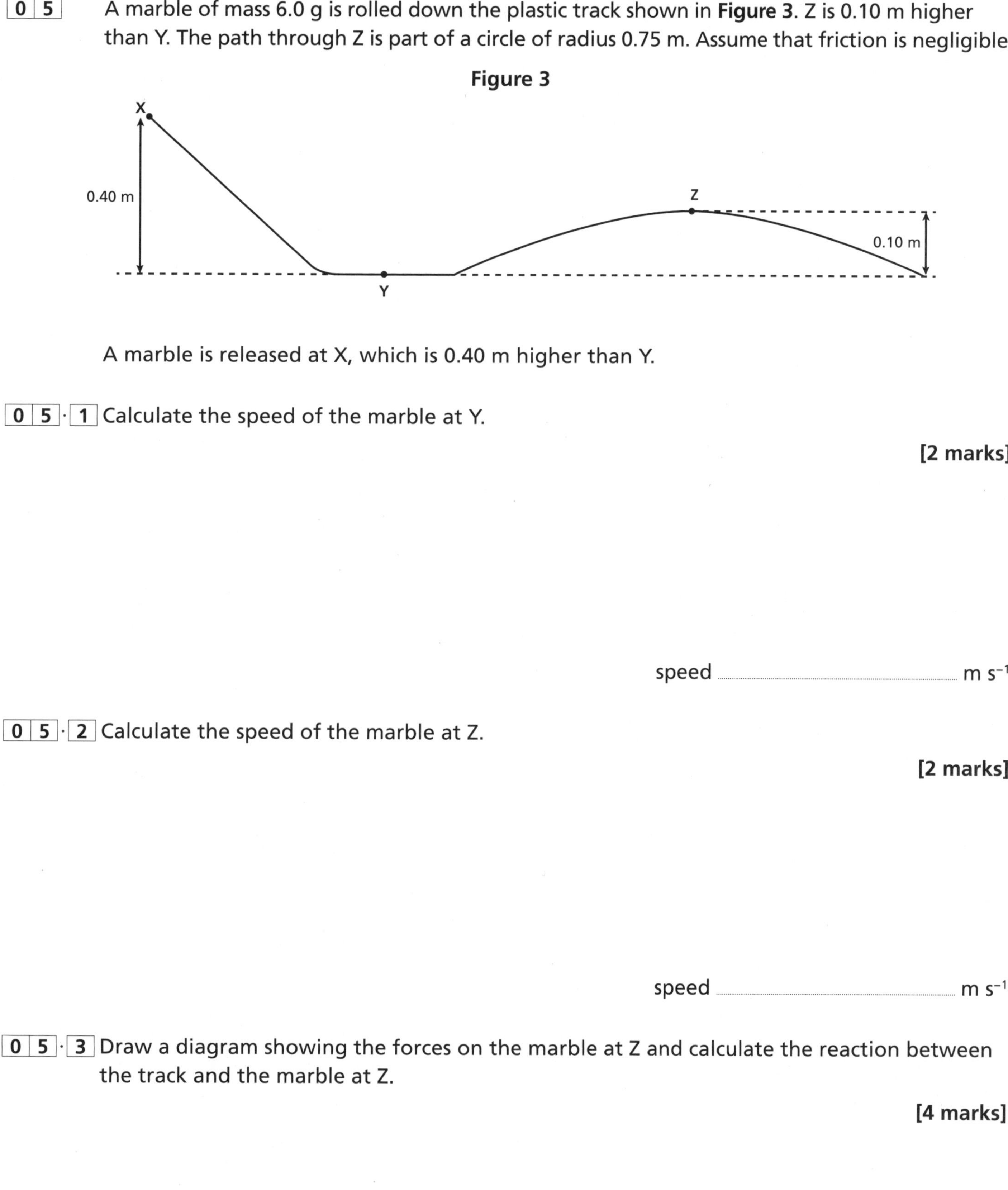

A marble is released at X, which is 0.40 m higher than Y.

0 5 · 1 Calculate the speed of the marble at Y.

[2 marks]

speed .... m s^{-1}

0 5 · 2 Calculate the speed of the marble at Z.

[2 marks]

speed .... m s^{-1}

0 5 · 3 Draw a diagram showing the forces on the marble at Z and calculate the reaction between the track and the marble at Z.

[4 marks]

reaction .... N

0 6 Read through the following passage and answer the questions that follow it.

The invention of the blue LED

Light-emitting diode (LED) technology is based on electroluminescence, which is a phenomenon discovered in 1907 by Henry Joseph Round. Electroluminescence is light emitted when an electric current passes through a material. In 1955 Rubin Braunstein reported that some simple semiconductor diodes emit radiation when current passes through them, but it was not until 1961 that the first practical device – a pure gallium arsenide (GaAs) crystal with a 900 nm wavelength output – was reported.

In 1962 Nick Holonyack developed the first visible red LED, with a wavelength of 660 nm. New semiconductor materials led to LEDs with other colours, but the blue LED was more difficult to achieve. In 1979, Shuji Nakamura invented the first blue LED using gallium nitride (GaN), but it was too expensive for commercial use. He improved the design and in 1994 he invented the first low-cost bright blue LED.

The blue LED made white light possible because our eyes see a combination of red, green and blue, or of yellow and blue, as white light. One way to make a white LED is to use a phosphor coating to absorb some of the blue light and emit yellow light. This results in a spectrum of yellow (maximum output at a wavelength of 580 nm) and blue (maximum output at 450 nm), which we see as white light.

0 6 · 1 State the region of the electromagnetic spectrum that is emitted by the first practical device (line 6).

[1 mark]

....

0 6 · 2 Calculate the energy of a photon emitted by the first visible red LED. Use the wavelength of red light given in line 8.

[3 marks]

energy .... eV

0 6 · 3 Describe the process that takes place in an atom in the phosphor coating so that yellow light is produced (line 14).

[2 marks]

....

....

....

0 6 · 4 A student suggests that the red LED could be used with phosphor coatings that emit green light of wavelength 550 nm, and blue light of wavelength 450 nm to produce white light.

Explain whether this is possible.

[2 marks]

....

....

....

0 6 · 5 The white light LED described in lines 13 to 16 is viewed using a spectrometer and a diffraction grating with 1500 lines per mm.

Calculate the first order angle at which the centre of the blue line is seen.

[2 marks]

angle .... °

0 6 · 6 Describe the spectrum that would be seen with the spectrometer.

[2 marks]

....

....

....

END OF SECTION A

Section B

Each of questions 7 to 31 is followed by four responses, A, B, C and D. For each question select the best response.

Only **one** answer per question is allowed.

For each answer completely fill in the circle alongside the appropriate answer.

CORRECT METHOD WRONG METHODS

If you want to change your answer, you must cross out your original answer as shown.

If you wish to return to an answer previously crossed out, ring the answer you now wish to select as shown.

0 7 A nucleus of $^{204}_{82}\text{Pb}$ absorbs an alpha particle and emits a positron.

What is the product nucleus?

[1 mark]

A $^{206}_{85}\text{At}$

B $^{208}_{85}\text{At}$

C $^{208}_{83}\text{Bi}$

D $^{207}_{84}\text{Po}$

0 8 The drag force F on a spherical object of radius r falling with terminal velocity v is given by:

$$F = 6\pi\eta rv$$

What are the units of η?

[1 mark]

A kg m^{-1}

B kg m^{-1} s^{-1}

C kg m^{2} s^{-1}

D m s^{-2} kg^{-1}

0 9 A metal sheet is placed in a beam of electromagnetic radiation. Photoelectrons are emitted from the surface of the metal.

Which list contains all the factors that determine the maximum speed of the emitted electrons?

[1 mark]

A The frequency of the electromagnetic radiation. 

B The frequency and the intensity of the electromagnetic radiation. 

C The frequency of the electromagnetic radiation and the work function of the metal. 

D The intensity of the electromagnetic radiation and the work function of the metal. 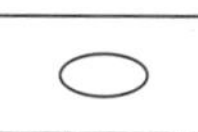

1 0 The diagram shows three energy levels for the outermost electron in an atom. λ_A λ_B and λ_C are the wavelengths of the photons emitted when the electrons drop from one energy level to another.

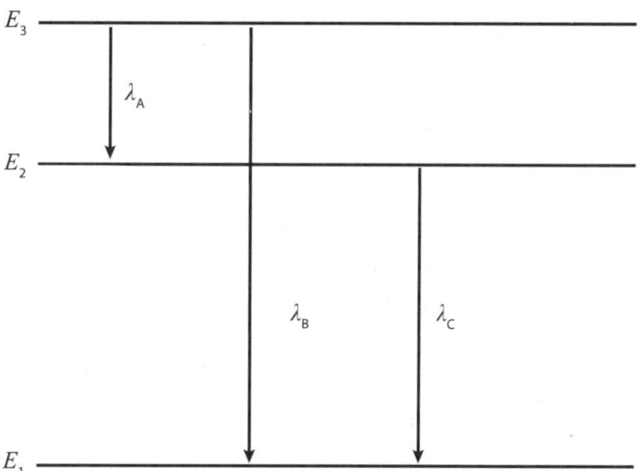

Which of the following statements is correct?

[1 mark]

A $\lambda_B = \lambda_A + \lambda_C$ 

B If λ_A is in the visible region, then λ_C could be in the infrared region.

C The frequency of the radiation with wavelength λ_A is less than the frequency of the radiation with wavelength λ_B.

D If λ_B is in the visible region, then λ_A could be in the ultraviolet region.

1 1 The diameter of a sphere is measured to be 0.025 (±0.001) m. The volume of the sphere is correctly calculated to be

$$V = \frac{4\pi}{3}\left(\frac{d}{2}\right)^3 = 8.81 \times 10^{-6}\ \text{m}$$

How should the percentage uncertainty in the volume, resulting from the uncertainty in the diameter, be calculated?

[1 mark]

A $\frac{0.001}{0.025} \times 100\%$ ⬭

B $3 \times \frac{0.001}{0.025} \times 100\%$ ⬭

C $\frac{0.001}{8.181 \times 10^{-6}} \times 100\%$ ⬭

D $3 \times \frac{0.001}{8.181 \times 10^{-6}} \times 100\%$ ⬭

1 2 Considering the alpha particle, the proton and the positron, which particle has the largest specific charge and which has the smallest?

[1 mark]

	Largest specific charge	**Smallest specific charge**	
A	alpha particle	positron	⬭
B	positron	alpha particle	⬭
C	positron	proton	⬭
D	proton	alpha particle	⬭

1 3 The frequency of the first harmonic of a string fixed at both ends is 200 Hz. The tension in the wire is doubled.

What is the new fundamental frequency?

[1 mark]

A 283 Hz

B 141 Hz

C 400 Hz

D 800 Hz

1 4 A wire with resistance R and length l has a circular cross-section with diameter d. A second wire with resistance R is made of the same material and has a square cross-section of side d.

What is the length of this second wire?

[1 mark]

A $2\pi l$

B $\frac{2l}{\pi}$

C $4\pi l$

D $\frac{4l}{\pi}$

1 5 A beam of light passes through a polarising filter with its axis of polarisation at 0° and a second polarising filter with its axis of polarisation at 90°. No light is transmitted. A third polarising filter is placed between the two crossed filters and rotated through 360°.

As the third filter is rotated, which of the following is true?

[1 mark]

A No light is transmitted at any angle.

B Some light is transmitted at all angles.

C Some light is transmitted, but only when the third filter has its axis of polarisation at 0°, 45°, 225° or 315°.

D Some light is transmitted whenever the axis of polarisation of the third filter is not 0° or is a multiple of 90°.

1 6 A light ray incident on the cladding of an optical fibre refracts along the core-cladding boundary as shown.

What is the critical angle at the boundary between the core and the cladding?

speed of light in the core = 2.02×10^8 m s^{-1}

speed of light in the cladding = 2.08×10^8 m s^{-1}

[1 mark]

A 14° ⬭

B 42° ⬭

C 44° ⬭

D 76° ⬭

1 7 An experiment in which microwaves pass through two narrow slits is done in a vacuum.

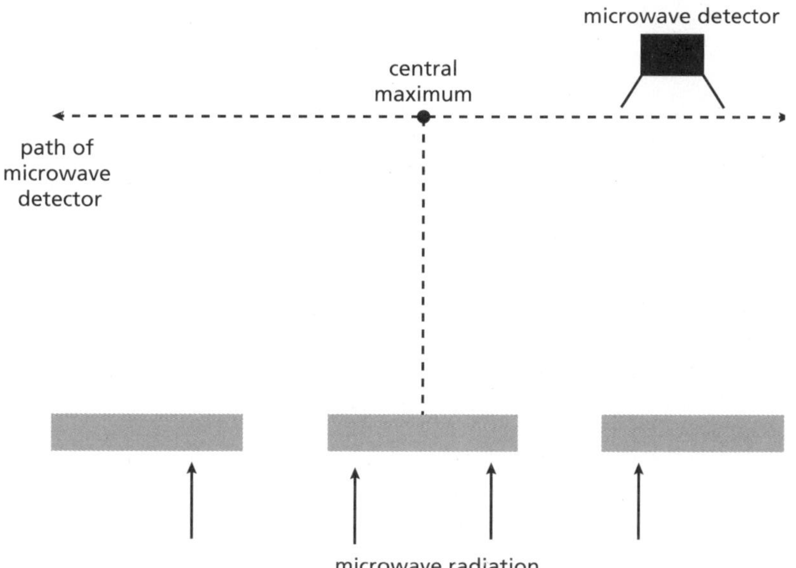

The slits act as coherent sources. The microwave detector is moved along the path shown. There is a central maximum intensity. On either side there are evenly spaced intensity maxima and minima.

When the microwave frequency is halved, what change in the pattern is observed?

[1 mark]

A The pattern is unchanged.

B The spacing of the maxima is unchanged, but there is a central minimum.

C The spacing of the maxima is doubled.

D The spacing of the maxima is halved.

1 8 A uniform 1.0 m beam of weight W is supported on a pillar 10 cm from one end and by a rope attached 30 cm from the other end.

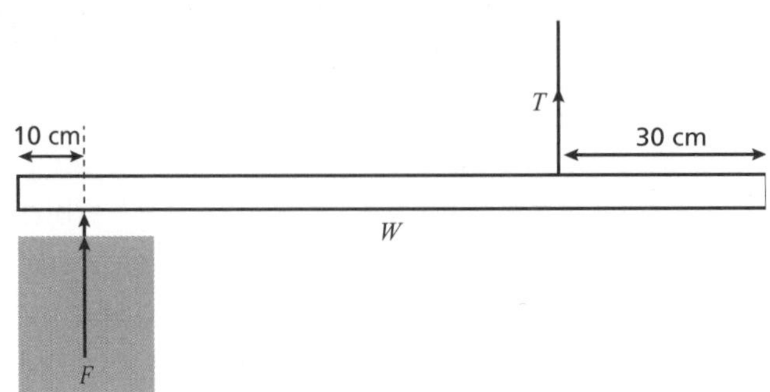

The reaction force from the pillar is F and the tension in the rope is T.

What is the ratio $T : F$?

[1 mark]

A 1 : 3 ⬭

B 1 : 2 ⬭

C 2 : 1 ⬭

D 3 : 1 ⬭

1 9 Three forces A, B and C act on the rim of a disc. Forces A and B are both 10 N and form a couple.

Which diagram shows the correct force C that prevents the disc from rotating?

[1 mark]

A

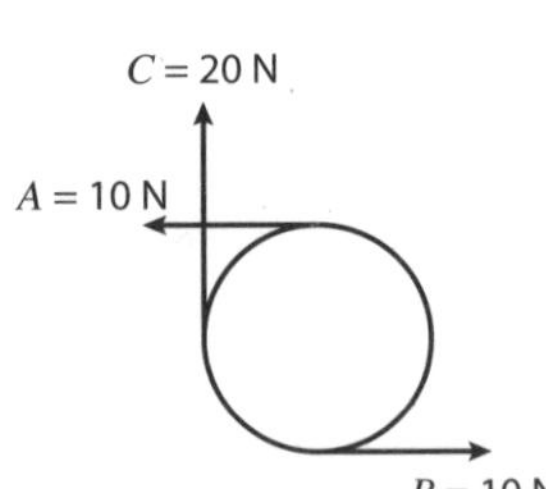

B

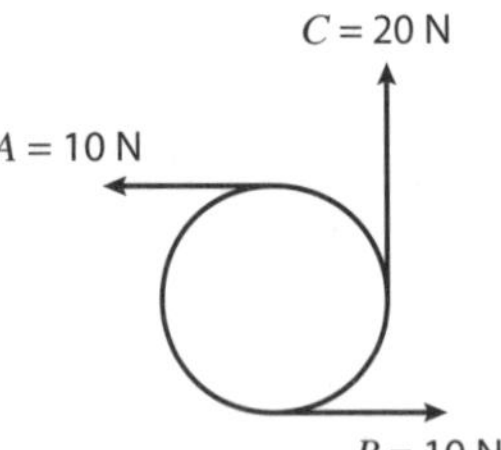

C

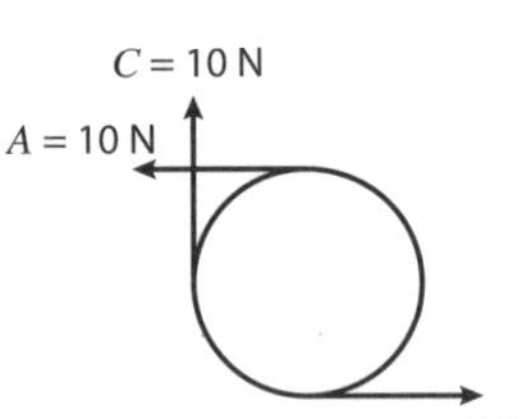

D

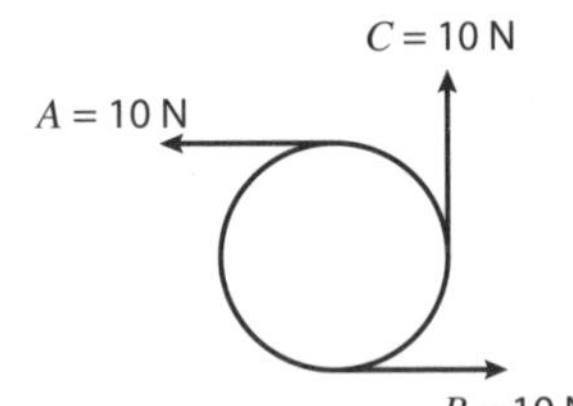

A ⬭

B ⬭

C ⬭

D ⬭

20 An object of mass 0.50 kg moves due South on a horizontal frictionless table with a speed of 3.0 m s^{-1}. A constant force of 0.20 N due East acts on it for 10 s.

What is the resultant velocity of the object?

[1 mark]

A 3.6 m s^{-1} due East 

B 3.6 m s^{-1} 53° East of South 

C 5.0 m s^{-1} due East 

D 5.0 m s^{-1} 53° East of South 

21 Two identical springs with spring constant k can be joined in parallel or in series.

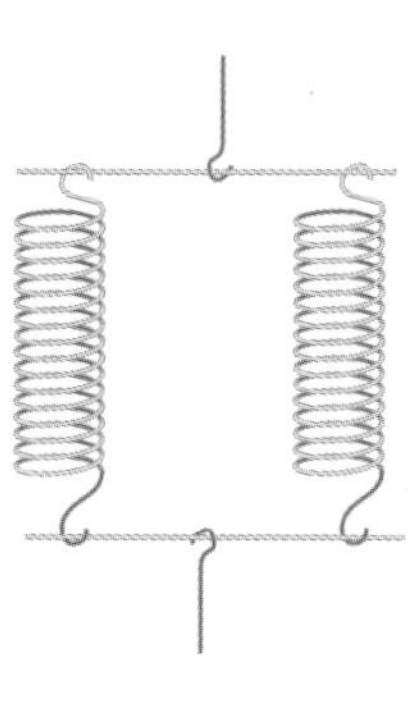

Which line of the table correctly shows the spring constant in each case?

[1 mark]

	Series combination	Parallel combination	
A	$2k$	$2k$	⬭
B	$2k$	$\frac{k}{2}$	⬭
C	$\frac{k}{2}$	$2k$	⬭
D	$\frac{k}{2}$	$\frac{k}{2}$	⬭

2 2 Two spheres of equal volume, one plastic and one metal, are projected horizontally from the top of a tall building at the same time and with the same velocity. Air resistance is negligible.

Which statement correctly describes when and where they will land?

[1 mark]

A The metal sphere will land first and closer to the building. ⬭

B The metal sphere will land first and further from the building. ⬭

C The plastic sphere will land first and closer to the building. ⬭

D They will both land at the same time and at the same distance from the building. ⬭

2 3 Two projectiles P and Q are projected upwards at an angle with the same speed v. The ground is horizontal. Projectile P is projected at angle θ to the horizontal and projectile Q at angle $(90° - \theta)$ to the horizontal. The time of flight of projectile P is t_p.

What is the time of flight of projectile Q?

[1 mark]

A t_p ⬭

B $t_p \tan\theta$ ⬭

C $\frac{t_p}{\tan\theta}$ ⬭

D $t_p \frac{2v}{g} \tan\theta$ ⬭

2 4 A person travels up and down in a lift, stopping at each floor of the building.

Which statement about the reaction force from the floor on the person is true?

[1 mark]

Compared to the reaction force when the lift is stationary:

A the reaction force is greater when the lift is going down and slowing down. ⬭

B the reaction force is greater when the lift is going down and speeding up. ⬭

C the reaction force is greater when the lift is going up and slowing down. ⬭

D the reaction force is less when the lift is going up and speeding up. ⬭

2 5 A rope is used to vertically raise a large crate of mass M to a platform at a height h above the ground. A ramp with negligible friction is set up at an angle of 45°, so that the rope can be used to pull the same mass up the ramp from the ground to the platform.

What effect does using the ramp have on the work done in raising the crate?

[1 mark]

A The work done will be less. ⬭

B The work done will be more. ⬭

C The work done will be the same. ⬭

D The work done will depend on how quickly the crate is raised. ⬭

2 6 A crane motor X raises 30 kg a height of 120 m in 2.0 minutes. A winch motor Y raises 8.0 kg a height of 6.0 m in 1.5 s and a lift motor Z raises 4.0 kg a height of 15 m in 10 s.

Which motor delivers the most output power?

[1 mark]

A crane X ⬭

B winch Y ⬭

C lift Z ⬭

D They are all the same. ⬭

2 7 In an open circuit the potential difference across the terminals of a cell is 9.0 V and when a current of 1.5 A passes through it is 7.8 V.

What is the internal resistance of the cell?

[1 mark]

A 0.8 Ω ⬭

B 1.8 Ω ⬭

C 5.2 Ω ⬭

D 6.0 Ω ⬭

2 8 This circuit is used to automatically turn on a light.

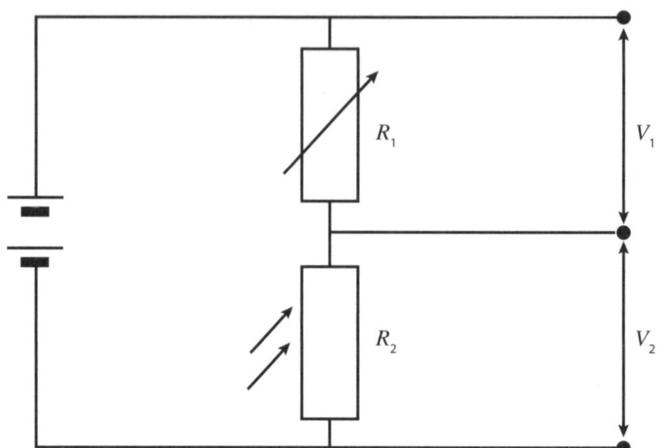

Which of the following statements correctly describes what happens as the amount of light and the resistance of R_1 is changed?

[1 mark]

A It gets dark, V_1 increases and can be used to switch on a lamp. When R_1 is decreased it is darker before the lamp switches on.

B It gets dark, V_1 increases and can be used to switch on a lamp. When R_1 is increased it is darker before the lamp switches on.

C It gets dark, V_2 increases and can be used to switch on a lamp. When R_1 is decreased it is darker before the lamp switches on.

D It gets dark, V_2 increases and can be used to switch on a lamp. When R_1 is increased it is darker before the lamp switches on.

2 9 A simple pendulum, consisting of a small mass on the end of an inextensible string, swings with simple harmonic motion.

Which of the following statements correctly describes the total energy in the system?

[1 mark]

A The total energy is at its maximum as the mass passes through the mid-point of the oscillation. ⬭

B The total energy is at its minimum as the mass passes through the mid-point of the oscillation. ⬭

C The total energy is at its maximum as the mass reaches the highest point of the oscillation. ⬭

D The total energy will not change with the position of the mass. ⬭

3 0 An object oscillates with damped simple harmonic motion.

Which of the following statements about the damping force is true?

[1 mark]

A It is always in the opposite direction to the displacement. ⬭

B It is always in the opposite direction to the velocity. ⬭

C It is always proportional to the displacement. ⬭

D It is always in the same direction as the acceleration. ⬭

3 1 An object travels around a circle with radius r. The centre of the circle is at O.

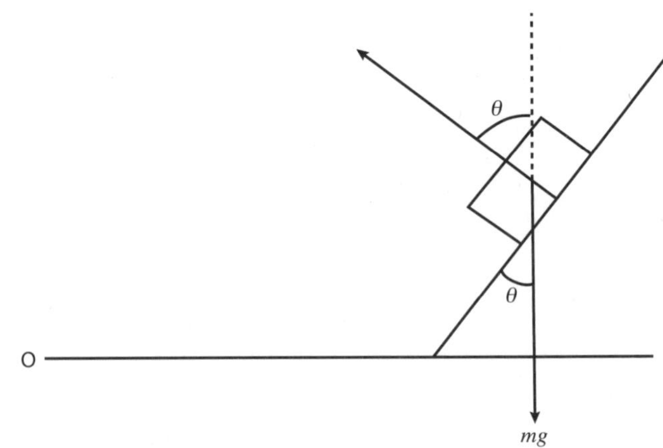

The edge of the circle is banked at an angle θ so that, at speed v, the object cannot slip.

What is the value of $\tan \theta$?

[1 mark]

A $\frac{mg}{rv^2}$ ⬭

B $\frac{rg}{v^2}$ ⬭

C $\frac{rv^2}{mg}$ ⬭

D $\frac{v^2}{rg}$ ⬭

END OF QUESTIONS

Collins

A-level

Physics

Practice paper for AQA

Paper 2

Time allowed: 2 hours

Materials

For this paper you must have:

- a pencil
- a ruler
- a calculator
- a data and formulae booklet (see pages 229–232).

Instructions

- Answer **all** questions.
- Show **all** your working.

Information

- The maximum mark for this paper is 85.

Name: ....

Section A

Answer **all** questions in this section.

---

0 1 A solid 'phase change material' (PCM) that melts at 37 °C is used where incubators are unavailable to keep small babies at the right body temperature of 37 °C.

In a test 400 g of the PCM is heated from 15 °C until it is all molten and its temperature has increased to 39 °C. The test is done in an insulated glass container with mass 240 g and specific heat capacity 840 J kg^{-1} K^{-1}. The thermal energy transferred to or from the surroundings during the test is negligible.

Table 1 shows some technical data for the PCM.

Table 1

Melting point	**37 °C**
Specific heat capacity when solid	2200 J kg^{-1} K^{-1}
Specific heat capacity when liquid	2600 J kg^{-1} K^{-1}

0 1 · 1 Calculate the thermal energy required to raise the temperature of the PCM **and** the container from 15 °C to 37 °C.

[2 marks]

energy .... J

0 1 · 2 The 12 V heating element used had a current of 1.7 A and took 90 minutes to raise the temperature of the PCM and the container 15 °C to 39 °C.

Determine the latent heat of fusion of the PCM.

[4 marks]

latent heat of fusion .... $J\ kg^{-1}$

0 1 · 3 In use, the PCM is enclosed in a quilt – it is heated so that it has partially melted and the quilt is wrapped around the baby.

Suggest, in terms of energy transfer, how this helps to stabilise the baby's body temperature.

[1 mark]

....

....

....

0 2 · 1 A student writes, "The gas laws are empirical. Kinetic theory is theoretical."

Explain what these statements mean.

[2 marks]

1. ....

....

2. ....

....

0 2 · 2 Kinetic theory assumes that the pressure of an ideal gas of molecules of mass m is

$$p = \frac{1Nm}{3V}(C_{rms})^2$$

State the physical significance of $\frac{Nm}{V}$ and explain your answer.

[2 marks]

....

....

....

0 2 · 3 Show how $(C_{rms})^2$ is calculated for four particles with velocity v_1, v_2, v_3 and v_4.

[1 mark]

0 2 · 4 The rms speed of nitrogen molecules is 520 m s^{-1}.

Determine the temperature of the nitrogen gas. The molar mass of nitrogen is 28 g/mol.

[3 marks]

temperature .... K

0 3 · 1 The electron and the proton in a hydrogen atom are separated by a mean distance of about 5.3×10^{-11} m.

Calculate the ratio of the magnitudes of the electrostatic force and the gravitational force between the two particles and comment on the effect of the gravitational force on subatomic particles.

[4 marks]

0 3 · 2 Other than the magnitudes of the forces, compare and contrast gravitational and electrostatic fields.

[5 marks]

0 4 A copper sheet is held between the two poles of an electromagnet, as shown in **Figure 1**.

Figure 1

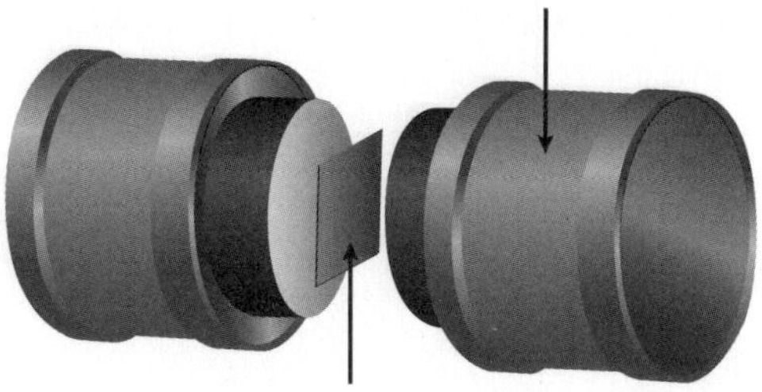

electromagnet

copper sheet

An alternating current flows through the coils of the electromagnet.

0 4 . 1 Explain why the temperature of the sheet increases.

[4 marks]

0 4 . 2 State **two** ways of increasing the rate of heating without changing or moving the sheet. Explain your answers.

[2 marks]

1.

2.

0 4 . 3 The sheet is replaced with a sheet of the same size and shape but made of a metal with higher resistance.

Explain how the rate of heating is changed.

[2 marks]

0 5 A cyclotron, shown in **Figure 2**, is a device for accelerating charged particles. It has two D-shaped containers where there is a magnetic field, provided by magnetic poles above and below the Ds. Across the 2.0 cm gap between the Ds there is an alternating electric field. There is no electric field in the Ds.

Figure 2

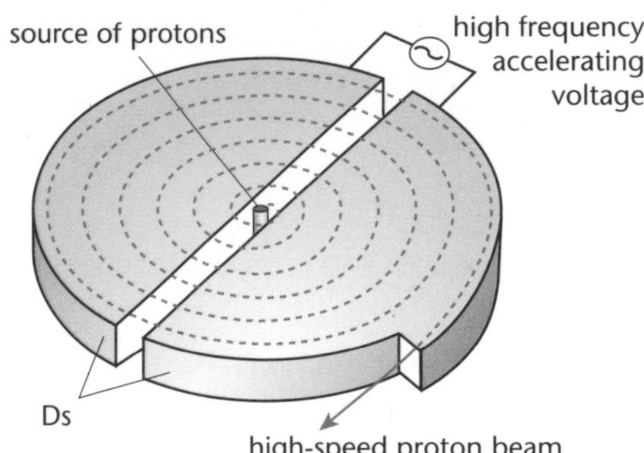

0 5 · 1 The source at the centre of the gap releases protons that are accelerated and enter the first D. The potential difference across the gap is 10 kV.

Show that the initial force on the proton is 8×10^{-14} N. (Assume the electric field across the gap is uniform.)

[2 marks]

0 5 · 2 A proton starts at rest at the centre of the gap and is accelerated to the first D.

Show that its acceleration is about 5×10^{13} m s^{-2} **and** that when it enters the D for the first time its speed is about 1×10^{6} m s^{-1}.

[3 marks]

0 5 · 3 The proton enters the first D and starts making a number of laps around the Ds.

It is accelerated across the 2.0 cm gap twice on each lap. It travels at constant speed in the Ds.

This makes a total distance over which it is accelerated of ($2n \times 2.0$) cm, where n is the number of laps.

Calculate the total number of laps to reach 10% of the speed of light.

[3 marks]

number of laps, n ....

0 5 · 4 Inside the Ds the protons are in the vertical magnetic field and move in a circular path. On **Figure 2** mark a proton inside a D on one of the dotted paths and draw labelled arrows showing the direction of the force on the proton and its direction of motion.

State the direction of the magnetic field and deduce which pole of the magnet is a north pole.

[2 marks]

....

....

....

....

0 5 · 5 By considering the magnetic force on the proton moving it in a circular path, show that the radius of the path r is

$$r = \frac{mv}{Be}$$

where m is the mass and e the charge on the proton, v is its velocity and B is the magnetic field.

[2 marks]

0 5 · 6 Before the proton source is opened, the inside of the cyclotron is a vacuum.

Suggest why a vacuum is required.

[1 mark]

....

....

0 6 Read through the following passage and answer the questions that follow it.

Many space probes use radioisotope thermoelectric generators (RTGs). In an RTG, radioactive decay transfers energy by heating the surroundings. It can be used to warm the electronics, or to generate electricity. The radioisotope used by NASA is plutonium-238, which is contained in pellets of plutonium dioxide. Plutonium-238 has a half-life of 88 years.

RTGs were used in the 1970s to power the Voyager and Pioneer deep-space probes that have now left the solar system. The Curiosity rover that explored Mars in 2012 had an RTG containing about 4.3 kg of plutonium to provide power and keep the electronics warm. (On Mars temperatures range from −133 °C to 27 °C and there are strong winds and dust storms.) It was designed to last for one Mars year (687 Earth days). Previous rovers have used some radioisotope heating, but relied on solar panels for their power.

In an RTG electricity is generated using a thermoelectric effect. A temperature difference is used to generate a potential difference and this is used to charge two rechargeable lithium-ion batteries.

The United States stopped producing plutonium-238 in 1988 and instead purchased it from Russia. Russia has now also stopped production and stocks are running low. In December 2015 the USA reported producing 50 g of plutonium-238 from neptunium-238 and they plan to increase production to about 1.5 kg a year.

0 6 · 1 Plutonium-238, ${}^{238}_{94}\text{Pu}$, decays to uranium-234, releasing an alpha particle.

Use the data in **Table 2** to calculate the energy released in joules by the decay of 1 nucleus of plutonium-238.

[3 marks]

Table 2

Nucleus	Mass / u
plutonium-238	238.04955
uranium-234	234.043924
helium-4	4.00151

energy .... J

0 6 . 2 Show that the number of atoms, N, in 4.3 kg of pure plutonium-238 is about 1×10^{25}. The molar mass of plutonium-238 is 238.05 g/mol.

[1 mark]

number of atoms, N ....

0 6 . 3 Use information about plutonium-238 (line 4) to calculate the initial activity of 4.3 kg of plutonium-238.

[2 marks]

activity .... Bq

0 6 . 4 Determine the initial power output of the RTG.

[1 mark]

power .... W

0 6 . 5 Suggest and explain the advantages of using RTGs instead of solar panels for powering deep-space probes and Mars rovers.

[2 marks]

....

....

....

....

0 6 · 6 Use the equation for the gravitational attraction between the Sun and a planet to show that $T^2 \propto r^3$, where T is the period and r the radius of orbit of a planet around the Sun.

[3 marks]

0 6 · 7 Using the information in lines 10–11, determine the ratio between the radii of the orbits of Mars and the Earth, $r_M : r_E$ and calculate the radius of the Mars orbit, r_M.

Earth's radius of orbit, $r_E = 1.50 \times 10^{11}$ m

[3 marks]

ratio ....

radius .... m

END OF SECTION A

Section B

Each of questions **7** to **31** is followed by four responses, **A, B, C** and **D**. For each question select the best response.

Only **one** answer per question is allowed.

For each answer completely fill in the circle alongside the appropriate answer.

CORRECT METHOD WRONG METHODS 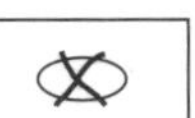   

If you want to change your answer, you must cross out your original answer as shown. 

If you wish to return to an answer previously crossed out, ring the answer you now wish to select as shown.

0 7 A fixed mass of gas occupies a constant volume. The temperature is T in degrees Celsius. The pressure p is doubled.

What is the new temperature in degrees Celsius?

[1 mark]

A $2T$

B $\frac{1}{2}T$

C $2T + 273$

D $\frac{T - 273}{2}$

0 8 Which statement is true for an ideal gas?

[1 mark]

A The average internal energy of the atoms is zero.

B The internal energy decreases when work is done on the gas.

C The internal energy equals the average kinetic energy of the atoms.

D The internal energy equals the average potential energy of the atoms.

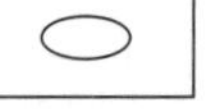

0 9 Which graph correctly shows how the gravitational force, F, between two masses varies with the distance between them, r?

[1 mark]

A

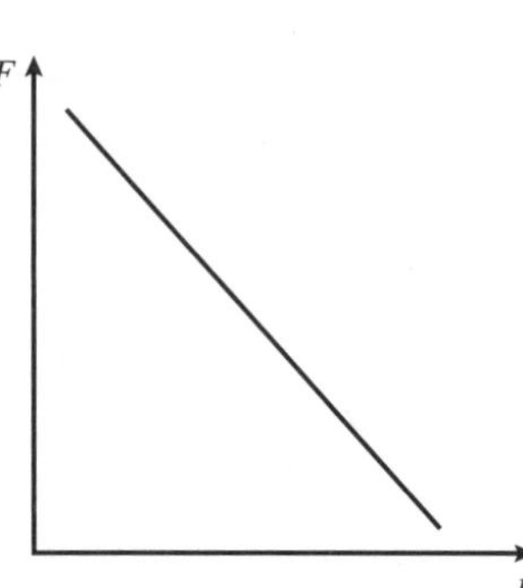

B

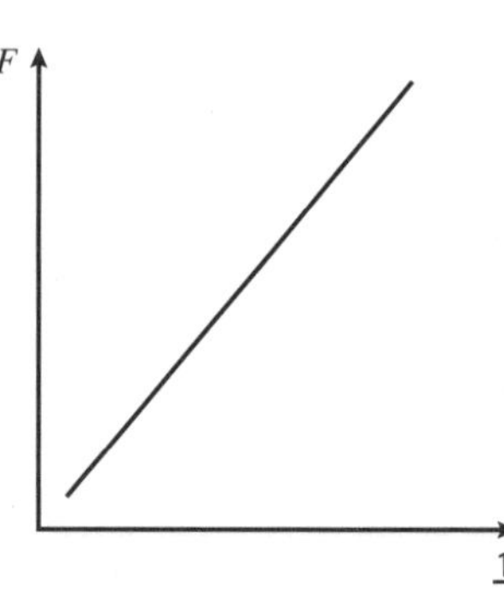

C

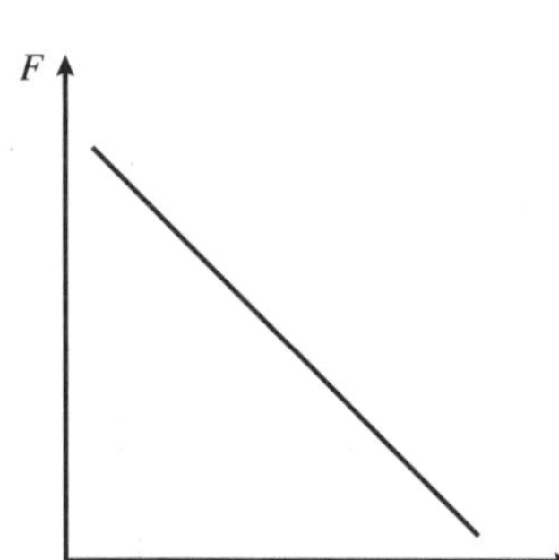

D

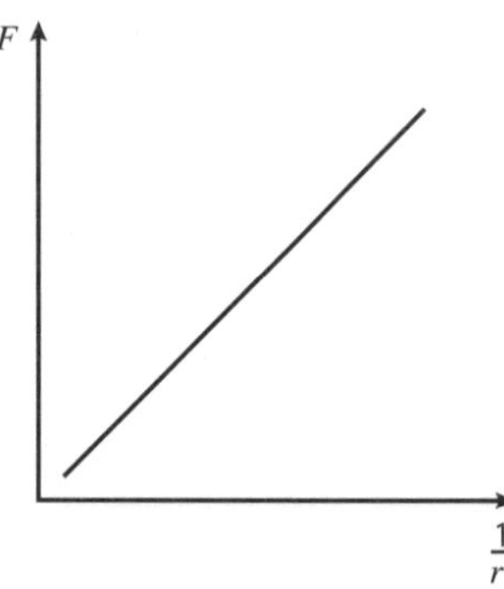

A 

B

C

D

1 0 Which statement correctly defines the gravitational potential at a point in a gravitational field?

[1 mark]

A The work done in moving any mass from infinity to that point. 

B The work done in moving any mass to infinity from that point.

C The work done in moving a unit mass from infinity to that point.

D The work done in moving a unit mass to infinity from that point. 

1 1 Jupiter has a radius about 11 times that of the Earth, and a mass of about 320 times that of the Earth. The gravitational potential at the Earth's surface is -6.3×10^7 J kg^{-1}.

What is the approximate value of the gravitational potential at the surface of Jupiter?

[1 mark]

A -1.8×10^9 J kg^{-1} ⬭

B -1.7×10^8 J kg^{-1} ⬭

C -2.4×10^7 J kg^{-1} ⬭

D -2.2×10^6 J kg^{-1} ⬭

1 2 A point X is a distance $3r$ from a large point mass $3M$. The gravitational potential at X due to this mass is V. A second large point mass $10M$ is placed a distance $4r$ from the first mass and $5r$ from point X.

What is the new value of the gravitational potential at X?

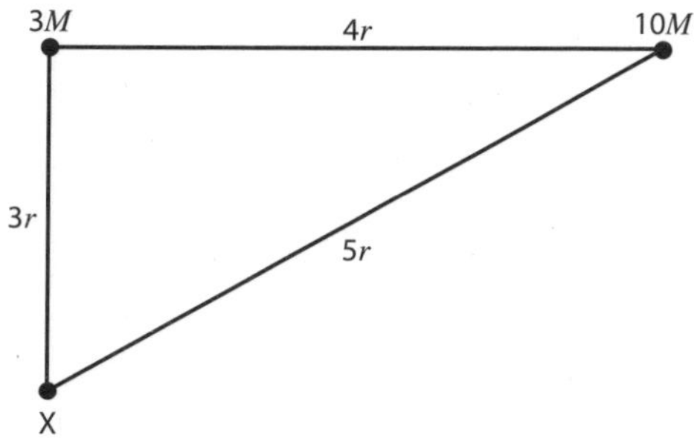

[1 mark]

A $\frac{11V}{15}$ ⬭

B $2V$ ⬭

C $3V$ ⬭

D $\frac{23V}{3}$ ⬭

13 Which line of the table is correct for a geostationary satellite and a geosynchronous satellite of the Earth?

[1 mark]

	Geostationary	Geosynchronous	
A	Orbital period is always one day. Plane of orbit is always the equatorial plane.	Orbital period is always one day. Stays over a fixed point on the Earth.	⬭
B	Orbital period is always one day. Stays over a fixed point on the Earth.	Orbital period is always one day. Plane of orbit is always the equatorial plane.	⬭
C	Orbital period is always one day. Plane of orbit is always the equatorial plane. Stays over a fixed point on the Earth.	Orbital period is always one day.	⬭
D	Orbital period is always one day. Stays over a fixed point on the Earth.	Orbital period is always one day. Plane of orbit is always the equatorial plane.	⬭

14 Two particles are a distance d apart. One has a charge of $+Q$ and the other has a charge of $-4Q$. The attractive force between them = F.

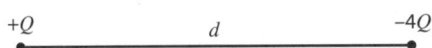

$+Q$ ——— d ——— $-4Q$

The particles are moved closer together so that the distance between them is $\frac{1}{2}d$. Both particles are given an additional charge of $+Q$.

What is the new force between the particles?

[1 mark]

A $2.5F$ ⬭

B $3F$ ⬭

C $5F$ ⬭

D $6F$ ⬭

 Electrons in a vacuum start from rest and are accelerated through a potential difference V.

Which graph shows how their velocity v varies with the potential difference?

[1 mark]

A

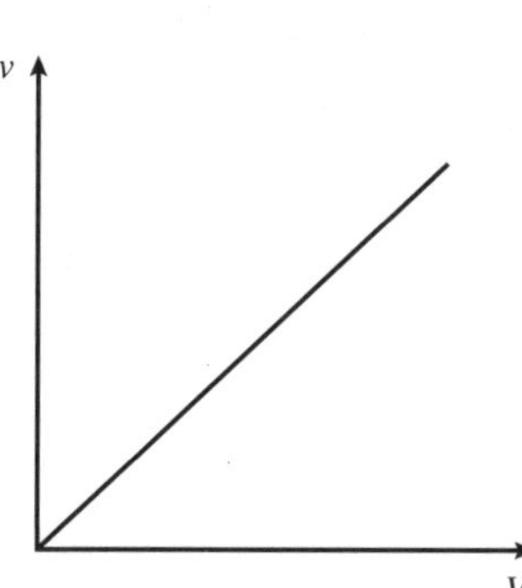

B

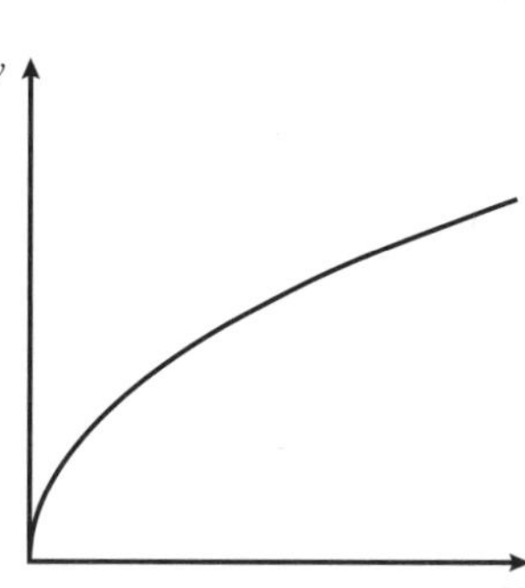

C

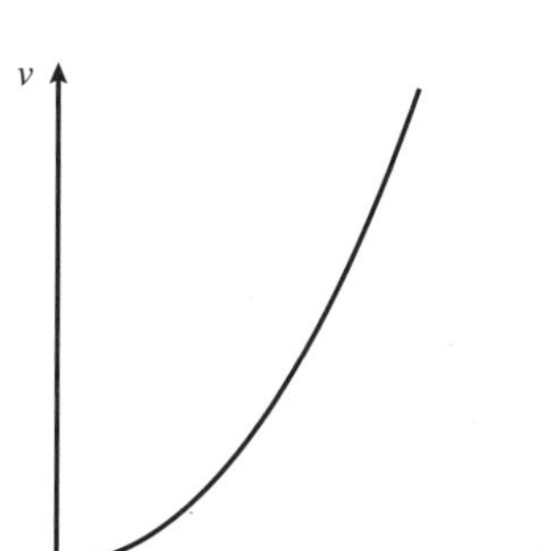

D

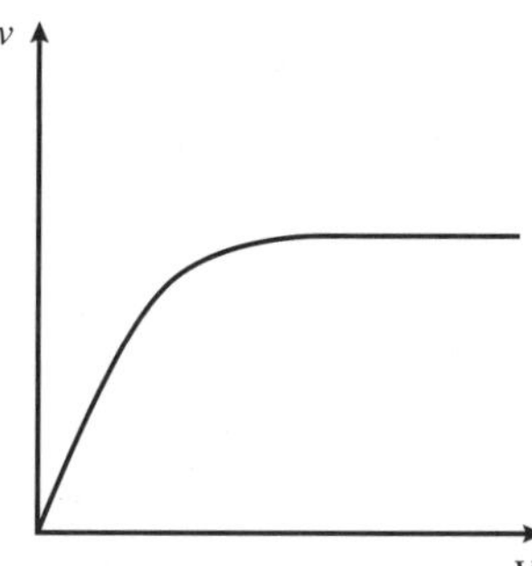

A 

B 

C 

D 

1 6 Two parallel metal plates 50 mm apart are charged so that one has a potential of 500 V and the other a potential of 0 V. There is a uniform field between them. The position of points X, Y and Z are shown on the diagram.

Which row of the table correctly shows the work done in moving an electron from point X to point Y and from point X to point Z?

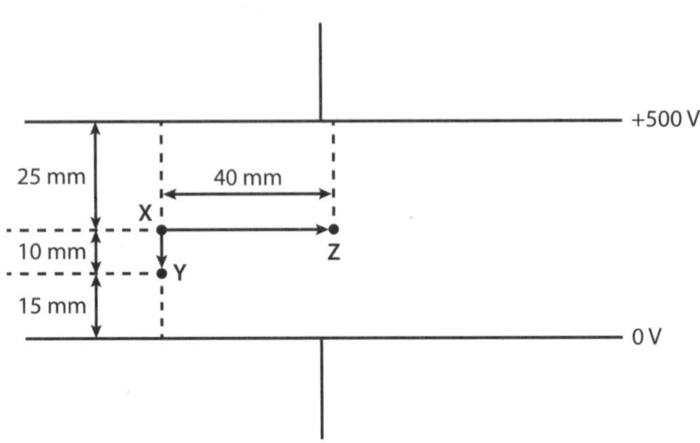

[1 mark]

	Work done moving from X to Y / J	Work done moving from X to Z / J	
A	1.6×10^{-16}	0	⬭
B	1.6×10^{-17}	0	⬭
C	1.6×10^{-16}	1.6×10^{-15}	⬭
D	1.6×10^{-17}	1.6×10^{-15}	⬭

1 7 A parallel plate capacitor with an air gap has capacitance C. It is connected to a battery with potential difference V so that there is a charge Q on the capacitor and it stores energy E. The air gap is gradually filled with oil that has a relative permittivity of 2, while the capacitor is still connected to the battery.

Which row of the table correctly shows what will happen to the charge on the capacitor and the energy stored by the capacitor?

[1 mark]

	New charge on capacitor	New energy stored by capacitor	
A	$\frac{Q}{2}$	$\frac{E}{4}$	⬭
B	$\frac{Q}{2}$	$\frac{E}{2}$	⬭
C	$2Q$	$2E$	⬭
D	$2Q$	$4E$	⬭

1 8 A charged capacitor is discharged through a resistor. Data is collected for the potential difference V across the capacitor at a number of times t after the start of the discharge.

Which variables should be plotted to give a graph with a straight line?

[1 mark]

A V against t

B V against $\frac{1}{t}$

C V against $\ln t$

D $\ln V$ against t

1 9 The charge on a fully charged capacitor is 10 μC. It is discharged through a resistor. The time constant of the circuit is 47 s.

What is the charge remaining after 47 s?

[1 mark]

A 0.21 μC

B 3.7 μC

C 3.9 μC

D 5.0 μC

2 0 The S.I. unit for magnetic flux density is the tesla (T).

What is 1 T in base units?

[1 mark]

A 1 kg A m

B 1 kg A^{-1} s^{-2}

C 1 kg A m s^{-2}

D 1 kg A^{-1} m s^{-2}

2 1 A square coil of side l with N turns is placed in a uniform magnetic field B so that its plane is perpendicular to the field. The coil is replaced with a square coil with sides $\frac{l}{2}$ and $2N$ turns.

What is the new flux linkage?

[1 mark]

A Half the original flux linkage.

B The same as the original flux linkage.

C Double the original flux linkage.

D Four times the original flux linkage.

2 2 An aircraft is flying perpendicular to the Earth's magnetic field at a place where the field is 5.0×10^{-5} T. It has a wingspan of 25 m and is flying at 125 m s^{-1}.

What is the induced emf in the wing?

[1 mark]

A 1.6×10^{-8} V

B 1.0×10^{-5} V

C 2.5×10^{-4} V

D 0.16 V

2 3 What is the root mean square value of a sinusoidal alternating current?

[1 mark]

A $\sqrt{2}$ (the mean value of the current over a half cycle)

B $\sqrt{2}$ (the peak value of the current)

C $\frac{1}{\sqrt{2}}$ (the mean value of the current over a half cycle)

D $\frac{1}{\sqrt{2}}$ (the peak value of the current)

2 4 A step-down transformer is used with the mains to supply a low voltage. A replacement is required to give the same input and output voltages and improved efficiency.

Which of the following changes would increase the efficiency of the transformer?

[1 mark]

A Improve the insulation of the wire used to make the coils. ⬭

B Increase the number of turns in the primary coil. ⬭

C Increase the number of turns in the secondary coil. ⬭

D Replace the solid iron core with one made of laminated layers of iron. ⬭

2 5 In the alpha particle scattering experiment, alpha particles are scattered from gold foil.

What model of the atom is suggested by the results of the experiment?

[1 mark]

A The atom has a nucleus of large radius and high density. ⬭

B The atom has a nucleus of large radius and low density. ⬭

C The atom has a nucleus of small radius and high density. ⬭

D The atom has a nucleus of small radius and low density. ⬭

2 6 At a certain time a radioactive sample X contains N radioactive nuclides with a half-life $T_{1/2}$ and a second radioactive sample Y contains $2N$ radioactive nuclides with half-life $3T_{1/2}$. The activity of sample X is A.

What is the activity of sample Y?

[1 mark]

A $\frac{2}{3}A$ ⬭

B $\frac{3}{2}A$ ⬭

C $6A$ ⬭

D $\frac{1}{6}A$ ⬭

2 7 Before measuring the count rate of a radioactive source, a student measures the background count in the laboratory.

How would this background count compare now to 100 years ago?

[1 mark]

A No change will have occurred.

B The background count rate will have decreased because naturally occurring radioactive isotopes will have decayed.

C The background count rate will have decreased because fewer cosmic rays are reaching Earth.

D The background count rate will have increased due to human activities like nuclear medicine and waste from nuclear power.

2 8 The radioactive decay constant of a free neutron is 1.13×10^{-3} s^{-1}.

What percentage of a large number of free neutrons will still remain after 15 minutes?

[1 mark]

A 0%

B 36%

C 64%

D 98%

2 9 How does the density of the nucleus depend on the number of nucleons forming the nucleus?

[1 mark]

A It is directly proportional to the number of nucleons in the nucleus.

B It is directly proportional to the number of protons in the nucleus.

C It is independent of the number of nucleons in the nucleus.

D It is inversely proportional to the number of nucleons in the nucleus.

3 0 This table shows some suggestions of how the binding energy per nucleon of the product changes compared to the initial nuclide, when nuclear fusion and nuclear fission occur.

Which row of the table is correct?

[1 mark]

	Binding energy per nucleon when nuclear fusion occurs	Binding energy per nucleon when nuclear fission occurs	
A	decreases	decreases	⬭
B	decreases	increases	⬭
C	increases	decreases	⬭
D	increases	increases	⬭

3 1 The table shows some factors to be considered when choosing materials for use in a nuclear reactor.

Which row of the table correctly shows the most important factors to be considered for the moderator, the control rods and the coolant for the reactor?

[1 mark]

	Elastic collisions between neutrons and material	Neutrons are absorbed and resulting nuclide fissions	Good absorber of neutrons	High specific heat capacity	
A	coolant	moderator		control rods	⬭
B	control rods	coolant	moderator		⬭
C	moderator		control rods	coolant	⬭
D		moderator	coolant	control rods	⬭

END OF QUESTIONS

THIS PAGE HAS DELIBERATELY BEEN LEFT BLANK

Collins

A-level

Physics

Practice paper for AQA

Paper 3 – Section A

Time allowed: 2 hours

Materials

For this paper you must have:

- a pencil
- a ruler
- a calculator
- a data and formulae booklet (see pages 229–232)
- a question paper/answer book for Section B.

Instructions

- Answer **all** questions.
- Show **all** your working.
- The total time for both sections of this paper is 2 hours.

Information

- The maximum mark for this section is 45.

Name: ....

Section A

Answer **all** questions in this section.

---

0 1 A student carries out an experiment to measure the Young modulus of a metal wire.

0 1 . 1 List **two** safety precautions the student should take while doing this experiment and explain why they are necessary.

[3 marks]

....

....

....

....

0 1 . 2 State the name of an instrument that a student could use to accurately measure the diameter of the wire.

[1 mark]

....

0 1 . 3 **Table 1** shows three measurements of the diameter.

Table 1

	First reading	Second reading	Third reading
Diameter of wire d / mm	0.77	0.77	0.79

Calculate the mean diameter of the wire **and** the absolute uncertainty in the measurement.

[2 marks]

diameter of wire .... ± .... mm

0 1 · 4 Calculate the cross-sectional area of the wire in metres^2 **and** its percentage uncertainty.

[3 marks]

cross-sectional area of wire .... m^2 ± .... %

0 1 · 5 The student wants to plot a stress–strain graph.

List the measurements the student must make to calculate values for stress and strain.

[3 marks]

....

....

....

0 1 · 6 **Figure 1** shows the graph that the student plotted of stress against strain.

Figure 1

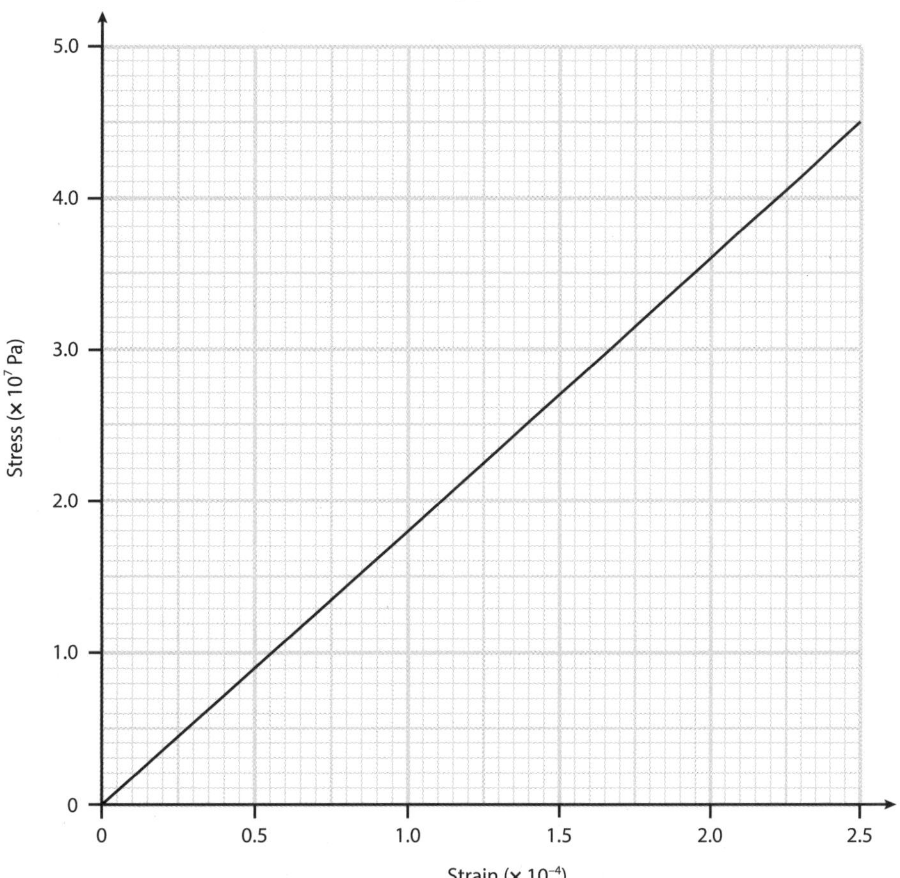

Use the graph to calculate the value of the Young modulus.

[3 marks]

Young modulus .... Pa

0 2 The value of the acceleration due to gravity, g, can be determined by using a simple pendulum.

The equation is $T = 2\pi\sqrt{\frac{l}{g}}$

A student times the swings of a mass hanging from a string and measures the length of the string. The experiment is repeated with different lengths of string.

0 2 · 1 Explain why the student swings the pendulum through a very small angle.

[1 mark]

0 2 · 2 **Table 2** shows the student's results.

Table 2

Length, l / m	Time for 10 swings / s	Period, T / s
0.8	18.4	1.84
1.0	20	2.0
1.1	21.4	2.14
1.2	23	2.3

Comment on these results, and suggest how you would improve them.

[4 marks]

0 2 · 3 The student measured the 10 swings using a stopwatch.

Outline the method you would use to do this accurately.

[2 marks]

....

....

....

0 2 · 4 The student:

- calculates values of T^2
- plots a graph of T^2 on the y-axis against l on the x-axis
- draws a straight line of best fit through the origin
- measures the gradient of the graph to be 4.2 $s^2\ m^{-1}$.

Show that, for motion described by the equation in 02, the graph of T^2 against l is a straight line through the origin and calculate a value for g.

[3 marks]

acceleration due to gravity, g .... $m\ s^{-2}$

Another student carries out the same experiment with the arrangement shown in **Figure 2** to measure the length of the pendulum.

Figure 2

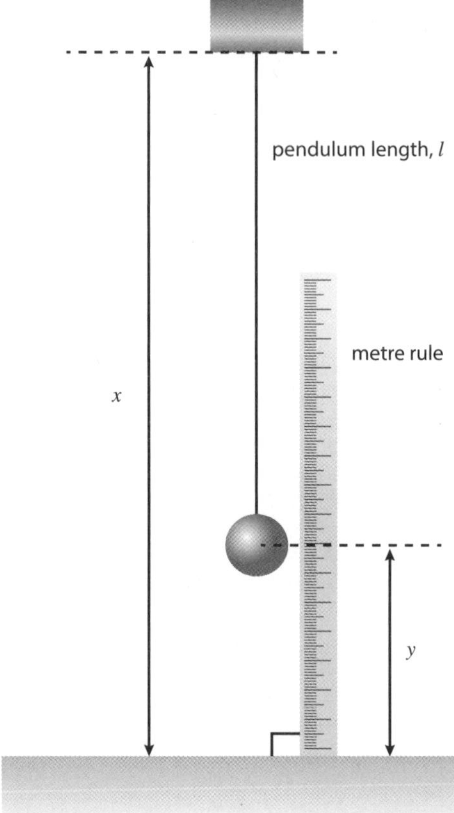

The length x is measured multiple times at the start of the experiment and the range of results gives an absolute uncertainty of $\pm$ 2 mm. The length y is measured once with a standard metre rule marked in millimetres.

The length of the pendulum $l = x - y$.

0 2 · 5 Estimate the uncertainty in the length of the pendulum as a result of using these measuring instruments. Explain your answer.

[2 marks]

uncertainty in $l = \pm$ .... mm

....

....

0 2 · 6 Due to a mistake, the recorded measurement of x is 2 cm too large, leading to an error in the measured pendulum lengths.

State the name given to this type of error.

[1 mark]

....

0 2 · 7 Without further calculation, describe the effect this error has on the graph the student plots **and** on the value of g calculated from the graph.

[2 marks]

....

....

....

0 3 Boyle's law states that the volume of a fixed mass of gas is inversely proportional to the pressure applied to it if the temperature is kept constant.

Figure 3 shows an experiment to test the law.

Figure 3

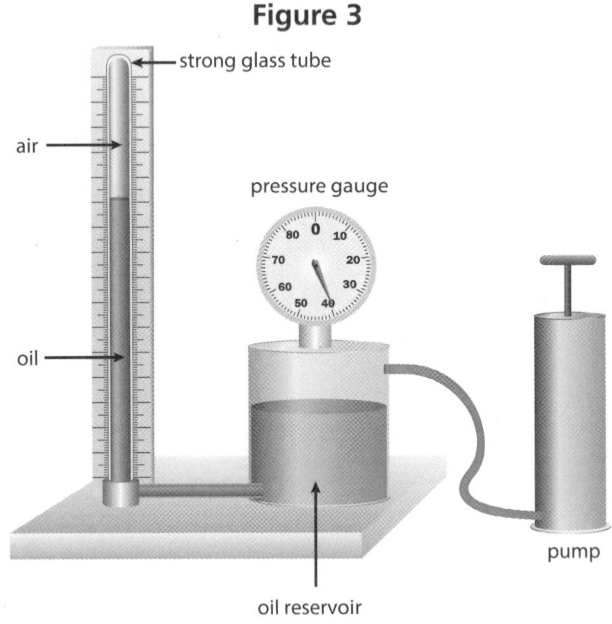

The pump is used to raise the pressure on the air in the tube.

0 3 · 1 State and explain **one** safety precaution you would take when using this equipment.

[2 marks]

....

....

0 3 · 2 Explain why it is important to wait between increasing the pressure and reading the volume.

[1 mark]

....

....

0 3 · 3 Describe how you would make sure that you read the volume scale accurately.

[1 mark]

....

Table 3 shows results from the experiment.

Table 3

Pressure, p / $\times 10^5$ Pa	**Volume, V / cm^3**		
1.0	40.0		
1.4	29.0		
1.8	22.0		
2.2	18.0		
2.5	16.0		
3.0	13.0		

0 3 · 4 You are to show whether Boyle's law is true for this gas by plotting a suitable graph with pressure on the x-axis.

Make any calculations that you need in order to plot your graph. The columns in **Table 3** are for you to use to calculate and tabulate the derived data that you need.

[3 marks]

0 3 · 5 Plot your graph on **Figure 4**. The values of p are provided on the x-axis.

Figure 4

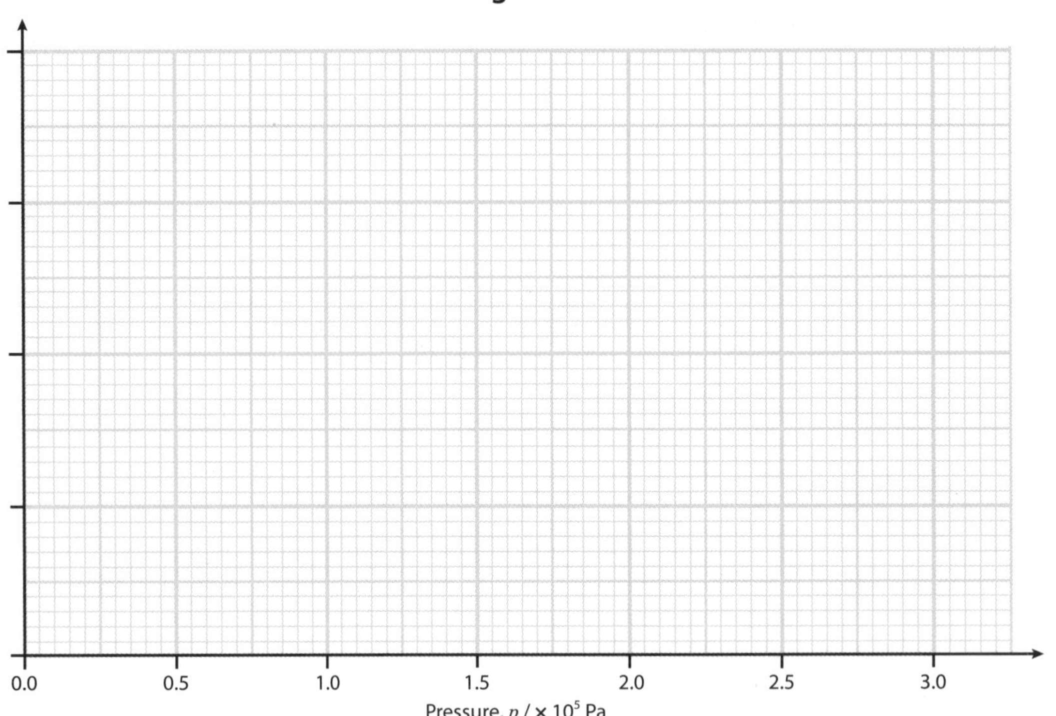

[3 marks]

0 3 · 6 Comment on whether Boyle's law is true for this gas.

[1 mark]

0 3 · 7 Charles's law states that the volume of a fixed mass of gas at constant pressure is proportional to temperature measured in kelvin.

Describe an experiment to demonstrate Charles's law. Include in your answer:

- a description of the equipment (which may include a diagram)
- an outline of the procedure
- an explanation of how you would use the data to demonstrate whether Charles's law is true for the gas.

[4 marks]

END OF SECTION A

Collins

A-level

Physics

Practice paper for AQA

Paper 3 – Section B (Astrophysics)

Materials

For this paper you must have:

- a pencil
- a ruler
- a calculator
- a data and formulae booklet (see pages 229–232)
- a question paper/answer booklet for Section A.

Instructions

- Answer **all** questions.
- Show **all** your working.
- The total time for both sections of this paper is 2 hours.

Information

- The maximum mark for this section is 35.

Name: ....

Section B

Answer **all** questions in this section.

---

0 1 The glass lenses used in some optical refracting telescopes can suffer from chromatic aberration.

0 1 · 1 Draw a diagram to show how light rays are affected by chromatic aberration in a lens.

[1 mark]

0 1 · 2 Suggest **one** way that chromatic aberration can be reduced or avoided in a refracting telescope.

[1 mark]

....

....

A 0.25 m diameter refracting telescope is used to observe the Moon. It has an objective lens with a focal length of 0.60 m. It is set up in normal adjustment and the angular magnification is ×20.

0 1 . 3 Calculate the distance between the two lenses when the telescope is in normal adjustment.

[3 marks]

distance apart ____________ m

0 1 . 4 Calculate the minimum resolvable angle of the telescope at a wavelength of 5.0×10^{-7} m.

[2 marks]

angular resolution ____________ unit ____________

0 2 Reflecting telescopes are used to observe the Sun in both the radio wave and the X-ray regions of the electromagnetic spectrum.

0 2 . 1 State a suitable site for a radio telescope and an X-ray telescope. Explain why the site is suitable in each case.

[4 marks]

....

....

....

....

0 2 . 2 Compare features of these reflecting telescopes, explaining how the wavelength range affects the design.

[4 marks]

....

....

....

....

0 3 Rigel and Procyon are two stars visible from the Earth. **Table 1** gives some data for these stars.

Table 1

Star	Apparent magnitude	Absolute magnitude	Spectral class
Rigel	+0.12	−7.8	B
Procyon	+0.38	2.6	F

0 3 · 1 By considering the data deduce which star is closer to the Earth and explain your answer.

[2 marks]

0 3 · 2 Describe the spectrum of radiation received from each of the stars.

[4 marks]

Spectrum from Rigel:

Spectrum from Procyon:

The intensity of the radiation from a third star S is measured from a space telescope and plotted in **Figure 1**.

Figure 1

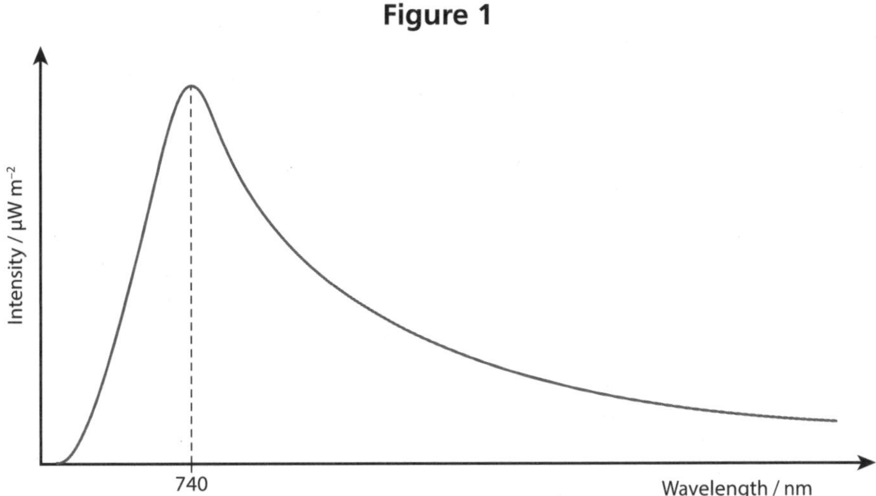

0 3 · 3 Show that the temperature of star S is about 4000 K.

[2 marks]

0 3 · 4 Star S is 6.5 ly from the Earth and an intensity of 4.2 μW m^{-2} reaches the Earth from star S.

Show that the power output from star S is about 2×10^{29} W and calculate its area.

[4 marks]

area of star S ________________ m^2

0 4 Edwin Hubble made use of standard candles in his observations of galaxies.

0 4 · 1 State what astronomers mean by a standard candle, and state an example.

[2 marks]

0 4 · 2 Explain how Edwin Hubble determined the distances and velocities of galaxies and how he deduced that the Universe was expanding.

[6 marks]

END OF QUESTIONS

Data and formulae booklet

DATA – FUNDAMENTAL CONSTANTS AND VALUES

Quantity	Symbol	Value	Units
speed of light in vacuo	c	3.00×10^{8}	m s^{-1}
permeability of free space	μ_0	$4\pi \times 10^{-7}$	H m^{-1}
permittivity of free space	ε_0	8.85×10^{-12}	F m^{-1}
magnitude of the charge of electron	e	1.60×10^{-19}	C
the Planck constant	h	6.63×10^{-34}	J s
gravitational constant	G	6.67×10^{-11}	N m^{2} kg^{-2}
the Avogadro constant	N_A	6.02×10^{23}	mol^{-1}
molar gas constant	R	8.31	J K^{-1} mol^{-1}
the Boltzmann constant	k	1.38×10^{-23}	J K^{-1}
the Stefan constant	σ	5.67×10^{-8}	W m^{-2} K^{-4}
the Wien constant	α	2.90×10^{-3}	m K
electron rest mass (equivalent to 5.5×10^{-4} u)	m_e	9.11×10^{-31}	kg
electron charge/mass ratio	$\frac{e}{m_e}$	1.76×10^{11}	C kg^{-1}
proton rest mass (equivalent to 1.00728 u)	m_p	$1.67(3) \times 10^{-27}$	kg
proton charge/mass ratio	$\frac{e}{m_p}$	9.58×10^{7}	C kg^{-1}
neutron rest mass (equivalent to 1.00867 u)	m_n	$1.67(5) \times 10^{-27}$	kg
gravitational field strength	g	9.81	N kg^{-1}
acceleration due to gravity	g	9.81	m s^{-2}
atomic mass unit (1u is equivalent to 931.5 MeV)	u	1.661×10^{-27}	kg

ALGEBRAIC EQUATION

quadratic equation $x = \frac{-b \pm \sqrt{b^2 - 4ac}}{2a}$

ASTRONOMICAL DATA

Body	Mass/kg	Mean radius/m
Sun	1.99×10^{30}	6.96×10^{8}
Earth	5.98×10^{24}	6.37×10^{6}

GEOMETRICAL EQUATIONS

arc length	$= r\theta$
circumference of circle	$= 2\pi r$
area of circle	$= \pi r^2$
curved surface area of cylinder	$= 2\pi rh$
area of sphere	$= 4\pi r^2$
volume of sphere	$= \frac{4}{3}\pi r^3$

Particle physics

Class	Name	Symbol	Rest energy/MeV
photon	photon	γ	0
lepton	neutrino	ν_e	0
		ν_μ	0
	electron	$e^\pm$	0.510999
	muon	$\mu^\pm$	105.659
mesons	π meson	$\pi^\pm$	139.576
		π^0	134.972
	K meson	$K^\pm$	493.821
		K^0	497.762
baryons	proton	p	938.257
	neutron	n	939.551

Properties of quarks

antiquarks have opposite signs

Type	Charge	Baryon number	Strangeness
u	$+\frac{2}{3}e$	$+\frac{1}{3}$	0
d	$-\frac{1}{3}e$	$+\frac{1}{3}$	0
s	$-\frac{1}{3}e$	$+\frac{1}{3}$	−1

Properties of Leptons

		Lepton number
Particles:	e^-, ν_e ; μ^-, ν_μ	+1
Antiparticles:	e^+, $\overline{\nu_e}$, μ^+, $\overline{\nu_\mu}$	−1

Photons and energy levels

photon energy $E = hf = hc / \lambda$

photoelectricity $hf = \phi + E_{k(max)}$

energy levels $hf = E_1 - E_2$

de Broglie wavelength $\lambda = \frac{h}{p} = \frac{h}{mv}$

Waves

wave speed $c = f\lambda$ *period* $f = \frac{1}{T}$

first harmonic $f = \frac{1}{2l}\sqrt{\frac{T}{\mu}}$

fringe spacing $w = \frac{\lambda D}{s}$ *diffraction grating* $d \sin\theta = n\lambda$

refractive index of a substance s, $n = \frac{c}{c_s}$

for two different substances of refractive indices n_1 *and* n_2,

law of refraction $n_1 \sin\theta_1 = n_2 \sin\theta_2$

critical angle $\sin\theta_c = \frac{n_2}{n_1}$ for $n_1 > n_2$

Mechanics

moments moment = Fd

velocity and acceleration $v = \frac{\Delta s}{\Delta t}$ $a = \frac{\Delta v}{\Delta t}$

equations of motion $v = u + at$ $s = \left(\frac{u+v}{2}\right)t$

$v^2 = u^2 + 2as$ $s = ut + \frac{at^2}{2}$

force $F = ma$

force $F = \frac{\Delta(mv)}{\Delta t}$

impulse $F\Delta t = \Delta(mv)$

work, energy and power $W = F s \cos\theta$

$E_k = \frac{1}{2}mv^2$ $\Delta E_p = mg\Delta h$

$P = \frac{\Delta W}{\Delta t}$, $P = Fv$

efficiency = $\frac{\text{useful output power}}{\text{input power}}$

Materials

density $\rho = \frac{m}{V}$ *Hooke's law* $F = k\,\Delta L$

Young modulus = $\frac{\text{tensile stress}}{\text{tensile strain}}$ tensile stress = $\frac{F}{A}$ tensile strain = $\frac{\Delta L}{L}$

energy stored $E = \frac{1}{2}F\Delta L$

Electricity

current and pd	$I = \frac{\Delta Q}{\Delta t}$ $\quad V = \frac{W}{Q}$ $\quad R = \frac{V}{I}$
resistivity	$\rho = \frac{RA}{L}$
resistors in series	$R_T = R_1 + R_2 + R_3 + \ldots$
resistors in parallel	$\frac{1}{R_T} = \frac{1}{R_1} + \frac{1}{R_2} + \frac{1}{R_3} + \ldots$
power	$P = VI = I^2R = \frac{V^2}{R}$
emf	$\varepsilon = \frac{E}{Q}$ $\quad \varepsilon = I(R + r)$

Circular motion

magnitude of angular speed	$\omega = \frac{v}{r}$
	$\omega = 2\pi f$
centripetal acceleration	$a = \frac{v^2}{r} = \omega^2 r$
centripetal force	$F = \frac{mv^2}{r} = m\omega^2 r$

Simple harmonic motion

acceleration	$a = -\omega^2 x$
displacement	$x = A \cos(\omega t)$
speed	$v = \pm\omega\sqrt{(A^2 - x^2)}$
maximum speed	$v_{max} = \omega A$
maximum acceleration	$a_{max} = \omega^2 A$
for a mass-spring system	$T = 2\pi\sqrt{\frac{m}{k}}$
for a simple pendulum	$T = 2\pi\sqrt{\frac{l}{g}}$

Thermal physics

energy to change temperature	$Q = mc\Delta\theta$
energy to change state	$Q = ml$
gas law	$pV = nRT$
	$pV = NkT$
kinetic theory model	$pV = \frac{1}{3}Nm(c_{rms})^2$
kinetic energy of gas molecule	$\frac{1}{2}m(c_{rms})^2 = \frac{3}{2}kT = \frac{3RT}{2N_A}$

Gravitational fields

force between two masses	$F = \frac{Gm_1m_2}{r^2}$
gravitational field strength	$g = \frac{F}{m}$
magnitude of gravitational field strength in a radial field	$g = \frac{GM}{r^2}$
work done	$\Delta W = m\Delta V$
gravitational potential	$V = -\frac{GM}{r}$
	$g = -\frac{\Delta V}{\Delta r}$

Electric fields and capacitors

force between two point charges	$F = \frac{1}{4\pi\varepsilon_0}\frac{Q_1Q_2}{r^2}$
force on a charge	$F = EQ$
field strength for a uniform field	$F = \frac{V}{d}$
work done	$\Delta W = Q\Delta V$
field strength for a radial field	$E = \frac{1}{4\pi\varepsilon_0}\frac{Q}{r^2}$
electric potential	$V = \frac{1}{4\pi\varepsilon_0}\frac{Q}{r}$
	$E = \frac{\Delta V}{\Delta r}$
capacitance	$C = \frac{Q}{V}$
	$C = \frac{A\varepsilon_0\varepsilon_r}{d}$
capacitor energy stored	$E = \frac{1}{2}QV = \frac{1}{2}CV^2 = \frac{1}{2}\frac{Q^2}{C}$
capacitor charging	$Q = Q_0(1 - e^{-t/RC})$
decay of charge	$Q = Q_0e^{-t/RC}$
time constant	RC

Magnetic fields

force on a current	$F = BIl$
force on a moving charge	$F = BQv$
magnetic flux	$\Phi = BA$
magnetic flux linkage	$N\Phi = BAN\cos\theta$
magnitude of induced emf	$\varepsilon = N\frac{\Delta\Phi}{\Delta t}$ $N\Phi = BAN\cos\theta$
emf induced in a rotating coil	$\varepsilon = BAN\,\omega \sin \omega t$
alternating current	$I_{rms} = \frac{I_0}{\sqrt{2}}$ $V_{rms} = \frac{V_0}{\sqrt{2}}$
transformer equations	$\frac{N_s}{N_p} = \frac{V_s}{V_p}$
	$efficiency = \frac{I_s V_s}{I_p V_p}$

Nuclear physics

the inverse square law for γ radiation	$I = \frac{k}{x^2}$
radioactive decay	$\frac{\Delta N}{\Delta t} = \lambda N$, $N = N_0 e^{-\lambda t}$
activity	$A = \lambda N$
half-life	$T_{1/2} = \frac{\ln 2}{\lambda}$
nuclear radius	$R = R_0 A^{1/3}$
energy-mass equation	$E = mc^2$

Astrophysics

1 astronomical unit = 1.50×10^{11} m

1 light year = 9.46×10^{15} m

1 parsec = 2.06×10^{5} AU = 3.08×10^{16} m

= 3.26 light years

Hubble constant, H = 65 km s^{-1} Mpc^{-1}

$$M = \frac{\text{angle subtended by image at eye}}{\text{angle subtended by object at unaided eye}}$$

telescope in normal adjustment	$M = \frac{f_0}{f_e}$
Rayleigh criterion	$\theta \approx \frac{\lambda}{D}$
magnitude equation	$m - M = 5 \log \frac{d}{10}$
Wien's law	$\lambda_{max} T = 2.9 \times 10^{-3}$ m K
Stefan's law	$P = \sigma A T^4$
Schwarzschild radius	$R_s \approx \frac{2GM}{c^2}$
Doppler shift for $v << c$	$\frac{\Delta f}{f} = -\frac{\Delta\lambda}{\lambda} = \frac{v}{c}$
red shift	$z = -\frac{v}{c}$
Hubble's law	$v = Hd$

Answers

Page 7

1. The joule [1]
2. 9×10^4 cm [1]
3. a) kg m s^{-2} [1] b) kg m^2 s^{-2} [1]
   c) kg m^2 s^{-3} [1] d) kg m^{-1} s^{-2} [1]
4. a) 1.8×10^3 A [1] b) 4.5×10^{-7} m [1]
   c) 8.2×10^{-4} s [1] d) 2.5×10^2 m^2 [1]
   e) 7.4×10^2 m^3 [1] f) 1.6×10^3 m^3 [1]

Page 9

1. a) 1.21 A [1] b) 0.06 A [1]
   c) 0.050 [1] d) 5.0% [1]
   e) $\frac{0.08}{3.20} \times 100$ [1]
   = 2.5% [1]
   f) $R = \frac{V}{I} = \frac{3.20}{1.21} = 2.64\,\Omega$ [1]
   $\varepsilon R = 5.0 + 2.5 = 7.5\%$ [1]
   g) 0.20 Ω [1]
2. a) 20.1 mm [1]
   b) $\Delta d = 0.3$ mm [1]
   $\varepsilon d = \frac{0.3}{20.1} \times 100 = 1.5\%$ [1]
   c) $A = \pi r^2 = \pi \left(\frac{20.1}{2}\right)^2 = 317.3$ mm^2 (317 mm^2 to 3 s.f.) [1]
   $\varepsilon A = 2 \times \varepsilon d = 3.0\%$ [1]
   d) $\frac{0.02}{1.48} \times 100$ [1]
   = 1.4% [1]
   e) $V = A \times h = 317.3 \times 1.48 = 470$ mm^3 [1]
   $\varepsilon V = 3.0 + 1.4 = 4.4\%$ (4.3% if unrounded numbers used) [1]
   f) 21 mm^3 (20 mm^3 if unrounded numbers used) [1]

Page 11

1. 10^6 J [1]
2. a) Axes labelled correctly [1]
   Points plotted correctly [1]
   Error bars drawn correctly [1]
   Line of best fit drawn correctly [1]
   b) 1.1 Ω (accept between 1.05 and 1.15 Ω) [1]
   c) Shallowest line of fit drawn correctly [1]
   1.0 Ω (accept between 0.95 and 1.05 Ω) [1]
   d) $\frac{0.1}{1.1} \times 100$ [1]
   = 9% (accept between 7% and 11%) [1]

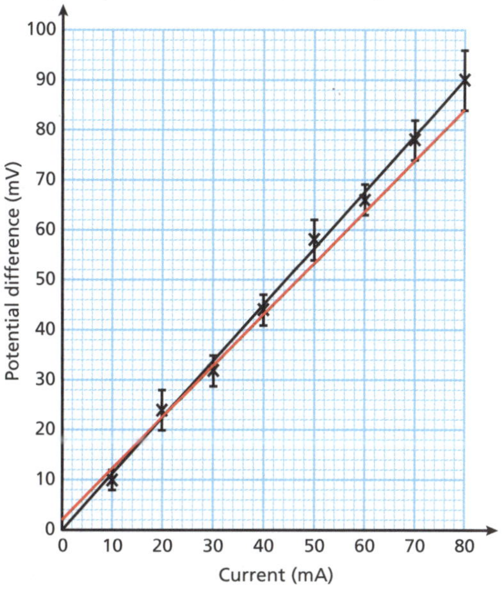

Page 13

1. An electron [1]
2. a) Total charge = $26 \times 1.6 \times 10^{-19}$ C = 4.16×10^{-18} C [1]
   $m = \frac{Q}{\text{specific charge}} = \frac{(4.16 \times 10^{-18})}{(4.45 \times 10^7)} = 9.35 \times 10^{-26}$ kg [1]
   $\frac{(9.35 \times 10^{-26})}{(1.67 \times 10^{-27})} = 56$ nucleons
   56 nucleons – 26 protons = 30 neutrons [1]
   b) The strong nuclear force is repulsive at distances below 0.5 fm [1]
   and attractive at distances between 0.5 and 3 fm. [1]
3. a) Similarity: both isotopes have 6 protons. [1]
   Difference: carbon–12 has 6 neutrons, while carbon–13 has 7 neutrons. [1]
   b) Total charge = $6 \times 1.6 \times 10^{-19}$ C = 9.6×10^{-19} C [1]
   Total mass = $12 \times 1.67 \times 10^{-27}$ kg = 2.0×10^{-26} kg [1]
   Specific charge = $\frac{Q}{m} = \frac{(9.6 \times 10^{-19})}{(2.0 \times 10^{-26})} = 4.8 \times 10^7$ C kg^{-1} [1]
   c) The specific charge of carbon–13 would be less [1]
   as carbon–13 has the same number of protons, but one more neutron. [1]
   d) Nucleon number = 14 [1]
   Atomic number = 7 [1]
   e) The diagram shows that the beta particles have a range of energies. [1]
   In a decay, energy should be conserved. Antineutrinos carry the missing energy. [1]

Page 15

1. Only photon A [1]
2. a) An antiparticle has the same mass as the corresponding particle. [1]
   An antiparticle has the opposite charge as the corresponding particle. [1]
   b) The positron [1]
   c) The electron and its antiparticle annihilate, [1]
   and create two gamma photons. [1]
   d) One of either: $0.510\,999 \times 10^6 \times 1.6 \times 10^{-19}$
   = 8.18×10^{-14} J [1]
   Or $E = mc^2 = 9.11 \times 10^{-31} \times (3.0 \times 10^8)^2$
   = 8.20×10^{-14} J [1]
3. a) Pair production involves the energy of a gamma photon [1]
   being converted into a particle-antiparticle pair. [1]
   b) To conserve momentum [1]
   c) An antiproton [1]
   d) Rest energy of proton and antiproton
   = $2 \times 938.257 \times 10^6 \times 1.6 \times 10^{-19}$ [1]
   = 3.0×10^{-10} J [1]
   $f = \frac{E}{h} = 4.5 \times 10^{23}$ Hz [1]
   e) Any extra energy beyond the minimum becomes kinetic energy of the proton and antiproton produced. [1]

Page 17

1. W boson [1]
2. Weak nuclear [1]
3. a) Virtual photon [1]

b) Exchange particles carry force, energy, charge and momentum [1]
from one particle to another. [1]

c) The strong nuclear force [1]
And any two of:
which has an exchange particle of a pion [1]
and has a range of 3 fm (while the electromagnetic force is long range). [1]
The strong nuclear force is also repulsive at separations below 0.5 fm. [1]

4. a) $p \rightarrow n + e^+ + \upsilon_e$ [1]

b) Any of beta-minus decay, electron capture or electron-proton collision. [1]
Either of $n \rightarrow p + e^- + \bar{\upsilon}_e$ (for beta-minus decay) or $p + e^- \rightarrow n + \upsilon_e$ (for electron capture or electron-proton collision. [1]

c) Proton and neutron correctly shown on left-hand side of the diagram. [1]
Positron and electron neutrino correctly shown on right-hand side of the diagram. [1]
Correct exchange particle (W^+ boson) [1]

Page 19

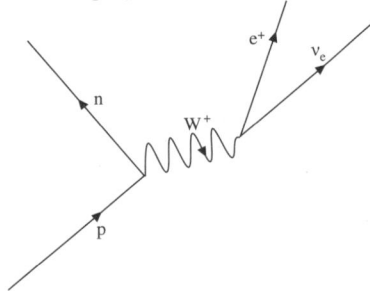

1. An antineutron has a baryon number of +1 [1]

2. a) Strangeness = +1 [1]
Charge = 0 [1]

b) Neutral kaon/K^0 [1]

3. a) A meson consists of a quark and an antiquark. [1]

b) $u\bar{s}$ [1]

c) $u\bar{d}$ [1]

d) $u\bar{u}$ (accept $d\bar{d}$) [1]

4. a) A particle that consists of three quarks. [1]

b) Neutron: udd [1]
Negative pion: $d\bar{u}$ [1]

c) ddd [1]

d) A hadron is a particle that is made of quarks. [1]

Page 21

1. a) $p \rightarrow n + e^+ + \upsilon_e$ [1]

b) The weak interaction [1]
as there is a change in quark character. [1]

2. a) The weak interaction [1]
And one of:
As there is a change in strangeness. [1]
As strange particles decay through the weak interaction. [1]

b) dds [1]

c) Due to conservation of charge, charge of X is –1. [1]
Due to conservation of baryon number, X is not a baryon. [1]
Due to conservation of lepton number, X is not a lepton. [1]
Therefore, X is a π^-. [1]

3. a) Charge = 0 [1]

b) The strong interaction [1]

c) Charge before interaction = +1. Charge after interaction = 0. Charge is not conserved. [1]
Baryon number before interaction = +2. Baryon number after interaction = +1. Baryon number is not conserved. [1]
Strangeness before interaction = 0. Strangeness after interaction = –1. Strangeness is not conserved. Strange particles are only made through the strong interaction, so strangeness needs to be conserved. [1]
Therefore, the particle interaction is not possible. [1]

d) Charge is conserved. [1]
Baryon number is conserved. [1]
Strangeness goes from –1 to 0, but this is allowed as it is a weak decay. [1]
This particle interaction is possible. [1]

Page 23

1. a) Both the metal rod and gold leaf are negatively charged. Like charges repel. [1]

b) When photons above the threshold frequency are incident onto a metal surface, [1]
photoelectrons are emitted from the metal surface. [1]

c) The frequency/energy of photons in the ultraviolet light is above the threshold frequency/work function and so photoelectrons are released and the gold leaf becomes less charged. [1]
The frequency/energy of photons in the white light is below the threshold frequency/work function and so charge remains on the gold leaf. [1]

2. a) The minimum photon energy needed to release an electron [1]
from a metal surface. [1]

b) $\phi = 4.2 \times 1.6 \times 10^{-19}\,\text{J} = 6.72 \times 10^{-19}\,\text{J}$ [1]
$f_0 = \frac{\phi}{h} = \frac{(6.72 \times 10^{-19})}{(6.63 \times 10^{-34})} = 1.0 \times 10^{15}\,\text{Hz}$ [1]

c) $E_{k(\text{max})} = hf - \phi = (6.63 \times 10^{-34}) \times (1.3 \times 10^{15}) - 6.72 \times 10^{-19}$ [1]
$= 1.9 \times 10^{-19}\,\text{J}$ [1]

d) $V_s = \frac{E_k}{e} = \frac{(1.9 \times 10^{-19})}{(1.6 \times 10^{-19})}$ [1]
$= 1.2\,\text{V}$ [1]

Page 25

1. a) 4.5 eV [1]

b) $E = 4.5\,\text{eV} = 4.5 \times 1.6 \times 10^{-19}\,\text{J} = 7.2 \times 10^{-19}\,\text{J}$ [1]
$f = \frac{E}{h} = \frac{(7.2 \times 10^{-19})}{(6.63 \times 10^{-34})} = 1.1 \times 10^{15}\,\text{Hz}$ [1]

c) Electron at infinity has zero (potential) energy. [1]
Energy needs to be transferred to electron to take it to infinity/cause ionisation. [1]

2. a) The energy difference between energy levels is 12.09 eV. [1]
Photons are absorbed and so need exactly 12.09 eV. [1]
Electrons transfer part of their kinetic energy and so need a minimum of 12.09 eV. [1]

b) Longest wavelength means smallest frequency and energy. [1]
$E = 3.4 - 1.51 = 1.89\,\text{eV} = 1.89 \times 1.6 \times 10^{-19}\,\text{J} = 3.02 \times 10^{-19}\,\text{J}$ [1]
$\lambda = \frac{hc}{E} = \frac{(6.63 \times 10^{-34}) \times (3.0 \times 10^{8})}{(3.02 \times 10^{-19})} = 6.6 \times 10^{-7}\,\text{m}$ [1]

c) An emission spectrum is formed by the de-excitation of electrons, which emits photons. **[1]**
An absorption spectrum is formed when a continuous spectrum passes through atoms, **[1]**
which excites electrons into higher energy levels, absorbing photons. **[1]**

d) Line spectra consist of discrete wavelengths. **[1]**
These discrete wavelengths correspond to an exact energy difference between energy levels. **[1]**

3. Any six from:
Thermionic emission releases electrons. **[1]**
These electrons collide with mercury atoms, **[1]**
and excite electrons in the mercury atoms. **[1]**
The mercury atoms de-excite, **[1]**
and emit UV photons. **[1]**
The UV photons get absorbed by a phosphor coating. **[1]**
The phosphor coating emits lower frequency visible photons. **[1]**

Page 27

1. a) Electrons demonstrate both wave-like and particle-like behaviour. **[1]**

b) The pattern is a diffraction pattern, only waves diffract. **[1]**
The bright rings occur when electrons are arriving in phase with each other and constructively interfering. **[1]**

c) The electron collision causes an electron in the phosphor to become excited to a higher energy level. **[1]**
It then de-excites, emitting a photon in the process. **[1]**

d) $E_k = 5.0\,\text{keV} = (5.0 \times 10^3) \times (1.6 \times 10^{-19})\,\text{J} = 8.0 \times 10^{-16}\,\text{J}$ **[1]**
$E_k = \frac{1}{2}mv^2$, $v = \sqrt{\frac{2E_k}{m}} = \sqrt{\frac{2 \times (8.0 \times 10^{-16})}{9.11 \times 10^{-31}}}$
$= 4.2 \times 10^7\,\text{m s}^{-1}$ **[1]**

e) $\lambda = \frac{h}{mv} = \frac{6.63 \times 10^{-34}}{(9.11 \times 10^{-31}) \times (4.2 \times 10^7)} = 1.7 \times 10^{-11}\,\text{m}$ **[1]**

f) The spacing between the maxima would increase. **[1]**
As the velocity of the electrons would be lower, meaning a smaller de Broglie wavelength. **[1]**
Diffraction is maximised when the wavelength is close in size to the space of the gap (nuclei spacing is of the order of 10^{-10} m). **[1]**

g) The photoelectric effect **[1]**

2. a) Molecules have a (de Broglie) wavelength. **[1]**
Waves undergo interference. **[1]**

b) $\lambda = \frac{h}{mv} = \frac{6.63 \times 10^{-34}}{(4.2 \times 10^{-23}) \times (150)} = 1.1 \times 10^{-13}\,\text{m}$ **[1]**

c) The larger the mass, the smaller the de Broglie wavelength. **[1]**

Page 29

1. a) 450°, $\frac{5\pi}{2}$ radians **[1]**

b) 630°, $\frac{7\pi}{2}$ radians **[1]**

c) 180°, π radians **[1]**

d) $0.45\,\text{m} = \frac{\lambda}{2}$
$\lambda = 0.90\,\text{m}$ **[1]**

2. a) Any three from:
Electromagnetic waves are transverse, **[1]**
the particles of the medium oscillate perpendicular to the direction of energy transfer. **[1]**
Electromagnetic waves travel at the speed of light, **[1]**
and can travel through a vacuum. **[1]**
Electromagnetic waves have electric and magnetic field components, which are perpendicular to each other. **[1]**

b) $f = \frac{c}{\lambda} = \frac{(3.0 \times 10^{-8})}{(532 \times 10^{-9})} = 5.64 \times 10^{14}\,\text{Hz}$ **[1]**
$\frac{(5.64 \times 10^{14})}{10^{12}} = 564\,\text{THz}$ **[1]**

c) $\frac{\pi}{2}$ radians is equivalent to $\frac{\lambda}{4}$ **[1]**
$\frac{\lambda}{4} = 133\,\text{nm}$ **[1]**

3. a) The particles of the medium oscillate, **[1]**
parallel to the direction of energy transfer. **[1]**

b) $T = 2.5\,\text{ms} = 0.0025\,\text{s}$ **[1]**
$f = \frac{1}{T} = \frac{1}{0.0025} = 400\,\text{Hz}$ **[1]**

c) $\lambda = \frac{c}{f} = \frac{340}{400} = 0.85\,\text{m}$ **[1]**

d) 180° is equivalent to $\frac{\lambda}{2} = 0.43\,\text{m}$ (to 2 s.f.) **[1]**

Page 31

1. Sound **[1]**
2. 90° **[1]**
3. Any six from:
Shine a light source through two polarising filters. **[1]**
Rotate the second filter (the analyser) relative to the first filter. **[1]**
Observe the brightness of light emerging from the second filter. **[1]**
When the transmission axes of the filters are aligned, the light intensity is maximised. **[1]**
As the analyser is rotated, the light intensity decreases. **[1]**
When the analyser is at 90° to the polariser, no light is transmitted. **[1]**
The first polarising filter polarises the light, allowing only oscillations in a single plane to pass through. **[1]**
The second filter blocks or transmits the polarised light based on its orientation relative to the first filter. **[1]**
The changes in transmitted intensity confirm that the light's oscillations are confined to a single plane. **[1]**
Light is a transverse wave as only transverse waves can be polarised. **[1]**

4. a) Polarised light consists of waves oscillating in a single plane, **[1]**
perpendicular to the direction of wave travel. **[1]**

b) Reflected light from the water is partially polarised. **[1]**
The polarising filter is rotated to align its axis perpendicular to the partially polarised light, blocking the reflection. **[1]**

c) Any one from: polaroid sunglasses, 3D glasses, aligning TV/radio aerials (or other correct answer). **[1]**

5. Sinusoidal graph **[1]**
with zero intensity at 0°, 180° and 360° and maximum intensity at 90° and 270°. **[1]**

Page 33

1. 1.20 m **[1]**
2. 80 Hz **[1]**
3. a) Any three from:
Incoming wave reflects from the metal plate. **[1]**
The incoming and reflected waves overlap and interfere. **[1]**

As the incoming and reflected waves have the same frequency, wavelength and amplitude, a stationary wave is formed. [1]

Nodes are formed by destructive interference and antinodes are formed by constructive interference. [1]

b) Node-node distance = $\frac{\lambda}{2}$ [1]

λ = 12.2 cm = 0.122 m [1]

$c = f\lambda = 2.45 \times 10^9 \times 0.122 = 2.99 \times 10^8\,\text{m s}^{-1}$ ($3.0 \times 10^8\,\text{m s}^{-1}$ to 2 s.f.) [1]

4. a) Three loops correctly drawn and equally spaced. [1]

Antinodes labelled at positions of maximum displacement. [1]

Nodes labelled at positions of zero displacement. [1]

b) Nodes are formed by destructive interference (when the incoming and reflected waves overlap while completely out of phase). [1]

Antinodes are formed by constructive interference (when the incoming and reflected waves overlap while in phase). [1]

c) $f = \frac{3}{2l}\sqrt{\frac{T}{\mu}}$ [1]

$T = \frac{f^2 \times 4l^2 \times \mu}{9} = \frac{36^2 \times 4 \times 0.8^2 \times 0.0018}{9} = 0.66\,\text{N}$ [1]

Page 35

1. Decreasing the width of the slits, keeping the slit separation the same [1]

2. Minima as the phase difference is 180° [1]

3. a) $w = \frac{\lambda D}{s} \frac{(532 \times 10^{-9}) \times 1.50}{500 \times 10^{-6}}$ [1]

$= 1.60 \times 10^{-3}\,\text{m}$ [1]

b) Light from the two slits overlaps and superposes. [1]

When light arrives in phase, constructive interference creates a bright fringe. [1]

When light arrives completely out of phase, destructive interference creates a dark fringe. [1]

c) Red light has a longer wavelength than green light. [1]

Therefore, the interference pattern will be more spread out. [1]

4. a) $\lambda = \frac{c}{f} = \frac{3.0 \times 10^8}{10 \times 10^9} = 0.030\,\text{m}$ [1]

$w = \frac{\lambda D}{s} = \frac{0.030 \times 1.5}{0.050}$ [1]

= 0.90 m [1]

45 cm = 0.45 m, so distance is half the fringe spacing. [1]

Therefore, destructive interference will occur. [1]

b) Coherent waves have the same frequency and wavelength, [1]

and a constant phase difference. [1]

Page 37

1. The maxima for 500 nm are closer to the central maximum. [1]

2. Longer wavelengths diffract more, causing the central maximum to appear white and other maxima to form spectra. [1]

3. a) $d = \frac{1}{500} = 2.0 \times 10^{-3}\,\text{mm}$ [1]

$= 2.0 \times 10^{-6}\,\text{m}$ [1]

b) $\theta = \sin^{-1}\left(\frac{n\lambda}{d}\right) = \sin^{-1}\left(\frac{2 \times 650 \times 10^{-9}}{2.0 \times 10^{-6}}\right)$ [1]

= 40.5° [1]

Angle between the two second order maxima = 2 × 40.5 = 81° [1]

c) $n_{max} = \frac{d}{\lambda} = \frac{2 \times 10^{-6}}{650 \times 10^{-9}}$ [1]

= 3.08 (round down to maximum order = 3) [1]

d) The central maximum is twice as wide as other maxima. [1]

The central maximum is much brighter than other maxima. [1]

4. a) $d = \frac{1}{1000} = 1.0 \times 10^{-3}\,\text{mm} = 1.0 \times 10^{-6}\,\text{m}$ [1]

$\lambda = \frac{d\sin\theta}{n} = \frac{(1.0 \times 10^{-6})\sin 22}{1}$ [1]

$= 3.7 \times 10^{-7}\,\text{m}$ [1]

b) Similarity, one of: transverse; travel at speed of light; can travel through vacuum; electromagnetic; both consist of photons. [1]

Difference, one of: X-ray has a higher frequency/lower wavelength; X-ray is ionising; X-ray has higher photon energy. [1]

Page 39

1. 1.4 [1]

2. a) Light travels from a higher refractive index to a lower refractive index, [1]

at an angle of incidence exceeding the critical angle. [1]

b) $\theta_c = \sin^{-1}\left(\frac{n_2}{n_1}\right) = \sin^{-1}\left(\frac{1}{2.42}\right)$ [1]

= 24.4° [1]

3. a) $c_s = \frac{c}{n} = \frac{(3.0 \times 10^8)}{1.33}$ [1]

$= 2.26 \times 10^8\,\text{m s}^{-1}$ [1]

b) $\theta_2 = \sin^{-1}\left(\frac{n_1 \sin\theta_1}{n_2}\right) = \sin^{-1}\left(\frac{1 \times \sin 50}{1.33}\right)$ [1]

= 35.2° [1]

c) Angle of incidence onto vertical glass surface = 90 – 35.2 = 54.8° [1]

$\theta_2 = \sin^{-1}\left(\frac{n_1 \sin\theta_1}{n_2}\right) = \sin^{-1}\left(\frac{1.33 \times \sin 54.8}{1.70}\right)$ [1]

= 40° (to 2 s.f.) [1]

4. Any four of:

Direct a named light source (e.g. laser or ray from ray box) onto the glass block [1]

Using a protractor, measure the angle of incidence and angle of refraction from the normal. [1]

Repeat for different angles of incidence (e.g. in 10° intervals). [1]

Plot a graph of $\sin\theta_1$ vs $\sin\theta_2$ (or $\sin\theta_2$ vs $\sin\theta_1$). [1]

The gradient gives the refractive index of the glass block (or $\frac{1}{n}$). [1]

Page 41

1. Lower refractive index than the core [1]

2. Any six from:

Pulse broadening is the spreading out of a pulse over time. [1]

Material and modal dispersion contribute to pulse broadening. [1]

Material dispersion occurs as different wavelengths experience different refractive indices, [1]

which leads to different wavelengths travelling at different speeds through the core. [1]

Material dispersion can be minimised by using monochromatic light. [1]

Modal dispersion is caused by light taking different paths through the core. [1]

A ray that travels a longer distance will take longer to leave the fibre. [1]

Modal dispersion can be reduced by using single-mode fibres that have a narrow core, [1] and by having a cladding that has a very similar refractive index to the core. **[1]**

3. a) To protect the fibre from damage **[1]**
   b) $n_2 = \frac{n_1 \sin\theta_1}{\sin\theta_2} = \frac{1 \times \sin 15.5}{\sin 10.5}$ **[1]**
   $= 1.466$ **[1]**
   $\theta_c = \sin^{-1}\left(\frac{1.4}{1.466}\right)$ **[1]**
   $= 73°$ (to 2 s.f.) **[1]**
   c) $c_s = \frac{c}{n} = \frac{(3.0 \times 10^8)}{1.466} = 2.05 \times 10^8\,\text{m s}^{-1}$ **[1]**
   Speed along axis of fibre = $2.05 \times 10^8 \times \cos 10.5 = 2.01 \times 10^8\,\text{m s}^{-1}$ **[1]**
   $t = \frac{s}{v} = \frac{5500}{2.01 \times 10^8} = 2.7 \times 10^{-5}\,\text{s}$ **[1]**
   d) A larger angle of incidence means a larger angle of refraction and so a greater distance travelled. **[1]**
   Violet light experiences a larger refractive index and so travels more slowly through the core. **[1]**
   These effects mean that the violet light will take a longer time to travel through the core. **[1]**
   e) Some light is absorbed in the core. **[1]**
   To reduce this, the core can be made of a material that is highly transparent. **[1]**
   Repeaters can be used to amplify the signal. **[1]**

Page 43

1. Horizontal component = 45cos 30 = 39 N (to 2 s.f.) **[1]**
   Vertical component = 45sin 30 = 23 N (to 2 s.f.) **[1]**
2. Vertical force drawn correctly to scale (e.g. 5.0 cm for 5.0 N) **[1]**
   4.0 N force drawn correctly to scale (e.g. 4.0 cm for 4.0 N) and at correct angle of 20° above the horizontal. **[1]**
   Resultant force measured to be in range 7.1–7.7 N **[1]**
   Angle measured to be in range 58–62° **[1]**
3. a) Weight = 5.0 × 9.81 = 49.05 N **[1]**
   49.05sin 30 = 24.5 N (25 N to 2 s.f.) **[1]**
   b) 24.5 N (25 N to 2 s.f.) **[1]**
   c) 49.05cos 30 **[1]**
   = 42.5 N (43 N to 2 s.f.) **[1]**
4. $T_1\cos 50 = T_2\cos 40$ **[1]**
   $T_1\sin 50 + T_2\sin 40 = 9.5$ **[1]**
   $T_1 = 7.3\,\text{N}$ **[1]**
   $T_2 = 6.1\,\text{N}$ **[1]**

Page 45

1. 30 N **[1]**
2. 20 N **[1]**
3. a) Taking moments about B:
   Clockwise moment = $4.0R_A$ **[1]**
   Anticlockwise moment = (120 × 2.0) + (25 × 1.5) **[1]**
   $4.0R_A$ = (120 × 2.0) + (25 × 1.5) **[1]**
   R_A = 69 N **[1]**
   b) One of $4.0R_B$ = (120 × 2.0) + (25 × 2.5) or 69 + R_B = 120 + 25 **[1]**
   R_B = 76 N **[1]**
4. Angle when centre of mass is over edge of box = $\tan^{-1}\left(\frac{0.80}{2.0}\right) = 21.8°$ **[1]**
   30° > 21.8° so, yes, the box will topple over. **[1]**
5. Clockwise moment = (85 × 0.30) + (75 × 0.60) **[1]**
   Anticlockwise moment = Tsin 30 × 0.60 **[1]**
   Tsin 30 × 0.60 = (85 × 0.30) + (75 × 0.60) **[1]**
   T = 235 N (240N to 2 s.f.) **[1]**

Page 47

1. The object is decelerating. **[1]**
2. a) Linear relationship with a constant gradient **[1]**
   Going to 49 m s^{-1} at a time of 5.0 s **[1]**
   b) Area under graph = 0.5 × 5.0 × 49 **[1]**
   = 123 m **[1]**
   c) Curved line with decreasing gradient **[1]**
   Always staying below the original line **[1]**
3. a) $a = \frac{\Delta v}{\Delta t} = \frac{6.9}{0.70}$ **[1]**
   = 9.9 m s^{-2} **[1]**
   b) Area under graph = 0.5 × 0.32 × 3.1 **[1]**
   = 0.50 m (accept between 0.48 m and 0.52 m) **[1]**
   c) Distance fallen between 0.32 s and 0.70 s = 0.5 × 0.38 × 3.8 = 0.72 m **[1]**
   0.72 – 0.50 = 0.22 m (accept between 0.18 m and 0.26 m) **[1]**
   d) Energy is dissipated to the surroundings. **[1]**

Page 49

1. a) Use of $s = ut + \frac{1}{2}at^2$ to obtain $45 = 0 + \frac{1}{2} \times 9.81t^2$ **[1]**
   $t = 3.0\,\text{s}$ **[1]**
   b) Use of $v^2 = u^2 + 2as$ to obtain $v^2 = 0 + 2 \times 9.81 \times 45$ **[1]**
   $v = 30\,\text{m s}^{-1}$ (to 2 s.f.) **[1]**
2. a) Use of $v^2 = u^2 + 2as$ to obtain $0 = 12.5^2 + 2 \times (-9.81) \times s$ **[1]**
   $s = 7.96\,\text{m}$ **[1]**
   b) Use of $v = u + at$ to obtain $0 = 12.5 - 9.81t$ **[1]**
   Double the time to reach maximum height to obtain 2.55 s. **[1]**
3. a) Use of $v = u + at$ to obtain $v = 0 + 0.5 \times 10$ **[1]**
   $v = 5.0\,\text{m s}^{-1}$ **[1]**
   b) Use of $s = ut + \frac{1}{2}at^2$ to obtain $s = 0 + \frac{1}{2} \times 0.5 \times 10^2$ **[1]**
   $s = 25\,\text{m}$ is the distance travelled in the first 10 seconds. **[1]**
   Distance travelled in next 2.0 minutes is 600 m, giving a total distance of 625 m. **[1]**

Page 51

1. 5.2 m **[1]**
2. a) Horizontal velocity = 25cos 5.0 = 24.9 m s^{-1} **[1]**
   Vertical velocity = 25sin 5.0 = 2.18 m s^{-1} **[1]**
   b) $t = \frac{s}{v} = \frac{12}{24.9}$ **[1]**
   = 0.48 s **[1]**
   c) $s = ut + \frac{1}{2}at^2 = 2.18 \times 0.48 + \frac{1}{2} \times 9.81 \times 0.48^2$ **[1]**
   = 2.2 m **[1]**
   No, the ball will not clear the net as it will reach the net at a height of 2.3 – 2.2 = 0.1 m **[1]**
3. a) Use of $s = ut + \frac{1}{2}at^2$ to obtain $-85 = 45\sin 20 \times t + \frac{1}{2} \times (-9.81) \times t^2$ **[1]**
   $t = 6.0\,\text{s}$ **[1]**
   b) $s = vt = 45\cos 20 \times 6.0$ **[1]**
   = 250 m (to 2 s.f.) **[1]**
   c) Horizontal velocity constant at 45cos 20 = 42.3 m s^{-1} **[1]**
   To calculate vertical velocity, use of $v^2 = u^2 + 2as$ to give $v^2 = (45\sin 20)^2 + 2 \times (-9.81) \times (-85)$ leading to $v = 43.8\,\text{m s}^{-1}$ **[1]**
   Use of Pythagoras to give resultant velocity of $\sqrt{42.3^2 + 43.8^2} = 60.9\,\text{m s}^{-1}$ (61 m s^{-1} to 2 s.f.) **[1]**
   $\theta = \tan^{-1}\left(\frac{43.8}{42.3}\right) = 46°$ below the horizontal (to 2 s.f.) **[1]**

Page 53

1. A rocket accelerating upwards after its engines fire. **[1]**
2. Both skaters exert equal and opposite forces on each other. **[1]**
3. **a)** Resultant force = 4000 – 800 – 400 = 2800 N **[1]**
   $a = \frac{F}{m} = \frac{2800}{1800} = 1.56\,\text{m s}^{-2}$ **[1]**
   b) Resultant force on trailer = ma = 600 × 1.56 **[1]**
   Tension = resultant force + 400 = 1300 N (to 2 s.f.) **[1]**
4. Resultant force = 150 – 10 – (12 × 9.81)sin 20 = 99.7 N **[1]**
   $a = \frac{F}{m} = \frac{99.7}{12} = 8.3\,\text{m s}^{-2}$ **[1]**
5. Any five of:
   The blades of a helicopter exert a downwards force on air particles **[1]**
   Due to Newton's third law, the air particles exert an equal and opposite force on the helicopter. **[1]**
   If the helicopter is hovering, the upwards force must be equal to the weight, **[1]**
   so that the resultant force is zero. **[1]**
   Newton's first law says that an object at rest remains at rest unless a resultant force acts on the object. **[1]**
   Due to Newton's second law ($F = ma$), if there is no resultant force on an object it experiences no acceleration. **[1]**

Page 55

1. Both momentum and kinetic energy **[1]**
2. 5.0 m s^{-1} **[1]**
3. **a)** Impulse = area under graph **[1]**
   = 2 × (0.5 × 45 × 0.20) = 9.0 kg m s^{-1} **[1]**
   b) 9.0 = 0.45Δv **[1]**
   Δv = 20 m s^{-1} **[1]**
4. **a)** Momentum before collision
   = (2.0 × 5.0) + (–3.0 × 2.0) = 4.0 kg m s^{-1} **[1]**
   Momentum after collision = 4.0 kg m s^{-1}
   = (–2.0 × 1.0) + 3.0v_B **[1]**
   v_B = 2.0 m s^{-1} **[1]**
   b) Initial kinetic energy = (0.5 × 2.0 × 5.0^2) + (0.5 × 3.0 × 2.0^2) = 31 J **[1]**
   Final kinetic energy = (0.5 × 2.0 × 1.0^2) + (0.5 × 3.0 × 2.0^2) = 7.0 J **[1]**
   Inelastic as kinetic energy is not conserved. **[1]**
   c) $F = \frac{m\Delta v}{\Delta t} = \frac{2.0 \times (-6.0)}{0.10}$ **[1]**
   = –120 N **[1]**
5. Initial momentum east = 1500 × 20 = 30000 kg m s^{-1} **[1]**
   Final velocity east = $\frac{30\,000}{1500 + 1000}$ = 12 m s^{-1} **[1]**
   Initial momentum north = 1000 × 15 = 15000 kg m s^{-1} **[1]**
   Final velocity north = $\frac{15000}{1500 + 1000}$ = 6.0 m s^{-1} **[1]**
   Resultant velocity = $\sqrt{12^2 + 6.0^2}$ = 13.4 m s^{-1} **[1]**
   At an angle of $\theta = \tan^{-1}\left(\frac{6.0}{12}\right)$ = 26.6° north of east **[1]**

Page 57

1. **a)** $\Delta E_p = mg\Delta h$ = 70 × 9.81 × 500sin 20 **[1]**
   = 1.17 × 10^5 J (1.2 × 10^5 J to 2 s.f.) **[1]**
   b) $W = Fs$ = 250 × 500 = 1.25 × 10^5 J (1.3 × 10^5 J to 2 s.f.) **[1]**
   c) Some energy is used to overcome resistive forces. **[1]**
   The cyclist has some energy in the kinetic energy store. **[1]**
2. **a)** $F = \frac{P}{v} = \frac{120\,000}{24}$ = 5000 N **[1]**
   b) 4200 × 9.81 × sin 2.5 **[1]**
   = 1800 N (to 2 s.f.) **[1]**
   c) Total force against motion = 5000 + 1800 = 6800 N **[1]**
   $P = Fv$ = 6800 × 24 = 163 kW (160 kW to 2 s.f.) **[1]**
3. **a)** $m = \frac{2E_k}{v^2} = \frac{(2 \times 22)}{18^2}$ **[1]**
   = 0.136 kg (0.14 kg to 2 s.f.) **[1]**
   b) $\Delta h = \frac{\Delta E_p}{mg} = \frac{120}{(0.136 \times 9.81)}$ **[1]**
   Δh = 90 m **[1]**
   c) Work done against resistive forces = 120 – 22 = 98 J **[1]**
   $F = \frac{W}{s} = \frac{98}{90}$ = 1.1 N (to 2 s.f.) **[1]**

Page 59

1. $\frac{\Delta L}{4}$ **[1]**
2. **a)** $\frac{1}{2}k(\Delta L)^2 = \frac{1}{2}$ × 200 × 0.15^2 = 2.25 J (2.3 J to 2 s.f.) **[1]**
   b) 0.5 × 0.50 × v^2 = 2.25 **[1]**
   v = 3.0 m s^{-1} **[1]**
3. **a)** F = 75 × 9.81 = 735.8 N **[1]**
   $\Delta L = \frac{F}{k} = \frac{735.8}{150}$ = 4.9 m **[1]**
   b) Initial gravitational potential energy
   = 75 × 9.81 × 45 = 3.31 × 10^4 J **[1]**
   $\frac{1}{2}k(\Delta L)^2 = \frac{1}{2}$ × 150 × $(\Delta L)^2$ = 3.31 × 10^4 **[1]**
   ΔL = 21 m **[1]**
4. Any six from:
   Using a ruler/metre rule, measure the unstretched length of spring. **[1]**
   To measure the extension of a spring with a mass on it, subtract the unstretched length from the extended length. **[1]**
   Repeat for different masses at regular intervals (e.g. 100 g intervals). **[1]**
   Calculate the force by multiplying by 9.81 (or by measuring weight using newton meter). **[1]**
   Plot a graph of force on the y-axis vs extension. **[1]**
   Gradient gives the spring constant. **[1]**
   To find the limit of proportionality, find where the graph stops being linear. **[1]**

Page 61

1. Ductile **[1]**
2. Density of alloy = (0.7 × 8900) + (0.3 × 7300) **[1]**
   = 8420 kg m^{-3} **[1]**
   Volume of sphere = $\frac{4}{3}\pi r^3 = \frac{4}{3}\pi(0.05)^3$
   = 5.24 × 10^{-4} m^3 **[1]**
   $m = \rho V$ = 8420 × 5.24 × 10^{-4} = 4.4 kg **[1]**
3. **a)** $V = \pi r^2 L = \pi \times (0.015)^2 \times 2.5$ = 1.77 × 10^{-3} m^3 **[1]**
   $m = \rho V$ = 7800 × 1.77 × 10^{-3} = 13.8 kg (14 kg to 2 s.f.) **[1]**
   b) $A = \pi r^2 = \pi \times (0.015)^2$ = 7.07 × 10^{-4} m^2 **[1]**
   Stress = $\frac{F}{A} = \frac{1200}{(7.07 \times 10^{-4})}$ = 1.7 × 10^6 Pa **[1]**
   c) 8.8 × 10^{-4} m **[1]**
   d) During elastic deformation, the rod will return to its original shape when the force is removed. **[1]**
   During plastic deformation, the rod is permanently deformed and does not return to its original shape when the force is removed. **[1]**
   e) F = (600 × 10^6) × (7.07 × 10^{-4}) **[1]**
   = 4.2 × 10^5 N **[1]**

Page 63

1. 1.8×10^{11} Pa [1]
2. Initial length of cable = $\frac{0.50}{\cos 30} = 0.577$ m [1]
   Clockwise moment = (65 × 0.25) + (105 × 0.50) [1]
   Anticlockwise moment = $T\sin 30 \times 0.50$ [1]
   $T\sin 30 \times 0.50 = (65 \times 0.25) + (105 \times 0.50)$ [1]
   $T = 275$ N [1]
   $\Delta L = \frac{275 \times 0.577}{(1.5 \times 10^{-6}) \times (2.0 \times 10^{11})} = 5.3 \times 10^{-4}$ m [1]
3. a) Attempt to find gradient of linear section [1]
   Young modulus = 5.7×10^{11} Pa
   (allow $5.6–5.8 \times 10^{11}$ Pa) [1]
   b) Attempt to find area under graph. [1]
   Answer of $1.1–1.2 \times 10^{5}$ J m^{-3} [1]
   c) Line going down from 3.4×10^{8} Pa with similar gradient to initial linear section. [1]
   d) The energy per unit volume required for permanent deformation. [1]
   e) Ductile material shows a large increase in strain after linear section. [1]
   Brittle material shows only a small increase in strain after linear section (before fracture). [1]

Page 65

1. B [1]
2. a) Correct shape between 0 and 15 V, starting linearly and then decreasing gradient [1]
   Correct shape between 0 and −15 V, starting linearly and then decreasing gradient [1]
   Goes through 0.5 A, 2.5 V [1]
   Goes through 1.0 A, 15 V [1]
   b) Straight line of constant gradient [1]
   Goes through 1.0 A, 15 V [1]
   c) Circuit contains correct symbols for cell/power supply, variable resistor, ammeter, filament lamp and voltmeter. [1]
   Ammeter in series with filament lamp; voltmeter is parallel across filament lamp. [1]
   d) For an ohmic conductor, the resistance is constant and therefore the potential difference is directly proportional to the current. [1]
   As the current increases for a filament lamp, the temperature of the lamp increases. [1]
   This increases the resistance of the filament lamp as the ions vibrate more and there are more collisions with electrons. [1]

Page 67

1. Halved [1]
2. a) $A = \pi(0.001)^2 = 3.14 \times 10^{-6}$ m^2 [1]
   $R = \frac{\rho L}{A} = \frac{(1.7 \times 10^{-8}) \times 5000}{(3.14 \times 10^{-6})}$ [1]
   $= 27\,\Omega$ [1]
   b) Superconductors have zero resistance below the critical temperature [1]
   So that there are no energy losses due to heating. [1]
   c) Any one from: MRI scanners/maglev trains/particle accelerators [1]
   All require large magnetic fields from large currents. [1]
   d) Line/curve with positive gradient. [1]
   Steep transition to zero resistance at temperature of 90 K. [1]
   e) Cooling to temperatures below critical temperature requires energy. [1]
   Liquid nitrogen or helium can be used to cool superconductors. [1]
3. As temperature increases, the resistance of a metal increases. [1]
   This is because increased temperature causes more frequent collisions between electrons and vibrating metal ions. [1]
   As temperature increases, the resistance of an NTC thermistor decreases. [1]
   This is because the thermal energy releases more charge carriers in the material, increasing its conductivity. [1]

Page 69

1. $10\,\Omega$ [1]
2. a) $A = \pi(5.0 \times 10^{-4})^2 = 7.85 \times 10^{-7}$ m^2
   $R = \frac{\rho L}{A} = \frac{(2.7 \times 10^{-8}) \times 50}{(7.85 \times 10^{-7})}$ [1] [1]
   $= 1.72\,\Omega$ [1]
   b) $P = I^2R = 200^2 \times 1.72$ [1]
   = 69 kW (to 2 s.f.) [1]
   c) $\frac{1}{R_T} = \frac{100}{1.7}$ [1]
   $= 0.017\,\Omega$ [1]
   d) As the resistance of the entire cable is (100 times) lower, [1]
   the power lost due to heating is also (100 times) lower. [1]
3. Resistance on lower path = $12\,\Omega$ [1]
   Current on lower path = $\frac{6.0}{12} = 0.50$ A [1]
   Due to Kirchhoff's first law, current on upper path = 1.5 − 0.50 = 1.0 A [1]
   $R_1 = \frac{2.0}{1.0} = 2.0\,\Omega$ [1]
   Due to Kirchhoff's second law, missing potential difference on upper = 6.0 − 2.0 = 4.0 V [1]
   $R_2 = \frac{4.0}{1.0} = 4.0\,\Omega$ [1]

Page 71

1. a) Maximum potential difference across variable resistor is when $R = 10\,\Omega$ [1]
   $V_1 = \frac{R_1}{R_1 + R_2} V_{in} = \left(\frac{10}{10 + 2.0}\right) \times 12$ [1]
   $= 10$ V [1]
   b) Use of $\frac{V_1}{V_2} = \frac{R_1}{R_2}$ leading to $\frac{8.0}{4.0} = \frac{R_1}{2.0}$ [1]
   $R_1 = 4.0\,\Omega$ [1]
2. a) Due to Kirchhoff's second law, potential difference across thermistor = 6.0 − 4.5 = 1.5 V [1]
   $I = \frac{V}{R} = \frac{1.5}{1800} = 8.3 \times 10^{-4}$ A [1]
   b) Use of $\frac{V_1}{V_2} = \frac{R_1}{R_2}$ leading to $\frac{4.5}{1.5} = \frac{R_1}{1800}$ [1]
   $R_1 = 5400\,\Omega$ [1]
   c) Use of $\frac{V_1}{V_2} = \frac{R_1}{R_2}$ leading to $\frac{5.0}{1.0} = \frac{5400}{R_2}$ [1]
   $R_2 = 1080\,\Omega$ ($1100\,\Omega$ to 2 s.f.) [1]
   d) To calculate equivalent resistance of R_1 and voltmeter, use of $\frac{1}{R_T} = \frac{1}{5400} + \frac{1}{900}$ [1]
   To give $R_T = 771.4\,\Omega$ [1]
   $V_1 = \left(\frac{771.4}{771.4 + 1080}\right) \times 6.0$ [1]
   $V_1 = 2.5$ V [1]

Page 73

1. 2.0 A **[1]**
2. a) $r = \frac{\varepsilon - V}{I} = \frac{15.0 - 13.5}{3.0}$ **[1]**
   $= 0.50\,\Omega$ **[1]**
   b) $R = \frac{V}{I} = \frac{13.5}{3.0}$ **[1]**
   $= 4.5\,\Omega$ **[1]**
   c) $P = I^2 r = 3.0^2 \times 0.50$ **[1]**
   $= 4.5\,\text{W}$ **[1]**
3. a) $I = \frac{12.0}{5.4}$ **[1]**
   $= 2.22\,\text{A}$ (2.2 A to 2 s.f.) **[1]**
   b) $V = \varepsilon - Ir = 12.0 - (2.22 \times 0.40)$ **[1]**
   $= 11.1\,\text{V}$ (11 V to 2 s.f.) **[1]**
   c) Total power supplied by battery $= I \times \varepsilon$
   $= 2.22 \times 12.0 = 26.64\,\text{W}$ **[1]**
   Power dissipated in internal resistance
   $= I^2 \times r = 2.22^2 \times 0.40 = 1.97\,\text{W}$ **[1]**
   Percentage dissipated as heat $= \frac{1.97}{26.64} \times 100$
   $= 7.4\%$ **[1]**
4. To calculate equivalent resistance of parallel resistors, use of $\frac{1}{R_T} = \frac{1}{R_1} + \frac{1}{R_2}$ to give
   $\frac{1}{R_T} = \frac{1}{4.0} + \frac{1}{6.0}$ **[1]**
   $R_T = 2.4\,\Omega$ **[1]**
   $I = \frac{6.0}{2.6} = 2.31\,\text{A}$ **[1]**
   $V = \varepsilon - Ir = 6.0 - (2.31 \times 0.20) = 5.54\,\text{V}$ (5.5 V to 2 s.f.) **[1]**

Page 75

1. 12.6 rad s^{-1} **[1]**
2. 614 N **[1]**
3. a) $F = \frac{mv^2}{r} = \frac{0.50 \times 6.0^2}{1.2}$ **[1]**
   $= 15\,\text{N}$ **[1]**
   b) $T = 15 - (9.81 \times 0.50)$ **[1]**
   $= 10.1\,\text{N}$ (10 N to 2 s.f.) **[1]**
   c) Resolving forces vertically: $T\sin 50 = 0.50 \times 9.81$ **[1]**
   $T = 6.40\,\text{N}$ **[1]**
   Centripetal force = 6.40cos 50 = 4.12 N **[1]**
   $\omega = \sqrt{\frac{F}{mr}} = \sqrt{\frac{4.12}{0.50 \times 1.2}} = 2.6$ rad s^{-1} (to 2 s.f.) **[1]**
4. a) $F = \frac{mv^2}{r} = \frac{1000 \times 20^2}{45}$ **[1]**
   $= 8889\,\text{N}$ (8900 N to 2 s.f.) **[1]**
   b) Resolving forces perpendicularly to the slope:
   Normal reaction = 1000 × 9.81cos 5 **[1]**
   Component of normal reaction horizontally
   = 1000 × 9.81cos 5 × sin 5 = 852 N **[1]**
   Horizontal component of friction = Fcos 5
   = 8889 − 852 = 8037 N **[1]**
   Friction $= \frac{8037}{\cos 5} = 8068\,\text{N}$ (8100 N to 2 s.f.) **[1]**

Page 77

1. 2.5 m s^{-2} **[1]**
2. The acceleration is always directed towards equilibrium and is proportional to the displacement. **[1]**
3. a) $\omega = 2\pi f = 2\pi \times 5.0$ **[1]**
   $v_{max} = \omega A = 2\pi \times 5.0 \times 0.30 = 9.4\,\text{m s}^{-1}$ **[1]**
   b) Particle is at equilibrium position at a time of
   $\frac{T}{4} = \frac{0.20}{4} = 0.050\,\text{s}$ **[1]**
   $-0.20 = 0.30\cos(10\pi t)$, leading to displacement of −0.20 at a time of 0.073 s **[1]**
   0.073 − 0.050 = 0.023 s **[1]**
   c) $x = 0.30\cos(10\pi \times 0.025) = 0.212\,\text{m}$ **[1]**
   $v = -\omega\sqrt{A^2 - x^2} = -10\pi\sqrt{0.30^2 - 0.212^2}$ **[1]**
   $= -6.7\,\text{m s}^{-1}$ **[1]**
   d) Sinusoidal graph of time period = 0.20 s **[1]**
   and amplitude 9.4 m s^{-1} **[1]**
   Negative sine graph so that $v = 0\,\text{m s}^{-1}$ at $t = 0\,\text{s}$ and $v = -9.4\,\text{m s}^{-1}$ at $t = 0.050\,\text{s}$ **[1]**

Page 79

1. 8.0 s **[1]**
2. a) $T = \frac{30}{20} = 1.5\,\text{s}$ **[1]**
   $l = \frac{1.5^2}{4\pi^2} \times 9.81$ **[1]**
   $= 0.56\,\text{m}$ **[1]**
   b) Increasing the mass of the pendulum has no effect on the time period **[1]**
   as the equation for time period only depends on the length of the string and the gravitational field strength. **[1]**
3. a) $T = 2\pi\sqrt{\frac{0.20}{150}}$ **[1]**
   $= 0.23\,\text{s}$ **[1]**
   b) $v_{max} = \omega A = \frac{2\pi}{T}A = \frac{2\pi}{0.23} \times 0.15$ **[1]**
   $= 4.1\,\text{m s}^{-1}$ **[1]**
   $E_k = \frac{1}{2}mv^2 = \frac{1}{2} \times 0.20 \times 4.1^2 = 1.7\,\text{J}$ **[1]**
   c) $E_k = \frac{1}{2}m\omega^2(A^2 - x^2)$ is equal to $E_p = \frac{1}{2}m\omega^2x^2$ **[1]**
   so that $(A^2 - x^2) = x^2$ and $\frac{A}{\sqrt{2}} = x$ **[1]**
   $x = 0.11\,\text{m}$ **[1]**
4. a) Potential energy drawn to be at 1.4 J at displacements of −4.0 and 4.0 cm and 0 J at a displacement of 0 cm. **[1]**
   b) $E_T = \frac{1}{2}m\omega^2A^2$ leading to $1.4 = \frac{1}{2} \times 0.50\omega^2 \times 0.04^2$ **[1]**
   $\omega = 59.2$ rad s^{-1} **[1]**
   $T = \frac{2\pi}{\omega} = \frac{2\pi}{59.2} = 0.11\,\text{s}$ **[1]**

Page 81

1. a) $T = 2\pi\sqrt{\frac{1.0}{9.81}}$ **[1]**
   $= 2.01\,\text{s}$ **[1]**
   $f = \frac{1}{T} = 0.50\,\text{Hz}$ **[1]**
   b) Pendulum E will oscillate with the largest amplitude **[1]**
   as it has the same length as the driving pendulum and so the same natural frequency. **[1]**
   Therefore, pendulum E is resonant with the driving frequency. **[1]**
   c) Free vibrations occur when an object oscillates at its natural frequency without an external force. **[1]**
   Forced vibrations occur when an external driving force is applied to an object. **[1]**
   d) Light damping occurs when a resistive force **[1]**
   causes the amplitude of oscillations to decrease gradually. **[1]**
2. a) Resonance occurs when the driving frequency matches the natural frequency of an object. **[1]**
   This causes a significant increase in the amplitude of oscillation. **[1]**
   If resonance occurs in a bridge, the oscillations can become large enough to cause structural damage or even collapse. **[1]**
   b) Any two from:
   Damping introduces resistive forces that dissipate the energy of oscillations. **[1]**
   Damping reduces the amplitude of oscillations. **[1]**
   Damping reduces the sharpness of resonance. **[1]**

c) Breaking step randomises the frequency of the forces applied to the bridge. [1]

Without a consistent driving frequency, it is less likely that the frequency of the steps will match the natural frequency of the bridge. [1]

This prevents sustained oscillations and reduces the likelihood of resonance. [1]

Page 83

1. The temperature of the substance remains constant. [1]
2. Energy needed to heat ice from –30°C to 0°C $= 1.2 \times 2100 \times 30 = 75600\,J$ [1]

   Energy needed to melt ice at 0°C $= 1.2 \times 334000 = 400800\,J$ [1]

   Energy needed to heat water from 0°C to 25°C $= 1.2 \times 4200 \times 25 = 126000\,J$ [1]

   Total energy required $= 75600 + 400800 + 126000 = 602400\,J$ [1]

   $t = \frac{E}{P} = \frac{602400}{400} = 1506\,s$ (1500 s to 2 s.f.) [1]
3. Thermal energy lost by metal $= 0.50 \times 900 \times (150 - T)$ [1]

   Thermal energy gained by water $= 2.0 \times 4200 \times (T - 20)$ [1]

   $0.50 \times 900 \times (150 - T) = 2.0 \times 4200 \times (T - 20)$ [1]

   Leading to $T = 26.6$°C [1]
4. $\Delta\theta = 10$°C [1]

   In first set of readings, electrical energy transferred $= 2.5 \times 12 \times 180 = 5400\,J$ [1]

   In second set of readings, electrical energy transferred $= 3.0 \times 14 \times 180 = 7560\,J$ [1]

   $c = \frac{Q_2 - Q_1}{(m_2 - m_1)\,\Delta\theta} = \frac{7560 - 5400}{(0.54 - 0.45) \times 10}$ [1]

   $= 2400\,J\,kg^{-1}\,K^{-1}$ [1]

Page 85

1. The volume is halved at constant temperature. [1]
2. Temperature in kelvin = 27 + 273 = 300 K [1]

   $V = \frac{nRT}{p} = \frac{3.0 \times 8.31 \times 300}{450\,000}$ [1]

   $= 0.017\,m^3$ [1]
3. a) Use of $P_1V_1 = P_2V_2$, leading to $100 \times 0.15 = P_2 \times 0.12$ [1]

   $P_2 = 125\,kPa$ (130 kPa to 2 s.f.) [1]

   b) $T = \frac{PV}{nR} = \frac{100\,000 \times 0.15}{5.0 \times 8.31}$ [1]

   = 361 K (360 K to 2 s.f.) [1]
4. Any three from:

   When the temperature increases, the mean kinetic energy and the mean speed of gas molecules increases. [1]

   There are therefore more collisions per second [1]

   and each collision causes a larger change in momentum. [1]

   Force is equal to the rate of change of momentum, and so the force and therefore pressure both increase. [1]
5. a) $W = P\Delta V = 250000 \times (0.080 - 0.030)$ [1]

   = 12 500 J (13 000 J to 2 s.f.) [1]

   b) $n = \frac{60}{40} = 1.5\,mol$ [1]

   $T_1 = \frac{PV_1}{nR} = \frac{250\,000 \times 0.030}{1.5 \times 8.31} = 601.7\,K$ [1]

   $T_2 = \frac{PV_2}{nR} = \frac{250000 \times 0.080}{1.5 \times 8.31} = 1604.5\,K$ [1]

   $\Delta T = 1003\,K$ (1000 K to 2 s.f.) [1]

Page 87

1. Collisions between gas particles are perfectly inelastic. [1]
2. $N = \frac{3pV}{m(c_{rms})^2} = \frac{3 \times 200\,000 \times 0.050}{(4.0 \times 10^{-26}) \times 2500^2}$ [1]

   $= 1.2 \times 10^{23}$ molecules [1]
3. Mass of a single molecule $= \frac{0.032}{6.02 \times 10^{23}} = 5.32 \times 10^{-26}\,kg$ [1]

   $c_{rms} = \sqrt{\frac{3kT}{m}} = \sqrt{\frac{3 \times (1.38 \times 10^{-23}) \times 300}{5.32 \times 10^{-26}}}$ [1]

   $= 483\,m\,s^{-1}$ ($480\,m\,s^{-1}$ to 2 s.f.) [1]
4. a) Any two from:

   The gas consists of a large number of identical particles. [1]

   The particles travel in straight lines and are in constant, random motion. [1]

   Collisions between particles and with container walls are perfectly elastic. [1]

   The time of collisions is negligible compared to the time between collisions. [1]

   No intermolecular forces act except during collisions. [1]

   b) $\Delta p = mu - (-mu) = 2mu$ [1]

   $F = \frac{\Delta p}{t} = \frac{2mu}{\frac{2L}{u}} = \frac{mu^2}{L} = \frac{m(u_1^2 + u_2^2 + u_3^2 + ...u_N^2)}{L}$ [1]

   $\overline{u^2} = \frac{(u_1^2 + u_2^2 + u_3^2 + ...u_N^2)}{N}$ [1]

   $p = \frac{F}{A} = \frac{\frac{Nm\overline{u^2}}{L}}{L^2} = \frac{Nm\overline{u^2}}{L^3} = \frac{Nm\overline{u^2}}{V}$ [1]

   $\overline{c^2} = 3\overline{u^2}$ and so $pV = \frac{1}{3}Nm\overline{c^2}$ [1]

   $c_{rms} = \sqrt{\overline{c^2}}$ and so $pV = \frac{1}{3}Nm(c_{rms})^2$ [1]

   c) Mass of a single particle $= \frac{0.040}{6.02 \times 10^{23}}$

   $= 6.64 \times 10^{-26}\,kg$ [1]

   $c_{rms} = \sqrt{\frac{3pV}{Nm}} = \sqrt{\frac{3 \times 250000 \times 0.020}{(2.5 \times 10^{23}) \times (6.64 \times 10^{-26})}}$ [1]

   $= 951\,m\,s^{-1}$ ($950\,m\,s^{-1}$ to 2 s.f.) [1]

Page 89

1. It increases by a factor of 16. [1]
2. $M = \frac{gr^2}{G} = \frac{15.0 \times (6.5 \times 10^6)^2}{6.67 \times 10^{-11}}$ [1]

   $= 9.5 \times 10^{24}\,kg$ [1]
3. a) The attractive force between two masses is proportional to the product of the masses [1]

   and inversely proportional to the square of their separation. [1]

   b) $F = \frac{Gm_1m_2}{r^2} = \frac{(6.67 \times 10^{-11}) \times (5.97 \times 10^{24}) \times (7.35 \times 10^{22})}{(3.84 \times 10^8)^2}$ [1]

   $= 1.98 \times 10^{20}\,N$ [1]

   c) The gravitational force per unit mass experienced by a small test mass placed in the field. [1]

   d) $g_E = \frac{G \times (5.97 \times 10^{24})}{r^2}$ [1]

   $g_M = \frac{G \times (7.35 \times 10^{22})}{(3.84 \times 10^{8-r})^2}$ [1]

   $\frac{G \times (5.97 \times 10^{24})}{r^2} = \frac{G \times (7.35 \times 10^{22})}{(3.84 \times 10^{8-r})^2}$ [1]

   $r = 3.46 \times 10^8\,m$ [1]

   e) At surface of Earth $g = 9.81\,N\,kg^{-1}$; at surface of Moon $g = 1.6\,N\,kg^{-1}$ [1]

   Curve that decreases and then increases [1]

   Curve that reaches $g = 0$ at a position roughly 90% of the way to the surface of the Moon [1]

Page 91

1. $-\frac{2GM}{R}$ [1]
2. $-40\,MJ\,kg^{-1}$ [1]
3. a) The work done per unit mass [1]

   to move an object from infinity to that point in the field. [1]

   b) $V = -\frac{GM}{r} = -\frac{(6.67 \times 10^{-11}) \times (5.97 \times 10^{24})}{(6.37 \times 10^6) + (400 \times 10^3)}$ [1]

   $= -5.88 \times 10^7\,J\,kg^{-1}$ [1]

c) The ISS orbits along an equipotential. [1]
As there is no change in potential, there is no work done due to $\Delta W = m\Delta V$ [1]

d) $\Delta W = m\Delta V = 450000 \times (5.88 \times 10^7)$ [1]
$= 2.65 \times 10^{13}$ J [1]

4. a) Gravitational potential is defined to be zero at infinity. [1]
Work must be done against a gravitational field to move the object to infinity. [1]

b) $V_A = -\frac{GM_A}{r_A} = -\frac{(6.67 \times 10^{-11}) \times (2.2 \times 10^{30})}{(5.0 \times 10^{10})}$ [1]
$= -2.93 \times 10^9$ J kg^{-1} (-2.9×10^9 J kg^{-1} to 2 s.f.) [1]

c) $V_B = -\frac{GM_B}{r_B} = -\frac{(6.67 \times 10^{-11}) \times (1.5 \times 10^{30})}{(1.5 \times 10^{11})}$
$= -6.67 \times 10^8$ J kg^{-1} [1]
$V_{total} = -2.93 \times 10^9 + (-6.67 \times 10^8)$
$= -3.60 \times 10^9$ J kg^{-1} [1]
$\Delta W = m\Delta V = 12000 \times (3.60 \times 10^9) = 4.3 \times 10^{13}$ J [1]

Page 93

1. $v_{esc} \geqslant \sqrt{\frac{2GM}{r}}$ [1]

2. a) $\frac{GMm}{r^2} = \frac{mv_{orb}^2}{r}$ [1]
$v_{orb} = \sqrt{\frac{GM}{r}}$ [1]
$\frac{2\pi r}{T} = \sqrt{\frac{GM}{r}}$ [1]
$T^2 = \left(\frac{4\pi^2}{GM}\right)r^3$ [1]
$\frac{4\pi^2}{GM}$ is constant and so $T^2 \propto r^3$ [1]

b) $r = \sqrt[3]{\frac{GMT^2}{4\pi^2}} = \sqrt[3]{\frac{(6.67 \times 10^{-11}) \times (5.97 \times 10^{24}) \times (24 \times 3600)^2}{4\pi^2}}$ [1]
Orbital radius of satellite $= 4.223 \times 10^7$ m [1]
$(4.223 \times 10^7) - (6.37 \times 10^6) = 3.59 \times 10^7$ m
(= 36 000 km to 2 s.f.) [1]

c) $v_{orb} = \frac{2\pi r}{T} = \frac{2\pi \times (4.223 \times 10^7)}{24 \times 3600}$ [1]
$= 3070$ m s^{-1} (to 3 s.f.) [1]

d) For LEO satellites, any one from:
Earth observations as the satellites are closer to Earth, the images are high resolution. [1]
Communications. Due to their closeness to Earth, signal travel time is low. [1]
For geostationary satellites, any one from:
For TV/radio/Internet. Fixed position allows for continuous communication. [1]
Weather forecasting as they continuously observe the same region of Earth. [1]
GPS and navigation. [1]

3. a) $v_{esc} \geqslant \sqrt{\frac{2GM}{r}} = \sqrt{\frac{2 \times (6.67 \times 10^{-11}) \times (5.97 \times 10^{24})}{(6.37 \times 10^6)}}$ [1]
$= 11200$ m s^{-1} [1]

b) $E_k = \frac{1}{2}mv^2 = \frac{1}{2} \times 1200 \times 11200^2$ [1]
$= 7.5 \times 10^{10}$ J [1]

4. $E_k = \frac{1}{2}mv_{orb}^2 = \frac{GMm}{2r}$ [1]
$E_p = m\Delta V = -\frac{GMm}{r}$ [1]
$E_T = \frac{GMm}{2r} - \frac{GMm}{r} = -\frac{GMm}{2r}$ (which is half of its gravitational potential energy) [1]

Page 95

1. a) $F_g = \frac{Gm_p^2}{r^2} = \frac{(6.67 \times 10^{-11}) \times (1.673 \times 10^{-27})^2}{(1.5 \times 10^{-15})^2}$ [1]
$= 8.3 \times 10^{-35}$ N [1]

b) $F_e = \frac{1}{4\pi\varepsilon_0}\frac{e^2}{r^2} = \frac{1}{4\pi \times (8.85 \times 10^{-12})} \times \frac{(1.6 \times 10^{-19})^2}{(1.5 \times 10^{-15})^2}$ [1]
$= 102$ N (100 N to 2 s.f.) [1]

c) $\frac{F_e}{F_g} = 1.2 \times 10^{36}$ [1]

d) The strong nuclear force [1]

2. a) The resultant force is zero, [1]
as it is repelled by both other charges so it experiences two equal and opposite forces. [1]

b) Horizontal force is still zero [1]
Vertical force =
$2 \times \sin 60 \times \frac{1}{4\pi \times (8.85 \times 10^{-12})} \times \frac{(5.0 \times 10^{-6})^2}{(0.0040)^2}$ [1]
$= 24300$ N (24000 N to 2 s.f.) [1]

3. Resolving forces vertically: $T\cos\theta = mg$ [1]
$T = \frac{mg}{\cos\theta} = \frac{0.050 \times 9.81}{\cos 10} = 0.498$ N [1]
Resolving forces horizontally: $F_e = T\cos 80$
$= 0.498 \times \cos 80 = 0.0865$ N [1]
$Q = \sqrt{4\pi\varepsilon_0 F_e r^2}$
$= \sqrt{4\pi \times (8.85 \times 10^{-12}) \times (0.0865) \times (0.35)^2}$ [1]
$= 1.1 \times 10^{-6}$ C [1]

Page 97

1. 4.3×10^5 N C^{-1} directed towards the $-1.0\,\mu$C charge [1]

2. a) Force per unit charge [1]
acting on a positive charge [1]

b) $Q = 4\pi\varepsilon_0 Er^2 = 4\pi \times (8.85 \times 10^{-12}) \times 450 \times (0.30)^2$ [1]
$= 4.5 \times 10^{-9}$ C [1]

c) $F = EQ = 450 \times (2.0 \times 10^{-9})$ [1]
$= 9.0 \times 10^{-7}$ N [1]

d) Electric field strength due to 2.0 nC charge $= \frac{1}{4\pi\varepsilon_0}\frac{(2.0 \times 10^{-9})}{r^2}$ [1]
Electric field strength due to 4.5 nC charge $= \frac{1}{4\pi\varepsilon_0}\frac{(4.5 \times 10^{-9})}{(0.30 - r)^2}$ [1]
$\frac{1}{4\pi\varepsilon_0}\frac{(2.0 \times 10^{-9})}{r^2} = \frac{1}{4\pi\varepsilon_0}\frac{(4.5 \times 10^{-9})}{(0.30 - r)^2}$ [1]
$r = 0.12$ m [1]

3. a) At least three equally spaced and parallel lines [1]
With arrows going from the 1200 V plate to the 0 V plate. [1]

b) $E = \frac{V}{d} = \frac{1200}{0.050} = 24000$ V m^{-1} [1]
$F = EQ = 24000 \times (1.6 \times 10^{-19})$ [1]
$= 3.84 \times 10^{-15}$ N (3.8×10^{-15} N to 2 s.f.) [1]

c) Vertical acceleration $a = \frac{F}{m} = \frac{3.84 \times 10^{-15}}{9.11 \times 10^{-31}}$
$= 4.22 \times 10^{15}$ m s^{-2} [1]
To calculate the time it takes to hit plates, use of $s = ut + \frac{1}{2}at^2$ leading to
$0.025 = 0 + \frac{1}{2} \times (4.22 \times 10^{15})t^2$ [1]
$t = 3.44 \times 10^{-9}$ s [1]
Minimum length of plates:
$s = vt = (1.0 \times 10^6) \times (3.44 \times 10^{-9}) = 3.4 \times 10^{-3}$ m [1]

Page 99

1. It is zero at infinity. [1]

2. They are perpendicular to electric field lines. [1]

3. a) Work done per unit positive charge [1]
to bring a small test charge from infinity to that point. [1]

b) $r = \frac{1}{4\pi\varepsilon_0}\frac{Q}{V} = \frac{1}{4\pi(8.85 \times 10^{-12})}\frac{3.0 \times 10^{-6}}{4500}$ [1]
$= 6.0$ m [1]

4. a) Potential due to $+2.0\,\mu$C charge
$= \frac{1}{4\pi(8.85 \times 10^{-12})}\frac{2.0 \times 10^{-6}}{0.15} = 1.2 \times 10^5$ V [1]

Potential due to $-1.0\,\mu C$ charge

$= \frac{1}{4\pi(8.85 \times 10^{-12})}\left(\frac{-1.0 \times 10^{-6}}{0.15}\right) = -6.0 \times 10^4 V$ [1]

Combined potential = $(1.2 \times 10^5) - (6.0 \times 10^4)$

$= 6.0 \times 10^4 V$ [1]

b) $\Delta W = Q\Delta V = (1.0 \times 10^{-9}) \times (6.0 \times 10^4)$ [1]

$= 6.0 \times 10^{-5} J$ [1]

5. a) $\Delta W = Q\Delta V = (2 \times 1.6 \times 10^{-19}) \times 1500 = 4.8 \times 10^{-16} J$ [1]

$v = \sqrt{\frac{2E_k}{m}} = \sqrt{\frac{2 \times (4.8 \times 10^{-16})}{4 \times (1.67 \times 10^{-27})}}$ [1]

$= 3.8 \times 10^5 m\,s^{-1}$ [1]

b) $4.8 \times 10^{-16} = \frac{1}{4\pi\varepsilon_0}\frac{Q_\alpha Q_{gold}}{r}$ [1]

$r = \frac{1}{4\pi\varepsilon_0}\frac{Q_\alpha Q_{gold}}{4.8 \times 10^{-16}} = \frac{1}{4\pi(8.85 \times 10^{-12})}\frac{(2 \times 1.6 \times 10^{-19})(79 \times 1.6 \times 10^{-19})}{4.8 \times 10^{-16}}$ [1]

$= 7.6 \times 10^{-11} m$ [1]

Page 101

1. a) Similarity: Both forces obey the inverse square law. [1]

Difference: Gravitational forces are always attractive; electrostatic forces can be attractive or repulsive. [1]

b) $\frac{GM^2}{r^2} = \frac{1}{4\pi\varepsilon_0}\frac{Q^2}{r^2}$ [1]

$GM^2 = \frac{1}{4\pi\varepsilon_0}Q^2$ [1]

$\frac{M^2}{Q^2} = \frac{1}{4\pi\varepsilon_0 G}$ leading to $\frac{M}{Q} = \sqrt{\frac{1}{4\pi\varepsilon_0 G}}$ [1]

c) $M = Q\sqrt{\frac{1}{4\pi\varepsilon_0 G}}$

$= (6.4 \times 10^{-11})\sqrt{\frac{1}{4\pi(8.85 \times 10^{-12})(6.67 \times 10^{-11})}}$ [1]

$= 0.74 kg$ [1]

2. a) Upwards [1]

b) Force per unit charge, [1]

acting on a test positive charge. [1]

c) $F_g = mg = 0.0010 \times 9.81 = 0.0098 N$ (downwards) [1]

$F_e = EQ = 100 \times (20.0 \times 10^{-6}) = 0.0020 N$ (upwards) [1]

Resultant force = 0.0098 – 0.0020 = 0.0078 N (downwards) [1]

d) $\Delta V_g = -g\Delta r = -9.81 \times (-50)$ [1]

$\Delta W_g = m\Delta V_g = m(-g\Delta r) = 0.0010 \times -9.81 \times (-50)$

$= 0.49 J$ [1]

$\Delta V_e = E\Delta r = 100 \times (-50)$ [1]

$\Delta W_e = Q\Delta V_e = QE\Delta r$

$= (20.0 \times 10^{-6}) \times 100 \times (-50) = -0.10 J$ [1]

Total work done on the particle = 0.49 – 0.10

= 0.39 J [1]

Page 103

1. $8C$ [1]

2. a) The capacitor stores 10.0 pC of charge [1]

for every 1.0 V of potential difference applied across it. [1]

b) $A = 0.050^2 = 0.0025 m^2$ [1]

$d = \frac{A\varepsilon_r\varepsilon_0}{C} = \frac{0.0025 \times 1 \times (8.85 \times 10^{-12})}{10.0 \times 10^{-12}}$ [1]

$= 2.2 \times 10^{-3} m$ [1]

c) $Q = C \times V = (10.0 \times 10^{-12}) \times 2500 = 2.5 \times 10^{-8} C$ [1]

d) The dielectric consists of polar molecules. [1]

These polar molecules align when an electric field is between the parallel plates of a capacitor, [1]

and produce an electric field in the opposite direction to that produced by the parallel plates. [1]

The alignment of the polar molecules allows more charge to be stored on the plates for the same applied potential difference. [1]

e) $\varepsilon_r = \frac{25.0}{10.0} = 2.5$ [1]

f) Increasing the area of overlap of the plates. [1]

Decreasing the distance between the plates. [1]

Page 105

1. a) $\tau = RC = (10 \times 10^3) \times (5.0 \times 10^{-6})$ [1]

$= 0.050 s$ [1]

b) $V = V_0\left(1 - e^{-\frac{t}{RC}}\right) = 12.0\left(1 - e^{-\frac{0.020}{0.050}}\right)$ [1]

$= 3.96 V$ (4.0 V to 2 s.f.) [1]

c) $E = \frac{1}{2}CV^2 = \frac{1}{2} \times (5.0 \times 10^{-6}) \times (12.0)^2$ [1]

$= 3.6 \times 10^{-4} J$ [1]

d) The total energy transferred by the power source is equal to $E = QV$ [1]

Half of the total energy is lost in heating any resistance in the circuit. [1]

2. $0.20I_0 = I_0 e^{-\frac{1.5}{(20.0 \times 10^{-6})R}}$ [1]

$\ln 0.20 = -\frac{1.5}{(20.0 \times 10^{-6})R}$ [1]

$R = 4.7 \times 10^4\,\Omega$ [1]

3. $V_0 = I_0R = 0.0050 \times 2000 = 10 V$ [1]

$3.0 = 10\left(1 - e^{-\frac{4.0}{2000 \times C}}\right)$ [1]

$\ln 0.7 = -\frac{4.0}{2000 \times C}$ [1]

$C = 5.6 \times 10^{-3} F$ [1]

Page 107

1. $6.5\,\mu F$ [1]

2. 78 ms [1]

3. a) $\tau = RC = 50 \times (100 \times 10^{-6})$ [1]

$= 0.0050 s$ [1]

b) $1000 = 5000e^{-\frac{t}{0.0050}}$ [1]

$\ln\left(\frac{1000}{5000}\right) = -\frac{t}{0.0050}$ [1]

$t = 8.0 \times 10^{-3} s$ [1]

c) Initial energy $= \frac{1}{2} \times (100 \times 10^{-6}) \times 5000^2 = 1250 J$ [1]

Potential difference across capacitor after 2.0 ms $= 5000e^{-\frac{0.0020}{0.0050}} = 3352 V$ [1]

Energy stored by capacitor at 2.0 ms =

$\frac{1}{2} \times (100 \times 10^{-6}) \times 3352^2 = 562 J$ [1]

Energy delivered = 1250 – 562 = 688 J (690 J to 2 s.f.) [1]

4. a) $\frac{1}{2} \times (330 \times 10^{-6}) \times 300^2 = 14.85 J$ (14.9 J to 3 s.f.) [1]

b) Energy after 5.0 ms = 1.485 J [1]

Potential difference after 5.0 ms $= \sqrt{\frac{2 \times 1.485}{330 \times 10^{-6}}}$

$= 94.9 V$ [1]

$94.9 = 300e^{-\frac{0.005}{R \times (330 \times 10^{-6})}}$ [1]

$\ln\left(\frac{94.9}{300}\right) = -\frac{0.005}{R \times (330 \times 10^{-6})}$ [1]

$R = 13.2\,\Omega$ (13 Ω to 2 s.f.) [1]

Page 109

1. Down [1]

2. 0.59 T [1]

3. $2F$ [1]

4. a) A wire of length 1.0 m, carrying a current of 1.0 A perpendicular to the field, [1]

experiences a force of 0.25 N. [1]

b) $F = BIl\sin\theta = 0.25 \times 3.5 \times 0.5 \times \sin 60$ [1]

$= 0.38 N$ [1]

c) The magnetic force decreases until it becomes zero [1]

as there is no component of the current that is perpendicular to the magnetic field. [1]

d) Any one from:
Reducing the magnetic flux density **[1]**
Reducing the current in the wire **[1]**
Reducing the length of wire in the field **[1]**

Page 111

1. a) $\Delta W = Q\Delta V = (3.2 \times 10^{-19}) \times 5000$ **[1]**
$= 1.6 \times 10^{-15}$ J **[1]**
$v = \sqrt{\frac{2 \times (1.6 \times 10^{-15})}{3.3 \times 10^{-26}}} = 3.1 \times 10^5$ m s^{-1} **[1]**

b) Forces due to electric field and magnetic field act in opposite directions. **[1]**
The magnetic force is velocity dependent, while the electric force is not. **[1]**
Particles only pass through undeflected when the electric force is equal and opposite to the magnetic force. **[1]**

c) $BQv = \frac{mv^2}{r}$ **[1]**
$r = \frac{mv}{BQ}$ **[1]**

d) $B = \frac{mv}{rQ} = \frac{(3.3 \times 10^{-26}) \times (3.1 \times 10^5)}{0.20 \times (3.2 \times 10^{-19})}$ **[1]**
$= 0.16$ T **[1]**

2. a) Uniform magnetic field within two semi-circular dees causes charged particles to move in circular motion. **[1]**
Two dees are separated, with an alternating electric field in the gap between them. **[1]**
The electric field accelerates the charged particles. **[1]**

b) $BQv = \frac{mv^2}{r}$ **[1]**
$r = \frac{mv}{BQ}$ **[1]**
$T = \frac{2\pi r}{v} = \frac{2\pi m}{BQ}$ **[1]**
$f = \frac{BQ}{2\pi m}$ and so is independent of the radius of orbit and the particle velocity. **[1]**

Page 113

1. 2.6 Wb **[1]**

2. The magnetic flux density is parallel to the coil. **[1]**

3. a) $A = 0.20 \times 0.20 = 0.040$ m^2 **[1]**
$\Phi = BA = 0.25 \times 0.040 = 0.010$ Wb **[1]**

b) $N\Phi = 50 \times 0.010 = 0.50$ Wb **[1]**

c) Initially, the flux linkage is a maximum when the coil is perpendicular to the magnetic field. **[1]**
As the coil rotates, the flux linkage decreases. **[1]**
The flux linkage is zero after it has been rotated by 90°. **[1]**
Between 90 and 180° of rotation, the flux linkage increases again but in the opposite direction. After the coil has been rotated by 180° it reaches a negative maximum when the coil is perpendicular to the field. **[1]**

4. a) $A = \pi r^2 = \pi \times 0.15^2 = 0.0707$ m^2 **[1]**
Magnetic flux linkage $= BAN = 0.40 \times 0.0707 \times 500$ **[1]**
$= 14.1$ Wb (14 Wb to 2 s.f.) **[1]**

b) $BAN \cos \omega t = 14.1 \cos(2.0 \times 1.0)$ **[1]**
$= -5.9$ Wb **[1]**

Page 115

1. 3.0 V **[1]**

2. a) Any five from:
Faraday's law states that the induced emf is directly proportional to the rate of change of flux linkage. **[1]**
When the strong magnet falls through the copper pipe, the pipe experiences a change in flux linkage. **[1]**
Therefore, an emf is induced. This causes a current in the copper pipe as the pipe creates a complete circuit. **[1]**
The current creates its own magnetic field. **[1]**
Due to Lenz's law, this magnetic field opposes the falling magnet. **[1]**
This means the resultant force downwards on the magnet is lower, which means that it falls at a slower rate. **[1]**

b) The induced emf would be the same. **[1]**
The resistance is higher and so the current is lower. **[1]**
The upwards magnetic force would be weaker and so the magnet would fall through in a shorter time. **[1]**

c) The cut acts as a break in the 'circuit' and so there would be no induced current. **[1]**
There would be no magnetic field and so no upwards magnetic force. **[1]**
The magnet would fall through the pipe in the same time as the non-magnetic cylinder. **[1]**

3. Sinusoidal graphs for both ϕ–t and ε–t graphs. **[1]**
Maximum flux linkage $= BAN = 0.020 \times 0.10^2 \times 200$
$= 0.040$ Wb **[1]**
Maximum emf $= BAN\omega = 0.020 \times 0.10^2 \times 250$
$\times \left(\frac{2\pi}{0.10}\right) = 2.51$ V (2.5 V to 2 s.f.) **[1]**
ϕ–t graph starts at a maximum (0.040 Wb) and then decreases. **[1]**
ε–t graph starts at 0 and then increases to a maximum (2.51 V) after a time of 0.025 s. **[1]**

Page 117

1. 3.5 A **[1]**

2. 50 Hz **[1]**

3. 7.1 V **[1]**

4. a) Time for 4 wave cycles $= 9.0 \times 0.2 = 1.8$ s **[1]**
$T = \frac{1.8}{4} = 0.45$ s **[1]**
$f = \frac{1}{0.45} = 2.2$ Hz **[1]**

b) Any three from:
Turn the time base off. **[1]**
Increase the vertical gain so the trace takes up a larger amount of the oscilloscope screen. **[1]**
Count the number of vertical squares and multiply by the volts/division setting. **[1]**
This gives the peak-to-peak potential difference. Halve this to find the peak emf. **[1]**

c) Maximum emf $= BAN\omega = 0.12 \times A \times 400$
$\times \left(\frac{2\pi}{0.45}\right) = 4.0$ V **[1]**
$A = 6.0 \times 10^{-3}$ m^2 **[1]**

d) The maximum induced emf will increase. **[1]**
Therefore, the Y-gain will need to be increased to fit the peak-to-peak potential difference on the oscilloscope screen. **[1]**
The time period will decrease. **[1]**
Can either change the time base to fit one wave cycle on the screen or leave the time base and measure the time period over multiple wave cycles. **[1]**

Page 119

1. a) A step-up transformer decreases the current. **[1]**
This reduces the power lost due to heating ($P = I^2R$). **[1]**

b) $0.95 = \frac{I_s \times 275000}{800 \times 25000}$ **[1]**
$I_s = 69$ A **[1]**

2. a) Laminating the core reduces eddy currents, [1] which reduces the energy lost due to heating the core. [1]

b) $V_s = V_p \times \frac{N_s}{N_p} = 230 \times \frac{200}{5000}$ [1]

$V_s = 9.2\,\text{V}$ [1]

c) An alternating current in the primary coil produces a changing magnetic flux in the iron core. [1]

This changing flux induces an alternating emf in the secondary coil. [1]

The lower number of turns in the secondary coil decreases the flux linkage in the secondary coil, inducing a lower emf. [1]

d) $0.90 = \frac{8.0 \times 9.2}{I_p \times 230}$ [1]

$I_p = 0.36\,\text{A}$ [1]

e) A d.c. power supply will supply a constant current, leading to a constant magnetic flux. [1]

Without a change in flux, no emf is induced in the secondary coil. [1]

Page 121

1. All alpha particles would pass straight through with little deflection. [1]
2. Most of the atom is empty space. [1]
3. Any six from:

Alpha particles are directed at a thin gold foil. [1]

Most of the alpha particles pass straight through, [1]

meaning that most of the atom is empty space. [1]

Some alpha particles are deflected through small angles, [1]

meaning that there is a positively charged nucleus. [1]

A small number of alpha particles are reflected backwards, [1]

meaning that the positive charge and most of the mass of the atom is in a small central nucleus. [1]

4. a) In the plum pudding model, the atom is modelled as a ball of positive charge, [1]

with negatively charged electrons scattered throughout. [1]

In the nuclear model, atoms consist of a small and dense, positively charged nucleus, [1]

with negatively charged electrons orbiting the nucleus. [1]

b) New (experimental) evidence is required to update a model. [1]

Peer review is used so that other experts in the field evaluate the new work and come to a consensus. [1]

Page 123

1. a) Geiger–Müller tube/detector [1]

b) Any two from:

Radon gas [1]

Certain rocks [1]

Certain foods [1]

Medical uses of radiation [1]

Nuclear fallout or waste [1]

c) Background count rate = $\frac{1140}{60}$ = 19 counts/minute [1]

Contribution to the count rate of only the radioactive source = 1550 − 19 = 1531 counts/minute [1]

Count rate from the radioactive source at a distance of 1.0 m = 61 counts/minute [1]

Total count rate (including background) = 61 + 19 = 80 counts/minute [1]

2. a) Cell damage/mutations/increased risk of cancer [1]

b) Isotope C is the most suitable. [1]

Gamma radiation is sufficiently penetrating to be detected outside the body. [1]

The half-life of isotope C is long enough to complete measurements but not too long to cause unnecessary exposure. [1]

3. a) Radon gas can be inhaled and cause cell damage in the lungs. [1]

b) Beta radiation can partially penetrate aluminium foil. [1]

Alpha radiation would be entirely absorbed by aluminium foil. [1]

Gamma radiation would penetrate through aluminium foil. [1]

Page 125

1. 0.49 [1]
2. a) A half-life of 5730 years means that it will take 5730 years for half of the carbon-14 nuclei to decay. [1]

b) $T_{\frac{1}{2}} = 5730 \times 365 \times 24 \times 60 \times 60 = 1.81 \times 10^{11}\,\text{s}$ [1]

$\lambda = \frac{\ln 2}{T_{\frac{1}{2}}} = \frac{\ln 2}{1.81 \times 10^{11}} = 3.8 \times 10^{-12}\,\text{s}^{-1}$ [1]

c) $0.18N_0 = N_0 e^{-(3.8 \times 10^{-12})t}$ [1]

$\ln 0.18 = -(3.8 \times 10^{-12})t$ [1]

$t = 4.5 \times 10^{11}\,\text{s}$ (14 000 years) [1]

d) 100 years is much shorter than one half-life and therefore not much of the carbon-14 will have decayed. [1]

3. a) A decay constant of $2.0 \times 10^{-3}\,\text{s}^{-1}$ means that there is a probability of 2.0×10^{-3} that a nucleus will decay in a second. [1]

b) Number of moles in sample = $\frac{5.0 \times 10^{-3}}{230}$ = 2.17×10^{-5} mol [1]

$(2.17 \times 10^{-5}) \times (6.02 \times 10^{23})$ = 1.31×10^{19} nuclei (1.3×10^{19} nuclei to 2 s.f.) [1]

c) Initial activity = $(2.0 \times 10^{-3}) \times (1.31 \times 10^{19})$ = 2.62×10^{16} Bq [1]

$A = A_0 e^{-\lambda t} = (2.62 \times 10^{16}) e^{-(2.0 \times 10^{-3}) \times 2.0 \times 60}$ [1]

= 2.1×10^{16} Bq [1]

Page 127

1. a) Graph is linear until $N = 20$, $Z = 20$. [1]

After this, the graph curves upwards until $N = 120$, $Z = 80$. [1]

Beta-minus emitter labelled above the stability curve. [1]

Beta-plus emitter labelled below the stability curve. [1]

Alpha emitter labelled below stability curve for $Z > 60$. [1]

b) Any four from:

Both protons and neutrons experience the attractive strong nuclear force. [1]

Only protons experience electrostatic repulsion. [1]

The strong nuclear force has a range of 3 fm. [1]

Electrostatic repulsion is longer range. [1]

Therefore, more neutrons are needed for large nuclei to compensate for the shortness of the strong nuclear force range. [1]

2. a) ${}^{99}_{42}\text{Mo} \rightarrow {}^{99}_{43}\text{Tc} + {}^{0}_{-1}e^{-} + {}^{0}_{0}\bar{\upsilon}_e$ [1]

b) $140\,\text{keV} = 140 \times 10^3 \times (1.6 \times 10^{-19}) = 2.24 \times 10^{-14}\,\text{J}$ [1]

$f = \frac{E}{h} = \frac{2.24 \times 10^{-14}}{6.63 \times 10^{-34}}$ [1]

$= 3.4 \times 10^{19}\,\text{Hz}$ [1]

c) Technetium–99m is a pure gamma emitter which is penetrating enough to be detected outside the body and will not damage cells unnecessarily. [1]

The half-life of technetium-99m is long enough to take measurements, but not so long to cause unnecessary exposure. [1]

d) $\lambda = \frac{\ln 2}{T_{\frac{1}{2}}} = \frac{\ln 2}{66} = 0.0105\ \text{hours}^{-1}$ [1]

$m = 5.0e^{-0.0105 \times 7 \times 24}$ [1]

$= 0.86\,\text{g}$ [1]

e) Any two from:

Use thick lead shielding to reduce exposure to radiation. [1]

Reduce time near the radioactive source. [1]

Maintain a distance from the radioactive source. [1]

Page 129

1. a) $E_k = 5.0 \times 10^6 \times (1.6 \times 10^{-19}) = 8.0 \times 10^{-13}\,\text{J}$ [1]

$r = \frac{1}{4\pi\varepsilon_0}\frac{Q_{\text{gold}}Q_\alpha}{E_k}$ [1]

$= \frac{1}{4\pi(8.85 \times 10^{-12})}\ \frac{(79 \times 1.6 \times 10^{-19}) \times (2 \times 1.6 \times 10^{-19})}{8.0 \times 10^{-13}}$

$= 4.5 \times 10^{-14}\,\text{m}$ [1]

b) The distance of closest approach would decrease, [1] as there would be a weaker electrostatic repulsion force. [1]

c) Closest approach of alpha particles is an upper bound estimate, [1] while electron diffraction is a measurement. [1]

d) Curve that decreases to a non-zero minimum, [1] and then increases again. [1]

2. a) $R = R_0 A^{\frac{1}{3}} = \left(1.2 \times 10^{-15}\right) \times 27^{\frac{1}{3}} = 3.6 \times 10^{-15}\,\text{m}$ [1]

$V = \frac{4}{3}\pi R^3 = \frac{4}{3}\pi(3.6 \times 10^{-15})^3$ [1]

$= 1.95 \times 10^{-43}\,\text{m}^3$ [1]

b) $\rho = \frac{m}{V} = \frac{27 \times 1.67 \times 10^{-27}}{\frac{4}{3}\pi(3.6 \times 10^{-15})^3}$ [1]

$= 2.31 \times 10^{17}\,\text{kg m}^{-3}$ [1]

c) $\rho = \frac{Am}{\frac{4}{3}\pi\left(R_0 A^{\frac{1}{3}}\right)^3} = \frac{m}{\frac{4}{3}\pi R_0^{\,3}}$ [1]

All terms in this expression are constants and it is independent of A. [1]

Page 131

1. a) $8.8 \times 56 = 493\,\text{MeV}$ [1]

b) The products would have a lower binding energy/nucleon. [1]

c) Curve that increases to iron–56 and then decreases (at a slower rate) [1]

Fusion labelled up until iron-56. [1]

Fission labelled after iron-56. [1]

2. Mass of reactants = 235.0439u + 1.00867u = 236.05257u [1]

Mass of products = 140.9144u + 91.9263u + 3(1.00867u) = 235.86671u [1]

Mass difference = 236.05257u – 235.86671u = 0.18586u [1]

Energy released = 0.18586 × 931.5 = 173 MeV [1]

3. a) Mass defect = 2(1.00867u) + 2(1.00728u) – 4.0015u = 0.0304u [1]

Binding energy = 0.0304 × 931.5 = 28.3 MeV [1]

Binding energy per nucleon = $\frac{28.3}{4}$ = 7.1 MeV / nucleon [1]

b) Mass of reactants = 2.0136u + 3.0155u = 5.0291u [1]

Mass of products = 4.0015u + 1.00867u = 5.01017u [1]

Mass difference = 0.01893u [1]

Energy released = 0.01893 × 931.5 = 17.6 MeV [1]

Page 133

1. Boron [1]

2. a) The fuel rods contain the material that undergoes fission. [1]

The moderator slows down fast neutrons to thermal energies, increasing the likelihood of absorption by uranium nuclei. [1]

The control rods absorb neutrons to reduce the rate of reaction. [1]

The coolant transfers heat from the reactor core. [1]

b) Graphite or water is used as the moderator. [1]

Their low masses mean that energy transfer is maximised in elastic collisions. [1]

c) Spent fuel rods/fission products [1]

d) High-level waste is left in cooling ponds for several years to allow the activity to decrease and for the waste to cool. [1]

It is then vitrified and stored in steel containers [1] before being buried deep underground in a geologically stable region. [1]

e) Any one from:

Reliable source of energy [1]

Low carbon dioxide emissions [1]

Large amount of energy per kilogram of fuel [1]

3. a) Each fission event releases neutrons that cause further fission reactions. [1]

If each fission event releases at least one neutron that causes another fission event, the reaction continues. [1]

b) A smaller mass means more neutrons escape the material rather than causing further fission. [1]

c) Any two suitable points, e.g.

In an emergency, control rods are fully inserted into the core to absorb all neutrons and stop fission. [1]

Thick concrete shielding surrounds the reactor and absorbs radiation. [1]

Page 135

1. a) Angle subtended without telescope $= \frac{15000}{1.0 \times 10^9} = 1.5 \times 10^{-5}$ rad (note that the small angle approximation of $\tan\theta \approx \theta$ has been used here) [1]

Magnification of telescope $= \frac{f_o}{f_e} = \frac{2.0}{0.05} = 40$ [1]

Angle when viewed through telescope $= (1.5 \times 10^{-5}) \times 40 = 6.0 \times 10^{-4}$ rad [1]

b) Three parallel rays drawn onto objective lens that converge to a focus. [1]

Rays continue correctly onto eyepiece lens and emerge parallel to each other. [1]

Focal lengths of the objective lens and eyepiece lens are labelled, with the focal length of the objective lens greater than the eyepiece lens. [1]

Construction line drawn, with emergent rays parallel to the construction line. [1]

c) Different wavelengths of light refract by different amounts when passing through a lens. [1]

2. a) Two parallel rays drawn onto primary concave mirror. [1]

Before the rays come to a focus, they reflect from a convex secondary mirror and pass through a hole in the primary mirror. [1]

The rays cross before meeting an eyepiece lens and emerge parallel to each other. [1]

b) Advantages:

Reflecting telescopes are more compact. [1]

Reflecting telescopes do not suffer from chromatic aberration. [1]

Reflecting telescopes do not suffer from spherical aberration if the mirrors are parabolic. [1]

Disadvantage:

The secondary mirror blocks some of the incoming light. [1]

Page 137

1. a) Similarity: both telescopes have primary concave reflectors. [1]

Difference: radio telescopes have a receiver instead of a secondary mirror. [1]

b) collecting power α diameter^2 [1]

$\frac{100^2}{2.5^2}$ = 1600. Radio telescope has a collecting power that is 1600 times larger than the optical telescope. [1]

c) For radio telescope: $\theta = \frac{\lambda}{D} = \frac{0.21}{100} = 2.1 \times 10^{-3}$ rad [1]

For optical telescope: $\theta = \frac{\lambda}{D} = \frac{500 \times 10^{-9}}{2.5}$

$= 2.0 \times 10^{-7}$ rad [1]

d) Optical telescopes are best placed in space or at high altitudes as the atmosphere absorbs some visible light. [1]

Radio telescopes can be placed on the Earth's surface but in remote locations to minimise interference from human-made signals. [1]

2. a) Infrared radiation is absorbed by the atmosphere. [1]

b) Angular size of exoplanet $= \frac{1.5 \times 10^{-7}}{5.0 \times 10^{-17}}$

$= 3.0 \times 10^{-11}$ rad [1]

Minimum resolvable angle $= \frac{\lambda}{D} = \frac{4.5 \times 10^{-6}}{6.5}$

$= 6.9 \times 10^{-7}$ rad [1]

The minimum resolvable angle is greater than the angular size of the exoplanet, so the exoplanet cannot be resolved. [1]

c) Two stars can just be resolved when the central maximum of the diffraction pattern (Airy disc) from one object [1]

overlaps with the first diffraction minimum of the other. [1]

d) A quantum efficiency of 80% means that 80% of the photons incident onto the detector are detected. [1]

Page 139

1. a) How bright a star appears, [1]

when observed from Earth. [1]

b) $\frac{B_1}{B_2} = 2.51^{(m_2 - m_1)} = 2.51^{1.49}$ [1]

= 3.94 times brighter (3.9 times brighter to 2 s.f.) [1]

2. a) Absolute magnitude is the brightness of a star from a distance of 10 parsecs. [1]

Apparent magnitude is the brightness of a star when observed from Earth. [1]

b) $M = -5\log\left(\frac{d}{10}\right) + m = -5\log\left(\frac{50}{10}\right) + 2.3$ [1]

$= -1.2$ [1]

3. a) A parsec is the distance at which an object would have a parallax angle of 1 arcsecond, [1]

when viewed from Earth. [1]

b) 20 pc [1]

c) $5.2 - 1.8 = 5\log\left(\frac{d}{10}\right)$ [1]

$10^{\frac{3.4}{5}} = \frac{d}{10}$ [1]

$d = 47.9$ pc (48 pc to 2 s.f.) [1]

Page 141

1. a) The peak wavelength of a black body spectrum is inversely proportional to its temperature. [1]

b) $T = \frac{2.9 \times 10^{-3}}{\lambda_{max}} = \frac{2.9 \times 10^{-3}}{450 \times 10^{-9}}$ [1]

$= 6440$ K [1]

c) $A = 4\pi r^2 = 4\pi(7.0 \times 10^8)^2 = 6.16 \times 10^{18}$ m^2 [1]

$P = \sigma AT^4 = (5.67 \times 10^{-8}) \times (6.16 \times 10^{18}) \times (6440)^4$ [1]

$= 6.0 \times 10^{26}$ W [1]

d) $I = \frac{P}{4\pi r^2} = \frac{6.0 \times 10^{26}}{4\pi(1.5 \times 10^{17})^2}$ [1]

$= 2.1 \times 10^{-9}$ W m^{-2} [1]

2. a) $P = I \times 4\pi r^2$

$= (3.0 \times 10^{-9}) \times 4\pi(150 \times 3.08 \times 10^{16})^2$ [1]

$= 8.05 \times 10^{29}$ W [1]

$T = \frac{2.9 \times 10^{-3}}{\lambda_{max}} = \frac{2.9 \times 10^{-3}}{600 \times 10^{-9}} = 4833$ K [1]

$A = \frac{P}{\sigma T^4} = \frac{8.05 \times 10^{29}}{(5.67 \times 10^{-8}) \times (4833)^4} = 2.60 \times 10^{22}$ m^2 [1]

$r = \sqrt{\frac{A}{4\pi}} = \sqrt{\frac{2.60 \times 10^{22}}{4\pi}} = 4.5 \times 10^{10}$ m [1]

b) Two curves, labelled A and B and of correct shape. [1]

Curve A has a peak wavelength at 600 nm and Curve B has a peak wavelength at 290 nm. [1]

Curve B has a higher intensity at all wavelengths. [1]

Page 143

1. a) Use of $\lambda_{max}T = 2.9 \times 10^{-3}$ to determine surface temperature of each star. [1]

For star X: $T = \frac{2.9 \times 10^{-3}}{\lambda_{max}} = \frac{2.9 \times 10^{-3}}{320 \times 10^{-9}} = 9060$ K [1]

For star Y: $T = \frac{2.9 \times 10^{-3}}{\lambda_{max}} = \frac{2.9 \times 10^{-3}}{680 \times 10^{-9}} = 4260$ K [1]

b) Star X is spectral class A. [1]

Star Y is spectral class K. [1]

c) Star X will have the strongest Balmer lines, [1]

as it is in spectral class A. [1]

d) The star emits a continuous spectrum. [1]

When this passes through hydrogen atoms, it excites electrons from the n = 2 state to a higher energy level. [1]

This absorbs light at discrete wavelengths. [1]

2. a) The star in spectral class B. [1]

b) The star in spectral class B has a higher surface temperature. [1]

Due to $P = \sigma AT^4$, the star in spectral class B will have a higher luminosity. [1]

Therefore, the star in spectral class B will be further away as the stars have the same apparent magnitude. [1]

3. Stars in spectral class G appear yellow-white, [1]

as they have a surface temperature between 5000 and 6000 K. [1]

Due to their surface temperature, they emit a peak wavelength of 480–580 nm. **[1]**

Prominent absorption lines are ionised and neutral metals. **[1]**

Page 145

1. a) Main sequence area drawn correctly, with shallower gradient in middle of curve. **[1]**
   Giants in the top right of the diagram. **[1]**
   White dwarfs in the bottom left of the diagram. **[1]**
   Temperature scale from 50000 to 2500 K (from left to right) **[1]**
   Absolute magnitude scale from +15 to −10 (from bottom to top) **[1]**
   b) Any three from:
   A nebula collapses under gravity and heats until nuclear fusion starts. **[1]**
   The star stays on the main sequence until its hydrogen runs out. **[1]**
   After the main sequence, the star expands and cools to form a red giant. **[1]**
   The outer layers of the red giant drift out in a planetary nebula, leaving behind a white dwarf. **[1]**
2. a) Star B is the white dwarf, **[1]**
   as it is dim and has a surface temperature of 10000 K. **[1]**
   b) Star A is the red giant, **[1]**
   as it is bright and has a surface temperature of 4500 K. **[1]**
   c) Star C is the main sequence star, **[1]**
   as it has an absolute magnitude of +4.5 **[1]**

Page 147

1. a) Type 1a supernovae have a known peak absolute magnitude (of −19.3) **[1]**
   b) Use of $m - M = 5\log\left(\frac{d}{10}\right)$, leading to $29.3 = 5\log\left(\frac{d}{10}\right)$ **[1]**
   $10^{\frac{29.3}{5}} \times 10 = d$ **[1]**
   $= 7.24 \times 10^6$ pc **[1]**
   c) Observations of type 1a supernovae in distant galaxies show that the rate of expansion of the Universe is accelerating. **[1]**
   A force must be responsible for this (proposed to be dark energy). **[1]**
   d) A curve that rapidly rises in absolute magnitude over time and then falls. **[1]**
   The peak absolute magnitude of −19.3 is at a time of 0 days. **[1]**
2. a) Once the main sequence star runs out of hydrogen, it expands and cools into a red supergiant. **[1]**
   Heavier elements are fused until iron, at which point the star undergoes supernova. **[1]**
   What is left behind then forms a black hole. **[1]**
   b) The Schwarzschild radius is the distance from the centre of a black hole for which the escape velocity is more than the speed of light. **[1]**
   c) $R_s = \frac{2GM}{c^2} = \frac{2 \times (6.67 \times 10^{-11}) \times (10 \times 2.0 \times 10^{30})}{(3.0 \times 10^8)^2}$ **[1]**
   $= 2.96 \times 10^4$ m (3.0×10^4 m to 2 s.f.) **[1]**

Page 149

1. a) $z = \frac{\Delta\lambda}{\lambda} = \frac{18}{600}$ **[1]**
   $= 0.030$ **[1]**
   b) $v = -zc = -0.030 \times 3.0 \times 10^8$ **[1]**
   $= -9.0 \times 10^6$ m s^{-1} **[1]**
   c) $v = 9.0 \times 10^3$ km s^{-1} **[1]**
   $d = \frac{v}{H_0} = \frac{9.0 \times 10^3}{70} = 129$ Mpc (130 Mpc to 2 s.f.) **[1]**
   d) The red-shift of light from galaxies shows that they are moving away from us. **[1]**
   More distant galaxies have higher red-shifts, meaning they are receding faster. **[1]**
   e) Cosmic microwave background radiation. **[1]**
   Relative abundance of hydrogen and helium in a 3 : 1 ratio. **[1]**
2. a) $H_0 = 72.6$ km s^{-1} Mpc^{-1} = 72600 m s^{-1} Mpc^{-1} **[1]**
   $H_0 = \frac{72600}{3.08 \times 10^{16} \times 10^6} = 2.357 \times 10^{-18}$ s^{-1} **[1]**
   $t = \frac{1}{H_0} = \frac{1}{2.36 \times 10^{-18}} = 4.242 \times 10^{17}$ s **[1]**
   $t = \frac{4.242 \times 10^{17}}{365 \times 24 \times 60 \times 60} = 13.5$ billion years **[1]**
   b) If two stars orbit around their common centre of mass, their light spectrum changes over time due to the Doppler effect. **[1]**
   If one star moves towards Earth, its light is blue-shifted. If one star moves away from Earth, its light is red-shifted. **[1]**
   If one star passes in front of the other, it causes periodic dips in brightness. **[1]**
   A deeper dip in brightness occurs if the cooler star passes in front of the hotter star. **[1]**

Page 151

1. a) Exoplanets are much dimmer than their parent star. **[1]**
   They are small and distant, making them hard to resolve with telescopes. **[1]**
   b) Radial velocity method. **[1]**
   Star and exoplanet orbit around their common centre of mass. **[1]**
   The movement of the star causes a varying red/blue-shift of spectral lines. **[1]**
   Transit method. **[1]**
   Exoplanet passing in front of star, **[1]**
   causes a dip in brightness. **[1]**
   c) The radial velocity shifts are much smaller for a low-mass planet like Earth, making them harder to measure. **[1]**
   The brightness dip due to transit of a low-mass exoplanet is small. **[1]**
   Planets can have long orbital periods, requiring observations over years to confirm their presence. **[1]**
2. a) A quasar forms from an active galactic nucleus/feeding black hole. **[1]**
   b) $v = zc = 0.11 \times 3.0 \times 10^8 = 3.30 \times 10^7$ m s^{-1}
   $= 3.30 \times 10^4$ km s^{-1} **[1]**
   $d = \frac{v}{H_0} = \frac{3.30 \times 10^4}{70} = 471.4$ Mpc (470 Mpc to 2 s.f.) **[1]**
   c) Use of $m - M = 5\log\left(\frac{d}{10}\right)$ **[1]**
   $9.0 - M = 5\log\left(\frac{471.4 \times 10^6}{10}\right)$ **[1]**
   $M = -29.37$ (−29 to 2 s.f.) **[1]**
   d) $2.51^{4.8-(-29.37)}$ **[1]**
   $= 4.5 \times 10^{13}$ times brighter **[1]**

PRACTICE PAPERS

Note: 'ecf.' stands for 'error carried forward'. If you get the wrong answer for part of a question and carry this mistake through to the next part of the question, 'allow ecf.' indicates that you can still get full marks if you do this part correctly.

Paper 1A

01.1 $K^- + p \rightarrow X + K^+$ **[1 mark]**

01.2 Charge: LHS (–1 e) + (+1 e) = 0 so RHS = 0 = (charge on X) + (+1 e) so charge on X = (–1 e) **[1 mark]**

01.3 Baryon no.: LHS (0) + (1) = +1 so RHS = +1 = (baryon no. of X) + (0) so baryon no. of X = (+1) **[1 mark]**

Strangeness: LHS (–1) + (0) = –1 so RHS = –1 = (strangeness of X) + (11) so strangeness of X = (–2) **[1 mark]**

01.4 Baryon no. = 1 so 3 quarks **[1 mark]** strangeness = –2 so 2 strange quarks, which have charge $(-\frac{1}{3}\text{ e}) + (-\frac{1}{3}\text{ e}) = (-\frac{2}{3}\text{ e})$ **[1 mark]** X has charge (–1 e) so third quark has charge $(-\frac{1}{3}\text{ e})$ so is a down quark **[1 mark]** **[dss scores 3 marks]**

02.1 Cell/Battery/Power supply and ammeter in series **[1 mark]** and voltmeter in parallel with thermistor **[1 mark]**

02.2 Resistance: $\frac{1}{R} = \frac{1}{(200 + 100)} + \frac{1}{(200 + 100)} = 150\ \Omega$, $R = 150\ \Omega$ **[1 mark for series (200 + 100), 1 mark for parallel ($\frac{1}{R} = \frac{1}{R_1} + \frac{1}{R_2}$ used with 300, 200 or 100), 1 mark for 150 Ω]**

Current: $I = \frac{(3\text{ V})}{(150\ \Omega)} = 0.020\text{ A} = 20\text{ mA}$ **[1 mark]**

02.3 Zero OR 0 A **[1 mark]** because there is no potential difference between A and B (because the potential difference between the battery and A and the battery and B is the same) **[1 mark]**.

02.4 Temperature increased **[1 mark]**; this releases more charge carriers and so the resistance of the thermistor decreases. **[1 mark]**.

02.5 Now lower resistance path through X than W **[1 mark]**, so more current through X than W **[1 mark]** (OR p.d. across X lower than across W so p.d. between A and B) so current in direction from A to B **[1 mark]**.

03.1 By conservation of momentum, momentum after collision = momentum before **[1 mark]** momentum before = (0.40 kg) × (0.30 m s^{-1}) + 0 = 0.12 kg m s^{-1} = (0.40 kg + 0.25 kg) × v **[1 mark]** v = 0.18 m s^{-1} **[1 mark, no marks for 0.2 as this is given in the question]**

03.2 Initial momentum = 0.12 kg m s^{-1}
final momentum (same mass and same speed but opposite direction) = –0.12 kg m s^{-1}
so change in momentum = –0.24 kg m s^{-1}
[1 mark, allow calculation using speed of 0.18 gives 0.23 kg m s^{-1} or speed of 0.2 gives 0.26 kg m s^{-1}, allow ecf. from 03.1]

03.3 Elastic collision – kinetic energy is conserved; in inelastic collision – kinetic energy is not conserved **[1 mark, mark not awarded for 'energy is not conserved']**. Momentum is conserved in both elastic and inelastic collisions **[1 mark, must say both]**.

03.4 Momentum before = (0.20 kg) × (0.30 m s^{-1}) + (0.20 kg) × (–0.20 m s^{-1}) **[1 mark]** = (0.060 – 0.040) = (0.020 kg m s^{-1}). By conservation of momentum, momentum after collision = momentum before, momentum after =
(0.20 kg) × v + (0.20 kg) × (0.30 m s^{-1}) **[1 mark]**
0.020 = 0.20v + 0.060 so 0.20v = –0.040 so
v = –0.20 m s^{-1} **[1 mark]**

E_K before = ½ (0.20)(0.30)^2 + ½ (0.20)(–0.20)^2 = 0.0090 + 0.0040 = 0.013 J

E_K after = ½ (0.20)(–0.20)^2 + ½ (0.20)(0.30)^2 = 0.0040 + 0.0090 = 0.013 J **[1 mark for E_K 'before' or 'after']**

E_K before = E_K after **[1 mark for showing this]** so elastic **[no mark for just writing this, i.e. guessing]**

04.1 $F = k\,\Delta L$, $k = \frac{mg}{\Delta L} = \frac{(0.31 \times 9.81)}{0.14}$ **[1 mark]**
k = 21.7 N m^{-1} (or 22 N m^{-1} (2 s.f.)) **[1 mark]**

04.2 $T = 2\pi\sqrt{\frac{m}{k}} = 2\pi\sqrt{\frac{0.31}{22}} = 0.75\text{ s}$ **[1 mark, allow using k = 20 N m^{-1} gives 0.78 s]**

04.3 Maximum tension will occur when the extension is the greatest value **[1 mark]**. This is when the mass is at the lowest point **[1 mark, OR when extension = 0.14 m + 0.025 m = 0.165 m]**.

$F = k\,\Delta l$ = 22 × 0.165 = 3.6 N **[1 mark]**
(OR 20 × 0.165 = 3.3 N)

04.4 Both m and k are constants **[1 mark]** so the period will not change **[1 mark]**. The initial extension will be less, hence the maximum tension will decrease because g is less on the Moon **[1 mark]**.

05.1 Loss of E_P between **X** and **Y** = gain in E_K at **Y**
$mg\Delta h = \frac{1}{2}mv^2$ so that (9.81 m s^{-2})(0.40 m) = $\frac{1}{2}v^2$ **[1 mark]** $v = \sqrt{(2 \times 9.81 \times 0.40)}$ m s^{-1} = 2.8 m s^{-1} **[1 mark]**

05.2 Loss in E_K between **Y** and **Z** = gain in E_P between **Y** and **Z** so overall loss in E_P between **X** and **Z** = E_K at **Z**. Δh = 0.30 m so that $mg\Delta h$ = ½ mv^2
(9.81 m s^{-2})(0.30 m) = ½ v^2 **[1 mark]**

$v = \sqrt{(2 \times 9.81 \times 0.30)}$ m s^{-1} = 2.4 m s^{-1} **[1 mark]**

OR using value from 5.1 **[allow incorrect value]**: loss in E_K between **Y** and **Z** = gain in E_p at **Z**. Δh = 0.10 m so that $mg\Delta h = ½ mv_Y^2 - ½ mv_Z^2$

(9.81 m s^{-2})(0.10 m) = ½ (2.80)^2 – ½ v^2 **[1 mark]**

$v = \sqrt{((2.80)^2 - 2 \times 9.81 \times 0.10)}$ m s^{-1} = 2.4 m s^{-1} **[1 mark]**

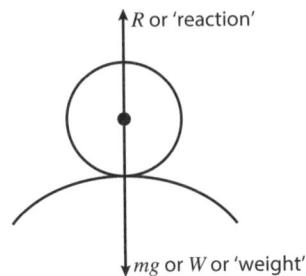

05.3

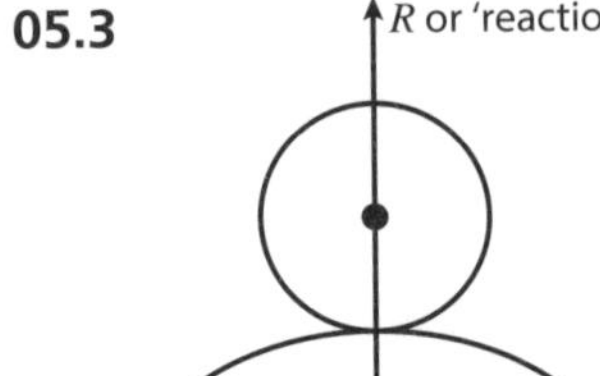

[1 mark]

$mg - R = \frac{mv^2}{r}$ **[1 mark]**

$(0.0060\,\text{kg})(9.81\,\text{m s}^{-2}) - R = \frac{(0.0060\,\text{kg})(2.43\,\text{m s}^{-1})^2}{(0.75\,\text{m})}$

[1 mark, allow incorrect v from 1.2]

R = 0.012 N **[1 mark]**

06.1 Infrared **[1 mark]**

06.2 $f = \frac{c}{\lambda}$ $f = \frac{(3.0 \times 10^8\,\text{m s}^{-1})}{(660 \times 10^{-9}\,\text{m})}$ = 4.5 × 10^{14} Hz **[1 mark]**

$E = hf$ E = (6.63 × 10^{-34} J s) × (4.5 × 10^{14} Hz) **[1 mark]** = 3.0 × 10^{-19} J

In eV: $E = \frac{(3.0 \times 10^{-19}\,\text{J})}{(1.6 \times 10^{-19}\,\text{C})}$ = 1.9 eV **[1 mark]**

06.3 Blue light excites an electron in phosphor atom to a higher energy level **[1 mark]**. The electron then drops to a lower energy level emitting a photon of longer wavelength/lower energy in the yellow part of the spectrum **[1 mark]**.

06.4 No **[0 marks for this, marks are for explanation]** because the red photon has less energy than the green and blue photons **[1 mark]** and cannot excite the electron to a high enough energy level for it to drop down emitting green light or blue light **[1 mark, allow explanation using a calculation showing energy of green or blue photon and comparing with energy of red photon]**.

06.5 $\sin\theta = \frac{n\lambda}{d} = 1 \times \frac{(450 \times 10^{-9}\,\text{m})}{\frac{1.0 \times 10^{-3}\,\text{m}}{1500}}$ **[1 mark]**

θ = 42° **[1 mark]**

06.6 Central white maxima, with higher diffraction orders showing separate blue and yellow lines **[1 mark]**. Blue has a lower wavelength so it will have smaller diffraction angles than yellow **[1 mark, allow a labelled diagram]**.

Paper 1B

07 **C:** $^{204}_{82}\text{Pb} + ^{4}_{2}\text{He} \rightarrow ^{208}_{83}\text{Bi} + ^{0}_{1}\text{e}^{+}$ **[1 mark]**

08 **B:** $\eta = \frac{F}{6\pi rv}$ units: $\frac{\text{N}}{(\text{m})(\text{m s}^{-1})} = \frac{\text{kg m}}{\text{s}^2} \times \frac{\text{s}}{\text{m}^2} = \frac{\text{kg}}{\text{s m}}$ = kg m^{-1} s^{-1} **[1 mark]**

09 **C:** Energy of photon, which depends on its frequency = work function of metal + max. kinetic energy of electron (which = ½ mv^2) **[1 mark]**

10 **C:** λ_B has the greatest energy **[1 mark]**. Since $E = hf = \frac{hc}{\lambda}$ it must also have the highest frequency. λ_A is the longest wavelength and λ_B is the shortest wavelength. The length of the lines on the diagram are proportional to energy and frequency, not wavelength.

11 **B:** $V \propto d^3$, % error in V = 3 × % error in d because d is cubed when calculating V **[1 mark]**

12 **B:** Note that positron is the same size mass and charge as electron (only sign is different) so either look up Q and m for electron and proton in data booklet and calculate alpha (roughly) from $\frac{(2 \times 1.6 \times 10^{-19})}{(4 \times 1.67 \times 10^{-27})}$ = 4.8 × 10^7 OR use electron mass $= \frac{1}{2000}$ × proton mass and alpha particle mass = 4 × proton mass together with electron charge = proton charge and alpha particle charge = 2 × proton charge to get the ratio positron: proton: alpha particle = 2000:1:0.5 **[1 mark]**.

13 **A:** Use $f = \frac{1}{2l}\sqrt{\frac{T}{\mu}}$, $f \propto \sqrt{T}$, when T changed to $2T$, f changed to $\sqrt{2}f = \sqrt{2}$ × 200 Hz **[1 mark]**

14 **D:** Use $R = \frac{\rho l}{A} = \frac{\rho l}{\pi d^2/4} = \frac{\rho l_2}{d^2}$ so length $l_2 = \frac{4l}{\pi}$ **[1 mark]**

15 **D:** As the third filter is rotated from 0° some light is transmitted through it except at 0° and multiples of 90°; some of this light is then transmitted through the final filter except (again) at 0° and multiples of 90° **[1 mark]**.

16 **D:** $\sin\theta_c = \frac{n_{\text{cladding}}}{n_{\text{core}}}$ and $n_{\text{cladding}} = \frac{c}{c_{\text{cladding}}}$ and $n_{\text{core}} = \frac{c}{c_{\text{core}}}$ so $\sin\theta_c = \frac{c_{\text{core}}}{c_{\text{cladding}}} = \frac{(2.02 \times 10^8)}{(2.08 \times 10^8)}$ = 0.971, θ_c = 76° **[1 mark]**

17 **C:** Width of fringes $w = \frac{\lambda D}{s}$ frequency is × $\frac{1}{2}$ so wavelength will be × 2 ($c = f\lambda$) and w will be × 2 **[1 mark]**

18 **C:** Taking moments about the centre of the beam – so that its weight has no effect. 40 × F = 20 × T so T:F = 40:20 = 2:1 **[1 mark]**

19 **A:** A and B have anticlockwise moment, total = 2 × 10 × radius = 20 × radius. For equilibrium C has clockwise moment 20 × radius **[1 mark]**

20 **D:** Motion at 90° is independent. East: $a = \frac{F}{m} = \frac{0.20}{0.50} = 0.40\ \text{m s}^{-2}$
$v = u + at = 0 + (0.40)(10) = 4.0\ \text{m s}^{-1}$
Resultant velocity of 3.0 m s^{-1} S + 4.0 m s^{-1} E cannot be East (or = $\tan^{-1}\frac{4.0}{3.0} = 53°$ East of South) magnitude using Pythagoras = $\sqrt{3.0^2 + 4.0^2}$ = 5.0 m s^{-1} **[1 mark]**

21 **C:** For one spring $k = \frac{F}{\Delta L}$. In series both springs extend so the extension is doubled, $k_s = \frac{F}{2\Delta L}$ or use $\frac{1}{k_s} = \frac{1}{k} + \frac{1}{k} = \frac{2}{k}$, $= k_s = \frac{k}{2}$, in parallel each spring supports half the load, so extension is halved $k_p = \frac{F}{0.5x}$
(or use $k_p = k + k = 2k$) so $k_p = 2k$ **[1 mark]**

22 **D:** Both will fall with vertical acceleration g. Both will have constant horizontal velocity **[1 mark]**.

23 **C:** Time of flight for P should be twice time to greatest height, so vertically $u = v\sin\theta$ and $v = 0$ and $t_p = \frac{2v}{g}\sin\theta$; for Q $t_q = \frac{2v}{g}\sin(90-\theta) = \frac{2v}{g}\cos\theta$.

Dividing two equations gives $\frac{t_p}{t_q} = \frac{\frac{2v}{g}\sin\theta}{\frac{2v}{g}\cos\theta} = \tan\theta$

so $t_q = \frac{t_p}{\tan\theta}$ OR use time of flight is time for vertical distance to reach 0. Use $s = ut + \frac{1}{2}at^2$ with $s = 0$ $g = -9.81$ gives $ut = \frac{1}{2}(9.81)t^2$ so $u = \frac{1}{2}(9.81)t$.

For P: $v\sin\theta = \frac{1}{2}(9.81)t_p$. For Q: (use $\sin\theta = \cos(90° - \theta)$) $v\cos\theta = \frac{1}{2}(9.81)t_q$.

Dividing two equations gives
$\frac{v\cos\theta}{v\sin\theta} = \frac{\frac{1}{2}(9.81)t_q}{\frac{1}{2}(9.81)t_p} = \frac{t_q}{t_p} = \frac{1}{\tan\theta}$ so $t_q = \frac{t_p}{\tan\theta}$ **[1 mark]**

24 **A:** Reaction force is greater when the lift is either accelerating upwards (speeding up) or decelerating downwards (slowing down). Reaction force is only less when the lift is accelerating downwards (speeding up) or decelerating upwards (slowing down) **[1 mark]**.

25 **C:** On a frictionless ramp, the work done is only against the weight of the crate. The work done is Mgh in both cases (and equal to the increase in potential energy) **[1 mark]**.

26 **B:** Power is $\frac{mgh}{t}$, X: $\frac{(30g \times 120)}{(2.0 \times 60)} = 30g$,
Y: $\frac{(8.0g \times 6.0)}{1.5} = 32g$, Z: $\frac{(4.0g \times 15)}{10} = 6.0g$ **[1 mark]**

27 **A:** Use $\varepsilon = I(R + r)$ $\varepsilon = V + Ir$ $9.0 = 7.8 + 1.5r$
$r = \frac{1.2}{1.5} = 0.8\ \Omega$ **[1 mark]**

28 **D:** Use potential divider equations; the ratio of p.d.s $\frac{V_1}{V_2}$ is the same as the ratio of resistances $\frac{R_1}{R_2}$ and $V_1 + V_2$ = constant. As it gets darker resistance of LDR R_2 increases so V_2 increases. Similarly, when R_1 is increased V_1 increases and V_2 decreases, which has the effect that it must get darker (so that R_2 increases more before the light switches on) **[1 mark]**.

29 **D:** The question is about the total energy, which does not change. If it was potential energy, B and C would be correct and if it was kinetic energy A would be correct **[1 mark]**.

30 **B:** Because it is a friction force it opposes motion and is always opposite to the velocity **[1 mark]**.

31 **D:** Vertical component of reaction $R\cos\theta = mg$ horizontal component $R\sin\theta = \frac{mv^2}{r}$ (the centripetal force on m) dividing the two equations $\tan\theta = \frac{\frac{mv^2}{r}}{mg} = \frac{v^2}{rg}$ **[1 mark]**

Paper 2A

01.1 $Q = mc\Delta\theta = (mc\Delta\theta)_{PCM} + (mc\Delta\theta)_{container}$
$= 0.4 \times 2200 \times (37 - 15) + 0.24 \times 840\ (37 - 15)$ **[1 mark]**
$= 19\,360 + 4435$
$= 23\,800$ J (24 000 J to 2 s.f.) **[1 mark]**

01.2 $E = IVt = 1.7 \times 12 \times 90 \times 60 = 110\,160$ J **[1 mark]**

States or shows that electrical energy transferred = thermal energy transferred to raise temperature of solid PCM and container to 37 °C, to then raise temperature of PCM and glass container from 37 °C to 39 °C and to melt the PCM **[1 mark]**.

$Q = 23\,800 + (0.4 \times 2600 \times (39 - 37)) + (0.24 \times 840\ (39 - 37)) + (0.4)L$ **[1 mark]**

$110\,160 = 23\,800 + 0.4L + 2080 + 403.2$, $0.4L = 83\,876.8$

$L = 210\,000$ J kg^{-1} (to 2 s.f.) **[1 mark]**

01.3 If the body temperature goes above 37 °C, energy is transferred to the PCM to melt it and if the body temperature falls below 37 °C, energy is transferred from the PCM to warm the body **[1 mark]**.

02.1
1. Empirical means observed from the results of experiment OR the gas laws are based on observations from experiments **[1 mark]**. (They predict results but don't explain why.)
2. Kinetic theory is based on assumptions leading to deductions using other knowledge and theories **[1 mark, allow any equivalent statements]**.

02.2 Density **[1 mark]**. N = number of molecules, m = molecular mass, V = volume of gas, Nm = total mass, $\frac{Nm}{V} = \frac{\text{mass}}{\text{volume}}$ = density **[1 mark]**

02.3 $[(v_1)^2 + (v_2)^2 + (v_3)^2 + (v_4)^2] \div 4$ **[1 mark]**

02.4 Use $\frac{1}{2}m(c_{rms})^2 = \frac{3}{2}kT$ (OR = $\frac{3\,RT}{2N_A}$) m

$= \frac{0.028}{(6.02 \times 10^{23})}$ kg **[1 mark]**

$T = \frac{m(c_{rms})^2}{3k}$

$= \frac{0.028 \times 520^2}{3 \times 6.02 \times 10^{23} \times 1.38 \times 10^{-23}}$ **[1 mark]**

= 304 K (300 K to 2 s.f.) **[1 mark]**

03.1 $F_G = \frac{Gm_1m_2}{r^2}$

$= \frac{(6.7 \times 10^{-11})(9.11 \times 10^{-31})(1.673 \times 10^{-27})}{(5.3 \times 10^{-11})^2}$

= 3.6×10^{-47} N **[1 mark]**

$F_E = \frac{1}{4\pi\varepsilon_0}\frac{Q_1Q_2}{r^2} = \frac{1}{4\pi(8.85 \times 10^{-12})}\frac{(1.6 \times 10^{-19})^2}{(5.3 \times 10^{-11})^2}$

= 8.2×10^{-8} N **[1 mark]**

Ratio: $\frac{F_E}{F_G} = \frac{8.2 \times 10^{-8}}{3.6 \times 10^{-47}}$

N = 2.3×10^{39} (to 2 s.f.) **[1 mark, no units]**

The gravitational force between a proton and an electron is of the order of 10^{39} times smaller than the electrostatic force, so is negligible and can be ignored when calculating the forces on subatomic particles **[1 mark]**.

03.2 **[Must give both statements for each mark]** Differences: 1. Gravity is always attractive, electrostatic is attractive or repulsive. 2. Gravity acts on all matter (objects with mass), electrostatic acts only on charged matter (charged objects). 3. You can shield objects from electrostatic forces, but not from gravitational forces. 4. Permittivity for electric fields depends on the medium in which the field exists, but for gravitational fields there is no difference in any material. 5. Gravitational field always directed towards mass producing it, electric is towards a negative charge but away from a positive charge. 6. Mass of 1 kg produces a small field, 1 C produces a much stronger field. 7. Gravitational potential is always negative, but electric potential is negative for negative charges and positive for positive charges.

Similarities: 1. In a radial field force varies as inverse square of the distance between objects. 2. Force between two objects proportional to the product of both (charges for electrostatic, masses for gravitational). 3. The field strength in a radial field is proportional to the mass/charge producing it. 4. Spherical and point objects have a radial field. 5. Work done in moving a mass or charge across a potential difference is calculated by multiplying the mass/charge by the potential difference. 6. Both types of potential are proportional to $\frac{1}{r}$ in a radial field. 7. In a uniform field the potential is proportional to the distance. 8. In a uniform field, the field has the same magnitude and direction at all points. **[5 marks: 1 mark for a difference, 1 mark for a similarity, 3 marks for additional similarities or differences]**

04.1 The changing electric current in the coils produces a changing magnetic field so there is changing magnetic flux through the sheet **[1 mark]**. The changing magnetic flux induces an emf in the copper sheet **[1 mark]**. The emf produces currents in the sheet **[1 mark]** and this has a heating effect due to the resistance of the sheet **[1 mark]**.

04.2 **[Either order]** 1. Increase the frequency of the alternating current. The induced emf is proportional to the rate of change of flux linkage, so by increasing the frequency of the alternating current the induced emf will be increased **[1 mark]**. 2. Increase the current in the coils, which will increase the magnetic field, increasing the maximum flux so that the rate of change of flux linkage is larger **[1 mark]**.

04.3 The emfs induced will be unchanged, but the currents will be reduced **[1 mark]**, although resistance is increased. (Thermal energy transfer = V^2/R.) Net effect will be a decrease in the rate of heating due to reduced current **[1 mark]**.

05.1 $E = \frac{V}{d} = \frac{10 \times 10^3}{0.020} = 5.0 \times 10^5$ N C^{-1} **[1 mark]**

$F = EQ = 5.0 \times 10^5 \times 1.6 \times 10^{-19} = 8.0 \times 10^{-14}$ N **[1 mark]**

05.2 $F = ma$, $a = \frac{8.0 \times 10^{-14}\text{ N}}{1.673 \times 10^{-27}\text{ kg}}$ **[1 mark]**

= 4.78×10^{13} m s^{-2}

$v^2 = u^2 + 2as = 0 + (2 \times 4.78 \times 10^{13} \times 0.010)$ **[1 mark, allow ecf. for *a*]**

$v = 9.8 \times 10^5$ m s^{-1} **[1 mark for correct evaluation of both to more than 1 s.f.]**

05.3 Use of $v^2 = u^2 + 2as$

$(3.0 \times 10^7)^2 = (9.8 \times 10^5)^2 + (2 \times 4.78 \times 10^{13})(2n \times 0.020)$ **[1 mark for attempt to use with speed acceleration and distance, 1 mark for correct use]**

Gives n = 235 laps needed **[1 mark, allow ecf. for own values calculated in 05.2, allow use of values given in 05.2]**

05.4 Proton marked on track with direction of motion tangent to track in direction from source to target. Force at right angles to track, directly towards source **[1 mark]**. Magnetic field is vertically upwards (left-hand rule) so north pole is below the Ds, south pole above **[1 mark]**.

05.5 F is at 90° to B so $F = Bev$ AND $F = \frac{mv^2}{r}$ **[1 mark]**

$Bev = \frac{mv^2}{r}$ **[1 mark]**

05.6 So that the protons do not collide with air molecules and be stopped or deflected **[1 mark]**

06.1 Mass defect = 238.04955 u – (234.043924 u + 4.00151 u) = 4.116×10^{-3} u **[1 mark]**

$E = mc^2$

Energy = 4.116×10^{-3} u × 1.661×10^{-27} kg × $(3.0 \times 10^8)^2$ (m s^{-1})^2 = 6.2×10^{-13} J

OR = 4.116×10^{-3} u × 931.5 MeV × 1.6×10^{-13} (J per MeV) **[1 mark]**

= 6.1×10^{-13} J **[1 mark]**

06.2 238 g of Pu238 contains 6.02×10^{23} atoms

4300 g contains $\frac{4300}{238.05} \times 6.02 \times 10^{23}$ **[1 mark]**

= 1.09×10^{25} (1.1×10^{25} to 2 s.f.)

06.3 Half-life = 88 years

$\lambda = \frac{\ln 2}{T_{1/2}} = \frac{\ln 2}{(88 \times 365 \times 24 \times 60 \times 60)}$

= 2.50×10^{-10} s^{-1} **[1 mark]**

$A = \lambda N = 2.50 \times 10^{-10} \times 1.09 \times 10^{25}$

= 2.7×10^{15} Bq (to 2 s.f.) **[1 mark]**

OR $\lambda = 7.88 \times 10^{-3}$ y^{-1} $A = \lambda N$

= 7.88×10^{-3} y^{-1} × $\frac{1.09 \times 10^{25}}{(365 \times 24 \times 60 \times 60)}$

[allow $N = 1 \times 10^{25}$ or ecf. from 06.2]

06.4 Total energy = energy per decay × number of decays

Power = energy per second = energy per decay × number of decays per second

Power = 6.2×10^{-13} J **[allow ecf. from 06.1]** × 2.7×10^{15} Bq **[allow ecf. from 06.3]** = 1700 W (to 2 s.f.) **[1 mark]**

06.5 Deep-space probes are far from the Sun and little solar energy is available. Dust storms on Mars can cover panels. During the night or when probes are behind planets they will not receive radiation **[1 mark for two points made]**.

So batteries will not charge and electronics will shut down. RTGs provide a continuous supply that will not be interrupted **[1 mark for a suitable explanation]**.

06.6 $F = m_p r\omega^2 = \frac{Gm_p m_s}{r^2}$ **[1 mark [allow equivalent derivation using $F = \frac{mv^2}{r}$]**

$r^3 = \frac{Gm_s}{\omega^2}$

$\frac{1}{\omega^2} = \frac{r^3}{Gm_s}$

Use of $\omega = 2\pi f$ and $f = \frac{1}{T}$ (or $T = \frac{2\pi}{\omega}$) **[1 mark]**

$T^2 = 4\pi^2 \left(\frac{1}{\omega^2}\right)$

$T^2 = 4\pi^2 \left(\frac{r^3}{Gm_s}\right)$

$T^2 = \left(\frac{4\pi^2}{Gm_s}\right) r^3$ AND π, G and m_s are constants

[1 mark] so $T^2 \propto r^3$

06.7 T_{Earth} = 365 days T_{Mars} = 687 days. Use

$$\frac{T_M^2}{T_E^2} = \frac{\left(\frac{4\pi^2}{Gm_s}\right) r_M^3}{\left(\frac{4\pi^2}{Gm_s}\right) r_E^3} = \frac{r_M^3}{r_E^3}$$

$\frac{T_M^2}{T_E^2} = \frac{687^2}{365^2} = \frac{r_M^3}{r_E^3}$ **[1 mark]**

ratio $\frac{r_M}{r_E} = \left(\frac{687}{365}\right)^{\frac{2}{3}} = 1.52$ **[1 mark]** …

radius $r_M = 1.52 \times (1.50 \times 10^{11})$ m = 2.3×10^{11} m **[1 mark]**

Paper 2B

07 **C:** $\frac{p_1}{T_1} = \frac{p_2}{T_2}$ when the temperature is the absolute temperature in kelvin **[1 mark]**

$\frac{p}{(T + 273)} = \frac{2p}{(T_{new} + 273)}$ when T and T_{new} are in °C. Rearranging: $(T_{new} + 273) = 2(T + 273)$ so $T_{new} = 2T + 273$

08 **C:** The internal energy of a system is the sum of the average kinetic energies and the potential energies of the atoms. For an ideal gas the potential energy is zero **[1 mark]**.

09 **D:** $F = \frac{GmM}{r^2}$ so $F \propto \frac{1}{r^2}$ **[1 mark]**

10 **C:** The work done in moving a unit mass from infinity to that point **[1 mark]**.

11 **A:** $V_{Earth} = \frac{-GM}{R} = 6.3 \times 10^7$ J kg^{-1}

$V_{Jupiter} = \frac{-G(320M)}{11R} = \frac{320}{11}\left(\frac{-GM}{R}\right) = (29.09)$ $(-6.3 \times 10^7$ J kg$^{-1}) = -1.8 \times 10^9$ J kg^{-1} **[1 mark]**

12 **C:** $V = \frac{-G(3M)}{3r} = \frac{-GM}{r}$

The total potential is the sum of the potential at X due to both masses = $\frac{-GM}{r} + \frac{-G(10M)}{5r}$

$= \frac{-GM}{r} - \frac{2GM}{r} = \frac{-3GM}{r} = 3V$ **[1 mark]**

13 **C:** Geosynchronous and geostationary orbits both have a period of 24 hours, and geosynchronous orbits will be overhead at a point in the orbit once a day. Geostationary is the special orbit that follows the equator (in the equatorial plane) and so is overhead at all times **[1 mark]**.

14 **D:** $F = \frac{-(Q)(-4Q)}{d^2} = \frac{4Q^2}{d^2}$

$F_{new} = \frac{-(2Q)(-3Q)}{(d/2)^2} = \frac{6Q^2}{(d^2/4)} = \frac{24Q^2}{d^2} = 6F$ **[1 mark]**

15 **B:** $\frac{1}{2}mv^2 = eV$ so $v \propto \sqrt{V}$ **[1 mark]**

16 **B:** Work done moving X to Y: Field is uniform so X and Z are at 250 V and Y at 150 V. Difference = 100 V (or $E = \frac{500 \text{ V}}{50 \text{ mm}} = 10$ V mm^{-1} and XY = 10 mm gives 100 V). Work done = $QV = (1.6 \times 10^{-19})(100) = 1.6 \times 10^{-17}$ J, X to Z is along an equipotential surface (250 V) so work done = 0 **[1 mark]**

17 **C:** From $C = \frac{A\varepsilon_0\varepsilon_r}{d}$ using a dielectric with relative permittivity $\varepsilon_r = 2$ will double the capacitance to $C_{new} = 2C$. $Q_{new} = (2C)V = 2Q$ and $E_{new} = \frac{1}{2}(2Q)V = 2E$ **[1 mark]**

18 **D:** $V = V_0 e^{\frac{-t}{RC}}$ to get an expression in the form $y = mx + c$ where $y = V$ and $x = t$. Take logs of both sides: $\ln V = \ln V_0 - \frac{t}{RC} = -\left(\frac{1}{RC}\right)t + \ln V_0$ so $y = \ln V$ and $x = t$ **[1 mark]**

19 **B:** $\tau = RC$ so τ is the time for the charge to fall to $\frac{1}{e}$ times the initial value. After 47 s the charge will be $(\frac{1}{e} \times 10\mu C) = 3.68\mu C \sim 3.7\mu C$ **[1 mark]**

20 **B:** Use an equation containing flux density B. $F = BIl$ is good as I and l are base units already. LHS = N = kg m s^{-2} RHS = (units of B) (A) (m) so units of B = kg m s^{-2} A^{-1} m^{-1} = kg A^{-1} s^{-2} **[1 mark]**

21 **A:** flux linkage $N\Phi = BAN\cos\theta$

$A = l^2$ and $\cos\theta = 1$ so $N\Phi = Bl^2N$

new flux linkage = $B\left(\frac{l}{2}\right)^2(2N) = \frac{1}{2}Bl^2N$

= ½ original flux linkage **[1 mark]**

22 **D:** emf $\varepsilon = \frac{\Delta\Phi}{\Delta t}$ so $\frac{\Delta\Phi}{\Delta t} = \frac{\Delta(BA)}{\Delta t} = \frac{B\Delta A}{\Delta t}$ the change in area is the area swept out by the wing in a time that depends on its speed so $\frac{\Delta A}{\Delta t} = 25 \times 125 = 3125$ m^2 s^{-1}

$\varepsilon = 5.0 \times 10^{-5} \times 3125 = 0.156$ V = 0.16 V (to 2 s.f.) **[1 mark]**

23 **D:** Remember: the rms value is related to the peak value, and will be less than the peak value **[1 mark]**

24 **D:** Changing the number of turns changes the output voltage. Improving the insulation will increase the running temperature so the resistance of the coils increases – leading to increased energy transfer as heat. An iron core made of layers will reduce eddy currents, and reduce energy transfers to the core **[1 mark]**.

25 **C:** The Rutherford model is that the atom has a small central nucleus of high density **[1 mark]**.

26 **A:** Using $\lambda_X = \frac{\ln 2}{T_{1/2}}$ and $A = \lambda_X N$ for X. For Y $\lambda_Y = \frac{\ln 2}{3T_{1/2}} = \frac{\lambda_X}{3}$ and $A_Y = \lambda_Y 2N = \frac{\lambda_X}{3}2N = \frac{2}{3}A$ **[1 mark]**

27 **D:** The background count rate will have increased due to human activities like nuclear medicine and waste from nuclear power. **[1 mark]**

28 **B:** Fraction remaining is $\frac{N}{N_0} = e^{-\lambda t} = e^{-(1.13 \times 10^{-3} \times 15 \times 60)} = 0.36$, as a percentage = 36% **[1 mark]**

29 **C:** From the equation for the radius, $R \propto A^{\frac{1}{3}}$ so volume $V = \frac{4}{3}\pi R^3 \propto R^3 \propto A$. Density = $\frac{M}{V}$ and as mass and volume are both proportional to A, density is independent of A **[1 mark]**.

30 **D:** Think of the binding energy per nucleon curve. Fe-56 is the most stable and has the greatest binding energy per nucleon. Light nuclides (less than iron) can fuse by increasing their BE per nucleon – the product is closer to Fe-56. Heavy nuclides can fission by increasing their BE per nucleon to give to lighter nuclides – products closer to Fe-56 **[1 mark]**.

31 **C:** Moderator is used to slow neutrons, so elastic collisions are required. Control rods are used to absorb neutrons to slow the rate of reaction. Coolant is required to transfer energy so a high specific heat capacity leads to large energy transfer with small change in temperature **[1 mark]**.

Paper 3A

01.1 Precautions: Wear eye protection. Check the breaking stress of the wire and ensure it is not exceeded. Explanation: If the wire breaks, the potential energy transferred may make the end of the wire move quickly.

Precaution: If heavy masses are being used ensure they can fall safely, e.g. into a bucket. Explanation: so they don't damage floor/feet. **[3 marks: 1 mark for each safety precaution, 1 mark for an explanation of one of the precautions stated]**

01.2 A micrometer **[1 mark]**

01.3 Diameter = $\frac{(0.77 + 0.77 + 0.79)}{3}$ mm = 0.777 ± $\frac{(0.79 - 0.77)}{2}$ = 0.01 so value (with appropriate s.f.) = 0.78 (± 0.01) mm **[2 marks: 1 mark for mean value, 1 mark for uncertainty]**

01.4 Cross-sectional area = $\frac{\pi d^2}{4} = \frac{\pi(0.78 \times 10^{-3})^2}{4}$ = 4.8×10^{-7} m^2 **[1 mark]** % uncertainty = 2 × % uncertainty in d = 2 × $\frac{0.01}{0.78}$ × 100 **[1 mark, ecf. for uncertainty in *d*]** = 2.56% = 3% **[1 mark]**

01.5 Tension in wire OR mass hung on wire; original length of wire; extended length of wire (not extension, unless indicated how this is to be measured directly, rather than calculated); diameter of cross-section (not area). **[3 marks for all four points made, 2 marks for three points made, 1 mark for two points made, 0 marks for one point made.]** Note that area is incorrect as it cannot be measured directly.

01.6 Attempt to calculate a gradient from a large triangle, using at least half of the line **[1 mark]** Gradient = $\frac{\Delta y}{\Delta x}$ with a pair of correct values from the graph **[1 mark]**

Young modulus = 1.8×10^{11} Pa (or correct equivalent, e.g. 180 GPa) **[1 mark, answers that round to 180 GPa are acceptable]**

02.1 So that the pendulum swings with SHM and equation can be used. OR The derivation of the equation for the time period relies on the small angle approximation. **[1 mark]**

02.2 More readings **[1 mark]** OR smaller intervals between lengths **[1 mark]** / larger range of lengths **[1 mark]**. Measure the length to the nearest mm **[1 mark]**. Measure the times to the nearest 0.01 s **[1 mark]**. Repeats and mean of values taken **[1 mark]**.

02.3 Time from the centre of the swing **[1 mark]**. Use a fiducial mark **[allow description of this, 1 mark]**.

02.4 $T = 2\pi\sqrt{\frac{l}{g}}$, $T^2 = 4\pi^2(\frac{l}{g})$, $T^2 = (\frac{4\pi^2}{g})$ compare with straight line $y = mx + c$ shows graph will be straight line with gradient $m = (\frac{4\pi^2}{g})$ **[1 mark]** and intercept $c = 0$ **[1 mark]**, i.e. through origin

$(\frac{4\pi^2}{g}) = 4.2$, $g = \frac{4\pi^2}{4.2} = 9.4 \text{ m s}^{-2}$ **[1 mark]**

02.5 Uncertainty ± 3 mm **[1 mark]** uncertainty using metre rule = 0.5 mm at each end = 1 mm add to uncertainty in x = 3 mm **[1 mark]**

02.6 Systematic error **[1 mark]**

02.7 The line does not go through the origin **[1 mark]** (straight line of same gradient). Value of g is unchanged **[1 mark]** (because gradient unchanged) **[allow explanation that if the line is forced through the origin the gradient will be shallower so the value of g will be increased (because $g = \frac{4\pi^2}{\text{gradient}}$)]**.

03.1 Safety precaution, **any one from**: wear eye protection OR use a plastic tube, not glass OR stand clear of the tube when using the pump or similar suggestion.

Explanation: because the high pressure may rupture the tube or cause the equipment to come apart suddenly **[2 marks: 1 mark for one safety precaution, 1 mark for explanation]**.

03.2 To keep temperature constant OR to let temperature return to room temperature **[1 mark]**

03.3 Read at eye level OR use a no parallax method **[1 mark]**

03.4 Column heading for $\frac{1}{V}$ with unit as shown below **[1 mark]**, calculations correct as shown in the table **[1 mark]** to 3 s.f. **[1 mark]**

Pressure, p / × 10^5 Pa	Volume, V / cm^3	**$\frac{1}{\text{Volume}}$ $\frac{1}{V}$ / cm^{-3}**
1.0	40.0	**0.0250**
1.4	29.0	**0.0345**
1.8	22.0	**0.0455**
2.2	18.0	**0.0556**
2.5	16.0	**0.0625**
3.0	13.0	**0.0769**

03.5 Vertical axis labelled: $\frac{1}{\text{Volume}}$ $\frac{1}{V}$ cm^{-3} **[1 mark]**. Correct plotting to 0.5 square **[1 mark]**. Best-fit line by eye **[1 mark]**

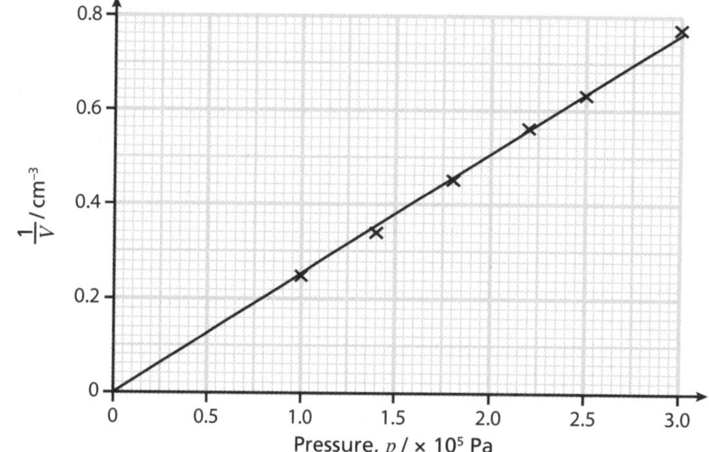

03.6 Appropriate comment **[1 mark]**, e.g. If the graph is a straight line: this shows that the pressure is proportional to $\frac{1}{V}$, i.e. inversely proportional to V and the gas obeys Boyle's law.

[ecf.: If incorrectly plotted the line does not give a straight line and so a mark would be awarded for saying that the pressure is not proportional to $\frac{1}{V}$, i.e. not inversely proportional to V and the gas does not obey Boyle's law]

03.7 **Any 4 marks**: Description/labelled diagram of closed glass capillary tube containing gas (air) V, sealed with 'bead' of sulfuric acid and a scale behind to measure V **[1 mark]** in a water bath with thermometer to measure temperature **[1 mark]**. Heat water and measure temperature and volume **[1 mark]**. Wear safety goggles **[1 mark]**. Plot values of volume against kelvin temperature **[1 mark]**. Charles's law is shown by a straight line through zero volume at 0 K **[allow 0 volume at –273 °C, 1 mark, allow a workable safe alternative experiment to measure V and T]**.

Paper 3B (Astrophysics)

01.1

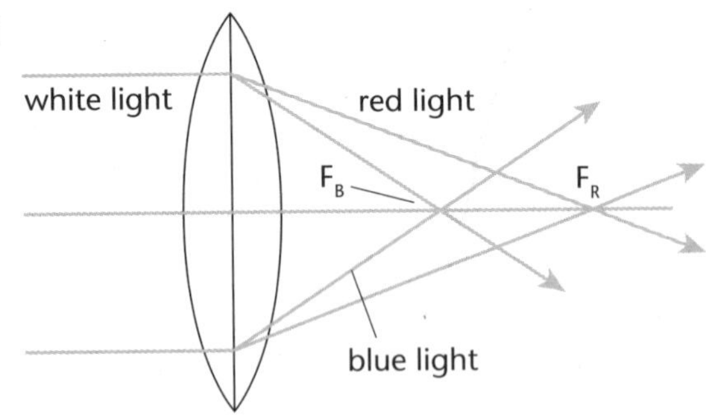

Colours (or correct f or λ) labelled, rays focused, blue/violet focal point closer to lens than red **[1 mark]**

01.2 **Any one from**: view monochromatic light (through a filter). Use achromatic lenses **[1 mark for one suggestion]**

01.3 $M = \frac{f_o}{f_e}$, $20 = \frac{0.60}{f_e}$ **[1 mark]** $f_e = 0.030$ m **[1 mark]**

distance apart = $f_o + f_e$ = 0.60 + 0.030 = 0.63 m **[1 mark]**

01.4 θ in radians $\approx \frac{\lambda}{D}$. For λ use 5.0×10^{-7} m as light from the Moon, (same as Sun) so use middle of visible spectrum. D is diameter of lens = 0.25 m.

$\theta = \frac{5.0 \times 10^{-7}}{0.25} = 2.0 \times 10^{-6}$ rad **[1 mark]** use of formula with 5.0×10^{-7} m value for wavelength and 0.25 m for D **[1 mark, correct answer and unit needed]**

02.1 Radio telescope site: Terrestrial and far from population centres **[1 mark]**. Terrestrial because large and heavy OR it needs to be far from population to avoid interference from human sources of radio waves **[1 mark]**.

X-ray telescope site: In space **[1 mark]** because X-rays are absorbed by the atmosphere **[1 mark]**.

02.2 Radio telescope detects radio waves that have longer wavelengths (~ metres) rather than X-ray wavelengths (~10^{-9}/10^{-10} m) **[1 mark]**; collecting power proportional to diameter^2 so large for radio telescopes but very small for X-ray telescopes **[1 mark]**; X-rays use grazing mirrors to focus whilst radio telescopes use parabolic dish to focus **[1 mark]**; resolving power proportional to $\frac{\lambda}{D}$ so small wavelength small D (X-ray) or large wavelength large D (radio) for same resolving power **[1 mark]**.

03.1 Correct use of $m - M = 5 \log(\frac{d}{10})$ **[1 mark]** to show that Procyon is closer to Earth. **[1 mark]**

03.2 Rigel: Blue star **[1 mark]** with strong Balmer absorption lines **[1 mark]**. Procyon: White star **[1 mark]** with strong absorption lines for metal ions **[1 mark]**.

03.3 $\lambda_{max} T = 2.9 \times 10^{-3}$ m K. $T = \frac{2.9 \times 10^{-3}}{740 \times 10^{-9}}$ **[1 mark]** = 3900 K (to 2 s.f.) **[1 mark, quote your answer to a greater accuracy than the 4000 given in the question to show you have calculated it]**

03.4 $I = \frac{P}{4\pi d^2}$ I from graph = 4.2 μW m^{-2}

$d = 6.5 \times 9.46 \times 10^{15}$ m

leads to $4.2 \times 10^{-6} = \frac{P}{4\pi(6.5 \times 9.46 \times 10^{15})^2}$

[1 mark]

$P = 1.996 \times 10^{29}$ W $\approx 2.0 \times 10^{29}$ W **[1 mark]**

$P = \sigma A T^4$ $1.996 \times 10^{29} = 5.67 \times 10^{-8} A (3900)^4$

[1 mark] $A = 1.5 \times 10^{22}$ m^2 (to 2.s.f) **[1 mark]**

04.1 A standard candle is an astronomical object of known absolute magnitude **[1 mark, 'constant'/'fixed luminosity' will not be allowed]**, example = Type 1a supernova **[1 mark, not just 'supernova', allow Cepheid variable star]**.

04.2 Little or no relevant information **[0 marks]**. One aspect partially covered **[1 mark]**. Two aspects partially covered **[2 marks]**. All three aspects partially covered, some detail missing from each OR one aspect covered and little or no information about the other two aspects **[3 marks]**. One aspect fully covered and two aspects partially covered OR two aspects fully covered and little or no information about the third aspect **[4 marks]**. Two of the three aspects fully covered with some detail missing from the third **[5 marks]**. All three aspects fully covered **[6 marks]**.

Aspect 1: Distance is measured by comparing the luminosity/power of a standard candle/star of known luminosity in the galaxy to the intensity received on the Earth. An inverse square law with distance relates intensity to luminosity.

Aspect 2: Doppler shift of wavelengths received from galaxy (change in wavelength/frequency of spectral lines of known wavelength) gives the velocity of the galaxy. Results showed that all the distant **[must be distant]** galaxies are moving away/receding.

Aspect 3: The results showed that the further away a distant galaxy was, the faster it was moving away from us. This can be explained by the fact that all distant galaxies are moving away from each other. In other words, the Universe is expanding.